ENCYCLOPEDIA OF MUSLIM-AMERICAN HISTORY

VOLUME II

ENCYCLOPEDIA OF MUSLIM-AMERICAN HISTORY

VOLUME II

Edited by Edward E. Curtis IV

Facts On File
An imprint of Infobase Publishing

ENCYCLOPEDIA OF MUSLIM-AMERICAN HISTORY

Facts On File, Inc.
An imprint of Infobase Publishing
132 West 31st Street
New York NY 10001

Library of Congress Cataloging-in-Publication Data

Encyclopedia of Muslim-American history / edited by Edward E. Curtis, IV.
p. cm.
Includes bibliographical references and index.
ISBN 978-0-8160-7575-1 (acid-free paper) 1. Muslims—United States—
History—Encyclopedias. I. Curtis, Edward E., 1970–
E184.M88E876 2010
973'.088297—dc22   2009024875

Facts On File books are available at special discounts when purchased in bulk
quantities for businesses, associations, institutions, or sales promotions.
Please call our Special Sales Department in New York
at (212) 967-8800 or (800) 322-8755.

You can find Facts On File on the World Wide Web at
http://www.factsonfile.com

Text design by Erika K. Arroyo
Composition by Hermitage Publishing Services
Cover printed by Sheridan Books, Ann Arbor, Mich.
Book printed and bound by Sheridan Books, Ann Arbor, Mich.
Date printed: June 2010

Printed in the United States of America

10 9 8 7 6 5 4 3 2 1

This book is printed on acid-free paper.

Contents

Entries M–Z

Majid, Satti (1883–1963) *Sudanese missionary to the United States*

By the 1920s, the United States had become home to competing strands of Islamic religion. There is perhaps no better illustration of this religious diversity than the reaction of Sudanese missionary Satti Majid to the teachings of the MOORISH SCIENCE TEMPLE of America, an African-American Muslim group established in CHICAGO in 1925 by NOBLE DREW ALI. Majid's opposition to the Moorish Science Temple anticipated the tensions between immigrant and indigenous, Sunni and non-Sunni forms of Islam that would arise later in the 20th century.

Born in al-Ghaddar, Sudan, in 1883, Satti Majid Muhammad al-Qadi, known more commonly as Satti Majid, memorized the QUR'AN at an early age. Little is known about why he eventually left his native land. Sometime after 1900, Majid traveled to England, then, in 1904, set sail for the United States. He later wrote that he traveled to America to correct the poor image of Islam in the West. Majid likely entered the United States through the port of New Orleans, where dozens of Muslim sailors who served on British merchant ships were disembarking at the time. Whether he stayed in New Orleans is not known. In fact, there is virtually no trace of him until 1921, when he resurfaced in NEW YORK CITY.

Serving as an imam, or religious leader, to Muslim sailors and other visitors stranded in New York during WORLD WAR I, Majid began a lengthy correspondence with the British consulate in the city and the British embassy in Washington, D.C. In his letters, Majid detailed the plight of Yemeni sailors from the city of Aden, which was controlled by the British, whose ships had been sunk by the Germans during the war. They had been unable to find work on other ships and were now poor and hungry. "In the name of humanity and renowned English justice," he wrote, "[I] beg of you . . . to graciously help them in obtaining employment on British steamers." What came of the correspondence is unclear, though Majid's letters establish that by the early 1920s, he had become a leader of Muslim Americans in New York.

Majid's missionary career in the United States in the 1920s is in need of further research, but it seems safe to conclude that his influence went beyond New York, as he established a series of benevolent societies devoted to the welfare of Muslims in various U.S. cities. These associations ministered not only to African and Middle Eastern immigrants but to African-American Muslims as well. In 1922, he traveled to DETROIT, where he sought incorporation papers for the benevolent association Moslem Welfare Society. There is also evidence that he established the Moslem Unity Association in New York in 1927. Then, in 1928, he created the African Moslem Welfare Society in Pittsburgh, an event confirmed by a letter from the Pennsylvania secretary of state's office dated January 15, 1928.

During the 1920s, Majid also came in contact with the Moorish Science Temple (MST), and his reaction to this indigenous group of Muslims was apoplectic. According to Majid's Arabic memoir, housed in the National Record Office in Khartoum, Sudan, Majid attempted to contact MST founder Noble Drew Ali and even attempted to sue the MST to "correct" the movement's teachings about Islam. After reading the *Holy Koran of the Moorish Science Temple of America*, a sacred text published in 1927 by Ali, he discovered that Ali considered himself a prophet, which was in violation of the Sunni Islamic tradition that Muhammad was the last of God's prophets. Majid wrote to Ali, challenging him to produce a miracle, as other prophets had done, and advised Ali to burn his book. He also tried to contact the government and wrote to various newspapers to correct what he considered to be Ali's errors.

On January 31, 1929, having failed in his attempts to prevent the rapid rise and popularity of the Moorish Science Temple, Majid left New York for Cairo, Egypt, where he hoped to gain the support of Islamic scholars at al-Azhar University for his campaign against Ali. In his letter to this international body of religious scholars, whom many Sunni Muslims considered the authoritative voices of Islam, Majid pointed out that Noble Drew Ali believed himself to be "the prophet promised at the end of time who was announced by Jesus." He also noted that Ali's book contained neither Qur'anic verses nor sayings of the prophet Muhammad.

In November 1931, 78 scholars at al-Azhar responded by both issuing a fatwa, or religious ruling, and creating a translated version of their religious opinion to be distributed in the United States. Signed by Muhammad al-Ahamadi al-Dawahiri, the head of al-Azhar, this document declared Ali to be "an imposter and disbeliever." Adding that the "truth and clear signs of Islam have been definitively established," the official translation of the fatwa stated that Ali's claims "could only be made by an unbeliever or a mentally-deranged person, and only those of like mentality would follow him."

Majid hoped to gain the support of al-Azhar to become an officially sanctioned Islamic missionary in the United States. But on December 17, 1934, Azhar officials wrote a letter denying Ali's request. "We declare," the letter said, "that he does not have the scholarly qualifications to be appointed to a religious mission such as al-Azhar is accustomed to send abroad." Though Majid's dream of returning to the United States as an Islamic authority was thwarted, he continued to correspond with his American followers.

Several letters addressed to the "Rev. Magid" and the "Respectable Father Sheich [sheikh, or leader] of Islam in America" were sent to him by members of the African Welfare Society in Pittsburgh in the 1930s. One letter, dated February 29, 1932, asked for news from Majid, reporting that Pittsburgh followers remained in contact with Muslims in CLEVELAND and New York. Helena Kleely, secretary of the Pittsburgh group, coauthored a letter on May 18, 1932, asking for Majid to provide English translations of the Arabic literature that he had sent. A 1935 letter discussed the Italian occupation of Ethiopia and looked forward to the day when African Americans could "return back to our homeland Africa," mentioning Abyssinia (Ethiopia) as a place that African Americans could colonize. Several of the writers complained that they had not received prompt replies to their correspondence.

Majid remained in Cairo, still hoping that he might procure the necessary funds to return to the United States and resume his missionary work. Such financial support never materialized, and when he applied for permission to return to the United States in the late 1930s, his request was denied. Majid moved to Sudan in the 1940s after an absence of decades and died in his native land on March 17, 1963.

Though Majid's impact on the country of his birth seems to have been minimal, the country where he lived for perhaps 25 years was changed as a result of his missionary activities. During the 1920s, his missionary efforts among both immigrant and indigenous Muslims contributed to a burgeoning Sunni Muslim–American community in cities such as Pittsburgh, Cleveland, New York, and Detroit. Like other Sunni Muslim leaders, including Daoud Ahmed Faisal and DUSÉ MOHAMED ALI, Majid served both immigrant and indigenous Muslims. He was also an uncompromising critic of homegrown American Islam, which he—and other Sunni Muslims after him—could do little to stop.

Edward E. Curtis IV

Further Reading

Ahmed I. Abu Shouk et al. "A Sudanese Missionary to the United States: Satti Majid, Shaykh al-Islam in North America, and His Encounter with Noble Drew Ali, Prophet of the Moorish Science Temple." *Sudanic Africa* 8 (1997): 137–191.

Malcolm X (1925–1965) *religious and political leader*

Thinker, agitator, speaker, and organizer, Malcolm X changed the way that Americans in the 1960s thought about civil rights and the struggle for black liberation. He also influenced the growth and development of Islamic religion among African Americans. Though his life was cut short by assassination, his memory, made popular first through the publication of his autobiography then later by a 1992 film directed by Spike Lee, became a powerful force in American religious and political life.

CHILDHOOD AND ADOLESCENCE

Malcolm X was born Malcolm Little on May 19, 1925, in Omaha, Nebraska. His parents—Louise, an immigrant from Grenada, and Earl, an organizer for the Universal Negro Improvement Association—raised him and his seven siblings to value their racial identity. Their defiant stance toward the racism and harsh discrimination against black people in the North led to the first tragedy of Malcolm's life. After moving to Lansing, Michigan, Earl Little was killed, most likely murdered, in 1931 while Malcolm was still a boy. Malcolm heard rumors his father had died for being too "uppity."

His mother struggled to raise her eight children in the midst of the GREAT DEPRESSION, and in 1939, she was declared legally insane by state health officials and sent to an asylum. This was the second tragedy of young Malcolm's life as he spent several years in and out of foster homes, away from his mother and siblings. In his teenage years, Malcolm moved to the East Coast and, from 1940 to 1944, lived in NEW YORK CITY and BOSTON.

In this period, "Detroit Red," as he was called, joined thousands of black youth who wore zoot suits, danced the lindy hop, and created a youth culture that defied the expectations of their parents and certainly of white Americans. Malcolm entered the underworld, doing drugs, gambling, and hustling to make ends meet. In 1946, he was arrested for stealing, convicted, and committed to the Massachusetts state prison system.

CAREER IN THE NATION OF ISLAM

In 1947 or 1948, in the Concord Reformatory, Malcolm converted to Islam as taught by ELIJAH MUHAMMAD, leader of the NATION OF ISLAM (NOI). He gave up the "slave name" Little for an "X," which signified his desire for a new identity. A voracious reader and talented prison debater, Malcolm became convinced that the NOI offered the only solution to the problem of racism in America. Paroled in 1952, he quickly established himself as a powerful advocate for Elijah Muhammad's vision, which called for black people to separate from whites, establish their own businesses and schools, convert to Islam, and practice clean living.

During the middle 1950s, Malcolm became an itinerant preacher and temple organizer, leading the NOI's effort to establish mosques and build attendance in Boston, PHILADELPHIA, and New York. Known for using sophisticated missionary, or "fishing," techniques, Malcolm also became known as a principled and brave civil rights leader on the East Coast. In 1957, he organized a NOI-led protest against the treatment of a fellow Muslim who had been beaten by police officers from New York's 28th precinct. The New York Police Department agreed to Malcolm's demand that the man receive immediate medical attention, and Malcolm's fame quickly spread among black Harlemites and New York City officials.

In 1958, Malcolm married the former Betty Sanders, another member of the NOI whom he knew through his work with the temple in Harlem. They had six daughters: Attallah in 1958; Qubilah in 1960; Ilyasah in 1962; Gamilah in 1964; and Malaak and Malikah, twins born after Malcolm's death in 1965.

In 1959, WCBS-TV news reporter Mike Wallace introduced Malcolm X to the nation in an exposé entitled "The Hate the Hate Produced." Offering an explanation of the NOI's appeal echoed by both white and black liberals, including the Reverend Martin Luther King, Jr., and scholar C. Eric Lincoln, Wallace depicted the NOI as the sad, dysfunctional product of poor American race relations. The NOI became a symbol of the need for stronger civil rights legislation that would guarantee legal equality.

Handsome, fiery, and articulate, Malcolm became a favorite on various TV and radio shows in the early 1960s. Attacked by whites and those whom Malcolm called "Uncle Tom Negroes," he was Elijah Muhammad's most committed defender and spokesman. He rejected the idea of racial integration with the "white devil," instead telling African Americans to rely only on themselves for their salvation. An uncompromising critic of racism, Malcolm's critics called him the "angriest Negro in America."

BREAKING AWAY

Among Elijah Muhammad's critics were AFRICAN-AMERICAN MUSLIMS and Muslim immigrants from abroad who rejected

Born Malcolm Little, Malcolm X became a central figure in the civil rights era. Converting to Islam first as a member of the Nation of Islam in the late 1940s, he became a Sunni Muslim in 1964, went on pilgrimage to Mecca, and changed his name to El Hajj Malik El-Shabazz. He was assassinated in 1965. *(Library of Congress)*

the NOI's doctrinal teachings about the divinity of W. D. FARD and Elijah Muhammad's status as a prophet. The same foreign Muslim students who would support the founding of the MUSLIM STUDENTS ASSOCIATION in 1963 confronted Malcolm along the college lecture circuit, trying to protect the image of Islam, as they understood it, from the likes of Elijah Muhammad.

In 1963, though Malcolm stalwartly defended Elijah Muhammad against his critics in the *New York Times Magazine,* it was already clear that he was questioning certain elements of NOI teachings. During March 3 and May 12 media appearances in Chicago and Washington, Malcolm said, for example, that whites were not devils because of who they were—that is, their genes—but because of what they did—that is, their abuse of black people.

When later that year it was discovered that Elijah Muhammad, who preached sexual restraint and monogamy, had fathered several children with his young secretaries, Malcolm rebelled. On December 1, 1963, he disobeyed

Muhammad's directive that all NOI ministers remain silent on the November 22, 1963, assassination of President John F. Kennedy. Speaking to the press, Malcolm said that the murder was the "chickens coming home to roost."

On December 4, 1963, the NOI suspended Malcolm from his duties as a spokesman for Elijah Muhammad. Three months later, on March 8, 1964, Malcolm officially announced his independence from Muhammad at the Park Sheraton Hotel in New York. He revealed his plan to create a new mosque called Muslim Mosque, Inc., and at a speech at Harvard University on March 18, he stated that black nationalism was still needed to solve the problem of racism.

THE FINAL YEAR

Reaching out to immigrant and foreign Muslims who had previously criticized him, Malcolm sought to learn more about Sunni Islam. On April 13, 1964, after making connections with supporters of the Muslim World League, a Saudi-financed missionary organization, Malcolm set out on the pilgrimage to Mecca, a journey movingly described in his autobiography. Becoming an official guest of the Saudi Arabian state, Malcolm was overwhelmed by the hospitality of his hosts, including Prince Faysal, who granted him an audience.

During his pilgrimage, Malcolm adopted a new name: El-Hajj Malik El-Shabazz. Like many who performed the hajj, Malcolm took on the honorific title hajji, or one who has made the pilgrimage. He translated Malcolm to Malik and embraced a new last name, Shabazz, after the black tribe of Shabazz that Elijah Muhammad had taught originally inhabited Mecca. Though non-Muslims would continue to refer to him as Malcolm X, many Muslim Americans, especially African-American Sunni Muslims, used his new name henceforth as a sign of respect and recognition.

As he circumambulated the Ka'ba in Mecca and performed the other rituals of the hajj, Malcolm was exposed to the multiracial nature of the worldwide community of Muslims. He wrote to his wife Betty and his followers, sharing the news that he had broken bread with blue-eyed, white Muslims. He praised Islam's ability to create racial equality and unity among its believers. Islam, he said, seemed to erase racial prejudice from the hearts of human beings.

Though Malcolm no longer believed that the white man was literally the devil, a teaching that he had already started to question publicly long before his official break with Elijah Muhammad, he remained convinced that America was a racist, inhospitable country for black people. On Mt. Arafat, the place from which Muslim pilgrims asked to be forgiven for their sins, Malcolm preached to his fellow Muslims about the "evils and indignities that are suffered by the black man in America." Indeed, though Malcolm was convinced that Islam could rid humanity of racial prejudice and discrimination, he also said that most blacks and whites in America were unlikely to become Muslims.

He was now committed to the same basic teachings of Islam as his Saudi hosts and other Sunni Muslims around the world, but he disagreed with many of them about the liberating potential of Islamic religion for political life. The problems of black people, he said, "go beyond religion."

Instead, Malcolm looked to sub-Saharan Africa for inspiration to create black self-determination in the United States. From Mecca and Medina, Malcolm flew to Beirut, Lebanon, on April 30, 1964, then to Lagos, Nigeria, on May 8. Two days later, he became a guest of Kwame Nkrumah, president of Ghana. Then he visited Senegal, Morocco, and Algeria. Praising the newly independent African states and basking in a welcome that went, as he wrote, "beyond words," Malcolm said that African Americans must join the movement of formerly colonized peoples in Africa and Asia for true independence.

Finally returning home on May 21, 1964, Malcolm became a leading advocate of pan-Africanism, the movement to unite all people of African descent in a common struggle for economic, political, and social liberation. On June 28, he established the Organization of Afro-American Unity (OAAU), which was to cooperate with the Organization of African Unity. Malcolm asked his allies from abroad to help him convince the United Nations to take up the cause of African Americans.

During the spring and summer, Malcolm and former colleagues in the NOI, including Minister LOUIS FARRAKHAN, traded jabs about his break from the movement. Malcolm publicly criticized his mentor, Elijah Muhammad, and Muhammad's followers responded by calling Malcolm a hypocrite. Malcolm's friends advised him to leave the country again because of the death threats he was receiving. On July 6, he left for Cairo, and there, on July 17, 1964, attended the African Summit Conference as a representative of his OAAU. He remained in Cairo through August, meeting with Egyptian officials, including the Supreme Council of Islamic Affairs, which granted him 20 scholarships so that some of his followers could study at the University of al-Azhar, one of most prestigious seminaries in the Islamic world.

In September, Malcolm performed an 'umra, or lesser pilgrimage, to Mecca, where he was hosted by the Muslim World League and offered training as a Muslim missionary. Malcolm maintained throughout this period that "my fight is two-fold, my burden is double, my responsibilities multiple." He meant to be both a Muslim leader and a black leader in the United States and saw these tasks as complementary but separate. African Americans would not convert to Islam en masse, he maintained, and he must find other tools in the struggle for freedom besides Islam.

After traveling to sub-Saharan Africa another time and meeting with 11 heads of state, Malcolm finally returned to New York on November 24, 1964. For the next couple of months, Malcolm maintained his usual frenetic schedule, giving speeches at various colleges and making a number of public appearances. He also attempted to nurture the growth of the OAAU and the Muslim Mosque and welcomed the placement of a Saudi-funded missionary in his nascent Muslim religious community. Surprisingly few donations, however, were forthcoming during a series of February talks in New York, and Malcolm worried about the future of these organizations.

HIS ASSASSINATION AND HIS LEGACY

Malcolm's life ended before this phase of his career could flower. On February 21, 1965, former NOI member Talmadge Hayer gunned down Malcolm as he was making a speech at the Audubon Ballroom in Harlem; Norman 3X Butler and Thomas 15X Johnson were also convicted for the murder, though they—and Hayer—maintained their innocence over the next three decades. Though Elijah Muhammad was never accused of the murder, Louis Farrakhan (who later formed his own version of the Nation of Islam) apologized in 2000 for helping to create the poisonous atmosphere that led to Malcolm's death.

Many African Americans believed that the FBI was complicit in the assassination. While the FBI defended itself against such charges, it is possible, if not probable that the FBI knew about the assassination and did nothing to stop it. Malcolm, like other black nationalist leaders of the time, was officially designated as an enemy of the state, and the FBI kept a close watch on him, as his FBI file makes clear. In addition to running surveillance on Malcolm, the FBI also had informants and even agents inside the NOI, a fact that has led many scholars to conclude that the FBI may have had information about the plots against his life.

If the assassins hoped to silence Malcolm's voice, however, they failed. In many ways, Malcolm became more powerful in death than he was in life. Only months after his assassination, journalist Alex Haley, his coauthor, released *The Autobiography of Malcolm X*, which, along with Franz Fanon's *Wretched of the Earth*, became a manifesto of the Black Power movement in the late 1960s. Malcolm was also adopted as the patron saint of young black leaders such as JAMIL ABDULLAH AL-AMIN, who, rejecting the middle-class Civil Rights movement, focused on the problems of black poverty, police violence, and extralegal discrimination.

Echoing Malcolm's simultaneous focus on local activism and international vision, these Black Power advocates rejected the legitimacy of the American nation-state, opposed the Vietnam War, armed themselves against police violence, fed the poor, and opened schools, all the while celebrating their history and heritage as people of African descent. Malcolm's image would remain potent in black American culture for the rest of the 20th century.

Malcolm's legacy for Muslims in the United States was similarly profound. African-American Sunni Muslims, or those who became Sunnis, were inspired by Malcolm's journey from the Nation of Islam to Sunni Islam. Seeing in him someone who triumphed over adversity and found the truth, Muslims in the United States adopted Malcolm as a model. W. D. MOHAMMED, leader of the NOI after Elijah Muhammad's death in 1975, named Temple No. 7 after Malcolm to honor his contributions to the movement.

But Malcolm's legacy was also relevant to the American people as a whole. His life had exposed the failures of a Civil Rights movement that, as Martin Luther King, Jr., admitted in the middle 1960s, put its hopes primarily in legal equality and voting rights. Malcolm taught that economic, social, and psychological reforms were all essential elements in the struggle for equality. Conservatives, liberals, and leftists alike would echo his views by the 1970s.

Malcolm X also became part of the pantheon of black historical figures who forced America to confront its past as a nation founded as much in slavery as in freedom. Malcolm's dramatic life story, enshrined in his now classic autobiography, echoed the enduring theme that Americans could reinvent themselves in their struggle for self-fulfillment, but reminded readers as well that their individual lives would always be tied to the lives of others.

Edward E. Curtis IV

Further Reading

Carson, Clayborne. *Malcolm X: The FBI File*. New York: Carroll & Graf, 1991.

Curtis, Edward E., IV. *Islam in Black America: Identity, Liberation, and Difference in African-American Islamic Thought*. Albany: State University of New York Press, 2002.

DeCaro, Louis A., Jr. *On the Side of My People: A Religious Life of Malcolm X*. New York: New York University Press, 1996.

Malcolm X, with Alex Haley. *The Autobiography of Malcolm X*. New York: Ballantine Books, 1987.

Malcolm X with Mrs. Fannie Lou Hamer (1964)

On December 20, 1964, African-American Muslim leader Malcolm X (1925–65), also known as El Hajj Malik El-Shabazz, spoke at a Harlem rally in support of Fannie Lou Hamer, the leader of Mississippi's Freedom Democratic political party. After hearing Hamer recount incidents of discrimination and violence that she had suffered at the hands of whites, Malcolm X rose to address the crowd at the Williams Institutional CME Church in Harlem. Obviously enraged, Malcolm restated his famous cry that blacks must be liberated "by any means necessary." His remarks, given approximately two months before his assassination, illustrate his ceaseless campaign in the last year of his life for a unified black response to antiblack violence and oppression. Though he believed that Islam was a religion that guaranteed racial equality, he said that the problems of American racism "went beyond religion" and required an uncompromising political response from people of African descent, wherever they resided.

When I listen to Mrs. Hamer, a black woman—could be my mother, my sister, my daughter—describe what they had done to her in Mississippi, I ask myself how in the world can we ever expect to be respected as men when we will allow something like that to be done to our women, and we do nothing about it? How can you and I be looked upon as men with black women being beaten and nothing being done about it, black children and black babies being beaten and nothing being done about it? No, we don't deserve to be recognized and respected as men as long as our women can be brutalized in the manner that this woman described, and nothing being done about it, but we sit around singing "We Shall Overcome". . . .

When I was in Africa, I noticed some of the Africans got their freedom faster than others. Some areas of the African continent became independent faster than other areas. I noticed that in the areas where independence had been gotten, someone got angry. And in the areas where independence had not been achieved yet, no one was angry. They were sad—they'd sit around and talk about their plight, but they weren't mad. And usually, when people are sad, they don't do anything. They just cry over their condition.

But when they get angry, they bring about a change. When they get angry, they aren't interested in logic, they aren't interested in odds, they aren't interested in consequences. When they get angry, they realize the condition that they're in—that their suffering is unjust, immoral, illegal, and that anything they do to correct it or eliminate it, they're justified. When you and I develop that type of anger and speak in that voice, then we'll get some kind of respect and recognition, and some changes from these people who have been promising us falsely already for far too long.

So you have to speak their language. The language that they were speaking to Mrs. Hamer was the language of brutality. Beasts, they were, beating her. . . . And when you and I begin to look at him and see the language he speaks, the language of a brute, the language of someone who has no sense of morality, who absolutely ignores law—when you and I learn how to speak his language, then we can communicate. But we will never communicate talking one language while he's talking another language—and think that he's going to understand.

Let's learn his language. If his language is with a shotgun, get a shotgun. Yes, I said if he only understands the language of a rifle, get a rifle. If he only understands the language of a rope, get a rope. But don't waste time talking the wrong language to a man if you want to really communicate with him. Speak his language—there's nothing wrong with that. If something was wrong with that language, the federal government would have stopped the cracker from speaking it to you and me. . . .

The brothers and sisters in Mississippi are being beaten and killed for no reason other than they want to be treated as first-class citizens. There's only one way to be a first-class citizen. There's only one way to be independent. There's only one way to be free. It's not something that someone gives to you. It's something that you take. Nobody can give you independence. Nobody can give you freedom. Nobody can give you equality or justice or anything. If you're a man, you take it. If you can't take it, you don't deserve it. Nobody can give it to you. So if you and I want freedom, if we want independence, if we want respect, if we want recognition, we obey the law, we are peaceful—but at the same time, at any moment that you and I are involved in any kind of action that is legal, that is in accord with our civil rights, in accord with the courts of this land, in accord with the Constitution—when all of these things are on our side, and we still can't get it, it's because we aren't on our own side.

We don't yet realize the real price necessary to pay to see that these things are enforced where we're concerned. And until we realize this, they won't be enforced where we're concerned. We have to let the people in Mississippi as well as in Mississippi, New York, and elsewhere know that freedom comes to us either by ballots or by bullets. That's the only way freedom is gotten. Freedom is gotten by ballots or bullets. These are the only two avenues, the only two roads, the only two methods, the only two means—either ballots or bullets. And when you know that, then you are careful how you use the word freedom. As long as you think we are going to sing up on some, you come in and sing. I watch you, those of you who are singing—are you also willing to do some swinging?

They've always said that I'm anti-white. I'm for anybody who's for freedom. I'm for anybody who's for justice. I'm for anybody who's for equality. I'm not for anybody who tells me to sit around and wait for mine. I'm not for anybody who tells me to turn the other cheek when a cracker is busting up my jaw. I'm not for anybody who tells black people to be nonviolent while nobody is telling white people to be nonviolent. I know I'm in the church, I probably shouldn't be talking like this—but Jesus himself was ready to turn the synagogue inside out and upside down when things weren't going right. In fact, in the Book of Revelations, they've got Jesus sitting on a horse with a sword in his hand, getting ready to go into action. But they don't tell you or me about that Jesus. They only tell you and me about that peaceful Jesus. They never let you get down to the end of the book. They keep you up there where everything is, you know, nonviolent. No, go and read the whole book, and when you get to Revelations, you'll find that even Jesus' patience ran out. And when his patience ran out, he got the whole situation straightened out. He picked up the sword.

I believe that there are some white people who might be sincere. But I think they should prove it. And you can't prove it to me by singing with me. You can't prove it to me by being nonviolent. No, you can prove it by recognizing the law of justice. And the law of justice is "as ye sow, so shall ye reap." The law of justice is "he who kills by the sword shall be killed by the sword." This is justice. Now if you are with us, all I say is, make the same kind of contribution with us in our struggle for freedom that all white people have always made when they were struggling for their own freedom. You were struggling for your freedom in the Revolutionary War. Your own Patrick Henry said "liberty or death," and George Washington got the cannons out, and all the rest of them that you taught me to worship as my heroes, they were fighters, they were warriors.

But now when the time comes for our freedom, you want to reach back in the bag and grab somebody who's nonviolent and peaceful and forgiving and long-suffering. I don't go for that—no. I say that a black man's freedom is as valuable as a white man's freedom. And I say that a black man has the right to do whatever is necessary to get his freedom that other human beings have done to get their freedom. I say that you and I will never get our freedom nonviolently and patiently and lovingly. We will never get it until we let the world know that as other human beings have laid down their lives for freedom—and also taken life for freedom—that you and I are ready and willing and equipped and qualified to do the same thing.

It's a shame that Mrs. Hamer came out here this afternoon where there are so few people. It's a shame. All of our people in Harlem should have heard her describe what they did to her down there. Because I think the people in Harlem are more capable of evening the score than people are anywhere else in this country. Yes, they are, and they need to hear her story. They need to know more, first hand, about what's happening down there, especially to our women. And then they need some lessons in tactics and strategy on how to get even. I, for one, will make the first contribution to any fund that's raised for the purpose of evening the score. Whenever someone commits murder, what do you do? You put out a "reward, wanted—dead or alive" for the murderer. Yes, learn how to do it. We've had three people murdered. No reward has been put on the head of the murderer. Don't just put a reward—put "dead or alive, dead or alive." And let that [Ku Klux] Klan know that we can do it tit for tat, tit for tat. What's good for the goose is good for the gander.

And if you all don't want to do it, we'll do it. We'll do it. We have brothers who are equipped, and who are qualified, and who are willing to—As Jesus said, "Little children, go thee where I send thee." We have brothers who can do that, and who will do that, and who are ready to do that. And I say that if the government of the United States cannot bring to justice people who murder Negroes, or people who murder those who are at the forefront fighting in behalf of Negroes, then it's time for you and me to retire quietly to our closets and devise means and methods of seeing that justice is executed against murderers where justice has not been forthcoming in the past.

I say in my conclusion that if you and I here in Harlem, who form the habit ofttimes of fighting each other, who sneak around trying to wait for an opportunity to throw some acid or some lye on each other, or sprinkle dist on each other's doorsteps—if you and I were really and truly for the freedom of our people, we wouldn't waste all of that energy thinking how to do harm to each other. Since you have that ingenuity, if you know how to do it, let me know; I'll give you some money and show you where to go, and show you who to do it to. And then you'll go down in history as having done an honorable thing.

Source: "With Mrs. Fannie Lou Hamer." *Malcolm X Speaks*, edited by George Breitman. New York: Grove Weidenfeld, 1990, pp. 107–108, 111–114.

Mamout, Yarrow (Mamout Yarrow or Mahmoud Yaro) (ca. 1736–1823) *slave, entrepreneur, portrait subject*

Yarrow Mamout, a Muslim born around 1736 in what is now the West African nation of Guinea, was possibly of Fulbe (Fulani) lineage. Literate in ARABIC and trained in Islamic studies, Mamout was captured and brought to America as a slave when he was approximately 14 years old. Purchased by Samuel Beall (or Bell) of Montgomery County, Maryland, Mamout was later inherited by Samuel's son, Brooke. He worked for the Beall family for nearly the entire second half of the 18th century; Brooke Beall promised Mamout his freedom when he finished making bricks for a new house in Georgetown, a neighborhood of Washington, D.C.

According to a report in *A Chorographical and Statistical Description of the District of Columbia* (1816), Mamout told General John Mason of Analostan Island (now Theodore Roosevelt Island), located in the Potomac River in Washington, D.C., in 1811 that he had convinced Beall that his working days were over: "Olda massa been tink he got all de work out of a Yaro bone. He tell a Yaro, go free Yaro; you been work nuff for me, go work for you now," Mamout said. Brooke Beall died before the house was completed, but Margaret Beall, his widow, freed Mamout, as promised, in 1796.

Within four years of gaining his freedom, Yarrow purchased a house and lot in what is now Dent Place in Georgetown. He saved enough money to secure his retirement, hiring himself out in the day for wages, then weaving baskets and nets at night. According to Mamout, "Yaro work a soon, a late, a hot, a cold. Sometime he sweat. Sometime he blow a finger." Twice he saved $100 for his retirement and entrusted it to ship captains. Each time the money was lost—one captain died broke and the other went bankrupt. But Yarrow earned another $200 and, after receiving advice on the matter, put his money in the stock of the Columbia Bank, founded by Alexander Hamilton in 1771. The proceeds allowed him to live in relative comfort to the end of his days.

Much of what is known about Mamout comes from the painter Charles Willson Peale (1741–1827), a renowned portrait painter of prominent politicians, who asked Mamout to sit for his portrait in 1819. Peale was intrigued when he heard a rumor that Mamout was 140 years old. The inflated age seems to have been the product of a cultural misunderstanding. According to Margaret Beall, Yarrow counted his own age based on the ISLAMIC CALENDAR, a lunar calendar, rather than on the Gregorian (solar) calendar—an estimate that likely led to miscalculations. Mamout was in his 80s at the time, according to the Beall estate records.

In producing what has been called one of the most sensitive portraits of an African American in the 19th century, Peale spent two days with Mamout, and spoke to the

Yarrow Mamout was a slave for almost half a century. After gaining his freedom in 1796, he became an entrepreneur, investor, and landholder in Washington, D.C. In 1819, artist Charles Willson Peale painted his portrait. *(Courtesy of Historical Society of Pennsylvania Collection, The Bridgeman Art Library)*

Beall family and others who knew him. Peale wrote in his diary that Mamout had a "good temper," was a sober man, and "professes to be a mahometan [Muslim]." According to Peale, Mamout was "often seen & heard in the Streets singing Praises to God—and conversing with him." Mamout told Peale that "man is no good unless his religion comes from the heart." Though General Mason reported that Mamout would shoot a gun on Christmas day to get a dram of alcohol, Mamout told Peale that "it is no good to eat Hog—& drink whiskey is very bad."

Peale, whose painting is owned by the Historical Society of Pennsylvania, was not the only painter to render a portrait of Mamout. A second, by James Alexander Simpson, hangs in the Peabody Room of the Georgetown Library. The second portrait, completed three years after the Peale painting, is said by critics to be a more lifelike portrait of Mamout since it depicts his clothes as worn and includes more blemishes on his face.

Mamout died on January 19, 1823. According to his obituary, which appeared in the *Gettysburg Compiler* on February 23, 1823, Mamout was buried "in the corner of his garden, the spot where he usually resorted to pray." He had a son, Aquilla Yarrow, who died in 1832. Yarrow also had a sister whose name was not known. Her daughter, Yarrow's niece, Nancy Hillman, died in 1843. Yarrow's name survived into modern times as Aquilla's wife, Mary (or Polly) Turner Yarrow, was a midwife in the area of Washington County, Maryland, in which she lived. That area, which was named after her, is now known as Yarrowsburg.

Tahira Abdul-Jalil

Further Reading

Allan D. Austin. *African Muslims in Antebellum America*. New York: Routledge, 1997.

Gomez, Michael A. *Black Crescent: The Experience and Legacy of African Muslims in the Americas*. Cambridge: Cambridge University Press, 2005.

Johnston, James H. "The Man in the Knit Cap," *Washington Post*, 5 February 2006, p. W16. Available online. URL: http://www. washingtonpost.com/wpdyn/content/article/2006/02/03/ AR2006020300827_4.html. Accessed April 7, 2009.

Turner, Richard Brent. *Islam in the African-American Experience*. Bloomington: Indiana University Press, 2003.

marriage

Since the first Muslims arrived as slaves in the Thirteen Colonies, marriage has been a highly meaningful institution among Muslim Americans. Throughout the 20th century, the practices associated with marriage—from how one should meet a spouse to what kind of dress should be worn on the wedding day—became diverse. By the late 20th and early 21st centuries, marriage was understood inside Muslim-American communities as an overall barometer for the moral character and social vigor of the community, which sought to encourage, protect, and nurture what it long considered to be a vital social institution.

MARRIAGE ACCORDING TO ISLAMIC SHARI'A

Historically speaking, marriage in Muslim lands has often been treated as a social institution governed by SHARI'A, or Islamic LAW and ethics, that involves the making of a legal contract guaranteeing the rights of both husband and wife. According to the shari'a, MEN may marry non-Muslim women who were "People of the Book," that is, Christians, Jews, and others. WOMEN were not supposed to marry non-Muslim men, since in Islam the religious identity of children is determined by the religion of the father. Men were allowed to take up to four wives, though they had to treat their wives equally financially, emotionally, and sexually. Women could include in the contract stipulations to secure rights within marriage, including the right to religious DIVORCE, to work outside the home, and to clarify how housework would be shared. Marriage contracts included *mahr*, money that the groom paid to the bride. That money remained hers if her husband divorced her or if she divorced him because he harmed her.

MUSLIM MARRIAGE IN SLAVERY

One of the earliest Muslim marriages of record in the United States took place in 1794 or 1795 when Muslim slave ABDUL RAHMAN IBRAHIMA (ca. 1762–1829) married a fellow slave, Isabella, in Natchez, Mississippi. Isabella was Baptist, and together the couple reportedly attended Christian religious services, though Ibrahima seemed to have remained a Muslim. Ibrahima may or may not have been able to choose whether to attend these services, but his attendance explains why his children understood themselves to be Christians rather than Muslims.

Sometime in the late 18th or early 19th century, BILALI OF SAPELO ISLAND (ca. 1760–1859) married a woman named Phoebe and raised a family of 12 sons and seven daughters with her. Bilali was an overseer of hundreds of slaves along the GEORGIA seacoast and a veteran of the War of 1812. Partly because of his relative privilege and isolation from the mainland, he likely raised his children either to practice Islam or at least to identify with their Muslim heritage.

Because slave marriages were constantly broken apart by masters who sold a husband or wife with little or no regard for the feelings of the spouses, it is likely that many Muslim slaves in the United States formally and informally married several times. There is no evidence to indicate that shari'a guidelines governing marriage were observed, at least not on a wide scale by the thousands of Muslim slaves.

EARLY SYRIAN-AMERICAN MARRIAGES IN THE MIDWEST

In the late 19th and early 20th centuries, some Syrian and Lebanese married couples such as the Juma family of Ross, NORTH DAKOTA, immigrated to the United States together. But in many other instances, women in the Middle East were discouraged from immigrating, and men, Muslims and Christians alike, came alone to seek what they believed would be riches in America and then return with their newfound wealth to the Old Country. According to a 1915 article in *Al-Bayan,* an American ARABIC-language newspaper founded in NEW YORK CITY by members of the DRUZE COMMUNITY, some men left their wives behind in their villages and took second wives in America. Although it is unknown how many men abandoned their first wives for American spouses, the newspaper condemned the practice.

Some single Muslim men married non-Muslim women. In North Dakota, for example, several mixed marriages between Muslim men and Irish-Catholic women took place. The same pattern also obtained for many early SOUTH ASIAN–AMERICAN MUSLIM male immigrants who married Roman Catholic Latinas in California and Spanish Harlem in New York City. These men cited several reasons for mixed marriages beyond the fact that few Muslim women were available. An example is the case of Abe, a SHI'A MUSLIM AMERICAN whose last name was withheld by author Alixa Naff in her book, *Becoming American* (1985). He married a Polish woman in 1933, explaining that he did not want to pay *mahr.* "This is America," he said. "If we love each other, we should marry, but they [the parents of prospective brides] asked and asked [for money]. Because of that, I did not marry a Syrian girl." According to Kahlil Bazzy, a sheikh, or leader, in Highland Park, Michigan, men did not marry Muslim women because they were not allowed to date them, whereas they could date Christian women.

MARRIAGE AFTER 1965

Muslim-American marriages after 1965 reflected the expanding diversity of the Muslim-American community in this period of tremendous growth. In addition to the multi-generational Arab, South Asian, and African-American Muslim communities, the IMMIGRATION ACT OF 1965 led to the immigration of approximately 1 million new Muslims to the United States from 1968 to the 2000. Many of them were Arab and South Asian, though Iranians, sub-Saharan Africans, southeastern Europeans, Southeast Asians, and other Muslims came in significant numbers as well. The presence of a Muslim community that was diverse by language, national origin, class, ethnicity, and generation translated into sometimes vastly different ideas about marriage.

Dating

Most Muslim-American religious leaders in the 20th century, regardless of sect or ethnicity, frowned on DATING as a religiously acceptable practice. In the NATION OF ISLAM (NOI), for example, if male or female members were caught dating, and even worse, fornicating, they would often be tried by their local mosque and suspended or expelled from the group. The NOI's socially conservative approach to dating was echoed in the era of religious revivalism in the 1970s, as many Sunni and Shi'a immigrant imams, or religious leaders, cited dating and sex out of wedlock as one of the evil aspects of American society.

Despite religious prohibitions, many Muslim Americans in the second half of the 20th century dated anyway. Some completely ignored the taboo of sex before marriage, while others were careful to marry before having sexual intercourse with their spouse. Some religious leaders, concerned about Muslims marrying non-Muslims, encouraged a form of chaperoned, religious dating, often sponsored by a mosque or Muslim organization.

In the early 21st century, mosques such as the All Dulles Area Muslim Society in Sterling, Virginia, created singles programs and premarital counseling. The MUSLIM ALLIANCE IN NORTH AMERICA, an African-American Sunni Muslim group, expressed concern about couples rushing into marriage to have sex or because individuals lacked communities to screen potential spouses. In 2008, an Alliance spokesperson argued that couples should be encouraged to date before marrying. Secular Muslims were more comfortable dating but often were still interested in meeting a Muslim spouse. They, like many other Americans, used INTERNET dating sites in which they might meet potential mates.

Weddings

Both before and after 1965, Muslim-American WEDDINGS did not follow any one ceremonial protocol. Because there were few religious protocols on Muslim wedding ceremonies, brides, grooms, and their families were free to choose among a variety of ritual options. At times, these followed the ethnic rituals of first-generation immigrants from places such as Bosnia or India. At other times, they were completely American in nature. In the Nation of Islam, for example, brides in the middle 1970s often wore elaborate, frilly wedding gowns with veils; grooms donned a tuxedo; and the couple was inevitably pictured jointly cutting a large wedding cake, generally baked by one of the NOI's many professional bakeries.

After 1965, Muslim brides who traced their ethnic roots to Arab, South Asian, or East African cultural traditions sometimes had their hands and feet decorated with henna a night or two before the wedding. This practice then spread to the rest of the Muslim-American community, becoming increasingly popular by the first decade of the 21st century with indigenous

Wedding of Harvey 2X and Marjorie X, 1972. Harvey 2X and Marjorie X cut their wedding cake—made with whole wheat flour in accordance with Nation of Islam dietary laws—during their wedding reception at Muhammad's Mosque No. 4 in Washington, D.C. After becoming Sunni Muslims in 1975, the couple became known as Ahmad and Marjorie Karim, names that were given to them by religious leader W. D. Mohammed. *(Photograph Courtesy of Jamillah Karim)*

Muslims. Generally all-female events, the henna party became a ritual of sisterly solidarity with the bride.

Though Muslim Americans have not traditionally exchanged wedding vows—which is accomplished by the signing of the wedding contract—they have held wedding celebrations of various sorts. Muslim-American wedding receptions, which can be separated by gender depending on the religious orientation, ethnicity, and class of the couple's friends and family, have included dancing and serving food to guests. Participants have worn a variety of outfits, often blending various forms of indigenous and immigrant styles of dress. Dancing at weddings can include the dabka, or Arab line dance, and the Electric Slide, a now venerable American tradition.

Polygamy

Though polygamy is against the law in the United States, and most mosques and Muslim-American organizations have discouraged the practice, it has been estimated that by the early 21st century, there were 50,000 to 100,000 Muslim

Americans living in polygamous households (including children). Generally speaking, men engaged in polygamy avoided confrontation with authorities by having one civil marriage and additional religious marriages. Polygamous marriages have led to the abuse or neglect of women in several cases, though some women have reported that they are highly satisfied with their husbands and gain contentment through their relationships with their fellow wives. Muslim-American women's activists such as Aziza al-Hibri and Daisy Khan encouraged Muslim women to add stipulations against polygamy to their marriage contracts, thus preventing their husbands from taking additional wives.

Healthy Marriages

Echoing general trends in American publishing, a huge religious literature has poured forth from various Muslim-American media about how to strengthen one's marriage. Marriage had been depicted as an aspect of life in which religious teachings are extremely relevant. Some Muslim-American women, for example, have used their own readings of the Qur'an and the hadith, or reports of the saying and deeds of the prophet Muhammad and his companions, to battle traditional American and Muslim notions about the privileges of husbands. Though PROGRESSIVE MUSLIMS of both genders have been at the forefront of calling for gender equality inside marriages—in addition to calling for the institution of marriage to be extended to LESBIAN, GAY, BISEXUAL, AND TRANSGENDER MUSLIMS—many socially conservative Muslim Americans have continued to assert the right of men to be the leaders of households.

Whether socially conservative or liberal, however, Muslim Americans in the first decade of the 21st century were unified in their absolute rejection of domestic violence. In 2005, for example, the MUSLIM ALLIANCE IN NORTH AMERICA (MANA) introduced the Healthy Marriage Initiative, designed to combat the presence of "broken homes, spousal abuse, children raised by one parent, and emotional turmoil in the community." In 2009, MANA was one of many organizations that reacted strongly to the murder of Bridges-TV cofounder Aasiya Hassan by her husband. Calling for a zero-tolerance policy for domestic violence, ISLAMIC SOCIETY OF NORTH AMERICA Vice President Mohamed Hagmagid Ali outlined a series of steps that all Muslim Americans, and particularly male imams, must take to prevent domestic violence and protect its victims.

CONCLUSION

During the several centuries of Muslim-American history, the meanings and functions of marriage have varied considerably. Struggling to protect their marriages and their families from the threat of sale and other violence, Muslim-American slaves were denied basic human rights to life and liberty. Muslim-American male immigrants who came by choice to the United States in the late 19th and early 20th centuries often married non-Muslim women because there were few Muslim women to marry. The proliferation of Muslim-American converts from the 1920s onward and the increased immigration of Muslims after 1965 led to the widely held sense that marrying another Muslim was vital to the perpetuation of Muslim-American identity, however one defined it. Marriage became a symbol for the health of the community as a whole, even as it was practiced and interpreted in a variety of ways.

Samira Mehta with Hanifa Abdul Sabur

Further Reading

Abdul-Ghafur, Saleemahm, ed. *Living Islam Out Loud: American Muslim Women Speak.* Boston: Beacon Press, 2005.

Abugideiri, S. "A Perspective on Domestic Violence in the Muslim Community." *Working Together* (Fall 2005): 1–4.

Alford, Terry. *Prince among Slaves: The True Story of an African Prince Sold into Slavery in the American South.* New York: Harcourt Brace Jovanovich, 1977.

Aswad, Barbara C., and Barbara Bilgé, eds. *Family and Gender among American Muslims: Issues Facing Middle Eastern Immigrants and their Descendants.* Philadelphia: Temple University Press, 1996.

Cateura, Linda Brandi. *Voices of American Muslims: 23 Profiles.* New York: Hippocrene Books, 2005.

Majeed, Debra Mubashshir. "The Battle Has Been Joined: Gay and Polygynous Marriages Are Out of the Closet and in Search of Legitimacy." *Cross Currents* 54, no. 2 (2004): 73–81.

Naff, Alixa. *Becoming American: The Early Arab Immigrant Experience.* Carbondale: Southern Illinois University Press, 1985.

Rouse, Carolyn Moxley. *Engaged Surrender: African American Women and Islam.* Berkeley: University of California Press, 2004.

Salaam, Aliyyah. "Children of Polygamy Speak." *Azizah* (Summer 2002): 106.

Matrimonials from *Islamic Horizons* (2007)

Islamic Horizons, the attractive glossy magazine of the Islamic Society of North America (ISNA), includes news about the ISNA, the largest Islamic organization in the United States, articles on various aspects of Muslim-American life, opinion pieces, personality profiles, book reviews, and advertisements of Islamic finance companies, food suppliers, and Muslim children's literature. It also features a matrimonials section in which prospective brides and grooms can advertise for a wife or husband—much like other Americans use personal ads in weekly newspapers to find marriage or romance. A large percentage of these advertisements are placed by highly educated, upwardly mobile Muslim Americans, often from a South Asian background. One explanation for the predominance of South Asian–American Muslims in this forum is the cost; South Asian–American Muslims are among the wealthiest of all Muslim-American ethnic groups and can thus afford to place such ads. Another factor may be that many South Asian–American Muslims live in isolated suburbs, where the pool of available spouses is smaller than it would be if they lived in ethnic enclaves such as Dearborn, Michigan. A final reason, apparent in the ads themselves, is that many of these persons are looking to marry someone of the same educational, ethnic, religious, and class background.

And of His signs is this; He created for you
  spouses
From yourselves that you might find peace in
  them,
And He ordained between you love and mercy.
Lo, herein indeed are signs for people who
  reflect.
(Qur'an 30:21)

Seeking Husband

Hyderabadi Sunni Muslim physician parents seek MD husband for their 24 year old daughter (3rd year medical student in Chicago, IL). Wears hijab.

Sunni Muslim Indian parents invite correspondence for their U.S.-born/raised daughter, 28, medical resident, from a medical doctor or professional, 28–32.

Sunni Muslim moderately religious parents invite correspondence for their Pakistan-raised daughter, 30, pretty, fair, 5'4", M.A., residing in CA, from highly educated Muslim professionals with strong family background.

Sunni Muslim Indian parents invite correspondence from professional or medical doctor for their U.S.-born/raised physician daughter, pretty, religious, in final year of residency program.

Middle Eastern parents of a hijab-wearing daughter, beautiful, 27 years old, U.S.-born and resident MD, looking for religious, 27–33, dynamic, and ambitious MD/professional.

Sunni Muslim parents of a U.S.-educated and citizen daughter, MD, second-year resident, invite correspondence from moderately religious professionals under 30.

Parents invite photo and correspondence for their U.S.-born daughter, 28, very accomplished, attractive, well-traveled, and outgoing lawyer who wears hijab.

Sunni Muslim Hyderabadi parent of hijab-wearing daughter, 22, citizen, and college junior invite correspondence from doctors/masters, practicing Muslims.

Parents of college-going educated daughters, 20 and 22, seek correspondence from never married, educated professionals, 25–28, religiously oriented, Pakistani origin. Family values are a must. Send resume and photo.

Sunni Muslim parents invite correspondence for their U.S. born/raised-daughter, 25, beautiful and tall, student at a prestigious medical school, from a practicing, highly educated professional.

Sunni Muslim Indo/Pak parents of U.S.-raised daughter, 26, law graduate from a prestigious U.S. university, invite correspondence from a professional Muslim, 26–29, of similar background.

Sunni Muslim Indiana-origin parents invite correspondence for their daughter 23, 5′5″, wears hijab, third-year MD student at a prestigious medical school, from an individual with an MD degree. Contact with photo and resume.

Muslim Bangladeshi parents (recognized by UN) invite correspondence from compatible match for their U.S.-raised, Ivy League engineer daughter, 29, currently holding position as certified project manager in a Fortune 100 company.

Sunni Muslim parents seeking a religiously-inclined match for their U.S. born, 21 year old, educated, pretty, hijabi, daughter.

Seeking Wife

Highly educated family of a practicing Sunni Muslim, intelligent, and handsome doctor from top-ranked medical school in a prestigious residency, 28, born in U.S. Seeks life partner: a professional with a similar level of education and religious commitment.

Sunni Muslim, never married, 40 years old, Ph.D., engineer, seeks educated, religiously oriented, U.S. resident, 31–35, India/Bangladesh/Pakistan origin.

Sunni Muslim parents of a U.S.-educated son, M.D., doing residency in a highly completive specialty, invite correspondence (with photo and short resume) from moderately religious, non-hijibi professionals 26 and under.

Pakistani Sunni Muslim parents of a medical resident, 30, seeking a beautiful, highly educated, and practicing Muslimah.

Source: Islamic Horizons (September–October 2007): 74.

Maryamiyya Sufi Order

The Maryamiyya, or Miriamiyya, Order was founded by the author, poet, painter, and Sufi teacher Frithjof Schuon (1907–98), known among his followers as 'Isa Nur al-Din. An outgrowth of the 'Alawiyya-Shadhiliyya, a North African Sufi lineage into which Schuon was initiated in Algeria, the Maryamiyya, as a distinct order, seems to have emerged from a series of powerful visions of the Virgin Mary that occurred to Schuon beginning in 1965.

Born in Basle, Switzerland, on June 18, 1907, into a German Catholic family, Schuon became interested in spiritual matters at an early age and first encountered Islam while working as a textile designer in Paris. Late in 1932, he traveled to Algeria, where the next year he was initiated into Sufism by the Shadhili Sufi master Ahmad al-'Alawi. For many years, Schuon led a small, secretive group of European Sufi disciples based mainly in Lausanne and Basle, Switzerland, although he counted followers from across Europe.

In 1946, Schuon was declared an independent master by his disciples rather than just a *muqaddam,* or "deputy," of the Algerian Sufi order into which he was originally initiated. In effect, this allowed Schuon to create his own Sufi order. He traveled widely from the 1950s to the early 1970s, a period during which he studied Native American art, religion, and culture among the Sioux and Crow Indians in the western United States. In 1980, Schuon and his wife, Catherine (1924–), moved from Switzerland to Bloomington, Indiana, where he quietly taught a small circle of American followers in the forested residential community of Inverness Farms.

On Christmas Eve 1985, Schuon experienced a particularly powerful vision of the Virgin Mary in which she appeared to him disrobed, an experience that appears to have led him to begin promoting mystical exercises involving ritual nudity among his disciples. In 1991, a disillusioned member of the order brought a legal case against Schuon, who was subsequently indicted by a grand jury on felony charges of child molestation and sexual battery. A number of Schuon's more prominent followers vocally denounced the charges in the local press as false, and the prosecutor eventually dropped the case, citing insufficient evidence. Schuon died in his home at Inverness Farms in Bloomington on May 5, 1998.

A prolific author, Schuon published works with a marked, although not always explicit, impact on the Western academic study of SUFISM and other mystical traditions as well as, to a lesser extent, on Muslim intellectualist circles in the West, largely through the aegis of scholars such as Seyyed Hossein Nasr (1933–   ) and Houston Smith (1919–   ). Deeply influenced by the thought of the French metaphysician René Guénon, Schuon's writings championed two interrelated ideas. First was the doctrine of the *sophia perennis,* or the "perennial wisdom," which was understood to animate all authentic systems of religious expression. This is normally called Perennialism. Second, there was the idea that secular modern life must be rejected in favor of traditional sacred doctrines. This is normally called Traditionalism. Among his many works addressing Islam, his *Understanding Islam* (1963) was particularly well received in both the Muslim world and the West.

Erik S. Ohlander

Further Reading

Aymard, Jean-Baptiste, and Patrick Laude. *Frithjof Schuon: Life and Teachings.* Albany: State University of New York Press, 2004.

Frithjof Schuon Estate. Available online. URL: http://www.frithjof-schuon.com. Accessed February 25, 2009.

Schuon, Frithjof. *Understanding Islam.* London: Allen and Unwin, 1963.

Sedgwick, Mark. *Against the Modern World: Traditionalism and the Secret Intellectual History of the Twentieth Century.* New York: Oxford University Press, 2004.

masjid   See MOSQUES AND ISLAMIC CENTERS.

Mattson, Ingrid (1963–   ) *Islamic Society of North America president*

Ingrid Mattson's election in 2001 to the vice presidency of the ISLAMIC SOCIETY OF NORTH AMERICA (ISNA) and her election in 2006 to the presidency marked the first time a woman or a convert to Islam has led the organization. These events have been widely viewed as symbols of the progressive nature of Islam in North America. Mattson has used her position to press for WOMEN's rights at mosques across the continent, in addition to advocating for Muslims' civil rights in the United States.

Born on August 24, 1963, in Kingston, Ontario, she was raised Roman Catholic and converted to Islam during her college years after a period of agnosticism. While an art student living in Paris during summer 1986, she was emotionally moved by kindnesses of poverty-stricken West African Muslims she encountered. Returning to the University of Waterloo in Ontario, Canada, she began listening to cassettes

Ingrid Mattson, the first female president of the Islamic Society of North America, is a professor of religious studies at Hartford Seminary in Connecticut.   *(Stephen J. Carrera/AP Images)*

with recitations of the QUR'AN. She converted to Islam before receiving her degree in philosophy and fine arts in 1987.

Before attending graduate school, Mattson moved to Peshawar, Pakistan, to work in a refugee camp, helping provide aid to Afghan refugees from late 1987 to early 1989. There she met and married a fellow aid worker, Amer Aatek, an Egyptian. Mattson has written about how several female refugees generously supplied her with an elaborate wedding outfit when they heard she was going to wear regular clothes to her wedding. The couple has two children: a daughter, Soumayya, and a son, Ubayda.

Enrolling at the University of Chicago in fall 1989, Mattson earned a Ph.D. in Islamic studies in 1999 and has since been a professor at the Macdonald Center for Islamic Studies and Christian-Muslim Relations at Hartford Seminary in Hartford, Connecticut. She became director of the center in 2008. She also directs the Islamic Chaplaincy program there, the first of its kind in the United States. As a professor, her courses have covered SHARI'A (a Muslim code of LAW and ethics), rituals, theology, history, female spirituality, and the life of the prophet MUHAMMAD. In 2007, she published a book entitled *The Story of the Qur'an: Its History and Place in Muslim Life.*

Her 2001 election to the vice presidency of ISNA provided a broader platform for her work as a Muslim-American public intellectual. A theme of her leadership has been her belief that it is more important to build the North American Muslim community into a model for Muslims worldwide than to criticize U.S. government policies, both foreign and domestic, that, many Muslims contend, are discriminatory against followers of their religion. In writings and lectures, she has challenged the male leadership of American mosques to provide women with improved PRAYER space so they can better hear sermons and announcements. She has advocated for women to be fully engaged in the management of their mosques and for their participation in decisions and discussions on religious rulings. To the chagrin of some liberal Muslim groups in the United States, however, she has not called for Muslim women to lead nonrelated Muslim men in prayer.

In 2007, she engaged in high-level interreligious dialogue with Rabbi Eric Yoffie, president of the Union for Reform Judaism (URJ). Yoffie delivered an address at an ISNA conference in CHICAGO, and Mattson did the same at a URJ conference in San Diego.

On January 18, 2009, Mattson was among several clergy who spoke at the inaugural prayer service for president-elect Barack Obama at the National Cathedral in Washington, D.C. She prayed that "[o]n this day of new beginnings, with hearts lifted high in hope, may we be a people at peace among ourselves and a blessing to other nations."

Jeff Diamant

Further Reading

Abdo, Geneive. *Mecca and Main Street: Muslim Life in America after 9/11.* New York: Oxford University Press, 2006.

Haddad, Yvonne, Kathleen Moore, and Jane Smith. *Muslim Women in America: The Challenge of Islamic Identity Today.* New York: Oxford University Press, 2006.

Mattson, Ingrid. *The Story of the Qur'an: Its History and Place in Muslim Life.* Malden, Mass.: Blackwell, 2008.

"A New Voice for Islam." National Public Radio. April 19, 2007. Available online. URL: http://www.speakingoffaith.public radio.org. Accessed May 19, 2009.

Mayfield, Brandon (1966–) *attorney*

In 2004, the Federal Bureau of Investigation (FBI) arrested Muslim-American Brandon Mayfield as a material witness in connection with the deadly 2004 train bombings in Madrid, Spain. Mayfield spent more than two weeks in detention but was eventually freed when it was discovered that the FBI had mistaken him for another person. For critics of the USA PATRIOT ACT, Mayfield's ordeal emerged as a sad symbol of U.S. law enforcement failures in the era after SEPTEMBER 11, 2001.

Brandon Bieri Mayfield was born in Coos Bay, Oregon, on July 15, 1966, and was raised in Halstead, Kansas. Mayfield served in the U.S. Army Reserve from 1985 to 1989. He met his wife, Mona, an Egyptian national, on a blind date in 1987. He converted to Islam shortly after their marriage. Mayfield served as a U.S. Army officer in Bitburg, Germany, from 1992 to 1994 and received a law degree from Washburn University

in Topeka, Kansas, in 1999. He passed the Oregon Bar in 2000 and began work on family law, civil law, and immigration law cases. Mayfield also worked with programs that offer reduced rates for low-income clients.

On March 11, 2004, a carefully planned series of explosions in the commuter train system in Madrid, Spain, killed 191 people and injured 2,000. Spanish National Police found a blue plastic bag in a van parked near the Acala de Henares train station that contained similar detonation devices used in the train bombings. Several latent fingerprints were found on this bag, and on March 17, a digital image of latent fingerprint No. 17 was sent to the FBI crime lab in Quantico, Virginia.

The FBI's Latent Print Unit conducted an examination of the latent fingerprint by running the image through the Automated Fingerprint Identification System, which produced 20 possible matches. FBI senior fingerprint examiner Terry Green manually compared the potential matches and, according to FBI claims, "found a '100 percent' match with the fourth ranked print on the list." The fourth-ranked matching print was identified as Brandon Mayfield. Mayfield's prints were on file from a burglary arrest in 1984. This match was confirmed by at least two other FBI fingerprint examiners.

Based on this evidence, Mayfield was arrested on May 6, 2004, and held in custody for 19 days without bond. Those 19 days were spent in solitary "lock-down" where he was not allowed contact with his family. A month earlier, however, Spanish authorities had examined the fingerprint and determined that it was "conclusively negative" to Brandon Mayfield, meaning the print was not Mayfield's. The Forensic Science Division of the Spanish National Police had verified that latent fingerprint No. 17 belonged to Algerian national Ouhnane Daoud. Spanish authorities stated that the fingerprints matched Daoud's right thumb and middle finger. Based on this information, Mayfield was released from prison on May 24, 2004.

In explaining its actions, a December 2005 FBI report from U.S. attorney Karen Immergut defended the arrest of Mayfield, stating that the evidence "demonstrates that the government and its agents were acting in good faith" when they imprisoned Mayfield. According to Immergut, Mayfield was believed to pray at a mosque in Oregon where some Muslims had pled guilty of conspiring to help the Taliban. Mayfield also wrote a letter in support of the Taliban, according to the FBI, and helped to organize a branch of the MUSLIM STUDENTS ASSOCIATION. Mayfield advertised his law practice with someone "directly linked in business dealings" with terrorist Osama bin Laden's former personal secretary. He had also represented Jeffrey Battle in a child custody case. Battle was later sentenced to 18 years in prison for conspiring to wage war against the United States. Mayfield's home computer, which was seized during a raid of his home, contained information on travel to Madrid, rental housing in Spain, and a Web site connected to the Spanish National passenger rail system.

Mayfield argued that he had not traveled to Spain and that the "Spanish documents" found by the FBI during a raid of his home were, in fact, Spanish homework belonging to his son. He called his imprisonment "an abuse of the judicial process" and described it as a "harrowing ordeal" in which he was "subject to lock-down, strip searches, sleep deprivation, unsanitary living conditions, shackles and chains, threats, physical pain and humiliation." Mayfield firmly believed that his warrantless surveillance and arrest, part of the USA PATRIOT Act, were a violation of his Fourth Amendment rights.

In November 2006, the U.S. government agreed to pay Mayfield $2 million and issued a formal apology for his arrest in connection with the Madrid bombings.

Britney J. McMahan

Further Reading

"Brandon Mayfield." National Association of Criminal Defense Lawyers. Available online. URL: http://www.nacdl.org. Accessed April 13, 2008.

"FBI Apologizes to Lawyer in Bombing Case." MSNBC. May, 25 2004. Available online. URL: http://msnbc.com. Accessed April 13, 2008.

Jacklet, Ben, and Todd Murphy. "Now Free, Attorney Brandon Mayfield Turns Furious." *Washington Report on Middle East Affairs* 23, no. 6 (July-August 2004): 68.

Lichtblau, Eric. "U.S. Will Pay $2 Million to Lawyer Wrongly Jailed," *New York Times,* 30 November 2006. Available online. URL: http://www.nytimes.com/2006/11/20/us/30settle.html. Accessed April 13, 2008.

Murr, Andrew, Michael Isikoff, Eric Pape, and Mike Elkin. "The Wrong Man." *Newsweek* 143, no. 23 (June 7, 2004): 30–31.

"Oregon Man Arrested in Spain Bombings Probe." Fox News. May 7, 2004. Available online. URL: http://www.foxnews.com. Accessed April 13, 2008.

media   See *Azizah;* FILM; INTERNET; *MUHAMMAD SPEAKS; MUSLIM SUNRISE;* POETRY; RADIO.

Melungeons

On the periphery of Muslim-American history are the Melungeons, a group with possibly Moorish ancestry and Muslim roots. Melungeons represent a mysterious chapter of Islamic history tucked away in the Appalachian Mountains of the eastern United States. Although these communities incorporated escaped Muslim slaves and possibly Muslim immigrants from the 16th to the 19th centuries, present-day Melungeons show little sign of Islamic roots. DNA evidence has also suggested that the vast majority of present-day Melungeons trace their genetic roots to European ancestry.

The term *melungeon* refers to a triracial person usually of European, African, and Native American descent. Melungeons are also loosely connected communities living predominantly in the Appalachian Mountains of Tennessee, Virginia, North Carolina, and Kentucky. These communities have traditionally been isolated and introverted. Melungeons married within their own community and had little contact with outsiders. Myths of their origins have abounded in the history of the South.

At times these myths turned to racial stereotypes and discrimination, as in the 1845 court case of eight Melungeons who were initially denied the right to vote in Hancock County, Tennessee, because some of them may have had African ancestry. The eugenics testing of the early 1900s that singled out multiracial peoples marks the most devastating form of racial discrimination. Largely targeting Melungeon communities, eugenics scientists sterilized thousands of multiracial people in the American South under false pretenses. Melungeons sought to protect themselves from discrimination by appealing to various myths of their origins, including that they are of Portuguese, Phoenician, or Jewish and Muslim descent.

The theory invoked most frequently to argue against their possible African-American ancestry was that the Melungeons were not in fact multiracial but, rather, of Portuguese origin. Although this claim appears to have no factual evidence, it has been suggested in numerous court cases. For instance, in the 1890s in Rhea County, Tennessee, Melungeons sued for the right to attend white schools based on their Portuguese roots. The 1845 right-to-vote suit was also won by arguing that the eight Melungeons were Portuguese. In 1872, lawyer Lewis Shepherd chose to capitalize on another Melungeon myth by arguing successfully for a Melungeon woman's right to the inheritance of her white father by suggesting that she was not multiracial but rather of Carthaginian or Phoenician origin. Melungeon historian Brent Kennedy suggests in *Melungeons* (1997) that Shepherd himself was most likely of Melungeon descent. Other possible Melungeons include President Abraham Lincoln, his Confederate counterpart, Jefferson Davis, and explorer Daniel Boone.

In 1885, North Carolina assemblyman Hamilton McMillan claimed that Melungeons were descendants of Sir Walter Raleigh's lost colony of Roanoke, Virginia. Melungeon historian Elizabeth Hirschman argues in *Melungeons* (2005) that the colonists of Roanoke Island, in present-day North Carolina, were predominantly Sephardic Jews and Muslim Moors. Both groups settled at Roanoke in 1587 rather than return to Europe and face the Spanish Inquisition. If this theory is true, the colony of Roanoke was the first Melungeon community, implying that the first American colony was both a Muslim and a Jewish settlement.

Hirschman also suggests that Roanoke began a long trend of predominantly crypto-Muslim and Jewish immigration to Melungeon communities lasting into the 1700s ("crypto" typically meaning to profess to be Christian while hiding a Muslim or Jewish identity). In the 17th and 18th centuries, South Carolina was an entry point for Moors and Sephardic Jews who could have assimilated into Melungeon communities. Many of these Muslim and Jewish immigrants, like their Roanoke predecessors, may have immigrated from Portugal and Spain. Both countries had a long and tenuous relationship with the Moors and Sephardic Jews who have settled and at times dominated Portugal and Spain, at times causing mass migrations of Moors and Sephardic Jews from the Iberian Peninsula.

In this case, Melungeons may be Portuguese and Muslim or Jewish, and this would support both origin theories. Although there is little evidence for the theory that these immigrants to South Carolina migrated to Melungeon communities, Melungeon scholars such as N. Brent Kennedy, Tim Hashaw, and Wayne Winkler demonstrate that Melungeon communities did integrate with Iberian, African, Native American (specifically Cherokee, Yuchis, Creeks, Powhatans, and others), and other peoples who were not of Anglo-European origin. DNA tests in the late 1990s suggested that approximately 17 percent of present-day Melungeons' genetic pool could be traced to American Indians, African Americans, and Middle Easterners, while 83 percent of their DNA was of European origin.

Hirschman has claimed that Melungeon communities remained predominantly Jewish but also Muslim into the 1900s while appearing outwardly Christian. The largest religious organization of Melungeon communities has been Primitive Baptist, a church known for a disdain of outside leadership and choosing ministers from their own congregations. Freemasons, a once secretive fraternal organization that became an open community-service organization in the 20th century, are another group popular among Melungeon communities. Melungeons could have conceivably maintained Muslim and Jewish beliefs and practices under the guise of Christianity through the lenient and closed Primitive Baptist church and the elite Freemasons, though this hidden religious life, if it once existed, appears to have gradually dissipated into a Christian identity as religious and ethnic roots were suppressed.

Today Melungeon enclaves have for the most part integrated into mainstream society. Few Melungeons are aware of their mysterious roots, their past being lost to history. A few notable scholars who themselves are Melungeons, however, such as N. Brent Kennedy, Elizabeth Hirschman, and Wayne Winkler, along with other scholars, are recovering the Melungeons' place in American history. Muslim-American authors such as Jerald F. Dirks have celebrated the Melungeons as one of the many signs of the "forgotten legacy" of Muslim Americans. Dirks points to the Melungeons, among other groups, as evidence for the continual presence of Muslims in North America. Ironically while Islam secured its place among 20th-century religions in the United States, the partially Islamic roots of Melungeon communities became part of history.

David Walsh

Further Reading

Dirks, Jerald F. *Muslims in American History: A Forgotten Legacy.* Beltsville, Md.: Amana, 2006.

Gomez, Michael Angelo. *Black Crescent: The Experience and Legacy of African Muslims in the Americas.* Cambridge and New York: Cambridge University Press, 2005.

Hashaw, Tim. *Children of Perdition: Melungeons and the Struggle of Mixed America.* Macon, Ga.: Mercer University Press, 2006.

Hirschman, Elizabeth Caldwell. *Melungeons: The Last Lost Tribe in America.* Macon, Ga.: Mercer University Press, 2005.

Kennedy, N. Brent. *The Melungeons: The Resurrection of a Proud People.* Macon, Ga.: Mercer University Press, 1997.

Mira, Manuel. *The Forgotten Portuguese.* Franklin, N.C.: Portuguese American Historical Association, 1998.

Patterson Bible, Jean. *Melungeons: Yesterday and Today.* Rogersville, Tenn.: East Tennessee Printing Company, 1975.

Winkler, Wayne. *Walking toward the Sunset: The Melungeons of Appalachia.* Macon, Ga.: Mercer University Press, 2004.

men

Studying Muslim-American history through the category of gender requires attention to men as well as WOMEN. As an analytic category, "gender" rejects assumptions about natural and unchanging social roles and instead focuses on the ways in which such roles have developed over time and across space. From romanticized figures of Orientalist "sultans" and peasant immigrants in the late 19th century to grotesque "terrorists" and al-Qaeda operatives in the 21st, these dominant caricatures dissolve religious identities within ETHNICITY, while failing to capture the realities of life experienced by Muslim-American men in different historical moments and geographic locations.

These caricatures also fail to recognize the earliest Muslims in America—African slaves—as well as the legacy of 20th-century black political groups drawing on Islamic vocabularies, symbols, myths, and images. Many Muslim-American men—like their non-Muslim counterparts—have embraced ideas of patriarchy by organizing their families and communities around male interests. But this social and historical fact should not exclude them from historical, ethnographic, or sociological investigation. Understanding patriarchy among Muslims in America requires attention to the wide spectrum of experiences and ideas of both men and women, while understanding gender among Muslims in America requires going beyond "patriarchy" as the single interpretive lens.

MUSLIM MALE SLAVES

Most records of Muslim life in the United States before the 20th century are from the perspectives of men. Testimonies of enslaved Africans whom scholars have identified as probable Muslims, for instance, are almost all from the lips of men. JOB BEN SOLOMON (ca. 1701–ca. 1773), ABDUL RAHMAN IBRAHIMA (1762–1829), LAMEN KEBE (1767–?), and OMAR IBN SAID (ca. 1770–1864) are such figures whose testimonies establish Muslim practice in the United States well before the 20th century—daily PRAYERS, dietary restrictions, even recitation and transcription of the Fatiha, the opening chapter of the QUR'AN. Nevertheless, that Job Ben Solomon and Abdul Rahman Ibrahima were both African royalty who eventually returned to their homelands—in Ibrahima's case by presidential directive—suggest that such records not only did not speak for all enslaved Muslims but that neither did they speak for all enslaved Muslim men. More common than these princes of Africa were the thousands of AFRICAN-AMERICAN MUSLIM SLAVES who practiced Islam and who, against many odds, passed on some elements of their Islamic traditions to subsequent generations.

Though enslaved Muslims of African descent were raised with the idea that they should provide economically for their families as the head of household, their ability to accomplish this task was severely handicapped by their enslavement. Not only were they forced to work for their owner rather than for themselves or their families, they were also unable to prevent their families from dismemberment through sale. Slave owners could sell any family member at will, thus tearing children from parents, husbands from wives, and siblings from one another.

Men also had limited power to protect daughters and wives against sexual predation. Attempting to prevent white overseers and owners from committing such acts could have severe consequences for men: They could be sold or tortured to death. The memory of such male "impotence" (the sexual imagery is significant) in the face of slave-owner power would later haunt African-American Muslims such as ELIJAH MUHAMMAD (1897–1975) and MALCOLM X (1925–65), both of whom saw the inability of black men to protect black women as an immoral act of cowardice brought about partly by the male slaves' denial of their true Islamic—and

manly—heritage. Although by the time of emancipation in 1865, most freed slaves who claimed a religious faith were Christian, not Muslim, the tendency of later generations to locate black manhood in a lost or abandoned non-Christian faith was important not only for the creation of African-American political identities but also for the creation of new forms of African-American manhood.

IMMIGRANT MUSLIM MEN

Despite a history of Muslim presence in America since its colonial days, not until the 20th century did immigrants from nations with significant Muslim populations begin to arrive voluntarily in the United States in statistically significant numbers. Echoing broader patterns in U.S. immigration history, immigrants in the earliest waves of this voluntary migration were predominantly male. Since the United States did not explicitly identify the religiosity of incoming migrants, it is impossible to state with complete certainty how many Muslims participated in the massive immigrations of the late 19th and early 20th centuries. Moreover, the majority of immigrants from nations with Muslim populations were Christian, not Muslim.

The pattern of immigration from regions with large numbers of Muslims followed, in three key aspects, that of other groups immigrating in large numbers at the same time. First, despite variations in nationality, sect, occupation, marital status, and age, throughout this century of Muslim immigration the vast majority of immigrants were men, with ratios reaching to more than 1,000 males to every 100 female immigrants. Second, in terms of occupation, until the 1960s most immigrant Muslims worked as common laborers, peddlers, and small-business owners. Third, many came to the United States expecting to return permanently to their homelands after making enough money to support their families, although in reality few were able to do so. As these men began to send for their wives or to visit home to wed, Islam became more firmly entrenched in the American landscape.

Not only did this trend contribute to the development of Muslim neighborhoods, the establishment of permanent MOSQUES AND ISLAMIC CENTERS, and the diversification of Islam in America, it also transformed the faith from predominantly male social environments to increasingly family-oriented communities. Living as fathers and husbands necessitated different sets of social practices from those of single men. As greater numbers of students and professionals began to immigrate after WORLD WAR II, the economic and professional base of Muslim Americans began to expand, thus generating even more ways of negotiating religion with gender.

One way of measuring changes in the way gender was understood is by examining the increase in rates of intermarriage between Muslim men and non-Muslim women in the second half of the 20th century. In *Family and Gender among American Muslims* (1996), Barbara Bilgé discusses intermarriages between men born in Turkey and women born in the United States and Canada. She divides these "heterogamous" marriages into three categories: working-class, middle-class/ ex-military, and affluent families. Her data expose how such variables as ethnicity, education, occupation, and religion affected understandings of gender roles within the family.

In the middle-class families Bilgé studied, it was commonly understood that the husband would be the provider, even if the wife had a comparable education or career before marriage. Patriarchal Turkish gender roles also often prevailed, particularly the expectation of respect for fathers and husbands, demonstrated by wives and children through obedient conduct both in private and in public. Among the working-class and affluent couples, Turkish culture was less present in their daily lives, although the gender roles of husband and wife were still clearly defined. For instance, working-class and affluent husbands were often more permissive about their wives' and daughters' DRESS and EDUCATION, even if the ideal of a solitary male provider prevailed.

Although many Muslim men have modified traditional gender roles—particularly ideas about male dominance—through interactions with American culture, this is not to say that Muslim manhood has "secularized"—become less "authentically" Muslim—in the United States. Interactions between men and women in Muslim communities have always been saturated with possibility—capable of taking on untold varieties of forms—regardless of the dominant narratives and ideals. Moreover, the popular prototypes of the submissive, veiled female and the authoritative, uncompromising male are in many ways products of the conservative turn in Islam during the last half of the 20th century.

As with REVIVALISM movements in other religious traditions, the ideological development of groups such as the Muslim Brotherhood testify as much to a rearticulation of Islamic manhood as they do to religious revival. Thus, even as some segments of the Muslim-American male population have increased their participation in American culture by establishing, directing, and participating in social, political, academic, and multireligious/interfaith organizations, others have distinguished themselves from the dominant public sphere by accentuating the distinctive attributes of their faiths. This splintered interaction with American culture helps explain the diversity of Islam in America, as well as the particular roles that individual Muslim men play in its multiple communities.

AFRICAN-AMERICAN MUSLIM MANHOOD

During the 20th century, African Americans constituted the single-largest ethnic group of Muslim Americans. Distinct

from the Islam practiced by slaves, however, until late in the century the category of "black Muslims" referred to several movements of 20th-century design that linked the symbols, myths, and practices of conventional Islam (especially Sunni and Shi'a) with quests for racial equality, liberation, or territorial emancipation. During the earliest decades of the 20th century, moreover, both NOBLE DREW ALI's MOORISH SCIENCE TEMPLE of America and Elijah Muhammad's NATION OF ISLAM were instrumental in the negotiation of African-American manhood. Later in the century, other movements, such as the FIVE PERCENTERS, offered explicit, gender-based cosmologies drawn from idiosyncratic interpretations of Islamic teachings. Certainly each of these groups provided forums for women to exercise and manipulate power within their respective communities. Nevertheless, participants in each of these movements authored and celebrated distinct forms of black manhood that conditioned group cohesion and worked toward meeting the broader social demands of a highly racialized society.

The Moorish Science Temple and the Nation of Islam developed in a period of heightened racial consciousness in the urban North. During the 1910s, when Noble Drew Ali (born Timothy Drew) first established in NEWARK, NEW JERSEY, what would later become the Moorish Science Temple, thousands of African Americans from the South migrated to urban centers in the North, such as NEW YORK CITY, DETROIT, and CHICAGO. Men as well as women made this journey and, upon arrival, transformed the religious culture of their destinations. While some "New Negroes" during the 1920s repudiated all religion as a pernicious invention of their former enslavers, others sought to salvage their faith by locating it in either rehistoricized or non-Christian form; that is, many African Americans joined "restorationist" Pentecostal churches (the most popular of which was the Church of God in Christ) that privileged the ancient church and scorned the church that sanctioned slavery, while others discarded Christianity altogether. Among the latter, many African Americans created and embraced forms of Judaism and Islam.

Surveillance documents gathered by the Federal Bureau of Investigation (FBI) during the 1940s indicate that many male members of the Moorish Science Temple then living in the North were in fact born in the South and thus participated in the Great Migration of the 1910s through the 1930s. As the sons and grandsons of slaves, these "Moorish Americans" were invested not in merely faulting their historical and contemporary oppressors but in constructing a response that proved their identities as men. One way of doing this was to reject the vernacular of race—they were neither black, negro, colored, nor Ethiopian, for each of these concepts, according to Moorish Science teaching, denied that they were "made in the Image and after the likeness of God, Allah." Another way of defining their humanity was to put into practice a system of gender that clearly defined the expectations for men and women, both individually and in relation to one another. The Divine Constitution and By-Laws of the movement clearly stated, for instance, that "husband, you must support your wife and children; wife, you must obey your husband and take care of your children and look after the duties of your household." Though this instruction reflected conventional (frequently rendered "patriarchal") gender roles, it also admonished an impoverished social group to industry, which had been a signature criterion for "manhood" among several different populations, throughout American history.

The Moorish Science Temple's key text, *The Holy Koran of the Moorish Science Temple of America* (1927), which was not derived from the historical Qur'an, also presented "holy instruction and warnings for all young men" as well as teachings on "the duty of a husband." Written by Noble Drew Ali, who was understood to be "ALLAH'S Prophet," the *Holy Koran* was the scriptural pillar of the movement and would have been read with the reverence and promise accorded other sacred texts, such as the Bible among Christians or the Torah among Jews. In any case, the specific appeal to gendered conduct was imbued with the status of scripture. The instructions to young men warned of "all the allurements of wantonness" and of the "harlot" who would "tempt thee to the excess in her delights." Not only would pursuit of these ephemeral pleasures desiccate the "foundation of health which must supply the stream of pleasure," but it would also perpetuate the reign of the "lower-self" and thereby preclude the union with Allah that came only by mastering the flesh. Like industry, or useful occupation that signified social and economic independence, self-mastery had been understood as a defining element of American manhood since the antebellum period.

Because stepping out from under the long shadow of slavery required moving into a new social identity of one's own construction, the Moorish Science Temple placed a premium on "becom[ing] a faithful member of society" through a properly regulated marriage. Thus the instructions to young men folded into the prescribed duties of a husband. The onus of a successful marriage was placed on the husband's selection of a suitable companion, one who did not "destroy" her time "in dress and adornment," who was not "enamoured with her own beauty," whose "foot abideth" firmly "in her father's house," and who possessed "a form agreeable to thy fancy." At a time when many domestic relations among urban African Americans lacked the permanency of legal marriages, this injunction to careful selection of one's spouse amounted to a revision of expected male behavior along more socially stable lines. Similarly, instead of celebrating the urban bachelor culture burgeoning in the 1920s, Moorish Science instructed its male members to "Be faithful to her [one's wife's] bed, for she is the mother of thy children."

Historical consensus identifies Moorish Science as the ideological progenitor of the far more popular Nation of Islam (NOI). Although the NOI, under the leadership of Elijah Muhammad, eventually transformed much of Moorish Science's doctrine and practice, nevertheless the NOI continued the Temple's legacy of constructing black manhood. Masculine language permeated the written record of the NOI in documents such as *Message to the Blackman in America* (1965) and the movement's periodical, MUHAMMAD SPEAKS, and the all-male FRUIT OF ISLAM (FOI) division provided rituals of masculinity that members lived every day of their lives. Members of the FOI were models of proper male conduct for others in the community, from matters of dress to regulated drills. Though changing over time, uniforms consisted of either dark suit and bow tie or militaristic garb complete with fez and three-button coat. One scholar has argued that the FOI emerged as a "private security force" during the ministry of the Nation's founder, W. D. FARD (ca. 1877–ca. 1934?), while the FBI identified the group as the "military section" of the Nation. Whether a defensive security force or an offensive military, the FOI certainly engaged in militaristic activity, such as disciplined drills aiming toward synchronicity and training exercises that, according to the movement's periodical, conditioned "absolute fitness and precision." In addition to sartorial and physical discipline, members of the FOI were also expected to discipline their time by selling copies of *Muhammad Speaks*.

Whereas the Moorish Science Temple produced the NOI, the NOI generated another movement, the Five Percenters, or the Nation of Gods and Earths. The Five Percenters were founded in Harlem in 1963 by a former Nation member, Clarence "Pudding" 13X. Whereas the NOI had taught that "the black man" was the "original man," and thus that God must himself be black, Clarence 13X taught that black men themselves were God. According to Five Percenter theology, "Allah" was proven the rightful name for black men by linking the letters in the anglicized term to anatomical parts: *arm, leg, leg, arm, head*. This theologizing of the black male body was codified in the movement's anthropology, which divided humanity into classifications based on percentages. According to this theory, 85 percent of humanity is incapable of salvation because they do not know God; 10 percent know God but deny his physical incarnation, teaching instead that he is a "spook"; and the remaining 5 percent know God as the black man. While men are Gods, women are Earths who become Muslim by acknowledging the divinity of their male counterparts and bearing the children of Gods.

CONCLUSION

Experiences of men and Islam in the United States vary according to a wide range of racial, ethnic, occupational, sectarian, and familial paradigms. While not all members of each community would recognize others as similarly "Muslim," each community nevertheless has participated in creations of masculinity that draw from and in turn shape religious knowledge and practice. It is thus important not to reduce understandings of "men and Islam" to specific stereotypes or caricatures but instead to keep in mind this spectrum of experience and circumstance.

Rachel McBride Lindsey

Further Reading

Bilgé, Barbara. "Turkish-American Patterns of Intermarriage." In *Family and Gender among American Muslims,* edited by Barbara C. Aswad and Barbara Bilgé, 59–106. Philadelphia: Temple University Press, 1996.

Curtis, Edward E., IV. *Black Muslim Religion in the Nation of Islam, 1960–1975.* Chapel Hill: University of North Carolina Press, 2006.

Ferris, Marc. "To 'Achieve the Pleasure of Allah': Immigrant Muslim Communities in New York City, 1893–1991." In *Muslim Communities in North America,* edited by Yvonne Yazbeck Haddad and Jane Idleman Smith, 209–230. Albany: State University of New York Press, 1994.

Gomez, Michael A. *Black Crescent: The Experience and Legacy of African Muslims in the Americas.* New York: Cambridge University Press, 2005.

———. *Exchanging Our Country Marks: The Transformation of African Identities in the Colonial and Antebellum South.* Chapel Hill: University of North Carolina Press, 1998.

Haddad, Yvonne Yazbeck, and Jane Idleman Smith. *Mission to America: Five Islamic Sectarian Communities in North America.* Gainesville and Tallahassee: University Press of Florida, 1993.

Nuruddin, Yusuf. "The Five Percenters: A Teenage Nation of Gods and Earths." In *Muslim Communities in North America,* edited by Yvonne Yazbeck Haddad and Jane Idleman Smith, 109–132. Albany: State University of New York Press, 1994.

Smith, Jane I. *Islam in America.* New York: Columbia University Press, 1999.

Mevlevi Sufi Order

Mevlevi refers to a form of SUFISM in which participants use dance as part of their primary religious ritual, called the *SEMA.* Also known as "whirling dervishes," a term that was regularly used in 19th-century English to denote spiritual ecstasy and even madness, Mevlevis are perhaps the most famous Sufi order in the United States. In addition to being part of the American cultural imagination for two centuries, Mevlevis began to tour as performers in the 1950s. Sponsored by the Turkish government, the "troupe" played to sold-out audiences across the United States. Since then,

an indigenous group of Americans have become devotees of the Sufi order.

Founded in honor of the poet Mevlana Jalal al-Din Rumi (?–1273) in 13th-century Anatolia, part of present-day Turkey, the Mevlevi Order strives to achieve total abandonment of worldly passions through a form of ritual dance. Rumi wrote that "dancing is when you rise above both worlds tearing your heart to pieces and giving up your soul." The dance, music, and poetry utilized in Mevlevi rituals attempt to stimulate an emotional approach to reality and are intended to develop an emotional link with God. The doctrine advocated by Rumi and adopted by Mevlevis is one of religious tolerance and acceptance, combined with a belief in goodness, charity, and awareness through love.

As with many American Sufi movements, the Mevlevi Order became attractive to Americans interested in an esoteric form of Islam that heightens the experience of the divine to achieve transcendence. The Mevlevi Order of America was founded in 1978 by Jeladdudin Loras, son of Suleyman Dede, who was the late sheikh, or leader, of the order in Turkey. Appointed by his father to bring the practices and teachings of the Mevlevi to the West, Jeladdudin first began teaching the Mevlevi way to students in the San Francisco Bay Area. The Mevlevi Order of America has since expanded to have a following in many cities on the West Coast, Hawaii, and also upstate New York. The order has also maintained a Web site and offered regular classes, seminars, and public viewings of the traditional whirling prayer ceremony on December 17 each year to mark the death of Rumi.

The Mevlana Foundation was founded in 1976 by Reshad Feild, who was born in London and was the first sheikh of the Mevlevi Order to venture to the United States. Feild also studied under VILAYAT KHAN and was initiated as a Sufi sheikh by him in the early 1960s. Feild has taught disciples in the American Southwest, although he lived mostly in Switzerland.

Another Mevlevi organization in the United States is the Threshold Society, led by Edmund Kabir Helminski, a Mevlevi sheikh appointed by Celattin Celebi, which has offered seminars and programs in North America and around the world. Celebi, who was regarded by his followers as a descendant of Rumi, was the late international head of the Mevlevi Order. The Threshold Society has maintained a center in Brattleboro, Vermont, where the group has met since the 1990s.

As with other Sufi groups, the Mevlevi Order has included the participation of women and has also appealed to Americans otherwise repelled by membership in other organized religious groups, whether Christian, Jewish, or Muslim. The Mevlevis have generally welcomed religious seekers who do not otherwise identify as Muslims. While their practices may seem exotic at first, some scholars have argued, the Mevlevis are a quintessentially American religious movement, part of a broader alternative American religious history that traces its lineage from 19th-century theosophy to 21st-century New Age groups.

Natalia Slain

Further Reading

And, Metin. "The Mevlana Ceremony." *Drama Review* 21, no. 3 (September 1977): 83–94.

Hermansen, Marcia. "Hybrid Identity Formations in Muslim America: The Case of American Sufi Movements." *Muslim World* 20 (2000): 158–197.

Mevlevi Order of America Web site. Available online. URL: http://www.hayatided.org. Accessed May 19, 2009.

military   See UNITED STATES MILITARY.

Million Man March

On October 16, 1995, between 700,000 and 1 million African-American men gathered in Washington, D.C., to attend one of the largest marches of African Americans in the history of the United States. Called the Million Man March, this day-long assembly was organized by LOUIS FARRAKHAN, leader of the NATION OF ISLAM. Men from around the country responded to Farrakhan's call to atone for their past mistakes and to unite for positive social change.

Arriving by bus, train, airplane, and car, some men came the night before the march and slept outside on the historic mall of the nation's capital. They awoke in the morning to the sounds of the *adhan,* the Islamic call to PRAYER. "As the sun grew warmer against a bracing morning chill," journalist Charlayne Hunter-Gault reported, "so did the mood. . . . The growing crowd of black men of all ages and walks of life, friends and strangers, acknowledged each other and seemed to celebrate this call for black men to stand up."

Coordinated by Benjamin Chavis Muhammad, former executive director of the National Association for the Advancement of Colored People (NAACP), the march was attended by black men of all faiths and no particular faith at all. Historically African-American Christian churches organized caravans and bus trips that accounted for thousands of those in attendance. The Reverend Jesse Jackson, an African-American civil rights leader and head of the National Rainbow Coalition, addressed the crowd.

Long a controversial figure especially among white Americans, Farrakhan became the center of various calls to boycott the march. Prominent politicians and community leaders, both black and white, urged people not to attend. Some called Farrakhan an anti-Semite, racist bigot, and

In 1995, the Million Man March, led by Nation of Islam leader Louis Farrakhan, drew hundreds of thousands, if not more than a million, black men to the historic Mall in Washington, D.C. *(Tim Sloan/AFP/Getty Images)*

sexist. W. D. MOHAMMED, the popular African-American Muslim leader whose leadership Farrakhan had rejected in the late 1970s, criticized Farrakhan's motives in his newspaper, the *Muslim Journal,* arguing that Farrakhan was leading African Americans "further and further into darkness."

But only 5 percent of marchers said that Farrakhan was their main reason for coming, according to a *Washington Post* survey. Harvard law professor Charles Ogletree, who attended the march with his college-age son, said that he was "particularly disturbed that so many of our black leaders, so-called leaders told people to stay away." Clarence Page, a prominent African-American reporter and columnist, argued that Farrakhan deserved credit for the march, no matter what his faults. "Since black men, particularly young black men are the most feared and loathed creatures on the urban streets today," Page explained, "we need self-esteem more than most."

Though the march was geared toward men, some women came in support. Dorothy Height, president of the National Council on Negro Women, addressed the crowd. Maya Angelou composed a poem for the occasion, noting that in spite of the great suffering of African Americans, "we are a going-on people who will rise again."

But Minister Farrakhan, who spoke for more than two hours, had the last word. Beginning and ending his speech with Islamic prayers, Farrakhan argued that the redemption of African Americans and America's atonement for the sin of slavery were necessary preconditions for healing the racial divide in the United States. Citing both Muslim and Christian scriptures, he called for black men to take responsibility for any violent and immoral acts in their past. The minister also asked participants to join a black political organization such as the NAACP or the Urban League, and he suggested that all black men attend a church, mosque, synagogue, or any other house of worship that would help them lead a more moral life.

The march was an important turning point in several respects. It inspired and provoked several other marches on Washington, including the 1999 Million Mom March against gun violence. The march built a coalition of African-American leaders that would eventually form the Millions More Movement, which has remained committed to many of the principles that Minister Farrakhan articulated in his 1995 address. Finally, the event also showcased a Farrakhan with whom many Muslim Americans were unfamiliar. Though

The Million Man March has been commemorated in film, literature, and material culture, including buttons. *(Corbis)*

many Muslim Americans continued to distance themselves from the controversial leader, others lauded his incorporation of Sunni Islamic teachings into his rhetoric, call for equality among people of all racial backgrounds, and praise for the virtues of personal responsibility and social justice.

Edward E. Curtis IV

Further Reading

CNN. "Million Man March." CNN.com. Available online. URL: http://www.cnn.com/US/9510/megamarch/march.html. Accessed November 13, 2008.

"Farrakhan Berated by W. Deen Mohammed." *Christian Century* 112, no. 34 (November 22, 1995).

PBS Newshour. "Million Man March." Online Newshour. Available online. URL: http://www.pbs.org/newshour/bb/race_relations/race_relations_10-16a.html. Accessed November 13, 2008.

missionaries

Some Muslims Americans believe that *da'wa*, or inviting people to Islam, is a duty spelled out in the QUR'AN 16:125: "Call thou to the way of thy Lord with wisdom and good admonition and dispute with them in the better way." Still, only a small minority of Muslim Americans have perceived active proselytization as an individual religious duty. Particular individuals, movements, and organizations have led the way in Muslim missionary endeavors. Muslim missionaries in the United States have adhered to a variety of traditions within Islam and have engaged in a variety of approaches. In addition to trying to convert non-Muslims to Islam, their mission work has targeted nonpracticing Muslims and those they feel practice a sectarian or unorthodox Islam. Debating what missionary methods to adopt, many missionaries have said that living faithfully as a Muslim is the single-best technique. Others have claimed missionary work must be pursued aggressively through direct encounter. In addition, missionaries have engaged in social service, community development, education, publishing, and political attempts to transform the United States into an Islamic society.

EARLY MUSLIM MISSIONARIES

ALEXANDER RUSSELL WEBB (1846–1916) was the first well-known Muslim-American missionary. A white American who converted to Islam in 1887, Webb drew attention on his return to the United States in 1893 after his travels in Asia. He optimistically believed that if he could educate Americans about the benefits of Islam, they would convert in large numbers. He initiated the American Muslim Propagation Movement and founded the American Islamic Mission in NEW YORK CITY in 1893. He published numerous newspaper articles and lectured throughout the country promoting Islam. He may be best remembered as the only Muslim to speak at the World's Parliament of Religions held in CHICAGO in 1893. Webb also opened a number of Islamic study circles in major American cities. Despite his optimism, he faced financial hardship and a lack of converts. Although he remained a significant figure in Muslim missions, he proved largely unsuccessful.

With their arrival in America in 1920, the Ahmadi missionaries became the first community to engage in Muslim missions on a large scale. Originating in the late 19th century in South Asia, many Sunni Muslims came to consider the Ahmadi movement sectarian and unorthodox. The Ahmadis have played a major role in propagating Islam in America, however, especially among African Americans. Sent abroad specifically as missionaries, they adopted a highly organized methodology. (See AHMADI MUSLIM AMERICANS.)

For example, Muhammad Sadiq, the first Ahmadi missionary to the United States, engaged in widespread circulation of the first English editions of the Qur'an and hadith, the reports of sayings and deeds of the prophet MUHAMMAD and his companions. Settling in Chicago in 1920, he quickly established a mosque and also began publishing an English-language Muslim journal, MUSLIM SUNRISE, appealing to a non-Muslim Western audience. Through testimonies of converts, defense of Islam against Western prejudices, and exposition of Qur'anic texts, the journal invited the reader to consider Islam.

Sadiq used the journal and numerous speeches to target explicitly African Americans in the northern urban centers of the country. Sadiq claimed that in contrast to the racism of American Christianity, Islam offered equality. By 1925, he had made 1,025 converts, primarily African Americans. He set up an organizational structure to maximize opportunities for mission. He appointed new converts as sheikhs, or leaders, to enlist others, establish mosques, and collect funds for the movement. This localization eventually led to diverse understandings of Islam within the Ahmadi movement, but it also allowed for continued growth. While the Ahmadi movement came to be overshadowed by other Muslim groups in America by the 1950s, it was a key missionary voice, especially in developing a large African-American Muslim population.

AFRICAN-AMERICAN MUSLIM MISSIONS

Among the indigenous Muslim-American population, the greatest growth has been among African Americans, who have played a major role in the story of Muslim missionaries. While Ahmadi missionaries had some initial success, other movements have presented other options. For example, DUSÉ MOHAMED ALI offered a different missionary approach. Involved in the Pan-Africanist movement of the early 20th century, he served as a mentor for Jamaican native and black nationalist leader Marcus Garvey and his Universal Negro

Improvement Association. While mostly residing in Great Britain, Ali came to the United States on at least three occasions in the late 19th and early 20th centuries. In the 1920s, he helped found the Universal Islamic Society in Detroit, using his mission to promote a universal Pan-Islamic movement. Ali saw his mission as offering a modernized Islam that could be a uniting movement for people of color as an alternative to Western imperialism. While the Universal Islamic Society remained small, it became a foundation for later Pan-Islamic and Pan-Africanist movements. Other Muslim missions in America were homegrown. NOBLE DREW ALI founded the MOORISH SCIENCE TEMPLE of America in Chicago in 1925. While incorporating influences from a variety of religions and secular movements, the group claimed to be Muslim. Drew Ali appealed to African Americans by giving them a new identity and homeland, claiming they were Asiatics descended from the Moors of Morocco. Speaking as a prophet, Ali taught that returning to Islam, their original faith, was the only way African Americans could escape racism. The movement spread to a number of cities in the 1920s and reached a membership of perhaps 30,000 at its height, but it lost ground after the 1940s.

The NATION OF ISLAM (NOI) may be the most successful missionary movement among African-American Muslims. Founded in 1930 by W. D. FARD, the NOI began to grow considerably under the leadership of ELIJAH MUHAMMAD (1897–1975). Differing in significant aspects from Sunni Islam, the NOI preached racial separation and black pride. Similar to Noble Drew Ali, Elijah Muhammad called on African Americans to reclaim Islam, the original faith of their fathers, and overthrow white control.

The NOI achieved large-scale growth in the period after WORLD WAR II. Part of its success was due to its PRISON ministry. In 1942, the movement began to preach in prisons among incarcerated African Americans. Among the many new converts was MALCOLM X (1925–65), who became the chief spokesman for Elijah Muhammad and a national figure who brought additional converts and publicity to the movement. In 1961, the NOI also began publishing a newspaper, MUHAMMAD SPEAKS, which became one of the largest minority weekly publications in the country and served as a vital medium for the group's message. While estimates vary, the NOI may have counted 20,000 members at its peak, but its influence far outstripped its numbers. With a firmly established mission, the NOI enlisted new members into its ranks but also reached those outside the movement with a message of black pride and resistance to American mainstream politics.

SUNNI MISSIONS TO AFRICAN-AMERICAN MUSLIMS

With the growth of Ahmadi and NOI missionary movements in the United States, a number of new Muslim missionaries sought to respond to what they considered to be these sectarian Islamic movements, and they began to encourage specifically indigenous African-American Muslims to adopt the Sunni tradition.

One such example was the work of WALI AKRAM (1904–94). An African-American convert to the Ahmadi tradition, Akram helped establish the First Cleveland Mosque in 1937. As Akram embraced Sunni Islam, he encouraged other African Americans to do the same. He conceived the mission of Islam in America not only as spiritual liberation but also as political and economic development within the African-American community. To achieve this mission, Akram established the Muslim Ten Year Plan in 1937 to advocate both religious revival and economic empowerment by working through established social structures.

Another Muslim missionary intent on spreading Sunni Islam among African Americans was MUHAMMAD EZALDEEN (1886–1957). A former leader within the Moorish Science Temple, Ezaldeen, like Akram, came to criticize his past tradition while embracing and proclaiming the Sunni tradition as an answer for spiritual and economic development among African Americans. Ezaldeen developed a religious curriculum that educated African Americans about Sunni Islam while also addressing political issues. In 1938, Ezaldeen established the ADDEYNU ALLAHE UNIVERSAL ARABIC ASSOCIATION (AAUAA). In promoting community development, Ezaldeen's AAUAA took an opposite approach from Akram's Muslim Ten Year Plan. Instead of engaging society, Ezaldeen separated from it by purchasing land and creating an independent Muslim community. Both approaches, however, demonstrated Muslim missionaries' interest in social issues.

A third figure, Sheikh Daoud Ahmed Faisal, was also an African-American Muslim missionary intent on converting Americans to Sunni Islam. Sometime before World War II, he established the Islamic Propagation Center of America in Brooklyn, New York. Faisal also illustrated his insistence on missionary work by referring to his State Street Mosque as the Islamic Mission of America. Constantly speaking and authoring pamphlets to inform and persuade Americans to embrace Islam as well as criticizing Christianity and American politics, he found his greatest audience among African Americans. The Islamic Mission of America achieved early success in integrating indigenous and immigrant Muslims in one mosque.

SUFISM

Sufi missionaries to America have also achieved success among non-Muslims, largely through their willingness to adapt their traditions to the West. The first Sufi missionary to the United States was INAYAT KHAN (1882–1927), the Hindustani musician and Sufi master who arrived in the United States for a tour in 1910. Averse to formal doctrine, Khan did not require his followers to convert officially to Islam and embraced a more universal approach to religion. Under the leadership of his son, VILAYAT INAYAT KHAN (1916–2004), the organization gained a greater audience in the 1960s among the educated elite and religious seekers. It has found particular success among WHITE MUSLIM AMERICANS.

Another one of many Sufi missionary movements in America is the BAWA MUYAIYADDEEN FELLOWSHIP. Established in Philadelphia in 1971 when its founder, Muhammed Raheem Bawa Muyaiyaddeen, came to the United States, the group attracted members drawn to its mystical tradition and its embrace of universal religious values. Over time, the fellowship has become more formally rooted as a Sufi movement while also adopting the basic tenets of Sunni Islam. The movement is most notable for its racial and ethnic diversity as well as its integration of men and women within the public practices of the community.

INTERNATIONAL MISSIONS TO MUSLIM AMERICANS

In the second half of the 20th century, Muslims around the world became more concerned that Muslims immigrating to America would lose their commitment to the faith. As a part of a growing Islamic REVIVALISM, Muslim missionaries came to the United States in greater numbers. One explicitly proselytizing movement was the TABLIGHI JAMAʿAT. Claiming that the propagation of Islam was the duty of all Muslims and not just the learned elite, its first missionaries entered the United States in 1952. While the movement now also attempts to convert non-Muslims, it originally concentrated on direct encounter with fellow Muslims to preach spiritual revival and a return to conservative ideals while avoiding ASSIMILATION to Western culture.

Islamist missionaries, or those Muslim missionaries who teach that Islam is both a religion and a state, have played a prominent missionary role as well. Many have advocated Islam as a total way of life and hope that through their missionary efforts that the United States might one day become a Muslim country. The followers of prominent Muslim thinkers such as Hasan al-Banna and Sayyid Qutb of the Muslim Brotherhood and Abdul A'la Mawdudi of the Jamaat-i Islami in Pakistan have translated a number of their writings into English, and they can be found as books and pamphlets in Islamic bookstores, mosques, and other public places. Of particular note for Americans is the Islamic Foundation led by Khuram Murad. While based in the United Kingdom, the Islamic Foundation has followed Jamaat-i Islami's ideology and financed a large number of English-language Islamic tracts written by Murad to be spread throughout the United States.

Another organization with a similar missionary purpose is the Muslim World League (MWL). Founded in 1962 by a number of Muslim nations, the MWL is one of the largest nongovernmental Islamic organizations. While the MWL serves many functions, missionary work is one chief aim. Financed largely by Saudi Arabia, the MWL has funded English-language pamphlets and volumes of the Qur'an, the building of mosques, and the education of potential Muslim-American clerics and leaders. The first director of the MWL, Ahmad Satr, continued to serve as a professor, prolific writer, and speaker in the United States. Satr has identified his purpose as strengthening Muslims' identity and building greater understanding of Islam among a larger American audience. Often associated with WAHHABISM, a modern reformist version of Islam based on the thought of an 18th-century Arabian cleric, the MWL has been charged by conservative critics of Islam with having ties to terrorists. While terrorism committed by Saudi Muslims is clearly a fact of American life, no connection has been found between the MWL and terrorism, and the MWL, sponsored by countries that are often the target themselves of al-Qaeda and other Muslim extremists, has little to gain by promoting terrorism.

LOCALES FOR MUSLIM MISSIONS IN AMERICA
Mosques and Islamic Centers

One major locale for Muslim missions in America is MOSQUES AND ISLAMIC CENTERS. In addition to serving the ritual religious needs of the Muslim community, these centers serve as a public presence for Muslims in America. They have also striven to educate both Muslims and non-Muslims in the faith. Many have maintained bookstores that carry a wide selection of mission literature. They have also engaged the community in dialogue on wider religious and public issues. The ISLAMIC CENTER OF WASHINGTON, D.C., and the Islamic Da'wah Center in Houston are prominent examples.

Paramosque Organizations

While mosques and Islamic centers are one important aspect of Muslim mission, American paramosque organizations have also become vitally important. These largely national organizations unaffiliated with a local mosque often include missionary activity as a specific aspect of their organization. International Muslim university students funded the MUSLIM STUDENTS ASSOCIATION (MSA) in 1963 to focus on retaining and strengthening their faith while studying in the United States. By 2007, the MSA maintained more than 250 affiliate chapters in the United States and Canada. Over time, the organization's focus has shifted from Muslim students intent on returning to their native countries to a new generation of students developing a specific Muslim-American identity. The MSA has also sought to present Islam to non-Muslims through befriending and inviting fellow students into community, publishing literature, and educational events. The

MSA created an Islamic Teacher Center and Islamic Book Service to assist in their publication and educational efforts. While they have designed brochures such as *Islam at a Glance* and *Ten Unique Features of Islam* for explicit proselytizing efforts, the MSA also pursues mission through general community dialogue.

Another organization, the ISLAMIC SOCIETY OF NORTH AMERICA (ISNA), grew out of the MSA in 1982. ISNA has served as an umbrella organization for many Muslims in the United States and has multiplied and subsumed many of the tasks begun by the MSA. While ISNA has offered a number of services to Muslim Americans, one of its tasks has been providing resources for missions. It has worked to engage in interfaith dialogue, educate the American pubic concerning Islam, and provide missionary literature for Muslim Americans.

The ISLAMIC CIRCLE OF NORTH AMERICA (ICNA), established in the early 1970s to promote Muslim-American religious education, social services, and missionary work, has been successful in adapting mission to new technologies. In the 21st century, ICNA melded mission with advertising, launching a campaign in New York City subways prompting citizens to call a toll-free hotline, 1-877-Why-Islam, or visit a Web site to learn more about Islam. ICNA has also found U.S. prisons to be a major area for missionary activity. While accurate numbers of converts are difficult to obtain, some experts estimate that 300,000 people have converted to Islam while in U.S. prisons.

OTHER STRATEGIES FOR MUSLIM MISSIONS IN AMERICA

In addition to standard proselytizing literature, direct preaching, and opportunities for education and dialogue, missionaries employed by local mosques and national paramosque organizations have continued to adapt other approaches. One such missionary is South African Ahmed Deedat (1918–2005), who was a major influence on Muslim Americans by perfecting a form of Muslim apologetics, the art of defending one's position through persuasive argument. Best known for public debates with evangelical Christians and lectures that discussed Islam, Christianity, and the Bible, he attempted to equip Muslims to defend their faith against Christian missions while living faithfully in a Christian-majority society.

Another approach was that of ISMA'IL AL-FARUQI (1921–86), who founded the INTERNATIONAL INSTITUTE OF ISLAMIC THOUGHT in 1981. Al-Faruqi advocated for what he called the "Islamization of Knowledge," which he saw as the key to bringing Islam into conversation with modern Western philosophies. In cross-training traditional Islamic scholars with modern Western social and physical science methodologies, al-Faruqi felt that his Islamization of Knowledge would make

Islam a recognizable and viable religious option for the West. Without advocating direct conversion of non-Muslims, al-Faruqi argued that reason had a strong foundation in the Qur'an, whose teachings supported this academic approach to Muslim mission.

The Aga Khan Development Network (AKDN) is another example of missions among ISMA'ILI MUSLIM AMERICANS. Under the leadership of the AGA KHAN, the network in the United States has funded educational youth programs for immigrant Muslims, attempts at interfaith and inter-Muslim dialogue, and humanitarian aid for victims of disasters such as Hurricane Katrina in 2005.

Another recent type of Muslim mission has developed among those who advocate a strongly Muslim-American identity, or what might even be called an American form of Islam. Muslim-American converts such as JEFFREY LANG (1954–) and HAMZA YUSUF (1960–) have begun to address how Islam must change to become a vibrant tradition in America while retaining the Muslim faith of the younger generation. These new voices have served as Muslim missionaries preaching a message of change.

CONCLUSION

Throughout the history of Muslim Americans, Muslim missionaries have not always agreed on who should be a missionary, what mission methods should be employed, and who is to be the focus of their missionary efforts. Many missionaries have embraced the religious freedom guaranteed in the U.S. Constitution to maximize their missionary efforts. Some are hopeful that they can turn the United States into an Islamic country. Others have wanted to establish Muslim enclaves in the United States, seeking protection from racism and discrimination. Most Muslim-American missionaries, however, have assumed a lower profile for inviting people to become Muslims. Asking fellow Muslims to become model Americans—to work hard and give back—these Muslim-American missionaries envision a future in which Muslims compete in goodness, as a popular Qur'anic verse exhorts, with other Americans.

David P. King

Further Reading

Abd-Allah, Umar F. *A Muslim in Victorian America: The Life of Alexander Russell Webb.* New York: Oxford University Press, 2006.
Curtis, Edward E., IV, ed. *The Columbia Sourcebook of Muslims in the United States.* New York: Columbia University Press, 2008.
Dannin, Robert. *Black Pilgrimage to Islam.* New York: Oxford University Press, 2002.
Esposito, John L. *The Islamic Threat: Myth or Reality?* New York: Oxford University Press, 1999.
al-Faruqi, Ismail R. "On the Nature of Islamic Da'wah." *Christian Mission and Islamic Da'wah: Proceedings of the Chambesy Dialogue Consultation.* London: Islamic Foundation, 1976.
GhaneaBassiri, Kambiz. *Competing Visions of Islam in the United States.* Westport, Conn.: Greenwood, 1997.
Haddad, Yvonne Yazbeck, ed. *The Muslims of America.* New York: Oxford University Press, 1991.
Haddad, Yvonne Yazbeck, and Jane Idleman Smith, eds. *Muslim Communities in North America.* Albany: State University of New York Press, 1994.
Malik, Jamal, and John Hinnells, eds. *Sufism in the West.* New York: Routledge, 2006.
Murad, Khurram. *Da'wah among Non-Muslims in the West.* London: Islamic Foundation, 1986.
Poston, Larry. *Islamic Da'wah in the West.* New York: Oxford University Press, 1992.
Turner, Richard Brent. *Islam in the African American Experience.* Bloomington: University of Indiana Press, 2003.

Mohammed, W. D. (Wallace Delaney)
(1933–2008) *religious leader*

W. D. Mohammed assumed leadership of the NATION OF ISLAM (NOI) after his father's death in 1975. Undertaking a series of reforms, he radically changed the religious doctrines of the movement and its advocacy of racial separation and black nationalism. He encouraged his followers to adhere to the five pillars of Islam as practiced by Sunni Muslims, who constitute approximately 80 to 85 percent of all Muslims, and changed the name of the group to WORLD COMMUNITY OF al-ISLAM IN THE WEST in 1976. In 1992, he became the first imam, or Muslim religious leader, to offer the invocation before a session of the U.S. Senate. Regarded by at least tens of thousands, perhaps hundreds of thousands of Muslim Americans as their religious leader, he remained a central religious force in American religion until his death in 2008.

GROWING UP IN THE NATION

Wallace Delaney Mohammed was born in DETROIT, MICHIGAN, on October 30, 1933. He was the seventh child of CLARA MUHAMMAD and ELIJAH MUHAMMAD, who was leading the NOI at the time of Wallace's birth. Although he grew up as a member of this "royal family"—his father would lead the NOI for more than 40 years—Wallace was raised largely by his mother. In 1934, the family moved to Chicago, and shortly thereafter Elijah Muhammad became a traveling preacher until his arrest in 1942 during WORLD WAR II for sedition and draft resistance. Wallace's father remained in prison until 1946.

After Elijah Muhammad was released from prison, he initiated a period of institutional growth within the NOI that included the opening of the University of Islam, as well

W. D. Mohammed greeted followers at a Saviour's Day convention in Chicago, Illinois, on February 26, 1975, the year he inherited the leadership of the Nation of Islam from his father, Elijah Muhammad, who is depicted in a large banner behind the stage.   *(AP Images)*

as an elementary and a high school. Mohammed attended the school from 1952 to 1954, during which time he began learning Arabic. His high school experiences prepared him for the various roles he played within the NOI after graduation, including as a member of the FRUIT OF ISLAM (FOI), the all-male auxiliary of the movement. During a period spent as minister of the Philadelphia temple in 1958, Mohammed put his Arabic skills to use and delved into the teachings of the QUR'AN. He was careful to do so in ways that did not challenge his father's teachings, many of which conflicted with standard interpretations of Islam.

Mohammed's leadership of the Philadelphia temple ended on October 31, 1961, when he entered the Sandstone Correctional Institution in Minnesota to serve a prison term for draft evasion. Becoming eligible for the military draft in 1953, Mohammed had requested and was granted conscientious objector status. In 1957, however, he did not report for the civilian position he was assigned at a hospital in lieu of his service in the U.S. MILITARY. After a long legal battle, a U.S. District Court sentenced him to three years for draft evasion in 1960. He served fewer than 15 months and was paroled on January 10, 1963.

QUESTIONING AND SEPARATION

According to Mohammed, his time in prison marked a period of personal spiritual growth, inspired by a close study of the Qur'an and the Bible. He saw prison as an opportunity to deepen his understanding of these texts and to read additional Islamic texts, and came to the believe that there was a serious conflict between his father's teachings and those of the larger Sunni Muslim community. When he was paroled in early 1963, Mohammed did not immediately break with his father's organization.

Not until questions of Elijah Muhammad's sexual improprieties arose later that year did significant tensions develop between father and son. By May 1964, Wallace had officially separated from the NOI. During this period of estrangement, he founded the Afro-Descendant Upliftment

Society, an organization that he hoped would provide him with the necessary financial base to remain separate from his father. But the organization failed to gather much support.

Mohammed's relationship to the NOI continued to be strained, and he feared for his life to such an extent that he sought FBI protection. When the prominent NOI speaker MALCOLM X was murdered in February 1965, Wallace returned to the NOI fold. This was not the end of his questioning and dissenting, however. In the following six years, he was banned from the NOI another two, three, perhaps four times. He was readmitted to the NOI in 1974 and quickly established himself as the successor to his ill father. No scholarly account has established how this prodigal son was able to regain his father's confidence late in life and rise above all the other would-be successors to Elijah Muhammad, including Muhammad's National Spokesman LOUIS FARRAKHAN (1933–   ).

CHANGING THE NATION

When Elijah Muhammad died on February 24, 1975, Mohammed had already positioned himself as the new leader of the NOI. He was supported, at least initially, by important NOI figures such as Louis Farrakhan, MUHAMMAD ALI, and his brother, Elijah Muhammad, Jr. The initial transition to his leadership, which many had feared would be tumultuous, was without incident.

But the following years were anything but placid, as Mohammed staged a massive upheaval of NOI structures and beliefs. Only two days after his father's death, Mohammed began addressing what he saw as problematic beliefs within the NOI, starting with the belief in the divinity of W. D. FARD, who had founded the NOI in 1930. Fard was a great spiritual master, he said, but he was not God.

Similarly, Mohammed explained that the NOI's teaching that white people were devils was allegorical, not literal. The apocalyptic belief that white people would be destroyed by a "mother ship" before the end of the world was reinterpreted by Mohammed as a belief that the "white mind"—that is, the racist mind—must be destroyed in all people. On June 15, 1975, before a crowd of 20,000 followers at Chicago's McCormick Place, Mohammed formally invited white people to join the NOI. Through all these changes, Mohammed argued that he was not rejecting his father's teachings but rather fulfilling his father's prophetic vision for the organization.

In October 1975, Mohammed instructed his believers to perform the *salat,* the daily PRAYER involving a series of prostrations and recitation of Qur'anic verses. He also asked all Muslims in Chicago to come together for prayer during Eid al-Fitr, the holiday marking the end of the dawn-to-sunset fasts during the month of Ramadan. In 1977, hundreds of his followers went on pilgrimage to Mecca. Over the following years, he asked ministers to call themselves imams, or Muslim religious leaders, and he said that temples should become mosques, or *masjids,* after the original Arabic. He referred to himself as a *mujaddid,* an Islamic term meaning "renewer of the faith."

Instead of calling themselves Afro-Americans, in November 1975 Mohammed asked African Americans to label themselves "Bilalian," after the Muslim-African ancestor Bilal ibn Rabah. Bilal, the first person to issue the ADHAN, or call to prayer, was an Ethiopian slave in the 7th century who became one of the prophet Muhammad's companions. Mohammed's use of the "Bilalian" label paralleled other efforts in the era of black consciousness and ethnic revival to celebrate the African past of African Americans.

In addition, Mohammed and his followers began to adopt Muslim names, replacing the X that had stood in for the surname of most NOI members. Harvey 2X of Atlanta, for example, became Ahmad Karim. In 1976, Mohammed distributed a list of Muslim names with their meanings in English and invited followers to pick a name that suited them. Mohammed himself retained his last name—at the time spelled Muhammad rather than Mohammed—but he also adopted the name Warith Deen, meaning "inheritor of the faith." Later, he decided to be known simply by his initials, W. D., and spelled his last name as it had been spelled when he was a child: Mohammed.

This was not the only change in nomenclature instituted by Mohammed. In late 1976, he announced that the NOI would henceforth be known as the World Community of al-Islam in the West. Louis Farrakhan, who had initially supported Mohammed's leadership, broke with him in 1978 to reconstitute the Nation of Islam. Farrakhan returned to many of the original belief structures of the NOI, including the idea of black separatism. This split initiated more than two decades of rivalry between these leaders and their organizations, but in February 2000, the two reconciled in an attempt by Farrakhan to bring the NOI more in line with Sunni Islamic practices. Over the years, Farrakhan garnered the most media attention, but Mohammed drew the most followers.

Mohammed continued to experiment with new names for his community of followers. In 1980, the World Community of al-Islam in the West became the American Muslim Mission (AMM). In 1997, the AMM became known as the American Moslem Society and then, in 2002, as the American Society of Muslims.

MUSLIM-AMERICAN SUNNI LEADER

From the 1980s until his death in 2008, W. D. Mohammed remained a popular leader in the African-American Muslim community, even if many African-American Muslims, including his own followers, may have disagreed with one or another of his views—especially his support of the U.S.-led coalition to remove the Iraqi army from Kuwait in 1991. Thousands of followers regularly attended his speeches at universities and convention centers, often traveling great distances to see their imam share his thoughts on various topics during talks that would last two hours or more. Like his father, Mohammed was not a skilled orator. His charisma arose from different attributes. Many found him to be an excellent model by virtue of his unassuming and authentic manner. Sometimes appearing with pencil and a notepad at his lectures, followers would take careful notes on his comments about how the Qur'an and the Sunna, or Tradition, of the prophet Muhammad should be applied to everyday life.

Mohammed consistently emphasized that he did not desire a cult of personality, encouraging Muslims to devote themselves instead to reading the Qur'an and following its guidance. A sometimes reluctant leader of his community, he moved on two separate occasions, once in 1985 and again in 2003, to relinquish organizational responsibility so that he could focus on teaching, preaching, philanthropy, and business activities. Though he remained the de facto leader of an informal network of mosques around the country until his death in 2008, he encouraged each community to take responsibility for its own fate and to hold elections for a board of directors.

Mohammed's work was frequently praised in this period for its focus on reconciliation. He strove to bring SUNNI MUSLIM AMERICANS together as a community, serving in honorary positions or attending the meetings of the ISLAMIC SOCIETY OF NORTH AMERICA and the MUSLIM AMERICAN SOCIETY. He was also a leading figure in global INTERFAITH MOVEMENTS and became involved in the Focolare movement, a Roman Catholic group that has stressed unity and love among all peoples, regardless of religious identity. In 1997, after establishing a friendship with Chiara Lubich, Focolare's leader, Mohammed invited Lubich to speak to Muslims at the Malcolm Shabazz Mosque in NEW YORK CITY. The two had an affinity for each other and appeared at several events together. Mohammed also communicated with Pope John Paul II on at least two occasions. In 1996, he led a small delegation of Muslims in an audience with the pope. Mohammed visited the Vatican again in 1999 and gave an address with both Pope John Paul II and the Dalai Lama present.

The powerful presence Mohammed commanded within the Muslim-American community is illustrated further by the public events in which he was asked to represent Muslim Americans. In 1992, he became the first Muslim to give the invocation in the U.S. Senate. One year later, and then again in 1997, Mohammed was invited to read verses from the Qur'an during President Bill Clinton's inaugural interfaith prayer service.

Mohammed was married at least four times, including two marriages to his first wife, Shirley, and a final marriage to Khadijah Siddeeq. One of Mohammed's nine children, NGina Muhammad-Ali, worked on the *Muslim Journal*. Another of his progeny, Wallace Mohammed II, served in a leadership role in his father's charitable organization, Mosque Cares.

CONCLUSION

W. D. Mohammed played a formative role in the religious history of the Muslim-American community. From bringing the majority of NOI followers to identify with Sunni Islam to representing the community at public events, Mohammed had a profound impact. His tireless work included bridging the gaps between Muslim Americans, meeting with leaders of different faiths, and promoting the faith across the world. His death on September 9, 2008, marked a great loss for the Muslim-American community.

See also FARD, W. D.

Shawntel L. Ensminger

Further Reading
Curtis, Edward E., IV. *Islam in Black America: Identity, Liberation, and Difference in African-American Islamic Thought.* Albany: State University of New York Press, 2002.
Gardell, Mattias. *In the Name of Elijah Muhammad: Louis Farrakhan and the Nation of Islam.* Durham, N.C.: Duke University Press, 1996.
Faith Project, Inc. "This Far by Faith. Warith Deen Mohammed." PBS. Available online. URL: http://www.pbs.org/thisfar byfaith/people/warith_deen_mohammed.html. Accessed March 24, 2009.

W. D. Mohammed
First Muslim Invocation in the U.S. Senate (1992)

Imam W. D. Mohammed (1933–2008), the son of Elijah Muhammad, aligned the Nation of Islam more closely with Sunni Islamic religious practices in the 1970s. On February 6, 1992, Mohammed became the first Muslim imam to offer the invocation before a daily session of the U.S. Senate. The tradition of opening meetings of the Senate with prayer dates to 1789, the first year that the Senate met. As one of its first acts, the Senate elected a chaplain, who ministered to senators and their families in addition to offering prayers before Senate sessions. Though all of the elected chaplains in the 19th and 20th centuries were Protestant Christians, by the late 20th and early 21st centuries, the Senate invited guest chaplains of every world religious tradition, including Judaism, Islam, and Hinduism, to give the prayer. According to the comments of Senators Paul Simon (D-Ill.) and Orrin Hatch (R-Utah), W. D. Mohammed's advocacy of interreligious and interracial harmony made him an appropriate choice as the first Muslim to do so.

The Imam Wallace D. Mohammed, Calumet City, IL, offered the following prayer:

Our Creator, the merciful benefactor, the merciful Redeemer who opens for all people a way to have good conscience and a good life:

Grant to this Nation that Americans continue to live as a prosperous nation of "many in one" and as a people of faith taking pride in human decency, industry, and service.

Let us pray that this great Nation's two centuries of national life may inspire other nations to move toward social and economic justice for all.

Grant that her big heart for charity, compassion, repentance, and mercy continue to beat strongly within all of us. Grant that Americans always have more hope than troubles and ever grow in goodness and in wisdom.

Bless Americans to always cherish our freedom and the noble essence of the American people.

Grant that we Americans understand better our brothers and sisters around the world and reject unsuitable national pride for a global community of brotherhood and peace.

Bring all citizens and Government together, those of great means and small means, to appreciate more our Nation's solemn pledge of liberty, peace, and justice for all.

Bless our homes and our schools.

Bless the parents, our troubled youth, our burdened inner cities to never be without hope or direction. Bless Americans to keep to the best of our ways.

Bless Americans to cherish more the pride of industry.

Bless the efforts of the President and all other efforts in progress for more jobs and more opportunity to be in this great society for more of us.

Bless matrimony and families here and in all the world.

Increase for the President of the United States, for every Member of the Senate, and for every Member of the House of Representatives, the excellence of man's spirit and the excellence of the intellect of the statesmen so that they may build a better America for us all. Amen.

* * *

Mr. SIMON. Mr. President [of the Senate], history was made in a small way this morning. We had an invocation by Imam Mohammed, the first Muslim to offer an invocation here in the U.S. Senate.

I think it is important that we reach out to one another, whether we are Christians, Jews, Muslims, Buddhists, whatever our belief or lack of belief. This morning's *Washington Post* has a story about Muslims fleeing persecution from what we have generally called Burma in the past.

The intolerance that is around the world in too many places is a cause for grief and is a cause for bloodshed and tragedy. What has happened this morning is the Imam Mohammed, is known in the Chicago area and around the Nation for reaching out to people of other beliefs and for preaching tolerance and understanding—his presence here today is, first of all, a tribute to him. I was pleased to join my colleagues, Senator [Alan] Dixon [D-Ill.] and Senator Hatch, in co-hosting his presence here today.

But it is a reminder to all of us, whatever our beliefs; yes, be firm in your beliefs, but also do not let excessive pride cause disruptions in our society, whether it is on the basis of religion, race, national background, or what it is. I hope today is one more small step in creating a nation and a world where there is more understanding.

* * *

Mr. HATCH. Mr. President, I would like to join in the remarks of my distinguished and great colleagues from Illinois. This is a great day for the U.S. Senate and for our country in having Imam Wallace Mohammed with us today, the first Muslim to pray in the U.S. Senate. We could not have made a better choice. There is not a better man in America or better religious leader who is trying to do what is right for his people in the inner cities, in jobs, in teachings of morality and decency, and in so many ways that help those who need help, to lend a helping hand.

Mohammed is a great man. He is a kind man. He is a compassionate man. He is a decent man. And it is an honor for us to have him in the Senate this day. I think it is fair to note that some of his greatest friends are sitting in the gallery today, some of whom are known by people all over the world, people of all faiths, of all religions. So we have made great strides today in the Senate, and I think the Senate is honored to have this great religious leader with us. I look forward to continuing an association and friendship with him and with his people for many years to come in the future.

⬥

Source: Congressional Record (Senate) 138, no. 14, 102nd Congress 2nd Session, February 6, 1992, S1103-S1104.

Moorish Science Temple

The Moorish Science Temple of America (MSTA) began in 1925 in CHICAGO, ILLINOIS, under the leadership of Timothy Drew (1886–1929), more commonly known within his religious community as NOBLE DREW ALI. Ali founded the Canaanite Temple, a precursor to the MSTA, in Newark, New Jersey, in 1913. It was in Chicago, however, where the MSTA would make its mark on Muslim-American history. The MSTA was initially incorporated as the Moorish Holy Temple of Science before being renamed in 1928. It would grow to include followers throughout urban and rural regions in the northern, Midwestern, and southern states. The history and development of the MSTA has been largely shaped by its message of a Moorish, Islamic heritage for blacks, respect for other religions, and an emphasis on social uplift.

BEGINNINGS

Ali was born Timothy Drew in North Carolina, eventually making his way to Chicago in his adult years. The details of Ali's early life are unknown. He claimed to have traveled to Egypt to study with a mystical teacher from whom he received esoteric knowledge of divine truths. It is evident from his theology and the MSTA's early development, however, that American religious traditions of Islam and Freemasonry were the basis for Ali's religious leadership. The MSTA emerged in the post–World War I years of growing urbanization, as hundreds of thousands of African-American southerners streamed to the northern urban centers seeking better jobs and relief from white mob violence, especially lynching. Ali was among these migrants. Northern cities like Chicago, DETROIT, NEW YORK CITY, and Philadelphia seemed to offer a needed change and greater opportunity. In addition, religious and social influences like Marcus Garvey's Universal Negro Improvement Association had introduced to millions of blacks the idea that they should actually take pride in their racial identity instead of internalizing self-hatred and a sense of inferiority. Most important, in the 1920s, the U.S. Supreme Court continued to interpret segregation law as constitutional, and white public officials typically viewed the nation as properly white, denying basic rights to blacks. Into this environment Ali entered with a message proclaiming an ethnic religion of Islam for black Americans.

TEACHINGS

Timothy Drew would come to identify himself as "Noble" Drew Ali, a prophet whose message of salvation to "so-called Negroes" claimed for them a rich history based on their own culture with distinctive clothing, geographic origin, and, most important, their own religion—Islam. Although Ali desired to create pride among blacks, he rejected America's racial labels like "black," "colored," and "Negro." Most essential was his message that these "so-called Negroes" were in fact Moorish Americans, descended from the ancient Moabites described in the Bible. Their homeland was Morocco. Because of their religious and geographic roots, Ali emphasized to his followers that they should properly recognize themselves as members of the larger "Asiatic" race, a category in which Ali included all peoples of color. Every nation or race, according to Ali, possessed its own national religion. So Christianity belonged to Europeans. Ali taught that he had been chosen to deliver a divine message to Moorish Americans, reminding them of their true identity (Moorish) and true religion (Islam). He introduced a Moorish national flag, a red banner bearing a five-pointed green star. Ali also presented to these Moorish Americans their own "divinely prepared" scriptures, the *Holy Koran of the Moorish Science Temple of America*, also called the *Circle Seven Koran*. This text related a history of the Moabites and other Canaanite peoples and also described the activities of Jesus in Asiatic lands. The oppressed status of blacks as second-class citizens was the fundamental problem to which Ali responded; white Americans treated blacks as if they did not belong in the United States, as an unwanted "white man's burden." Ali believed that if black Americans embraced their true Moorish "nationality" (as he termed it), the U.S. government under which they lived and all other nations would respect so-called Negroes and regard them as a people with a history and who merited dignity.

Since most early converts to the MSTA were former Protestants, Ali's teachings about Jesus and Christianity were especially important. Ali emphasized the origins of Christianity within the ancient Roman Empire. Christianity, he taught, was the religion of the "pale skin" European Romans who executed Jesus, whom Ali identified as a member of the Moabite nation, one of the Asiatic races. Jesus was a prophet whose mission, according to Ali, was to rescue the Jewish nation from rule by the "pale skin nations of Europe." As the *Circle Seven Koran* explained to its readers, European Christians, after executing Jesus, enjoyed a peaceful existence for many centuries until "Muhammad the first" (i.e., Muhammad ibn Abdallah of seventh-century Arabia) arrived on the scene to "fulfill the will of Jesus" by formally establishing the first Muslim community. In this way, Ali attempted to reclaim Jesus as a person of color from his symbolic use by white American Christians who typically promoted anti-black racism with no hint of irony.

This picture of the 1928 convention of the Moorish Science Temple in Chicago featured movement founder Noble Drew Ali (*first row, standing, fifth from left*). Ali's Islamic symbols and clothing were generally adapted from the Black Shriners, an African-American fraternal organization.   *(Photographs and Prints Division, Schomburg Center for Research in Black Culture, The New York Public Library, Astor, Lenox, and Tilden Foundations)*

The response to Ali's message of Moorish redemption was considerable. In Chicago, where the MSTA headquarters was established, Moorish Americans commanded public respectability until Ali's suspicious death in 1929. Working with his wife, Pearl Jones Drew Ali, Noble Drew Ali and other MSTA members organized parades and public celebrations of an ancient Moorish heritage that drew large crowds, including local political leaders. The pages of the *Chicago Defender* provided positive coverage of the movement, which was a major public relations asset. The MSTA also established the Moorish Manufacturing Company to produce oils, incense, soaps, and other Moorish products, the sales from which buoyed the religion's financial base. From New York City to Kansas City, Kansas, to Belzoni, Mississippi, MSTA converts established temples and vibrant communities of faith with a resounding message of renewal through reclaiming a religious heritage that stretched from ancient Palestine to Arabia to the empires of northern Africa.

Especially important were elements of the religion that communicated as sense of ethnic identity. Followers received new names ending in "Bey" or "El" to denote their Moorish ancestry. They paid nominal membership dues (ranging from 50 cents to two dollars in the 1920s and 1930s) and, in exchange, received membership cards certifying that their identity was not Negro but "Moorish American." Male members wore the fez to distinguish themselves. During formal events, men and women donned robes that suggested an Eastern style of dress. The *Circle Seven Koran,* along with other instructional literature of the MSTA, grounded followers in a compelling worldview that emphasized the value of having a heritage and gaining respect for themselves.

Many members of the MSTA were inspired by these teachings to defy segregation laws, claiming that such laws did not apply to them since they were Moors and not "so-called Negroes." Like all other religious movements throughout history, including earlier expressions of Islam, the MSTA drew on their immediate environment to express their religion. The public parades and attire of Shriners influenced Ali's choice of clothing, and the swell of interest in "lost traditions" about Jesus, especially Levi Dowling's *Aquarian Gospel* (1908), provided the basis for the *Holy Koran* that Ali published.

The MSTA departed from the sexist leadership pattern that dominated most American religious establishments. Although Ali did not formally stipulate shared authority among women and men, he chose from the beginning to include women in leadership. In 1928, he ordained and appointed M. Whitehead-El (the aunt of his wife, Pearl) to lead one of the Chicago temples. In the 1930s, three of the MSTA's "Grand Governors" were women; in this capacity, they held either regional or state authority in Illinois, Tennessee, and New Jersey.

The MSTA, under Noble Drew Ali's leadership, also introduced the American religious public to the first institutional critique of American slavery as a process of religious cultural destruction. Instead of celebrating the Christianization of blacks, the MSTA lamented that Islam had been stripped from American's black slaves. This analysis of slavery would be followed most notably by the NATION OF ISLAM beginning in the 1930s and by Yoruba revivalism in the 1950s. The MSTA also instituted holidays that continue to be observed today. These include January 8, the birthday of Prophet Noble Drew Ali, and January 15, the Moorish New Year. In addition, the MSTA holds an annual national convention in September.

NOBLE DREW ALI'S DEATH AND FACTIONS

Most of the formal assemblies of the Chicago Moors occurred in Unity Hall, a brick building on Chicago's Indiana Avenue that the MSTA purchased in 1926 for such purposes. The MSTA enjoyed general favor in the public eye until the time of Ali's suspicious death. In March 1929, Claude Greene, who had formerly worked with Ali as a business manager for the MSTA, was shot and stabbed. His violent death led the Chicago police to arrest Ali along with dozens of other Moors. Ali was suspected to be behind the murder because of testimony that he and Greene had parted ways and were competing for followers. Meanwhile, public sentiment soured as local media produced negative reports of the prophet, alleging sex scandals and financial exploitation. Ali was eventually released on $10,000 bail, but within days he was found dead in his apartment. The cause of his death was never resolved, but his followers suspected police abuse.

Noble Drew Ali's untimely death brought competing interests to the surface of the religious community. During his lifetime, some MSTA members had begun flashing their membership cards before whites to protest racist treatment, and others had become vocally critical of the federal government. Ali had sought to dampen both of these trends. After his death, some followers insisted that they had inherited Ali's spirit and should be recognized as his successor. Among these was Ali's chauffeur, Timothy Givens-El. He assumed the name Noble Drew Ali Reincarnated Muhammad III, and he led a faction of followers to organize a formally separate body of Moors, which he called the Moorish Science Temple Divine and National Movement of North America. After his arrest, Ali had appointed a follower named Ford-El to lead the main temple in Chicago. But Ford-El moved to Detroit and, under the name W. D. FARD, organized what became the Nation of Islam. E. Mealy-El, as governor and supreme grand sheik of Temple No. 1 in Chicago, also led a competing faction. Eventually, however, the majority of Moors would recognize the leadership of Charles Kirkman-Bey, who was supreme grand adviser of Chicago's Temple No. 9. Until his death in 1959, Kirkman-Bey traveled to temples throughout the country to reestablish unity and to rebuild the MSTA's momentum, which had floundered under the impact of Ali's death.

DEVELOPMENT AND GOVERNMENT SUPPRESSION: 1940s TO 1970s

The most tumultuous period for the MSTA began in the 1940s as the United States enforced the Selective Service Act and instituted the draft, preparing to enter WORLD WAR II. The MSTA, since its origins, had emphasized loyalty to the federal government while calling for worldwide unity among peoples of color and fair treatment as citizens. By 1941, however, many MSTA temples encouraged their male members to refuse registration for the draft in a war against Japan, a "colored" nation, because African Americans themselves were denied citizenship rights by a federal government that openly espoused white supremacy and enforced racial discrimination in the military, public education, voting, public transportation, and other aspects of life. The result was a decades-long process whereby the Federal Bureau of Investigation (FBI) suppressed the MSTA, classifying Moors as a threat to national security, claiming they were sponsored by Japan, and describing them as poorly educated fanatics because of their belief in racial equality.

The FBI successfully planted numerous informants in local temples, threatened to prosecute local Moorish leaders to frighten them into ceasing their religious work, and eavesdropped on the MSTA's religious meetings. The MSTA's national leader, Kirkman-Bey, like other members of the Moorish Science Temple, predictably became a frequent target of FBI surveillance. Most devastating was a series of mass arrests by the FBI in the 1940s, which took its toll on the religious community. During this time, the leadership of women in the MSTA, formally organized as the Sisters National Auxiliary, was crucial in sustaining the work and worship of the temples. In the 1950s and 1960s, FBI repression against a number of black religious and secular organizations was intensified under the implementation of the U.S. Department of Justice's Counter-Intelligence Program (COINTELPRO), and the MSTA continued to suffer severe repression. Some minor progress was made, however, as federal authorities gradually began to regard the MSTA more seriously as a bona fide religious community. For the first time, a few MSTA members were legally permitted to petition their status as conscientious objectors to war.

INSTITUTIONAL CONTINUITY:
1970s TO PRESENT

In 1975, one of the smaller sects of the Moorish Science Temple, led by Richardson Dingle-El, relocated their headquarters from Illinois to Maryland. Sheik Richardson Dingle-El, who had led the Moorish Science Temple National and Divine Movement during the era of the Civil Rights movement, devoted much of his work to seeking reparations for blacks from the federal government of the 1950s and 1960s. His brother, Timothy Dingle-El, wrote a history of this particular Moorish American group, *The Resurrection of the Moorish Science Temple*. This smaller group has continued to publish its organ *Moorish Voice* from its Chicago center.

Meanwhile, the larger body of Moors continued under the national leadership of R. Love-El, who in 1971 followed J. Blakely-Bey as the supreme grand adviser and moderator. With the ongoing struggle to implement desegregation in the 1960s and 1970s and the rapid urbanization of blacks, more African Americans encountered racist police departments; imprisonment was becoming the fate of numerous urban blacks. In this context, Love-El led the MSTA to develop a formidable prison ministry network, which continues today. Since its beginning, the MSTA has published periodicals to communicate with membership and to represent its religious interests, including the *Moorish Review, Moorish American Voice*, and *Moorish Guide National Edition*. Such publications continue to serve a vital function. Like other organizations, the MSTA has established an Internet presence as well. In 2002, R. Jones-Bey became the grand sheik and moderator (national leader) of the MSTA, following the death of R. Love-El. The slate of local and national leaders, moreover, has fully retained its commitment to a balance of men and women.

The contemporary concerns of African-American Islam, as with other religious communities, continue to shift over the decades. Nevertheless, the continuity of the MSTA is evident in the Moors' abiding emphasis on the importance of possessing a heritage, since Ali taught that an ethnic heritage affords a people the ability to command respect as Americans. Although its most dynamic years of growth seem to have passed, the MSTA, with more than 40 temples and a few thousand members, continues to thrive as a vital part of the varieties of Islamic faiths in the United States today.

Sylvester Johnson

Further Reading

Clegg, Claude Andrew, III. *An Original Man: The Life and Times of Elijah Muhammad.* New York: St. Martin's Press, 1997.

Curtis, Edward E., IV. *Islam in Black America: Identity, Liberation, and Difference in African-American Islamic Thought.* Albany: State University of New York Press, 2002.

Dannin, Robert. *Black Pilgrimage to Islam.* New York: Oxford University Press, 2002.

Evanzz, Karl. *The Messenger: The Rise and Fall of Elijah Muhammad.* New York: Pantheon, 1999.

McCloud, Aminah Beverly. *African American Islam.* New York: Routledge, 1995.

"Moorish Science Temple of America." In *Encyclopedia of African American Religions,* edited by Larry J. Murphy, Gordon Melton, and Gary L. Ward. New York: Garland, 1993.

Mubashshir, Debra Washington. "Forgotten Fruit of the City: Chicago and the Moorish Science Temple of America." *Cross Currents* 51, no. 1 (Spring 2001): 6–20.

Nance, Susan. "Mystery of the Moorish Science Temple: Southern Blacks and American Alternative Spirituality in 1920s Chicago." *Religion and American Culture* 12, no. 2 (Summer 2002): 123–166.

———. "Respectability and Representation: The Moorish Science Temple, Morocco, and Black Public Culture in 1920s Chicago." *American Quarterly* 54, no. 4 (December 2002): 623–659.

Turner, Richard Brent. *Islam in the African-American Experience.* 2d ed. Bloomington: Indiana University Press, 2003.

Wilson, Peter Lamborn. *Sacred Drift: Essays on the Margins of Islam.* San Francisco: City Lights Books, 1993.

Juanita Richardson-Bey, "Dio de Mio" (1929)

The success of Islamic movements among African Americans has often been explained partly as a result of these movements' attractiveness to men. The Nation of Islam in the 1960s and some late 20th-century Sunni Muslim communities have been viewed as groups in which men attempt to assert their patriarchal authority over women—reclaiming the black manhood, as Malcolm X described it, that they had lost during the era of slavery. But the association of

African-American Islamic communities with men wrongly ignores the history of African-American women, who have helped to build and sustain black Muslim groups since the 1920s. One such movement is the Moorish Science Temple of America, established by Noble Drew Ali in 1925. In his organization, women ascended to the highest levels of authority next to Ali himself. C. Alsop Bey was a governess in Chicago, while Sister Lomax Bey was grand governess of Detroit. Sister Whitehead-El was the head of a temple located at 862 Townsend Street in Chicago. Juanita Mayo Richardson-Bey played a different role. As managing editor of the newspaper Moorish Guide, *she helped to shape the news that the movement reported to the outside world. She was also a poet who recited her own work and the poems of others at organizational gatherings. In the 1929 poem below, Richardson-Bey expresses thanks for the comfort that faith in God/Allah gives her and asks for God's presence in the year ahead, the very year in which Noble Drew Ali, her prophet, would be killed.*

Dio de Mio [God of Mine]

There's peace within thy walls—Almighty Allah
   The prayers of Israel's children soothe my mind;
And all the restlessness of me is calmed;
   My futile heartaches vanish as I pray
The loneliness that haunted all my days,
   E'en when I mingled with the crowds, is gone;

I feel the force and strength of calm companionship,
   Uniting me with all Thy quiet strength.
Oh all these years I battled with myself,
   Denying fiercely there was any God-Allah;
And all I found was emptiness in life,
   Until today when something led me here,
And midst the prayers of Israel I find peace.

My Allah—and Allah of all my fathers
   Hear my supplication—In the coming year
Be with me, with me when the road is dark with
   doubt,
   Be with me when the haunting loneliness
Would crush my spirit down to the depths.
   Oh! Never let me know the emptiness.

Source: Moorish Guide, 1929.

Moorish Science Temple, Inc. v. Smith

Moorish Science Temple, Inc. v. Smith (1982) is among the most significant court cases dealing with dietary restrictions among Muslim prison inmates. This case, which was decided by the U.S. Court of Appeals for the Second Circuit in NEW YORK CITY in 1982, determined that prison authorities must provide diets consistent with their inmates' religious beliefs while they are incarcerated. The court ruled that failure to accommodate religious dietary restrictions is a violation of First Amendment rights to the free exercise of religion.

In *Moorish Science Temple, Inc. v. Smith,* R. Smallwood-El alleged that his First Amendment rights to freedom of religion had been violated while he was incarcerated at Attica Correctional Facility in New York for burglary. He filed a suit against Harold J. Smith, superintendent of the prison, and argued his case before the United States District Court for the Western District of New York in 1976. Smallwood-El, a member of the MOORISH SCIENCE TEMPLE of America, claimed that prison officials provided Jewish inmates with alternative diets that conformed to the requirements of their religion but refused to accommodate the dietary restrictions of members of his religion. In addition to his charge about his rights to practice his religion, Smallwood-El also challenged the state proceedings leading to his arrest and alleged that his constitutional rights had also been violated because he was held in isolation for 23 hours per day without a hearing. Smallwood-El contended that the state had not complied with habeas corpus requirements in his case. These requirements stipulate that the state must bring prisoners before the court to decide whether the state has the proper authority to confine them. The district court determined that Smallwood-El had failed to exhaust all available state remedies for his habeas corpus claims and dismissed his petition.

Smallwood-El appealed the court's decision. In 1982, the appellate court upheld the lower court's decision that Smallwood-El had failed to exhaust all available state remedies for his habeas corpus claims but reversed its decision regarding the conditions of his confinement. The appellate court determined that Smallwood-El's constitutional rights had been violated because he was denied a diet that conformed to his religious beliefs and was held in isolation without a proper disciplinary hearing. The court maintained that the state must provide Muslim inmates with diets that conform to Islamic dietary requirements.

This decision affirmed the precedent set in 1975 with *Kahane v. Carlson,* in which the U.S. Court of Appeals for the Second Circuit determined that the denial of kosher food in prison was a violation of the First Amendment, and extended the same considerations to Muslim prisoners. Two similar cases, however, challenged the legal interpretations set forth in *Kahane v. Carlson* and *Moorish Science Temple, Inc. v. Smith.* In *Jihaad v. Carlson* (1976), the U.S. District Court for Eastern Michigan ruled that prisoners cannot be forced to eat pork products but are not entitled to a special diet. The court cited an earlier case, *Knuckles v. Prasse* (1970), as the precedent for its decision. In *Barnes v. Virgin Islands* (1976), the U.S. District Court for the Virgin Islands urged prison officials to make reasonable efforts to provide Rastafarian and Muslim inmates with diets that conformed to their religious dietary restrictions but did not require them to do so.

Tammy Heise

Further Reading

Moore, Kathleen M. *Al-Mughtaribun: American Law and the Transformation of Muslim Life in the United States*. Albany: State University of New York Press, 1995.

Mos Def (1973–) *rap singer, actor*

Mos Def is an American rapper and actor from Brooklyn, New York. Born Dante Terrell Smith on December 11, 1973, Mos Def emerged as a major force in the underground hip-hop scene in the late 1990s as a part of a new wave of socially conscious rappers who celebrated political consciousness and Afrocentric themes. In 1998, he received widespread acclaim for his breakthrough album with the group Black Star, formed with rapper Talib Kweli and producer Hi-Tek, entitled *Mos Def and Talib Kweli Are Black Star*. His performances on that album achieved fame for their complex freestyles (improvisations), the distinctive quality of his voice, and cogent, pro-black political messages. In 1999, Mos Def produced a solo album, *Black on Both Sides,* which further cemented his reputation as one of the most talented rappers of his time. Both albums are widely regarded as hip-hop classics. Since then, he has released three albums, *The New Danger* (2004), *True Magic* (2006), and *Mos Definite* (2007), though the latter was not released in the United States.

Following the release of *Black on Both Sides,* Mos Def turned the bulk of his professional attentions toward acting, and he is one of the few rappers to transition successfully into stage, screen, and film work. Since 2000, he has enjoyed critical and commercial success as an actor, costarring in films such as Spike Lee's *Bamboozled* (2000), the Oscar-nominated *Monster's Ball* (2001), and Hollywood blockbusters *The Italian Job* (2003) and *16 Blocks* (2006). In 2002, he made his Broadway debut in Suzan Lori-Park's Tony-nominated, Pulitzer Prize–winning play, *Topdog/Underdog,* and in 2005 garnered an Emmy nomination for his role in the made-for-TV movie *Something the Lord Made.* He has also served as host for HBO's award-winning spoken word series, *Def Poetry Jam,* since its debut in 2001.

Mos Def has been an outspoken social critic and political activist throughout his career, speaking frequently on issues of black empowerment and America's involvement in the War on Terror. In 2004, he released "Bin Laden" (recorded with rapper Eminem), a controversial song that blamed the terrorist attacks of SEPTEMBER 11, 2001, on what he viewed as the destructive policies of Republican presidents Ronald Reagan, George H. W. Bush, and George W. Bush. Released the following year, his single "Katrina Clap" criticized the government's response to Hurricane Katrina. He has also worked extensively on campaigns protesting the prison sentences of African-American journalist Mumia Abu-Jamal and African-American Muslim imam JAMIL ABDULLAH AL-AMIN (formerly known as H. Rap Brown). A devout Sunni Muslim, Mos Def's father, a former member of the NATION OF ISLAM who later joined the congregation of Imam W. D. MOHAMMED, first introduced the rapper/actor to Islam at age 13. He became a Muslim six years later at age 19, after meeting other Muslim rappers such as Q-Tip and Ali Shaheed Muhammad from A TRIBE CALLED QUEST.

Mos Def opens many of his albums and performances with the words "Bismallah ar-Rahman ar-Raheem" (In the name of God, the most gracious, the most merciful) and credits his Islamic faith as the driving force behind his involvement with social issues, declaring in an interview with Beliefnet.com, "If Islam's sole interest is the welfare of mankind, then Islam is the strongest advocate of human rights anywhere on Earth."

Sylvia Chan-Malik

Further Reading

Abdel-Alim, Hesham Samy. "Hip Hop Islam." *Ah-Ahram Weekly* 7, no. 740 (2005). Available online. URL: http://weekly.ahram.org.eg/2005/750/feature.htm. Accessed January 21, 2008.

Asadullah, Ali. "You're Gonna Serve Somebody." Beliefnet.com. Available online. URL: http://beliefnet.com/story/75/story_7526.html. Accessed January 17, 2008.

Birchmeier, Jason. "Mos Def." In *All Music Guide to Hip Hop: The Definitive Guide to Rap & Hip Hop,* edited by Hal Leonard Corporation. San Francisco: Backbeat Books, 2003.

Mosque of Islamic Brotherhood   See AFRICAN-AMERICAN MUSLIMS.

mosques and Islamic centers

Most simply defined, a mosque, or *masjid,* is a place where Muslims perform the *salat,* the prayer in which they prostrate themselves in the direction of Mecca as many as five times per day. Muslims also pray in other spaces, which are sometimes known by different names. For example, the recitation of DHIKR, or litanies reciting the names of God in addition to other rituals of piety, can take place in Sufi lodges, often called *tekkes* or *khanaqas.* Shi'a Muslims, in addition to praying in mosques, also conduct a number of PRAYER rituals in IMAMBARGAHS, husayniyas, and JAMAATKHANAS.

The Druze community offers its prayers in the *majlis*. For most Muslims in the United States, however, the mosque is the primary space for weekly congregational prayer and the preferred site for daily prayer.

By the beginning of the 21st century, there were more than 2,000 mosques and Islamic centers throughout the United States. From its modest beginning as an informal space of gathering for America's first Muslims in the 17th and 18th centuries, to elaborate, architecturally sophisticated structures confidently proclaiming Muslims as permanent citizens in the United States, the mosque has provided a space for spiritual reflection, congregation, education, and social and cultural activities for Muslim Americans. Mosques and Islamic centers have built and reinforced communal, ethnic, and religious solidarity. For Muslims and non-Muslims alike, the mosque has become an important symbol of Islam in the United States and a marker of the religion's presence in the country.

A number of terms have been used historically for "mosque" among Americans, ranging from *"masjid,"* a word derived from Arabic but also prevalent in a number of other languages of the Muslim world, to the more generic "temple," preferred by some early groups of African-American Muslims such as the Moorish Science Temple of America and the Nation of Islam. Serving a variety of urban and rural communities, ethnic groupings, and a range of Muslims from diverse branches of Islam, the mosque is for many Muslims the center not only of their religious and cultural life but also a marker of their Muslim-American identity and a reminder of the religion's continued presence in the United States.

THE FIRST AMERICAN MOSQUES

While the first purpose-built mosques were constructed in the early decades of the 20th century, Muslims had been gathering in temporary spaces since their earliest days in the Thirteen Colonies and, later, the United States. The earliest Muslim-American prayer spaces were used by African-American Muslim slaves from the 17th to the 19th centuries. The earliest Muslim Americans practiced their religion and maintained their identities mainly by praying informally in their living quarters, in the woods, or in nearly any other place. Without the means or freedoms to build designated spaces, these Muslims "created" spaces in which to contemplate and pray.

These were the earliest of American *masjids* in the technical sense—literally places of prostration—and they served the thousands of Muslim slaves who were brought to the United States from sub-Saharan West Africa, which itself had seen the spread of Islam before and during the period of the transatlantic slave trade. While some slaves were illiterate and had limited access to education, others were leaders of their communities and teachers of the Qur'an. As a result, their religious practices and systems of prayer varied from the recitation of the *salat,* one of the pillars of Sunni Islamic practice, to the recitation of *dhikr,* or religious litanies.

EARLY TWENTIETH-CENTURY INSTITUTIONAL FOUNDATIONS

Between 1875 and 1912, immigration to the United States from various regions of the Ottoman Empire was set in motion, as many sought to make their fortunes in America. Most of these early Muslim immigrants were from former Ottoman territories today known as Lebanon, Syria, Jordan, Israel, and Palestine. Following the pattern of emigration in the 19th century, Arab Christians arrived in larger numbers first, being exposed more readily to prospects of moving westwards and aware that their religion was shared outside their own borders and boundaries. They were soon joined by an increasing number of Sunni and Shi'a Muslims, as well as by their Druze and Alawi coreligionists.

Early Arab-American Muslims settled first in the Midwest, including North Dakota; Cedar Rapids, Iowa; Michigan City, Indiana; and Detroit, Michigan. Since many planned at some point to return to their homelands, they did not build stand-alone mosques but instead used simple, informal, or rented spaces such as converted firehalls, churches, basements, theaters, and warehouses. With the eventual collapse of the Ottoman Empire and the turmoil brought on by World War I, however, many more immigrant Muslims made the United States their permanent homes and invited their relatives to settle in their newfound land. As a result, individuals gradually formed large family networks and began to focus on practical and religious needs such as sanctifying marriages and burying their dead in Islamic cemeteries. Accordingly, it became necessary to think about more permanent structures to facilitate the religious needs of the community.

A number of buildings—most of which were in the Midwestern United States—emerged during this period as America's first purpose-built mosques. With the intention of blending into their environment, each of these buildings resembled their architectural surroundings. In 1921, Detroit's Muslim leaders celebrated the opening of the Moslem Mosque with a parade that attracted hundreds from the local Muslim community. Shi'a imam Kalil Bazzy, Ahmadi Muslim–American leader Muhammad Sadiq, and others were on hand to thank Lebanese-American real estate developer Muhammad Karoub for building the mosque. Karoub's brother, Hussien Karoub (1892–1973), a Sunni Muslim, became the mosque's leader.

Despite the fanfare that greeted the mosque's opening, it operated for only a few years, then was purchased by the city of Highland Park in 1926. But Karoub remained a popular pastor, often traveling to offer guest lectures or raise money for other Muslim-American imams. One of the legacies of this mosque and of other early mosques was to establish its prayer leader as a congregational minister in the mold of other American pastors, including Christian-American ministers and Jewish-American rabbis. Like his pastoral compatriots, Karoub and the early generation of Muslim imams often oversaw the weddings of Muslims and their burials, offered advice and informal counseling, raised money for other congregations and various causes, and acted as liaisons between Muslims and non-Muslims. The mosque and its imam became quintessentially American institutions.

American influences also appeared in the architectural styles of mosques. In 1929, in Ross, North Dakota, a building set into a shallow trench in the earth and reminiscent of a granary or other farm structure became the only purpose-built mosque for Muslim Americans in North Dakota. It was used by the town's Muslim community until the 1960s but was never completed because of the GREAT DEPRESSION and later because of a number of other social and economic pressures on Ross's Muslim community. Over time, as the small Muslim prairie community struggled to maintain its numbers and through an increasing number of marriages to Christians as well as conversions, the mosque fell out of use and was eventually torn down.

In 1919, Muslims in Michigan City, Indiana, began to meet for congregational prayer on a regular basis through their organization, the Modern Age Arabian Islamic Society.

But they did not build their own mosque until 1934. That same year, the "Mother Mosque of America" was completed in Cedar Rapids, Iowa. It was begun as the Rose of Fraternity Lodge in 1925, and its supporters later erected a simple white two-story rectangular building with an iconic green dome over the front door. In its design and shape, it was akin to and drew on the models of a country schoolhouse or rural church. It was marked by a sign in English and Arabic announcing it as a space for Muslim prayer. The first floor was used extensively as a prayer space, while the second floor hosted social and cultural events.

During the Great Depression the mosque quickly fell into disuse and disrepair. Only in 1991, after it was vacated and then used as a Pentecostal church and teen center was it repurchased and renovated. In 1992, a rededication ceremony saw it open its doors again, although most Muslims attended the city's larger, more modern Islamic center, which had opened in 1992 to serve the city's 700 Muslim families from more than 30 countries. This "Mother Mosque" was listed in the National Register of Historic Buildings in 1996.

In the 1920s, after successfully bringing their missionary movement to Europe one decade earlier, Ahmadi Muslims began to proselytize in the United States, first in New York and later in Detroit and Chicago, where they established their first "mission house," which included a mosque. With limited success in converting "white Americans" to Islam,

Unique for its architectural style, this mosque in Ross, North Dakota, was used by the town's Muslim community from 1929 through the 1960s. Muslims from Ross, who traced their roots to Syria, built the mosque to withstand the harsh winters of the American Plains.   *(AP Images/Minot Daily News)*

the charismatic Muhammad Sadiq, the representative of the Ahmadi movement in the United States, turned to African Americans and converted hundreds, if not thousands to Islam. He won the most converts in Detroit and CHICAGO, with lesser but notable successes in Gary, Indiana, and St. Louis, Missouri.

Supported primarily by community members in the Indian subcontinent, the Ahmadi Muslim mission set up and financed a network of "mission houses" and mosques in the United States, bringing together Muslims of various ethnicities as well as immigrants and native-born Americans. By the 1940s, the Ahmadiyya movement claimed more than 2 million adherents worldwide, of which as many as 10,000 could be found in the United States. Their primary missions and mosques were located in Chicago, CLEVELAND, Kansas City, WASHINGTON, D.C., and Pittsburgh. Though the movement declined later years, it continued its tradition of sustaining mission houses in various cities, using converted one-story houses to host its prayers and other activities.

1945 TO 1965: A CHANGING SCENE

If measured by the establishment of mosques, the fastest-growing Muslim-American organization in the era immediately following WORLD WAR II was the Nation of Islam (NOI). Rather than building its own congregational spaces, however, the NOI generally rented and then often purchased converted storefronts, churches, and, for its Chicago headquarters, a former synagogue. NOI founder W. D. FARD created the first Temple of Islam in Detroit in 1930, followed quickly by Temple No. 2 in Chicago. Milwaukee and Washington, D.C., were added to the list during the 1940s. By 1973, the NOI claimed more than 70 mosques and temples—terms that were used interchangeably by thousands of members from coast to coast.

A number of activities occurred throughout the week in NOI mosques, which unlike most mosques featured benches on which members could sit. In Chicago's Temple No. 2 in the late 1950s, Wednesday and Friday lectures started with prayers that combined verses from the Qur'an, recited in English, with blessings on NOI leader ELIJAH MUHAMMAD,

Located in Chicago, Mosque Maryam, named after the Qur'anic (and biblical) Mary, was originally a Greek Orthodox church. Purchased by Elijah Muhammad, leader of the Nation of Islam and then repurchased by Louis Farrakhan, the mosque differed from most other American mosques in that it contained pews and, later, seats. *(Daniel Lainé)*

Islamic Society of North America headquarters, Plainfield, Indiana. Located next to Interstate Highway 70 and rising above corn and bean fields, the headquarters and mosque of the Islamic Society of North America was built in the early 1980s. Architect Gulzar Haider used abstract geometric patterns to express Islamic themes such as God's Oneness.   *(Edward E. Curtis IV)*

whom members believed to be a prophet. Hands outstretched and palms facing upward—a gesture common among Muslims in prayer—members bowed their heads, closed their eyes, and recited these prayers. When finished, they passed their palms over their faces, saying Amen using the Arabic pronunciation.

But in addition to explicitly religious meetings, NOI temples and mosques hosted special events such as jazz concerts and became entrepreneurial sites in which the selling of MUHAMMAD SPEAKS, the group's newspaper, was coordinated. Perhaps most important, NOI temples and mosques were spaces for meetings of the FRUIT OF ISLAM (FOI) and the MUSLIM GIRLS TRAINING (MGT), the all-male and all-female auxiliaries of the NOI. On various nights throughout the week and during weekends, the FOI taught its members military protocol, self-defense, and hygiene in addition to conventional academic subjects such as math and English. Similarly, the MGT turned the temple and mosque into a

home economics school, teaching its members sewing, cooking, penmanship, nutrition, and hygiene, in addition to organizing all-female drill teams.

During this era, then, Muslim-American mosques became more than simply places for congregational prayers. Like Christians and Jews in this period, Muslims used their spaces for worship as community centers that often housed classes, social gatherings, fund-raisers, and dances. One could live one's waking life in and around the mosque, a practice that some Muslims subscribed to both historically and in a number of Muslim-majority countries in the contemporary world.

Unlike the modest Midwestern mosques of the 1920s and 1930s, a few Sunni Muslim mosques in this period came to emulate the architectural styles of mosques in the Middle East. Combining various styles into one building, the ISLAMIC CENTER OF WASHINGTON, D.C., featured an Egyptian Mamluk edifice, Andalusian arches, and Ottoman-style glazed tiles. Supported by the many ambassadors from various Muslim countries and designed by Italian architect Mario Rossi, the building was dedicated in 1957 by President Dwight Eisenhower and other dignitaries.

In this period, SHI'A MUSLIM AMERICANS also erected their first purpose-built mosque. Led by Lebanese-American MOHAMAD JAWAD CHIRRI (1913–94), the Islamic Center of Detroit, later called the Islamic Center of America, opened its doors in 1963. Its appearance marked the beginning of a period of massive growth for Shi'a spaces of worship. By the first decade of the 21st century, the United States had more than 250 Shi'a mosques, *imambargahs*, and *jamaatkhanas*.

GROWTH AFTER 1965

Following the IMMIGRATION ACT OF 1965, over a million Muslims immigrated to the United States by the end of the 20th century. These immigrants, in tandem with African-American, white, Hispanic, Arab-American, South Asian–American, and other Muslims, changed the physical landscape of the United States by building hundreds of new mosques—more than 313 from 1980 to 2000. During this period, the architectural styles of mosques became even more varied. In addition to the converted storefronts and grand Middle Eastern–style buildings that already existed, several marquis mosques were built using modernistic designs, often improvising on geometric patterns drawn from medieval Islamic art and architecture.

Prime examples of this modernistic mosque architecture included the headquarters of the ISLAMIC SOCIETY OF NORTH AMERICA in Plainfield, Indiana, and the Islamic Cultural Center in NEW YORK CITY, located on 96th Street and Third Avenue, which was designed by the architectural firm of Skidmore, Owing, and Merrill. Like many mosques, the Islamic Cultural Center features verses from the Qur'an a decorative element both inside and outside the mosque. But rather than using a floral or circular font, the script of the Qur'anic verses is rendered in completely horizontal and vertical patterns. As architectural critic Akel Ismail Kahera pointed out in *Deconstructing the American Mosque* (2002), this "angular" script "produces a visual affinity" with the geometric patterns found in the dome of the mosque and in its other structures.

As the forms of mosques diversified after 1965, so did their functions. Mosques and Islamic centers offered Muslim Americans an increasing range of activities. Friday congregational prayers remained the best-attended weekly event in the mosque, but some practitioners came to prayer more often at the mosque, sometimes more than once a day. Men, women, and children often attended the Arabic and Islamic studies classes offered on the weekends and weeknights. Some Sufi mosques also featured weekly and sometimes daily sessions of *dhikr,* reciting the names of God or repeating other auspicious words, phrases, and formulas.

Study circles, support groups, and missionary committees met at mosques, and mosques also offered funeral services, washing, clothing, and praying for the body in accordance with Muslims traditions.

Acting as community centers and expanding on what earlier Muslim-American mosques had done, mosques in this period fielded teams in local youth sports competitions, coordinated fitness programs for female members, held potluck or pitch-in dinners, sponsored FOOD pantries, and set up public health clinics. If located in working-class neighborhoods plagued by crime or illegal drug use, mosques also staged rallies against substance abuse, offered drug rehabilitation services, and organized job fairs.

During this period, the organizational and leadership structures of mosques also became more diverse. As in the past, a number of mosques continued to be led by an often charismatic leader or by a central organization, as in the case of the Ahmadi missions or Nation of Islam mosques. But more and more mosques also established either boards of directors or executive committees vested with ultimate authority; in many cases, board members were elected by fellow mosque members. According to a 2001 survey, *The Mosque in America: A National Portrait,* most African-American mosques, which by and large had a small annual budget, were led by imams with final decision-making authority, while 62 percent of immigrant-dominated mosques utilized a board of directors.

Most Muslim-American mosques were led by part-time or volunteer imams. In fact, according to *The Mosque in America,* only 33 percent of all Muslim-American mosques had paid, full-time imams, and most of these were in immigrant-led mosques. The survey also found that mosques with volunteer or part-time imams were more active in formal community engagement and outreach activities than mosques with full-time, paid imams, while mosques with full-time imams were more active in offering weekend Islamic studies classes and other mosque-based activities to their congregants. This difference reflected, among other factors, the high levels of voluntarism and community involvement in predominantly African-American mosques, most of which were led by volunteer or part-time imams.

In the late 20th century, many Muslim Americans, of various political and religious persuasions, called on their communities to address the increasing demand for gender equality in the mosque. Muslim-American leaders such as INGRID MATTSON, later elected president of the Islamic Society of North America, observed that the space set aside for women in most American mosques was woefully inadequate. She also encouraged women to assume greater leadership roles in the community by joining the boards that were in charge of many mosques.

Akel Ismail Kahera pointed out that the design of many Muslim-American mosques—unlike many American

Sufi lodges or *jamaatkhanas*—relegated women to separate spaces far away from the imam, or prayer leader, and *khatib,* or sermonizer. This spatial discrimination, Kahera claimed, violated the tradition of the prophet Muhammad, whose mosque in Medina offered equal space to men and women. It also undermined the mosque's function as Muslim Americans' primary space for community making.

In the first decade of the 21st century, some Muslim-American FEMINISTS and PROGRESSIVE MUSLIMS went further, calling for women to lead mixed-gender congregational prayer as imams, rejecting the interpretation of SHARI'A, or Islamic law, that forbade women from doing so. But many, if not most Muslim Americans, like many Roman Catholics and Missouri Synod Lutherans, reiterated their belief that while women could participate in worship in many ways, they should not lead it. Some moderate Muslims, including Ingrid Mattson, warned that such an innovation would pit the Muslim-American community against the vast majority of the world's Muslims and render their activism ineffective in making positive change for Muslim women around the world.

AFTER 9/11

Immediately following the al-Qaeda attacks of SEPTEMBER 11, 2001, dozens of mosques and Islamic centers were either vandalized or attacked. In many instances, non-Muslim Americans attempted to help Muslim Americans protect these symbols of religious diversity in the United States. In TOLEDO, OHIO, for example, Chereffe Kadri, the president of the Islamic Center of Greater Toledo, joined hands with 2,000 community members as they surrounded and prayed for the mosque—whose stained-glass windows had been damaged by gunfire. Mosques and Islamic centers also became open houses, hosting thousands of information sessions on the Muslim faith and practice, terrorism, and Muslims in America.

Various Muslims and non-Muslims engaged in a struggle to define the meaning and functions of mosques. After the passage of the USA PATRIOT ACT in October 2001, for example, an increasing number of undercover FBI agents and police officers infiltrated mosques, viewing them as potential hotbeds of terrorism. Muslims attempted to reassure government officials and their non-Muslim neighbors that their spaces of worship were just that.

The mosque after 9/11 became more visible and vulnerable, like the Muslim-American community as a whole. There was no untangling this Muslim-American institution from the larger pressures faced by Muslim Americans in American society. But mosques and Islamic centers also offered a sense of pride and accomplishment to those who had built, renovated, and sustained what were now symbols of Muslims' abiding place in the American religious landscape.

Edward E. Curtis IV and Rizwan Mawani

Further Reading

Abdo, Geneive. *Mecca and Main Street: Muslim Life in America after 9/11.* New York: Oxford University Press, 2006.

Bagby, Ihsan, Paul M. Perl, and Bryan T. Froehle. *The Mosque in America: A National Portrait.* Washington, D.C.: Council of American-Islamic Relations, 2001.

Curtis, Edward E., IV. *Black Muslim Religion in the Nation of Islam, 1960–1975.* Chapel Hill: University of North Carolina Press, 2006.

Kahera, Akel Ismail. *Deconstructing the American Mosque: Space, Gender and Aesthetics.* Austin: University of Texas Press, 2002.

Mattson, Ingrid. "Women, Islam and Mosques." In *Encyclopaedia of Women and Religion in North America,* edited by Rosemary Skinner Keller and Rosemary Radford Ruether, 615–619. Bloomington: Indiana University Press, 1996.

Metcalf, Barbara Daly, ed. *Making Muslim Space in North America and Europe.* Berkeley: University of California Press, 1996.

Nimer, Mohamed. *The North American Resource Guide: Muslim Community Life in the United States and Canada.* New York: Routledge, 2002.

Mount Vernon

Mount Vernon, located in Fairfax County, Virginia, belonged to the Washington family from 1674 until its sale in 1858 (with its final closing in 1860), just before the Civil War, to the Mount Vernon Ladies' Association, the first national preservation group in the United States. The 8,000-acre plantation is best known as the home of George Washington, commander in chief of the Continental Army during the American Revolution (1775–83), president of the Constitutional Convention (1787), and first president of the United States (1789–97). Less well known is the fact that it was also home to more than 300 enslaved African and African-American people—some of whom may have been Muslim—at the time of Washington's death in 1799.

To a great extent, the religious life of the Mount Vernon plantation mirrored its social makeup. At the top were George and Martha Washington and their family, following the formal and rather reserved pattern of 18th-century Anglicanism, which stressed the need for private devotions and service to one's church and community through work on the vestry and charitable contributions. They, in turn, supported the religious needs of their employees, who were primarily from England, Ireland, Scotland, and Germany and probably represented a wide variety of Christian denominations, by giving time off to attend church services and occasionally purchasing devotional materials for their use.

In contrast to the whites at the top and middle of the social scale, who, whether they practiced it or not, came out of a Christian background, were the African and African-American slaves who made up roughly 90 percent of Mount Vernon's population. By 1799, most of the enslaved at Mount Vernon were second- or third-generation Americans. While at least some were involved with Christian denominations in the area, including Episcopalians, Baptists, Methodists, and Quakers, elements of both Islam and traditional African religions survived among Mount Vernon's enslaved population. Documentary and archaeological evidence of similar cultural survivals have been found elsewhere in Virginia, Maryland, and the Carolinas, and, according to historian Peter Kolchin, African-born slaves generally continued to practice the religions with which they had grown up, after their enslavement and transportation to the Americas. These traditions survived longest in areas where the population had a high concentration of Africans. It is clear that Washington did not care what religion was practiced by the people who worked for him. As he wrote in March 1784, when he was trying to hire skilled workmen for Mount Vernon, all he was concerned with was their work skills, not their religion: "If they are good workmen, they may be of Asia, Africa, or Europe. They may be Mahometans [Muslims], Jews, or Christians of any Sect, or they may be Atheists."

Despite Washington's supposedly tolerant outlook, there would have been challenges to anyone trying to practice a non-Christian religion, especially certain elements of Islam. The degree of supervision by an overseer or master might well have interfered with the requirement to pray five times each day. Some white persons made fun of or thought Islamic PRAYER to be evil, as was shown by the case of JOB BEN SOLOMON (1701–73), whose prayers were continually interrupted by a boy who insisted on throwing dirt on him. Despite Islamic prohibitions against both pork and alcohol, on most plantations pork formed a major part of the food provided for slaves, and alcohol was often used as a reward or was given out during times of especially hard work. Slaves were allowed to raise domestic fowls in their quarters, hunt and trap wild game at night and on their days off, and raise additional food in the garden plots designated by masters. Such efforts to procure food that followed Islamic DIETARY LAWS added to an already long workday.

Much of the evidence for the presence of Muslim slaves at Mount Vernon comes from naming practices, as well as personal histories and marriage practices. The names of at least three female slaves at Mount Vernon indicate a Muslim influence on the estate, if not the actual practice of Islam, over a period of roughly 30 years. Two women, presumably a mother and daughter, called "Fatimer" and "Little Fatimer," were included on a 1774 "titheables list," a document prepared for local authorities showing the people on his estate for whom George Washington's had to pay taxes.

These names appear to be a variation of the popular Muslim woman's name, Fatima, which in Arabic means "Shining One," and was the name of the prophet MUHAMMAD's daughter. Similarly, a young, supposedly unmarried mulatto woman named Letty, who lived at Washington's Muddy Hole Farm (one of five farms making up the Mount Vernon plantation), gave birth in 1800 to a little girl she called "Nila." This unusual name is a known variant of an Islamic woman's name, "Naailah," which means "someone who acquires something" or "someone who gets what he or she wants."

In accordance with her late husband's final wishes, Martha Washington had taken steps at the end of 1800 to free those slaves who had belonged to him, including Letty, her three children, both her parents, and all her siblings. It may be that "Nila" was an old name, remembered in Letty's family, or that of her baby's father, from Africa. Maybe she simply knew someone named Nila and wanted her daughter to carry the name of her friend. Given the timing of the girl's birth, however, it is also possible that this baby's name was bestowed in commemoration of her family's newly acquired freedom. Even if no one was actually practicing Islam, this child's name provides evidence that some knowledge of Islamic tradition or a familiarity with the Arabic language could still be found in the larger African-American community in Fairfax County or Alexandria, if not at Mount Vernon itself, at the beginning of the 19th century.

The documented history of an African-born carpenter at Mount Vernon, known as Sambo Anderson, suggests that he was a practicing Muslim. Even today, the name Sambou is very common in West Africa, where people are often named for either the day of the week on which they were born or for their birth order within their family. Sambou is a name used primarily for a second son among the Hausa people of what is now northwestern Nigeria and southern Niger, although it can also be found among other ethnic groups in this part of Africa. Sambo Anderson was described as having mahogany-colored skin, with high cheekbones and a stout build. His face was marked by both tribal cuts and tattooing, and he wore gold rings in both ears. Sambo told several people that he was of royal birth and that his father was a king.

It is not clear exactly when Sambo came to Mount Vernon, but plantation records indicate that he was a boy in 1776 and only about 20 years old in 1781. Once there, he was trained as a carpenter by William Bernard Sears, an English-born craftsman who originally came to Virginia as a young indentured convict in 1752. Sambo was one of 17 slaves—14 men and three women—who voluntarily left Mount Vernon in April 1781 during the American Revolution (1775–83), when the British warship Savage anchored in the Potomac River and the enemy was furnished with provisions from the estate. George Washington was understandably upset when he learned of this incident, noting in a letter to the cousin who was managing the estate that he would have preferred that his home be burned and the estate ransacked, rather than providing assistance to the enemy. A little less than half of this group of 17 slaves was eventually returned to Washington's estate. Sambo got as far as Philadelphia before he was recovered, along with four of the other men from Mount Vernon.

Sambo was likely Muslim. The ethnic group from which he most likely came, the Hausa, bore a strong Islamic influence, which had come to them from Mali, beginning in the late 14th century. Evidence about Sambo's family life strengthens the notion that he, and very likely others, had not given up Islam when he came to America.

According to Washington's 1799 slave list, Sambo was married to a 36-year-old woman named Agnes, with whom he had three children, ranging in age from 17 to 11. Also on that list were three other children, Ralph (9), Charity (2), and Charles (1), whose mother, Sall, had died not long before. Sambo was among the slaves freed by the terms of Washington's will; however, Agnes, her children, and Sall's children, as "dower slaves" who belonged to the estate of Martha Washington's first husband, could not be freed and were eventually divided among the latter's four grandchildren.

Eleven years later, in summer 1810, a local newspaper alerted its subscribers to the escape of a young man named Ralph, then about 21 years old, from his owner, who was the husband of Martha Washington's second granddaughter. Ralph was believed to be heading for the home of his father, who was described as a freeman by the name of Sambo, living at Mount Vernon. It is possible that Sambo had two wives, both Agnes and Sall, a fact George Washington might not have recognized because it was outside the scope of his experience and cultural expectations.

Polygamy, while probably not common among Virginia slaves, was not completely unknown either. At least one African-born slave on a plantation belonging to Robert Carter had two wives. Besides polygamy, however, there may be other explanations for Sambo's family situation, including an extramarital relationship between Sambo and Sall, or the informal adoption of Sall's children by Sambo and Agnes. It is impossible to do more than speculate, but the possibility that Sambo may have been practicing the marriage pattern he knew as a child in Africa is certainly intriguing and should not be overlooked. Either Islam, which permitted up to four wives, or a more traditional African religion, some of which allowed hundreds and even thousands of wives for those who could afford them, would have given him both a tradition of and clear conscience to practice polygamy. Given the likelihood that Sambo was a Hausa, most of whom were Muslim, his polygamy, if any, was probably a reflection of an Islamic background.

Sambo was one of 123 slaves freed by the terms of George Washington's will on January 1, 1801. As a free man, he took the last name Anderson, perhaps a reflection of positive feelings toward Washington's Scottish farm manager, James Anderson, or his son John. Sambo made his home on Little Hunting Creek near Mount Vernon and supported himself by hunting game and wildfowl, which he sold to private customers and hotels in Alexandria. With the money he earned, he is said to have purchased two slaves himself. County records show that Sambo emancipated two slaves, but at least one is known to have been his son, William Anderson, born about 1812, while the other, a young woman named Eliza Anderson, who was six years younger, was probably his daughter. Sambo and his son William were among 12 former Washington slaves and their descendants who voluntarily returned to the estate in 1835 to work on George Washington's tomb, offering their services as a way of honoring the man who had freed them from slavery.

Given recent research by historians documenting the practice of Islam by enslaved people throughout North America, the idea that there may have been Muslim slaves at Mount Vernon should come as no surprise. Although definitive evidence is lacking, the likely presence of Muslims at this most prominent 18th-century plantation reminds us that America was built by people with a variety of faiths. In considering the practice of religion at Mount Vernon, one is struck by the thought that when George Washington spoke of the need for religious toleration and freedom, when he wrote in May 1789 of his belief that "every man, conducting himself as a good citizen" was "accountable to God alone for his religious opinions" and should "be protected in worshipping the Deity according to the dictates of his own conscience," perhaps he was extrapolating from the situation at his own home to the country at large.

Mary V. Thompson

Further Reading

Curtin, Philip D. *Africa Remembered: Narratives by West Africans from the Era of the Slave Trade.* Madison: University of Wisconsin Press, 1967.

Diouf, Sylviane A. *Servants of Allah: African Muslims Enslaved in the Americas.* New York: New York University Press, 1998.

"George Washington to Tench Tilghman, March 24, 1784." In *The Papers of George Washington, Confederation Series,* Vol. 1, edited by W. W. Abbot, 232. Charlottesville: University Press of Virginia, 1992.

"George Washington to the United Baptist Churches of Virginia, [May 1789]." *The Papers of George Washington, Presidential Series,* Vol. 2, edited by W. W. Abbot, 424. Charlottesville: University Press of Virginia, 1987.

Gomez, Michael A. "Muslims in Early America." *Journal of Southern History* (November 1994): 671–710.

Kolchin, Peter. *American Slavery, 1619–1877.* New York: Hill and Wang, 1993.

Thompson, Mary V. "'And Procure for Themselves a Few Amenities': The Private Life of George Washington's Slaves." *Virginia Cavalcade* 48, no. 4 (Autumn 1999): 178–190.

———. "Religious Practice in the Slave Quarters at Mount Vernon." *Colonial Williamsburg Interpreter* 21, no. 1 (Spring 2000): 10–14.

Walsh, Lorena S. *From Calabar to Carter's Grove: The History of a Virginia Slave Community.* Charlottesville: University Press of Virginia, 1997.

Muhammad Ali v. United States   See CLAY, AKA ALI V. UNITED STATES.

Muhammad, Clara (1899–1972) *matriarch of the Nation of Islam*

Clara Belle Evans Muhammad was matriarch of the original NATION OF ISLAM (NOI) and, as wife of NOI leader Elijah Muhammad, one of the group's most influential women. Clara Muhammad was born in Wenona, Georgia, in 1899 (the exact date is unknown) to farmer Quartus Evans and his wife Mary Lue Thomas. She attended school up to the eighth grade in Cordele, Georgia.

In 1919, Muhammad married Elijah Poole, who would later change his last name to Muhammad. To escape the perils of Southern racism, they moved to DETROIT in 1923, where Clara found work as a maid in white homes. Her husband worked in various industrial jobs but was unable to remain steadily employed and increasingly drank to excess. Clara and their children, who ultimately numbered eight, continually lived at the poverty level.

During the 1920s, the couple became interested in Islam and were sporadically involved with the MOORISH SCIENCE TEMPLE of America. In spring 1931, Clara heard a talk by W. D. FARD, a Muslim gaining local recognition as a religious speaker. Inspired, she became convinced that Fard was a prophet. Clara invited Fard to dinner at the Poole home so that she could introduce her husband to his teachings.

After the introduction, the Pooles' family life was reoriented by Fard's guidance. Elijah believed Fard to be not only a prophet but God himself. He was taught to preach, and in 1933, Fard rewarded him with the new surname Muhammad. Their small group of followers was renamed the Nation of Islam. Fard disappeared the following year, and Elijah Muhammad assumed the leadership role. Clara believed her husband had been chosen as the Messenger of Allah, and she supported his leadership. Her 1972 obituary in *MUHAMMAD SPEAKS,* the NOI newspaper, said that she "recreated the very definitions of devotion and righteousness, [and] submission," adding that she had "manifested a new path for the Black woman."

One of Clara Muhammad's most important roles in the NOI came during the period from 1942 to 1946, when her husband was imprisoned for violating the Selective Service Act. Clara Muhammad became the supreme secretary of the NOI in his absence. Through regular prison visits, she delivered Elijah's instructions to ministers and offered her own guidance about completion of their tasks. Although the NOI membership shrank considerably during this time, if not for her dedication the movement might have disintegrated completely.

Clara and Elijah experienced domestic trouble over the years, especially in the early 1960s when she discovered the births of several of his illegitimate children. The FBI had leaked information about his extramarital affairs, apparently hoping that a shadow on Elijah Muhammad's character would cause both divorce and the tarnishing of his reputation. While his activities did not cause excessive discord within the NOI, they did cause distress and depression for Clara. She left Elijah for months at a time, but their troubles were kept relatively private within the organization.

Clara Muhammad died on August 12, 1972, from stomach cancer. Her husband died in 1975 and left the leadership of the NOI to one of their sons, W. D. MOHAMMED. The legacy of her interest in children's education is preserved in the Clara Muhammad Schools, a national system of ISLAMIC SCHOOLS named in her honor. Originally called the University of Islam, these schools began as a parochial school for NOI members' and other African-American children in 1932. Clara Muhammad was among the first to remove her children from public schools and enroll them in the new program, thus setting the example for other NOI families. By the 21st century, the accredited school system, located in dozens of North American cities, included elementary and secondary schools as well as weekend programs.

Marie W. Dallam

Further Reading

Evanzz, Karl. *The Messenger: The Rise and Fall of Elijah Muhammad.* New York: Pantheon Books, 1999.

Gardell, Mattias. *In the Name of Elijah Muhammad: Louis Farrakhan and the Nation of Islam.* Durham: Duke University Press, 1996.

Muhammad, Elijah (Elijah Mohammed, Elijah Poole) (1897–1975) *leader of the Nation of Islam, 1934–1975*

For four decades, Elijah Muhammad led the NATION OF ISLAM, the largest, most recognizable, and most influential Muslim organization in the United States. To his followers, he became known as the Honorable Elijah Muhammad, Messenger of Allah. When he began his ministry in the mid-1930s, there were perhaps a few thousand African-American Muslims in the United States. By the time of his death in 1975, there were a few hundred thousand. Through the efforts of followers such as MALCOLM X, LOUIS FARRAKHAN, and his son W. D. MOHAMMED, he is indirectly responsible for the million-plus African Americans who call themselves Muslim. Even though these three other Muslim leaders eventually attained greater fame than he did and two of them rejected his formulation of Islam, it was Elijah Muhammad who brought each of them to Islam.

There would be no doubt that Elijah Muhammad was the most influential African-American Muslim, or even the most influential American Muslim, were it not for the question of whether he actually was a Muslim. On the one hand, his personal commitment to Allah and his emphasis on the Qur'an seem to place him clearly within the religion of Islam. On the other hand, Muhammad claimed that his mentor W. D. FARD was "Allah in person," that he was Allah's apostle, that the white man is the devil, and that heaven and hell are states of mind on earth rather than a place to which one goes after death. These teachings seem to contradict some of the basic teachings of Islam as traditionally understood, and so many Muslims outside the Nation of Islam vehemently objected to the description of Muhammad as a "Muslim" and his religion as "Islam."

THE LIFE OF ELIJAH MUHAMMAD

Elijah Muhammad was born Elijah Poole in Sandersville, Georgia, in October 1897—the exact date is unknown since Georgia did not keep birth records for black people. His father and grandfather were untrained Baptist preachers. From an early age he was given to Bible study, and it was assumed that he would follow their footsteps and become a Christian preacher. He questioned Christian doctrine, however, especially in light of the virulent white racism in the South in the early 20th century. He even witnessed two lynchings and later said that Christians, black or white, had done little to stop them. These experiences were evidence to him that Christianity, as practiced in America, was antiblack.

In 1919, he married Clara Evans and eventually had eight children: Emmanuel, Ethel, Lottie, Nathaniel, Herbert, Elijah, Jr., Wallace, and Akbar. His first contact with Islam occurred well after he migrated to Detroit in 1923 with his wife and family. In Detroit, according to an interview that Muhammad gave to the Federal Bureau of Investigation (FBI) in 1942, he worked at the American Nut Company, the American Copper and Brass Company, and finally as an auto worker for Chevrolet Axle. When the GREAT DEPRESSION began in 1929, he lost his job.

In 1931, he met W. D. Fard (also known as Wali Fard Muhammad), a preacher who taught that the "so-called Negroes" were originally part of the Asiatic race and the religion of Islam. Freedom and justice, said Fard, required abandoning Christianity—the religion of the "white devil"—and returning to their religion, Islam. Fard also taught that the present world would be consumed in an apocalyptic battle between Christianity and Islam. In addition, Fard told his followers to avoid pork and alcohol, both of which were traditional Islamic teachings. Such lessons had a profound effect on Elijah Muhammad. Even before Fard gave him permission to preach this message, he began transmitting what he had learned from Fard to others, often sharing his own reading of the Bible to support Fard's Islamic teachings; it was he who first called Fard Muhammad a prophet and later came to believe that Fard was God or Allah in person. He eventually became Fard's chief minister, and sometime from 1931 to 1934, Fard gave Elijah Poole two new surnames to replace his "slave name" that he had been given by a former slave owner. The first was Karriem. The second was Muhammad, the name he used for the rest of his life.

In 1933, Fard was arrested by the police in Detroit on the suspicion that he had ordered a man to kill someone in a ritual sacrifice. Robert Harris, the killer who said he was acting on Fard's orders, was committed to a hospital for the mentally insane and the charges were dropped. But the police still ordered Fard to leave Detroit, and he complied. He moved to Chicago, where Elijah Muhammad saw him for the last time in 1934. According to the Nation of Islam's official history, Fard gave him two copies of the Qur'an and a list of 104 books to read. Elijah Muhammad returned to Detroit, and Fard then mysteriously disappeared.

A power struggle erupted within the movement. Harassed by the police and, according to Muhammad, threatened by rivals, he escaped to Chicago. There, one of his own brothers challenged his authority, and in 1935, Muhammad fled again. Of the estimated 5,000 to 8,000 followers of Fard, fewer than 200 gave their allegiance to his chief minister. Elijah Muhammad spent the next seven years proselytizing in East Coast cities with significant African-American populations.

As WORLD WAR II approached, the FBI came to suspect that Muhammad was preaching a revolutionary, antiracist message and that some sort of alliance might form between the empire of Japan and African Americans. In 1942, he was arrested and accused of sedition. Although acquitted of this charge, he was convicted of failing to register for the military draft and sentenced to one to five years in prison. From 1943 to 1946, Muhammad was incarcerated in a federal correctional institution in Milan, Michigan, but remained in contact with his followers through his wife, Clara. By the time of his release, he had only 1,000 followers in four temples, but his sense of mission was strengthened and his rivals had all but disappeared. During his imprisonment, he also saw that no one was seeking to reform African-American prisoners. His decision to give attention to this group brought to his movement its most charismatic spokesmen and missionary, Malcolm Little, who was incarcerated in Massachusetts from 1946 to 1952.

From 1952 to 1963, with the help of Malcolm Little, who had changed his name to Malcolm X, Muhammad oversaw the growth of the Nation of Islam from approximately 10 to 50 temples or mosques. The movement attracted national and even international attention and was famously criticized in 1959 by CBS reporter Mike Wallace as the "hate that hate produced." In 1961, the movement remained in the spotlight as African-American sociologist of religion C. Eric Lincoln published the first major academic study of the movement, *The Black Muslims in America*. It was a label that stuck, and for decades afterward, Americans would still refer to members of the Nation of Islam as "Black Muslims."

In 1963, the partnership between Elijah Muhammad and Malcolm X, often the cause of jealousy among other movement leaders, unraveled. That year, when allegations emerged that Muhammad had fathered several children with mistresses, Malcolm X first sought to mitigate the damage by devising explanations and discussing them with other ministers. But Muhammad came to believe that Malcolm was spreading rumors, and he and Malcolm's rivals sought to curtail his influence and public appearances. When President John F. Kennedy was assassinated in November 1963 and Muhammad ordered his followers to make no comment, Malcolm broke Elijah's commandment, saying Kennedy's violent death was an example of America's "chickens coming home to roost." Muhammad ordered him to be silent for 90 days as punishment, but Malcolm soon declared that members of the Nation of Islam were plotting against his life.

Malcolm X left the Nation of Islam and rapidly moved to a more SUNNI, or what he called a more "orthodox," formulation of Islam. His subsequent criticism of the Nation of Islam greatly angered Elijah Muhammad and others in the movement. In February 1965, Malcolm X was assassinated by several gunmen alleged to be part of the Nation of Islam. Muhammad seems to have had no involvement in the assassination, but it has been argued that he inadvertently set the stage by attacking Malcolm as the "chief hypocrite" and a "traitor."

Malcolm X was not Elijah Muhammad's sole difficulty. His sons Akbar Muhammad and Wallace D. Muhammad (later known as W. D. Mohammed) also broke with their father over his teachings, which they believed did not accord with those of the Qur'an and Sunni Islam. Akbar was declared a heretic, but Wallace was readmitted into the Nation after Malcolm X's assassination.

Despite these difficulties, the final decade of Elijah Muhammad's life was characterized by continued growth of his movement. As the number of mosques increased, do did Muhammad's personal wealth. In addition to buying a small bank, he owned a multimillion-dollar fish import business, grocery stores, farms, a newspaper, and other small businesses. By the time of his death in 1975, some estimated his estate to be worth more than $60 million, while other observers noted that there were massive debts against his significant assets. More important to the growth of the Nation of Islam, many of these businesses provided both employment opportunities and a sense of pride to movement members who worked in them.

This period saw the rise of Louis Farrakhan, a Nation of Islam minister who assumed the title of National Spokesman for the Honorable Elijah Muhammad. In the early 1970s, rivalries within the Nation of Islam and with rival Muslim organizations again brought turmoil to the movement. As Muhammad neared the end of his life, he never explicitly named a successor, thinking it unnecessary. Others, including Farrakhan and Muhammad's son W. D. Mohammed, began maneuvering to succeed him. When Elijah Muhammad died on February 25, 1975, just one day before the annual Savior Day's rally in Chicago, his son W. D. Mohammed prevailed and was proclaimed the new supreme minister. Almost immediately, W. D. Mohammed began the process of transforming his father's Nation of Islam into a far more Sunni Muslim movement.

ELIJAH MUHAMMAD'S FORMULATION OF ISLAM
Elijah Muhammad and his followers considered themselves to be Muslims who practiced the correct form of Islam, and many of his teachings and the practices of his followers were easily identifiable as Islamic. He taught the belief that God was One, that God had sent prophets such as Moses, Jesus, and Muhammad to humankind, that the Qur'an was the word of God, and that there would be rewards and punishment on Judgment Day. Some of his followers prayed five times a day, fasted, and abstained from pork and alcohol. In sum, many basic beliefs and practices of Sunni and Shi'a Islam were advocated by Elijah Muhammad.

And yet each of these beliefs and practices had a racial (and, for most Muslims, an unorthodox) component. Instead of one god who was wholly different from his creation, Muhammad taught that Allah was a black man, the most recent of whom was W. D. Fard, his minister in the 1930s. Such a belief violated the strong prohibition in Islamic history against associating anything or anyone with Allah. Moreover, Muhammad taught that a mad, evil scientist named Yakub had bred the "devil white race" out of the original black humanity 6,600 years ago and that these devils—that is, whites—would be killed in a Day of Judgment in which black greatness would be restored to the earth.

In Elijah Muhammad's Islamic teachings, the historical role of Moses, Jesus, and even Muhammad were largely confined to their largely futile efforts to reform or confine the white race. Muhammad's tendency to read references in the Qur'an to "Allah" and the "messenger of Allah" as references to both W. D. Fard and himself were also problematic. Likewise, Muhammad's denial of a bodily resurrection on the Last Day as taught by most other formulations of Islam and his description of Heaven and Hell as contemporary situations and resurrection as a mental condition were all novel interpretations. Muhammad also understood and practiced Islamic rituals differently from other Muslims. For example, he advocated fasting, not during the month of Ramadan in commemoration of the initial revelation of the Qur'an to Muhammad, but in December to focus his followers' minds on W. D. Fard instead of Christmas.

Similarly troubling for some Muslims was Elijah Muhammad's tendency to focus on racial conflict in the United States, especially when he portrayed his racial political and economic policies as inseparable from Islam. Many of Elijah Muhammad's contemporary Muslim rivals also focused on racial issues. They argued that Islam taught the equality of all humankind, however, regardless of race. Muhammad's efforts toward economic independence from white America and demands for territorial separation within the continental United States for African Americans were not only no less important than teaching prayer, but also he claimed that this was for him what Islam taught. That is to say, Muhammad insisted that Islam was the original religion of black humanity (which he thought, at least at first, comprised all nonwhites). The primary context of the Qur'an was not seventh-century Arabia (where Islam first emerged), but 20th-century America. Therefore, he interpreted historical references in the Qur'an as prophecies. For instance, passages about "hypocrites" in the Qur'an were interpreted to be prophecies against opponents such as Malcolm X, and the many passages about the Last Day were interpreted to be prophecies about the coming "Fall of America."

ELIJAH MUHAMMAD AND OTHER MUSLIMS
From the late 1950s onward, Elijah Muhammad experienced increasing hostility from other Muslims. Many of them, not surprisingly, charged him with not being a "real" Muslim. They focused on the novel beliefs and practices of the Nation of Islam. Initially, these Muslims were African-American converts to Sunni Islam whose own movements were in direct competition with the Nation of Islam or were Muslim immigrants from the Middle East. They even objected to Muhammad's use of the words "Muslim" and "Islam." Later, Muhammad had to contend with former followers, most notably Malcolm X and his own sons.

Elijah Muhammad's earliest comments on Arab Muslims sought to minimize differences. At the same time, he tried to adopt some orthodox practices and went on pilgrimage to Mecca to demonstrate his Islamic credentials. Ironically, his travels within the Muslim world also disabused him of his utopian image of other Muslims that he had had and made the later break with them easier. Initially, however, he criticized them mainly for continuing to try to convert whites to Islam—a task he thought to be completely pointless. Thus, he considered "Eastern Muslims" merely conservative or confused. After being criticized by these Muslims, he increasingly came to believe that Muslims from the East had been corrupted and were, in fact, hypocrites. In the early 1970s, he used even stronger language, criticizing "old-world" Muslims for following an "old Islam led by Whites" and claiming that they were no better than white Christians. It is noteworthy that Muhammad abandoned these other Muslims, but he never abandoned Islam. In fact, the centrality of Islam in his personal life and to his movement is demonstrated by his taking criticism from other Muslims so seriously.

Of course, Muhammad's claim to be Muslim and his authority to lead his Muslim followers was never based on being accepted by "orthodox" Muslims. For him, his authority came directly from Allah himself. Muhammad believed that Allah in the person of W. D. Fard had appointed him. For more than three years in the early 1930s, he had been trained personally by Fard. Then, for the remainder of his life, Muhammad claimed that Allah continued to speak to him at least once a year. Scripture, both the Bible and the Qur'an, also confirmed for him everything he had been taught about Islam and the black and white races.

CONCLUSION
The autonomous black state and the racial separation that Elijah Muhammad had long advocated never occurred, and his enormous business empire was quickly dismantled after his death in 1975. His son W. D. Mohammed changed the beliefs, practices, and even the name of his father's movement in 1976 from the Nation of Islam to the World Community of al-Islam in the West. By the 1990s, W. D. Mohammed argued that the move of the Nation of Islam to Sunni Islam had always been part of W. D. Fard's plan. First he had to free the minds of African Americans, and then they would be ready to embrace Islam. W. D. Mohammed believed his father died an orthodox Sunni Muslim.

Elijah Muhammad's importance to "orthodox" Islam in America need not depend on this type of revisionist history, however. First, despite being considered a heretic by many other Muslims, he accomplished what no other Muslim had done: directly and indirectly Elijah Muhammad brought thousands of African Americans to Islam, and this made him the most successful Muslim missionary in American history.

Second, Muhammad's use of the Qur'an to justify his own teachings not only gave an advantage to his Sunni opponents who were far more familiar with the text but also eventually affected key figures within the Nation of Islam, most notably his own sons and his first protégé, Malcolm X. Thus, Elijah Muhammad's own profound attachment to Islam and its scripture made the eventual move to some form of orthodoxy, while unpremeditated, much more likely.

Elijah Muhammad's historical legacy also extends beyond Muslim America. His radical criticism of the United States and Christianity as inherently racist and his calls for racial separatism made civil rights activists such as Martin Luther King, Jr., look politically moderate by comparison. Muhammad's successful building of a national religious movement marked as much by business activity as by prayer was a source of pride to many African Americans, whether they agreed with his Islamic teachings or not. Upon his death, the *New York Times* remarked on its editorial pages that Muhammad had improved the lives of African Americans who had been largely abandoned. Few figures have had a greater impact on Muslim-American history than Elijah Muhammad.

Herbert Berg

Further Reading

Berg, Herbert. *Elijah Muhammad and Islam.* New York: New York University Press, 2009.

Clegg, Claude Andrew, III. *An Original Man: The Life and Times of Elijah Muhammad.* New York: St. Martin's Press, 1997.

Curtis, Edward E., IV. *Black Muslim Religion in the Nation of Islam, 1960–1975.* Chapel Hill: University of North Carolina Press, 2006.

Jackson, Sherman A. *Islam and the Blackamerican: Looking toward the Third Resurrection.* Oxford: Oxford University Press, 2005.

Lincoln, C. Eric. *The Black Muslims in America.* 3d edition. Grand Rapids: Wm. B. Eerdmans, 1994 (1961).

Malcolm X and Alex Haley. *The Autobiography of Malcolm X.* New York: Ballantine Books, 1965.

Muhammad, Elijah. *Message to the Blackman in America.* Newport News, Va.: United Brothers Communications Systems, 1992 (1965).

———. *The Supreme Wisdom: The Solution to the So-Called Negroes' Problem.* Newport News, Va.: National Newport News and Commentator, 1957.

Elijah Muhammad
"What the Muslims Want" and
"What the Muslims Believe" (1965)

Elijah Muhammad (1897–1975), longtime leader of the Nation of Islam, won over thousands of African-American converts with teachings that responded to the social, religious, political, and economic hopes and needs of black Americans after World War II. These teachings appeared each week on the back page of Muhammad Speaks, *one of the most popular black national newspapers of the 1960s and early 1970s. "What the Muslims Want" and "What the Muslims Believe" presented the simplified version of Elijah Muhammad's doctrines about the beginning and end of the world, as well as his formula for black political and economic power. Men wearing bow ties and dark suits sold* Muhammad Speaks *door-to-door and on the streets of urban black America—using the sale of the newspaper as a chance to promote Muhammad's message as well. That message contained religious doctrines that combined Sunni Islamic beliefs with Muhammad's unique prophecies and mythological teachings. It also embodied hopes for freedom, equality, and economic success that had been central to African-American culture since the 19th century.*

What the Muslims Want

1. We want freedom. We want a full and complete freedom.

2. We want justice. Equal justice under the law. We want justice applied equally to all, regardless of creed, or class, or color.

3. We want equality of opportunity. We want equal membership in society with the best in civilized society.

4. We want our people in America whose parents or grandparents were descendants from slaves, to be allowed to establish a separate state or territory of their own . . . either on this continent or elsewhere. We believe that our former slave masters are obliged to provide such land and that the area must be fertile and minerally rich. We believe that our former slave masters are obligated to maintain and supply our needs in this separate territory for the next 20 to 25 years . . . until we are able to produce our own needs.

Since we cannot get along with them in peace and equality, after giving them 400 years of our sweat and blood, and receiving in return some of the worst treatment human beings have ever experienced, we believe our contributions to this land and the suffering forced upon us by white America, justifies our demand for complete separation in a state or territory of our own.

5. We want freedom for all Believers of Islam now held in federal prisons. We want freedom for all black men and women now under death sentence in innumerable prisons in the North, as well as the South.

We want every black man and woman to have the freedom to accept or reject being separated from the slave-masters' children and establish a land of their own.

We know that the above plan for the solution of the black and white conflict is the best and only answer to the problem between two people.

6. We want an immediate end to the police brutality and mob attacks against the so-called Negro throughout the United States.

We believe that the Federal government should intercede to see that black men and women tried in white courts receive justice in accordance with the laws of the land, or allow us to build a new nation for ourselves, dedicated to justice, freedom and liberty.

7. As long as we are not allowed to establish a state or territory of our own, we demand not only equal justice under the laws of the United States, but equal employment opportunities—NOW!

We do not believe that after 400 years of free or nearly free labor, sweat and blood, which has helped America become rich and powerful, that so many thousands of black people should have to subsist on relief or charity or live in poor houses.

8. We want the government of the United States to exempt our people from ALL taxation as long as we are deprived of equal justice under the laws of the land.

9. We want equal education—but separate schools up to 16 for boys and 18 for girls on the condition that the girls be sent to women's colleges and universities. We want all black children, educated, taught and trained by their own teachers.

Under such schooling systems we believe we will make a better nation of people. The United States government should provide, free, all necessary text books and equipment, schools, and college buildings. The Muslim teachers shall be left free to teach and train their people in the way of righteousness, decency and self respect.

10. We believe that intermarriage or race mixing should be prohibited. We want the religion of Islam taught without hindrance or suppression.

These are some of the things that we, the Muslims, want for our people in North America.

What the Muslims Believe

1. We believe in the One God Whose proper Name is Allah.

2. We believe in the Holy Qur-an and in the Scriptures of all the Prophets of God.

3. We believe in the truth of the Bible, but we believe that it has been tampered with and must be reinterpreted so that mankind will not be snared by the falsehoods that have been added to it.

4. We believe in Allah's Prophets and the Scriptures they brought to the people.

5. We believe in the resurrection of the dead—not in the physical resurrection but in mental resurrection. We believe that the so-called Negroes are most in need of mental resurrection; therefore, they will be resurrected first.

Furthermore, we believe we are the people of God's choice, as it has been written that God would choose the rejected and the despised. We can find no other persons fitting this description in these last days more than the so-called Negroes in America. We believe in the resurrection of the righteous.

6. We believe in the judgment. We believe this first judgment will take place in America.

7. We believe this is the time in history for the separation of the so-called Negroes and so-called white Americans. We believe the black men should be freed in name as well as in fact. By this we mean that he should be freed from the names imposed upon him by his former slave-masters. Names which identified him as being the slave of a slave-master. We believe that if we are free indeed, we should go in our own people's names—the black people of the earth.

8. We believe in justice for all whether in God or not. We believe as others that we are due equal justice as human beings. We believe in equality—as a nation—of equals. We do not believe that we are equal with our slave master in the status of "Freed slaves."

We recognize and respect American citizens as independent people and we respect their laws which govern this nation.

9. We believe that the offer of integration is hypocritical and is made by those who are trying to deceive the black people into believing that their 400-year-old open enemies of freedom, justice and equality are, all of a sudden, their "friends." Furthermore, we believe that such deception is intended to prevent black people from realizing that the time in history has arrived for the separation from the whites of this nation.

If the white people are truthful about their professed friendship toward the so-called Negro, they can prove it by dividing up America with their slaves.

We do not believe that America will ever be able to furnish jobs for her own millions of unemployed, in addition to jobs for the 20,000,000 black people as well.

10. We believe that we who declared ourselves to be righteous Muslims should not participate in wars which take the lives of humans. We do not believe this nation should force us to take part in such wars, for we have nothing to gain from it unless America agrees to give us the necessary territory wherein we may have something to fight for.

11. We believe our women should be respected and protected as the women of their nationalities are respected and protected.

12. We believe that Allah (God) appeared in the Person of Master Fard Muhammad, July, 1930—the long-awaited "Messiah" of the Christians and the "Mahdi" of the Muslims.

We believe further and lastly that Allah is God and besides HIM there is no God and He will bring about a universal government of peace wherein we all can live in peace together.

❖

Source: Muhammad, Elijah. "What the Muslims Want" and "What the Muslims Believe." In *Message to the Blackman in America,* 161–164. Chicago: Mohammed's Temple of Islam, 1965.

Muhammad, Prophet of Islam

The earliest Muslim Americans to speak about the prophet Muhammad (570–632), the central figure in the rise of Islam, were likely slaves from West Africa. Some, such as ABDUL RAHMAN IBRAHIMA (1762–1829), who was captured and enslaved in Mississippi, were graduates of leading Muslim academies in Africa. These slaves often had training in SHARIʿA, a Muslim code of law and ethics, in addition to detailed knowledge of the QURʾAN and of the life of Muhammad. Some of them prayed five times a day, invoking peace and blessings on "Muhammad, his descendants and followers." YARROW MAMOUT (ca. 1736–1823) was said to do so on the streets of Washington, D.C. Some slaves were familiar with the pious account of Muhammad's life from the earliest *sira,* or biographies of the Prophet, as well as from the hadith literature, the sayings and deeds of Muhammad and his companions. At the time, very little of this literature was known in the West.

When Muslims first came to America, most English-language books on Islam and on Muhammad were written from a polemical perspective, ridiculing Muhammad as a false prophet, a womanizer who composed the Qurʾan to justify his and his followers' polygamy and the use of the sword. This view of Muhammad stands in sharp contrast with how slaves saw him. For them, Muhammad was God's prophet, the last in a line of prophets that began with Adam, who was followed by Abraham, Moses, and Jesus. They revered all these prophets, uttering "peace be upon them" after mentioning their names. Like all prophets, Muhammad committed no major sin. In their view, he did not compose the Qurʾan but received this through the Angel Gabriel from God in a series of revelatory experiences.

In the midst of the stereotypes about the prophet Muhammad popular in 19th-century America, Muslim-American convert ALEXANDER RUSSELL WEBB (1846–1916) attempted in his book *Islam in America* (1893) to correct what he regarded as common falsehoods about Muhammad. He refuted some "popular errors," claiming that no existing book on Muhammad in English represented a true account. According to Webb, Christians had "persistently . . . misrepresented and misunderstood Muhammad," calling Islam "the religion of the sword." Webb challenged that view by arguing that both Muhammad and the first caliph, Abu Bakr, laid down humane rules of military engagement insisting on "mercy and kindness." Muhammad was generous and forgiving when Mecca surrendered in the seventh century, Webb wrote, and not a single home was plundered. In addition, he said, Muhammad condemned the use of the sword to proselytize, as well as to commit "violence and [the] taking of life in any form."

In Webb's view, Muhammad fought only defensive wars and, "above all" else, wanted peace. Though given permission by God to fight because Muslims had been attacked and driven from their homes, Webb declared, Muhammad was tolerant of other religions. On slavery, Muhammad and the Qurʾan encouraged emancipation and took several steps to "abolish future slavery," he wrote. In addition, on a chapter about "Polygamy and Purdah [gender segregation]," Webb argued that neither of these was truly Islamic but that the former paled in moral significance compared with marital infidelity and prostitution common in the West. He did not discuss Muhammad's marriages. In summary, Webb wrote, Muhammad taught "nothing new" but revived the "one eternal truth which has been preserved" for humankind from the beginning of the world. Like Jesus, he never claimed to be God or the Son of God. In fact, according to Webb's reading of Islamic tradition, Jesus prophesied Muhammad's coming. The true teachings of Jesus and Muhammad are identical, he concluded, yet Christians describe Muhammad as an imposter.

When Ahmadi missionaries came to the United States in 1921, they were anxious to defend Muhammad from misunderstanding and criticism. Speaking in a Chicago church to a large gathering sometime after 1928, Sufi missionary M. R. Bengalee outlined what Muhammad's message would be to the people of Chicago. According to Bengalee, Muhammad would ask them to pray to the one God and to respect all prophets including Krishna, Buddha, and Jesus, as well as the Ahmadi prophet, Ghulam Ahmed. Muhammad would ask them to be true democrats, to open their doors to people of all colors and races, to give generously to the needy, and to pray several times a day. Muhammad would ask them to forgo drinking alcohol. He would enthusiastically support prohibition. He would invite people to find happiness in serving God and humanity.

For members of the NATION OF ISLAM (NOI), founded by W. D. FARD in 1930, the prophet Muhammad was the messenger to whom God had revealed the Qur'an, and Muhammad's religion was the same as that of Jesus and of all the prophets. Muhammad succeeded in setting "darkness back 1,000 years" until the white race reached America and enslaved Africans. At the same time, members of the NOI did not regard Muhammad as the final prophet of God. The Muhammad of 1,400 years ago was not the "prophet like unto Moses" (Deuteronomy 18:18), they thought; that prophet was ELIJAH MUHAMMAD, who led the NOI from the 1930s until his death in 1975. Some NOI members have suggested that Elijah Muhammad performed more impressively than "the Muhammad of 1,400 years ago" because he revived a forgotten and lost nation. When NOI members recited the Islamic profession of faith, "There is no god but God; Muhammad is the Messenger of God," most were referring to W. D. Fard, who was believed to be God, and Elijah Muhammad, who was God's messenger.

Sheikh Daoud Ahmed Faisal (1891–1980), the leader of the State Street mosque in Brooklyn, New York, challenged that view. In 1950, he argued that Muhammad of Arabia was the final messenger of God, countering claims by Muslim-American prophets Noble Drew Ali and Elijah Muhammad, as well as the arguments of the Ahmadis. He also stressed that the prophet Muhammad did not preach a new message but taught exactly what Abraham, Moses, and Jesus had preached—all of whom were Muslim, he said. Through Muhammad, the religion of all humanity had spread across the world, said Faisal; Muhammad's mission was to establish global harmony.

When W. D. MOHAMMED led the majority of NOI members into Sunni Islam after Elijah Muhammad's death in 1975, the pious account of Muhammad's life replaced the version taught by his father. The simultaneous growth of Sunni Muslim communities not associated with W. D. Mohammed's leadership in the 1960s and 1970s led to a consolidation of Sunni views of Muhammad among African-American Muslims. Often joining with other Muslim Americans, most African-American Muslims identified the life example of the prophet Muhammad as a primary source of their religious values.

By the end of the 20th century and the beginning of the 21st, Muslim Americans often united to respond to specific criticisms of Muhammad that emanated from conservative critics of Islam. When Iranian leader Ayatollah Khomeini approved the killing of author Salman Rushdie for making derogatory comments about Muhammad in his 1988 novel, The Satanic Verses, Muslim Americans gained several allies, including former President Jimmy Carter, in their rejection of the call for Rushdie's death and their condemnation of the stereotypical depictions of Muhammad.

After the terrorist attacks of SEPTEMBER 11, 2001, criticisms of Muhammad as intolerant, deceitful, and violent only increased. For example, anti-Muslim critic Robert Spencer's The Truth about Muhammad: Founder of the World's Most Intolerant Religion (2006), stated that Muhammad ordered the murder of critics, especially of poets. The COUNCIL ON AMERICAN-ISLAMIC RELATIONS (CAIR) and numerous other Muslim-American groups strongly challenged these views. Citing Muhammad's tolerance of criticism, for example, CAIR argued that Muhammad would not condone violence in response to novels. Instead, CAIR said, he would gently point out the need for respect of people's beliefs and for truth and accuracy in what is written. Asking whether Muslim reactions were consistent with "what Muhammad would have done," CAIR stated that when he had the opportunity to "strike back at those who attacked him," he refrained from doing so.

In a 2003 INTERNET article, "The Legacy of prophet Muhammad," Muslim-American political scientist Muqtedar Khan discussed the accusation that Muhammad was a pedophile. This view, long a part of Christian criticisms of Muhammad, arose from the tradition that Muhammad is said to have married his wife, Aisha, when she was only six years old. Jerry Vines, a former president of the Southern Baptist Convention, set off debate and controversy surrounding this issue in a speech in June 2002 during which he called Muhammad a "demon-possessed pedophile." Khan responded that such criticisms are part of a campaign by American evangelicals to demonize Islam and, by extension, Muslims. Khan pointed out that there is disagreement on Ayesha's age at marriage. She may have been between 14 and 21. In any case, Muslims are squarely against child marriage, said Khan.

After the publication of cartoons of Muhammad in a Danish newspaper in September 2005, CAIR also launched the campaign Explore the Life of Muhammad. As part of this campaign, CAIR recommended Muhammad: Legacy of a Prophet (2002), a film produced by Muslim-American

Michael Wolfe, which initially aired on PBS stations. The documentary, also promoted by the National Council of Churches, sought to show what Muhammad means to typical Muslim Americans by interviewing Muslims in their homes, place of business, and mosques.

That CAIR, one of the leading Muslim-American public affairs groups, had to launch a full-blown public relations campaign to defend Muhammad spoke to the precariousness of Muslim-American life in the first decade of the 21st century. Stereotypes about Islam and Muslims showed no sign of abating, and in one 2006 poll, 45 percent of Americans said that they had an unfavorable impression of Islam. Though the legacy of Muhammad continued to have multiple meanings among Muslim-American communities, many Muslim Americans could not help feeling that an attack on their prophet was also an attack on them.

Clinton Bennett

Further Reading

Austin, Allan D. *African Muslims in Antebellum America: A Sourcebook.* New York: Garland, 1984.

Bengalee, M. R. "What Would Muhammad Say to Chicago?" *Muslim Sunrise* 7 (1930): 18–19.

Faisal, Daoud Ahmed. *Al-Islam: The Religion of Humanity.* Brooklyn: Islamic Mission of America, 1950.

Hooper, Ibrahim. "What Would Muhammad Do?" *About Islam.* February 4. Available online. URL: http://islam.about.com/od/currentissues/a/cartoon.htm. Accessed April 30, 2009.

Khan, Muqtedar. "The Legacy of prophet Muhammad and the Issues of pedophilia and polygamy." *Ijtihad.* June 9. Available online. URL: http://www.ijtihad.org/women2.htm. Accessed April 30, 2009.

Kronemer, Alexander, Michael Wolfe, Michael Schwarz et al. *Muhammad: Legacy of a Prophet.* Menlo Park, Calif.: Kikim Media, 2003.

Muhammad, Elijah. *Message to the Blackman in America.* Chicago: Mohammed's Temple of Islam, 1965.

Rushdie, Salman. *The Satanic Verses.* New York: Viking, 1989.

Spencer, Robert. *The Truth about Muhammad: Founder of the World's Most Intolerant Religion.* Washington, D.C.: Regnery, 2006.

Webb, Alexander Russell. *Islam in America* New York: Oriental Publishing Company, 1893.

Muhammad Speaks

Muhammad Speaks, possibly the most popular source for news of the developing world among African Americans in the 1960s, was the official weekly newspaper of the NATION OF ISLAM (NOI) from 1961 to 1975.

In the 1950s, NOI leader ELIJAH MUHAMMAD (1897–1975) published his own pamphlets such as "Muslim Daily Prayers" (1957) and articles in black newspapers such as the *Pittsburgh Courier.* Male members of the NOI sold copies of these pamphlets and newspapers in predominantly African-American neighborhoods to spread Muhammad's message and generate revenue for the organization. But Muhammad did not approve of some of the content in the non-Muslim newspapers that carried his articles. Rejecting what he believed to be the black media's use of indecent and harmful materials, he directed his followers to establish their own newspaper. In 1960, MALCOLM X (1925–65) was a leading figure in founding the New York–based newspaper *Mr. Muhammad Speaks.* At the time, he attributed the idea for the paper to Elijah Muhammad, but he later took sole credit for its establishment. In 1961, the paper became known simply as *Muhammad Speaks,* and its main offices moved to CHICAGO.

With help from non-Muslim editor Dan Burley, artist Eugene Majied, and South Asian–American columnist and editor Abdul Basit Naeem, *Muhammad Speaks* became a widely read newspaper among African Americans. The newspaper performed two primary functions. On the one hand, it was the official medium through which the NOI could present itself to the outside world. As such, *Muhammad Speaks* contained Elijah Muhammad's teachings, a column on prayer and other religious matters, hundreds of personal testimonies from NOI members, photographs of members' activities, a Muslim women's column, reports on the movement's schools, and other information on the NOI. On the other hand, the paper also published articles by many non-Muslim syndicated journalists and employed numerous non-Muslims as editorial staff, becoming a trusted source of news among African Americans on matters such as the VIETNAM WAR and the perpetuation of social inequality and racism after the passage of civil rights legislation in 1964 and 1965.

In 1964, author and playwright Richard Durham replaced Burley as editor. Under his leadership from 1964 to 1969, the publication grew significantly. Elijah Muhammad purchased a new printing press, which allowed the staff to produce the periodical completely in-house. The press could print 50,000 copies per hour, and by 1969 the press was printing 400,000 issues of *Muhammad Speaks* per week. It was during the 1960s and under Durham's direction that the paper also became known for its coverage of black history and international news, especially in Africa. Black Power advocates, African-American intellectuals, and others read the paper to follow events in the Congo, learn about the latest developments in the case of Muhammad Ali's conviction for refusing to serve in Vietnam, and ponder comic strips that addressed great heroes in African Islamic history.

In 1969, John Woodford, former editor of *Ebony* magazine, took over as editor. Expanding the newspaper's coverage beyond hard news, he included additional photography and features on music and art. During his time at *Muhammad*

Speaks, Woodward reported a regular circulation of 650,000, though editor Leon Forrest later wrote that the actual number was around 70,000. In 1972, Woodford left to join the staff on the *Chicago Sun Times* and later moved to the *New York Times.* Forrest, a novelist and professor, became the next editor. He stayed for about a year before he was succeeded by the first Muslim editor, Askia Muhammad, then known as Charles 67X.

Under Askia Muhammad, the newspaper began to narrow its focus, and the balance between movement news and outside news in the 20- to 30-page paper tipped in favor of the former. During the 1970s, the NOI underwent a dramatic economic expansion. Elijah Muhammad purchased new farms, a Chicago bank, real estate, and other holdings. The NOI also launched an international fish import business, Whiting H & G, which imported fish from Peru and distributed it in African-American neighborhoods through its extensive network of mosques and temples. *Muhammad Speaks* chronicled these activities and reported an increase in circulation to more than 800,000 copies per week. Though exaggerated, there may indeed have been a rise in circulation due to the increasingly efficient organization of the newspaper's distribution and the movement's purchase of additional vans and trucks to deliver papers in a timely fashion to mosques and temples.

For some members of the FRUIT OF ISLAM (FOI), the movement's all-male auxiliary, selling the paper was a religious ritual and a sacred duty. Dressing immaculately in suit and tie, smiling, and showing great respect to their customers, FOI members used their sale of the paper as a chance to "fish" for new members. They testified to what they touted as the high morals and industriousness of NOI members. Each member had a weekly sales quota, often in the hundreds, and the NOI used a combination of incentives and shame to encourage young male believers to sell their copies of the paper. Members who met or exceeded their weekly quotas were regularly featured in the paper itself, and some were flown to Chicago headquarters to meet Elijah Muhammad as a reward for their work. Memorializing members of the FOI who sold the paper in 1969, NOI member George X (George E. Berry) wrote, "They walk the streets, with 'Muhammad Speaks,' / To turn the opposing tide. / 'Muhammad Speaks' to the wealthy; / 'Muhammad Speaks' to the poor. / His 'Message to the Blackman' / Is to live forever more."

In 1975, *Muhammad Speaks* was renamed the *Bilalian News* by W. D. MOHAMMED (1933–2008), Elijah Muhammad's son and successor. The new name referenced Bilal ibn Rabah, a companion of the prophet MUHAMMAD who was the first *muadhdhin,* or prayer caller, in Islam. In 1981, it was again renamed, becoming the *Muslim Journal.* Unlike his father, W. D. Mohammed did not pressure his members to sell the paper. Quotas were abandoned and circulation fell.

A member of the Nation of Islam sells *Muhammad Speaks,* the organization's newspaper, outside the Chicago Coliseum in 1964. *(Bettmann/CORBIS)*

Though the *Muslim Journal* and the *Final Call,* the paper of the Nation of Islam group led by LOUIS FARRAKHAN (1933–), continued to serve as vital media for Muslim Americans, no Muslim-American newspaper has ever matched the impact of *Muhammad Speaks* on American society and U.S. politics. Perhaps no Muslim-American periodical has ever been regarded with the same devotion or imbued with the same sense of religious meaning for its producers and distributors. The success of *Muhammad Speaks* in the 1960s and early 1970s represents a key moment in U.S. history when a medium became the message of a religious and social movement.

Monica C. Reed with Edward E. Curtis IV

Further Reading

Curtis, Edward E., IV. *Black Muslim Religion in the Nation of Islam, 1960–1975.* Chapel Hill: University of North Carolina Press, 2006.

Forrest, Leon. *Relocations of the Spirit.* Wakefield, R.I.: Asphodel Press, 2004.

Muhammad, Wallace D.   See W. D. MOHAMMED.

music

Music has played an important role in Muslim-American communities from slavery to the present day. Representing the diversity of Muslims themselves, the range of music has been vast—from traditional Sufi devotionals to rap. Muslim Americans have also disputed the ethics of music. While some have claimed that music is prohibited in Islam, others have seen it as a form of worship. This variety of musical expression sheds light on both the diversity of Muslim Americans and their enduring contribution to American artistic culture.

SLAVE MUSIC AND BLUES

Muslims taken as slaves brought their traditional West African music to the Americas in the 17th through 19th centuries. Although many slaves eventually adopted Christianity, remnants of Muslim influence remained in their music. For instance, the Harvest Festival celebrated on the Georgia seacoast by slaves and former slaves was largely influenced by African and Muslim traditions. Once a year around harvest time, the community on Sapelo Island, who traced their ancestry to a Muslim slave from West Africa, would gather to pray and sing throughout the night. After the sun appeared, they would bow while it ascended in the sky. Then singing and dancing would commence to the beat of drums, the rattle of gourd maracas, and the clapping of flat tin plates. The celebration was to honor and give thanks for the annual crop.

Blues also showed African and Muslim influence. Like music from Muslim West Africa, blues featured a style called melisma, or attaching several notes to a single lyrical syllable, and wavy intonation, a series of notes that shift from major to minor scale. The solo singers and stringed instruments featured in slave music and blues also resembled those from Muslim West Africa used in musical storytelling. Historian Sylviane A. Diouf has also compared the *adhan*, the Muslim call to PRAYER, to "Levee Camp Holler," a song written and sung by former slaves. Both used "the same ornamental notes, tortuously elongated sounds, pauses, nasal humming, simple melody, and impression of human loneliness."

JAZZ

Throughout its history, JAZZ has incorporated various religious and cultural influences. Muslim influence began immediately after WORLD WAR II, when many jazz musicians began converting to Islam. In particular, the Ahmadiyya Movement, which began in the 19th century in present-day Pakistan and spread to the United States in the 1920s, was a popular means through which jazz musicians came to Islam.

In the mid-20th century, ART BLAKEY, whose Muslim name was Abdallah ibn Buhaina, formed a Muslim group called the Jazz Messengers. The Jazz Messengers toured extensively, spread the message of Islam through their music, and developed some of the most talented jazz musicians of the era. Prominent members included YUSEF LATEEF and Sahib Shihab. Wynton Marsalis, one of the most popular jazz musicians, was also connected with the Jazz Messengers. The Muslim influence on Marsalis can be seen in his 1996 album *In This House, On This Morning,* which features a piece celebrating the *adhan.*

John Coltrane, another one of the most popular jazz musicians, was also influenced by Islam both musically and personally. His acclaimed 1964 album, *A Love Supreme,* was composed and performed as a devotional to God that incorporated many different religious influences, including Islam. In the poetic accompaniment of the album's liner notes, Coltrane clearly used language influence by the QUR'AN and Islam. Additionally, Coltrane's pianist McCOY TYNER was Muslim, as was his first wife, Juanita Naima Grubb. After Coltrane's death in 1967, Tyner and another of Coltrane's protégés, Pharoah Sanders, released albums with distinct religious, including Muslim, influence. In 1969, Sanders released the album *Jewels of Thought,* which included a chant for peace, "Hum-Allah-Hum-Allah-Hum-Allah." Sanders also worked with other Muslim-American musicians like Idris Muhammad and pianist AHMAD JAMAL, and international Muslim musicians like Mahmoud Guinia.

Islam's influence on the musical structures of jazz has been subtle. In general, Muslim-American jazz musicians have not used classical Islamic music or its motifs but have defined their own relationship between Islam and music. For instance, some jazz artists have incorporated African, Middle Eastern, or South Asian styles and instruments to connote their Muslim identity, while others have used their albums' liner notes to discuss religion.

SUFI MUSIC

Many Sufi Muslim Americans have used *dhikr,* the "remembrance of God" through recitation, singing, playing instruments, and dancing, as a form of spiritual expression. The pioneering Sufi musician in America was INAYAT KHAN, born into a family of prominent Indian musicians. Khan first traveled to the United States in 1910. As explained in his autobiography, he planned to communicate Sufism through music: "I came to America with the Sufi Message, but the only means which I had to carry out my mission was by music, my profession." During his tour, perhaps a few dozen or fewer Americans converted to Sufism. Khan married Ora Ray Baker, a relative of Mary Baker Eddy, the founder of Christian Science. Later, his family followed in his footsteps and returned to the United States as Sufi leaders.

After Khan, other foreign Sufi musicians traveled to America. Their objective was not explicitly religious, and their visits did not often result in more conversions to Islam. Rather, their presence in America contributed to the growing popularity of world and fusion music as they collaborated with non-Muslim American musicians. In 1975, the Pakistani group Sabri Brothers introduced Qawwali Sufi music to Americans at a sold-out concert in NEW YORK CITY's Carnegie Hall. As the *New York Times* reported: "the audience was clapping and shouting deliriously . . . it was really a reaffirmation of the power of music." In the 1990s, another Pakistani Qawwali musician, Nusrat Fateh Ali Khan, achieved fame in the United States. Besides performing traditional music, Khan collaborated with Eddie Vedder from Pearl Jam for the soundtrack to the 1995 movie *Dead Man Walking* and with Peter Gabriel for the soundtrack to the 1988 movie *The Last Temptation of Christ*. Sufi music also influenced classical musicians. In 1998, cellist Yo-Yo Ma began the Silk Road Project, a multicultural music program that features Sufi musicians and songs from Eurasia.

RAP / HIP-HOP

In the 1990s, music journalist Harry Allen called Islam the "official religion" of HIP-HOP. Indeed, since its emergence in the mid-1970s, rap and hip-hop have borne indisputable marks of Muslim influence. The NATION OF ISLAM (NOI) has been particularly important because several of its members became mainstream musicians, and because this music became a vehicle to popularize its message of Islam and black nationalism. For instance, Public Enemy, one of the first rap groups to achieve superstar status, is affiliated with the NOI, discusses its ideas in their lyrics, and samples audio clips of MALCOLM X and LOUIS FARRAKHAN in their songs. Farrakhan, also a musician (a former calypso singer and classical violinist), reciprocated this relationship with the music world: In 2001, he delivered the keynote speech at the National Hip-Hop Summit and has featured a weekly music column in the NOI newspaper, *The Final Call*.

Sunni Muslims have also been influential in mainstream rap and hip-hop. MOS DEF, a Grammy Award–winning musician, asserted the intimate relationship between music and Islam: Both rap and the Qur'an use language in a similar manner. Mos Def and other Sunni rappers have also woven Islamic sounds of worship into their melodies. Mos Def opened his 1999 album, *Black on Both Sides,* with the *basmallah,* a Muslim invocation meaning "in the name of God, the Compassionate, the Merciful." Everlast repeatedly sings the first half of the *shahadah,* the Muslim testament of faith, in his 1999 Grammy Award–winning song, "Put Your Lights On." And Lupe Fiasco, a Grammy-nominated musician, plays off Kanye West's "Jesus Walks" with the song "Muhammad Walks." In this song, Lupe recites the *basmallah* and samples the *adhan.*

Other musicians influenced by Islam include Jurassic 5, Afrika Bambaata, Common, The Roots, Ice Cube, Beanie Sigel, Napoleon of Outlawz, Rza of WU-TANG CLAN, and Q-Tip and Ali Shaheed Muhammad of A TRIBE CALLED QUEST.

TAQWACORE / PUNK MUSIC

TAQWACORE is a subculture of Muslim punk music that emerged after Michael Muhammad Knight's novel *The Taqwacores.* Knight, a white American convert to Islam, wrote the book in 2002 and initially distributed photocopies of his work. It was eventually published in 2005. The book describes a fictitious group of Muslim punks in New York City whose lives included prayer, parties, music, and Mohawk haircuts, as they searched for "what it means to be young and Muslim in modern-day America." The term *taqwacore* combines the Arabic word *taqwa,* "God-consciousness," and the slang word "hardcore," a subcategory of punk rock. After the release of Knight's novel, several taqwacore bands emerged, including the Kominas, Vote Hezbollah, 8-bit, Al-Thawra, Diacritical, and Secret Trial Five. The Kominas have arguably become the most famous taqwacore band. This group of Punjabi musicians living in the Boston suburbs recorded their first song, "Rumi Was a Homo (But Wahhaj Is a Fag)," a musical response to homophobic comments made by Imam Siraj Wahhaj.

Much of taqwacore music has ridiculed prominent Muslim-American leaders and the traditions of the Muslim-American mainstream. For instance, to coincide with the 2005 annual ISLAMIC SOCIETY OF NORTH AMERICA Convention, several taqwacore bands collaborated to produce a compilation CD called *Hamza Don't Surf* (a reference to an article that described Hamza Yusuf as a surfer-turned-sheikh). But taqwacore has also ridiculed American culture and U.S. foreign policy with songs like the Komina's "Suicide Bomb the Gap" and 8-bit's "I'll Be Your Terrorist." Taqwacore has rebelled against both American and traditional Muslim establishments. As Knight explained, "In this so-called clash of civilizations, Taqwacore is about sticking the middle finger in both directions." However, Knight and taqwacore musicians have made it clear that the music is not about blasphemy or attacking Islam; rather, taqwacore has created an alternative to the Muslim-American mainstream and the moral rigidity associated with it.

MUSIC FOR MUSLIMS

Muslim Americans have also created a new music genre specifically for their community. Like those in the mainstream, these musicians have drawn on both Islamic and American styles. For these musicians, however, Islam is the central theme, and Muslims are the primary audience.

The Islamic Society of North America has promoted many of these musicians through performances at its annual national convention and MYNA-RAPS, a project that produces the albums of Muslim musicians. Its most prominent musicians are NATIVE DEEN, an African-American hip-hop trio. Native Deen uses only vocals and percussion in their music, in accordance with MYNA-RAPS's prohibition on wind and string instruments, which are considered impermissible by some Islamic scholars because they are thought to arouse passions and encourage sinful actions. Like mainstream secular musicians, Native Deen boasts several albums, music videos, an elaborate Web site, an online store, and an international concert tour. Prominent musicians outside MYNA-RAPS production include Tyson, Brother Dash, Seven8Six, and Kareem Salama. European Muslim musicians such as Sami Yusuf, Yusuf Islam, Outlandish, and Mecca2Medina also frequently perform in the United States and have many listeners.

This new music genre is also supported by the emergence of Muslim record labels. Anas Canon, founder of the label Remarkable Current, has explained this need: "When presenting on someone else's stage, we will never be able to fully express the true beauty and balance of Islam. But when WE control our presentation, we have command over the world's perception of Islam as displayed through Muslim culture." Some international Muslim labels, such as Meem Music and Global One Records, have branches in the United States and sign American musicians. Other labels, like Jamal Records, are widely distributed in the United States. Muslim music has not been a unified genre. Instead, Islamic themes, symbols, and multiple musical genres have influenced many different musical styles throughout U.S. history. Muslim influence in African-American music began as a faint echo of Muslim ancestry and has grown over the centuries. Today, Muslim musicians enjoy mainstream success and their own music niche among Muslim Americans. This mutual exchange between Islam and American music has not only had an impact on the history of Muslim-American music culture but also on American music culture as a whole.

Caitlin Yoshiko Buysse

Further Reading

Abdalla, May. "On Tour with the Taqwacores." BBC Newsnight. Available online. URL: http://news.bbc.co.uk/2/hi/pro grammes/newsnight/7024784.stm. Accessed May 21, 2009.

Abdel-Alim, Hesham Samy. "Hip Hop Islam." Al-Ahram Weekly Online. Available online. URL: http://weekly.ahram.org. eg/2005/750/feature.htm. Accessed May 21, 2009.

Curiel, Jonathan. "Muslim Roots of the Blues." San Francisco Chronicle Online. August 15, 2004. Available online. URL: http://sfgate.com/cgi-bin/article.cgi?f=/c/a/2004/08/15/ INGMC85SSK1.DTL. Accessed May 21, 2009.

Diouf, Sylviane A. *Servants of Allah: African Muslims Enslaved in the Americas.* New York: New York University Press, 1998.

Floyd-Thomas, Juan M. "A Jihad of Words: The Evolution of African American Islam and Contemporary Hip Hop." In *Noise and Spirit: The Religious and Spiritual Sensibilities of Rap Music,* edited by Anthony B. Pinn. New York: New York University Press, 2003.

Georgia Writers' Project. *Drums and Shadows: Survival Studies among the Georgia Coastal Negroes.* Athens: University of Georgia Press, 1986.

Khan, Inayat. "Autobiography: America, 1910–1912." Wahiduddin's Web: Living from the Heart. Available online. URL: http://wahiduddin.net/mv2/bio/Autobiography_1.htm. Accessed January 20, 2008.

Kubik, Gerhard. *Africa and the Blues.* Jackson.: University Press of Mississippi, 1999.

MuslimHipHop.com. Available online. URL: http://www. muslimhiphop.com/. Accessed January 20, 2008.

Remarkable Current. Official Remarkable Current Site. Available online. URL: http://www.remarkablecurrent.com/. Accessed January 20, 2008.

Rockwell, John. "Qawwali Music Stirs the Audience; Pakistanis Bring Drums and Chants to Carnegie." *New York Times,* 5 March 1975, p. 30.

Muslim Alliance in North America

Formally organized in 2005 after several years of planning, the Muslim Alliance in North America (MANA) is a Muslim-American religious organization that focuses on the religious, political, and social concerns of American-born Muslims. It quickly emerged as a leading umbrella organization for black Sunni Muslim mosques, individuals, and organizations not associated with the leadership of W. D. MOHAMMED (1933–2008), the leader who transformed the original Nation of Islam into a Sunni Muslim group.

The first elected leader, or *amir,* of MANA was SIRAJ WAHHAJ (1950–   ), the Brooklyn-based African-American Muslim leader. Its secretary-general, responsible for administration, was University of Kentucky religious studies professor Ihsan Bagby. Other leading figures in the establishment and operation of MANA have included University of Michigan religious studies professor Sherman Jackson, religious leader Talib Abdur Rashid, Zaytuna Institute founder HAMZA YUSUF (1960–   ), prison chaplain R. Mukhtar Curtis, and religious scholar ZAID SHAKIR (1956–   ). Though led primarily by men, the executive committee of MANA has explicitly sought to include women, and social worker Aneesa Nadir and English instructor Halima Toure have been members.

Reflecting the viewpoints of several of these scholars and religious leaders, MANA has focused on providing mosque-based solutions to social and economic problems, especially in urban areas; increasing the number of conversions to Islam; and taking a critical stance on aspects of U.S. domestic and foreign policy that the group believes is unjust. Many of MANA's leader, including Ihsan Bagby, Zaid Shakir, and Hamza Yusuf, have been interviewed by mainstream media outlets on issues pertaining to Muslim-American affairs. Its leaders have also been active writers whose publications have appeared in peer-reviewed journals and books, as well as on the organization's Web site. To cite one example, Sherman A. Jackson's *Islam and the Blackamerican* (2005) articulates a vision for American Islam that preserves African-American Muslim concerns with social justice while also making certain that personal piety and spirituality never become subordinate to politics.

In 2008, MANA held its first national conference during Thanksgiving weekend in PHILADELPHIA, the same city in which the organization was first launched. During the conference, a lifetime service award was given to Muhammad Ali (1942–   ) and a community service award was presented to Tayyibah Taylor, founder of *AZIZAH* magazine. Conference topics included Muslim-American history, criminal justice, mission work, Islamic jurisprudence, mosque development, Muslim-American YOUTH, HEALTH CARE, EDUCATION, POLITICS, FAMILIES, and WOMEN. The group also sponsored an evening comedy show, *Allah Made Me Funny*.

Edward E. Curtis IV

Further Reading

Jackson, Sherman A. *Islam and the Blackamerican: Looking toward the Third Resurrection.* New York: Oxford University Press, 2005.

"Muslim Alliance in North America." Available online. URL: http://www.mana-net.org/index.php. Accessed March 20, 2009.

Muslim American Society

Emerging from a Chicago-based organization founded in 1969 called the "Cultural Society," the Muslim American Society (MAS) was formally established in 1992 and 1993 by a group of predominately ARAB-AMERICAN MUSLIMS who hoped to create an "Islamic revival and reform movement that uplifts the individual, family, and society." In 1998, the MAS opened a national office in Falls Church, Virginia, and by the beginning of the 21st century, it grew to include thousands of Muslim Americans who were members of approximately 40 local chapters across the nation.

In 1999, MAS launched its own magazine, *The American Muslim,* a bimonthly glossy publication that includes features on ISLAMIC THOUGHT and RELIGIOUS LIFE, children's cartoons and stories, Muslim involvement in politics both at home and abroad, the arts and culture, and advertisements from travel agencies, charities, and Muslim publishers. The November/December 2003 issue, for example, discussed the impact of the USA PATRIOT Act on Muslim Americans, the use of herbs and other natural remedies for healing, a comic strip called Maged and Mazen, and the growing "trialogue of the Abrahamic faiths [Judaism, Christianity, and Islam]."

In the 21st century, its Web site has offered users news and information of concern to the Muslim-American community, information about Islamic civilization and religion, and an "Ask the Imam" feature. From 2004 to 2006, the organization's Web site actively hosted online chats with Muslim-American imams, or religious leaders, in which Internet users could ask for an online FATWA, or religious opinion, on questions ranging from the circumstances under which one can seek an Islamic divorce to the permissibility of drawing a nude model for a college class.

In 2002, MAS registered its own online educational institution, the Islamic American University, as a tax-exempt agency. The institution, which is not accredited, has offered associate's, bachelor's, and master's degrees in Islamic studies, attempting to educate both Muslims and non-Muslims through its correspondence and online courses. Its Winter 2009 schedule, for example, included more than 30 distance-learning classes in ARABIC on *fiqh*, or Islamic jurisprudence, *da'wa*, or missionary work, hadith, or reports about prophet Muhammad and his companions, and the QUR'AN. The school also maintained a physical campus in Southfield, Michigan.

In 2002, MAS held a joint convention with the ISLAMIC CIRCLE OF NORTH AMERICA, a predominately SOUTH

Imam Mahdi Bray of the Muslim American Society Freedom Foundation leads a protest outside the Israeli embassy in Washington, D.C., against Israeli military operations in the Gaza Strip, on December 30, 2008. *(Courtesy of the Author)*

ASIAN–AMERICAN MUSLIM organization. Talk of a merger between the two organizations proceeded, but the two groups decided instead to coordinate their education campaigns and continue to hold joint conventions. The theme of their 2003 gathering at Hyatt Regency in CHICAGO was "Muslims, Citizens of the West: Rights, Duties, and Prospects." In 2007, the conference was devoted to the subject of "The Qur'an: Relevant Guidance for a Pluralistic America." The conference included lectures and workshops, a bazaar, prayers, and parenting clinics.

After the terrorist attacks of SEPTEMBER 11, 2001, the MAS also established the MAS Freedom Foundation whose goal was to protect the civil rights of Muslim Americans by partnering with like-minded organizations, lobbying Congress, and raising awareness. Its executive director in 2009 was Mahdi Bray, a religious leader and political activist from greater Washington, D.C., who has helped to organize the Muslim-American vote and led opposition to the IRAQ WAR. Like the COUNCIL ON AMERICAN-ISLAMIC RELATIONS, MAS Freedom Foundation also established local chapters. The North Carolina chapter, for example, was led by Khalilah Sabra, who participated in local interfaith dialogues and the activities of the National Association for the Advancement of Colored People and encouraged fellow Muslims to become more politically active.

Edward E. Curtis IV

Further Reading

Muslim American Society. Available online. URL: http://www.masnet.org/. Accessed March 25, 2009.

Nimer, Mohamed. *The North American Resource Guide: Muslim Community Life in the United States and Canada.* New York: Routledge, 2002.

Muslim Brotherhood　See REVIVALISM.

Muslim Girls Training—General Civilization Class

The Muslim Girls Training—General Civilization Class (MGT) trained female members of the NATION OF ISLAM (NOI) to embody the virtues of good Muslim women. According to Nation of Islam tradition, the MGT was established by W. D. FARD in the early 1930s. The female counterpart to the male FRUIT OF ISLAM (FOI), the MGT taught women life skills such as sewing, cooking, housekeeping, child rearing, hygiene, reading, writing, proper diet, and self-defense to prepare them as wives and mothers. The MGT also educated women about Islam and black history through the study of the QUR'AN, the Bible, and *Supreme Wisdom,* a 1957 text published by NOI leader ELIJAH MUHAMMAD.

The MGT prescribed strict rules of dress and diet to instill modesty, discipline, and bodily purification in women. Women in the MGT wore a fully covering white uniform consisting of a long gown, cape, gloves, and box hat. While symbols of sexual immodesty like makeup and high heels were prohibited, the MGT instructed women to behave in a ladylike manner. Theoretically speaking, women were to refrain from swearing and yelling and were to practice walking with good posture and grace. At the same time, historical films depict MGT members shouting, laughing, and "grooving" as they performed military-like drills and marches in some MGT meetings.

Women were also expected to follow a specific diet and abstain from what the NOI considered "slave food." Proper body weight was sometimes enforced through mandatory weight checks. While some members of the MGT found such discipline to be oppressive, others enjoyed the sisterhood and racial solidarity that it helped to produce.

Similar to the FOI, the MGT was responsible for NOI security and recruitment. All women who entered NOI temples and mosques were searched by the MGT; prohibited items like alcohol, cigarettes, nail files, and makeup were confiscated. The MGT also created links with women outside the NOI to recruit new members and to discuss mutual community concerns.

The organizational structure of the MGT paralleled the FOI. The MGT operated both nationally and locally; national headquarters were located in CHICAGO, while local branches were attached to each temple. The Supreme Captain headed the national MGT and resided in Chicago so she could take direct orders from Elijah Muhammad. The Supreme Captain then commanded the local captains of every temple. Each local captain also took orders from the temple's minister and subsequently directed the first, second, and third lieutenants in her local squad. This chain of command often broke down as local chapters either ignored or selectively enforced orders from headquarters in Chicago.

During the height of the NOI in the 1950s and early 1960s, Sister Lottie Muhammad, daughter of Elijah, served as the Supreme Captain of the MGT. The wives of many prominent male NOI members also led or participated in the MGT. CLARA MUHAMMAD, wife of Elijah, trained and taught women in Chicago. Ethel Sharrieff, wife of FOI Supreme Captain Raymond Sharrieff and daughter of Elijah, proposed and implemented the idea of an MGT bakery. The first bakery began in Ethel's home basement and eventually developed into a nationwide business. Betty Shabazz, wife of MALCOLM X, was an MGT instructor who lectured on hygiene and health, and Khadijah Farrakhan enrolled in the New York MGT while her husband, LOUIS FARRAKHAN, served as minister.

Female Nation of Islam members, also part of the Muslim Girls Training, attend a Muslim rally in New York in 1963.   *(Library of Congress)*

Since the NOI viewed women as the foundation of civilization, the MGT's role in strengthening, educating, and disciplining women was considered crucial. Led in 2008 by National Captain Aishah Muhammad and National Vanguard Captain Sharrieffah Muhammad in Louis Farrakhan's Nation of Islam, the MGT has remained active, participating in its traditional activities and offering supplementary programs for women and girls.

Caitlin Yoshiko Buysse

Further Reading

Curtis, Edward E., IV. *Black Muslim Religion in the Nation of Islam 1960–1975.* Chapel Hill: University of North Carolina Press, 2006.

Essien-Udom, Essien Udosen. *Black Nationalism: A Search for an Identity in America.* Chicago: University of Chicago Press, 1962.

Gardell, Mattias. *In the Name of Elijah Muhammad: Louis Farrakhan and the Nation of Islam.* Durham, N.C.: Duke University Press, 1996.

Muhammad, Nisa Islam. "Are You Living in the Light?" Final Call.com News. Available online. URL: http://www.final call.com/artman/publish/article_3443.shtml. Accessed March 4, 2009.

Muslim Public Affairs Council

Established in 1988 as a nonprofit organization, the Los Angeles–based Muslim Public Affairs Council (MPAC) has sought to further the interests of Muslim Americans in U.S. POLITICS, to encourage interfaith dialogues among Muslims and people of other faiths, and to fight STEREOTYPES of Islam and Muslims in American media and culture, especially FILM. Led by its longtime executive director Salam al-Marayati, by the 21st century MPAC had five chapters in addition to its main office in LOS ANGELES.

Since 1991, MPAC has issued media awards to various artists and filmmakers who are "voices of courage and conscience" in American society. Award winners have included Spike Lee for *Malcolm X* (1992), Warner Brothers for *Syriana*

(2005), and Lawrence Bender for *An Inconvenient Truth* (2006). In addition, MPAC has advised various television shows, including the CW's series *Alien in America,* on their portrayal of Muslims.

MPAC has sought to stake out political and social positions that emphasize what it considers to be the uniquely balanced perspectives of Muslim Americans toward controversial topics such as terrorism and UNITED STATES FOREIGN RELATIONS with the Muslim world. For example, in September 1990, the group wrote an op-ed article in *USA Today* that was titled "Middle Eastern Dictators Don't Speak for Islam," arguing that many Middle Eastern leaders abused Islam in justifying their policies. At the time, Iraq's army under Saddam Hussein was occupying Kuwait. MPAC both condemned the Iraqi invasion and called on the United States to withdraw its troops from the region, advocating a peaceful solution to the crisis.

In 2000, MPAC opened an office in Washington, D.C., where it hoped to influence domestic and foreign policies of concern to Muslim Americans. That year, MAHER MUHAMMAD HATHOUT (1936–   ), an MPAC board member, delivered an invocation at the Democratic National Convention. MPAC also denounced the Taliban government in Afghanistan and its destruction of the ancient Buddhist religious sites and statues in the country.

MPAC immediately condemned the terrorist attacks of SEPTEMBER 11, 2001, and in December 2001 staged a conference entitled "The Rising Voice of Moderate Muslims," trying to emphasize that violent extremists did not represent mainstream Muslims. It also sought to provide support to the thousands of foreign visitors from Arab and Muslim countries who faced increased scrutiny after 9/11. In 2003, MPAC joined with other civil rights and advocacy groups to monitor the Immigration and Naturalization Service's treatment of Arabs and Muslims.

In its publications and conferences after 9/11, MPAC consistently claimed, echoing a widespread view among Muslim Americans, that counterterrorism efforts must be careful to avoid demonizing all Muslims. Its 2004 conference, "Counterproductive Counterterrorism," outlined what it believed was the negative impact of "Islamophobia," the irrational fear of Islam and Muslims, on fighting religious extremism. In 2005, it launched a grassroots campaign to fight terrorism, giving suggested guidelines for both law enforcement and Muslim-American religious leaders in addressing the issue.

In 2007, MPAC joined the Progressive Jewish Alliance in sponsoring "NewGround: A Muslim-Jewish Partnership for Change," for blunt dialogue around controversial issues such as Israel/Palestine, women's rights, and religious pluralism. In 2009, NewGround launched a pilot program in which participants read and discussed each other's sacred scriptures.

Edward E. Curtis IV

Further Reading

Haddad, Yvonne Y. *Muslims in the West: From Sojourners to Citizens.* New York: Oxford University Press, 2002.
Muslim Public Affairs Council. Available online. URL: http://www.mpac.org/. Accessed April 15, 2009.

Muslim Students Association

The Muslim Students Association (sometimes also called the Muslim Students' Association or Muslim Student Association) of the United States and Canada, otherwise known as MSA National, or simply MSA, was created to strengthen ties among Muslim-American students in January 1963 at a conference at the University of Illinois at Urbana-Champaign. Though the organization included only 13 chapters during its first year of operations, by 1967, there were 36 chapters. By 1970, 68 campus chapters were affiliated with the organization. Such growth continued in the late 20th and early 21st centuries, and by 2010, there were more than 250 affiliated MSA chapters in the United States and Canada, in addition to many other Muslim student groups who maintained loose ties with MSA National but retained their official autonomy from the organization.

ORIGINS

The organization's founders included 75 students—most of whom were seeking graduate degrees—from Turkey, Pakistan, Iran, India, and various Arab countries. At least some MSA members were also Americans, as illustrated by the case of the MSA chapter at Southern Illinois University, which was led in 1966 by Linda Clark, a white woman. Following the initial conference in January 1963, a substructure soon developed, and local chapters were connected on both regional and national levels. Each year, MSA holds an annual convention that featured a menagerie of activities, all of which helps to bolster the influence of the organization.

While MSA shared many of the same goals as its organizational predecessors, including the FEDERATION OF ISLAMIC ASSOCIATIONS IN THE UNITED STATES AND CANADA (FIA), its focus on and connections to foreign and recently arrived immigrant Muslims gave the organization a recruitment advantage after 1965, when the liberalization of immigration policy led to a large influx of Muslim immigrants into the United States. In the 1970s, funded partly through the missionary outreach of Saudi Arabia and other oil-producing countries, MSA published books and pamphlets with the aim of helping new Muslim immigrants live an Islamic life in the West. For example, *Al-Ittihad* (The unity), which became a biannual journal, was first published in the 1970s.

Al-Ittihad frequently discussed the ideas of the most prominent Muslim intellectuals of the era, including Abu al-Ala Mawdudi, the founder of the Jamaat-i Islami

Muslim Students Association (MSA) chapter, Southern Illinois University, Carbondale, 1966. The MSA was launched as a national organization in 1963 at the University of Illinois, Urbana-Champaign. Headed by President Linda Clark *[front row, center]*, the MSA chapter at Southern Illinois University, Carbondale, hosted weekly prayers, celebrated Ramadan, and invited guest speakers to campus.   *(Special Collections Research Center, Morris Library, Southern Illinois University, Carbondale)*

in Pakistan, and Sayyid Qutb, a leader in the Muslim Brotherhood in Egypt. During the first years of the publication, almost every issue of *Al-Ittihad* contained favorable sentiments toward a number of Islamic revivalist movements throughout the world and at least one article by Mawdudi or Qutb. Both Mawdudi and Qutb advocated the application of Islamic teachings in private and public life, believing that Islam contained teaching on every aspect of life, from how to interact with one's spouse to how to run a government. Qutb was particularly critical of what he considered to be Western immorality and believed his own country to be un-Islamic and in need of an Islamic revolution. Many MSA members disagreed with Qutb's radical politics, but they admired his religious verve and commitment to leading a pious life.

In addition to *Al-Ittihad,* the widely distributed MSA *Newsletter,* first published in 1971, became a source of community news before it gave way to its successor, *Islamic Horizons,* in 1976. That year MSA also published *Parents Manual: A Guide for Muslim Parents Living in North America.* Additionally, individual MSA university chapters created publications of their own, including UCLA's *Al-Talib* (Student) magazine, which was founded in 1990, and the MSA chapter at Salisbury University in Maryland, which published a COOKBOOK of "Muslim family recipes from around the world."

In 1971, as an attempt to solidify MSA into an organization with strong, central governance, a rudimentary headquarters operating from Al-Amin Mosque was established in Gary, Indiana. Two years later, in 1973, a full-time executive director was appointed, and in September 1975, the constitu-

tion was revised, creating a staff of full-time workers. MSA left the mosque in Gary in order to establish a more permanent headquarters in Plainfield, Indiana, in 1983, and later moved to Falls Church, Virginia.

CHANGES AFTER 1975

The 1975 constitution no longer aimed primarily at providing guidance to new Muslim immigrants but instead adopted guidelines that applied to Muslims in the United States more broadly. The MSA shifted from a group of Muslim students with no plans of remaining in the United States to an organization that hoped to become a powerful voice for all Muslim Americans in both the United States and Canada. While MSA was initially influenced by the ideology of the Muslim Brotherhood of Egypt and the Jamaat-i Islami of the Indian subcontinent, such influences waned as it became larger and more heterogeneous. The organization gradually developed into a network of communities that challenged its members to put their Muslim identities before their loyalties to their particular ethnic and linguistic groups.

MSA spawned—both directly and indirectly—a number of other Muslim-American organizations, including the ISLAMIC MEDICAL ASSOCIATION OF NORTH AMERICA, the ASSOCIATION OF MUSLIM SCIENTISTS AND ENGINEERS, the ASSOCIATION OF MUSLIM SOCIAL SCIENTISTS, the FIQH COUNCIL OF NORTH AMERICA, and many more. Perhaps most notable, however, was the MSA's direct involvement in the genesis of the ISLAMIC SOCIETY OF NORTH AMERICA (ISNA), which became one of the most influential and largest Muslim organizations in the United States. In 1982, after approximately six years of discussions among 50 prominent Muslim-American leaders, former MSA leader Sayyid M. Syeed announced the formation of ISNA at the annual MSA convention in Bloomington, Indiana. Both ISNA and MSA grew in the last two decades of the 20th century and in September 1998 met jointly in St. Louis, Missouri, to celebrate MSA's 35th annual meeting. More than 100 sessions took place at the conference.

This era also saw a sea change in the leadership of the MSA. In the beginning of its history, MSA leaders were mainly men, while Muslim women assisted with typing, publishing, and fundraising. However, as more and more American women assumed positions of leadership in American society in the 1970s and beyond, the leadership of the MSA reflected these larger social changes. By 2001, well over half of MSA National's elected leadership were women, though the president's office had always been occupied by a male. On June 25, 2004, Hadia Mubarak, a graduate student at Georgetown University, became the first woman elected to the presidency of MSA National—and the first American-born student to hold the office.

Mubarak had run previously and lost, but her perseverance was eventually rewarded. Her election marked a doubly significant occasion, both as a symbol of the advancement of gender equality and of the growing American national identity of the organization. In the same year, the COUNCIL ON AMERICAN-ISLAMIC RELATIONS (CAIR) gave Mubarak their Islamic Community Service Award for her achievements and efforts. Since then, other women have become MSA leaders, including Asma Mirza, who was the second female president of MSA. A variety of MSA university chapters throughout the United States have also had women presidents, including Duke University and the University of California, Santa Barbara (UCSB). Some chapters of the MSA, such as MSA-Northwestern University, even created bylaws requiring copresidency to be shared by a female and male.

Since its establishment in 1963, the Muslim Students Association has become a visible presence on many college campuses. *(Tom Carter/PhotoEdit)*

LOCAL AUTONOMY AND NONALIGNED MSAS

Since 1963, several MSA organizations on American campuses have remained officially independent from MSA National. In addition, there have been splits from the MSA National organization, including the Persian-Speaking Group of the MSA (MSA-PSG), which was founded by SHI'A MUSLIM AMERICANS following the Iranian Revolution of 1979. Another organization that assumed the MSA title but never held official ties to MSA National was MSA West (which was different from MSA National's Western branch called "West Zone USA"). MSA West was founded in the late 1990s in order to serve Muslim students in the western United States, and while it has remained independent from MSA National, the two organizations have cooperated on a number of endeavors, including leadership training and joint conferences.

Individual MSA chapters have also engaged in community awareness and service projects that are specific to their campuses. In 1994, Muslim students at DePaul University in Chicago founded the Inner-city Muslim Action Network (IMAN), which consisted of a group of volunteers who would gather at a major Arab center in Chicago to help children with their homework and oversee recreational activities.

Some local MSA chapters have also struggled to fend off attacks from conservative critics of Islam such as David Horowitz, whose defamation campaigns have attempted to link the MSA with terrorism. Horowitz's criticism of the MSA are based largely on the organization's former links to overseas organizations such as the Muslim World League, the Muslim Brotherhood, and Jamaat-i Islami, which Horowitz considers to be terrorist organizations. Three of MSA's 75 founders in the 1960s were members of the Muslim Brotherhood, and Horowitz assumed that any organization once linked to these organizations must be anti-American.

In 2008, Horowitz published a paid advertisement in the UCSB's campus newspaper, *The Daily Nexus,* entitled, "Stop the Jihad on College Campuses," accusing the local chapter of the MSA of recruiting public speakers who "are calling for the execution of gays, killing of Jews and [who] support terrorist jihad against America." The ad appeared as part of Horowitz's third annual Islamo-Fascism Awareness Week. But UCSB's MSA chapter had no ties to terrorists, the Muslim Brotherhood, or the Jamaat-i Islami. It may have sponsored campus speakers who opposed aspects of UNITED STATES FOREIGN RELATIONS with the Muslim world, especially the IRAQ WAR, and advocated socially conservative family values, but there was no evidence that UCSB's MSA supported the execution of lesbian, gay, bisexual, and transgender persons or supported "terrorist jihads" against America. When Horowitz spoke at UCSB in May 2008, his list of MSA chapters comprising part of what he called a "jihad network" did not include the UCSB chapter, demonstrating further the gross generalities of his claims.

While MSA National's publishing house and book dissemination network once focused on what might be considered "fundamentalist" or revivalist literature, the autonomy of local MSA chapters and more than four decades of MSA National's evolution have made it impossible to characterize MSA with large brushstrokes. The various expressions of MSA, as well as MSA National itself, became too diverse and heterogeneous to be characterized by any single political ideology.

CONCLUSION

While its initial goals were shaped largely by foreign Muslim students who came to study in the United States during the 1950s and 1960s, the MSA evolved into a national organization with a broad reach throughout Muslim America. From a defensive organization concerned largely with preserving Islamic identity in what was seen as a hostile environment, it has evolved into a group focused on crafting a specifically Muslim-American identity. As a symbol of this change, in 2007 the MSA adopted a new red, white, and blue logo that fused elements of the U.S. and Canadian flags, including the maple leaf and the stars and stripes, into two Islamic crescent moons. In the middle of the logo, cradled by the two moons, is the word "salam," or peace. The success of the MSA as a national organization has led to the establishment of several other Muslim-American associations, which together have aided Muslim-American attempts to influence American society. From religious outreach efforts and political activism to community service projects that address issues of homelessness, youth violence, and failed schools, MSA has had an important impact on American society.

See also REVIVALISM.

Elliott Bazzano

Further Reading

Abdo, Geneive. *Mecca and Main Street: Muslim Life in America after 9/11.* New York: Oxford University Press: New York, 2006.

GhaneaBassiri, Kambiz. *Competing Visions of Islam in the United States: A Study of Los Angeles.* Westport, Conn.: Greenwood, 1997.

Haddad, Yvonne Y. "The Muslim Experience in the United States." *The Link* 2, no. 4 (1979).

Haddad, Yvonne Y., ed. *The Muslims of America.* New York: Oxford University Press, 1991.

Haddad, Yvonne Y., and Jane Smith, eds. *Muslim Minorities in the West: Visible and Invisible.* New York: AltaMira Press, 2002.

Smith, Jane. *Islam in America.* New York: Columbia University Press, 1999.

Muslim Sunrise

Founded in 1921, *The Muslim Sunrise: A Journal of the Islamic Renaissance in America* was one of the earliest Muslim publications originating in the United States. It took its name from the quote of the prophet Muhammad that the journal frequently displayed: "In the latter days, the sun shall rise from the west." Dr. Mufti Muhammad Sadiq (1872–1957), the first Ahmadiyya missionary to arrive in America, founded the magazine in DETROIT, MICHIGAN. As of 2010, it continued to appear as a quarterly journal of the American Ahmadiyya Muslim community, serving as a platform for discussions on Islam and other religions. The contemporary *Sunrise* offers an Islamic perspective on contemporary issues. Their official Web site highlights the role Islam plays within a "changing society" and the journal's particular interest in "rehabilitating the relationship" between Islamic and Western cultures.

The Ahmadiyya were a pioneering force in the history of Islam in the United States and led many African Americans to convert to Islam. The *Muslim Sunrise,* as an Ahmadiyya media outlet, is therefore an important source for the history of Islam in the United States during the first half of the 20th century. In its early decades, the format of the journal was fairly consistent: It featured a translated passage from the Qur'an, followed by sayings of the prophet Muhammad, excerpts from the writings of Hazrat Mirza Ghulam Ahmad (the founder and most important religious figure of the Ahmadiyya Movement in India), and an address, prayer, or lecture from a prominent Ahmadi leader or scholar. The articles consisted of theological material, stories from the Qur'an or Bible, and interpretations of Islamic principles or practices. There were also articles that addressed current world events, often from Southern Asia or the Middle East, and also on events from local Muslim American communities. The *Sunrise* published press notices, obituaries of prominent Muslims, a listing of recent American converts and their new Arabic names, and other statistics and reports of missionary work. It also published letters of congratulations and condolences sent to famous and well-connected individuals, their responses, and letters commenting on lectures given at churches and social gatherings.

More recently, the *Muslim Sunrise* organized articles around particular themes, providing commentary on current issues from varying Islamic perspectives. There have been regular features such as letters to the editor, reviews of books and other media, and an interview section in which the *Sunrise* staff has met with religious figures, scholars, and civic leaders from the United States and abroad. Some columns have discussed daily life and the personal practice of Islam from historical and contemporary viewpoints. The "Friday Sermon" and "Poetry Corner" sections have appeared regularly alongside a new feature, "Religion and Science," in which the *Sunrise* has argued that, although other religious teachings cannot be reconciled with scientific fact or evidence, the Ahmadiyya Muslim Community asserts that "the laws of nature and God are in harmony."

Karima W. Abidine

Further Reading

The Ahmadiyya Muslim Community U.S.A. Available online. URL: http://www.ahmadiyya.us. Accessed on May 26, 2009.

Al Islam: The Official Web Site of the Ahmadiyya Muslim Community. Available online. URL: http://www.alislam.org. Accessed on May 26, 2009.

"The Muslim Sunrise." Available online. URL: http://www.muslimsunrise.com. Accessed on May 26, 2009.

MuslimWakeUp!

MuslimWakeUp! was cofounded in January 2003 by Ahmed Nassef and Jawad Ali, two Muslim-American graduates from the University of California, Los Angeles, who wished to "reflect the voice of Muslim Americans" and to begin a dialogue among them in "a more open Islamic context." The organization began primarily as a Web site (www.muslim-wakeup.com), headquartered in Pleasantville, New York, which until 2007 functioned as "a progressive online Muslim-American magazine."

From the outset, the Web site gathered both praise and criticism as it tried to promote what it defined as a more progressive Islam that was contrasted to the views of more extremist groups. For example, the organization launched a campaign to "Hug a Jew," which attempted to displace the visceral idea that Jews and Israel were somehow anathema to the Muslim experience. In addition to proclaiming that Jews, too, were creatures of God and shared a common humanity with Muslims, the site argued that the Jewish experience provided opportunities for reflection and thought among Muslims. It also featured the stories of several Jewish Americans who were pro-Palestinian or anti-Zionist. Another feature, "Sex and the Umma," one of the most popular sections of the Web site, touched on issues such as abortion, polyandry, homosexuality, and same-sex marriage through fiction as well as editorial and opinion pieces.

MuslimWakeUp! also opposed "all forms of oppression, bigotry, sexism and racism" and aligned itself with other progressive Muslims, including the Progressive Muslims Union. On March 18, 2005, these groups sponsored mixed-gender Friday prayers in NEW YORK CITY led by Islamic studies professor and activist AMINA WADUD. The event, which violated the traditional Islamic prohibition against a woman leading men in prayer, was originally scheduled to take place in a mosque and then later an art gallery, but was moved to St. John the Divine, an Episcopalian cathedral, after a number of bomb threats. The event sparked intense debate and was both condemned and applauded by individuals and Muslim groups around the world.

In November 2007, the muslimwakeup.com Web site ceased to be active. Cofounder Ahmed Nassef stopped working on the site for unexplained reasons, and cofounder Jawad Ali left the United States to aid the victims of the 2006 earthquake in Pakistan. In addition, many of the participants on the site disagreed over the direction of the progressive movement, especially on their stances toward U.S. foreign policy. Various progressive Muslim groups, including the Progressive Muslim Union, Muslims for Progressive Values, and ProgressiveIslam.org provided venues and spaces for the ongoing debates. Though MuslimWakeUp! was short-lived, for four years it provided a rallying point for activists, students, journalists and young Muslim Americans hoping to counter stereotypical images of Muslims as socially conservative and to debate the future of Islam.

Rizwan Mawani

Muslim World League   See MISSIONARIES.

N

Naqshbandi Sufi Order

Naqshbandi Sufis practice a form of SUFISM in which participants use silence and internal contemplation in order to connect with God. The term Naqshbandi incorporates two ideas: the *naqsh* or "engraving" the name of Allah in the heart and the band or "bond" describing the link between the individual and the Creator. The Naqshbandis are also known as "silent Sufis" because of their practice of the silent meditation of the heart. The Naqshbandi Sufi Order traces its origins to Abu Bakr as-Siddiq, a seventh-century caliph who succeeded the prophet MUHAMMAD in leading the early Muslim community.

In the middle ages, the Naqshbandi school of thought flourished in central Asia and India, and in the 20th century spread to China, the Soviet Union, Western Europe, and the United States. Although Naqshbandis believe that other Sufi paths are able to find a path to God through DHIKR, the repetition of the names of God, the Naqshbandis believe there are 70,000 veils between the uninitiated and the station that prophet Muhammad reached and that *dhikr* should be practiced in silence. A Naqshbandi master "rends these veils in descending order," leaving one veil left to prevent strain on the person from "the contemplation of Divine Reality." A grand *shaykh*, or religious leader, in the Naqshbandi order does not rend that last veil until the highest state of perfection in the mind has been reached or until the grand *shaykh* has only seven breaths left on his deathbed.

Naqshbandis have a significant presence worldwide, with Shah Naqshband's (1317–?) school and mosque being the largest Islamic center of learning in Central Asia. By the 21st century, there were approximately 18 Naqshbandi centers in the United States and two in Canada. The Naqshbandi order was led by Muhammad Nazim al-Haqqani, the 40th member in a chain of Sufi leaders. His son-in-law, Sheikh Hisham Kabbani, was the Naqshbandi representative in the United States when he and his family relocated in 1990 and has since established an INTERNET site and classes to teach Americans about the order. The center for the Naqshbandi-Haqqani Sufi Order in America is in Fenton, Michigan. This fairly conservative Islamic spiritual movement has established itself as one of the fastest growing Sufi orders in North America.

In the first decade of the 21st century, an offshoot known as the Naqshbandiyaa-Mujaddidiyya Order maintained the Golden Sufi Center in Inverness, California. According to many community members, Irina Tweedie, a Russian woman who was taught by the Naqshbandi teacher Guru Bhai Sahib, brought the Naqshbandi Sufi movement to the West in 1985. The center in Inverness has overseen the task of presenting the teachings of the Naqshbandiyya-Mujaddidiyya Order to the public and has operated meditation groups in Northern California, NEW YORK CITY, LOS ANGELES, Seattle, Minnesota, CHICAGO, and in Canada. In addition to emphasizing the silent meditation of the heart, the order also places great importance on the use of dreams, which are seen as a form of guidance along the path. At meetings, practices usually include silent meditation followed by "dreamwork." Participants are encouraged to share their own dreams. The center has also sponsored retreats, lectures, and seminars, and maintained a trilingual Web site. Leader Irina Tweedie retired in 1992 and was succeeded by Llewellyn Vaughan Lee.

While there are no definitive figures on the size of these Naqshbandi orders, it is estimated that there are several thousand members in the United States. The Naqshbandis, like other Muslim-American groups, have benefited from their use of the Internet, which has enabled them to convert many nonimmigrant Americans to Islam. The high profile of women in the community and its critiques of consumerism and environmental degradation have also appealed to many American members. While Naqshbandi groups have succeeded in establishing a considerable following in the last 10 years, however, they have become increasingly alienated from some other Muslim-American associations, who do not consider the movement to be a legitimate representative of "mainstream" American Islam.

Natalia Slain

Further Reading

Malik, Jamal, and John Hinnells, eds. *Sufism in the West.* New York: Routledge, 2006.

Naqshbandi-Haqqani Sufi Order of America Web site. Available online. URL: http://www.naqshbandi.org. Accessed May 26, 2009.

Naqshbandiyya-Mujaddidiyya Order Web site. Available online. URL: http://www.goldensufi.org. Accessed May 26, 2009.

Nas (1973–) *rap singer*

Nas is a controversial rap singer whose lyrics and political views have engendered criticism from political leaders and media figures on both the left and the right.

Born on September 14, 1973, Nasir bin Olu Dara Jones, or "Nas," was raised in the Queensbridge Housing Projects in New York City. His parents were Olu Dara and Fannie Ann Jones. Nasir, which means "helper and protector" in Arabic, spent much of his formative years on the steps of his apartment building listening to his father play jazz on his trumpet. By the time his father left his household, relinquishing custody to Nas's mother, who was a postal employee, Nas had already been deeply influenced by both his father's musical tastes and religious beliefs. Nas later said that he was also influenced by Michael Jackson, Rick James, Run D.M.C., and three hip-hop artists—Erik B. and Rakim, G. Rap, and Kane—who have incorporated Muslim themes into their music.

As a child, Nas was fascinated with the Nation of Islam and the Five Percenters, the Nation of Islam breakaway group that was a central force behind East Coast hip-hop. Dropping out of school in the eighth grade, Nas embarked on a program of self-study that included African culture, the Bible, the Qur'an, and the history of hip-hop. Nas's music has reflected all of these influences.

His first album, *Illmatic,* was released by Columbia Records in 1994 to the wide acclaim of critics and became known as a classic of hip-hop. His subsequent releases, *It Was Written* (1996), *I am . . .* and *Nastradamus* (1999), *Stillmatic* (2001), *Hip Hop Is Dead* (2006), and the infamously "Untitled" album of 2008, cemented his reputation as a serious, if controversial artist. Nas had planned to call this 2008 album "Nigger," which incensed numerous African-American leaders such as Jesse Jackson and Al Sharpton. Nas dismissed them both as being culturally irrelevant and relics of a former age, but, bowing to the pressures from the music industry, he reluctantly consented to the change. He claimed that he wanted his fans to have access to his message and that they would understand that the "real" title of the album was in fact *Nigger* and not "Untitled," which is how it was released.

Nas also attracted considerable attention due to his televised dispute with Bill O'Reilly of Fox News, whom he accused of having racist agendas. O'Reilly publicly criticized the decision to allow Nas to perform at the benefit concert given at Virginia Tech after the tragic shootings there in 2007, condemning violent lyrics in songs such as "Shoot 'Em Up" and "Got Urself a Gun." During the 2008 presidential campaign, Nas joined forces with the activist groups MoveOn.org and ColorofChange.org and delivered a speech in front of the Fox News headquarters in which he demanded that the network "stop the racist smears on Obama and all black Americans." This was in direct response to Fox having run a graphic referring to Michele Obama as "Barack's Baby Mama."

On January 21, 2009, Nas performed his song "Black President" at Black Entertainment Television's ball honoring Barack Obama's inauguration as the 44th president of the United States.

Nicholas Boeving

Further Reading

Birchmeier, Jason. "Nas." All Music. Available online. URL: http://allmusic.com/cg/amg.dll?p=amg&sql=11:fxfexqe5ldde~T1. Accessed April 7, 2009.

Reid, Shaheem. "Nas and Bill O'Reilly Take Their Beef to the Air." MTV News. July 24, 2008. Available online. URL: http://www.mtv.com/news/articles/1591487/20080724/nas.jhtml. Accessed April 7, 2009.

———. "Nas Takes Jesse Jackson to Task for His Barack Obama Comments." MTV News. July 10, 2008. Available online. URL: http://www.mtv.com/news/articles/1590708/20080710/nas.jhtml?rsspartner=rssMozilla. Accessed April 7, 2009.

National Basketball Association (NBA)

The National Basketball Association (NBA) is America's premier basketball league and one of the most successful professional sports organizations in the United States. Since the 1960s, NBA teams have featured a number of Muslim players. The NBA has welcomed both foreign and African-American Muslim athletes into its ranks, coincidentally introducing the league's predominantly white, non-Muslim audience to multiple forms of Islamic identity. In this way, the NBA has been a vehicle for Muslim assimilation into American culture.

The Muslim presence in the NBA began in the mid-1960s, when Mahdi Abdul-Rahman (Walt Hazzard) and Wali Jones (Wally Jones) announced their conversions to Islam. They were followed by Zaid Abdul-Aziz (Don Smith), Shahid Abdul-Alin (Charlie Scott), Jamaal Wilkes (Keith Wilkes), and Kareem Abdul-Jabbar (Lew Alcindor) in the 1970s. These conversions reflected a broader trend in black America, which was increasingly turning to Islam as a political and spiritual alternative to Christianity. At a time when other Muslim athletes such as Muhammad Ali and Ahmad Rashad faced public hostility to their religious views, the

NBA's Muslim players reported few incidents of harassment from fans or journalists. Abdul-Jabbar later claimed that his talent protected him from religious criticism.

The NBA gained its first foreign-born Muslim player when the Houston Rockets drafted HAKEEM OLAJUWON of Nigeria in 1984. Olajuwon became more observant as his career progressed, and eventually he became a role model and religious ambassador for Muslim America. For many years he and Abdul-Jabbar presented non-Muslims with a positive view of Islam. The league aggressively marketed both players, and as two of the NBA's biggest stars, they received numerous offers to endorse products and even made appearances in movies and on television.

In 1996, relations between Islam and the NBA were strained when Denver Nuggets guard and Sunni Muslim convert MAHMOUD ABDUL-RAUF refused to stand for "The Star-Spangled Banner," which is played before every NBA game. Abdul-Rauf claimed that Islam forbade worship of any nationalist symbol as a form of idolatry. Fans, journalists, and even fellow Muslims—including Olajuwon—swiftly condemned his act. Abdul-Rauf refused to change his position even when the NBA suspended him indefinitely, prompting the league to offer a compromise that allowed him to pray visibly while the anthem played. He was booed at stadiums around the league and later blamed the incident for ending his NBA career.

Later that year, Craig Hodges, a former player for the Chicago Bulls and a supporter of the NATION OF ISLAM (NOI), filed suit against the NBA for "blackballing" him "because of his outspoken political nature." During a visit to the White House in 1992, Hodges had presented President George H. W. Bush with a letter asking him to improve the lives of African Americans. Hodges claimed that the NBA had felt embarrassed by the incident and by his affiliation with the NOI and that teams had therefore colluded to keep him out of the league. A Federal court rejected the case.

Despite the Abdul-Rauf and Hodges controversies, the NBA has continued to market a number of Muslim players as role models. Olajuwon and SHAREEF ABDUR-RAHIM represented the United States as members of the 1996 and 2000 Olympic Basketball Teams, respectively. After the terrorist attacks of SEPTEMBER 11, 2001, sportswriters and league officials turned to both players for an explanation of Islamic beliefs regarding terrorism. One columnist valorized Olajuwon as "a true face of Islam." While the American media have devoted much attention to Islamic extremism in the 21st century, the NBA, which benefits both economically and culturally from its Muslim players' achievements, has placed Islam in a more favorable light and given players a platform to represent their own understandings of their religion.

William Brown

Further Reading

Berkow, Ira. "The Case of Hodges vs. the NBA," *New York Times.* Available online. URL: http://query.nytimes.com/gst/fullpage.html?res=9906E3D71E31F936A15751C1A960958260&scp=3&sq=Craig%20Hodges&st=cse. Accessed August 23, 2008.

Blinebury, Fran. "Hakeem a True Face of Islam," *Houston Chronicle.* Available online. URL: http://www.chron.com/CDA/archives/archive.mpl?id=2001_3334868. Accessed August 23, 2008.

Carry, Peter. "Center in a Storm." *Sports Illustrated.* Available online. http://vault.sportsillustrated.cnn.com/vault/article/magazine/MAG1087055/1/index.htm. Accessed August 23, 2008.

Daulatzai, Shohai. "View the World from American Eyes: Ball, Islam, and Dissent in Post-race America." In *Basketball Jones: America above the Rim,* edited by Todd Boyd and Kenneth L. Shropshire. New York: New York University Press, 2000.

Fish, Mike. "More Than a Friend: Atlanta's Abdur-Rahim Stands by Convicted Muslim Leader." CNNSI.com. Available online. URL: http://sportsillustrated.cnn.com/inside_game/mike_fish/news/2002/03/12/fish_straightshooting/. Accessed August 23, 2008.

George, Nelson. "Afros and Islam." In *Elevating the Game: Black Men and Basketball.* Lincoln: University of Nebraska Press, 1992.

"On Being a Muslim in America" (interview with Kareem Abdul-Jabbar), *New York Times.* Available online. URL: http://video.on.nytimes.com/?fr_story=eef6468fdfb96df88cc04e71bc155ee161493dc2. Accessed August 23, 2008.

National Football League

There have been Muslims in the National Football League (NFL) since at least the 1970s. By 2008, approximately 50, or 3 percent, of players in the NFL were Muslim. Though small in number, these players have made an important impact on the history of football, both through their individual professional accomplishments and through their collective efforts to garner recognition for religious diversity in the NFL.

MUSLIM PLAYERS

The first prominent Muslim in the NFL was Ahmad Rashad, born Robert Earl Moore on November 19, 1949. A wide receiver, Rashad converted to Islam in 1972 and was the fourth overall draft pick for the St. Louis Cardinals. He played for the Buffalo Bills (1974–76), the Seattle Seahawks (1976), and the Minnesota Vikings (1976–82), earning four Pro-Bowl selections (1978–81). He later became an Emmy Award–winning sportscaster, most notably with NBC. He also made guest appearances in television sitcoms. Several NFL players have been named after him, including Ahman Rashad Green, a running back for the Houston Texans; Ahmad Rashad Merritt, a wide receiver for the Arizona Cardinals; and Ahmad Rashad Hall, a fullback for the Tennessee Titans.

There have been several other noteworthy Muslim players in the NFL. Ephraim Salaam (1976–   ), right and left tackle, was drafted in 1998 by the Atlanta Falcons. He played in Super Bowl XXXIII in 1999 and, since 2009, has been on the Detroit Lions' active roster. In addition to his NFL position, Salaam launched a successful career in the entertainment industry, with multiple television and film appearances, including an NFL advertisement.

Az-Zahir Ali Hakim (1977–   ), wide receiver, was drafted in 1998 by the St. Louis Rams. In 2000, he helped the Rams win Super Bowl XXXIV. He joined the Detroit Lions in 2002 and played for several different teams in subsequent years.

In addition, Abdul Raheeda Hodge (1982–   ), linebacker, was drafted in the third round of the 2006 league draft by the Green Bay Packers and played for the Cincinnati Bengals. Kareem Brown (1983–   ), defensive end, was drafted by the New England Patriots in 2007 and played for the New York Jets. Hamza Muhammad Abdullah (1983–   ), special teams and safety, was drafted in 2005 by the Tampa Bay Buccaneers and played for the Denver Broncos and the Cleveland Browns. Ahmad Brooks (1984–   ), linebacker, was drafted in 2006 for the Cincinnati Bengals and played for the San Francisco 49ers. Antwaan Randle El, who played special teams and wide receiver for the Pittsburgh Steelers and Washington Redskins, had family members who have had connections with the MOORISH SCIENCE TEMPLE of America, but he himself is a devout Christian.

RELIGION AND FOOTBALL

Many Muslims believe in maintaining sound bodies, minds, and morals and value the protection of life; such beliefs and values extend to the realm of professional sports. While many may consider a contact sport such as American football potentially fatal or life-threatening, and thus in conflict with practicing Islam, Muslims are not forbidden from such adventures, according to the SHARI'A, or Islamic law. If a sport is considered adventurous and safety measures are taken to protect one's life, then there is nothing morally wrong with Muslims playing the sport. Muslims in the NFL generally face the same challenges in integrating their religion into their professional careers that players of any other faith face. Most players keep their beliefs private and personal and do not partake in public displays of their religion beyond an occasional gesture toward the heavens or a prayer circle with their fellow teammates before or after a game.

The NFL has been studiously cautious and discreet when making statements, guidelines, or rules regarding religion. The league has refrained from specifically mentioning any particular religion in its official bylaws and rule books. It has also used secular language when addressing aspects of players' lives that relate to religion, issues that are generally managed by the NFL's Player Development Department. The NFL, like many other professional organizations, has sought to be inclusive and to respect the religious diversity of its players.

In 2003, the NFL amended Section 15.7b of its official rule book, which governs the guidelines for on-field demonstrations of religiosity. The policy stated, "On-field displays of religious expression will be allowed, as long as the following requirements are met: 1. No offensive displays or gestures are allowed, and 2. Representatives of more than one religion must be present, to convey the diversity of the league." Muslims, therefore, are often solicited by Christians (who represent the majority of NFL players) to join their on-field prayer circles before or after games. While some players have expressed discomfort with this policy, it serves to illustrate the caution and discretion the NFL uses concerning religion and in respect of the privacy of its players.

Christine Drewel

Further Reading

"National Football League." Available online. URL: http://www.nfl.com. Accessed January 2, 2009.

Rashad, Ahmad, and Peter Bodo. *Rashad: Vikes, Mikes, and Something on the Backside.* New York: Viking, 1988.

Nation of Gods and Earths   See FIVE PERCENTERS.

Nation of Islam

The "Lost-Found Nation of Islam in the Wilderness of North America," better known as the Nation of Islam (NOI), was established in 1930 by W. D. FARD, or Farad Muhammad, in DETROIT, MICHIGAN. After WORLD WAR II, it became the best known, and the most controversial, Muslim group in the United States. The NOI was a religious group that had a political impact far beyond its official membership. During the height of the Civil Rights movement in the 1950s and 1960s, it opposed the movement's struggle for racial integration. Instead, it advocated for the establishment of a separate black nation (to be carved out of the Deep South) and for self-defense against both police and mob violence. In the midst of the cold war with the Soviet Union and the war in Vietnam, it urged black Americans not to serve in the military, and it became the predominant domestic voice of Afro-

Asian unity in the face of U.S. and Soviet interference in the affairs of newly independent states of Asia and Africa.

But the NOI was not only a voice of political protest. It also spread a gospel of black pride, extolling the historic achievements of black people from ancient times to the present. It taught self-reliance and encouraged black men and women to obtain an education and establish their own businesses. The NOI was also a bastion of socially conservative ethics and clean living, putting an emphasis on healthy diet, modest dress, sexual propriety, patriarchy, thrift, hard work, discipline, punctuality, and other behaviors generally associated with "family values." As a religious organization, it established dozens of temples and mosques around the country and helped to spread its version of Islamic religion to thousands of African Americans.

ORIGINS AND DOCTRINES

NOI founder W. D. Fard, whose ethnic and racial origins are still hotly debated by historians, began the movement in 1930. A peddler of silks and other wares, he told his African-American customers that he was from the Holy City of Mecca and brought them good news of their true identity. They were originally followers of the religion of Islam, he said, and their original language was Arabic, which was stolen from them when they were enslaved and brought to America.

One of his early followers was Elijah Poole, a native of Sandersville, Georgia, who in 1923 migrated, like a million and a half black Southerners between WORLD WAR I and World War II, from the Deep South to the urban North. Poole, who changed his last name first to Karriem and then to Muhammad (after the seventh-century prophet MUHAMMAD), became one of Fard's most fervent followers. In fact, when Fard mysteriously disappeared in 1934, it was ELIJAH MUHAMMAD who claimed the leadership of the small organization. Muhammad testified that Fard was God-in-the-flesh and that he had been commissioned by God to lead African Americans from their state of mental slavery to the freedom of Islam.

The version of Islam taught by the man known as the Honorable Elijah Muhammad, Messenger of Allah, differed in several important respects from that of most Muslim Americans and other Muslims around the world. No other Muslims believed that W. D. Fard was God, and most others rejected the idea that Elijah Muhammad was a prophet. Though some NOI members used both the QUR'AN and the Bible as sacred scriptures, they read these texts through the revelations of Elijah Muhammad.

Teachings that were unique to the Nation of Islam included explanations of how the world began and how it would end. The NOI's creation story, called the "Myth of Yacub," explained that the original people of the Earth were black. Called the Tribe of Shabazz, these original people inhabited the Holy City of Mecca and ruled the world in peace and righteousness for millions of years until, 6,000 years ago, Yakub, a mad, evil scientist, rebelled and began to genetically engineer the white race, a people who were naturally inclined toward brutality. Using "tricknology," whites enslaved blacks, and made them "mentally dead, blind, deaf, and dumb" to the truth of their original status as rulers of the earth.

But God, the NOI taught, would not abandon God's people. Appearing in the person of W. D. Fard in 1930, God appointed Elijah Muhammad to "mentally resurrect" the black man, bring him back to Islam, and rid him of the names of the slave masters. The end of the world was near, according to NOI teachings, and black people needed to prepare for a coming apocalypse in which whites would be eliminated—either they would be killed or their "white" (that is, racist) hearts and minds would be changed.

In this version of Armageddon, which for some members was literal and for other allegorical, a dreadful wheel-shaped spaceship, called the Mother Plane or Mother Ship, would destroy white evil and restore the earthly paradise of blacks. Heaven and hell, according to NOI doctrines, did not exist someplace else; they were states of being on earth, and it was time for blacks to stop enduring so much hell. Beliefs in an unseen God, angels, devils, physical resurrection after death, and the existence of paradise and hellfire were all deemed "spooky." Although many Muslim Americans and scholars of Islam said that such teachings contradicted the basic tenets of Sunni Islam, the NOI argued that such discrepancies were only a matter of difference in *interpretation* of the message of Islam and that their Messenger, Elijah Muhammad, was uniquely qualified to interpret Islamic traditions.

GROWTH AFTER WORLD WAR II

The NOI remained a tiny group until the late 1930s and early 1940s when it began to spread from Detroit and Chicago to numerous cities and among incarcerated African Americans. The golden age of the movement can be dated to the early 1950s, when Malcolm Little, who was imprisoned in Massachusetts from 1946 to 1952, declared his allegiance to Islam. After his release, MALCOLM X, as he became known—the X symbolizing the African name lost when his ancestors were enslaved in America—rose through the ranks as an NOI minister in Boston, Harlem, and Philadelphia and became a chief spokesman for and adviser to Elijah Muhammad. Malcolm X was essential to the success of the movement in this era. Though the FBI estimated its membership total at only 5,000 people in 1965, the NOI claimed to have 100,000 members. An independent estimate by historian Claude Clegg has put the number of members at 20,000, though historians are in near unanimous agreement that the political, social, and cultural influence of the organization could be observed far beyond its card-carrying members. The

Members of the Nation of Islam, 1942, attending a hearing in the Chicago Federal Building during World War II in which Department of Justice officials asked for more time to prepare their case of sedition against movement leaders. Elijah Muhammad, the head of the organization, was eventually acquitted of sedition but convicted of draft evasion.   *(Bettmann/CORBIS)*

number of NOI businesses and temples continued to expand even after Malcolm X left in 1964, and by 1975, the NOI had approximately 75 mosques around the country. New converts to the NOI had to study and memorize catechisms attributed to W. D. Fard. Called various titles, including *Actual Facts* and *Student Enrollment,* these catechisms focused on the plight and history of the black people, the "devilishness" of the white man, the mission of W. D. Fard, and various statistics about astronomy, geography, and anatomy (all of which had numerological or hidden meanings). Once the student mastered those lessons, he or she was given an "X" to replace his or her "slave name" or an original Arabic last name. To receive an original name, the convert was required to copy a letter by hand in neat, error-free writing and mail it to Elijah Muhammad. To facilitate identification among Muslims who had the same first name and belonged to the same temple, numbers were prefixed to the X. For example, John Smith,

the first John to convert, became John X; after that, subsequent Johns were given numbers such as John 13X, according to the order of their admittance to the temple.

Once admitted to a local temple or mosque (the movement used both words for their places of worship), the NOI member often participated in activities throughout the week. Members attended Sunday worship services and lectures. Men joined the FRUIT OF ISLAM (FOI), the male auxiliary of the movement charged with protecting members and the temple, among other duties, while women joined the MUSLIM GIRLS TRAINING—GENERAL CIVILIZATION CLASS (MGT), the all female auxiliary that taught home economics and etiquette and organized various mosque activities. Children attended many temple activities and sometimes attended one of the parochial schools that were established alongside the mosque.

Both the FOI and MGT also enforced the strict behavioral rules of the organization, which banned smoking, dancing, drinking, overeating, gambling, doing drugs, dating, and fornication. FOI and MGT captains also ensured that mosque members were neat, clean, and well groomed. The NOI welcomed all African Americans, including ex-convicts and drug addicts, so long as they abided by these rules. If anyone violated these norms, they would be put on trial and either suspended or expelled from the temple.

MGT and FOI members joined other mosque members in supporting the businesses owned by Elijah Muhammad or established their own markets, salons, restaurants, bakeries, and laundries, often next to the local mosque. In the 1960s, FOI members famously marketed bean pies and the movement newspaper, MUHAMMAD SPEAKS, on the streets of black America. Their hard work to meet sales quotas resulted in a weekly circulation of approximately 60,000 copies, making *Muhammad Speaks* one of the most read newspapers among African Americans in that decade. In the 1970s, that same zeal helped members of the FOI and other black males sell millions of dollars worth of imported fish. During this period of expansion for the movement, Elijah Muhammad also purchased a local Chicago bank and farms in Michigan, Alabama, and Georgia, where NOI members worked. When Muhammad died in 1975, his assets were estimated to be worth approximately $60 million.

RADICAL POLITICS IN THE 1960s

Since the 1930s, the Federal Bureau of Investigation (FBI) carefully watched Elijah Muhammad and other members of the NOI, fearing that the spread of the movement would result in a violent revolt among African Americans against the U.S. government and white people. But Elijah Muhammad, who had served a federal prison sentence from 1943 to 1946 for refusing to register for the military draft during World War II, never advocated the breaking of other U.S. laws. Muhammad told his followers to observe all other laws and instructed them to focus on self-improvement. Even the fiery Malcolm X was not in favor of violent attacks against white people; he merely said that if white people attacked blacks, they should defend themselves "by any means necessary."

The NOI was not a terrorist group, but its radical politics and what many considered odd religious teachings about the end of the white race did provoke fear among many white Americans. In 1959, CBS News reporter Mike Wallace introduced the NOI to the public through a series of televised reports entitled "The Hate That Hate Produced." It was during this period that many Americans came to know the NOI as "Black Muslims," a term used frequently by journalist Louis Lomax and scholar C. Eric Lincoln to describe the group. Though the NOI disavowed the term, it stuck in the public consciousness and made it seem, incorrectly, as if all African-American Muslims were members of the NOI. During this time, the NOI also came to be widely known as a "black supremacist" group, which was criticized not only by whites but also by middle-class blacks, including the Rev. Dr. Martin Luther King, Jr., in his 1963 "Letter from a Birmingham Jail." Other Muslims, especially many Sunni Muslim Americans, also rejected the group as hateful and un-Islamic.

The movement's call for racial separation contradicted the aims of many white and black liberals who thought that the enactment of civil rights and voting rights would bring about equality for African Americans. The NOI's philosophy of black uplift instead echoed generations of African-American leaders from Edward Wilmot Blyden to Marcus Garvey, who had advanced the idea that only black people, creating their own institutions and even countries, could liberate blacks from racist oppression. When the Civil Rights Act of 1964 and the Voting Rights Act of 1965 failed to deliver racial equality, many advocates of black power adopted the rhetoric of the NOI and especially of Malcolm X—who was assassinated in February 1965—in advocating for black community and local control over every aspect of life that affected African Americans—from schools to food distribution.

But the Islamic identity of the NOI was radical in another way too. During a time when the U.S. government was locked in a struggle with the Soviet Union, the NOI questioned the claims of the U.S. government that it represented the forces of freedom and equality. At the height of the VIETNAM WAR, boxer MUHAMMAD ALI, the heavyweight champion and a follower of the NOI, willingly gave up his title in 1966 rather than serve in the U.S. military.

Even more, Elijah Muhammad, Malcolm X, Muhammad Ali, and the men and women of the NOI also rejected Christianity, the religion of most Americans, as a hypocritical tradition that justified slavery and racism. Instead, they associated themselves with Muslims around the world, declaring their allegiance to a faith seen as exotic, foreign, and scary to many Americans. As documented in internal FBI memoranda made available though the Freedom of Information Act, government officials suspected NOI members of disloyalty to the United States. Since black Muslims were not patriots, it was thought, they might be more likely to seek revenge for the injustices that they felt they had suffered. Though the NOI never directly threatened public security, its symbolic resistance to the hypocritical aspects of both U.S. foreign policy and Christian-American racism challenged the interests of the U.S. nation-state and its protectors.

AFTER ELIJAH MUHAMMAD

After Elijah Muhammad's death in 1975, his son, W. D. MOHAMMED, inherited the leadership of the movement and dramatically changed it. Steering the group toward Sunni Islam, he abandoned or reinterpreted many of the unique NOI teachings. The white man was no longer considered a devil. The demand for a separate state was dropped and the Fruit of Islam was disbanded. U.S. flags were placed in mosques. The Honorable Elijah Muhammad was respected, but the prophet Muhammad of Arabia was affirmed as the last messenger of God. The monthlong dawn-to-sunset fast of Ramadan, which had been observed during Yuletide in the Nation of Islam, was celebrated instead according to the Islamic lunar calendar. The name of the organization was also changed, first from the NOI to the WORLD COMMUNITY OF AL-ISLAM IN THE WEST in 1976, and then to the American Muslim Mission in 1980.

But W. D. Mohammed, who died in 2008, was not the only claimant to the legacy of W. D. Fard and Elijah Muhammad. In 1977 and 1978, Minister LOUIS FARRAKHAN, who replaced Malcolm X as the National Spokesman for the Honorable Elijah Muhammad in the middle 1960s and served in that capacity until 1975, rejected Mohammed's changes. Claiming to represent the original teachings of Elijah Muhammad, he re-formed the Nation of Islam and re-implemented many of the practices of the old NOI. This new version of the NOI published a newspaper, the *Final Call,* which was once again sold on the streets of black America by well-groomed men wearing suits and bow ties. In this new version of the NOI, women rose to greater positions of power than in the old one. Farrakhan's NOI also claimed the mantle of Elijah Muhammad's social and political activism and in 1995 staged a successful MILLION MAN MARCH in Washington, D.C., in which more than 700,000 African-American males pledged themselves to bettering themselves and their communities.

In addition to W. D. Mohammed and Louis Farrakhan, other relatives and students of Elijah Muhammad created new denominations of the NOI. The Lost-Found Nation of Islam was formed in 1977 by Silis Muhammad. In 1978, Minister John Muhammad, Elijah Muhammad's brother, formed a Nation of Islam. Though these organizations have survived, their growth has been small in comparison to the communities led by W. D. Mohammed and Louis Farrakhan.

CONCLUSION

The NOI has had a profound impact on the history of the United States. Its post–World War II protests against the social injustices faced by African Americans ignited hope, pride, and self-worth in the hearts of hundreds of thousands, perhaps millions, including many who never became Muslims. Its 1960s opposition to the Vietnam War and advocacy of black self-determination inspired and anticipated the battle cries of black power advocates such as Stokely Carmichael and H. Rap Brown (JAMIL ABDULLAH AL-AMIN). From the late 1950s until the 1970s and perhaps later, it was the domestic face of Islam with which most Americans were familiar. It popularized Islam in black America. Thousands

of Muslim Americans in the 21st century trace their Islamic lineage through the NOI even if they no longer agree with its teachings or orientation.

Edward E. Curtis IV and Mustafa Khattab

Further Reading

Barboza, Steven. *American Jihad: Islam after Malcolm X.* New York: Image Books Doubleday, 1994.

Clegg, Claude Andrew, III. *An Original Man: The Life and Times of Elijah Muhammad.* New York: St. Martin's Press, 1997.

Curtis, Edward E., IV. *Black Muslim Religion in the Nation of Islam, 1960–1975.* Chapel Hill: University of North Carolina Press, 2006.

———. *Islam in Black America: Identity, Liberation, and Difference in African-American Islamic Thought.* New York: State University of New York Press, 2002.

Dannin, Robert. *Black Pilgrimage to Islam.* New York: Oxford University Press, 2002.

Essien-Udom, Essien Udosen. *Black Nationalism: A Search for an Identity in America.* Chicago: University of Chicago Press, 1962.

Gardell, Mattias. *Countdown to Armageddon: Louis Farrakhan and the Nation of Islam.* London: Hurst & Company, 1996.

Jackson, Sherman A. *Islam and the Blackamerican: Looking toward the Third Resurrection.* New York: Oxford University Press, 2005.

Lee, Martha F. *The Nation of Islam: An American Millenarian Movement.* Syracuse, N.Y.: Syracuse University Press, 1996.

Lincoln, C. Eric. *The Black Muslims in America.* Boston: Bacon Press, 1961.

Malcolm X, with Alex Haley. *The Autobiography of Malcolm X.* New York: Ballantine Books, 1999.

Marsh, Clifton E. *From Black Muslims to Muslims: The Transition from Separatism to Islam 1930–1980.* Metuchen, N.J.: Scarecrow Press, 1984.

McCloud, Aminah Beverly. *African American Islam.* New York: Routledge, 1995.

Muhammad, Elijah. *Message to the Blackman in America.* Phoenix, Ariz.: Secretarius MEMPS Publications, 1965.

Turner, Richard Brent. *Islam in the African-American Experience.* Bloomington: Indiana University Press, 1997.

Allen 3X, "How Messenger Muhammad's Dietary Laws Saved My Life" (1971)

In the late 1950s and early 1960s, the Nation of Islam (NOI) came to the attention of most Americans—white, black, or brown—as a radical movement that preached racial separatism, black pride, an unorthodox version of Islamic religion, and the need for black self-determination. But for the thousands of African Americans who became actual members of the organization, it held other, less controversial attractions as well. NOI leader Elijah Muhammad offered his followers a way of life focused on the whole person; he not only outlined a strategy for black political empowerment and religious salvation but also gave practical advice on how to raise children, what kinds of clothes to wear, and how to seek career advancement. Elijah Muhammad's preaching focused a great deal on caring for the body, which he said had been abused, poisoned, and humiliated by white oppressors and blacks themselves. From the beginning of the movement in the 1930s, the NOI stressed the need for a healthy and well-regulated diet, which Muhammad taught would strengthen and purify the body physically and spiritually. In the late 1960s and early 1970s, Muhammad published two volumes of a book entitled How to Eat to Live. *The advice in those books, many NOI members said, changed their lives for the better. Allen 3X, whose story is recounted below in an article he wrote for the NOI newspaper,* Muhammad Speaks, *said that these dietary rules saved his life. This very personal account demonstrates how the lives of NOI members often revolved around mundane matters like health and wellness as much as they did around political protest.*

"You will not be sick often if you eat once a day and eat the proper food," states the Honorable Elijah Muhammad, Messenger of Allah, in *How to Eat to Live,* page 27. I bear witness that this is true. Prior to becoming a follower of the Honorable Elijah Muhammad, and eating the foods (and the way) he teaches us to eat, I was sick almost daily.

Perhaps I should start at the beginning. As far back as I can remember I suffered from headaches, heartburn and occasionally, hemorrhoids. I accepted them as being normal. I did not know how it felt to have a clear head. I existed on B.C. Stanback, and in later years, Dristan tablets [both of which are pain relievers].

Then in the spring of 1964, the headaches became unbearable. I would take the pills but got little or no relief. One night, while lying in bed restless with a severe headache, something seemed to have burst inside of my head.

The next morning I decided to have my head X-rayed. This was on a Saturday. I was living in Los Angeles at the time.

As I drove around looking for a medical office that was open, I passed Muhammad's Mosque. In the next block I saw a sign that read: X-Ray. I stopped, went in, and asked to see the doctor. Explaining what had happened the night before, I requested an X-ray of my head.

Luckily, this doctor was a chiropractor. After I had finished explaining he began to question me. One of the questions he asked me was concerning the last time excrementation had taken place. I answered that I thought it had been about two weeks. To this, he said, "the problem is not your head." I did not understand and was ready to leave, but I decided to hear him out.

Starting with the nervous system, he began to explain its function: how its branches (nerves) senses pain and pressure throughout the body, these nerves send signals to the head, caused by these signals, causes the head to hurt.

These signals will continue until the pressure is relieved or until the pain subsides. If nothing is done to correct the problem in the affected area, this state of agitation inside of the head, caused by these signals, causes the head to hurt.

He said that this stands true to most headache producing ailments. The problem is rarely in the head. The headache is only a symptom. If the cause is removed the symptom (headache) will disappear.

The headache in my case was caused by pressure due to excess excrement in the colon. This pressure was sensed by the nerves and transmitted to the central nervous system through the spinal cord.

We talked about the hemorrhoids which are caused by straining while constipated. This ruptures the rectal tissue. "Preparation H" and other ointments and suppositories are needed. Fasting relieves the constipation and the hemorrhoids will disappear as the Honorable Elijah Muhammad teaches us to fast once a month.

The skin rash, he explained, occurs when waste becomes petrified and seeks to be evacuated through the skin.

The last symptom we discussed was of a respiratory nature. Its symptom like asthma, characterized by part of the breathing passage being choked off, causing one to gasp for breath. I had experienced this symptom, but we did not get into a discussion as to the cause. Yet these symptoms have only occurred during periods of constipation.

Then in August of 1964, something wonderful happened. The Honorable Elijah Muhammad came to Los Angeles. He spoke at the Olympic Auditorium August 9. I went to hear him and came in the Nation the following week.

During the processing period, I attended the weekly Orientation classes. There I learned that

Muslims [who follow Elijah Muhammad] eat once a day. So I began this practice at once. At this time I was still making regular visits to the doctor.

After eating once a day for about a week, I noticed that, occasionally, my system worked naturally, with time it kept getting better. After a month or so I was able to stop going to the doctor altogether. This went on for about a year.

Then one week while reading the Honorable Elijah Muhammad's column on "How to Eat to Live" I was struck by something he said about eating one meal a day or one meal every other day. The result was amazing. My system began to work perfectly.

There were other symptoms of relief: my head cleared up and felt light, muscles and joints became limber, and I felt energetic and youthful—younger than I felt anytime in the past.

Though I ate every other day for only four months, I had a glimpse of what it feels like to be sixteen again. The Honorable Elijah Muhammad teaches us that in the hereafter we will be like sixteen again.

I eat once a day now, but as long as I stay off pastries and minimize my intake of starches which the Honorable Elijah Muhammad teaches us are not good for us anyway, unless we live in a frigid zone, I don't have any problems. I no longer need the doctor. If I have a problem, I fast and the problem disappears.

I write this article because I know that many Black people suffer needlessly from many symptoms that could be eliminated by putting into practice what the Honorable Elijah Muhammad teaches in *How to Eat to Live*.

This done, they would bear witness as I bear witness that the Honorable Elijah Muhammad, the last and greatest Messenger of Allah, is fulfilling that prophecy, attributed to Jesus, wherein it reads: "I am come that ye may have life and life more abundantly."

Source: Allen 3X. "How Messenger Muhammad's Dietary Laws Saved My Life," *Muhammad Speaks,* April 9, 1971, p. 8.

Native American Muslims   See AMERICAN INDIAN MUSLIMS.

Native Deen

Native Deen is a HIP-HOP MUSIC group composed of three African-American Muslims whose lyrics focus on Islamic themes. The group's name includes the Arabic word *deen,* which means "religion" or "way of life." Founded in 2000, the group has made frequent appearances at Muslim-American weddings, festivals, conferences, and fund-raisers. Its members, Joshua Salaam, Naeem Muhammad, and Abdul-Malik Ahmad, have collectively produced two albums, *Deen You Know* (2005) and *Not Afraid to Stand Alone* (2007). The group also contributed songs to *Night of Remembrance* (2004) by Yusuf Islam, the former Cat Stevens.

Native Deen has also developed an international following among Muslims. In 2003, it began performing around the world under the auspices of the U.S. State Department, which has viewed its popularity among Muslim Americans as a tool to improve U.S. relations with the Muslim world. On its Web site, the group's members have written that they are not associated with the NATION OF ISLAM or FIVE PERCENTERS, stressing that most AFRICAN-AMERICAN MUSLIMS are not members of these groups.

ORIGINS

Group members Joshua Salaam, Naeem Muhammad, and Abdul-Malik Ahmad were all born in the 1970s on the East Coast to parents who had converted to Islam. The three met each other in the late 1980s and 1990s at multiple gatherings of the Muslim Youth of North America (MYNA), a Muslim youth organization, where they performed for their peers as teenage solo artists and contributed to albums for a program called MYNA Raps. They selected their group's name to

One of many Muslim hip-hop artists to emerge in the late 20th and early 21st centuries, Native Deen, based in Washington, D.C., is a group that combines its African-American culture and Muslim faith to produce Sunni Islamic music. *(Reuters/HO/Landov)*

promote the Islamic belief that the "deen," or religion, native to all creation is Islam.

Salaam and Ahmad moved to the Washington, D.C., area as adults. Through its first decade Native Deen performed 30 to 60 times a year, and the members held full-time jobs unrelated to music. Salaam, who served four years in the U.S. Air Force as a police officer, later managed the civil rights division of the COUNCIL ON AMERICAN-ISLAMIC RELATIONS before accepting a job as youth director at the All Dulles Area Muslim Society, a mosque and Muslim community center in Sterling, Virginia. Muhammad has worked for Islamic Relief, a Muslim charity, and Ahmad has developed multimedia applications for the National Aeronautics and Space Administration (NASA).

MUSIC AND LYRICS

Native Deen's music has been classified as Islamic—in contrast to hip-hop performed by Muslims—since it avoids the glorification of sex and violence in its lyrics, seeks to comply with various religious standards in its music, and caters mostly to Muslim-majority audiences. Its recordings have been part of a musical trend in the United States in which religiously inspired groups, including the Christian rock groups Relient K and Switchfoot and the Jewish reggae artist Matisyahu, have promoted religious values while benefiting from the rhythms, sounds, and production quality associated with contemporary popular music.

The group's musical style is commonly described as a combination of rap, reggae, and rhythm and blues. During live performances, members wear kufis (caps) and loose-fitting clothing and avoid using wind and string instruments, which some Muslims have considered to be religiously taboo. Their songs instead rely on drums and other percussion instruments. They do not play in bars or dance clubs.

Native Deen's songs have held to religious, cultural, and political themes affecting Muslim Americans. Some have lyrics drawn from ARABIC phrases widely used in Muslim PRAYER. Songs such as "Subhan Allah" and "Sea of Forgiveness" rely on rhythmic chanting and repetition of phrases in Arabic such as *Alhamdulillah* (Praise God), *La ilaha illa Allah* (There is no god but God), and *Muhammadun rasulullah* (Muhammad is the Messenger of God).

The group became better known, however, for its English-language raps with rhyming lyrics designed to inspire religious pride, criticize anti-Muslim DISCRIMINATION, and allege religious profiling by U.S. law enforcement agencies after SEPTEMBER 11, 2001. For example, in a track entitled "M-U-S-L-I-M," the group chants proudly of the 1-billion-plus world Muslim population. In "Stand Alone," it sings in praise of a single Muslim mother who braved employment discrimination for wearing her *HIJAB,* or head scarf. In "Still Strong," the group sings about federal agents banging on a

man's door, handcuffing him in front of his family, and falsely accusing him of being on a "terrorist list." In "Intentions," it examines motives behind good deeds. In "I Am the Deen You Need," it implores Muslims who have strayed from the faith to return.

FOREIGN RELATIONS

Shortly after 9/11, the U.S. State Department enlisted Native Deen in its "Shared Values Initiative," designed to show residents of predominantly Muslim countries that Muslim Americans are largely happy with their lives in the United States. On the group's first government-sponsored trip in March 2003, it performed in Mali, Senegal, and Nigeria. In 2006, the group performed in London, Turkey, Dubai, Jerusalem, and the Palestinian Territories. In 2007, it traveled to Egypt and Tanzania. The group's members have said that these trips abroad have promoted tolerance and helped to improve the United States's image to Muslims around the world by showing that Muslim Americans practice their religion freely.

Jeff Diamant

Further Reading

Abdo, Geneive. *Mecca and Main Street.* New York: Oxford University Press, 2006.

Khabeer, Suad A. "Rep That Islam: The Rhyme and Reason of American Islamic Hip Hop." *Muslim World* 97, no. 1 (January 2007): 125–141.

"Native Deen Online." Available online. URL: http://www.native deen.com. Accessed April 8, 2009.

Navy　See UNITED STATES MILITARY.

Neshat, Shirin (1957–) *artist*

One of the most celebrated contemporary visual artists in the United States and around the world, Shirin Neshat has produced photographs, video installations, and films that explore themes related to women, Iran, Islam, tradition and modernity, and the use of space and architecture to think about freedom and constraint, and order and chaos.

Born to an upper-middle-class family in Qazvin, Iran, on March 26, 1957, Neshat had a secular upbringing in Iran, where she also attended a Catholic school. Prior to the 1979 Iranian Revolution, she moved to the United States in 1974 to pursue her education, graduating from University of California, Berkeley, with a B.A., M.A., and M.F.A. in painting in 1983. Upon graduation she moved to NEW YORK CITY, where she worked in several different jobs including at the nonprofit organization Storefront for Art and Architecture.

Artist Shirin Neshat, an Iranian-American artist based in New York City, has used the media of film, photography, and video installations to explore issues related to Islam and women. *(Reuters/Corbis)*

Inspired by the many post-revolution Iranian women she saw during her return to Iran in the early 1990s, Neshat began a series of photographs entitled *Women of Allah.* This was a personal exploration for her, and she claims the series had the naïveté of someone coming to terms with understanding the new Islamic Republic of Iran and its practice of gender segregation. Using Persian calligraphy, she explored the poetics and politics of the revolution and women's participation in it.

Neshat also began experimenting with FILM, a medium she said was the most complete because it included various other media, from photography to performance and MUSIC. She also said the medium allowed her to become more philosophical, lyrical, and poetic, since photography, through its single and still image, was often confining. Video and film also called people into participating more intimately with her work, according to Neshat. She produced a number of videos and films in the late 1990s, which firmly established Neshat in the New York art scene, and became one of the most sought-after artists in the United States and around the world. Her trilogy, *Turbulent* (1998), *Rapture* (1999), and *Fervor* (2000), followed by a fourth film, *Soliloquy* (2000), have not only been shown around the world but have been the subjects of many academic works on art.

Tooba (2003) was the first work that did not include women in veils. Shot in Mexico, *Tooba* was an attempt to think more about the meaning and less about the clichés of the veil. Inspired by the story called *Tooba and the Meaning of the Night* by Iranian novelist and memoirist Shahrnush Parsipur, Neshat's story examined the relationship of women, men, and a blessed tree in the garden of paradise. For Neshat, this work was a way of thinking about the events of

September 11, 2001, and an attempt at bringing back beauty to the world. It was, she said, her most Iranian, Islamic, and universal work.

Several more works inspired by Parsipur's *Women without Men,* an Iranian novel, were made into films by Neshat. All five films of this series, *Mahdokh* (2004), *Zarin* (2005), *Munis* (2008), *Faezeh* (2008), and *Farokh Legha* (2008), were premiered together, first at the ARoS Aarhus Kunstmuseum in Denmark from March to May 2008, and then at the National Museum of Contemporary Art in Athens, Greece, from March to May 2009.

Shirin Neshat has received numerous awards for her work and has exhibited at all the major art fairs around the world, and her solo and group show exhibits number into the hundreds all over the United States, Europe, Asia, and Africa. She was also a featured artist in the Museum of Modern Art's 2006 show in New York called "Without Boundary: Seventeen Ways of Looking," an exhibit on Islam and contemporary art and artists.

Munir Jiwa

Further Reading

Dabashi, Hamid. "Shirin Neshat: Transcending the Boundaries of an Imaginative Geography." In *The Last Word.* Museum of Modern Art: San Sebastian, Spain, 2005.

Daftari, Fereshteh. "Islamic or Not?" In *Without Boundary: Seventeen Ways of Looking.* New York: The Museum of Modern Art, 2006.

Jensen, Mona. *Shirin Neshat: Women without Men.* Denmark: Narayana Press and the ARoS Aarhus Kunstmuseum, 2008.

Newark, New Jersey

Newark, New Jersey, and its surrounding region have played a prominent role in AFRICAN-AMERICAN MUSLIM history. NOBLE DREW ALI is widely believed to have founded the Canaanite Temple, a precursor to the MOORISH SCIENCE TEMPLE of America (MST), in Newark in 1913, though details of the temple's origin and actual relationship to the MST are unclear. Since those days, the forms of Islam most popular in the Newark area have changed markedly every two or three decades. Notably, in the 1960s and 1970s, the membership of the NATION OF ISLAM (NOI) in Newark ranked among the most active NOI contingents of any city in the United States.

A lack of close ties between Newark's Muslims, who are predominately African-American, and nearby Muslim communities of other ethnicities is indicative of the sometimes racially and ethnically segregated nature of Islam in the United States. Although Newark is located close to South Brunswick and Piscataway, New Jersey, which have thousands of SOUTH ASIAN–AMERICAN MUSLIMS, and Paterson and Jersey City, which have thousands of Palestinian and Egyptian Muslims, the various communities interact very little. The same is true regarding the Newark community's relationship with Muslim communities of NEW YORK CITY, located only 10 miles from Newark. The community life and leadership of Newark's Muslims are largely distinct from those in New York.

BEFORE THE NATION OF ISLAM

The organized history of Islam in Newark mainly involves African Americans, though its origins are shrouded in doubt. While some historians have long placed the founding of the Moorish Science Temple in Newark and have often written that the founding of its predecessor, the Canaanite Temple, occurred in 1913, recent scholarship has questioned this claim, noting that historical proof is scant—limited to one secondary source and to the movement itself. The alternate theory is that the Moorish Science Temple was formally founded in 1925 in CHICAGO. How much the later Moorish Science Temple in Chicago shared with the Canaanite Temple in Newark is yet to be determined. More clear is that the movement did not become a national one until the 1920s and 1930s, when there were 4,000 registered members across New Jersey and Pennsylvania alone.

In 1941, a more Sunni Islamic influence gained a foothold in Newark due to the presence of MUHAMMAD EZALDEEN (ca. 1880–1957), a former leader in the MST, in which he was known as James Lomax Bey. Ezaldeen, like many others in the MST, had gravitated toward Sunni Islam. In 1938, he became the imam of the ADDEYNU ALLAHE UNIVERSAL ARABIC ASSOCIATION (AAUAA), which was incorporated in West Valley, New York. The AAUAA, which claimed its members were of Hamitic heritage—a term deriving from Ham, a son of the biblical Noah—helped to build Islamic communities and teach converts about Islam and the Arabic language. Over the years, it promoted the building of mosques for African-American Muslims in several other states, including Ohio, Pennsylvania, and Florida.

Although Ezaldeen later moved the organization's base to southern New Jersey, both he and the organization remained strong in Newark. Through the 1940s and 1950s, Ezaldeen served as a religious mentor to many converts in Newark. In the 1960s, AAUAA members interacted with both immigrant Muslims from the Middle East and members of the Nation of Islam (NOI). The AAUAA's view that the NOI's position regarding the status of W. D. FARD as God and the status of ELIJAH MUHAMMAD (1897–1975) as a prophet were not proper Islamic views caused occasional tension between the two groups.

After Ezaldeen's death in 1957, another AAUAA leader, Imam Heshaam Jaaber, born in North Carolina to Sudanese-American parents, followed him in promoting Sunni Islamic views to local African Americans. In the 1960s, Jaaber, a well-known figure in local circles, gained recognition and influence beyond Muslim communities in the area. In 1965, at age 34, he presided at the funeral of MALCOLM X (1925–65) in Harlem, braving security concerns related to the circumstances of Malcolm X's assassination. In 1967, wearing the red fez favored by his organization, Jaaber helped law-enforcement authorities control near-riot conditions in Elizabeth, New Jersey. His efforts were lauded by the 1968 report of the Kerner Commission, a federal panel appointed by President Lyndon B. Johnson to investigate race riots and civil disturbances in the nation's cities the previous year. The report stated that Jaaber drove in a car, bullhorn in hand, as more than 20 of his followers walked the streets trying to keep order. Jaaber died in 2007.

THE NATION OF ISLAM'S HEYDAY

The first Nation of Islam mosque in Newark, known as Temple No. 25, opened in 1958 on South Orange Avenue. Its membership and that of its satellite mosques in the area soon gained the reputation within the national organization as being among the most active and loyal, more so than NOI members in some larger cities. Temple No. 25 soon had several affiliated satellite mosques in the area. Many attributed the strength of local sentiment toward the NOI to the leadership of Minister James Shabazz, the imam of Temple No. 25, who preached loyalty to the national organization and whose dynamic preaching style earned him the nickname "Son of Thunder."

Following the organization's dictates of self-respect and economic self-sufficiency, many Newark-area members opened and managed new businesses, such as Steak-n-Take and Whiting H. & G. (headed and gutted) food stores, affiliated with the NOI. Others sold the NOI newspaper, MUHAMMAD SPEAKS, and bean pies on the streets. Female members managed family life, and many oversaw home-based businesses. University of Islam schools educated thousands of Newark children. Hundreds, probably thousands, of African Americans in the Newark area adhered to the self-discipline associated with the NOI and left the "street life." Male members of the NOI were known to be more likely than nonmembers in the area to be married.

The violence often associated in the popular imagination with the NOI affected some of Newark's members and also affected the reputation of Temple No. 25. The three men convicted of Malcolm X's assassination in 1965—Talmadge Hayer, Norman 3X Butler, and Thomas 15X Johnson—allegedly had ties to Temple No. 25, as did two other men later named as accomplices by Hayer. And in February 1973, Minister James Shabazz was assassinated in his driveway by four members of a splinter group called the New World of Islam.

LATE TWENTIETH CENTURY

In 1975, after the death NOI leader Elijah Muhammad, most NOI members in the Newark area joined the national organizational exodus away from Muhammad's theology. Led by his son, Imam W. D. Mohammed (1933–2008), they gravitated toward Sunni Islamic teachings and changed the name of Temple No. 25 to Masjid Mohammed.

Divisions over leadership and theology caused splits, however. Former NOI member Ahmed Burhani, an African American who was defeated in his effort in the mid-1970s to lead Masjid Mohammed, founded the Islamic Center of East Orange in 1980. At first, Burhani recognized the leadership of W. D. Mohammed but later decided to separate from him. Burhani's mosque thrived and by 1982 relocated to larger space.

Two years later, in 1984, another new predominantly African-American mosque with no ties to Mohammed opened in downtown Newark. This mosque, the Islamic Culture Center, was run by an Egyptian immigrant named Osman Ahmed, an engineering professor at Raritan Valley Community College, who persuaded the Muslim owner of a failing commercial building, a Saudi named Ali Habib, to donate space inside for local Muslims unaffiliated with the NOI or Mohammed who needed prayer space. The Islamic Culture Center's close proximity to Newark's busiest commercial centers helped attract large crowds for Friday prayers.

By 2010, there were no fewer than eight mosques in the area that could trace their roots to Temple No. 25. The neighboring towns of East Orange and Irvington joined Newark as relatively large centers for African-American Muslim life. Many mosques in the area remained affiliated with W. D. Mohammed, though their predominance was challenged in the 1990s by mosques associated with Salafi Muslims, who offered a stricter, more socially conservative version of Sunni Islam.

In 1997, the Islamic Center of East Orange was renamed the Islamic Center of America and relocated to an old armory building. This mosque rejected teachings of both Louis Farrakhan's Nation of Islam and W. D. Mohammed's community as insufficiently pious and authentic. Predominantly Guyanese and Nigerian mosques also opened in the area, reflecting new immigration patterns. By the first decade of the 21st century, between 10,000 and 20,000 African Americans in the Newark area were practicing Muslims, as were at least a few thousand Latina/os and immigrants from Guyana, the Middle East, and Nigeria. Many former NOI members who had become disaffected from that organization's teachings and who instead frequented Sunni Islamic mosques would still regard the NOI's local history as beneficial, on balance, for the growth of Islam in the area. In all its divergent strands and diverse origins, the Muslim-American community of Newark, New Jersey, has shaped the history of the city and surrounding area for almost a century.

Jeff Diamant

Further Reading

Nash, Michael. *Islam among Urban Blacks: Muslims in Newark, New Jersey, A Social History.* Lanham, Md.: University Press of America, 2008.

West, Cynthia S'thembile. "Revisiting Female Activism in the 1960s: The Newark Branch Nation of Islam." *Black Scholar* 26, nos. 3–4 (1996).

New York City

The first Muslims in New York City may have arrived when it was still New Amsterdam, a 17th-century Dutch colony. Some mixed-race settlers such as Anthony Jansen Van Salee (ca. 1607–1676), one of the largest landowners on Manhattan prior to 1639, may have been Muslim, and it is even more likely that some of the African slaves forcibly brought to New York were followers of Islam. Muslim sailors and freedmen such as Abdul Rahman Ibrahima (ca. 1762–1829) and Mahommah Gardo Baquaqua (ca. 1830–?) visited New York from the colonial era to the 19th century, though the first viable Muslim-American community in the city was likely established in the late 19th century when more than a million Eastern and Southern Europeans as well as Middle Easterners arrived in the United States.

Since then, the Muslim population has grown from a minuscule percentage to a significant minority of New Yorkers. Muslims have become involved in every aspect of life in the United States's largest city. By 2000, approximately 7 percent of the city's 8 million residents, or about 600,000 people, were Muslim, making New York the home of the largest Muslim-American community in the nation. In the first decade of the 21st century, around 102,000 Muslim children were enrolled in New York City public schools, constituting approximately 10 percent of all students. Nearly every type of American Islam has become represented in New York, though many "cultural" Muslim New Yorkers are not observant in their religious practices.

LATE NINETEENTH AND EARLY TWENTIETH CENTURIES

The most active missionary voices on behalf of Islamic religion in the 19th century were white American converts. Though white Muslim Americans have constituted a minority of all Muslim Americans, their relative social privilege has allowed them to establish the institutions and publications necessary to proselytizing on behalf of their faith. Alexander Russell Webb, a former U.S. consul to the Philippines and journalist born in the Hudson Valley, was the most prominent of these persons. After securing the financial support of a Muslim businessman from India, he established the "American Islamic Propaganda" in February 1893. That year Webb penned a book entitled *Islam in America,* published a glossy newspaper called the *Moslem World,* and set up an office in Manhattan.

Webb's goal was to recruit middle-class white people to the religion, as he explained to the *New York Times,* noting that he did not desire any sort of relationship with the Muslim peddlers and other working-class Muslim immigrants from the Middle East and South Asia who already lived in New York. After falling out with Webb, two other white Muslims, John A. Lant and British immigrant Emin Nabakoff, established a competing group, the First Society for the Study of Islam in America, in December 1893. The split attracted negative attention from the press and from the missions' foreign Muslim backers, who asked the three men to reconcile. But the fighting continued, and both missions failed by 1894, unable to attract followers or funding. Webb moved to Ulster Park, New York, and eventually to New Jersey, where he continued to write on behalf of Islam, but seemingly reached few persons with his message.

According to some sources, the next Muslim association to be established in New York City was the American Mohammedan Society in 1907. Lithuanian, Polish, and Russian Muslims who settled in Williamsburg, Brooklyn, likely met and prayed together in each other's homes or rented space until 1931, when they purchased three buildings on 104, 106, and 108 Powers Street. These Muslims, many of whom were ethnic Tatars, have been perhaps the least studied of all Muslim ethnic groups in New York.

Hundreds, if not thousands, of ARAB-AMERICAN MUSLIMS arrived in New York from 1878 to 1914. Some of them settled in "Little Syria," located on Washington Street in lower Manhattan, and later in South Ferry, Brooklyn; others used New York only as a point of disembarkation and headed west toward DETROIT, TOLEDO, NORTH DAKOTA, and other locations. By the 1920s, Arab-American Muslims from the

In the 1890s, the largest Syrian immigrant neighborhood in New York City, called the "Mother Colony," was located on Washington Street in Lower Manhattan. In the first decades of the 20th century, Atlantic Avenue in Brooklyn came to rival the Mother Colony as the largest enclave of Arabic-speaking Americans in New York.   *(Photolibrary)*

DRUZE COMMUNITY had established an Arabic newspaper called *al-Bayan,* located on 391 Fulton Street in Brooklyn, and some others founded a New York chapter of the Young Men's Moslem Association, which took an active interest in UNITED STATES FOREIGN RELATIONS, especially concerning the fate of Arabs in Palestine.

SOUTH ASIAN–AMERICAN MUSLIMS began to arrive in the late 19th century as well. Composed largely of male sailors, these Muslims from Bangladesh worked in the British merchant marine, occasionally leaving their ships for good when they docked in New Orleans or New York. Some married African-American and Hispanic women, settled permanently in the United States, and, if allowed by the authorities, became U.S. citizens. Some of them who had settled in New Orleans in the 1890s decided to come north between WORLD WAR I and WORLD WAR II.

These men, who had children with names such as Roheamon, Rostom, and Bahadour, moved to the so-called ghettoes of the city, including the Lower East Side of Manhattan, Harlem, or Hell's Kitchen. Ibrahim Choudry, for example, was a resident of Harlem who married a Puerto Rican woman and became director of the British Merchant Sailor's Club for Indian Seamen in 1943. The Indian Seamen's club served Indian FOOD to sailors and allowed Muslims to hold religious ceremonies, including Friday prayers, on premises. Another South Asian Muslim who married a Puerto Rican woman was Habib Ullah, a restaurateur who threw parties that featured both salsa music and Indian food spiced with ingredients purchased at Spanish Harlem's La Marqueta.

Some Muslim immigrants, identifying a potential advantage to their classification by Anglo-Americans as "colored" people, targeted both their businesses and their missionary activities toward black New Yorkers. As foreign affairs columnist for the *Negro World* and head of the African Affairs office of the New York–based Universal Negro Improvement Association (UNIA), Egyptian-born intellectual DUSÉ MOHAMED ALI (1866–1945) actively encouraged African Americans to support the liberation causes of other colonized peoples and explicitly linked the interests of Muslims abroad to African Americans at home.

Though his relationship with the UNIA began and ended abruptly in 1922, his activities in New York were by no means finished. In 1926, he tried to establish an import business to give West African farmers direct access to American markets while also continuing to raise awareness about African and Asian cultures through staged dramas and various publications. Similarly, though Sudanese Muslim missionary SATTI MAJID (1883–1963) began his career in New York by ministering to Yemeni sailors around 1921, he, too, finished his career in the United States as a missionary to a mainly indigenous group of African-American Muslims.

Of all immigrant Muslim missionaries, however, the most successful and important in this era was Daoud Ahmed Faisal, a black emigrant from the Caribbean, who in 1939 rented a brownstone at 143 State Street in Brooklyn Heights for his Islamic Mission of America. It would become New York's most successful Sunni Muslim mosque during and after World War II. Interracial and interethnic, this mosque tailored its message for African Americans but invited Muslims from all backgrounds, including diplomats from the United Nations, to attend its prayer services.

MID-TWENTIETH CENTURY

Despite his success, Daoud was not the public face of Islam in New York City. In fact, with the exception of Mohammad Webb, Muslims in the New York area attracted little attention from local media until the 1950s. The emergence of the NATION OF ISLAM (NOI) as a national movement changed that. In 1946, the NOI opened Temple No. 7 at the Harlem Young Men's Christian Association (YMCA) building and received a significant boost in 1954, when the charismatic NOI leader MALCOLM X (1925–65) was named to head the temple.

As the civil rights movement at home and the independence of former colonies abroad coincided in the late 1950s and 1960s, Malcolm X became an important voice in the lively intellectual and political life of Harlem. Noticed first by black New Yorkers, Malcolm X came to the attention of the entire city on April 14, 1957, when he gathered a group of Muslims outside the 123rd Street police station and demanded the release of Hinton Johnson, a black Muslim who had been beaten by the members of the New York police department.

In 1959, Malcolm X became a national figure when WNTA-TV journalist Mike Wallace featured him as a protagonist in an exposé on the NOI called "The Hate That Hate Produced." By the early 1960s, Malcolm X had become a Muslim celebrity in New York. Such coverage only increased when Malcolm famously split from the NOI in a news conference held on March 12, 1964, at the Park Sheraton Hotel, and when he was assassinated in Harlem's Audubon Ballroom on February 21, 1965.

Some Muslim immigrants in New York reached out to more famous Muslims in the NOI, especially Abdul Basit Naeem, a Pakistani entrepreneur whose journal, the *Moslem World,* covered the rise of the NOI and other Muslim groups in the 1950s. Despite the fact that he attended Friday prayers at Faisal's State Street mosque in Brooklyn, Naeem developed strong ties to NOI members, explaining that only differences in interpretations separated Sunni Islam from the NOI. Naeem performed Islamic marriage ceremonies, sold tapestries, books, and handbags, and taught Arabic and Islamic studies in Harlem. His life testified to the fluidity of Muslim cultures in the city as ideas and goods freely circulated among New York's Muslims.

A Muslim woman pushes a stroller along the Brooklyn Bridge in New York City.   *(Jason Florio/Corbis)*

This dynamic environment also fueled the proliferation of many different religious groups among Muslims in New York. In 1963, for example, CLARENCE 13X broke away from the NOI and began to form his own group, the FIVE PERCENTERS. Also called the Nation of Gods and Earths, this group of African Americans called themselves "poor righteous teachers," an elect group that could unlock the secret meanings of language and numbers. Around the city in the 1970s and 1980s, especially on public basketball courts, Five Percenters popularized their teachings and language among youth—introducing slang such as "G" for God—which greatly influenced the rise of rap and hip-hop during this era. The movement's founder, who had since come to call himself "Allah," also established a Five Percent school and worked on violence prevention programs with the administration of New York City mayor John Lindsay.

Sunni Muslim groups also multiplied in this period. In 1967, Khalid Ahmad Tawfiq, an African-American Muslim who had studied at al-Azhar University in Cairo, Egypt, cre-

ated the Mosque of Islamic Brotherhood (MIB) in Harlem. The MIB combined Sunni Islamic religious practice with an emphasis on black pride and self-determination. In 1968, other black Sunni Muslims broke away from the State Street mosque and established Darul Islam, or House of Islam, on 240 Sumpter Street in Brooklyn. This movement was utopian, and dreamed of the establishment of the kingdom of God on earth in which the SHARI'A, or Islamic law and ethics, would be the governing legislation of all humankind.

POST-1965 IMMIGRATION

By the late 1960s, Muslim immigrants and visitors had been arriving in New York City for hundreds of years—but in relatively small numbers. That changed after the passage of the IMMIGRATION ACT OF 1965, which liberalized the restrictions on immigrants from Africa and Asia. From 1968 until 1997, perhaps 1.1 million Muslim immigrants entered the United States. The result in New York City, which received hundreds of thousands of these immigrants, was that the face of Islam changed.

One new and prominent Muslim was Muhammad Abdul-Rauf, a graduate of al-Azhar University in Cairo, Egypt, and the British School of Oriental and African Studies in London, who became director of the Islamic Center of New York, located on Riverside Drive and 72nd Street. In response to the tensions between Jewish and Muslim New Yorkers in the wake of the 1967 Arab-Israeli war, Abdul-Rauf initiated interfaith dialogues with Jewish groups. Though Abdul-Rauf moved in five years to Washington, D.C., to serve as the Director of the ISLAMIC CENTER OF WASHINGTON, D.C., his son, FEISAL ABDUL RAUF, remained in New York and, in 1983, became the imam, or religious leader, of a Sufi mosque in lower Manhattan. He, too, supported various INTERFAITH MOVEMENTS in the city and founded his own organization called the ASMA Society, which was later taken over by his wife, Daisy Khan.

New York's physical landscape was altered as Muslims built a number of new mosques. In Queens, Pakistani Muslims built the Islamic Center of Corona on 42-12 National Street in 1983 and the Muslim Center of New York on 137-64 Geranium Avenue in 1991. In Manhattan, Muslims finished in 1991 what is likely the most prominent mosque in New York, the Islamic Cultural Center at Third Avenue and 96th Street. By the end of the 20th century, researchers for Columbia University's "Muslim in New York City" project, funded by the Ford Foundation, estimated that there were 140 Muslim places of worship in the city. Their architectural styles ranged from grand mosques to rented halls and converted storefronts.

Muslims also changed the city's look by participating in that most obvious sign of communal and ethnic arrival in New York: the staging of an annual parade. Beginning in

1986, the Muslim World Day Parade transformed the intersection of Lexington Avenue and 33rd Street into an outdoor mosque, where parade participants would prostrate themselves on sheets of plastic in the direction of the Ka'ba, Islam's most sacred shrine, in Mecca. Marching south down Lexington toward 23rd Street, participants carried banners with messages about God, the prophet MUHAMMAD, and the QUR'AN as they passed by Muslim-owned stores that sold South Asian food and DRESS. Floats in the parade included models of the Ka'ba, the grand mosque surrounding the Ka'ba, and the Dome of the Rock in Jerusalem.

The parade drew from a population of Muslim New Yorkers that was becoming increasingly diverse. By the end of the 20th century, nearly two-thirds of all Muslims in New York were immigrants, reflecting larger DEMOGRAPHIC patterns in the Muslim-American population as a whole. More than 35 different ethnic groups, speaking dozens of languages, were represented in New York's Muslim community. Muslims in New York came from sub-Saharan Africa, all parts of Asia and Europe, and from Latin America. Large Arab-American Muslim communities lived around Atlantic Avenue, Bay Ridge, Crown Heights, and Bedford-Stuyvesant in Brooklyn and around Jerome Avenue and the Grand Concourse in the Bronx. South Asian–American Muslims were more concentrated in Queens, largely in Flushing and Jamaica, which was headquarters of the ISLAMIC CIRCLE OF NORTH AMERICA (ICNA), a national Muslim-American organization run primarily by South Asians that began in 1974.

Beginning in the 1970s, it was impossible for non-Muslim New Yorkers to avoid daily, if casual contact with Muslims. Bangladeshi and other Muslims became known for driving the city's taxicabs. Muslim street vendors offered passersby HALAL, or religiously permissible, hot dogs and falafel sandwiches, and West African–Muslim immigrants developed networks of salesmen who hawked inexpensive knockoffs of watches and other luxury items. In Manhattan's financial district, Muslims became prominent investment bankers. Hundreds of Muslims served in the New York police and fire departments.

Though this era was dominated by immigrants, African-American Muslims remained some of the city's most prominent Muslim faces. South Asian immigrants associated with ICNA helped to fight drug use and engaged in community uplift efforts in neighborhoods around Brooklyn's Masjid al-Taqwa, or "Mosque of God-Consciousness," but the leader of the effort was an African-American Sunni, SIRAJ WAHHAJ (1950–   ). In legal circles, SHEILA ABDUS-SALAAM, a graduate of both Barnard College and Columbia University School of Law, steadily climbed from her position as staff attorney at Brooklyn's Legal Services office in the late 1970s to her eventual election as New York Supreme Court Justice in 1993.

IN THE AGE OF TERROR AND ANXIETY

But no matter how central Muslims had become to the life of the city in the late 20th century, their lives remained fraught with tension as they despaired over terrorist attacks against the World Trade Center (WTC), first in 1993 and then again on SEPTEMBER 11, 2001. On February 26, 1993, five Muslim extremists attempted to blow up the WTC. Although the buildings withstood the attack, the explosion killed six people and injured more than 1,000. Additional plots against city landmarks such as United Nations headquarters, 26 Federal Plaza, the George Washington Bridge, and the Lincoln and Holland tunnels had been planned by the conspirators, a group led by Egyptian preacher OMAR ABDEL-RAHMAN, a veteran of the U.S.-backed military campaign against the Soviet army in Afghanistan who came to live and work in New York and New Jersey in the early 1990s.

Though the association of Muslims with terrorism led to several incidents of anti-Muslim discrimination in the city after the 1993 bombing, the situation of Muslim New Yorkers became even more precarious after the 2001 attacks against the WTC, which led to the death of more than 2,700 people, great economic hardship, and personal tragedy. Despite the fact that Muslims were among those killed in these attacks and among the first-responders on the scene, hate crimes against Muslims rose nationally 1,700 percent, according to the FBI. At the same time, many Muslim and non-Muslim New Yorkers reached out to one another, holding an unprecedented number of interfaith meetings.

For example, New Yorkers Ranya Idibly, Suzanne Oliver, and Priscilla Warner—a Muslim, a Christian, and a Jew, respectively—tried to write an interfaith children's book in response to the tragedy but ended up having extended and extremely difficult conversations about the religious and political issues that separated them. Instead of producing a book for children, they wrote a memoir about their dialogues called *The Faith Club* (2006), which became a *New York Times* best seller and inspired women and men across the country to begin their own interfaith dialogues.

The 9/11 attacks also inspired more Muslim New Yorkers to enter law enforcement and especially counterterrorism. Even as many Muslim-American leaders, civil liberties advocates, and regular citizens questioned the law enforcement techniques used in the wake of 9/11, many Muslim-American New Yorkers volunteered to lead such efforts. Disregarding the policy of many federal intelligence agencies that restricts the hiring of foreign-born agents, the New York City Police Department (NYPD) recruited hundreds of foreign-born officers for a thousand-person counterterrorism and intelligence unit. Many of these officers were native speakers of Arabic, Urdu, and other languages in which terrorists have communicated. By 2006, while the FBI had only 33 agents

The annual American Muslim World Day Parade in New York City became a popular event in the late 20th century.   *(David Grossman/ Alamy)*

with "some proficiency" in Arabic, the NYPD had more than 65 fluent speakers of Arabic.

The NYPD used these intelligence capabilities to conduct undercover operations among various terrorism suspects and engaged in controversial sting operations, which led some observers to criticize the department for exaggerating threats and even encouraging the terrorist plots. Before the 2004 Republican National Convention in New York, for example, the department exposed a plot to bomb the Herald Square subway station. A Muslim undercover officer from Bay Ridge in Brooklyn provided evidence against the two plotters who some said were incompetent and only half serious in their intent to go through with the attack. Whether New Yorkers viewed these particular arrests as a success or failure, it helped to illustrate the advantage or perhaps the necessity of involving the city's large Muslim population in the struggle against terrorism.

CONCLUSION

In 2008, the Empire State Building, the tallest and one of the most recognizable buildings in New York and a symbol of the entire city, commemorated Eid al-Fitr, the HOLIDAY marking the end of the monthlong Ramadan fast from dawn to sunset, by turning its tower lights green, the color most associated with Islam. A few New Yorkers protested the decision by writing letters to various officials, but many welcomed the move, especially Muslim-American leader Daisy Khan, who saw the lights as she was walking down a New York street with her family. "I cannot tell you how grateful and how proud I am to be an American Muslim," she wrote to the *Washington Report on Middle East Affairs.*

Such public recognition also marked the changing nature of Muslims' historical presence in New York City. While Muslim New Yorkers were an oddity until the 20th century, in the past century they have made an indelible mark on the city. By the 1950s, African-American Muslims and Muslim immigrants established important ethnic enclaves in Harlem and in Brooklyn. After 1965, Muslim Americans came to inhabit all five boroughs of the city and participated in every aspect of its life. They helped to make New York City one of the most dynamic international crossroads in the United States.

Edward E. Curtis IV

Further Reading

Bald, Vivek. "Overlapping Diasporas, Multiracial Lives: South Asian Muslims in U.S. Communities of Color, 1880–1950." *Souls* 8, no. 4 (December 2006): 3–18.

Benson, Kathleen, and Philip M. Kayal, eds. *A Community of Many Worlds: Arab Americans in New York City*. New York: Museum of the City of New York/Syracuse University Press, 2002.

Dickey, Christopher. *Securing the City: Inside America's Best Counterterror Force—the NYPD*. New York: Simon & Schuster, 2009.

Ferris, Marc. "To 'Achieve the Pleasure of Allah': Immigrant Muslim Communities in New York City, 1893–1991." In *Muslim Communities in North America*, edited by Yvonne Y. Haddad and Jane I. Smith, 209–230. Albany: State University of New York Press, 1994.

Gomez, Michael A. "Muslims in New York." In *Black Crescent: The Experience and Legacy of African Muslims in the Americas*. New York: Cambridge University Press, 2005: 128–142.

Idibly, Ranya, Suzanne Oliver, and Priscilla Warner. *The Faith Club: A Muslim, A Christian, A Jew—Three Women Search for Understanding*. New York: Free Press, 2006.

Middle East Institute, Columbia University. "Muslims in New York City." Available online. URL: http://www.tc.edu/muslim-nyc/. Accessed February 20, 2009.

Singleton, Brent D. "Brothers at Odds: Rival Islamic Movements in Late Nineteenth Century New York City." *Journal of Muslim Minority Affairs* 27, no. 3 (December 2007): 473–486.

Slyomovics, Susan. "The Muslim World Day Parade and 'Storefront' Mosques of New York City." In *Making Muslim Space in North America and Europe*, edited by Barbara Daly Metcalf, 204–216. Berkeley: University of California Press, 1996.

Daoud Ahmed Faisal
Al-Islam: The Religion of Humanity (1950)

In 1939, Shaikh Daoud Ahmed Faisal (1891–1980), the founder of the Islamic Mission of America, leased a brownstone for his burgeoning Muslim community on 143 State Street in Brooklyn. By the 1950s and 1960s, he was one of New York's most prominent Sunni Muslim leaders. An African-American convert to Sunni Islam, Faisal ministered to Muslims from every part of the globe, including foreign visitors, businessmen, students, and some United Nations officials. His Islamic school, the Institute of Islam, offered daily classes on Islamic studies and Arabic, and hundreds came to pray each Friday at his mosque. An uncompromising missionary, Faisal exhorted all people to convert to Islam, which he believed was the one, true religion. In his 1950 book, Al-Islam: The Religion of Humanity, *from which an excerpt is reproduced below, he criticized the post–World War II emphasis among American politicians and religious leaders on interfaith dialogue. For the sake of their own salvation, he wrote, Jews and Christians should convert to Islam.*

For the assurance of everlasting *Peace* and *Security*, the people and the nations of the world, must accept "Al-Islam," the *Religion of humanity*, revealed by "Allah," the "Almighty God," unto His chosen Prophets, as the *Religion of humanity* in which to worship Him as their *Religion*. And they must also adopt and put in execution its Principles and its Laws as revealed by "Allah," the Lord of the worlds, unto His Holy Apostle Mohammed, for the one world government of the *brotherhood* of all humanity, as decreed by God, so that all men shall worship and be of one *God*, one *Religion* and one *Law*.

For The Benefit Of Humanity, "Al-Islam" is the Religion of the Peace of God, the Reward or the Attributes of obedience to the Commandments and the Laws of "Allah," the "Almighty God." "Al-Islam" is the *Religion of humanity*. It is the reward the gift from "Allah" to all who bowed down their will in *submission* to the *(Will)* of "Allah," the (one) God, in obedience to His Laws, His Commandments, His Prophets and what He hath revealed for the government and guidance of humanity, and as the Religion and the *Faith* in which to worship Him.

All the people and the nations of the world should know that *"Islam,"* the *Religion* of "Allah," the "Almighty God" is the *only* Religion of humanity. They should also know that "Islam" is the Religion of all the *Prophets* and *Messengers* of God, including Abraham, Isma'il, Isaac, Jacob, the Tribes, Moses, David, Jesus and Mohammed, and the Prophets of God were not Jews but *Muslims*. No one has Religion, and neither can any one worship God, unless he bows down his will in submission to the *(Will)* of "Allah," the "Almighty God," the Lord of the worlds, in obedience to His Laws, His Commandments, His Prophets and what He hath revealed for the benefit of humanity.

The Islamic Mission of America, Mosque and Institute, established in the name of "Allah," the "Almighty God" according to His own Divine revealed laws in the promotion of the highest human interest in the worship of "Allah," the (one) true God, designed especially for the propagation, teaching and defending "Al-Islam," the Religion of humanity, which "Allah," the Lord of the worlds, hath revealed unto His Chosen Prophets, as the Religion and the Faith in which all humanity shall worship Him. It appears to me as though the people of the Western parts of this world have no knowledge of the Religion of their Lord. Their constant *laughing* and *mocking* the *Muslims'* manner of worshipping God clearly proves this, because it is only fools who laugh and mock at things of which they have no knowledge. They have never been made to know that prostration is the proper manner of worshiping God. Prostration signifies humility and meekness of oneself before his or her creator. Muslims are the true believers who have never deviated in the slightest degree from "Islam," the Religion of God and His Prophets and mankind. We are in strict accordance and obedience with the laws of our Lord as revealed and as prescribed by His Holy Prophets.

It is deceiving and shameful on the part of the leaders of the Jews, the Catholics and the Protestants, to proclaim the so-called three Faiths at a time like this, to an enlightened and troubled world, to people who are seeking for the truth, peace, security and the brotherhood of man.

Faith is to believe in the oneness of God, obedience to His Commandments, His Laws, His Prophets and what He hath revealed. All who believe in the oneness of God, Who created the universe, His commandments and His Laws are of (one) Faith. The Jews know better because their religion is of the religion of Abraham. They are only leading the Christians on who are using the books of Moses, the law giver, and, a prophet of the Israelites. This is no way to establish brotherhood. Human brotherhood is a reality, because we are one human family. The brotherhood of man must be established in obedience to the Commandments and the laws of the (one) God of Abraham, which is a different thing all together. "Islam," our religion, mine and yours, is the Religion of humanity. The so-called three Faiths must find a different name for unification. But to call yourselves the three faiths when you believe in the one and the same God is deception in the highest degree. The Jews must return to "Islam," the religion of Abraham, and the Christians must accept "Islam," the Religion of humanity; that is if they hope to bring about peace and the one universal brotherhood of man.

It is my desire that the Christian people should know that I am not an enemy of theirs, but a friend of humanity, a lover of truth and human-ity, and a heralder of the truth as revealed by the "Almighty God." And should you find knowledge, guidance, peace, the blessings and the forgiveness of God through the pages of this book then I will have accomplished more than my object. I beg of you to read this book very carefully and then make a fair comparison of what you read and what you have been taught to believe. However, there are certain things you must know in relationship with your God before you die.

Christianity is not your Religion, and it is not the Religion of God, and it has no relationship with God, because its teachings and its philosophy are contrary to the revelations and the laws of the Almighty God and the teachings of His Holy Prophets. But "Islam" is your Religion, and unless you surrender your will to the WILL of "Allah," the Unity in the one God, in obedience to His commandments and His laws and observe the teachings of His Prophets, which will automatically make you a Muslim, the gates of Heaven and Paradise will be closed to you, because none goes to Heaven but Muslims who observe the Commandments and the Laws of their Lord.

We are asking the Christian people to stop making fools of themselves, because it is only fools who laugh and mock at things of which they have no knowledge. Why laugh at the Muslims, when the Muslims are the only true believers whose Religion has always been the Religion of God and His Prophets. The religious laws, habits and culture of the Muslims are in true accord with the revealed laws of God.

Source: Daoud Ahmed Faisal *Al-Islam: The Religion of Humanity.* Brooklyn, N.Y.: Islamic Mission of America, 1950, pp. 14–17.

Nimatullahi Sufi Order

The Nimatullahi Sufi Order is a Muslim mystical association from Iran with an established presence in the United States. Originally founded in the early 15th century by the mystic and poet Shah Niʿmatullah Wali, the Nimatullahi Sufi Order in the United States refers to Khaniqahi Nimatullahi, a registered charity and religious association that until 2008 was under the direction of the Iranian psychiatrist and Sufi master Javad Nurbakhsh, known also as Nur ʿAli Shah Kermani. Born in Kerman, Iran, on December 10, 1926, he became master of the order at the age of 27. An energetic and intellectually imposing figure, Nurbakhsh obtained an M.D. in 1952, pursued advanced medical studies in France, and eventually became professor and head of the Department of Psychiatry at the Tehran University School of Medicine and director of a nearby teaching hospital. He retired from medicine in 1977.

During his years in Iran, Nurbakhsh divided his time between his medical duties and his responsibilities as head of a Sufi order, expanding the presence of the Nimatullahi brotherhood throughout the country through building projects and a vigorous publications program. At the insistence of American disciples who had first met him in Tehran in the early 1970s, he visited the United States in 1974. In the following year, the first two American Nimatullahi Centers, or khanaqahs, were established in San Francisco and New York. Others quickly followed. Forced to flee Iran at the onset of the Islamic Revolution in 1979, Nurbakhsh lived in Los Angeles for a time and, in 1983, settled in London. In the early 1990s, he purchased a manor in the English countryside where he established the Nimatullahi Research Center. He spent the remainder of his life there, directing the affairs of the order, writing, and receiving disciples and visitors up until his death on October 10, 2008. In the years leading up to his death, his son, Alireza Nurbakhsh, had progressively taken on more responsibility for running the affairs of the order. With his father's death, he assumed the position of its master.

The Nimatullahi Sufi Order maintains centers throughout the United States, including New York City, Washington, D.C., Boston, Chicago, Santa Fe, Seattle, San Francisco, Los Angeles, Santa Cruz, and San Diego. Centers have also been established in Canada, Europe, West Africa, and Australia. In 2006, worldwide membership outside of Iran was estimated at 3,600. In the United States, the order's membership is generally composed of a mixture of Iranian expatriates and white Muslim-American converts. Members gather twice-weekly for meditational exercises led by a designated representative of Nurbakhsh. Individual centers are run as registered self-financing charities and normally have a full-time resident caretaker. Although the historical Nimatullahi Order is associated with Shi'a Islam, this association is not always explicit in the public face of Nurbakhsh's Khanaqahi Nimatullahi. Strict adherence to Islamic ritual and legal norms is not required of members.

A prolific compiler, author, and well-known editor of medieval Sufi texts, Javad Nurbakhsh and his order have pursued a vigorous publishing program under the auspices of the order's publishing house, Khaniqahi Nimatullahi Publications, which has offices in both New York and London. In addition to scores of volumes comprised of translated compilations of classical Sufi literature and essays and other writings by Nurbakhsh himself, since 1989, it has also published a journal entitled *Sufi*. Issued in both English- and Persian-language versions, this periodical includes scholarly essays, short fiction, book reviews, and translations from classical Sufi literature, as well as original artwork and poetry.

Erik S. Ohlander

Further Reading

Lewisohn, Leonard. "Persian Sufism in the Contemporary West: Reflections on the Ni'matu'llahi Diaspora." In *Sufism in the West,* edited by Jamal Malik and John Hinnells, 49–70. New York: Routledge, 2006.

Nimatullahi Sufi Order. Available online. URL: http://www.nimatullahi.org. Accessed February 25, 2009.

Rothschild, Jeffrey. *Bestower of Light: A Portrait of Dr. Javad Nurbakhsh, Master of the Nimatullahi Sufi Order.* New York: Khaniqahi Nimatullahi Publications, 1999.

Noor, Queen (Lisa Halaby) (1951–)   *Queen of Jordan*

Queen Noor was born Lisa Halaby on August 23, 1951, in Washington, D.C. Queen Noor's father, Arab-American Najeeb Halaby, was a successful attorney who led several organizations and worked under President John F. Kennedy as the director of the Federal Aviation Administration. Lisa Halaby lived a privileged life and attended numerous private schools. She was a member of the first coed class at Princeton University in 1969. After receiving a degree in architecture and urban planning, Halaby took a job with an architectural firm and worked in Europe, Australia, and the Middle East. As part of her work, she traveled to Jordan to meet her father, who was working with King Hussein on an aviation project. Najeeb Halaby talked his daughter into staying in Jordan, and during this period, she began a secret courtship with King Hussein.

The courtship between the 26-year-old Lisa Halaby and the 42-year-old King Hussein was brief and private. Their engagement lasted only a few months. Lisa Halaby married King Hussein ibn Talal on June 15, 1978, in a private ceremony at Zaharan Palace, in Amman, making her the king's fourth wife and stepmother to his eight children. (The king's former wives were either deceased or lived away from the palace when Halaby and King Hussein married.) The king gave his bride the name Noor al Hussein, Arabic for "light of Hussein." He also gave her the title of queen, and she became known as Queen Noor.

A Christian, Queen Noor took the *shahada,* the Islamic profession of faith, not long before she and the king married. Queen Noor gave birth to four children, two boys and two girls. Prince Hamzah, born in 1980, is the eldest son of Queen Noor and King Hussein. A year later, 1981, Prince Hashim was born. In 1983 Queen Noor gave birth to her first daughter, Princess Iman. In 1986 the king and queen had their fourth child, Princess Raiyah.

The queen directed several development projects throughout Jordan and worked for improvements in education. A supporter of microeconomic development, she promoted Jordanian goods such as Palestinian *jalabas* by wearing them herself and used her clout to provide Jordanian women with seed money to start handicraft projects. Noor was also instrumental in the founding of the Jerash Festival, which brought musical artists from around the world to perform in Jerash, one of the world's best preserved ancient Roman cities. Noor also promoted programs to disable land mines and supported efforts to establish peace in the Middle East. Finally, she spoke out in favor of increased women's rights in Jordan and, during the Islamic month of Ramadan, challenged a taboo by holding *iftar* dinners—the daily meal after sundown during Ramadan—for women.

Queen Noor's husband died of cancer in 1999, and his eldest son, Abdullah II, the son of Hussein's British wife, Tony Gardiner, became the king of Jordan in 1999. Abdullah II named Queen Noor's oldest son, Prince Hamzah, Crown Prince in 1999, but in 2004 removed him from the line of succession. Though Queen Noor still possesses the title of queen, she no longer lives in Jordan and, as of 2010, spends most of her days outside her adopted country.

Britney J. McMahan

Further Reading

Contreras, Joseph, Christopher Dickey, and Russell Watson. "The Light of His Life." *Newsweek* 133, no. 6 (February 1999): p. 42.

Donahue, Deirdre. "Noor Sheds Light on Her Life," *USA Today,* 8 March 2003.

Fenton, Matthew McCann. "A Revealing Talk with the American Who Became Queen of Jordan." *Biography* 7, no. 9 (September 2003): pp. 44–98.

Noor, Queen. *Leap of Faith: Memoirs of an Unexpected Life.* New York: Miramax, 2003.

Rompalske, Dorothy. "The All-American Girl Who Became Queen." *Biography* 1, no. 9 (September 1997): p. 72.

North Dakota

On a percentage basis, North Dakota was perhaps the largest Muslim-American enclave in the United States in the early 20th century. From the late 19th century until 1930, North Dakota became home to approximately 2,000 Syrian and Lebanese immigrants. Of those 2,000, an estimated 500 were Muslims. This was unusual, since, generally speaking, Muslims constituted only 10 percent of this wave of Arab-American immigration.

The first Syrian Muslim settlers reached North Dakota by the 1890s. The flow of Muslim settlers increased from 1900 to the 1930s as a continued stream of immigrants reached

North Dakota from the Levant through intermediary locations such as NEW YORK CITY and Montreal. Their presence encouraged further settlement by friends, family members, and fellow villagers from the home country to immigrate to North Dakota.

It is estimated that 35 to 40 percent of Syrian applicants for citizenship in North Dakota from 1899 to 1917 were Muslims. Syrian Muslim settlement was widespread throughout the state, usually as part of a homesteading or peddling enterprise. However, larger settlements clustered around Ross and Williston in the central and western areas of the state. As the 1920s and 1930s progressed, the trend toward a denser population pattern increased as many homesteaders migrated into more urban areas of the state.

One of the largest Muslim populations in the state was in the town of Ross. The Muslim settlement in Ross is the best example of the chain migration process. The first Muslim men were present in the Ross area in 1900 or 1901. According to the records of the Federal Land Office, by 1909 at least 66 men filed for land claims in the Ross area. What was initially a small Muslim settlement swiftly grew. By 1910, the census estimated that there were more than 100 Muslim settlers in the area. These settlers retained their traditional religion by meeting in informal home settings.

By 1920, the community established a Muslim cemetery whose 22 existing gravestones include Arabic inscriptions and Islamic symbols. Guest imams, or religious leaders, from the Canadian cities of Edmonton, Calgary, and Swift Current were sometimes invited to perform the Muslim prayer service for the dead. By 1929, the Ross Muslim community had begun construction on a mosque. Built with a large basement to withstand the harsh winters of North Dakota, the simple post-and-beam building looked nothing like the mosques of the Middle East. It rose only a few feet above ground. Called a *jima,* or religious gathering place, by Muslims in Ross, it was known as the Mohammedan church by Ross's Christian populations.

The Muslim community in Ross declined in the 1930s during the economic collapse of the Great Depression. Many farmers, both Muslim and non-Muslim, were forced to sell their livestock to the government for reduced prices. This out-migration of the population during the 1930s continued in the 1940s as North Dakotans more generally answered the call to work in war-related industries and serve in WORLD WAR II. After the 1940s, the mosque was seldom used and was dismantled in 1979.

Works Progress Administration (WPA) records provide a human context for the larger story of immigration and survival on the North Dakota plain in the early 20th century. These records suggest that Muslims in North Dakota did not have a fear of religious prejudice or feel a need to conceal their religious faith at this time. In one interview with

Muslim immigrant and homesteader Mary Juma in 1939, Juma told her interviewer that her "religion in the old country was Moslem. We attended church every Friday, just as we do now." In another interview with the WPA, Kassam Rameden related a similar experience. He told his interviewer in 1939 that "we attended the Mohammedan Church and we had church every day."

The existence of a larger Muslim community aided immigrants in their efforts to retain the religious and cultural traditions of their homelands. Adherence to some Islamic religious practices, such as prostrating oneself to pray, no doubt set the Muslims apart from their Christian neighbors. But other Islamic religious traditions would have blended in with Christian practices at the time. Since early 20th century North Dakota was a dry state where the consumption of alcohol was illegal, for example, the fact that Muslims refused to drink did not make them any different from the majority of Protestant Christians who also practiced prohibition. Muslims fasted and used prayer beads—like the state's many Roman Catholics. The fact that Muslims butchered their own meat in accordance with Islamic DIETARY LAWS would not have been strange in this agrarian state.

In their interviews with the WPA Writers' Project in 1938 and 1939, Muslim respondents were unanimous in their appreciation for their neighbors' acceptance of them. In his interview, Allay Omar of Ross wrote that "all the people in my neighborhood were very friendly, and they helped me whenever they could." Joe Albert of Williston reported a similar experience in his interview: "When I first came, everyone helped me all they could—more friendly here than in the old country." The experiences of Allay Omar and Joe Albert indicate that the Muslim populations of North Dakota assimilated into the fabric of North Dakota society as equals with other immigrant groups.

Patrick Callaway

Further Reading
Sherman, William C., Paul L. Whitney, and John Guerrero. *Prairie Peddlers: The Syrian-Lebanese in North Dakota.* Bismarck, N.Dak.: University of Mary Press, 2002.

WPA Interview with Mary Juma (1939)
In the 1930s, the Works Progress Administration employed writers in a national program to gather information on the vanishing ethnic cultures of immigrants who had arrived in the United States in the late 19th and early 20th centuries. Arab-American Muslims in North Dakota who were interviewed noted the differences between their lives in Lebanon and Syria and their lives on the American prairie. One of those interviewed was Mary Juma, a Syrian American who settled in the United States in 1901. In the excerpt below, fieldworker Everal J. McKinnon offers a summary of his interview with Juma, which took place on the Juma farm in Ross, North Dakota, in 1939.

I was born in Byria, Rushia, Syria. I don't know my exact age, but according to my naturalization papers, I am sixty-nine years old. I am sure that I am at least seventy-five years of age, however.

My home in Syria was a large, one-story, stone house. The floors were made of logs (about the size of our telephone poles), and the space between the poles was filled with smaller poles. Branches were used to fill small unfilled parts. A mixture of wet clay and lime was spread over the poles and branches, packed in hard, and smoothened by running a heavy roller over the floor. This was allowed to dry, and the result was a hard floor looking like cement. The roof was made in the same way.

Our village was located in a valley, and the land surrounding the village was level, extending two miles on each side of a river meeting rougher and more rolling land.

My religion in the Old Country was Moslem. We attended services every Friday, the same as we do here.

I received no education, as our people figured that it was a waste of time and money to teach a girl to read and write. There were no schools in our village, and those that were taught to read and write, were taught by a tutor.

Being a woman, I knew nothing about labor conditions, wages, renting, taxes, nor about farming methods. I know that everything was done the hard way. We didn't have machinery to farm, and used oxen on a walking plow. Seeding, harvesting, and threshing was done by hand.

Parties were given only to celebrate such an occasion as a wedding. The kind of party given would depend on the financial condition of the family giving it. If the people were well-off, they would prepare for many and invite the people from the nearby villages, and there would be much feasting and dancing. The table was set all the time and people ate whenever they felt like it. When dancing, everyone dance alone, not in couples. There was one dance where many joined hands and danced in a circle, a great deal like our square dances here. These parties for days sometimes.

A wedding in the Old Country was just the same as a Moslem wedding anywhere. There is no courting before the wedding. When a boy decides to marry a certain girl, he goes to her parents and tells them about it. If he is not of age, he tells his own mother and she goes to see the girl's parents.

They then have a private discussion as to whether or not they should marry. The girl is not consulted at all. She, in most cases, is but a young miss of only eleven or twelve years of age. The outcome of the decision depends on the financial status of the prospective groom. An agreed amount of money is to be put aside by the groom in case of a separation. The separation must not be culminated through the fault of the bride if she is to receive that dowry. This amount varies. After the preliminary agreements are made, the date of the wedding is set. If the family of the groom is wealthy, the people from all the neighboring villages are invited to the ceremony and a feast is prepared. The bride names two witnesses for the ceremony, and then all is ready. The bride goes to an enclosure away from the ceremony and her father acts in her place. He clasps the hand of the groom and a handkerchief is draped over the clasped hands, and thus the vows are exchanged. After the ceremony, the feasting and celebrating begins.

My husband's farm was very small. I don't know the number of acres, but it wasn't enough for us to but barely exist on. The people in our vicinity were migrating to America and kept writing back about the riches in America. Everyone wanted to move and we were a family of the many that contemplated leaving. We sold all our possessions and borrowed two-hundred dollars from a man, giving our land as a collateral.

A big farewell party was given in our honor, as there were twelve of us coming to America from that one village. It was a sad farewell as our relatives hated to see us leave. We feasted, danced, and played games at the party. The games were for men, which were feats of strength and endurance.

We left two daughters in the Old Country with relatives. One of the girls has died since, and the other one still lives there.

We went to Beirut, which was about thirty miles from our home, and caught a boat to France. It took us about three weeks to travel through France. I do not remember the name of the boat we took from there to America. It took us three weeks to come from France to Montreal, Canada.

We moved further inland and started to travel over that country with a horse and cart as peddlers. We stayed there only a few months, and then moved to Nebraska, in the United States. We traveled through the entire state in a year. We never had trouble making people understand what we wanted while peddling, but many times we were refused a place to sleep. We suffered the same conditions as the pioneers, and at times were even more uncomfortable.

We were in Canada in 1900, and in Nebraska in 1901. In 1902, we came to western North Dakota where we started to peddle. It was at the time when there was such an influx of people to take homesteads, and for no reason at all, we decided to try homesteading too.

We started clearing the land immediately, and within a year, had a horse, plow, disk, drag, and drill. We also had some cattle and chickens. When there was a very little work to do on the farm, my husband traveled to Minnesota and eastern North Dakota to peddle.

In 1903, my son, Charles, was born. He was the first Syrian child born in western North Dakota. We were the first Syrians to homestead in this community, but soon many people from that country came to settle here.

Our home has always been a gathering place for the Syrian folk. Not many parties or celebrations were held, except for occasions like a wedding or such. Before we built our church [mosque], we held services at the different homes. We have a month of fasting, after which everyone visits the home of another, and there was a lot of feasting.

I am pretty old now, and am confined to this wheel-chair because of my leg which was amputated two years ago. I miss my work, both indoor and outdoor, but still enjoy life.

We were always able to make a very good living by farming and raising livestock, until the death of my husband in February of 1918. My son then took over the management of the farm, and I have lived with his family since. The depression has made living hard, but I don't worry.

Charles went to school in Ross until my husband died, and was not able to even complete the eighth grade.

We always speak in our native tongue at home, except my grand-children who won't speak Syrian to their parents. They do speak in Syrian to me because I cannot speak nor understand English. My grand-children range from fourteen months of age to eight years, and there are four of them. . . .

I can't read at all, neither in English nor Syrian. My son and daughter-in-law tell me the news they think might interest me.

We don't have any recreation; we only work. Sometimes friends stop in to talk for awhile, and then we attend services every Friday too, but that is all. I sew a little occasionally, and like to hold the baby. . . .

There is too great a comparison to say much about America and my native land. This country has everything, and we have freedom. When we pay taxes, we get schools, roads, and an efficiency in the government. In the Old Country, we paid taxes and Turkey took all the money, and Syria receiving nothing in return. We were repaid by having Turkey force our boys to join her army. The climate in the Old Country was wonderful, but we [Americans] have such a climate down south.

If I had my life to live over, I would come to America sooner than I did. I would have liked to visit the people in Syria five or ten years ago, but now that I am helpless, I wouldn't care to go. I don't ever want to go back there to live.

Source: Works Progress Administration. North Dakota Writers' Project Ethnic Group Files, Series 30559, Roll 3, 1939.

Olajuwon, Hakeem (Akeem) (1963–)
professional basketball player

Hakeem Olajuwon is a former professional basketball player who spent 18 seasons with the Houston Rockets (1984–2001) and Toronto Raptors (2001–02) of the National Basketball Association (NBA). He received the league's Most Valuable Player Award in 1994, won consecutive championships with the Rockets in 1994 and 1995, and was named one of the NBA's 50 Greatest Players of all time in 1997. His on-court success and public devotion to Islam have made him a role model to young Muslims worldwide. Since retiring in 2002, he has become known for his charitable work and efforts to build an Islamic community in Houston.

Olajuwon was born Akeem Abdul Olajuwon in Lagos, Nigeria, on January 21, 1963, to a Muslim family of the Yoruba tribe. Though his parents were observant Muslims, Hakeem recalls that they did not pressure their children to practice Islam. The young Olajuwon was exceptionally tall—at age 15, he already stood six feet nine inches—but did not play basketball until a coach convinced him to try "the American game." Less than four years after shooting his first basket, he left Nigeria to pursue an athletic scholarship in the United States.

Olajuwon began his American career at the University of Houston. After starting on the practice team, he progressed well enough to become the Cougars' top center. In 1984, the media honored him as a first-team All-American, placing "Akeem the Dream" among the nation's best college players. Houston reached the championship game of the Final Four in both 1983 and 1984, losing twice. Following the second defeat, the Houston Rockets selected Olajuwon with the first overall pick in the 1984 NBA draft. He became the first foreign-born player in the NBA.

As his career blossomed, Olajuwon became more religiously observant. He had long been wary of getting caught up in black nationalist Muslim groups—more specifically the NATION OF ISLAM, whose teachings he considered un-Islamic—but in 1990 he started attending prayers when he learned of a Sunni mosque located near the Rockets' arena. "When they made the call to prayer, there were goose bumps all over me," he later recalled. "It was so emotional to hear that call again. I was like, wow, look what I've been missing!" To symbolize his newfound devotion, he added an "H" to his first name, making it similar to the ARABIC term for "all-wise." The following year he performed the hajj, or pilgrimage to Mecca.

Olajuwon spoke openly about his faith and committed himself to charity work and the establishment of a Muslim community in Houston. He also began taking Arabic lessons during his off-season trips to Nigeria and Jordan. Though teammates resisted his attempts to convert them, they claimed to respect his beliefs. For the remainder of his career, he strictly observed the Ramadan fast, even when bouts of weakness hindered his play—a situation the *Houston Chronicle* called "unfortunate" but "honorable."

Shortly after Olajuwon's rededication to Islam, the Rockets emerged as one of the league's elite teams. In 1994, Houston won a franchise-record 58 games and its first NBA championship, capping a season in which Olajuwon became the first and only player to win the Most Valuable Player Award, Defensive Player of the Year Award, and NBA Finals Most Valuable Player Award in the same year. The Rockets repeated as champions the following season. Though Olajuwon continued to be one of the league's best players for several more years—he received numerous All-Star and All-NBA selections and won a Gold Medal as a member of the 1996 United States Olympic Basketball Team—his abilities faded toward the end of the 1990s. He played his final season with the Toronto Raptors before retiring in 2002.

Since leaving basketball, Olajuwon has become a fixture in America's Muslim community. He has made appearances before the ISLAMIC SOCIETY OF NORTH AMERICA and the MUSLIM STUDENTS ASSOCIATION and has served as a spokesman for charitable causes, especially those relating to education. His own charity, the Dream Foundation, has awarded college scholarships to Houston-area students since 1995. He has also refused to promote products he sees as un-Islamic or immoral.

These efforts have made him the public face of Islam for many non-Muslim Americans. In 1996, when fellow Muslim and Denver Nuggets star MAHMOUD ABDUL-RAUF refused to stand for the national anthem on religious grounds, Olajuwon questioned his understanding of Islam and told reporters that "to be a good Muslim is to be a good citizen." After the terrorist attacks of SEPTEMBER 11, 2001, he called on the media to treat Muslims fairly. "The Muslims in America are now the face of the crime and that fulfills the stereotype," he said. "It puts us in a very bad position, all the way back to almost the beginning, to having to explain to a country where we are still in the great minority that the actions of a few cannot be allowed to represent all Muslims."

Olajuwon's Islamic activism has drawn much praise, but also some scrutiny. In February 2005, the U.S. Treasury Department discovered that he had raised money for two relief agencies suspected of funding al-Qaeda and Hamas, the Palestinian political party. Olajuwon denied any knowledge of the ties and expressed regret that his donations may have indirectly supported terrorist organizations. Federal officials chose not to investigate him.

In the first decade of the 21st century, Olajuwon developed a highly successful real estate business in Houston while also spending time with his wife, Dalia Asafi, and their two daughters. He was elected to the Basketball Hall of Fame in 2008.

William Brown

Further Reading

Associated Press. "Olajuwon says he didn't know of terrorism ties." *ESPN.* Available online. URL: http://sports.espn.go.com/nba/news/story?id=1987790. Accessed July 8, 2008.

Blinebury, Fran. "Hakeem a true face of Islam," *Houston Chronicle.* Available online. URL: http://www.chron.com/CDA/archives/archive.mpl?id=2001_3334868. Accessed July 8, 2008.

Caldwell, Deborah. "Hakeem Olajuwon: A Ramadan Interview." Beliefnet. Available online. URL: http://www.beliefnet.com/story/55/story_5556_1.html. Accessed July 8, 2008.

DeLong-Bas, Natana. "Hakeem Olajuwon." In *Notable Muslims: Builders of World Civilization and Culture.* Oxford: Oneworld, 2006.

Falsani, Cathleen. "Hakeem Olajuwon." In *The God Factor: Inside the Spiritual Lives of Public People.* New York: Farrar, Straus and Giroux, 2006.

Hedges, Michael. "In '95, Olajuwon said America had 'no morals,'" *Houston Chronicle.* Available online. URL: http://www.chron.com/CDA/archives/archive.mpl?id=2005_3845719. Accessed July 8, 2008.

Murphy, Kate. "A Slam-Dunk in Real Estate," *New York Times.* Available online. URL: http://www.nytimes.com/2006/12/06/realestate/commercial/06houston.html?_r=1&ore f=slogin. Accessed July 8, 2008.

NBA Encyclopedia. "Hakeem Olajuwon Biography." NBA.com. Available online. URL: http://www.nba.com/history/players/olajuwon_bio.html. Accessed July 8, 2008.

Picker, David. "Olajuwon Says He Trusted Charities," *New York Times.* Available online. URL: http://www.nytimes.com/2005/02/16/sports/basketball/16Hakeem.html. Accessed July 8, 2008.

Robertson, Dale. "Unfortunately but honorably, Olajuwon slowed by fasting," *Houston Chronicle.* Available online. URL: http://www.chron.com/CDA/archives/archive.mpl?id=1996_1325155. Accessed July 8, 2008.

O'Lone v. Estate of Shabazz (1987)

In 1987, the United States Supreme Court heard the case *O'Lone v. Estate of Shabazz.* Although the case was originally brought by a prison inmate named Ahmad Uthman Shabazz, he died on January 15, 1986, so the case was brought to the Supreme Court by his estate. This case came about after Muslim prisoners at New Jersey's Leesburg State Prison brought suit against Edward O'Lone, administrator of the Leesburg prison complex, arguing that newly instituted prison policies violated their rights to freedom of religion under the Free Exercise clause of the First Amendment to the U.S. Constitution. The policies required the inmates to leave the prison grounds during the day for work detail and also prohibited them from returning to the grounds during work hours. This meant that Muslim inmates assigned to these details were unable to attend Friday congregational prayers, which many Muslims understand to be religiously incumbent.

Leesburg State Prison had three custody classifications for inmates: maximum security, gang minimum security, and full minimum security. Maximum and gang minimum inmates were held in the main building, whereas full minimum prisoners were held in a separate building, known as "the Farm." In April 1983, the state instituted a policy that barred the movement of prisoners directly from maximum security to the Farm without first spending time housed under the middle classification. This resulted in an overwhelming number of inmates grouped under the two higher classifications and therefore overpopulation of the main prison building. In order to deal with the large number of prisoners, some were assigned to work outside the main building during the day, during which time eight to 15 inmates were supervised by one guard. This meant that if one inmate needed to return to the main building, then every member of the detail also had to return.

When the new work policy was first instituted, some Muslim inmates were permitted to work in the main building on Fridays so that they could attend congregational prayers, but this exception was eliminated in March 1984, and all gang minimum inmates were required to work outside the main building Monday through Friday. Muslim inmates asked that exceptions be made, but prison officials maintained that this would be too costly and would cause security risks. The prisoners proposed that inmates who wanted to attend Friday services be placed in all-Muslim work details so that they could all return for prayer. Prison officials argued that having inmates return during the day caused a security problem because all traffic in and out of the prison had to be put on hold while they were searched and processed. Officials were also concerned that creating work groups based on religious affiliation would create the appearance of favoritism.

The inmates also suggested that they be permitted to work outside of the main building on the weekend and remain in the building on Fridays. Again, officials argued that this would make problematic distinctions among various prison groups and that the cost of having increased security on the weekend made this option unreasonable. They also maintained that in order to rehabilitate prisoners and ready them for life in the outside world, where they would be expected to complete full workdays, they should not be released from their work assignments. For these reasons, no exceptions were made.

When the prisoners first brought suit in March 1984, the U.S. district court in New Jersey found that there was no violation of the prisoners' rights, holding that prohibiting inmates from returning during the day was valid in order to advance security and rehabilitation. The U.S. Court of Appeals for the Third Circuit overturned this decision. The circuit court held that the district court's decision did not adequately protect prisoners' rights to practice their religion, concluding that inmates' rights could be limited only if there was no reasonable alternative that could be instituted without causing a serious security risk. The court of appeals also held that the risk as described by prison officials was not sufficient to warrant limiting inmates' religious rights.

It was after the district court decision was reversed by the court of appeals that the Supreme Court heard the case and, in a 5–4 decision, overturned the Third Circuit's ruling. The opinion of the court was written by Chief Justice William H. Rehnquist, who was joined by Justices Byron White, Lewis F. Powell, Sandra Day O'Connor, and Antonin Scalia. Justice William J. Brennan authored the dissenting opinion, in which Justices Thurgood Marshall, Harry A. Blackmun, and John Paul Stevens joined.

The majority of the Court explained that its ruling was based on a balancing of two principles. The first was that inmates did not forfeit their First Amendment rights when they were incarcerated. The second, however, which was the guiding principle in the majority's decision, was that impris-

onment necessarily results in the limitation of rights and privileges. The court drew on an earlier decision, *Turner v. Safley* (1987), which held that prison officials had the right to anticipate security problems and limit inmates' rights as they saw necessary in order to avoid these problems. The Turner case also concluded that the courts should limit their role in evaluating the validity of the actions taken by prison officials in these situations.

Relying on the precedent articulated in Turner, the Court decided in *O'Lone v. Estate of Shabazz* that the court of appeals had erroneously placed the burden of proof on prison officials to show that there were no available alternatives that they could take in order to allow the prisoners to participate in Friday congregational prayers. The Court also held that the court of appeals should have accepted the assessment of prison officials and placed the burden of proof on the inmates who were arguing for an exception to be made. In a non-prison setting, when dealing with issues of religious freedom, the burden of proof is placed on the person or institution that is attempting to limit individuals' religious freedoms. By allowing prison officials to limit the inmates' religious rights, however, the Supreme Court concluded that when dealing with prisoners the burden should be placed on the petitioner. The Court also determined that because Muslims were not barred from participating in all Muslim religious practices, their rights were not being limited enough to warrant a change.

The dissenting opinion argued that the burden of proving the need for restricting the right to free exercise should remain on the prison officials, and they should be required to show that allowing prisoners to participate in Friday congregational prayers presented a valid security risk and that there was no reasonable way to allow them to participate in this religious practice.

Although the *O'Lone* decision made it easier for prison officials to limit the religious rights of inmates by requiring only that the prison's interest be "legitimate" in order to outweigh a prisoner's right to the free exercise of religion, the Religious Freedom Restoration Act (RFRA) of 1998, a federal law, required a "compelling" interest on behalf of the government or prison officials in order to limit inmates' practice. As a result of RFRA, the Supreme Court's decision in *O'Lone* was effectively nullified, and the First Amendment rights of prisoners were expanded.

Monica C. Reed

Further Reading

O'Lone v. Estate of Shabazz, 482 U.S. 342 (1987).

Rachanow, Shelly S. "The Effect of *O'Lone v. Estate of Shabazz* on the Free Exercise Rights of Prisoners." *Journal of Church and State* 40, no. 1 (1998): 125–149.

P

Padilla, José (Abdullah al-Muhajir) (1970–   )
"dirty bomb" suspect

José Padilla, a convert to Islam and of Puerto Rican descent, was publicly accused by U.S. Attorney General John Ashcroft in 2002 of plotting to detonate a radioactive "dirty bomb" in CHICAGO. He ultimately faced charges that did not mention a dirty bomb. A U.S. citizen, Padilla was transferred on June 9, 2002, a month after his arrest, to a Navy brig where he spent the next three years and seven months as an "enemy combatant." Convicted on August 16, 2007, of federal charges of conspiracy to murder, kidnap, and maim people in a foreign country, conspiracy to provide material support for terrorism, and providing material support for terrorists, he was sentenced on January 22, 2008, to 17 years and four months in federal prison. Critics of the U.S. government's response to the al-Qaeda attacks of SEPTEMBER 11, 2001, view his case as representative of other post-9/11 cases in which the government has made highly publicized terrorism accusations against individuals but ends up negotiating plea bargains or winning convictions for crimes of lesser magnitude.

Born on October 18, 1970, in Brooklyn, New York, Padilla grew up in Chicago, where his family attended a Pentecostal church. As a teenager, he joined a gang and spent several years in juvenile detention after participating in a robbery that turned into a homicide. At age 19, he moved to Florida with his mother. Around 1993, he converted to Islam after he and his girlfriend, Cherie Stultz, who would become his first wife, became friendly with their Muslim boss at a fast-food restaurant in Davie, Florida, where they both worked. According to his relatives and his lawyers, in 1998 he moved to Egypt, hoping to teach English and eventually become an imam, or religious leader, and in 2000, after making the pilgrimage to Mecca, he moved to Yemen and traveled to Pakistan to continue his studies. In Egypt, Padilla met a woman named Shamia'a, who became his second wife. (Stultz then filed for divorce.) Padilla has three sons: Hussein and Hassan, both with Shamia'a; and Joshua, with a woman he had known as a teenager in Chicago.

The U.S. government believed he was closely associated with al-Qaeda and met with senior members of that organization. Padilla was arrested on May 8, 2002, after arriving at O'Hare International Airport in Chicago from Islamabad, Pakistan. The government contended that Padilla was evasive with FBI interrogators about his time in the Middle East and that in 2000 he filled out an application form for an al-Qaeda training camp in Afghanistan.

The manner of his detention was a major point of contention. Shortly after Padilla's arrest he was transferred to military confinement at the Naval Weapons Station in Charleston, South Carolina, where the government kept him for three years and seven months as an "enemy combatant"— a status that allowed the administration to detain him indefinitely. Padilla eventually sued, seeking the right to challenge his detention in a U.S. court.

On February 28, 2005, he was ordered released by District Judge Henry F. Floyd of the U.S. district court in South Carolina, but on September 9, 2005, the U.S. Court of Appeals, Fourth Circuit, reversed that decision, saying Padilla could indeed be held as an "enemy combatant" without a charge. On November 22, 2005, shortly before the U.S. Supreme Court was expected to consider the manner in which he was detained, the government indicted Padilla on federal charges, paving the way for his transfer on January 3, 2006, to a federal prison in Miami, Florida, from the Navy brig.

In Padilla's three-month trial in the federal court system, the main piece of evidence against him was a form that prosecutors said was an application he had signed in 2000 to go to the training camp in Afghanistan. The application had his fingerprints on it, which Padilla's attorneys argued could have come from the defendant's handling of it while in custody. The government also claimed that they had recordings of Padilla talking with two codefendants, Adham Hassoun and Kifah Jayyousi, in allegedly coded conversations about planned terrorist acts, though Padilla participated in only a small minority of the recorded conversations. On August 22, 2007, a jury convicted him. During the sentencing phase of his trial, prosecutors tried unsuccessfully to include as evidence what they said was an al-Qaeda "graduation list" with Padilla's Muslim name on it. The judge questioned the form's validity and the prosecution's timing.

Details of Padilla's federal crimes remained unclear even after his conviction. His trial included no mention of a dirty bomb, despite Ashcroft's public statements of 2002. The government had said its information linking Padilla to a dirty bomb plot stemmed from interrogations of terrorism suspects overseas, but federal rules of evidence placed heavy restrictions on how such information could be used in court. In sentencing Padilla on January 22, 2008, to 17 years and four months, rather than to life in prison as the government wanted, U.S. District Judge Marcia Cooke said she considered the "harsh" conditions Padilla faced in the Navy brig. She also said she considered the fact that no evidence connected him to actual acts of terrorism or any plot to overthrow the U.S. government.

Critics of the government's handling of Padilla have argued that his original transfer to military custody owed less to specific circumstances of his case than to government frustrations in prosecuting terrorism cases through the court system. While federal authorities have claimed that battling terrorism in the public forum of a courtroom can hurt national security if sensitive evidence becomes public and confidentiality of informants is compromised, critics have answered that the convictions in Padilla's case showed that at least some terrorism suspects can be successfully prosecuted in the court system.

Jeff Diamant

Further Reading

Rumsfeld v. Padilla, 542 U.S. 426 (2004).

Sontag, Deborah. "Terror Suspects Path from Streets to Brig," *New York Times,* 25 April 2004, p. 1.

PATRIOT Act   See USA PATRIOT ACT.

Philadelphia, Pennsylvania

Philadelphia, Pennsylvania, played an important role in the growth of Islam in the United States throughout the 20th century. Like CLEVELAND, OHIO, it was one of the cities where Sunni Islam took root early among African Americans. In combination with other groups such as the MOORISH SCIENCE TEMPLE of America and the NATION OF ISLAM, these groups helped to make Philadelphia one of the most religiously diverse Muslim cities in the United States by the middle of the 20th century. That diversity only increased after the passage of the IMMIGRATION ACT OF 1965, as tens of thousands of Muslim immigrants from Asia and Africa came to make Philadelphia their new American home. By the 21st century, these immigrants, in combination with the large population of African-American Muslims, likely meant that Philadelphia became home to moer than 100,000 Muslim Americans.

MAJOR AMERICAN ISLAMIC MOVEMENTS SINCE THE EARLY TWENTIETH CENTURY

While the existence of Muslims in Philadelphia dates to the colonial era, when thousands of AFRICAN-AMERICAN MUSLIM SLAVES were transported to North America, there is scant documentation about the activities of such persons in the city. The story of Muslims in Philadelphia becomes clearer in the early 20th century, when African Americans in Philadelphia began to practice various forms of Islam, the growth of which eventually resulted in an entire street, Lancaster Avenue, becoming known as Philadelphia's Muslim Main Street.

Like other northern cities, Philadelphia became one of the destinations for the migration of 1.5 million southern black migrants who left the south between WORLD WAR I and WORLD WAR II. The "Great Migration," as it is called by many historians, resulted in an unprecedented period of religious and cultural activity among African Americans. Older religious institutions such as the Baptist and Methodist churches benefited from the influx of new residents, and new religious movements, including Muslim groups, also developed in this environment. Black religious institutions, no matter what their particular religious outlook, tended to address the whole person, offering economic, political, and social resources as well as religious doctrines and practices to people who were still the victims of legal and extralegal discrimination.

One of the new religious movements to take root in Philadelphia was the Moorish Science Temple (MST), founded in CHICAGO in 1925. Located at North Fifth Street, the Philadelphia chapter of the MST grew during the 1930s and 1940s. Though NOBLE DREW ALI, the founder of the movement, died in 1929, he remained the focus of the group's religious practices in the 1930s, when anthropologist Arthur Huff Fauset conducted research on the Philadelphia chapter for his groundbreaking *Black Gods of the Metropolis* (1944).

The only scholar to leave a detailed record of Moorish religious practice in this era, Fauset described Friday evening prayer services as quiet and contemplative. Though members did not sing lustily, they softly chanted a hymn called "Moslem's That Old Time Religion," using the tune of the Christian hymn, "Give Me That Old Time Religion." They recited parts of *The Holy Koran of the Moorish Science Temple of America,* a book published in 1927 by Ali and considered to be religious revelation by members. A male leader, often dressed in a fez or a turban, told them about the significance of their national origins in Morocco, the religion of Islam, and their great Asiatic (Asian) history in Canaan, Egypt, and North Africa. Participants then stretched out their arms in a salute and prayed: "Allah, Father of the Universe, the father of Love, Truth, Peace, Freedom, and Justice. Allah is my protector, my Guide, and my Salvation by night and by day, through His Holy Prophet, Drew Ali. Amen."

The Moorish Science Temple was not the only Muslim movement to become popular among African Americans in Philadelphia in this period. One of the unusual aspects of Muslim history in Philadelphia was the role the city played in spreading Sunni Islam among African Americans before 1945. The ADDEYNU ALLAHE UNIVERSAL ARABIC ASSOCIATION (AAUAA), formally established in 1938 in New York and New Jersey, quickly developed a presence in Philadelphia. Like the MST, the AAUAA taught that African Americans had an ethnic and racial connection to Islam (traced through the biblical figure of Ham). But unlike the MST, the AAUAA espoused a Sunni orientation. Founder MUHAMMAD EZALDEEN (1886–1957) lived in Philadelphia, and though it is not clear when, a chapter of AAUAA was founded there sometime in the late 1930s or early 1940s.

In 1943, Philadelphia also hosted what was one of the first national meetings of African-American Sunni Muslim groups in history. On August 18, Ezaldeen joined other leaders, including Cleveland's WALI AKRAM (1904–94) and Daoud Ahmed Faisal of NEW YORK CITY, to discuss their common goals and interests. The four-day meeting resulted in the formation of the Uniting Islamic Societies of America, an umbrella group that was supposed to further the coordination that had been initiated at the conference, but that effectively disbanded by 1946. Despite this national organization's lack of success, its mere formation indicated the extent to which Sunni Islam was growing among African Americans and also likely had ripples among Philadelphia's AFRICAN-AMERICAN MUSLIMS.

After World War II, Philadelphia saw the growth of still more Muslim groups. In addition to a local chapter of the Ahmadi Muslims, one of the first successful Muslim missionary groups among black Americans, the NATION OF ISLAM established a strong presence in Philadelphia. In 1954, MALCOLM X (1925–65), the foremost activist in the movement, came to Philadelphia to organize Temple No. 12, which later operated from 1319 West Susquehanna Avenue in North Philadelphia. The permanent leader appointed to lead the temple was W. D. MOHAMMED (1933–2008), the son of NOI leader ELIJAH MUHAMMAD (1897–1975). Mohammed, unlike many other ministers in the NOI, incorporated several teachings from the QUR'AN into his speeches and classes, anticipating the increased incorporation of Sunni Islamic texts and symbols among the NOI's intelligentsia in the 1960s and 1970s.

One sign of the temple's successful growth in Philadelphia was its hosting of two visits by Elijah Muhammad in 1960 and 1963, when thousands of people in Philadelphia gathered at 45th and Market Street to hear him speak. In the 1970s, five other temples opened in the city, referred to as Temple No. 12B, 12C, 12D, 12E, and 12F, with the headquarters being the temple on Susquehanna Avenue. In the 1970s, NOI members became known by Philadelphia's mainstream press for their economic and civic activities—both legal and illegal. On the one hand, the NOI staged highly successful three-day Muslim bazaars that offered tens of thousands Philadelphians the chance to purchase and exchange goods, see live performances, eat food, and hear political and religious speeches. In 1976, a year after W. D. Mohammed took over the NOI, local Muslims also opened a Sister CLARA MUHAMMAD School, a parochial school serving Muslim and non-Muslim children. On the other hand, some NOI members became known as the "black mafia," accused of dealing illegal drugs and shaking down merchants for protection money.

MUSLIM IMMIGRANTS AFTER 1965

One of the earliest Muslim immigrants in Philadelphia was Mohamed Ahmad, who arrived in Philadelphia from Palestine in 1908. Later, in the 1950s, he brought his son, family, cousins, and friends, who in turn established their own extended kinship network of Palestinians in Philadelphia. Such immigration was not unusual, though again, little is known about the activities of these early immigrants. After the passage of the Immigration Act of 1965, the presence and visibility of immigrant Muslims increased in Philadelphia.

Foremost among these immigrant Muslims was Imam Hatip Jemali, a pioneering leader who arrived in 1957 as a political exile from Yugoslavia, where he once served as a mayor of a small town near the Albanian border. Later obtaining U.S. citizenship, he brought his family to the United States in 1966. In 1974, he founded a mosque at 157 West Girard Avenue in order to meet the religious and cultural needs of the growing Muslim immigrant population. Gradually, the mosque became a center of the immigrant Muslim community and an important part of the national Albanian-American Muslim Society.

In 1986, Philadelphia's Muslim community was traumatized by the brutal murder of Muslim-American leader and Temple University professor Ismail al-Faruqi and his wife, Lamya, in their Cheltenham home. A leading figure in the establishment of several prominent Muslim-American institutions, including the INTERNATIONAL INSTITUTE OF ISLAMIC THOUGHT (IIIT), and an advocate of Palestinian nationalism, al-Faruqi had been warned by the Federal Bureau of Investigation (FBI) just a week before that his life may have been in danger due to his anti-Zionist politics. As rumors about the involvement of persons linked to the Jewish Defense League (JDL) in the murders spread among Arabs and Muslims in Philadelphia, the FBI said that the murders were the result of a botched robbery. More than 4,000 people attended al-Faruqi's funeral, held at Masjid Muhammad in West Philadelphia. The murders of al-Faruqi and his wife also led to a congressional hearing on hate crimes and terrorism waged against Muslims and Arab Americans.

In the face of this tragedy, many ARAB-AMERICAN MUSLIMS in Philadelphia adopted a two-tiered approach to their lives: attempting to preserve their communal solidarity while also reaching out to fellow residents of Philadelphia through civic engagement and interfaith dialogue. In 1989, Palestinian and other Arab-American Muslims built the Al-Aqsa Mosque at 1501 Germantown Avenue. Conducting prayers and sermons in ARABIC, the mosque has catered largely to first-generation Arab Americans. It has also attempted to develop outreach to other religious groups. By the beginning of the 21st century, participants in its Friday congregational PRAYER services numbered as many as 1,000 men, women, and children. The mosque also operated an Islamic bookstore, a Muslim grocery, and the Al-Aqsa Society, which worked to preserve the cultural and religious identity of Arab-American Muslims. In addition, it operated the Al-Aqsa Islamic Academy, a school with about 300 students in kindergarten through 12th grade.

The new wave of immigration after 1965 also led to the formation of Sufi communities in Philadelphia, including the BAWA MUHAIYADDEEN FELLOWSHIP. Sufi teacher M. R. Bawa Muhaiyaddeen arrived from Sri Lanka in 1971 and taught about Sufi practices such as DHIKR, the ritual remembrance of God, in the city until his death in 1986. In 1973, followers met at 5820 Overbrook Avenue; then in 1984, the Mosque of Sheikh M. R. Bawa Muhaiyaddeen was built in the same area. By the beginning of the 21st century, the group was estimated to have approximately 1,000 members and extended its reach from Philadelphia to other cities in the United States and abroad.

In addition, Philadelphia has become a home to the GÜLEN MOVEMENT, a Sufi-oriented group that emphasizes self-improvement and service. Led by Fethullah Gülen, who moved to the Pocono Mountains in northeastern Pennsylvania in 1999, the movement has established several organizations in Philadelphia, including the Philadelphia Dialogue Forum located at 700 Townshipline in Havertown, a suburb of Philadelphia approximately nine miles from the city center. Established in 2003, the forum maintains a membership consisting of hundreds of Turkish Muslim-American immigrants and students and offers activities such as an annual Ramadan interfaith dinner and interfaith trips to Turkey in order to foster dialogue between people of different faiths and backgrounds.

AFTER 9/11

In the aftermath of the terrorist attacks on SEPTEMBER 11, 2001, hate crimes and DISCRIMINATION against Muslim Americans in Philadelphia increased. In 2007, a local hotel worker was sentenced to eight months in a halfway house for writing a threatening note to her Arab-American boss that referenced the 9/11 attacks and said, "You and your kids will pay." The Philadelphia Police Department and the local office of the Federal Bureau of Investigation responded to increased threats by assisting the Al-Aqsa mosque and other Muslim institutions in increasing their security. When the so-called Fort Dix Six, all of whom lived and worked in or around Philadelphia, were arrested in 2007 for conspiring to kill U.S. soldiers at Fort Dix Army base in New Jersey, Philadelphia's Muslims worried about a potential backlash against them. Local Muslim leaders said that they had never seen the suspects and assured non-Muslims that intolerant and violent interpretations of Islam were unwelcome in Philadelphia.

Philadelphia's Muslims continued to reach out in the midst of these threats. In 2004, they organized the Interfaith Peace Walk in coordination with local religious leaders Rabbi Lynn Gottlieb and Imam Abdul Rauf Campus-Marquetti. In 2007, about 3,000 Muslims gathered to share their history, FOOD, and MUSIC during the annual Islamic Heritage Festival at Penn's Landing. The Al-Aqsa mosque has also served as an Election Day polling site and has hosted a number of forums for candidates for the Philadelphia City Council.

From its beginnings as a site for the early growth of Islam among African Americans to its more contemporary position as one of the largest and fastest growing Muslim cities in the country, Philadelphia has long been a site of Muslim diversity. Even when living in communities divided along racial and ethnic lines, Muslims in Philadelphia have sustained public lives that are deeply intertwined with those of non-Muslim residents. In business, EDUCATION, PHILANTHROPY, and other areas, Muslims in Philadelphia have contributed to the pluralistic spirit that is embodied in the city of brotherly love.

Heon C. Kim and Edward E. Curtis IV

Further Reading
Curtis, Edward E., IV. *Muslims in America: A Short History.* New York: Oxford University Press, 2009.

Fauset, Arthur Huff. *Black Gods of the Metropolis: Negro Religious Cults of the Urban North.* Philadelphia: University of Pennsylvania Press, 1944.

Haddad, Yvonne, ed. *The Muslims of America.* New York: Oxford University Press, 1991.

Haddad, Yvonne, and Jane Smith, eds. *Muslim Communities in North America.* Albany: State University of New York Press, 1994.

McCloud, Aminah Beverly. "This Is a Muslim Home." In *Making Muslim Space in North America and Europe,* edited by Barbara D. Metcalf, 65–73. Berkeley: University of California Press, 1996.

Padhdiwala, Tasneem. "The Aging of the Moors." *Chicago Reader* 37, no. 8 (November 15, 2007). Available online. URL:

http://www.chicagoreader.com/features/stories/moors/. Accessed May 5, 2009.

Shah, Tabassam, and Jeffrey Diamond. "The African-American Sunni Muslim Community of West Philadelphia: Institutional." Available online. URL: http://tyo.ca/islambank. community/modules.php?op=modload&name=News& file=article&sid=180. Accessed May 1, 2009.

philanthropy

Philanthropy has always been an important component of Muslim life, both in the United States and abroad. The very notion of giving is enshrined in the Islamic notion of *zakat*, a pillar of Islamic practice that requires Muslims to give a portion of their wealth to worthy causes. From the moment that AFRICAN-AMERICAN MUSLIM SLAVES arrived on American shores in the 16th and 17th centuries, Muslim Americans have contributed their energy and resources toward philanthropic endeavors in the Western Hemisphere. But the nature of Muslim-American philanthropy has changed dramatically since the colonial era. In the 20th century, Muslim-American philanthropy focused on a variety of activities. Muslim Americans contributed large sums of money and their own labor toward the building of MOSQUES AND ISLAMIC CENTERS, ISLAMIC SCHOOLS, and national organizations geared primarily toward serving the interests of the Muslim community. They also supported non-Muslim philanthropic organizations and developed social service institutions and charities that served Muslims and non-Muslims alike. In many ways, the Muslim-American experience, like the American experience overall, can be understood only through a close examination of its philanthropic elements. Philanthropy is an inextricable part of U.S. and Muslim-American history, since it has often been the object of people's greatest passions and voluntary commitments.

SLAVE TIMES

While philanthropy is generally understood to be a voluntary activity, the forced enslavement of Africans, including Muslims, is an important exception to this rule. Against their will, African-American slaves grew crops, tended animals, and contributed other forms of labor to the economic development first of American colonies and then to the United States. They also contributed to the success of the U.S. economy through the sharing of technical knowledge, teaching their owners and overseers how to cultivate rice or make dyes, for example. In addition, slaves themselves became chattel, a piece of property that was bought and sold, significantly increasing the net wealth of thousands of Americans who benefited from their purchase and sale.

Beyond this forced philanthropy, however, Muslim-American slaves practiced philanthropy as it is more commonly understood, voluntarily sharing their goods and labor with one another. The descendants of Muslim slaves on Sea Island, Georgia, recalled stories of their parents and grandparents about the celebration of certain West African holidays among the Muslim and non-Muslim slaves. During harvest festivals, African-American women would prepare sweet rice cakes called *saraka* or perhaps *sadaka,* an Islamic charitable gift that is not obligatory but is laudatory. One woman recalled that her grandmother would wash the rice to remove the starch, and then soak the rice in water overnight. She would then beat it into a paste, and add honey or sugar, forming this mixture into cakes. As the grandmother called the children to a table to partake of the sweets, she would bless the food by saying, *"Ameen, Ameen, Ameen,"* using the Arabic word for Amen.

In addition to serving one another through philanthropic activity, Muslim-American slaves were occasionally the beneficiaries of white philanthropy. The African-American Muslim slave community included several literate and highly educated Muslim scholars and students from West Africa who attracted the attention of slave owners, Christian missionaries, and journalists. For example, between 1731 and 1733, the Arabic letters of American slave JOB BEN SOLOMON, also known as Hyuba Boon Salumena Jallo, somehow came into the possession of James Oglethorpe, founder of the Georgia colony and a member of British Parliament. Oglethorpe purchased Job's bond, brought him to England, and toured him around British aristocratic circles. Job was eventually freed and offered a job for the Royal African Company in West Africa.

But perhaps the most successful fund-raiser among African-American Muslim slaves was ABDUL RAHMAN IBRAHIMA, who raised thousands of dollars to purchase the freedom not only of his wife but also of his eight children. Setting out on a national fund-raising tour in 1828, Ibrahima met some of the nation's most prominent white and black citizens during his tour. By 1829, after soliciting men such as abolitionist Arthur Tappan, philanthropist Thomas Gallaudet, Congressman Edward Everett, and writer David Walker, Ibrahima had raised the necessary funds to free his family and set sail for Liberia, the American colony of freed African Americans in West Africa.

FROM 1900 TO 1965: BUILDING MUSLIM INSTITUTIONS

No serious institution-building by Muslims occurred until the first two decades of the 20th century. During this era, many Muslims, who largely identified with one another based not on religion but on race or ethnicity, began to establish places of worship, cemeteries, and mutual aid societies. These organizations were essential to the development of Muslim-American religious identity but were often as focused on social networking, economic development, and political activism as they were on religious practice. In CHICAGO, for example, Bosnian-American Muslims created a mutual aid society around 1906. They helped pay each other's medical bills, celebrated Muslim holidays, purchased a Muslim cemetery, and drank lots of Turkish coffee together. In Michigan City, Indiana, ARAB-AMERICAN MUSLIMS created a group in 1907 that by 1924 was known as the Modern Age Arabian Islamic Society. In CEDAR RAPIDS, IOWA, Muslims rented space for communal gatherings and prayers in 1925 and built their own mosque in 1934.

In Seattle, Washington, some Druze Muslims, a Middle Eastern religious community seen as heretical by most Sunni Muslims, created the "First Fruit of the Druze," a group that had chapters around North America by the 1920s. In DETROIT, two Syrian immigrant brothers, Muhammad and Hussein Karoub, created a Sunni mosque in 1921. In nearby Dearborn, near the southeast corner of town where Ford Motor Company developed its gigantic Rouge plant, immigrants also established a Shi'a mosque called the Hashemite Hall.

African-American Muslims also established various mosques and Muslim organizations during this period. In 1925, NOBLE DREW ALI formed the MOORISH SCIENCE TEMPLE of America in Chicago, and in 1930, W. D. FARD created the NATION OF ISLAM in Detroit. Both of these organizations were missionary movements that hoped to bring black Americans back to what they argued was their original religion of Islam. But they were also political, economic, and social organizations that stimulated black entrepreneurship, increased the political clout of African Americans, defended African Americans against police violence, rehabilitated ex-convicts, and encouraged black solidarity. Though many immigrant Muslims later criticized these movements as unorthodox, they were the first Muslim philanthropic organizations that were national in scope. During the 1920s and 1930s, several Sunni Muslim mosques also took root in black America, though these communities were not able to develop a national network until after WORLD WAR II.

In the postwar period, both indigenous and immigrant Muslim movements and organizations grew at a much quicker rate. Muslim Americans continued to form groups along ethnic, racial, and national lines, but they also united to create pan-ethnic and even pan-racial Muslim-American organizations. Most prominent among them were the Nation of Islam; the FEDERATION OF ISLAMIC ASSOCIATIONS IN THE UNITED STATES AND CANADA, created in 1952; and the MUSLIM STUDENTS ASSOCIATION (MSA), established in 1963. Such internal institution-building bore fruit after 1965, when South Asian, Arab, and other immigrants used their philanthropic resources to contribute equally to Muslim-American and non-Muslim causes.

1965–PRESENT: A PHILANTHROPIC FLOWERING

The IMMIGRATION ACT OF 1965 and the continued proliferation of indigenous Muslim groups, especially African Americans, resulted in exponential growth, not only of the Muslim-American community, but also of mosques, schools, advocacy groups, charities, and other Muslim-American philanthropic causes. In 1971, Pakistani Americans with strong ties to the Jamaat-i Islami party of Pakistan established the ISLAMIC CIRCLE OF NORTH AMERICA. In 1982, major Muslim organizations including the Muslim Students Association formed the ISLAMIC SOCIETY OF NORTH AMERICA. In 1992, mostly Arabic-speaking leaders from the MSA and the Islamic Society of North America then established the MUSLIM AMERICAN SOCIETY. During this period, philanthropy was also directed toward the establishment of advocacy groups that defended Muslim rights and the image of Islam. Since 1990, a number of such organizations have also been established, including the COUNCIL ON AMERICAN-ISLAMIC RELATIONS (probably the largest with over 32 chapters), the MUSLIM PUBLIC AFFAIRS COUNCIL, MAS Freedom Foundation, and the AMERICAN MUSLIM ALLIANCE. This list does not include many smaller regional or local public advocacy organizations that have been established by Muslims.

Muslim-American mosques and other Muslim-American organizations addressed a growing number of social concerns, including domestic violence, education, poverty, homelessness, interfaith outreach, and media relations. According to a 2001 survey published by the Council on American-Islamic Relations, mosques serve as important conduits of philanthropy among Muslim Americans. Eighty-four percent of mosques were reported to give cash assistance to families or individuals; 74 percent provided counseling services; 60 percent had prison or jail programs; 55 percent had a food pantry, a soup kitchen, or collection of food for the poor; 53 percent had a thrift store or collected clothes for the poor; 28 percent had a tutoring or literacy program; 18 percent had an antidrug or anticrime program; 16 percent had a daycare or preschool program; and 12 percent had a substance abuse program.

In addition, nearly every college campus with a Muslim population has established a Muslim Students Association. YOUTH groups such as the Interfaith Youth Core in Chicago have encouraged high school and middle school youth to be more involved with civic engagement and to volunteer their time to service projects that benefit all Americans. Professional associations such as the National Association of Muslim Lawyers, Islamic Medical Association of North America, American Muslim Social Scientists, Islamic Social Services Association, Association of Muslim Mental Health Professionals, and American Muslim Scientists and Engineers ask for Muslim support in exchange for amplifying Muslim voices in the public sphere. Finally, Muslim Americans have established at least 12 major Muslim relief organizations in the United States that raise money to be spent on relief projects primarily in the Muslim world. These organizations reported raising more than $93 million in 2006.

Muslim Americans have also rallied around national or international calls for philanthropy. For example, in response to Hurricane Katrina and the 2005 Pakistani earthquake, major Muslim-American organizations raised $10 million for Katrina victims and at least $20 million for earthquake victims. These numbers include only direct financial assistance, not the countless voluntary hours spent at the mosque, community, and individual levels to aid victims of these disasters.

One poll conducted by the Zogby organization asked Muslim Americans if they were involved in various kinds of civic engagement. They defined "involved" as having donated time or money or having served as an officer of an organization. Seventy-seven percent reported being involved with organizations that help the poor, sick, elderly, or homeless; 71 percent volunteered for a mosque or religious organization; 69 percent served a school or youth program; 46 percent volunteered for a professional organization; 45 percent served a neighborhood, civic, or community group; and 42 percent helped an arts or cultural group.

Another poll reported on Muslim-American attitudes toward philanthropy. Seventy-six percent expressed the belief that making charitable contributions or giving *zakat* was very important; an additional 14 percent stated that it was somewhat important; and only 8 percent stated that it

was not too important or not at all important. When ranking the Islamic religious activities in order of importance, *zakat* was second only to fasting. Muslim Americans said that giving to worthy causes was more important than performing the pilgrimage to Mecca, reading the QUR'AN daily, or performing daily prayers.

According to scholar Adil Najam, Pakistani Americans, most of whom are Muslims, may be among the most philanthropic people in the United States. Approximately 500,000 Pakistani Americans donate more than $250 million in cash and kind on an annual basis. In addition, they contribute more than 43 million hours to volunteer work—which roughly translates into $750 million of labor. Of this giving, 40 percent goes to charities in Pakistan, while an additional 20 percent goes to Pakistani causes in this country. Forty percent is donated to causes that have no connection to Pakistan. The most striking finding, however, was that Pakistani Americans give 3.5 percent of their estimated household income to charity, whereas the national average in the United States is 3.1 percent.

AFTER 9/11

In the wake of the attacks of SEPTEMBER 11, 2001, the U.S. government launched a number of raids on high-profile Muslim-American charities on the suspicion that they had ties to terrorism. While such raids yielded no information about Muslim-American links to al-Qaeda or the 9/11 attackers—at least no information that the Federal Bureau of Investigation was willing to make public—they did lead to prosecutions of a small number of Muslim-American charities on other grounds. In December 2001, for example, President George W. Bush named the Holy Land Foundation of Richardson, Texas, as a specially designated terrorist organization. Its assets were frozen and the charity was shut down.

On July 24, 2004, U.S. Attorney General John Ashcroft announced that a grand jury in Dallas had indicted the Holy Land Foundation on 42 different counts related to the support of terrorism. "Today," Ashcroft said, "a U.S.-based charity, that claims to do good works, is charged with funding works of evil." Noting that the government's investigation would have been "difficult, if not impossible" without the new surveillance powers granted by the USA PATRIOT ACT, Ashcroft explained that the foundation had violated the law by contributing $12.4 million to Hamas, the Palestinian political party responsible both for providing social services to Palestinians and for conducting deadly attacks against Israeli civilians.

Three years later, in July 2007, in what the *Dallas Morning News* called the "biggest terrorist finance trial in history," the trial of Holy Land Foundation officials began. There were a total of 197 charges against them.

Hoori Sadler raised more than $700,000 for the University Muslim Medical Association (UMMA) Clinic in South Central Los Angeles, which began to offer free medical services to those in need in 1996. She is pictured here with Muslim-American comic Maz Jobrani. *(David Livingston/Getty Images)*

During the trial, the government admitted that the Holy Land Foundation had not directly funded suicide bombers but argued that the support of Hamas's charitable activities (including the building of hospitals and feeding of the poor) amounted to material support of a terrorist group. In October, the jury rendered its verdicts. Despite some convictions on minor charges, the jurors either acquitted the defendants or deadlocked on the major counts of the indictment. On these counts, the judge declared a mistrial. But on November 23, 2008, after retrying the case, federal prosecutors achieved a different result. Five Holy Land Foundation officials were found guilty of 108 criminal counts related to tax fraud, money laundering, and the support of terrorism.

As the Holy Land Foundation's lawyers planned their appeal, some critics of the government's prosecution of Muslim-American charities pointed out that no conviction related to the terrorist attacks of 9/11 had yet been obtained. The Department of Justice, they said, was casting an overly wide net in its attempt to convict and root out terrorists. In 2007, the American Civil Liberties Union filed a lawsuit against the department on behalf of the largest Muslim-American nonprofit group, the Islamic Society of North America, claiming that the government had damaged its reputation by listing it as an "un-indicted co-conspirator" in one of its cases.

The effect of the government's action on Muslim-American philanthropy was unclear. At the start of Ramadan in 2004, U.S. Secretary of the Treasury John W. Snow issued a "Ramadan" statement, cautioning Muslims against giving to questionable groups: "When you open your hearts to charity during Ramadan, we encourage you to educate yourself on the activities of the charities to which you donate, to help ensure that your generosity is not exploited for nefarious purposes." He noted that it was a crime to support any of the 27 groups designated by the U.S. government as supporting terrorism. In response, Muslim-American philanthropists expressed anxiety about donating to any foreign Muslim causes.

Remittances sent to family and associates in Muslim-majority countries seemed to have declined. In 2001, of the top 20 countries receiving remittances from people in the United States, eight of them—Morocco, Egypt, Turkey, Lebanon, Bangladesh, Jordan, Yemen, and Pakistan—were Muslim-majority countries, while three additional countries—India, the former Yugoslavia, and Sri Lanka—have significant Muslim populations. By 2007, though India was rated as the top recipient of remittances from the United States, not one Muslim-majority country remained on the list.

At the same time, individual donations reported by Muslim-American relief organizations showed growth.

While the events of 9/11 introduced anxiety among Muslim Americans about giving to Muslim causes abroad, they hardly dampened the enthusiasm of Muslim Americans for philanthropy overall. Muslim Americans continued to develop their own institutions, contributed to an increasing number of non-Muslim causes, and became even more central to American society. Such enthusiasm expressed the spirit of a Muslim-American past defined by giving.

Muslim Americans have given their minds and bodies to the building of America from its very beginning. Despite the fact that Muslim slaves were forced to do so, their contributions were nonetheless important to the nation's development. In the 20th century, Muslim Americans built institutions that served their own interests and contributed to the social and cultural diversity of the United States. Finally, in the post-9/11 world, governmental suspicions of Muslim-American charities challenged all Americans to face important questions about the meaning of being American in an era fraught with insecurity and even hope that Muslim-American philanthropists might offer a bridge between the United States and the Muslim world.

Edward E. Curtis IV and Shariq A. Siddiqui

Further Reading

Bagby, Ihsan, Paul M. Perl, and Bryan T. Froehle. *The Mosque in America: A National Portrait.* Washington, D.C.: Council on American-Islamic Relations, 2001.

Burlingame, Dwight. *Philanthropy in America: A Comprehensive Historical Encyclopedia.* Santa Barbara, Calif.: ABC-CLIO, 2004.

Curtis, Edward E., IV, ed. *The Columbia Sourcebook of Muslims in the United States.* New York: Columbia University Press, 2008.

———. *Muslims in America: A Religious History.* New York: Oxford University Press, 2009.

Diouf, Sylviane A. *Servants of Allah: African Muslims Enslaved in the Americas.* New York: New York University Press, 1998.

Eaton, Leslie. "No Conviction in Trial against Muslim Charity," *New York Times.* 22 October 2007.

Leonard, Karen Isaksen. *Muslims in the United States: The State of Research.* New York: Russell Sage, 2003.

McChesney, Robert D. *Charity and Philanthropy in Islam: Institutionalizing the Call to Do Good.* Bloomington and Indianapolis, Ind.: IU Center on Philanthropy, 1995.

Nyang, Sulayman. *Islam in the United States of America.* Chicago: Kazi Publications, Chicago, 1999.

Pew Research Center. *Muslim Americans: Middle Class and Mostly Mainstream.* Washington, D.C.: Pew Research Center, 2007.

Smith, Jane I. *Islam in America.* New York: Columbia University Press, 1999.

Zogby International. *Muslims in the American Public Square.* Washington, D.C.: Zogby International, 2001.
———. *Report on Muslims in the American Marketplace.* Washington, D.C.: Zogby International, 2001.

PIEDAD (Propagación Islámica para la Educación de Devoción a Ala' el Divino)

Founded in 1988 in New York by Khadijah Rivera, PIEDAD became the first Latina Muslim organization dedicated to Latina converts in the United States. PIEDAD stands for Propagación Islámica para la Educación de Devoción a Ala' el Divino (Islamic Propagation for the Education on the Devotion of Allah the Divine). Rivera started this organization to help non-Muslim Latinas married to Muslims understand Islamic culture better. While one of its initial tasks was the development of missionary activities for Latinas in the United States, PIEDAD also established programs to help women converts and non-Muslims address the issues related to marriage, FOOD preparation, and dealing with other family members that were suspicious about Islam.

As a volunteer-based organization, PIEDAD sought the help of other Muslim-American leaders and organizations in creating its programs and activities. Since its founding, it has developed programs and seminars for the International Islamic Federation of Student Organizations (IIFSO), established five toll-free nationwide phone lines to guide people to local *masjids,* and distributed free literature about Islam.

By 2009, PIEDAD had five chapters and 300 members around the country. Rivera has presided over the organization since its founding, supported in her work by Jill Finney, a white Muslim convert, who has also served as vice president. PIEDAD has continued to engage in missionary activities, though their main task has become aiding new converts with the transition into a Muslim lifestyle. PIEDAD members often consult with one another on everyday concerns such as how to DRESS, to strengthen their marriages, and to raise their children. The Tampa chapter, for example, meets once a month in one of the members' houses to pray, to hear presentations, and to have informal discussions.

Like other U.S. Latina/o Muslim groups such as LADO (LATINO AMERICAN DAWAH ORGANIZATION), PIEDAD performs community service in addition to cooperating with other local Muslim groups. For fund-raisers, they have sold T-shirts, handmade ponchos, and handbags. LADO members have translated and proofread literature about the QUR'AN as part of their commitment to teach about Islam, especially to other Latina/os in the United States. They have also encouraged Muslim-American imams, or religious leaders, to learn Spanish so that they can better serve all Muslim Americans.

Hjamil A. Martínez-Vázquez

Further Reading
Day, Sherri. "America's Muslim Population is Gaining a Hispanic Accent," *St. Petersburg Times,* 9 February 2008.
Rivera, Khadijah. "Empowering Latino Women." *Islamic Horizons* (July/August 2002): 37–38.

pilgrimage   See HAJJ.

poetry

Muslim-American poetry is multiethnic, multicultural, multilingual, and multiracial, and its history reveals how Muslims reacted to racism and slavery, demanded civil rights, remembered war-torn homelands and stranded families, and reflected on their RELIGIOUS LIFE amid the ebbs and flows of adversity and ease. Like other American poetry, Muslim-American poetry has been published in collections and periodicals but has also been performed in front of friends, family, and broader live audiences. These varying ways of being poetic have revealed diverse snapshots of Muslim-American life. While Muslim Americans have been making poetry since the first AFRICAN-AMERICAN MUSLIM SLAVES arrived in the colonial era, Muslim-American poets in the late 20th and early 21st centuries have contributed to what poet and scholar Mohja Kahf sees as an emerging and identifiable corpus of explicitly Muslim-American poetry. Though no anthology of Muslim-American poetry had yet been produced by 2009, the work of Muslim-American poets could be found in collections of their own work, poetry journals, Muslim periodicals, and in anthologies of African-American, ethnic, and multicultural literature.

MUSLIM-AMERICAN POETRY: 1900–1960
Since the emergence of Islam in the seventh century, poetry in Muslim cultures has been a vital mode of social communication, expression, criticism, and exploration. This literary genre, created and performed in oral and written forms, was used to chronicle history, teach Arabic grammar, entertain, romance, and inspire. Vibrant vernacular traditions developed alongside literary ones as Islam spread from Arabia to Persia, North Africa, and Spain and later to South Asia, Indonesia, and southern Africa, expanding a poetic repertoire rooted in pre-Islamic Arabia and the QUR'AN to include imagery, symbolism, and metaphor from every new land. These poetic traditions came to the Americas with the African-American Muslim slaves who arrived from the 17th to 19th centuries and with immigrants from the Balkans, the Near and Middle East, South Asia, and Africa during the 19th and 20th centuries, though little evidence has yet emerged of the perpetuation or adaptation of such traditions in the Americas.

It was not until the formation of early 20th century Muslim organizations that Muslim-American poets begin to appear regularly in print. Small communities of Polish, Russian, and Lithuanian Muslims in New York, Albanian Muslims in Maine, and others in the Midwest and California may have been writing or reciting poetry, but the earliest examples of Muslim-American poetry are found in the newspapers widely distributed in the 1920s by the Ahmadiyya movement and the MOORISH SCIENCE TEMPLE of America (MST). The *Moorish Voice,* the MST's primary publication, featured the work of male and female poets whose poems weave their tales of conversion and their penchant for racial justice into one solitary poetic expression. These poems provided the vernacular seeds of a determined and brutally honest verse that flowered decades later in the powerful poetry of the Black Arts Movement of the 1960s and 1970s. One poem by Sister Garret Bey published in February 1943 illustrates the changing meaning of race in the United States. Written during WORLD WAR II, the poem hails a future that is unencumbered by racial identity: "Time was, we thought in terms of race / . . . Now round the world our lads have gone / to set all people free / and everything they look upon / shows how deceived were we."

Another venue for the publication of Muslim-American poetry in the first half of the 20th century was the *MUSLIM SUNRISE,* the newspaper of AHMADI MUSLIM AMERICANS. After Muhammad Sadiq arrived in Chicago in 1920 from India as a missionary for the Ahmadiyya movement, he founded the periodical in order to refute misrepresentations of Islam and carry his mission's multiracial message to an eager and mostly African-American audience. The editors of the *Muslim Sunrise* printed translations of Urdu, Persian, and Arabic poetry written by Ghulam Ahmad (1835–1908), the founder of the Ahmadiyya movement, creating a direct link between the South Asian and Arabic poetic tradition and new Muslim Americans.

Traditional styles of *ghazal* (lyric) and *qasida* (panegyric, or praise) poetry were represented, including Muslim imagery of the soul being drawn to God like a moth to a flame and Muslim themes of God as desirous love and God's followers as persons intoxicated with the love of God. Alongside selections of Islamic classical poetry and some secular poetry, vernacular poets from all levels of the movement contributed poems using free verse and rhymed verse. These poems included reflections on the Qur'an, prayer, and conversion and often addressed such religious topics from a political angle. Ahmadi Muslim-American poets were also reading other classical material as a Mrs. Garber from New York City indicated in her poem entitled "The Beauties of Islam." Published in the October 1921 issue of the *Muslim Sunrise,* it concludes with two lines of the well-known 11th-century Muslim mystic and theologian al-Ghazali.

Other major influences on Muslim-American poetry were the *mahjar* (émigré) poets, also known as the New York Pen League (*al-Rabita al-Qalamiyah*), from Syria and Lebanon, and the free (verse) poetry movement in the Muslim Middle East. The Pen League Poets were Christian-Arab immigrants who embraced the free verse of Walt Whitman and American Romanticism, giving new life to Arabic poetry, but whose Arabic work contained substantial Muslim imagery and metaphor. Later Arab-Muslim poets like Adonis, Mahmoud Darwish, and Nazik al-Malaika would also influence Arab-American poets with their modern Arabic poetry that differed from classical verse in content and style and in structure and rhyme.

THE NATION OF ISLAM AND THE BLACK ARTS MOVEMENT

MUHAMMAD SPEAKS, the weekly newspaper of the NATION OF ISLAM founded in 1961, became another major outlet for Muslim-American poetry in the 1960s. Its editors published NOI members' poetry amid coverage of international and domestic current events, vivid political cartoons, and the messages of NOI leader ELIJAH MUHAMMAD. These poets used free and rhymed verse with some poetic prose to illustrate their Islamic religious imagination and hope in a time rife with racial violence and turmoil. Children also were encouraged to write and publish in the newspaper.

Among these poets was Sonia Sanchez, also known as Laila Mannan (1934–   ). Sanchez maintained a regular column of poetry in *Muhammad Speaks* called New Frontiers and published two independent collections of her own poetry during her three years in the NOI from 1972 to 1975. She had known MALCOLM X in New York and was influenced poetically by his oratorical style. Her poetry directly referenced the NOI, Allah, and Islam as viable responses to the cruel and difficult social realities she witnessed. She was active in the Black Arts Movement (BAM) established by poet, playwright, and NOI member AMIRI BARAKA (LeRoi Jones).

Though poetry ceased to have the same place in the NOI after the death of Elijah Muhammad in 1975, the practice of poetry as an art of liberation was perpetuated by individuals such as Marvin X. Another NOI poet and cofounder of BAM, Marvin X wrote poems addressing systemic poverty and disproportionate incarcerations of African Americans in the United States. Later, he also cited the poetry and teachings of 13th-century Persian Sufi poet Jalaluddin Rumi and the Sri Lankan–American Sufi Bawa Muhaiyaddeen as influential on his poetry.

LATE TWENTIETH- AND EARLY TWENTY-FIRST-CENTURY IMMIGRANT POETRY

The poetry of ARAB-AMERICAN MUSLIMS after 1965, when the IMMIGRATION ACT OF 1965 opened the doors to increased numbers of immigrants, documented stories of forced emigration and war, meditating on life as a refugee or an exile. But it also addressed other aspects of Arab-American and American life. Indiana-born poet H. S. Hamod (1936–), for example, penned an elegiac poem on musician Joe Williams and others on the politics of innocents in Iraq and Palestine. The poets of this era, including Etel Adnan (1925–), Fawaz Turki (1940–), and Elmaz Abinader (1954–), wrote primarily in free verse, sometimes referring to Muslim life and politics with nostalgia and at other times expressing an impatience with a lack of social and cultural reform in Middle Eastern societies.

Younger-generation poets of this era include Syrian-American Mohja Kahf (1967–), who has written with humor about the cultural contact between Muslim religious life and American secular culture. She has been a contributor to *Azizah*, a Muslim-American women's magazine that features a section of poetry in each issue.

Arab-American Muslim poets with ties to countries other than the United States have written insightfully into the complexities of being people betwixt and between their various homelands. Libyan-American Khaled Mattawa (1964–) and Palestinian-American SUHEIR HAMMAD (1973–), for example, have both reflected about their homelands' plight and the realities of having a multiple identity in the 21st century. Critical of UNITED STATES FOREIGN RELATIONS in the Middle East, their writing, like that of many other Muslim poets, has provided a perspective into the human quality of the life, dreams, and habits of Muslims.

SOUTH ASIAN–AMERICAN MUSLIMS have also been vital contributors to the lively Muslim-American poetry scene of the late 20th and early 21st centuries. Some of the poets have sought inspiration in vernacular poetic forms and languages from Pakistan, Bangladesh, Afghanistan, India, and Sri Lanka. Agha Shahid Ali (1949–2001), a Kashmiri-American poet, focused much of his work on *ghazal* poetry and published several volumes in English. The *ghazal* is a sixth-century pre-Islamic Arabic poetic form of rhyming couplets and a refrain that entered South Asia with Persian-speaking Muslims. It is written in Persian, Arabic, and Urdu. The *ghazal* has been attractive to Westerners for over a century, and although its traditional subjects of pain, separation, and love were more or less maintained, its form had been highly compromised for free verse. Agha Shahid Ali's work in English was instrumental in returning the *ghazal* back to its traditional form. His poetry used the *ghazal* to weave together his American social and natural landscape with his Muslim poetic consciousness.

In contrast, Indian-American Muslim Saleem Peeradina has not used traditional forms of poetry, instead writing in free verse replete with the imagery and metaphors of India. His poetry is not nostalgic but rather captures moments in the cross-cultural transformation of a South Asian man, husband, and father in America. Gender has been a vital area of poetic expression for South Asian–American men and women, and women's poetry is replete with the frustration, humor, and triumph that accompany their life stories. South Asian–Muslim Americans have charted the triumphs and trials of being a Muslim woman, mother, daughter, or sister in the United States.

Political events, sexuality, and social conditions have also been frequent topics as Tehmina Khan's poetic critiques of UNITED STATES MILITARY action in Iraq have demonstrated.

Iranian-American Muslims have comprised another significant ethnic group contributing to Muslim-American poetry. While Arabic holds poetic stature among Muslims, second to this, if only in deference to the language of the Qur'an, must be Persian poetry. Majid Naficy (1952–) published his first book of poetry in Persian in 1969. He was active in the revolution against the Shah but suffered under the Islamic revolution, when its leaders abandoned many of their leftist allies once they had consolidated power. He has continued to publish poetry in the United States as an Iranian exile and is intimately connected with Iranian-American poets through workshops and readings.

The Iranian Revolution of 1979 has left its mark on much of Iranian-American poetry though classical imagery; the scents of persimmon, jasmine, and roses have remained central as well. Poet Persis Karim's anthology of diaspora Iranian women writers contains a rich collection of Muslim-American poetry with Persian themes interpreting an American social landscape. Karim's poetry has lamented the innocent casualties of the war in Iraq and questions the patriarchal implementations and interpretations of Islamic law.

PERFORMANCE POETRY AND SUFISM

Iranian-American Haale Gafori grew up in the Bronx, New York, and has weaved classical and modern Persian poetry, including the works of Attar, Rumi, and Hafez, into English verse during musical performances. Gafori has also published her poetry, which also exhibits the influence of SUFISM, the mystical branch of Islam.

For some Muslim poets, jazz and blues music has emerged as a primary medium in which to express their poetic sensibilities. While a variety of wind, string, and percussive instruments have accompanied Muslim poetry for centuries, contemporary performances of classical and modern Sufi poetry have also adopted electric instruments and contemporary beats to accompany their rhythmical free verse. The roots of modern HIP-HOP and spoken-word performance have been located by some in the 1960s Muslim poet/musician group the Last Poets, who emerged out of a Harlem writers group. Still a vital part of the hip-hop poetry genre, NOI members have been joined by increasing numbers of Sunni and Shi'ai poets who have performed at open mics, poetry slams, and spoken-word gatherings. Artists Amir Sulaiman and Brother Dash, whose performances have attracted large audiences, often offer popular commentary on the Qur'an and critical social commentary. Calligraphy of Thought, a Muslim poetry collective in Oakland, California, has met for open mics, regularly providing a venue for young Muslims to express and listen to Muslim social, political, and spiritual concerns. These poets have challenged public stereotypes and religious dogmatism found in their own Muslim communities. While diverse, the group has included Cathy Espinoza, one of a growing number of LATINO/A MUSLIM AMERICANS.

WHITE MUSLIM AMERICANS have also been vital contributors to Muslim-American poetry, and none has had a larger impact than performance artist Daniel Abdal-Hayy Moore (1940–), who published his first book of poetry before his conversion to Islam in 1970. His poetry has included reflections on the Vietnam War, Muslim life, and Qur'anic verse and has itself been situated within an Islamic cosmology. Moore, like many other Muslim poets, also writes poetry containing no specific Islamic references.

Foreign Sufi groups have also introduced Americans to poetic traditions in Turkish, Urdu, Swahili, and Persian, and Sufi Muslim Americans have performed classical Sufi poetry during their DHIKR ceremonies. Among them are followers of the MEVLEVI SUFI ORDER, or so-called whirling dervishes, whose ritual dance incorporates both music and poetry. In addition, the BEKTASHI SUFI ORDER, whose headquarters is located in greater Detroit, has been reciting poetry as part of its religious practices since the 1950s.

CONCLUSION

Muslim-American poetry began with a distinctly African-American tone that then absorbed a complex immigrant narrative from the Middle East, South Asia, and Africa. These immigrants, who introduced new languages and cultural imagery into Muslim-American poetry, arrived voluntarily, but would often share the penchant for justice and political consciousness of African Americans. The history of Muslim-American poetry illustrates the struggles of Muslim Americans to combat racial discrimination, deal with the contradictory pressures of ASSIMILATION and alienation, and find religious meaning in their lives. This focus on particular concerns simultaneously raises universal concerns with love and loss, violence and peace, and the often absurd conditions of modern life. Muslim-American poetry is composed in a variety of poetic forms including rhymed and free verse, and it can be written or oral, and performed with music. Muslim-American poets can serve as carriers and transformers of religious tradition, radical social commentators, or pure entertainers.

Melinda Krokus

Further Reading

Afzal-Khan, Fawzia, ed. *Shattering the Stereotypes: Muslim Women Speak Out.* Northampton, Mass.: Olive Branch Press, 2005.

Ali, Agha Shahid. *Call Me Ishmael Tonight: A Book of Ghazals.* New York: W. W. Norton, 2003.

———. *Rooms Are Never Finished.* New York: W. W. Norton, 2002.

Ali, Agha Shahid, ed. *Ravishing DisUnities: Real Ghazals in English.* Hanover, N.H.: University Press of New England, 2000.

Ansari, Tiel Aisha. *Knocking from Inside.* Philadelphia: The Ecstatic Exchange, 2008.

Charara, Hayan. *Inclined to Speak: An Anthology of Contemporary Arab American Poetry.* Fayetteville: University of Arkansas Press, 2008.

Darraj, Susan Muaddi, ed. *Scheherazade's Legacy: Arab and Arab American Women on Writing.* Westport, Conn.: Praeger, 2004.

Delgado, Linda, et al. *Many Voices, One Faith: Islamic Writer's Alliance Anthology 1.* Heliographica Press, 2004.

Gillan, Maria Mazziotti, and Jennifer Gillan, eds. *Unsettling America: An Anthology of Contemporary Multicultural Poetry.* New York: Penguin, 1994.

Jubran, Sulaiman. "Classical Elements in *Mahjar* Poetry." *Journal of Arabic Literature* 38, no. 1 (2007): 67–77.

Karim, Persis. *Let Me Tell You Where I've Been: New Writing by Women of the Iranian Diaspora.* Fayetteville: University of Arkansas Press, 2006.

Moore, Daniel Abdal-Hayy. *Burnt Heart/Ode to the War Dead.* San Francisco: City Lights Books, 1971.

———. *The Chronicles of Akhira.* Santa Barbara, Calif.: Zilzal Press, 1986.

———. *The Ramadan Sonnets Long Days on Earth: Book V.* San Francisco: City Light Books, 1996.

Orfalea, Gregory, and Sharif Elmusa. *Grape Leaves: A Century of Arab American Poetry.* Salt Lake City: University of Utah Press, 1988.

Rustomji-Kerns, Roshni. *Living in America: Poetry and Fiction by South Asian American Writers.* Boulder, Colo.: Westview, 1995.

Sanchez, Sonia. *A Blues Book for Blue Black Magical Women.* Detroit, Mich.: Broadside Press, 1974.

———. *Love Poems.* New York: Third Press, 1973.

Srikanth, Rajini. *The World Next Door: South Asian American Literature and the Idea of America.* Philadelphia: Temple University Press, 2004.

Women of South Asian Descent Collective, eds. *Our Feet Walk the Sky: Women of the South Asian Diaspora.* San Francisco: Aunt Lute Books, 1993.

Internet Web Sites

www.iranian.com

www.iranianamericanwriters.org

www.islamicwritersalliance.net
www.muslimahwritersalliance.com
www.muslimhiphop.com
www.rawi.org/CMS/ Radius of Arab American Writers Inc.

Journals
MELA: Multiethnic Literatures of America
MELUS: Multiethnic Literatures of the United States
Mizna: Prose, Poetry, and Art Exploring Arab America

Poems of Daniel Abdal-Hayy Moore

Muslim-American poet Daniel Abdal-Hayy Moore (1940–   ), a native of Oakland, California, published his first book of poems, Dawn Visions (1964), before his conversion to Sufism, the mystical branch of Islam, in 1970. As a participant in the lively arts scene in Berkeley, the home of the University of California, Moore also established and directed the Floating Lotus Magic Opera Company. In 1972, he performed the pilgrimage to Mecca, one of the five pillars of Islamic practice, and, during the 1970s, traveled and lived in Morocco, Spain, Algeria, and Nigeria. In 1990, he moved to Philadelphia, where he continued his writing and editing of poetry. In a career that has spanned over four decades, he has written more than 50 collections of poetry. The excerpts from this body of work reprinted below include "Abdallah Jones—Takes the Antique Seller's Advice," the first chapter of Abdallah Jones and the Disappearing-Dust Cape, *an extended poem written for children and the young at heart in the early 1980s but published in 2006; "A Thousand Armies," a poem written in 2003 but published in 2006 during the Iraq War; and "The Heart Has Reason to Believe," a poem written in 2008 on the occasion of Barack Obama's election to the presidency.*

❖

Chapter 1: Abdallah Jones—Takes the Antique Seller's Advice (2006)

Abdallah Jones jumped off the train as it drew near
   the
      trestle with the glass ball of disappearing dust in
      his hand
which he had just snatched from the evil magi-
   cian who
      drew strange symbols on a tray of sand
preparing to make all the people in the world
disappear!
Abdallah had been trying to get into his castle for a
   whole year,
   finding out all he could, disguising himself as an
      idiot
      beggar in the marketplace,

standing close to the Caliph's horse when it went
   on
      parades, keeping an expressionless face
as the dust rose around him, trying to get clues.

Finally he found out, in a back-room antique
   shop,
      from one of those sinister marketplace sellers who
      sits in a broken-down chair and just chews,
the whereabouts of the Sorcerer's castle.

"But you cannot go alone, my boy, and if they catch
   you, what a hassle!
They usually throw people like you to the sharks,
or stretch you on a stretching rack, holding flares
   close
      to your face so the flying sparks
burn out your eyes,
or some such other unpleasant surprise.
He's the Caliph's man. You don't think you can reach
   him so easily!"
But then the man drew Abdallah toward him,
   cocking
      one eye and whispering sleazily
into his ear.
"Never fear—
for the right price I can get you in, but the rest is up to you!"

"What's the right price?" asked Abdallah. And
   then the
      old scoundrel curled his toes up in his pointed
      shoes
and became leeringly his most archetypical self, poor
   man,
looking like a gnarled and deformed elf more than
a man. He was all calculation, all scheming, all
   "opportunity knocking."

But Abdallah stayed cool. Even this experience he
   didn't
      let on was shocking
to him, here among the dusty bric-a-brac.

"I'll take all your money—*all of it!* Don't hold any
   of it
      back!
Only then will I get you into that Sorcerer's hall."
Abdallah trusted Allah. He reached into his
   pocket and
      pulled out *all,*
not a cent did he save behind.

"Are you sure that's all?" asked the man, "or
   Allah strike
      you blind?"

"Yes!" said Abdallah with absolute confidence.
"One thousand, seven hundred dollars, and
    eighty-seven cents.

It's what I needed to find the powder before that
    shaytan uses it.
It's a plot against mankind, and I'm the one sent
    by my
    Shaykh to be the one who defuses it,
insha'Allah! But I must hurry before he puts it to
    use!"

"Then put on this cloak, this hood, these rags,
    and take
    this jeweled box the magician bought—the ruse
is this! You've come from my shop and are delivering
    the box to his room.
Then you step out into the hallway and get
    behind one
    of the curtains, and quickly turn the rags
    inside-out.
    You'll then look like just another groom
for the Sorcerer's horses. That way you can remain in
    the castle for a little while.
But be quick! They're sure to notice you right
    away. Be
    sure not to smile!
They never smile there. It's a dark place, and
    they're all
    a gloomy lot."
"Don't worry," said Abdallah, "just give me the
    clothes
    and let me put them on. I feel I haven't got
much time. That madman may strike any moment!"

So he got into disguise, and was given the box, with a
    letter written by the antique dealer to be sent
with the delivery, to make it all look official.
Then Abdallah took a little white homeopathic pill
for the jitters and set off.
He made as long and gloomy a face as that of Boris
    Karloff
as he walked through the street studying the map the
    man had given him,

through the market, past a dark door, *one, two,
    three* paces,
    the wind having driven him
to a hole in a wall—*there!* With no one looking, he
    darted in
and walked tight-shouldered between narrow
    shrubbery,
    then came to a stream, and found a little boat he
    quickly departed in,

going along a shadowy channel, finally under another
    wall, into a kind of stone building,
then in total darkness, damp and spider-webby,
    all alone,
    mildewing
sides brushing his hands as he rowed, the only sound
    the splashing of oars.

Then he saw a tiny peep of light, and the sound of a
    waterfall cascade as it roars
down a huge chasm.
Suddenly the boat lurched forward in a strong
    spasm
and he found himself outside heading for a cliff!

Would he go off the edge, here all alone, and be
    found
    weeks later dead, and wet, and stiff?

*   *   *

A Thousand Armies (2003)
From *Psalms for the Brokenhearted* (2006)

And the hapless Soldier's sigh
Runs in blood down Palace walls

—William Blake

A thousand armies sat on a wall and
everyone of them was dead

eating sandwiches out of little tin boxes
yellow broken teeth and considerable chewing

But their eyes were not that interested in seeing
their eyes didn't follow anything moving in front
    of them
or look as they pulled the waxed paper away
    from their bread
or broke open their bottles of water or sat with
    their friends

There was a constant murmuring like a stomach
    churning its juices
a constant scratching like animals caught
    between walls
They sat on a wall overlooking an orchard and
each one of them was dead

But they watched the seasons come to life on the
vine in the vineyards and down the long
crop rows though their eyes barely took it in
and when the crops were harvested and the
snows came they barely blinked they barely noticed

Thousands of armies dangling their legs bootless
    in heaven

eating sandwiches out of little silver boxes
their eyes transformed from burning buildings
　　and people
running into the streets to
green fields full of lions and lambs and other
　　wingéd animals
lying together

though their eyes were always elsewhere

and their hearts were as round as the world

*　　*　　*

The Heart Has Reason to Believe (2008)

Le coeur a ses raisons que la raison ne connaît point
　　　　　　　　　　　　　　　　—Blaise Pascal

The heart has reason to believe its tropical
　　islands will bloom
giant scarlet palm trees whose
spraying spathes make golden pinwheels in a
bright blue sky

The heart has reason to believe the secret door to
　　Allah's private
chamber opens here without benefit of lock
but whose key is that murmur on the lips of a lover
that reverberates through our bones to the
earth-bound bottoms of our toes

The heart has reason to believe in a sky whose
　　opening eyelid
shows an eye that goes on and on into oracular
　　oblivion
seeing every creation He's ever created from
time before time to time after time has expired

The heart has reason to believe it's riding a
team of wild white horses going at full gallop
　　through all
the worlds and all the world's oceans at once
to run along a shore brought to life as we pass
whose faces open like white roses and whose
voices chime like silver bells

The heart has reason to believe the heart's God's
　　residence
and we enter it with caution and with care
with courage and bravado for He's waiting there
　　for our
entrance and His Face is already coming into
focus in our sphere

The heart has reason to believe all this by the
　　simple fact of being a heart

and not a steamboat or a plank of wood floating
　　on black water
where moonlight cannot reach

And the spaces between the heart's beats are
　　orbital dimensions
complete worlds come to birth in

and the beats themselves are His Name
as He names the worlds that come to birth

How can we not be delirious with love under
　　these
perfect climactic conditions!

When He beckons us toward Him by the very
organ that keeps us alive

in the very chambers He's created for His voice
to echo and reecho in

calling us home!

―――――――――――――――――――――

Source: Daniel Abdal-Hayy Moore, "Abdallah Jones—Takes
the Antique Seller's Advice," from *Abdallah Jones and the
Disappearing-Dust Cape,* Philadelphia: The Ecstatic Exchange,
2006; "A Thousand Armies," from *Psalms for the Brokenhearted,*
Philadelphia: The Ecstatic Exchange, 2006; and "The Heart
Has Reason to Believe," from *Through Rose Colored Glasses,*
Philadelphia: The Ecstatic Change, 2008.

politics

Understanding Muslim-American participation in U.S. politics depends on how one defines politics. In the broadest
sense, politics is the negotiation of power and the pursuit of
personal and collective interests at all levels of society. Human
beings are inevitably political, since they are social creatures
who figure out how to organize and govern themselves. In a
more narrow sense, politics is the art and science of governance involving the ways in which a political body such as a
state or nation is formed and managed. Muslim Americans
have played a role in U.S. politics since the birth of the republic, though their involvement in issues of governance, including elections, did not begin in earnest until the 20th century.

BLACK MUSLIM POLITICS
FROM SLAVERY TO FREEDOM

Using a broad definition of politics, it is possible to understand
how Muslims have contributed to U.S. politics since they first
arrived on American shores, mostly as slaves who, though
lacking the right to vote and most other rights afforded by
the Constitution, attempted to improve their living conditions

and gain their freedom. Without mounting a formal political campaign to abolish slavery, AFRICAN-AMERICAN MUSLIM SLAVES such as LAMEN KEBE (1767–?) and YARROW MAMOUT (ca. 1736–1829) used a variety of techniques to challenge the negative effects of the "peculiar institution" on their lives. Kebe, for example, used his literacy in ARABIC as a way to convince others of his human worth and became an ally of the American Colonization Society, which hoped to transport African Americans to Africa. His strategy worked, and he succeeded in returning home to Africa.

Yarrow Mamout, on the other hand, convinced his master, after decades of bondage, that he was no longer capable of working—that, as he put it, "Olda massa been tink he got all de work out of a Yaro['s] bone." Mamout knew that slaveholders often freed their older slaves to avoid paying for the slaves' food and housing. But after being freed around the age of 64, Mamout went to work for himself, earned $200, bought stock in Columbia Bank, and purchased property and a house in Washington, D.C.

As African Americans converted to various forms of Islam in the 1920s and 1930s, they did so partly to protest their lack of full citizenship rights in the United States—rights that had been guaranteed by the 14th and 15th amendments to the Constitution but which would not be enforced until the 1964 Civil Rights and 1965 Voting Rights Acts were passed and signed into LAW by President Lyndon Johnson. Facing DISCRIMINATION in employment, housing, and education in addition to police brutality and extralegal mob violence, some African Americans were attracted to the notion that by becoming Muslim, they might achieve the power and prestige that other ethnic minorities such as Italian Americans and Irish Americans had been able to gain. Others hoped to establish a nation within a nation, largely separating from whites in order to create a social space where they could achieve their version of the American dream. In both cases, ethnic and religious solidarity was seen as a weapon of the weak in a country dominated by an Anglo-Protestant majority.

In 1925, when NOBLE DREW ALI created the MOORISH SCIENCE TEMPLE of America, he told blacks that while they were citizens of the United States, their national origin was Moorish, or Moroccan. Ali issued identity cards indicating these Moorish national origins, echoing the idea that Moorish Americans, like other ethnic minorities in the United States, had a proud ethnic identity that white Americans ought to respect. This idea was repeated in 1930, when W. D. FARD created the NATION OF ISLAM (NOI), a simultaneously religious and political movement that sought self-determination for African Americans. Fard and his successor, ELIJAH MUHAMMAD (1897–1975), stressed the importance of totally separating from whites and forming alternative economic, political, and cultural institutions, including schools. He banned participation in U.S. elections.

While African-American Sunni Muslims such as MUHAMMAD EZALDEEN (1886–1957) and Wali Akram rejected the NOI's unique teachings about the divinity of W. D. Fard and the prophecy of Elijah Muhammad, they shared the NOI's emphasis on cultural and economic self-determination. They, too, advocated the building of a separate black "polis" within the United States that could provide the opportunities denied to them by white American society. In the 1940s, for example, some of Ezaldeen's followers established a farming community in West Valley, New York, called Jabul Arabiyya, the Mountain of Arabic-Speaking People. Approximately 40 residents owned 462 acres, a schoolhouse, a place of worship, and 15 houses, where they attempted to live outside the boundaries of mainstream American politics.

TWENTIETH-CENTURY FOUNDATIONS

As Muslim immigrants from Europe, Asia, and Africa came to the United States in the late 19th and early 20th centuries, their political involvement revolved largely around local and sometime regional groups focused on improving their living conditions. The informal politics of many ARAB-AMERICAN MUSLIMS, TURKISH-AMERICAN MUSLIMS, and SOUTH ASIAN–AMERICAN MUSLIMS in the early 1900s often inwardly focused on their own ethnic group. As Muslims volunteered to serve in the UNITED STATES MILITARY during WORLD WAR I, however, that situation began to change. Increasingly seeing themselves as Americans, for example, Muslim farmers in NORTH DAKOTA joined the major national political parties and voted in local and national elections.

In the 1920s, there was also briefly a convergence of immigrant and African-American politics, as an increasing number of Muslim Americans, of whatever ethnicity, spoke out against European and American colonialism and interventionism in what they called the "colored world"—that is, Africa, Asia, and Latin America. DUSÉ MOHAMED ALI, an Anglo-Egyptian actor and playwright, became head of the African Affairs division of the Universal Negro Improvement Association in 1922 and foreign affairs columnist for the *Negro World,* warning of a rise of Muslim opposition to Western imperialism across Africa and Asia. Arab-American Muslims became politically active in fighting Zionism, the movement to establish a Jewish national home in Palestine. In 1917, hundreds of Arab-American protesters, both Muslims and Christians, met at a hotel in Brooklyn to denounce the Balfour Declaration, which expressed Great Britain's support for a Jewish homeland in Palestine, and the Young Men's Moslem Association continued the struggle in the late 1920s, meeting with Secretary of State Henry Stimson to lobby the U.S. government to halt European Jewish immigration to Palestine.

Such protests, though expressing a certain degree of alienation, were also evidence that Muslim Americans were using mainstream political means to accomplish their ends.

For lighter-skinned Muslims, the lack of a racial stigma fostered their ASSIMILATION into mainstream politics, and Muslim Americans in places such as North Dakota and TOLEDO, OHIO, increasingly identified with the United States and its political system. While many African-American Muslims were willing during WORLD WAR II to go to jail rather than fight the Japanese, whom they considered to be fellow people of color, more than a thousand, mainly immigrant Muslim Americans, served in the war.

The fracturing of Muslim-American political interests along lines of race and ethnicity as well as political affiliation, class, religious identity, and other factors was a sign that the community was already too diverse to hold one single political platform or view. Much of the institution-building among Muslim immigrants after 1945 focused explicitly on integration into mainstream politics, while the black separatism of the Nation of Islam (NOI) helped to catapult it into a lofty position as the most popular of over a dozen different black Muslim groups during this era. The NOI became a place where African Americans could express their discontent with the ongoing scourge of Jim Crow segregation—not outlawed until passage of the Civil Rights Act in 1964—and their solidarity with the struggles of colonized people attempting to gain their independence. During the VIETNAM WAR, there was no more powerful symbol of protest than that of boxer MUHAMMAD ALI (1942–), one of many NOI members willing to go to PRISON rather than participate in what they considered to be an unjust war.

Muslim immigrant groups, often dominated by Arab Americans in this era, expressed support of Arab nationalism and protested the founding of the state of Israel in 1948, but were also focused on claiming an equal social and political status with other white Americans. For example, the FEDERATION OF ISLAMIC ASSOCIATIONS IN THE UNITED STATES AND CANADA (FIA), formed in 1952, actively lobbied government officials for recognition and accommodations for Muslim religious practices. In the early 1950s, FIA founder Abdullah Igram, a World War II veteran, convinced the Department of Defense to allow Muslim Americans to identify their religious identities on their "dogtags," the identity tags generally worn around a soldier's neck. These kinds of political engagements also led to the election of the first Muslims in public office. In 1963, James H. Karoub, of DETROIT, MICHIGAN—the son of religious leader HUSSIEN KAROUB (1892–1973)—was elected to the Michigan House of Representatives.

LATE TWENTIETH-CENTURY POLITICAL FLOWERING

Though many African-American Muslims stressed the need for separate black political institutions until the 1970s, and other Muslims, both immigrant and indigenous, advocated a healthy separation from what they saw as the corrupt world of politics, the last three decades of the 20th century were overwhelmingly characterized by increased mainstream political organizing among Muslim Americans. In 1975, W. D. MOHAMMED (1933–2008) inherited the leadership of the NOI from his father, Elijah Muhammad, and quickly reversed the organization's traditional boycott of electoral politics. Mohammed encouraged his members to vote in all elections and become active politicians themselves—a move that later led to the election of many African-American Muslims to public office.

In addition, the IMMIGRATION ACT OF 1965 led to the immigration of more than a million Muslims to the United States, and these Muslims achieved, on the whole, remarkable financial success. Using increased financial clout and social connections, many of these Muslims were able to organize a number of effective public affairs and lobbying groups. The largest of them, the ISLAMIC SOCIETY OF NORTH AMERICA (ISNA), was a grassroots organization formed out of the MUSLIM STUDENTS ASSOCIATION in 1982. Its headquarters were in Plainfield, Indiana—rather than in Washington, D.C.—and the group came to focus largely on responding to the needs of the growing number of individual MOSQUES AND ISLAMIC CENTERS, which were its institutional members. But like the ISLAMIC CIRCLE OF NORTH AMERICA, the MUSLIM AMERICAN SOCIETY, and other predominantly immigrant groups, it also encouraged the involvement of Muslim Americans in U.S. politics.

In the late 1980s and early 1990s, a number of Muslim-American public affairs and lobbying organizations emerged to influence U.S. politics. In addition to the MUSLIM PUBLIC AFFAIRS COUNCIL, the American Muslim Congress, and the AMERICAN MUSLIM ALLIANCE, the COUNCIL ON AMERICAN-ISLAMIC RELATIONS, established in 1994, attempted to gain access to elected and appointed officials in the executive and legislative branches of the federal government, issued press releases on their political positions, and organized letter-writing campaigns and protests on issues ranging from the employment discrimination faced by women who wore a HIJAB, or head scarf, to the Israeli occupation of the West Bank. In 1998, nearly every major Muslim-American national organization supported the founding of the American Muslim Political Coordinating Council (AMPCC), whose goal was to help present a united front on political issues of common interest.

Another measure of increased Muslim-American political engagement during this period was the increasing number of Muslims who ran for and were elected to public office at the local, state, and national level In 1991, Charles Bilal was elected mayor of Kountze, Texas. In 1993, SHEILA ABDUS-SALAAM (1952–) was elected to a 14-year term on New York State's Supreme Court for the County of New

Voters in Michigan have helped Muslim Americans emerge as a small but meaningful voting bloc in U.S. elections.   *(Jim West/Alamy)*

York. In 1996, Larry Shaw was elected to the North Carolina State Senate. In 2000, Saghir "Saggy" Tahir became the only Muslim Republican elected to a state office when he won a seat in the New Hampshire House of Representatives. That year, Tahir was only one of perhaps hundreds of Muslim Americans, according to the American Muslim Alliance, who were candidates for various public offices around the country.

In 2002, Yaphett El-Amin was elected to the Missouri House of Representatives—one of the first Muslim-American women to achieve this distinction. Then, in 2006, KEITH M. ELLISON (1963–   ) of Minneapolis, Minnesota, became the first Muslim elected to Congress, and in 2008, ANDRÉ D. CARSON (1974–   ) of Indianapolis, Indiana, became the second Muslim in the U.S. House of Representatives.

AFTER 9/11

As a result of the terrorist attacks of SEPTEMBER 11, 2001, Muslim Americans faced violent backlash, increased employment discrimination, and surveillance, detention, and extraordinary rendition authorized by the USA PATRIOT ACT signed into law on October 26, 2001. Muslim-American

political participation increased in the wake of the attacks, as Muslims sought to identify politicians and interest groups that would become allies in what they considered to be a struggle to defend their rights as Americans. The opposition of Muslim-American groups, in tandem with the efforts of civil liberties groups and groups representing ethnic minorities, led to widespread dissatisfaction with the USA PATRIOT Act. By 2003, over a hundred municipalities and counties passed resolutions criticizing or refusing to cooperate with the provisions of the law.

At the same time, a number of Muslim-American leaders also encouraged Muslims to become more involved in the war on terrorism. The FIQH COUNCIL OF NORTH AMERICA, a body of scholars trained in SHARI'A, a Muslim code of law and ethics, issued an opinion stating that Muslim-American involvement in the war on terrorism was justifiable on the grounds that as Americans, Muslims should help to defend the country in a just cause. Young Muslim-American men responded by joining the U.S. military and by joining the antiterror force of the New York City Police Department.

In 2003, AMPCC announced its position on the impending IRAQ WAR. Iraqi leader Saddam Hussein, the council declared, was a dictator whose actions were un-Islamic. Calling for the Iraqi president to resign, AMPCC also asked President George W. Bush not to go to war, explaining that the invasion would cause more problems than it would solve. It proposed instead that the United Nations should administer fair and free elections to decide the next government of Iraq.

The Bush administration's foreign and domestic policies caused a shift in Muslim-American party affiliation. In the 2000 election, AMPCC had endorsed Bush, the Republican candidate for president, largely because of his opposition to the use of secret evidence in federal terrorism trials. Muslim support may have been vital to Bush's victory in Florida—the state that ultimately tipped the election to Bush—according to the American Conservative Network. In the 2004 presidential contest, according to a 2007 Pew poll, approximately 85 percent of Muslim-American voters supported Democratic candidate John Kerry, U.S. senator from Massachusetts, over President Bush, who was running for reelection. But many Muslim Americans did not turn out to vote: 58 percent of U.S. Muslim citizens reported voting in the election, as compared to 74 percent of the general public.

According to the same Pew poll, the plurality of Muslim Americans (38 percent) identified themselves as political moderates, with 63 percent saying that they were Democrats or leaned Democratic. Only 11 percent identified themselves as Republicans, which indicated the strong opposition of Muslim Americans to the domestic and foreign policies of the Bush administration. Just 15 percent approved of the way President Bush was handling his job. The Pew report deemed Muslim Americans "big government social conservatives." While seven in 10 Muslim Americans favored "big government" with increased social service and especially federal assistance to the poor, 61 percent said that homosexuality was "a way of life that should be discouraged by society, not accepted" and 59 percent said that the government should do more to protect morality.

While Muslim Americans shared generally positive views about their experiences in the United States, they differed markedly from the general population in their views toward U.S. foreign policy. Approximately eight out of every 10 Muslims interviewed said that they were happy or very happy with their lives in the United States. A large majority (71 percent) said that hard work leads to success in the United States. Though 76 percent of those surveyed expressed a concern over the rise of Islamic extremism in the world, only 26 percent of Muslims, compared to 67 percent of the general population, viewed the U.S.-led war on terror as a "sincere effort to reduce terrorism." Approximately one out of 10 (12 percent) thought that the Iraq War was the "right decision," while 45 percent of the general populace supported the decision to go to war.

In the 2008 presidential campaign, Muslim Americans voted overwhelmingly for Democrat Barack Obama, who had positioned himself as one of the few candidates who had opposed the Iraq War before it began. One poll conducted in 10 states determined that 89 percent of Muslim voters had cast their votes for Obama. During the course of the campaign, many Muslim Americans kept their enthusiasm for the candidate quiet, fearing that their support would actually hurt his chances. Having felt the sting of anti-Muslim discrimination themselves, they feared that the rumors about his supposedly secret Muslim identity might keep others from voting for him. Oddly, this brand of politics had deep roots in the United States. It echoed a trend in the early republic when "Muslim" was used as an epithet, meant to discredit one's opponent.

CONCLUSION

But unlike in the early republic, Muslim Americans in the late 20th and early 21st centuries had organized politically to protect their rights and advance their social status in the United States. Their increased participation in U.S. politics was a vital sign of their historical journey in the United States. Enslaved at the beginning of U.S. history, some Muslim Americans used surreptitious politics to improve their living conditions and perhaps go back home. In the beginning of the 20th century, most were focused on local and informal politics, attempting to figure out their relationships to one another and the communities in which they lived. In the wake of World War I, however, both indigenous and immigrant Muslim Americans attempted to affect American government in a formal fashion. Those efforts blossomed in the late 20th century as Muslim Americans increased in number and in wealth. They created both grassroots organizations and Washington lobbies, built political alliances, and, by 2008, elected more than 20 different Muslim politicians to various posts, including city halls and state legislatures, around the country. Though still representing a small percentage of Americans by the beginning of the 21st century, their centrality to the battles over civil liberties and U.S. foreign policy, among other issues, made them a consequential presence in U.S. politics.

Edward E. Curtis IV

Further Reading

Ali, Lorraine. "Islam and Obama: American Muslims Overwhelmingly Voted Democratic." *Newsweek.* 7 November 2008. Available online. URL: http://www.newsweek.com/id/168062. Accessed May 5, 2009.

Curtis, Edward E., IV. *Muslims in America: A Short History.* New York: Oxford University Press, 2009.

Elkholy, Abdo. *The Arab Moslems in the United States.* New Haven, Conn.: College and University Press, 1966.

Gomez, Michael A. *Black Crescent: The Experience and Legacy of African Muslims in the Americas.* Cambridge: Cambridge University Press, 2005.

Nimer, Mohamed. "Social and Political Institutions of American Muslims: Liberty and Civic Responsibility." In *Muslims in the United States,* edited by Philippa Strum and Danielle Tarantolo, 45–61. Washington, D.C.: Woodrow Wilson International Center for Scholars, 2003.

Pew Research Center. "Muslim Americans: Middle Class and Mostly Mainstream." Washington, D.C.: Pew Research Center, 2007.

Sinno, A. H. *Muslims in Western Politics.* Bloomington: Indiana University Press, 2009.

Suleiman, Michael W., ed. *Arabs in America: Building a New Future.* Philadelphia: Temple University Press, 1999.

Zahid Bukhari on Muslims in American Politics (2000)

Zahid Bukhari, who graduated from the University of Connecticut with a Ph.D. in political science, has studied political engagement on two continents. From 1978 to 1983, he was executive director of the Pakistan Institute of Public Opinion in Islamabad. In the United States, he served as Secretary General of the Islamic Circle of North America from 1990 to 1995. From 1999 to 2004, he served as director of the Muslims in the American Public Square project, which was granted $1.25 million by the Pew Charitable Trust to study Muslim-American engagement in public life. He coedited one of the project's publications, Muslims' Place in the American Public Square, *which appeared in 2004, after which he became director of American Muslim studies at Georgetown University. In a 2000 interview with the Muslim American Society, excerpted below, Bukhari answered questions about the Muslim-American vote in the upcoming election, but rather than focusing on handicapping individual political races, Bukhari attempted to articulate a vision for Muslim-American political activism that encompassed religious ideals and political strategies.*

Q: What role do you see Muslims in America playing in the future affairs of the Muslim world? Do Muslims in your view have an opportunity to influence American foreign policy?

A: The last decade of the twentieth century has witnessed a thriving, vibrant, and expanding Muslim community on the American civic horizon. The Muslim community in America, six million in number, is a replica of the more than one billion Muslims of the world. The community has at least three roles to perform on this continent.

One is to function as a minority group seeking to protect its rights. Another is to represent the larger Muslim Ummah [the global community of Muslims] by struggling to help out Muslims around the world in difficult times. The third responsibility of Muslims and the Muslim Ummah in America is to bring the wisdom of Islam to promote social justice and political responsibility in America for all citizens, as well as to participate in ecumenical efforts to restore America's spiritual underpinnings. The combination of these three roles has made the Muslim community a multiple agenda group instead of a single-agenda political-community.

The Muslim community in America possesses more financial, human, and high tech resources than any other Muslim community in the world. It is a fact that there are more professional Muslims in the United States than in any Muslim country. Interestingly enough and it may seem strange: the Muslims in America are also more active politically and Islamically than are Muslims in any other country. All these characteristics, plus being strategically placed in the belly of the sole super power of the world today, would give the Muslim community in America added effectiveness in its role as guardian for the future affairs of the Muslim World.

The Muslims in America are becoming a source of ideas, actions, and leadership in the following four areas that are shaping the future of the Muslim World:

1. Helping in the development of the basic physical and culture infrastructure, including education, health, information technology, management, polity, and cultural development of various Muslim countries;

2. Restructuring the fields of communication and channeling the flow of news from a Muslim perspective;

3. Facilitating civilizational dialogues between Islam and the West in general and the Muslim World and the United States of America in particular; and

4. Affecting American foreign policy toward the Muslim World.

In order to influence American foreign policy, the Muslim community has to be involved in the domestic affairs of the United States. I would like to give one example to underscore this point. The Muslims have a universal belief that Jewish groups are controlling American foreign policy, at least in the Middle East. Half a century before achieving this "status," the Jewish intellectuals and activists were also instrumental in shaping the domestic agenda of President Roosevelt.

The Muslim community should try to have a significant impact on this society. Three steps are necessary to achieve this goal.

Along with having advanced education in medicine, business administration, and computer sciences, the Muslims should also excel in the social sciences, law, communications, journalism, media, political science, sociology, and international relations. During this era of institution building, we should also plan to establish Muslim universities and hospitals, as well as think tanks and research centers for public policy in America.

We have Muslim advocacy groups, and their achievements are remarkable. The next stage, however, is to establish institutions working for social justice, not only for Muslims but also for the whole society. There is obvious *zulm* [wrongdoing and oppression] in the society in the shape of police brutality, hunger, homelessness, and broken families. The country also faces natural disasters of various types. The Muslim community, especially the relief organizations, should act collectively to eradicate the zulm and compete with other like-minded people and groups in promoting the good. Commitment to this purpose of Islam and Muslims in America is the best form of da'wa [missionary work].

In order to do all this, however, we must strengthen a unified voice of the Muslim community of America. The joint forum of the National Islamic Shura Council, which consists of the leadership of all major organizations, should become functional and it should establish an effective secretariat in Washington, D.C. The Muslim leadership in America should present the Muslim agenda for domestic and international affairs, which consists of common principles derived from the Revelation of Tawhid [Oneness] as applied through mutual consultation in evaluating and addressing specific issues of conscience, so that Americans can better address the underlying causes rather than merely the effects of disharmony and injustice in their society.

Inward unity and outward caring for the society will ultimately give the Muslim community an opportunity to lead America and influence American foreign policy toward the other peoples of the world.

Q: What percentage of the Muslim American population do you believe is eligible to vote? What percentage do you believe would actually vote if the elections were held today? Considering that we have been witnessing a decline in American voting, do you believe that the Muslim vote has a possibility of being a swing vote?

A: It is not a question of belief but a question of an estimate. Rather, in the absence of any authentic data, it can only be a mere guesstimate. Nevertheless, I can give you observations on the voting patterns and potentials of Muslims in America.

If we just look at the minimum voting age requirement of eighteen years, a vast majority of the Muslim population is eligible to vote. But four factors have curtailed their effectiveness in casting votes: 1) Many Muslim families are in the process of immigration, and it will take some time for them to become eligible for naturalization; 2) A good number of Muslims do not want to become citizens, either because they fear losing their home country citizenship or because they are convinced that the Pledge of Allegiance is against Islam; they prefer to be only green card holders, although the recent immigration laws passed by Congress have reduced substantially the number of Muslims in this category; 3) Ongoing conceptual and theoretical discussion on the issue of Muslims participating in a non-Muslim political system, and even on the compatibility of democracy with Islam, has made some individuals and groups, especially among indigenous and second generation Muslims, refrain from the voting process; 4) A great number of Muslims, who are eligible to vote but do not have any strong Fiqh [Islamic legal] reservations, still will not become registered voters. Why? The reasons may range from lack of any democratic practices in their home countries, lack of education on the importance of civic participation, and lack of procedural knowledge, to general apathy toward the prevailing political process!

The good news is that those Muslims who become registered voters tend to vote more conscientiously than the average American voter. As things are moving, especially the implementation of the recent immigration laws and increasing awareness among the members of the community, the number of eligible and registered voters will grow rapidly in the near future. There is definitely great potential that the Muslim vote, in a narrow sense, may become a swing vote, but only after a concerted effort and a comprehensive strategy. In targeted primaries and constituencies, the Muslim voters could certainly affect the outcome of the elections.

Q: What is your opinion concerning the differences in the political ideals and methods of American-born Muslims and immigrant Muslims who are eligible to vote? Do you see one group as potentially more powerful than another? What are the common issues or views of these two groups as you see them?

A: The American Muslim community is diverse. First of all, it is divided into Ansar and Muhajir (indigenous and immigrant Muslims). Among the indigenous are Afro-American and Caucasian-American Muslims, and their aspirations vary. Among immigrants, there are Arab and Ajam (non-Arab) Muslims, who have different socio-political experiences. Second-generation Muslims are also an important element of the community composition. All these sub-groups of the Muslim community have their distinct political ideas and feelings. The alarming fact is that the two main groups, indigenous and immigrants are living side by side like *maraj al-bahrain,* two different oceans, with an invisible but strong barrier between them.

The Muslim immigrants are experienced and resourceful, and their suburban Islamic centers have grandiose structures. They have the habit of looking at a great variety of issues, both international and domestic. The indigenous Muslims, on the other hand, are less resourceful and their inner-city masjids [mosques] have more humble structures, but they have more connection with the masses. They tend to see problems from the domestic perspective. For immigrants, Palestine, Kashmir, Bosnia, Kosova, and disasters in the Muslim world are more important, whereas the indigenous Muslims would give more importance to the local community's socio-economic conditions. This does not mean that the immigrants do not care about the domestic problems, or that the indigenous Muslims do not bother with the Ummah's crisis. But they have different preferences.

My strong belief is that both groups of the Muslim community, immigrants and indigenous, need to learn from each other's experience. Only by working together will they be able to achieve any meaningful success in the political field.

Q: Will the American public view Muslim political participation as a threat to the secular establishment in America? Do you see Islamic political activism as secular or religious in nature?

A: Muslim political activism is a religious activism but it should encompass all faiths and all sectors of society. Public perception depends upon our behavior and how others will portray us in the media and other political channels. Much of the American public is hostile to any overly religious political overtures. We should adopt a strategy of selective alliance, working with various political and religious groups on different issues. If Muslims present themselves only as the champion of Muslims' rights and not as the champion of justice, domestically and internationally, the American public would certainly feel wary of us. I would suggest that Muslims should follow the fine balance of the American Constitution, which stands for separation of church and state, on the one hand, in order to protect religious minorities from political oppression by the majority, and, on the other hand, guarantees individual freedom for everyone to bring one's religious principles, wisdom, and commitment to bear in the public square.

Q: Are there any possibilities of reconciliation between Muslim Americans and the Christian Right? Do you see a faith-based coalition as a possible influence in the Year 2000 elections?

A: My answer to both of the questions is negative. I would not rule out any positive development in the long run, but any reconciliation between Muslims in America and the Christian Right is not possible in near future. In the same way, I do not see the development of an influential faith-based coalition, at least not in the Year 2000 elections.

Q: Which party would benefit the most from Muslim political participation, and why? In your opinion is Islamic politics more compatible with American liberalism or American conservatism?

A: Before determining which party would benefit the most from Muslim political participation, one should look at the basis of Muslim activism and also examine which party has more capacity to attract this activism.

Three sets of issues are significant in determining the political affiliation of Muslims in America:

1) race, rights, and welfare; 2) values and religious issues; and 3) American policy in foreign and international conflicts, especially where Muslims are involved, whether or not they identify ethnically with one side or the other. Two more factors, namely, the image of the party and personality of a candidate, are also important in determining the level of political participation by an ethno-religious group.

Both American parties have distinct policy-mixes in their bids for Muslim participation. Democrats have an edge through primarily "secular issues," as the champion of immigrants and minority rights, to attract more Muslim votes, although some traditionalist or paleo-conservatives are the most articulate in heralding the benefits of open immigration. Republicans could claim more Muslim affiliation as the party of values, family traditions, and religious rights. Its presidential hopeful, George Bush Jr., could charm more Muslim votes compared to any of his rivals. Looking at the year 2000, the Republican Party seems to be harvesting more fruit from Muslim participation at the presidential level, while the Democratic Party will enjoy more benefits at the level of Congress. If Muslims keep their options open, however, and are involved in both parties at the grassroots level, the American society would, ultimately, be the greatest beneficiary of their participation in the political arena.

In response to your second question about the relative attraction of liberalism versus conservatism for Muslim political activists, I do not see any Muslim politics here. There is Muslim activism on the basis of international issues, minority rights, and perhaps issues of a welfare safety net. Muslim politics would be compatible with either liberalism or conservatism depending upon the nature of the issue and the debate of the day. Islamic politics would seem to be more compatible with conservatism because of religious and value issues, but becomes more compatible with American liberalism when the issues of rights, race, and the welfare of small groups are taken into consideration.

Q: Comparing the Muslim American community with the American Jewish community, what are their commonalities and differences, particularly with respect to their foreign policy interests? Do you see Jews and Muslims sharing similar objectives on domestic issues?

A: Once an editor of *Newsday,* a major metropolitan newspaper of New York City, stated to a dele-

gation of Muslim leaders that Muslims in America are at the same stage where Jewish people were in 1920. My response, as a member of the delegation, was that, because of the advancements achieved by Jewish, Afro-American, and other minority groups, the Muslim community will be catching up very fast.

Jews suffered and struggled along with other minority groups and ultimately, after a long and continuous effort, they are now enjoying the present state of influence. Not only are they able to mold American foreign policy, but are successful in the fields of education, media, entertainment, medicine, health, law, and business. Advancement in all the nerve centers of a society is required in order to play a significant role in the decision-making process.

Both groups have faced the same problems during the immigration and post-immigration periods. Settling in a new and sometimes hostile cultural environment, establishing religious, educational, and political institutions, facing family problems, fulfilling the dietary requirements, and experiencing controversies over the opinions of imported scholars are all familiar stories for both of them. As I stated earlier, if Muslims adopt a strategy of selective alliance on domestic issues, they will soon see Jewish groups as effective partners.

Foreign policy interests are really thorny issues in the whole equation. The Jewish community, in contrast to the Muslim community, is a single-agenda entity in so far as it considers itself the sole guardian of Israel's security. Some of their individuals and groups have nourished, unfortunately, a conception of perpetual animosity for Palestinians, Arabs, Muslims, and even for Islam. I should also say that reciprocally this also is true for some of the Muslim individuals and groups. This state of affairs needs to be addressed. Because it is a multiple agenda community and because it focuses on bettering the larger society, the Muslim community in America is in a position to change this misconception and thereby benefit.

Source: Muslim American Society. "Muslims in American Society: Interview with Zahid Bukhari." Available online. URL: www.masnet.org/contempissue.asp?id=1763. Accessed February 10, 2009.

population   See DEMOGRAPHICS.

prayer

Muslims in the United States subscribe to diverse schools of ISLAMIC THOUGHT and come from a variety of cultural backgrounds. It is no surprise, then, that there are a variety of religious traditions of devotion and piety among them. While the prescribed prayer involving the prostration of the body toward Mecca, called *salat* or *namaz,* is most often associated with "Muslim prayer," Muslim Americans have prayed in a variety of ways since they first arrived on American soil centuries ago during the colonial era.

DIVERSITY OF MUSLIM PRAYER TRADITIONS

Prayer in Muslim experience is expressed though shared rituals of piety such as the recitation of the QUR'AN, acts of supplication *(du'a),* prayers asking for God's blessings upon the prophet MUHAMMAD *(salawat),* and rituals glorifying the Divine *(tasbih).* Prayer also includes practices that are particular to various Muslim communities. These include the *DHIKR* rituals of various Sufi and mystically oriented communities, 'Ashura commemorations of Twelver SHI'A MUSLIM AMERICANS, *majlis* gatherings of the DRUZE COMMUNITY, the recitation of religious poetry among various Muslim Sufi communities, including the BEKTASHI SUFI ORDER, and the canonic *du'a* among the Nizari branch of the ISMA'ILI MUSLIM AMERICAN community. Likewise, Muslim prayer does not only take place in MOSQUES AND ISLAMIC CENTERS but does and has historically occurred in the home and in spaces designated as Sufi lodges, *IMAMBARGAHS,* and *JAMAATKHANAS* in the American context.

PRAYERS OF AMERICA'S EARLIEST MUSLIMS

The first Muslim prayers in America were performed by the thousands of AFRICAN-AMERICAN MUSLIM SLAVES who arrived in the Thirteen Colonies and the United States from the 17th to the 19th centuries. For example, JOB BEN SOLOMON (ca. 1701–1773), a slave who lived in Maryland from 1730 to 1733, kept his daily prayers even in the midst of harassment; he told his biographer Thomas Bluett that when he would go to the woods to pray, a white boy would make fun of him and throw dirt in his face. Job, as he was commonly known, was only one of many literate, educated, and highly pious slaves who preserved their Islamic rituals after having been stolen away to the Americas.

Included in these rituals were various prayers that they had learned from West African SUFISM, the inclination and practice of mysticism in Islam. For example, BILALI OF SAPELO ISLAND (ca. 1760–1859) and his wife, Phoebe, "prayed on the bead," performing *dhikr,* a meditative form of prayer in which the believer recites the names of God or a series of prescribed formulas. According to one of his heirs, Bilali would repeat words of devotion to God and his prophet, Muhammad, pulling on a long string of prayer beads that was likely used by the Qadiri Sufi order in West Africa.

While the slave trade introduced America to many of its earliest Muslims, the first Muslim immigrants arrived in the late 19th century and later coalesced into communities based around linguistic affiliation—many coming from ARABIC-speaking regions that today would include Syria, Lebanon, Jordan, Israel, and Palestine. Many of these Arab pioneers settled in the American Midwest and on the East Coast. Some were Sunni Muslims, who constitute 80 to 85 percent of the world's Muslims, while others subscribed to Shi'a Ithna 'Ashari beliefs or belonged to the Druze faith, each of which had its own specific prayer systems and acts of devotion.

SUNNI PRAYERS

SUNNI MUSLIM AMERICANS, like their counterparts from other communities, hail from all parts of the Muslim world and include a large number of indigenous Americans who converted beginning in the early 20th century. While the earliest purpose-built mosques did not appear until the 1920s, it is clear that WHITE MUSLIM AMERICANS such as ALEXANDER RUSSELL WEBB, ARAB-AMERICAN MUSLIMS, and SOUTH ASIAN–AMERICAN MUSLIMS were performing the daily prayers in rented halls and homes by the late 19th century.

While the SHARI'A, or code of Muslim law and ethics, permits Muslims to perform the prayer individually, it is expected that Muslim males will come together to perform *salat al-jum'a,* the midday congregational prayers on Friday. This ritual, when performed in public, often begins with the ADHAN, or the call to prayer, in which a muezzin beckons the faithful to come to worship, adding in the early morning that "prayer is better than sleep." Though the call to prayer was surely performed before the 19th century in North America, some of the first recorded instances of its public performance came in 1893: once at the Chicago World's Fair, or the COLUMBIAN EXPOSITION OF 1893, and once from a third-story window of the Union Square Bank building in NEW YORK CITY.

Many Muslims also perform a series of ablutions, called *wudu,* in which they ritually purify themselves before making their prayers, washing their mouth, nose, ears, head, arms, and feet with water, or sand where water is not available. The prayer ritual then performed, called the *salat,* is the best-known form of Muslim prayer and is considered by Sunni Muslims to be incumbent upon all believers. The person offering prayers begins by positioning his or her body in the direction of Mecca, the holy city. He or she stands, hands held near the sides of one's head, and recites that "God is most great." Then, the hands are dropped to the side of the body or folded in front of the chest, and other verses from the Qur'an are recited. The believer next bows at the waist,

Prayer times, August 2008. Muslims who practice *salat,* prescribed prayers involving a series of prostrations and the recitation of Qur'anic passages and other holy words, often pray five times throughout the day. This sign also includes the time for *jumah,* the congregational prayers held each Friday in lieu of the *duhr* prayer.   *(Photograph courtesy of Edward E. Curtis IV)*

and then touches his or her head to the ground. Rising, but still sitting on the knees, he or she turns left and then to the right, and after reciting several additional lines of spoken prayer, concludes by saying to his or her fellow Muslims, "Peace and mercy of God be upon you." This is considered a prayer cycle and is performed throughout the day.

In addition to the *salat,* many Muslims participate in a range of additional prayers that form part of the ritual life of their communities. On auspicious days of the Muslim calendar, such as the birthday of prophet Muhammad, the night of power *(laylat al-qadr),* and the night journey of the Prophet from Mecca to Jerusalem to heaven and back *(laylat 'isra wa'l mi'raj),* many communities also observe special *salat,* supplicatory prayers, recitation of the Qur'an, and personal reflection and meditative contemplation.

SHI'A PRAYERS

Ithna 'Ashari, or Twelvers, the largest and most prominent Shi'a Muslim community, as well as a number of other Shi'a communities, also perform the *salat.* The majority combine their prayers into three sessions rather than five, although still observing five *salat* per day as Sunni Muslims do. Since the early 20th century, Shi'a Muslim Americans have also participated in religious processions and prayer gatherings organized during the month of Muharram and especially on its tenth day called 'Ashura. At this time a number of solemn observances take place to commemorate the seventh-century martyrdom of Husayn ibn Ali, the Shi'a imam and grandson

of the Prophet. This occasion, filled with intense emotion, was one of the most important days in the Shi'a calendar and has attracted men and women from the entire community.

In addition to the recitation of the *salat,* lamentation songs *(nawhas* and *rawzas)* were sung, extolling the virtues of the family of the Prophet and relating the tragic stories and events of Karbala leading to Husayn's death. Later, in the 1960s, when mosques, Islamic centers, and *imambargahs* were constructed, the ritual life of the Shi'a Twelvers expanded to formally include a range of other activities that were observed in addition to the daily *salat,* such as gathering to recite the prayers of *Kumayl,* believed to have been given by their first imam, Ali (father of Husayn ibn Ali), to one of his companions, and greetings of peace *(salam)* to the Shi'a imams. These institutions were further strengthened by the settlement of Iranian Shi'a Muslims beginning in the 1960s, followed by Twelvers from the Indian subcontinent.

The Nizari branch of the Isma'ilis, another Shi'a Muslim community, began arriving in the United States in the 1950s. This community, as part of their canonical prayers, observe the recitation of the *du'a,* an Arabic prayer of supplication recited in their own spaces of communal congregation known as the *jamaatkhana.* Introduced to the worldwide Isma'ili community beginning in 1954 by their 48th imam, AGA KHAN III, Sir Sultan Mohamed Shah, this unified prayer replaced a number of diverse supplications in a multitude of languages observed by the community based on their regional backgrounds.

MOORISH SCIENCE TEMPLE
AND THE NATION OF ISLAM

The MOORISH SCIENCE TEMPLE of America (MST), established by NOBLE DREW ALI in 1925 in Chicago, adopted most of the forms of their prayer rituals from African-American Christian traditions and those of the Shriners, an American fraternal organization. In their Philadelphia temple in the early 1940s, for example, they held Friday prayer services in which they chanted a song, "Moslem's That Old Time Religion" to the tune of a Christian hymn, "Give Me That Old Time Religion."

The service, which was described by anthropologist Arthur Huff Fauset as a generally quiet and contemplative religious service, also incorporated recitations of *The Holy Koran of the Moorish Science Temple of America* (1927), a sacred text composed by their prophet, Noble Drew Ali, with few similarities to the Qur'an. Participants concluded the service with the prayer: "Allah, Father of the Universe, the father of Love, Truth, Peace, Freedom, and Justice. Allah is my protector, my Guide, and my Salvation by night and by day, through His Holy Prophet, Drew Ali. Amen." Though many of those words may have been acceptable to other Muslims, the idea that Drew Ali was a prophet was rejected by many other Muslim Americans at the time, including Sudanese missionary SATTI MAJID.

The NATION OF ISLAM (NOI), founded by W. D. FARD in Detroit in 1930 and led for many decades by ELIJAH MUHAMMAD, incorporated a greater number of Sunni Muslim traditions in its prayer rituals, although it also developed its own words to the prayers. In 1957, Muhammad published a prayer manual that described each step of the *salat*, the prescribed prayer. He advised his believers to perform the prayer five times a day, but to do so in English rather than in Arabic. Some NOI members also learned the prayers in Arabic and performed them, although they did so alone rather than collectively.

Prayers at NOI temple meetings were said in English, and members performed them from their seats, not on the floor as many other Muslims do. In the 1960s, the NOI newspaper, *MUHAMMAD SPEAKS,* featured a regular column called "Prayer Service in Islam" that began to incorporate new and original prayers into the *salat,* including the recitation of beliefs that W. D. Fard was God. In the 1960s, NOI leaders explained the difference between their prayer rituals and those of other Muslims as those of interpretation. Unless the words of the prayer were understood, they said, it could become hollow and meaningless.

SUFI PRAYERS

American Sufi orders, organizations that often advocate a more emotional or mystical relationship with God through the use of various rituals, have cut across many Muslim-American social boundaries and have both Sunni and Shi'a Muslim adherents. The orders often differ over the question of whether members must formally commit to Islam as a religious conviction or simply remain true to its values while permitting individuals to belong to other traditions or faiths. The most common form of practice shared by most of these esoteric-oriented communities is the *dhikr,* or the remembrance of God through repetitions of God's names and through formulas that invoke God's beauty, uniqueness, and transcendent nature. These invocations can be recited silently or aloud, privately or collectively, and are sometimes accompanied by the recitation of religious songs *(nashid),* the playing of musical instruments, and through dance. For the HALVETI-JERRAHI ORDER, for example, it also involves rhythmic bodily movement and complex systems of breathing to further call upon God and induce a mystical encounter. In addition to the *dhikr,* another almost ubiquitous practice is the spiritual discourse or teaching lesson between spiritual leaders and their followers in hope of guiding them through the states of spiritual development and toward a closer relationship with the Divine. While some of these practices complement the *salat,* certain groups have their own canonical prayers which transcend the more common practices of Sunni and Shi'a Muslims.

CONCLUSION

The diverse forms of prayer among Muslim Americans are testament to the religious, ethnic, and social diversity of American Islam. Distinctly American prayers sit alongside prayer systems that are traced back to the time of the prophet Muhammad in the sixth and seventh centuries. The sheer variety of prayer among Muslim Americans shows that there is no one type of Muslim in the United States and suggests that the diversity of Islamic religious practice is one source of its growth and spread as an American religion.

Rizwan Mawani and Edward E. Curtis IV

Further Reading

Curtis, Edward E., IV. *Black Muslim Religion in the Nation of Islam, 1960–1975.* Chapel Hill: University of North Carolina Press, 2006.

Haddad, Yvonne Yazbeck, and Jane I. Smith. *Mission to America: Five Islamic Sectarian Communities in North America.* Gainesville: University Press of Florida, 1993.

Hermansen, Marcia. "In the Garden of American Sufi Movements: Hybrids and Perennials." In *New Trends and Developments in the World of Islam,* edited by Peter Clarke. London: Luzac, 1996.

Kassam, Tazim R. "The Daily Prayer (Dua) of Shi'a Ismaili Muslims." In *Religions of the United States in Practice,* Vol. 2, edited by Colleen McDanell. Princeton, N.J.: Princeton University Press, 2001.

Malik, Jamal, and John Hinnels, eds. *Sufism in the West.* London: Routledge, 2006.

Netton, Ian Richard. *Sufi Ritual: The Parallel Universe.* Richmond, Surrey: Curzon, 2000.

Renard, John, ed. *Windows on the House of Islam: Muslim Sources on Spirituality and Religious Life.* Berkeley: University of California Press, 1998.

Wallbridge, Linda. *Without Forgetting the Imam: Lebanese Shi'ism in an American Community.* Detroit: Wayne State University Press, 1996.

Webb, Gisela. "Sufism in America." In *America's Alternative Religions,* edited by T. Miller. Albany: State University of New York Press, 1995.

prison

Considering the large number of inmates who have converted to Islam in prison and later reentered society, a sizeable portion of the Muslim-American community has been shaped by America's penal system. America's state and federal prisons stand as a microcosm of the country's larger Muslim society and culture. As with the outside world, Islam within prison walls has given many men and women a source of hope, identity, and sense of community.

Yet incarcerated Muslims have faced many more difficulties than their free counterparts in gaining access to religious resources and the freedom to worship. Muslim Americans have often led the struggle for constitutional rights, protections, and the liberty to practice their religion inside prisons since the middle of the 20th century, and though many advances have been made, conditions are still often restricted. For just one example, a federal court ruled in 2003 that New Jersey State Prison is not obligated to supply Muslim prisoners with HALAL meals, or those that are permissible according to the SHARI'A, or Islamic LAW. Nevertheless, the history of Muslim-American involvement in the country's prisons provides a rich understanding of the community's ministry, practices, and engagement with the larger society and culture.

NATION OF ISLAM PRISON MINISTRIES

The Muslim American prison ministry began with NATION OF ISLAM (NOI) leader ELIJAH MUHAMMAD in the 1940s. Muhammad was arrested in 1942 along with several other NOI members for evading WORLD WAR II draft laws. Though most of the defendants were sentenced to three years in prison, the Federal Bureau of Investigation raised the charges to sedition against Muhammad and two other NOI followers.

Muhammad was subsequently housed at the federal correctional institution in Milan, Michigan, until his release in 1946. During this time, his wife, Clara, oversaw the NOI and relayed communications from Muhammad to his followers at Detroit's Temple No. 1. While in prison, Muhammad's experiences led to his desire for NOI independence and self-sufficiency as well as an interest in spreading his message through print and radio media. While in prison, moreover, Muhammad came to believe an insufficient amount of attention was given to rehabilitating African-American inmates. After his release, this concentration on prisoners became a central component of the NOI program.

The experiences of MALCOLM X in prison are undoubtedly the best-known of any Muslim American's. Malcolm X was arrested in January 1946 and charged with breaking and entering, larceny, and carrying firearms. Originally sentenced to Massachusetts's Charlestown Prison, Malcolm X was initially hostile toward religion until his brothers, Philbert and Reginald, introduced him to Elijah Muhammad's teachings. Beginning his conversion to Islam in 1947, Malcolm X started corresponding with Muhammad after his transfer to the more progressive Norfolk Prison Colony in 1948. In the following years, he became an ardent supporter of Muhammad, and on his parole and release in 1952, Malcolm X was integrated into the NOI community. Like Muhammad's, Malcolm X's experiences in prison convinced him of the need and fertile potential for outreach to African-American inmates.

Although more inmates were converting to Sunni Islam than to the NOI by the 21st century, the NOI was instrumental in establishing a uniquely Muslim-American prison ministry. One reason for this success—and still seen to this day in faith-based outreach to prisoners—was the NOI's consistent propagation carried out by members outside the prison as well as by those inmates who had already joined the faith. In the 1950s, the NOI built up its organization in the country's state and federal prisons, primarily by recruiting and educating new converts through the distribution of literature. NOI members wrote to inmates and encouraged further correspondence, often with Elijah Muhammad himself.

By the 1960s, the NOI was a powerful force in America's prison system and had the sympathy of many African-American prisoners. It is estimated that the NOI counted as many as 100,000 members by 1960, many of whom were in prison, though the FBI insisted that the organization had only 5,000 members. The NOI provided inmates with a sense of identity, belonging, and community; resources for education and rehabilitation; a highly organized protective network that offered security; and assistance for those reentering society. Yet the NOI also required inmates to embrace discipline and personal responsibility. Islam therefore played a significant part in the reform and personal transformation of countless prisoners.

Often, inside prisons the process of conversion and identification as Muslim followed a pattern. Generally, inmates considering converting to Islam were first provided with information familiarizing them with the faith. Then, once the decision to convert was made, inmates recited the *shahada,* or declaration of faith, in front of witnesses and thereby entered into the community of Muslim inmates. Next, recent converts normally changed their appearance in DRESS and facial hair (where allowed) as well as their names to match traditional standards. By this point, they would also participate fully in both individual and collective activities such as praying five times daily, attending Friday prayer, studying the Arabic language and QUR'AN, and fasting during Ramadan. Through all of these practices Muslim inmates demonstrated both a personal commitment to their faith and solidarity with the larger Muslim community.

GROWING DIVERSITY

Initially, prison administrators viewed Islam in general and the NOI in particular as problematic and even threatening movements and consequently attempted to restrict their practice. However, beginning in the 1960s and continuing into the 21st century, Muslim Americans frequently turned to the courts and filed lawsuits in their struggle for religious rights and freedom of practice with many cases settling in their favor. Several of these rulings, supported by legal and financial assistance from Muslim Americans outside prison, involved the definition of religion and application of the First Amendment pertaining to freedom of religion, with defendants arguing that prison authorities discriminated against non-Christian and non-Jewish faiths.

Claiming constitutional protection, Muslim Americans took legal action on several issues such as rights to PRAYER, diet, space for worship and services, literature, chaplains and religious counseling, grooming, and dress. Because of these cases, Muslim Americans in many states won the right to wear beards and kufis in addition to having pork-free diets, halal FOOD, and iftar (the daily meal held after sundown during Ramadan). Muslim-American efforts were largely responsible both for obtaining constitutional liberties and protections for prisoners of all faiths as well as bringing prison conditions to the attention of the general public. Furthermore, administrators came to see Islam positively and began to promote rather than hinder its practice in prisons. Ultimately, Muslim Americans, in challenging what they saw as the injustices of America's penal system, stood at the vanguard of this distinctive area in the civil rights movement.

The increase in Muslim immigrants and converts in America in the second half of the 20th century is paralleled in the country's prison population. By the first decade of the 21st century, America's prisons housed between 300,000 and 400,000 Muslims with approximately 30,000 or more added or converted each year. With this growth came a need for trained imams, material resources, and community support. Though more recently Muslim CHAPLAINS were working with those of other faiths to promote equal access and opportunity, this state of affairs did not always exist. Even at the turn of the century it was not uncommon for Christian and Jewish chaplains to fulfill the roles of spiritual mentors to Muslim inmates or for inmates to go without Qur'ans and spaces designated for Muslim worship and services.

As a result, Muslim Americans formed a number of organizations that existed at least in part to remedy this problem. The National Association of Muslim Chaplains, the Junior Association of Muslim Men, and the ISLAMIC SOCIETY OF NORTH AMERICA (ISNA) aimed to prepare men and women for prison ministry and counseling as well as to provide religious, educational, and post-prison support programs for inmates. Groups such as the Propagación Islámica para la Educación y Devoción de Ala' el Divino (PIEDAD) and the Alianza Islamica formed in the 1980s to assist incarcerated Latina and Latino Muslims. Many smaller Islamic centers, mosques, and Sufi groups were also involved with prison outreach.

AFTER 9/11

Since the al-Qaeda attacks of SEPTEMBER 11, 2001, the presence of some groups and individuals seeking to spread WAHHABISM, create terrorist cells, and generally radicalize

inmates came to the attention of both prison authorities and Muslim-American leaders. In 2004, the U.S. Department of Justice issued a report warning of the rise in Islamic extremism and fundamentalism among Muslim-American inmates that combined religious intolerance with racial hostility. Though the situation was difficult given the lack of qualified and eligible imams, Muslim-American organizations such as ISNA and Hartford Seminary's Muslim chaplaincy program, in addition to both state and federal prison chaplains, attempted to confront such extremism by providing religious guidance and religious literature and by assisting ex-prisoners with reintegration into society.

By the 21st century, incarcerated Muslim Americans were able to engage freely in a number of religious practices and represented a broad range of Islamic beliefs and groups. Religious affiliation inside America's prisons mirrored that of the larger culture, with Muslim inmates identifying as Sunni, Shi'a, Sufi, NOI, and MOORISH SCIENCE TEMPLE of America. Often each group had access to the resources particular to that affiliation. However, in many cases, such as in New York's Fishkill Correctional Facility and South Carolina state prisons, prison systems provided only Sunni chaplains, programs, and literature for their diverse population of Muslim inmates. Grouping together such diverse religious populations has sometimes resulted in lawsuits by non-Sunni Muslim prisoners fighting for the right to practice Islam in the way that they understood it. Muslim Americans in prison compose a distinctive and significant subculture within the larger community while simultaneously mirroring its diversity. At the beginning of the 21st century, it is as of yet unclear what effect the presence and fear of radical Islam will have on constitutional protections and rights to religious freedom in America's penal system. However, it is certain that Muslim Americans both inside and outside prison will continue to shape its history and development.

Daniel C. Dillard

Further Reading

Ammar, Nawal H., Robert R. Weaver, and Sam Saxon. "Muslims in Prison: A Case Study from Ohio State Prisons." *International Journal of Offender Therapy and Comparative Criminology* 48, no. 4 (2004): 414–428.

"Black America, Prisons and Radical Islam: A Report." Washington, D.C.: Center for Islamic Pluralism, 2008. Available online. URL: http://www.islamicpluralism.org/CIPReports/CIPPrisonReport.pdf. Accessed December 23, 2008.

Clegg, Claude A. *An Original Man: The Life and Times of Elijah Muhammad.* New York: St. Martin's Press, 1997.

Gottschalk, Marie. *The Prison and the Gallows: The Politics of Mass Incarceration in America.* New York: Cambridge University Press, 2006.

Malcolm X, with Alex Haley. *The Autobiography of Malcolm X.* New York: Grove Press, 1965.

Moore, Kathleen. "Muslims in Prison: Claims to Constitutional Protection of Religious Liberty." In *The Muslims of America,* edited by Yvonne Yazbeck Haddad. New York: Oxford University Press, 1991.

Muffti, Siraj Islam. "Islam in American Prisons." Available online. URL: www.islamonline.net/servlet/Satellite?c=Article_C&cid-1156077734147&pagename-Zone-English-Muslim_Affairs%2FMAELayout. Accessed December 23, 2008.

progressive Muslims

The proliferation of violent extremist groups such as al-Qaeda, which was responsible for the terrorist attacks of September 11, 2001, has been accompanied by a politically and religiously progressive response among Muslim Americans. In the period following 9/11, progressive Muslim voices in the United States have broadcast a very different understanding of Islam, using the Internet, public speeches, and Friday congregational prayer meetings to reach the general public and the Muslim-American community. Although one cannot point to a single progressive Muslim agenda, progressive Muslims became known for a willingness to question time-honored Islamic traditions that they found to be unjust. At the same time, they criticized the West's tendency to use violence and economic leverage to achieve its foreign policy objectives. This was an unusual political position that pitted progressive Muslims against those who were unwilling to question their views of Islam—whether these views were positive or negative.

Progressive Muslims wished to maintain continuity with the Islamic tradition, but they believed in the importance of examining tradition critically. The process of critical examination involves rethinking how to read and understand traditional sources such as the Qur'an and the hadith, the reports of prophet Muhammad's sayings and deeds and those of his companions. Progressive Muslims have advocated reading sacred texts in light of the historical context of their revelation. To read sources in reference to their historical context is to take account of the significant differences that exist between premodern and modern cultures.

Progressive Muslims have thought that such differences ought to and do affect how Muslims practice their religion. For example, they have argued that the status of women in many countries differs from the status of women in seventh-century Arabia, and thus Islamic laws and cultural attitudes should reflect this change. A historically contextualized type of reading is opposed to a literalist reading of sources, in which cultural norms and customs described in the Qur'an and hadith are interpreted as timeless norms. Progressive Muslims believe in the possibility of a multiplicity of interpretations inherent in the Qur'an and in the Islamic legal tradition. Dialogue and disagreement, they argue, are a vital part of the Islamic tradition as a living tradition.

In addition to producing scholarship on Islam, progressive Muslims have engaged in political activism. Progressive Muslims address not only Islam as it is practiced in the United States but also Islam as a global phenomenon. One reason for this is that many progressive Muslims were born overseas and then came to the United States as adults. Legal scholar Khaled Abou El Fadl (1963–   ), for example, was trained in shari'a, or the Islamic legal sciences, in Egypt and Kuwait before coming to the United States for graduate study. Abou El Fadl writes and teaches extensively on topics related to Islamic law and human rights. His books include *Speaking in God's Name: Islamic Law, Authority, and Women* (2001), *Religion and Violence in Islamic Law* (2001), and *Islam and the Challenge of Democracy* (2004). Abou El Fadl has claimed that Islam and democracy are compatible and complementary.

Another progressive Muslim whose thought has been very influential in the United States and abroad is Abdullahi Ahmed An-Na'im, who was born in Northern Sudan. Like Abou El Fadl, An-Na'im was trained in Islamic legal theory. He received his education in law from the University of Khartoum, Sudan, and during this time he joined the Islamic reform movement of Mahmoud Mohamed Taha of the Republican Brothers. During the late 1970s and early 1980s, Taha espoused a progressive approach to interpreting the Qur'an and shari'a in the Sudan.

But Taha's emphasis on reform clashed with Sudan's military regime of Ja'far Nimeiri, and Taha was executed in 1985. After Taha's death, An-Na'im moved to the United States, where he could pursue more freely scholarship and political activism involving human rights and Islamic legal theory. Becoming a professor at Emory University in Atlanta, An-Na'im has been engaged in worldwide human rights advocacy and written several books, including *Toward an Islamic Reformation: Civil Liberties, Human Rights, and International Law* (1990) and *Islam and the Secular State: Negotiating the Future of Shari'a* (2008).

Other progressive Muslims are indigenous to the United States, including Amina Wadud (1952–   ). Born in Maryland, Amina Wadud is an African-American Muslim who has written extensively on the topic of Islam and gender justice and published a book on feminist Qur'anic exegesis, *Qur'an and Woman: Rereading the Sacred Text from a Woman's Perspective* (1999). In that book, Wadud examines scriptures that have traditionally been read and interpreted as oppressive of women and writes with the explicit purpose of empowering women by offering new interpretations of the sacred text. A feminist activist, Wadud has also broken the taboo against women's leadership of mixed gender prayers. On March 18, 2005, Wadud led a Friday prayer service in the Episcopal Cathedral of St. John the Divine in New York City.

Wadud drew criticism from both moderate and conservative Islamic groups for her action, though the Progressive Muslim Union (PMU) endorsed her action.

The work of white Muslim American Kecia Ali has represented another angle on gender and Islamic cultures, specifically Islamic jurisprudence. In her book, *Sexual Ethics and Islam: Feminist Reflections on Qur'an, Hadith, and Jurisprudence* (2006), Ali has written about Islamic practices of marriage and divorce, calling attention to the ways in which traditional Islamic jurisprudence has privileged MEN over WOMEN.

Some progressive Muslims have created groups and Web sites as a form of political activism and social education. One such group is the Progressive Muslim Union (PMU). Originally founded in 2004, the PMU has since struggled due to a lack of consensus of its members regarding the approach that progressive Muslims should take to questions about religion, politics, and economics, especially with regard to UNITED STATES FOREIGN RELATIONS with the Middle East. Other progressive Muslim voices have chosen to express their views through a Web site, ProgressiveIslam.org, that is a self-described "super blog" for Muslims of theological and ethnic diversity. The Web site has articulated its purpose as an informal group of Muslims working together through intellectual debate and discussion. Another group represented on the Internet, Muslims for Progressive Values (MPV), has declared that Islam is compatible with progressive social views. This group has claimed that it is not interested in the reform of Islamic tradition, but rather that it wants to change how Muslims perceive their religion in terms of social justice issues and the separation of church and state.

Progressive Muslims in the United States have represented a constituency of Muslims who have voiced dissatisfaction with neoconservative and politically radical Islamic groups. They have sought to diminish the pervasive global influence of such groups through engagement with Islamic textual traditions as well as political and social activism. These scholars and activists have disagreed at times about the nature of reform in the Islamic tradition, but overall as a collective group they have espoused a pluralistic view in which identities that are both Western and Islamic are not only possible but inevitable.

Shannon Dunn

Further Reading

Abou El Fadl, Khaled. *Islam and the Challenge of Democracy.* Princeton, N.J.: Princeton University Press, 2004.

Ali, Kecia. *Sexual Ethics and Islam: Feminist Reflections on Qur'an, Hadith, and Jurisprudence.* Oxford: Oneworld, 2006.

An-Na'im, Abdullahi. *Islam and the Secular State: Negotiating the Future of Shari'a.* Cambridge, Mass.: Harvard University Press, 2008.

Kelsay, John. *Arguing the Just War in Islam.* Cambridge, Mass.: Harvard University Press, 2007.

Safi, Omid, ed. *Progressive Muslims on Justice, Gender, and Pluralism.* Oxford: Oneworld, 2003.

Wadud, Amina. *Qur'an and Woman: Rereading the Sacred Text from a Woman's Perspective.* New York: Oxford University Press, 1999.

punk music See TAQWACORE.

Qadiri-Rifa'i Sufi Order

One of the many manifestations of SUFISM, the mystical and pietistic branch of Islam that seeks to bring believers to closer, more personal relationship with God, the Qadiri-Rifa'i Sufi Order has a spiritual lineage reaching back to Abdul Qadir Geylani and Ahmed al-Rifa'i, the 12th-century founders of the two largest Sufi orders in the world, the Qadiris and Rifa'is. The joint Qadiri-Rifa'i Sufi Order was established in the early 20th century by religious master Muhammad Ansari in Istanbul. His goal was to teach *tasawwuf,* or Sufism, in a way that would make the tradition relevant in the modern world.

His school of thought was introduced to the United States in the 1980s by Turkish religious master Taner Ansari. The Qadiri-Rifa'i Order attracted its first members in Kalamazoo, Michigan, where Ansari had previously been a university student and founding member of the local chapter of the MUSLIM STUDENTS ASSOCIATION in the middle 1960s. The movement did not grow significantly until Ansari decided in the 1990s to relocate to Napa, California, where the order established a permanent center. There its membership numbered perhaps in the hundreds.

In the 1990s, the order also began to publish the *Call of the Divine,* a print newsletter. Ansari also formally incorporated his own press to publish works related to Sufism, including his original writings. He was a regular speaker at the annual Sufism Symposium hosted by the International Association of Sufism.

Members, who included converts to Islam and persons born Muslim from a variety of religious, national, and ethnic backgrounds, participated in local interfaith councils and community projects. Like many other Muslims, they observed various components typical of Muslim RELIGIOUS LIFE, including fasting during Ramadan, giving alms, and performing the *salat,* the form of prayer that involves a series of bodily prostrations and recitation of various Qur'anic verses and other sacred words. But as a Sufi order whose goal is to know God directly, the Qadiri-Rifa'i also emphasized the need for persistent reflection and the purification of the heart and the cleansing of the ego *(nafs)* through recitation of the 99 names of God. Qadiri-Rifa'i DHIKR, or prayer of remembrance, is often accompanied by poetry, music, and movement when performed in a congregation. In addition, the order put great emphasis on the relationship between the disciple and the teacher or spiritual master that is formally established when each member is initiated into the order.

During the first decade of the 21st century, the order moved its international headquarters to Nassau, New York, where as of 2009, it was still in the process of building an ecologically sustainable retreat center. Leader Taner Ansari also moved to upstate New York where, using the INTERNET and other media, he has continued to teach his followers about Sufi healing and sustainable living. There are at least 13 teachers or centers associated with the movement in New York, California, Massachusetts, and Michigan, and in Australia, Bosnia, Mexico, South Africa, Tanzania, and the United Kingdom.

Melinda Krokus

Further Reading

Ansari, Es-Seyyid Es-Shaykh Taner. *Alternative Healing: The Sufi Way.* Nassau, N.Y.: Ansari Publications, 2007.
———. *The Sun Will Rise in the West.* Napa, Calif.: Ansari Publications, 2000.
———. *What About My Wood! 101 Sufi Stories.* Nassau, N.Y.: Ansari Publications, 2005.
Ansari, Es-Seyyid Es-Shaykh Taner, trans. *Grand Masters of Sufism: Abdul Qadir Geylani Secret of Secrets and Ahmed er Rifai Guidance to Mysticism.* Nassau, N.Y.: Ansari Publications, 2008.
Qadiri Rifai Sufi Order. Available online. URL: http://www.qadiri-rifai.org. Accessed April 8, 2009.

Queen Noor   See NOOR, QUEEN.

Qur'an

The Qur'an is the sacred scripture of Islam. According to traditions accepted as authentic by both Sunni and Shi'a Muslims, the general outline of the origins and nature of the

Qur'an are uncontroversial: In the early decades of the seventh century C.E., MUHAMMAD ibn 'Abdallah, a pious merchant from a powerful tribe in the Arabian peninsula, began to receive visitations from a mysterious figure believed to be the angel identified as Gabriel in Jewish and Christian lore. The angel had been sent by God to Muhammad to vouchsafe to him an "ARABIC recitation," one that would not only communicate the Divine plan to Arabic-speaking peoples in their own tongue but that would also "correct" previous Near Eastern scriptures that had suffered corruption at the hands of unscrupulous sectarians.

Muhammad learned these recitations by heart and, in turn, taught them to a growing circle of followers. Throughout his prophetic career, which lasted from 610 to 632 C.E., literate members of Muhammad's circle wrote down portions of the recited text as an aid to memorization. Either during the Prophet's lifetime and under his direction, or shortly thereafter, the extant portions of the recitation were collected and arranged in substantially the form that was later officially recognized by the community of Muslim scholars. That authorized edition is the Qur'an in use among Sunnis and Shi'a today.

The word *qur'an* literally means "something recited" in Arabic. For the vast majority of Muslims around the world, the Qur'an is an aural experience that tends to supply the "soundtrack" for daily living. In Muslim-majority countries, one hears the Qur'an recited aloud in mosques during daily PRAYERS, in private homes on festive occasions (often performed by trained reciters), in shops, in taxicabs, on street corners—wherever a portable cassette or CD player may be found.

IN EIGHTEENTH- AND NINETEENTH-CENTURY AMERICA

The introduction of the Qur'an to the Western Hemisphere coincides with the importation of African slaves to both North and South America by European settlers. From the 15th to the 19th centuries, Spanish, Portuguese, French, Dutch, and British colonists imported some 10 million Africans to the Americas to serve as slave labor. Of these European imperial powers, the British maintained the most durable and extensively developed presence in North America. According to historian Michael Gomez, nearly half of the 481,000 slaves brought by the British to these shores during the course of the trans-Atlantic trade hailed from parts of Africa that contained significant Muslim populations. He therefore estimates that thousands, if not tens of thousands, of these slaves were Muslim at the time of their importation.

Despite the size of this population, the conditions of African slavery in the Americas were not conducive to the establishment, practice, or propagation of Islam: Slaveholders were not keen to permit their charges to practice a religion

unless it was one that the slaveholders themselves were competent to oversee and to interpret to their advantage. Therefore, little material culture survives to bear witness to the role that the Qur'an may have played among Muslim slaves.

It is possible, however, that amulets containing Qur'anic inscriptions either survived the middle passage or were reproduced on plantations by those slaves who were familiar with West African conjure culture. Moreover, interviews conducted among the descendants of African slaves still living in the sea islands of Georgia in the 1930s produced intriguing recollections of individuals from prior generations who would pray on mats, facing east, at specified intervals each day. Some of those who did so were remembered to have made devotional use of a book that they otherwise kept hidden. Of course, as noted above, a "book" in material form would not be necessary for those who had portions of the Qur'an committed to heart.

One piece of evidence to support the assertion that there were indeed Africans enslaved in the Americas who kept the Qur'an "hidden" in their memories—if not in tangible form secreted among their material possessions—consists of a single handwritten page. One side of the document reads as follows: "The Lord's Prayer written in Arabic by Uncle Moreau (Omar) a native African, now owned by General Owen of Wilmington N. C. He is 88 years of age & a devoted Christian. Given to Mary Jones, at the Rockbridge Alum Springs, Rockbridge County Va. by Genl Owen July 27, 1857." On the reverse side of the page, in large Arabic script, one finds not the Lord's Prayer but the 110th Surah, or chapter, of the Qur'an: hand-drafted in ink with some minor interpolation. "Uncle Moreau" is believed by scholars to be one OMAR IBN SAID (1770–1864), a West African Muslim scholar who was sold into slavery in 1807 and who later authored a surviving autobiography. What "Uncle Moreau" or Omar intended when he wrote this page is unclear since the circumstances surrounding its production are unknown; nevertheless, its very existence justifies the inference that the Arabic Qur'an was able to lead a clandestine life among Muslims enslaved in the Americas.

Where open access to the Qur'an *was* permitted in early American history, it was not among African slaves, nor self-identifying Muslims, but among non-Muslims such as Thomas Jefferson. As a young man, Jefferson purchased his edition of the Qur'an in 1765 while studying law at the College of William and Mary. Directly translated into English from the Arabic text by the British Oriental Studies scholar George Sale, Jefferson's Qur'an had been published in London the previous year. Originally issued in that same city in 1734, its full title was *The Koran, Commonly Called the Alcoran of Mohammed.* By 1764, Sale's translation had to be reissued in two volumes in order to make room for a "Preliminary

Discourse" authored by the translator himself. This introduction offered the reader a broad overview of Islam in the space of roughly 200 pages. Sale's translation was the first scholarly edition of Islamic scripture to appear in English and, as such, remained the standard version in the United States until the 20th century.

IN TWENTIETH-CENTURY BLACK AMERICA

Indigenous American representations of the Qur'an found new expression through the religious imaginations of African Americans within a few decades of their emancipation from slavery in 1865. The form that these representations assumed reflected the prevailing conditions of blacks in the post-Reconstruction period of U.S. history, and especially the conditions of the approximately 1 million who abandoned life in the rural segregated South as sharecroppers and laborers to resettle in America's new industrial heartlands of the North and Midwest between 1920 and 1930. Spurred by the hope of escaping the poverty and racism that characterized life in the states of the old Confederacy, many African Americans migrated north only to encounter social and economic impediments that rivaled the inequities experienced under sharecropping. For some former slaves and their descendants, the Qur'an's linguistic and religious foreignness offered an alternative space of imagination in which to express a different identity from that which race, poverty, and compelled servitude had thrust upon them.

Among the first to claim the Qur'an as an emblem of African-American difference was NOBLE DREW ALI (1886–1929) and his MOORISH SCIENCE TEMPLE of America. In 1927, Ali published his own *Holy Koran,* a book that owes far more to theosophical texts popular among American practitioners of metaphysical religions in the first third of the 20th century than to the Qur'an of the prophet Muhammad. In terms of content, Ali's *Holy Koran* bears little resemblance to the Arabic recitations of the seventh century, but Ali's choice of title for his own text reflects the significance with which he invested the foreign-sounding name. By identifying his community's scripture with the founding text of an alien tradition, Ali was able to underscore the radical difference that he believed distinguished Americans of African descent from the dominant white, Protestant culture into which, generations before, they had been transported as slaves.

A second milestone in the history of the Qur'an as an emblem of African-American difference arose from an equally unexpected quarter: South Asia. There the combined efforts of British colonists and associated Christian missionaries had prompted a vigorous response on the part of some Muslims. In the early 20th century, the Ahmadiyya, a modernist Messianic movement, produced numerous polemical and scholarly tracts and some formidable scholarship—including

a translation of the Arabic Qur'an into English. Although it is unlikely that this translation was undertaken with an eye to its eventual export to North America, this is precisely what took place. After the movement split into two branches in 1914, one branch attempted to look westward for its future. This decision would have a lasting impact upon African-American religiosity and upon the history of the Qur'an in the United States.

The Ahmadiyya mission to America began in 1920, when Mufti Muhammad Sadiq arrived in the United States. He soon moved to DETROIT, MICHIGAN, and then to CHICAGO, ILLINOIS, where the new headquarters of AHMADI MUSLIM AMERICANS was located.

One of the group's main missionary goals was to distribute copies of his movement's English translation of the Qur'an. First published in 1917, the Ahmadi Qur'an contained the Arabic text with English renderings as well as annotations reflecting the doctrinal stance of its translator, Maulana Muhammad Ali. Muhammad Ali did not share the theory of prophecy that characterized Mufti Sadiq's branch of the Ahmadiyya, but this difference of opinion did not prevent Sadiq from overseeing the importation and distribution of Muhammad Ali's translation. Indeed, Sadiq's ability to get a copy of Muhammad Ali's Qur'an into the hands of Americans (mostly African Americans), Muslim and non-Muslim, Ahmadi or not, constitutes one of the most enduring legacies of his mission. With its bright green cover and gilt calligraphy, the Ahmadi Qur'an has an attractive and distinctive appearance; it is often conspicuously present in photographs taken of black Muslims from the 1920s to the present.

Beginning in the 1930s, African-American Muslims who chose to practice Sunni Islam sought to become more knowledgeable about the Qur'an. Often using an Ahmadi translation of the Qur'an, they looked to the scripture for guidance on everything from politics to personal appearance. A few rare African Americans, such as MUHAMMAD EZALDEEN, traveled abroad in the 1930s to learn more about the rudiments of Sunni Islamic tradition, including the Qur'an. Perhaps the first African-American religious leader to articulate a full-blown social philosophy based on the Qur'an was Daoud Ahmed Faisal, whose 1950 book on Islam discussed how passages from the Qur'an related to interfaith encounters in America and other topics central to postwar culture.

Though black Sunni Muslims constituted a vital portion of the African-American community, it was ELIJAH MUHAMMAD's NATION OF ISLAM (NOI) that brought the Qur'an to the attention of most black Americans. Becoming leader of the Nation of Islam in the 1930s, Elijah Muhammad maintained a somewhat curious relationship to the holy book. While Muhammad relied heavily on the

Bible to explain his version of Islam, he also selected passages from the Qur'an to prove the Islamic authenticity of his message. In other words, the Qur'an served Muhammad as an emblem of African-American difference; the extent to which it may have formed his religious thinking, however, is open to question.

A similar stance toward the Qur'an can be observed in the career of Minister LOUIS FARRAKHAN (1933–   ). Since recreating a version of the Nation of Islam in 1978, Farrakhan has consistently used verses from the Bible in his speeches and writing. In public appearances, however, Farrakhan has also brandished his iconic copy of Maulana Muhammad Ali's translation of the Qur'an. Moreover, Farrakhan based key portions of his most important speech, the address to the hundreds of thousands of African-American men who attended the 1997 MILLION MAN MARCH, on passages from the Qur'an, and he has increasingly incorporated the reciting of the Qur'an at Nation of Islam functions.

LATE TWENTIETH CENTURY

Despite the fact that the Qur'an remained of somewhat limited use in the Nation of Islam late into the 20th century, the majority of African-American Muslims—and Muslims of every other ethnic background—devoted increasing time, energy, and financial resources to studying, listening to, writing about, and publicizing the Qur'an in the 1970s and 1980s. While Muslim immigrants from the Middle East and South Asia, who had been arriving on American shores since the late 19th century, always relied on the Qur'an in their religious rituals and for other purposes, the new attention given to the Qur'an in this period was different in both its intensity and scope.

This new Muslim-American devotion to the Qur'an coincided with a more general religious revival in the United States during the 1970s and with the global Islamic revival of the same period. Supported financially by the oil-rich Kingdom of Saudi Arabia, Muslim-American organizations and mosques began to distribute, often for free, English translations of the Qur'an and commentaries on the holy book. In addition to reciting and hearing others recite the Qur'an, an increasing number of Muslim Americans became devoted students of the text's meanings and their application to nearly any circumstance.

Though the Qur'an had been studied at American universities before this time, most leading scholars of the Qur'an worked in European universities. After 1965, however, increasing numbers of immigrants from Asia and Africa began to arrive in the United States, including notable scholars of Islam such as FAZLUR RAHMAN (1919–88). Rahman, who taught at the University of Chicago from 1969 to 1988, taught an entire generation of Muslim and non-Muslim

scholars about his own style of interpreting the Qur'an. By the end of the 20th century, several Muslim Americans had produced works of scholarship written for a general audience that often analyzed the potential meanings of particular Qur'anic passages illustrative of the Qur'anic message as a whole. Works representative of this genre included Fazlur Rahman's *Major Themes of the Qur'an* (1980), AMINA WADUD's *Qur'an and Woman: Rereading the Sacred Text from a Woman's Perspective* (1992), and Farid Esack's *The Qur'an: A Short Introduction* (2001).

In their sermons and books, Muslim-American leaders of every ethnic background urged their followers to study and follow the Qur'an. W. D. MOHAMMED (1933–2008), one of the most influential African-American Sunni leaders of the late 20th century, often relied on passages of the Qur'an as a guide to personal ethics and community improvement. Based on his reading of the Qur'an, for example, he supported interfaith dialogue and interracial harmony while also maintaining that a strong sense of ethnic solidarity and personal responsibility were essential to the advancement of his predominantly African-American community.

The devotion to understanding the Qur'an and applying its lessons to daily life also developed among local communities. African-American Muslim females in South Central LOS ANGELES, for example, studied the Qur'an for guidance on how to deal with patriarchy in their mosques and in their marriages. Similarly, South Asian–American writer Asma Gull Hasan used passages from the Qur'an to argue with her grandfather about his patriarchal views of women. According to Hasan, her old-fashioned grandfather thought that the Qur'an favored men over women in both earthly and spiritual matters. But when Hasan challenged him to cite the passages that established this male superiority, he balked. According to Hasan's reading of the Qur'an, such verses do not exist.

AFTER 9/11

After the al-Qaeda attacks of SEPTEMBER 11, 2001, non-Muslims seemed to develop an equally intense fascination with the Qur'an—albeit for different reasons. Translations of the Qur'an became best sellers at bookstores around the country as many Americans sought to read the book for clues on how the 9/11 terrorists could commit such evil acts or simply to understand more about the religion. Many conservative and liberal commentators alike saw the Qur'an as a source of what they deemed to be Islamic intolerance. When U.S. Representative KEITH M. ELLISON (D-Minn.), the first Muslim elected to Congress, sought to be sworn in using Thomas Jefferson's copy of the Qur'an in 2006, a fellow representative, Virgil Goode (R-Va.), criticized the move as an example of "infiltration by those who want to mold the United States into the image of their religion." Some members of the UNITED STATES MILITARY guarding Muslim prisoners at the detention center at GUANTÁNAMO BAY held similar views and desecrated the Qur'an by putting a volume of it in urine.

For Muslim Americans, protecting—at times, literally—the Qur'an after 9/11 became an important symbol of their struggle for recognition as full citizens and persons worthy of respect in the United States. Muslim Americans involved in INTERFAITH MOVEMENTS and other leaders sought to show that the Qur'an did not support the killing of innocents or the maltreatment of women or the forcible conversion of Jews and Christians. Muslim critics of terrorism often found fault in the improper interpretation of the Qur'an rather than in the text of the Qur'an itself. Through public speeches, outreach to schools, and the use of various media, Muslim Americans attempted to reassure their fellow citizens about their holy book. In its many translations and interpretations, the Qur'an remains the central text for Muslim Americans and Muslims around the world.

Peter Matthews Wright

Further Reading

Curtis, Edward E., IV. *Black Muslim Religion in the Nation of Islam, 1960–1975*. Chapel Hill: University of North Carolina Press, 2006.

———. *Islam in Black America: Identity, Liberation, and Difference in African-American Islamic Thought*. Albany: State University of New York Press, 2002.

Diouf, Sylviane A. *Servants of Allah: African Muslims Enslaved in the Americas*. New York: New York University Press, 1998.

Esack, Farid. *The Qur'an: A Short Introduction*. Oxford: Oneworld, 2001.

Gomez, Michael A. *Exchanging Our Country Marks: The Transformation of African Identities in the Colonial and Antebellum South*. Chapel Hill: University of North Carolina Press, 1998.

Hayes, Kevin J. "How Thomas Jefferson Read the Qur'an." *Early American Literature* 39, no. 2: 247–261.

The Holy Qur'an. 5th ed. Translation and commentary by Maulana Muhammad Ali. Columbus, Ohio: Ahmadiyyah Anjuman Isha'at Islam Lahore, Inc., 1963.

The Koran: Commonly Called the Alcoran of Mohammed. 5th ed. Translation, explanatory notes, and preliminary discourse by George Sale. Philadelphia: J. W. Moore, 1856.

Muhammad, Elijah. *Message to the Blackman in America*. Chicago: Muhammad Mosque of Islam No. 2, 1965.

Rahman, Fazlur. *Major Themes of the Qur'an*. Minneapolis: Bibliotheca Islamica, 1980.

Turner, Richard Brent. *Islam in the African-American Experience*. 2d ed. Bloomington: Indiana University Press, 2003.

Wadud, Amina. *Qur'an and Woman: Rereading the Sacred Text from a Woman's Perspective*. Oxford: Oxford University Press, 1999.

M. R. Bawa Muhaiyaddeen
"The Inner Qur'an" (1987)

From the beginning of Islamic history, Muslims have sought to imbibe the inner meaning of the Qur'an. From the seventh century until today, they have viewed the Qur'an as a revelation that offers moral guidance and brings human beings closer to God's presence. The cultivation of God's presence by meditating upon the Qur'an has been particularly important for Sufi Muslims, who emphasize the development of a personal relationship with God. While Sufism was likely first brought to the Americas by West African Muslim slaves in the colonial era, Sufi missionaries first appeared in the United States at the beginning of the 20th century. After immigration restrictions were lifted in 1965, more Sufi missionaries came, including Muhammad Raheem Bawa Muhaiyaddeen, a Sri Lankan Muslim Sufi teacher. In 1971, he founded a Sufi group in Philadelphia that catered to a racially integrated and ethnically diverse fellowship centered on his teachings about spirituality and its importance to peace and justice in the modern world. Muhaiyaddeen, who died in 1986, said that the Qur'an was the light of God in the world, and in "The Inner Qur'an," an essay published posthumously in 1987, he explained how this light would bring peace, both internal and external, to all those who sought to achieve a more intimate relationship with God.

I seek refuge in Allah from the evils of the accursed Satan.

In the name of Allah, Most Merciful, Most Compassionate. May all the peace, the beneficence, and the blessings of God be upon you.

Brothers and sisters in Islam, no matter what changes occur throughout the ages, the Qur'an is one thing that never changes. It is immutable. It offers an explanation appropriate for every period of time and for every level of understanding. All the meanings it contains could not be written down even if all the oceans of the world were made into ink and all the trees were made into pens.

To comprehend the Qur'an, first we must establish our absolute faith, certitude, and determination; then we must acquire wisdom; and finally we must delve deep inside and study it from within. If we look into the depths of the Qur'an, we will find the complete never-ending wealth and grace of Almighty God. We will find the light of Allah, the resplendence of Allah. We will not find racial or religious prejudices, battles, or fighting of any kind. We will find only the benevolence of all the universes.

The Qur'an appeared as the beginning, the emergence of creation . . . , as the eternal life, the emergence of the soul . . . , as the food, the nourishment for all creations . . . , as the innermost heart . . . , as the beauty of the face which is a reflection of the beauty of the heart . . . , and as the plenitude, the light which became completeness within Allah and then emerged. . . .

The Sufis also say that only when man comes to a realization of himself and dives deep within the inner Qur'an, drinking from its essence, will the truth of Muhammad be revealed to him in his meditation. Only when he reaches the state where he speaks to Allah alone, can he be said to truly exist in Islam. When he attains that state of communion with Allah, he will understand that the Qur'an and the holy books are his body, the inner mystical form of a human being. Such a man will understand the inner meaning of *al-hamdu lilla,* which is the praise of the inner form of man. Understanding the history of the One who is all praise, he will glorify Him alone. Only then can he see this history as one continuous study, an endless ocean of divine knowledge. Otherwise each book he reads will then refer him to yet another book. As long as he continues reading only those outer books, he will never reach his freedom.

My brothers, we must consider how the Qur'an came from Allah, and we must delve deep within it. In order to understand its true meaning, we must be in the same state as that original Qur'an was when it emerged from Allah. It came as a resplendence, a radiance, resonance, and a grace. Then it came as a light to Gabriel. And when it came to Muhammad, the Messenger, it came as the grace and attributes of Allah. Next Muhammad brought it to us as a revelation. Then the sound of these revelations was transformed into letters and formed into words. What was revealed in those words ultimately became public knowledge and part of history. The interpretations of this knowledge later gave rise to religious differences, divisions, and bigotry, which in turn gave rise to prejudice, fighting, and wars. This is the state the world has come to.

We, however, must delve into the depths of the Qur'an; we must experience each step of the way as it originally came from Allah. As we look deeper and deeper, we will see the Messenger of God, and once we see him, we will know how Gabriel came to him and how he received that grace. We will see the light, and if we look through that light we will experience the resonance of Allah within the Qur'an. As we understand that resonance, we will understand our life and our death; we will understand the Day of Judgment, the Day of Questioning, and the ninety-nine attributes of Allah.

Once we have this understanding, we will see that all men are our brothers just as the Qur'an teaches us. To truly see all people as our brothers is Islam. If we see anyone who is in need, we must offer him the water of the mercy of all the universes, the water of absolute faith, and the affirmation of that faith, the *kalima* [there is no god but God, Muhammad is the Messenger of God]. That water must be given to everyone who is hungry or thirsty. We must embrace them lovingly, quench their thirst, and wash away their dirt. We must offer them love, compassion, patience, and tolerance, just as the Prophet did. This is what will satisfy their needs and dispel the darkness in their hearts.

My brothers and sisters in Islam, if we offer peace, then justice will flourish. Love will cut away all enmity. Compassion will cause God's grace to grow in this world, and then the food of faith and the mercy of all the universes can be offered. When that food is given, hunger, disease, old age, and death will be eliminated, and everyone will have peace.

Allah and the state of a true human being are right here within us. It is a great secret, hidden within our hearts. . . . Only if we can study this divine knowledge can we attain our freedom. All who have faith must reflect upon this, understand it, and teach it to those who have less wisdom, to those who have no clarity of heart, to those whose minds oppose us, and to those who have no peace of mind. We must teach them these qualities, give them this food, this beauty, and this nourishment of grace and absolute faith. Every human being in the community of Islam, everyone who has faith,

all those who are learned and wise, all the leaders
of prayer and the teachers, all those who know
the Qur'an—all must understand this. This is what
I ask of you.

Amen. Allah is sufficient unto us all.

Source: M. R. Bawa Muhaiyaddeen, "The Inner Qur'an." In *Islam
and World Peace,* 133–138. Philadelphia: Fellowship Press,
1987.

Qureshey, Safi (1951–) *entrepreneur, philanthropist*

Safi Qureshey was the cofounder of the computer company
AST, which developed from a small firm to a Fortune 500
company, one of the 500 largest companies in the world. As a
philanthropist, he mentored young entrepreneurs, supported
brain research, and promoted understanding of Islam in the
United States.

Qureshey was born on February 15, 1951, in Karachi,
Pakistan, where he completed an undergraduate degree in
physics in 1971. After moving to the United States, he earned
a B.S. in electrical engineering at the University of Texas in
1975. In 1980, Qureshey and fellow entrepreneurs Albert
Wong and Thomas Yuen founded AST Research, a personal computer manufacturer in Irvine, California. Under
Qureshey's leadership, AST grew from a small start-up to
a Fortune 500 company. AST's first business opportunity
arose from the mutual incompatibility of the two most popular personal computers of the 1980s: IBM's PC and Apple's
Macintosh. AST manufactured microcomputer expansion
cards that allowed Macintosh computers to run Microsoft's
MS-DOS along with its own operating system. AST also
manufactured expansion cards to provide IBM PCs with
additional features such as a mouse port or a parallel printer
port. In the late 1980s, as IBM PCs integrated these features
into their motherboards, AST began to manufacture their
own line of personal computers for the desktop, mobile, and
server markets.

In 1987, in an attempt to maintain dominance in the computer market, IBM developed and patented MicroChannel
Architecture, a propriety operating system. IBM also imposed
strict licensing and royalty policies. Companies such as
AST, which produced IBM clones at a lower price, needed
an alternative system. In 1988, Qureshey banded together
with eight other manufacturers of PC clones to create the
"Gang of Nine," a group that created the Extended Industry
Standard Architecture (EISA) to compete with IBM's pro-
prietary MicroChannel Architecture. Essentially, the EISA
promised to perform the same tasks as MicroChannel at less
expense. Even so, EISA was expensive to implement. It did
not penetrate the desktop personal computer market, though
it gained some success in the server market.

At the height of Qureshey's success in 1991, AST had
operations in more than 100 countries and generated $2.5
billion in annual revenue. But in the coming years, AST's
sales declined. Rather than outsource the production of certain components, as other companies did, AST continued to
develop its own components in order to maintain control over
quality. In 1994, in a cost-cutting measure, Qureshey had to
lay off 440 workers, and in 1996, he sold AST research to
Samsung. A new company named AST Computers acquired
rights to AST's name and intellectual property in 1999.

In 2006, Qureshey launched a new venture called
Quartics, a wireless company that, like AST, found opportunity in the gap between two technologies—in this case,
wireless personal computers and television. Quartics has
produced microchips to allow consumers to broadcast media
content from their personal computers to their televisions or
other outlets of their choice. In 2008, Quartics reported $5.6
million in sales and employed 58 people. In 2008, Qureshey
resigned as chief executive officer of Quartics and focused
on PHILANTHROPY work in the Chief Executive Officer
Emeritus Club in Orange County, California, an organization
that mentored promising young entrepreneurs.

Qureshey's activities have also extended to politics
and international trade. From 1995 to 1999, Qureshey
served as one of President Bill Clinton's appointees to the
President's Export Council, a private advisory group seeking to increase American exports. Qureshey accompanied
the secretary of the treasury on trips abroad, especially to
Asia. In 2003, California governor Arnold Schwarzenegger
enlisted Qureshey to recruit talented people of all ethnicities
for the governor's new administration. Qureshey also served
as regent's professor at the Graduate School of Business
Management, University of California, Irvine (UCI), which
awarded him the UCI Medal in 1995. In 1997, a research
laboratory at UCI's Center for Neurobiology of Learning and
Memory was named in his honor.

Like several other high-profile SOUTH ASIAN–AMERICAN
MUSLIMS who arrived in the United States after the liberalization of immigration laws in 1965, Qureshey has been hailed
by other Muslim Americans as an example of how Muslims
have contributed to the building of the American economy.
He became one of Southern California's leading Muslim philanthropists, donating more than $1 million to support brain
research at UCI and additional seed money for a foundation
to make documentaries promoting public understanding of
Islam. His success has been put forward as an example for
other Muslim Americans to follow. Qureshey not only helped

to build a Fortune 500 company, he also attempted to share his wealth and expertise with others.

Sonja Spear with Nicholas P. Jackson

Further Reading

"AST Co-Founder Seeks Room Inside the PC." *Cnet News,* 11 November 2008. Available online. URL: http://news.cnet.com. Accessed February 13, 2009.

Hotch, Ripley. "Two Musketeers Take on the PC World." *Nation's Business* (December 1999). Available online. URL: http://findarticles.com/p/articles/mi_m1154/is_n12_v78/ai_9695871Bnet.com. Accessed February 14, 2009.

"Safi U. Qureshey: Executive Profile and Biography." BusinessWeek.com. Available online. URL: http://investing.businessweek.com/businessweek/research/stocks/private/person.asp?personId=714335&privcapId=27975311&previousCapId=20767&previousTitle=Greylock%20Partners. Accessed February 13, 2009.

R

radio

Muslim-American involvement in radio broadcasting reflects the diverse backgrounds and concerns of Muslim-American communities. From the 1960s until the beginning of the 21st century, radio developed as an important tool for Muslim community-building in the United States. Generally speaking, Muslims have not used radio as much as other American religious communities have, partially because of a lack of financial and human resources. Nevertheless, the use of new technologies, such as the INTERNET, has meant an increase in Muslim-American radio broadcasting.

In the 21st century, radio has become an increasingly important medium among Muslim Americans. The purpose of Muslim-American religious broadcasting, like that of other religious communities' radio broadcasts, has ranged from religious education and missionary work to bridge-building with other American populations. Whatever the purpose of these transmissions, Muslim involvement in radio broadcasting has shown the different ways in which Muslims shape and convey their community interests and, in turn, how this medium shapes and informs the ever-changing Muslim-American community.

TWENTIETH-CENTURY
MUSLIM-AMERICAN RADIO

Among the earliest Islamic communities to utilize radio technology was the NATION OF ISLAM (NOI), which began broadcasting radio programs in the early 1960s. Prior to using the radio for the propagation of the NOI's teachings, ELIJAH MUHAMMAD (1897–1975), the movement's longtime leader, reached out to the public via the use of pamphlets and newspapers. However, during the 1960s, Muhammad launched the NOI's first radio shows on CHICAGO airwaves, broadcasting the NOI's teachings and recipes for black uplift.

While Muhammad hosted weekly shows in Chicago, MALCOLM X (1925–65) broadcast from NEW YORK CITY and other American cities. From approximately 1965 to 1975, LOUIS FARRAKHAN (1933–   ) acted as the voice of the Nation of Islam on the radio. Following this period, W. D. MOHAMMED (1933–2008), son of Elijah and CLARA MUHAMMAD (1899–1972), assumed leadership of the community and of the NOI's radio broadcasts. According to the NOI newspaper, *MUHAMMAD SPEAKS,* more than 100 major American cities eventually broadcast the NOI's radio programming, with each local station determining the timing of the transmission.

After his father's death in 1975, W. D. Mohammed introduced various reforms to the NOI, bringing it closer to Sunni Islam and distancing it from the group's race-based theology and black separatism. When Elijah's son changed his name to Warith Deen Muhammad and renamed the Nation of Islam as the WORLD COMMUNITY OF AL-ISLAM IN THE WEST in 1976, the tradition of broadcasting the movement's teachings continued. From 2000 to 2003 and 2007 to 2008, *New Africa Radio,* an Internet radio station, developed an archive of Mohammed's radio broadcasts. These broadcasts were part of Mohammed's "Mosque Cares" project, part of a missionary effort to "invite" people to better understand Islam.

During the late 20th century, first-generation Muslim American immigrants also became more involved with the medium of radio. The IMMIGRATION ACT OF 1965 eased previous immigration restrictions in the United States, which resulted in an influx of more than a million Muslim immigrants from various Muslim countries, such as Pakistan, Bangladesh, Turkey, Iran, Egypt, and Iraq, in the late 20th century. As the influence of these new Muslim Americans was increasingly felt in the American society, several important radio programs developed amid growing feelings that Muslim Americans were being denied the right to speak on their own behalf. Muslim-American radio represented an opportunity for Muslim Americans to define their own concerns and share them with each other and the broader American public.

One program that sought to fill this need was Radio Tahrir, the project of producer and host Barbara Nimri Aziz, which began broadcasting over Pacifica-WBAI in New York City in 1980. Tahrir, which literally means "liberation," is dedicated to bringing the voices, histories, and concerns of Arab and Muslim communities in the United States into the sphere of public broadcasting. Continuous and weekly hour-long broadcasts began in 1989. Topics of interest included the arts and public affairs, civil rights, and social and legal issues, and Tahrir featured the voices of Muslim-American educators, musicians, leaders, thinkers, writers, and artists.

In the 1990s, Abdul Malik Mujahid, activist, scholar, and creator of the Sound Vision Foundation, launched Radio Islam as an online radio station. Later, the Chicago radio station, WCEV, began broadcasting the show for an hour once a week, with the aim of clarifying misunderstandings about Islam.

MUSLIM-AMERICAN RADIO SINCE 9/11

The al-Qaeda attacks on SEPTEMBER 11, 2001, raised a number of concerns that Muslim-American radio attempted to address on air. One of the first media campaigns undertaken by an Islamic organization after September 11 was developed by the COUNCIL ON AMERICAN-ISLAMIC RELATIONS (CAIR). CAIR initiated a campaign of radio public-service announcements condemning terrorism as part of their "Not in the Name of Islam" campaign. Many secular radio talk shows invited Muslim speakers to participate in their programming, answering questions that arose in the political climate of the time and clarifying common misconceptions about the religious tradition.

Weekly radio programs on the topic of Islam in America included True Talk, a weekly hour-long live public affairs show on Tampa's WMNF 88.5 FM that focused on Muslim Americans and the broader global Muslim community. WMNF's mission involves entertaining and educating the public around a set of "shared values." The "Crescent Report," another Muslim-American program, was begun by Imam Mahdi Bray and broadcast weekly over WUST 1120 AM in Washington, D.C. Its first guest was America's first Muslim congressman, KEITH M. ELLISON (1963–   ), elected to the U.S. House of Representatives in 2006. Topics of interest on the show have included religious and political issues such as Muslim-American civil rights.

Another radio program launched in the early 21st century was "Prophetic Echoes," a Harlem-based radio show hosted by Imam Al-Hajj Talib Abdul Rashid, the leader of the Mosque of Islamic Brotherhood in Harlem, which has aired every fourth Friday of the month on 90.3 FM in New York City, or via Internet stream. Another was "The Beauty of Islam," a program on KCAA Radio 1050 AM in Loma Linda, California, hosted by Imam J. D. Hall, which attempted to counter distorted perceptions of Islam in American society.

Muslim Americans have also broadcast programs regarding interfaith activities. For example, "Interfaith Voices," a program carried on 60 stations in the United States and Canada, began in 2006. In order to promote interfaith dialogue, the program has addressed issues such as social justice, war and peace, POLITICS, human rights, and sexuality. It attempts to engage a wider, non-Muslim public by discussing these issues from the viewpoint of different religious traditions.

While most Muslim-American radio broadcasts have been made available online as downloadable podcasts after their initial broadcast over the air, other shows have been created expressly for the Internet. For example, Radio al-Islam, founded in 1995, has provided live streams of QUR'AN recitations, recordings of the ADHAN, or call to PRAYER, discussions of Qur'anic interpretation, and traditional a cappella religious songs called *ansasheed,* as well as discussion on the Sunna, or the traditions of the prophet Muhammad, and Islamic POETRY.

The "American Muslim Radio Show" was created in 2008 and hosted by BlogTalkRadio, a Web site that allows anyone to set up a podcast or radio show over the Web. Led by Robert Salaam and Alia Sajid, the program has focused on the everyday lives of Muslim Americans. This technology has given Muslim Americans a relatively cheap and convenient method for developing community-based radio programming.

Muslim involvement in radio broadcasting reflects the diversity of Muslim-American communities and their concerns. In its short history, it has also highlighted the multiple functions of radio in the era of Web-based broadcasting. Radio offers Muslim Americans a forum for community-building and outreach, for educating one another and non-Muslims, and for conducting missionary work while also broaching issues that have little to do with religion.

Sajida Jalalzai

Further Reading

"American Muslim Radio Show." Available online. URL: http://www.blogtalkradio.com/theamericanmuslim. Accessed March 23, 2009.

Muslim Herald. "First Live Radio Talk Show Starts in Washington." Available online. http://www.muslimherald.com/English/EN_News/America/162605457.htm. Accessed March 23, 2009.

Radio Islam. Available online. URL: http://www.radioislam.com. Accessed March 23, 2009.

Rahman, Fazlur (1919–1988) *intellectual*

Known for rigorous academic knowledge in both Islamic and Western classical philosophy, Fazlur Rahman was a highly regarded thinker among both Muslim and non-Muslim academics.

He was born on September 21, 1919, in the Punjab region of India, son of Maulana Shihab al-Din, a well-known Islamic scholar who had studied SHARI'A, or Islamic law and ethics, at the Deoband seminary. After receiving his baccalaureate in Arabic at Punjab University, Rahman studied in England under S. Van den Bergh and H. A. R. Gibb at Oxford

University, earning his doctorate in 1949. His doctoral dissertation, which explored the philosophy of medieval Islamic philosopher Ibn Sina, was published in 1952 as *Avicenna's Psychology.* During the 1950s, he taught at the University of Durham in England and McGill University in Montreal, Canada. At McGill, Rahman staffed the faculty of its Institute of Islamic Studies and published one of his most important works, *Prophecy in Islam: Philosophy and Orthodoxy* (1958). This book, which referenced texts in Arabic, Persian, Greek, Latin, German, and French, showcased his command of both Western and Islamic philosophical sources and languages.

In 1961, Rahman became the head of the new Central Institute of Islamic Research in Karachi, Pakistan, where he founded the academic journal *Islamic Studies* and advised the government on Islamic affairs. After the 1964 elections, Pakistani president Ayyub Khan asked him to be a religious affairs adviser, but Khan began to lose control of the country in the 1960s, as Bangladesh threatened to secede from Pakistan. By 1968, Rahman's political alliances and unorthodox interpretations of religious tradition put him at risk, and he received various threats against his life. That year, he took a temporary teaching post to teach at the University of California, Los Angeles, and then, in 1969, was appointed Professor of Islamic Thought at the University of Chicago, where he stayed until his death in 1988. He was the first Muslim to be appointed to the faculty of the University of Chicago Divinity School.

Rahman excelled in both purely academic scholarship and interpretive debate with fellow Muslims about how best to understand Islam in a modern context. In the latter capacity, he is best known for his efforts to revive and maintain the liveliness of Islamic intellectual life by attempting to separate the core of Islamic tradition from the corpus of medieval Islamic interpretations. To understand and make the best use of the QUR'AN, Rahman argued, Muslims should understand the historical contexts in which the revelations came to the prophet MUHAMMAD in the seventh century. Once this interpretation was accomplished, he explained, the modern Muslim could see the larger principles at work and apply the larger moral and ethical principles in a dynamic way to contemporary problems.

Active in both the academic and Muslim communities, Rahman worked to bridge the two worlds. Since his death on July 26, 1988, Rahman's efforts have continued to wield influence over the field of Islamic studies and ISLAMIC THOUGHT, as can be observed in the work of feminist thinkers such as AMINA WADUD.

Hanifa Abdul Sabur

Further Reading
Denny, Frederick M. "The Legacy of Fazlur Rahman." In *Muslims of America,* edited by Yvonne Yazbeck Haddad, 96–108. New York: Oxford University Press, 1991.
Rahman, Fazlur. *Avicenna's Psychology.* London: Oxford University Press, 1952.
———. *Prophecy in Islam: Philosophy and Orthodoxy.* London: Allen and Unwin, 1958.

Ramadan   See HOLIDAYS; ISLAMIC CALENDAR.

religious life
Throughout their history in the United States, most religiously observant Muslims have structured their lives around a relationship to God and allegiance to the human example of the prophet MUHAMMAD (ca. 570–632), as expressed in the declaration, "There is no god but God. Muhammad is the messenger of God." Most have strived to follow the QUR'AN, which they believe Muhammad received from God through the angel Gabriel, as well as the example of Muhammad himself. Amid this striving, religious practices have been similar both within and between various Muslim groups in the United States, but they have also contained striking differences. The main Muslim groups in the United States are Sunnis, Shi'as, Sufis, and the Nation of Islam.

RELIGIOUS LIFE IN SUNNI ISLAM
The first Muslims to come to the Americas in any significant number arrived as slaves from West Africa in the 17th century. Approximately 10 percent of all West African slaves in America, these Sunnis generally adhered to fundamental Islamic practices including fasting and prayer. This early Sunni presence faded away, however, largely because many slave masters prohibited the practice of Islam and forced their slaves to convert to Christianity. Sunni Islam reappeared in the United States in the late 19th century through Arab and other immigrants.

In the first half of the 20th century, significant Sunni communities emerged. Many immigrants established Islamic centers or mosques in or near large cities such as NEW YORK CITY, DETROIT, and CHICAGO, and in smaller cities or towns including CEDAR RAPIDS, IOWA. Also in the first half of the 20th century, Muslim communities composed mostly of African Americans began to form. African Americans began to convert to various Sunni Islamic movements and mosques in the late 1920s and 1930s.

The number of Sunni immigrants increased greatly after the IMMIGRATION ACT OF 1965. Many of these immigrants held jobs in medicine, engineering, and other sciences, and they established hundreds of mosques and ISLAMIC SCHOOLS. Since 1965, immigrants have made up the majority of Sunni Muslims in the United States, yet American-born Sunnis, mostly African-American, have also been a very sizable and influential component of American Sunni Islam.

Certain practices have defined the lives of religiously observant Sunnis in the United States. *Salat,* a very structured form of prayer, requires specific bodily postures including kneeling and placing one's forehead on the ground, symbolizing submission before God. Sunni Muslims perform *salat* five times daily, facing the direction of Mecca in Saudi Arabia. Before praying, they purify themselves by washing their face and arms, a process that Muslims also undertake before handling the Qur'an. A weekly highlight is the noontime Friday *salat,* which includes a sermon.

Sunni religious life has also included fasting during the month of Ramadan, when Muslims refrain from food and drink from dawn until dusk. Upon sundown, Muslims often gather together for a fast-breaking meal, which may include reading a large portion of the Qur'an. Despite the challenges of fasting, many Muslims look forward to Ramadan and feel sad when it ends due to benefits they receive, such as growing closer to God, developing greater patience and discipline, and deepening their understanding of the poor and needy. Because Muslims follow a lunar calendar, Ramadan occurs during different seasons of the year.

The HAJJ, or pilgrimage to Mecca, has been another defining religious practice for American Sunnis. Muslims must make this pilgrimage once in their lifetime if physically and financially able. A powerful expression of Muslim unity, the hajj involves a series of rituals performed by approximately 2 million pilgrims during a five-day period. Among these rituals are walking around the Ka'ba, a black cubical structure believed by Muslims to have been built long before the time of Muhammad by Abraham and his son Ishmael, and throwing stones at a pillar to symbolize stoning the devil.

Although these defining practices have given American Sunni religious life a significant degree of similarity, important differences have emerged among American Sunni Muslims. Whereas some Sunni mosques in the United States have had full-time, trained leaders, others have not. Often this has been true in less wealthy, largely African-American communities, yet it has also occurred in more wealthy mosques, where Friday worshippers may listen to a sermon from a doctor who wants to understand his religion but lacks classical training in Islamic history and law.

Another significant issue of difference for American Sunnis has concerned WOMEN and *salat.* In many mosques

As part of the *salat* ritual, Muslims line up next to one another and bow in the direction of the Ka'ba in Mecca, which is also the site of the annual hajj, or pilgrimage. *(Bob Daemmrich/PhotoEdit)*

women pray behind or to the side of men, while in others they pray in a separate room, perhaps on a different floor. Sunnis have also differed regarding female leadership of *salat*. Opposing the regulation that women may not lead *salat* if at least one man is present, religious scholar AMINA WADUD led a mixed-gender *salat* in New York in 2005. This controversial event took place in a Christian cathedral after three mosques refused to serve as host. Additionally, the matter of women's DRESS has been a point of difference among Sunnis in the United States. Most have agreed that the Qur'an requires a woman to cover her body modestly not only at the mosque but in any setting in which she may be seen by a man who is not a close family member. The issue of which body parts must be covered has caused debate, with some mandating covering the face and others saying that the combination of a headscarf and modest dress is sufficient. Still others have disagreed with the need for any head covering at all, arguing that this is a cultural, unnecessary addition to Islamic devotion.

RELIGIOUS LIFE IN SHI'A ISLAM

Shi'a Muslims were among the immigrants who came to the United States during the late 19th and early 20th centuries. The first Shi'a immigrants arrived from Lebanon, and others came later from India, Iran, and Iraq. Similar to early Sunni immigrants, these Shi'as were generally economically and educationally disadvantaged, a trend that changed in the second half of the 20th century. From 1952 to 1979, a large number of Shi'as came to the United States as students from Iran during the rule of the Shah. Many returned to the United States after the Islamic Revolution in Iran in 1979. While Shi'as who live in smaller cities and towns have often participated in Sunni mosques, many have gathered in or near large cities in the United States and have established mosques of their own.

One important Shi'a center in the United States has been Dearborn, Michigan. Lebanese Shi'as gathered in Dearborn and constructed a mosque in 1940. At risk of losing their distinctiveness from the larger surrounding Sunni community, Shi'as in Dearborn grew in awareness of their uniqueness with the arrival of trained Shi'a leaders who taught them about their own history, beliefs, and practices. This awareness developed further with the arrival of thousands of Shi'as during the Lebanese Civil War (1975–90).

As a result of this activity over the decades, Shi'as in Dearborn have been rather diverse in their religious practice and interpretation of Islamic law. Stricter mosques have required women to wear head scarves inside the mosque and outside of the home. Other Dearborn Shi'as have identified this as unnecessary and possibly harmful to attracting new followers. The Islamic Center of America, a Shi'a mosque in Dearborn, claims to be the largest mosque in the United States. Sunday sermons at this mosque have been a distinct departure from Islamic tradition. Sunday attendees have outnumbered those on Fridays, primarily because women and children attend sermon services only on Sundays.

To a large extent, the American Shi'a practice of *salat*, fasting during Ramadan, and the hajj pilgrimage has been similar to American Sunni practice of these rituals. Differences include the times during which *salat* prayer occurs during the day and patterns of financial giving. Both Sunnis and Shi'as have commonly required payment of *zakat*, a fixed portion of a Muslim's wealth given to assist the poor and needy and to enable the spread of Islam. In addition to *zakat*, many Shi'as have also paid *khums*, a 20 percent tax given by Shi'as in the United States to pay salaries of religious teachers and leaders and to help with the building of mosques. An even more visible difference between Shi'as and Sunnis has been the Shi'a emphasis upon Ashura. On this day of mourning, commemorated on the 10th day of the month of Muharram on the ISLAMIC CALENDAR, Shi'as remember the death of Husayn, Muhammad's grandson, who was killed in 680 by the leader of the Islamic empire. Mourning occurs at special ceremonies in mosques and in processions that include rhythmic beating of the chest.

RELIGIOUS LIFE IN SUFI ISLAM

One of the earliest teachers of Sufi doctrine in the United States, INAYAT KHAN traveled across the nation in the 1910s and 1920s after studying with both Muslim and Hindu masters. Khan founded the SUFI ORDER OF THE WEST, a group that many Muslims have criticized. Criticism from other Muslims has been a common trend throughout SUFISM's history. Among other claims, many Muslims have declared that Sufis overstep the bounds of true Islam through their practice of DHIKR, a ritual practice often involving music or repetitive chanting to promote remembrance of God. Like many Sufi masters throughout history, Khan proclaimed the virtues of music. He taught that music puts one in harmony with life and allows one to appreciate every aspect of beauty. Many American Sunnis have taken exception to Khan's view of music, claiming that the Qur'an and the tradition of Muhammad prohibit Muslims from listening to instrumental music because it distracts Muslims from awareness of God. As demonstrated by contemporary Sunni HIP-HOP groups such as NATIVE DEEN, however, not all Sunni Muslims have shared this position.

In addition to simply performing music, some Sufi groups in the United States have featured dance as an important part of their practice of *dhikr*. The MEVLEVI SUFI ORDER, tracing their roots back to 13th-century Turkey, came to the United States by way of Suleiman Hayati Dede. This Sufi group has been commonly known as the "whirling dervishes" due to its unique form of dance, in which dancers silently chant the name of God and whirl around a center point, considered to be God, the spiritual center of the universe.

Another important connection between dance and Sufism in the United States has been Dances of Universal Peace, begun by SAMUEL LEWIS, or "Sufi Sam," in the late 1960s. Shaped by Inayat Khan as well as by other forms of religious expression such as Zen Buddhism, Lewis promoted spiritual meditative dances, involving a number of dancers in a circle and featuring some sort of sacred chant. According to Lewis, these dances manifest the truth that lies at the core of all religions and promote peace as dancers experience this universal truth.

Having emphasized Sufism's uniqueness, it should also be pointed out that many Sufi mosques and organizations in the United States have shared numerous beliefs and practices with Muslims not influenced by Sufism. The Mosque of Sheikh M. R. Bawa Muhaiyaddeen in PHILADELPHIA, founded upon the teaching of a Sri Lankan–born Sufi master who came to the United States in 1971, demonstrates Sufi belief and practice while following a Sunni interpretation of Islamic law. Like other mosques throughout the United States, this mosque is open for the five daily *salat* prayers; distinctively, though, it also offers early morning *dhikr* recitation. Furthermore, reflecting the common Sufi tendency to revere a group's founder or great master of the past, pilgrims visit the resting place of Sheikh Muhaiyaddeen outside of Philadelphia. Other Sufi mosques and organizations are connected to Shi'a Islam. Dr. Javad Nurbakhsh, a psychiatrist from Iran, brought the NIMATULLAHI SUFI ORDER to the United States in the 1970s. This group, like many other Sufi organizations, has emphasized love and respect for all people regardless of religious belief or affiliation.

RELIGIOUS LIFE IN THE NATION OF ISLAM

In 1930, W. D. FARD appeared in Detroit and claimed to have come from Mecca with a message specifically directed to African Americans, whom he identified as members of the lost ancient tribe of Shabazz. Elijah Poole, renamed ELIJAH MUHAMMAD, became the leader of Fard's movement, the NATION OF ISLAM. This movement emphasized inward and outward cleanliness, good manners and respect, modest dress by women, and avoidance of pork, alcohol, and smoking. While incorporating some elements of Sunni Islamic tradition, the Nation of Islam also featured elements that distinguished it sharply from mainstream Islam. Whereas many Muslims have taught the equality of all races, the Nation of Islam responded to racial discrimination against blacks by prohibiting whites from becoming members. Furthermore, contrary to the strong concern especially among Sunni Muslims not to make anyone or anything equal to God, the Nation of Islam declared that W. D. Fard held divine status.

After attracting many followers in the middle of the century, the Nation of Islam greatly felt the effects of the conversion of MALCOLM X, one of its most prominent leaders, to Sunni Islam in 1964. While performing the hajj, Malcolm X came to see Islam as a religion of racial unity and equality and no longer accepted the Nation of Islam's teachings of black superiority as the basis of his religious life. A decade later, Nation of Islam leader W. D. MOHAMMED, the son of Elijah Muhammad, redirected the organization toward a path of Sunni belief and practice. Opposing this, LOUIS FARRAKHAN then revived the original Nation of Islam, which continued to emphasize the teachings of Elijah Muhammad. Farrakhan cut off all ties with W. D. Mohammed's community in 1978, discouraged integration with whites, and taught that blacks should control their own resources, although he officially reconciled with Mohammed in 1999.

Consideration of *salat* and fasting can provide some insight into the complex relationship between the Nation of Islam and other forms of Islam in the United States. In the late 1950s, Elijah Muhammad taught his followers to perform *salat* in a traditionally Islamic manner, with the exception that they utter words in English rather than the traditional Arabic. In later comments on *salat,* however, he added more nontraditional elements and also broke radically from tradition by claiming that the required elements of *salat,* known as *fard* in Arabic, refer to W. D. Fard. As for fasting, Elijah Muhammad instructed his followers to practice the dawn-to-dusk fast during the Christian Advent season instead of the month of Ramadan, arguing that followers would benefit from having a cause for celebration in December as a substitute to Christmas. W. D. Mohammed changed this policy, calling upon black Muslims to observe the fast during Ramadan in unity with Muslims worldwide. Despite his many disagreements with W. D. Mohammed, Louis Farrakhan agreed, and later promoted fasting during Ramadan and Friday congregational prayers along the lines of Sunni Islam.

While striking differences between the Nation of Islam and other Muslim groups have caused some to question if the Nation of Islam can really be called true Islam, others have maintained that the differences illustrate the rich variety of Muslim groups in the United States. Certainly many characteristics of religious life have been similar throughout Muslim communities in the United States. Ultimately, these communities also reflect the varied population and history of the United States itself.

Steven Fink

Further Reading
Abdo, Geneive. *Mecca and Main Street: Muslim Life in America After 9/11.* New York: Oxford University Press, 2007.

Curtis, Edward E., IV. *Islam in Black America: Identity, Liberation, and Difference in African-American Islamic Thought.* Albany: State University of New York Press, 2002.

Denny, Frederick Mathewson. *Introduction to Islam.* 3d ed. Upper Saddle River, N.J.: Pearson, 2006.

Haddad, Yvonne Yazbeck, Jane I. Smith, and Kathleen M. Moore. *Muslim Women in America: The Challenge of Islamic Identity Today.* New York: Oxford University Press, 2006.

Kahf, Mohja. *The Girl in the Tangerine Scarf.* New York: Carroll & Graf, 2006.

Khan, M. A. Muqtedar. "Constructing the American Muslim Community." In *Religion and Immigration: Christian, Jewish, and Muslim Experiences in the United States,* edited by Yvonne Yazbeck Haddad, Jane I. Smith, and John L. Esposito, 175–198. Walnut Creek, Calif.: AltaMira Press, 2003.

McCloud, Aminah Beverly. *Transnational Muslims in American Society.* Gainesville: University Press of Florida, 2006.

Nimer, Mohamed. *The North American Muslim Resource Guide: Muslim Community Life in the United States and Canada.* New York: Routledge, 2002.

Schmidt, Garbi. *Islam in Urban America: Sunni Muslims in Chicago.* Philadelphia: Temple University Press, 2004.

Smith, Jane I. *Islam in America.* New York: Columbia University Press, 1999.

Turner, Richard Brent. *Islam in the African-American Experience.* 2d ed. Bloomington: Indiana University Press, 2003.

Walbridge, Linda. *Without Forgetting the Imam: Lebanese Shi'ism in an American Community.* Detroit: Wayne State University Press, 1997.

revivalism

Religious revivalism is a phenomenon in which people of faith call one another and others to renew and revive their religious traditions. Religious revivals have been a part of American history since the First Great Awakening in the 18th century, which occurred in the decades before the American Revolution. Though it is difficult to determine when each revival begins and ends, many scholars agree that the 1970s mark one such period of religious revival in the United States. Many Muslims, Christians, Jews, advocates of countercultural spiritual movements, and others called on fellow Americans to renew their ties with a religion or a spiritual practice that they generally believed would improve American society. Clearly affected by these larger American trends, Muslim Americans shared in this revival. But as part of a global Muslim community, they were also influenced by calls for reform and renewal, or *islah wa tajdid,* in Muslim-majority nations. Muslim-American revivalism brought together strands of this global Islamic revival with those of the American religious revival in the late 20th century.

ISLAMIC REVIVAL COMES TO AMERICA

As with many religious traditions, the history of Islam is replete with calls for reform and renewal of religious faith. In the late 19th and early 20th centuries, as Europeans came to militarily occupy most Muslim-majority countries, Muslim leaders said that such powerlessness was a sign of moral decline and, like earlier religious leaders, called for a religious revival. In Egypt, one of the most effective voices for Islamic reform was the Muslim Brotherhood, which was founded by Hasan al-Banna, a schoolteacher, in 1928. The organization first focused on popular morality and providing social services to the less fortunate, and then became active in Egyptian politics. From the 1940s through the 1960s, members were frequently imprisoned, and sometimes killed, for their various criticism of the Egyptian government.

The Brotherhood advocated an Islamist government in which Islamic ideas would form the foundation of government policies. The state's legal system, it said, should be based on the SHARI'A, or Islamic LAW and ethics. The Muslim Brotherhood also saw the potential of Islamic reform and renewal to reach beyond national borders, and sought allies for its approach across the Islamic world. After Egyptian president Gamal Abdel Nasser consolidated his control over the country by suppressing the organization in the late 1950s and early 1960s, the Muslim Brotherhood turned to the Kingdom of Saudi Arabia, an enemy of Egyptian expansion throughout the Middle East, for financial support and political refuge. Gaining Saudi support meant that the Muslim Brotherhood could broadcast their message to a much larger world audience.

The Muslim Brotherhood came to the United States during the 1950s and 1960s by way of immigrant students, visitors, and refugees who had been influenced by its ideas. These Muslims, often alienated at first by American culture and sometimes from second- and third-generation ARAB-AMERICAN MUSLIMS, rejected the differing religious culture of some Muslim-American organizations. As these immigrants established their own mosques and associations, they also began to influence indigenous Muslims. Cities such as PHILADELPHIA and NEW YORK CITY became places of interaction among Arab immigrants and indigenous African-American converts.

For example, Talib Dawud, a Caribbean immigrant, came originally to the United States to play JAZZ in the 1940s. He was among several African-American jazz musicians who converted to Islam. When Dawud lived in Philadelphia in the late 1950s, he met Mahmoud Alwan, an advocate for the Muslim Brotherhood's views. Eventually Dawud encouraged a group of followers who had gathered around him to join the International Muslim Brotherhood in Harlem, New York, and advocated a closer relationship between Muslim Americans and Muslims abroad. His efforts to expand the movement conflicted with other Muslim-American movements such as the NATION OF ISLAM (NOI). Dawud criticized the theology of the NOI and stressed the need for Muslim unity across racial and national lines.

Another Caribbean immigrant influenced by the Muslim Brotherhood was Sheikh Daoud Ahmad Faisal, who gave voice to Islamist ideas in the United States in the 1950s. Faisal founded the Islamic Mission to America, which became one of the most prominent mosques in New York City. This mosque was a gathering place for both Arab immigrants and indigenous African-American converts in the area, and Faisal consciously attempted to bring these two communities together. Faisal envisioned the renewal of a global Islamic civilization and he worked to strengthen international ties. In calling for an Islamic awakening, he traveled around the United States and preached to African Americans who had grown up as Christians. Faisal also espoused anticommunist rhetoric during the 1960s and stressed a political quietism in which he urged followers to obey the government and cooperate with police.

The Islamist message of the Muslim Brotherhood found resonance among AFRICAN-AMERICAN MUSLIMS who were interested in the global revival of Islam during the latter half of the 20th century. The 1960s was a politically tumultuous time for Muslims in other parts of the world. The Muslim Brotherhood USA viewed Algeria's war for independence against France, to name one example, as evidence of a global Islamic revival. Sayyid Qutb, who had become the major ideological figure of the Muslim Brotherhood in Egypt, was arrested several times for antigovernment political organizing and was eventually executed during this period. The involvement of Islamist ideas in other revolutionary political contexts reinforced a sense of solidarity among Muslims, both immigrant and indigenous, in the United States.

The Muslim Brotherhood also played a direct role in the development of student groups in the United States. The MUSLIM STUDENTS ASSOCIATION (MSA) was born in 1963 out of the collaboration of various Muslim student groups, including the Egyptian Brotherhood, on the campus of the University of Illinois, Urbana-Champaign. Muslim student immigrants from the Middle East were often well educated and were sometimes harshly critical of their home countries and Western culture. Supported in part by aid from Saudi Arabia, the MSA created an extensive networking system, in which every major college campus hosted a chapter.

By the 1970s, however, the MSA began to sever its ties to the Islamist group as the organization began to focus more on helping and working with students who planned to stay in the United States. The Islamic revival broadened its base both in the United States and abroad. More and more Muslims were participating in its various activities. But as its appeal increased, the call for renewal and reform could not be directed by any one organization or contained by any one single belief. The meaning of Islamic reform shifted depended on who was advocating it. In the United States, the Islamic revival took on a distinctively American flavor.

LATE TWENTIETH-CENTURY MUSLIM-AMERICAN AWAKENINGS

For many Muslim Americans in the late 20th century, a commitment to Islamic revival emphasized personal piety over any explicitly political agenda. For some, that meant regularly performing daily PRAYER, engaging in PHILANTHROPY, fasting more faithfully during Ramadan, or renewing their commitment to other aspects of Muslim RELIGIOUS LIFE. Some gave up interest-bearing savings accounts, trying to adhere to the Islamic prohibition against usury. Many men and women sought to DRESS more modestly, donning loose-fitting clothing and head cover of some kind. Muslim Americans sought to purchase FOOD that had been prepared according to Islamic DIETARY LAWS.

In response to the desire among Muslim Americans to lead a more religious life, a whole host of consumer products was introduced by Muslim and non-Muslim businesses. Midamar, founded in CEDAR RAPIDS, IOWA, in 1974 by a multigenerational Muslim-American family, offered HALAL, or permissible, food by mail order; eventually, pizza, chicken nuggets, and beef sausage became available. Muslim-American media, including books, newspapers, magazines, and radio, proliferated.

Sufi Muslim groups also fueled the revival, and an increasing number of Sunni religious practices, such as the reading and study of the QUR'AN and the performance of the daily prayer, were incorporated into the practices of such groups. For example, Sufi master M. R. Bawa Muhaiyaddeen, who founded a Sufi group in Philadelphia in 1971, took a gradual approach but by 1981 had introduced his followers, including many new converts, to the Qur'an and the pillars of Islamic religious practice, including the prescribed daily prayers.

Some Muslim Americans focused not only on inward renewal but also on outward reforms of U.S. society. Imam W. D. MOHAMMED (1933–2008), African-American Muslim leader of the NOI and WORLD COMMUNITY OF AL-ISLAM IN THE WEST, joined Christian and Muslim leaders in blaming illegal drugs, extramarital sex, and other signs of what he considered to be moral decay for larger social problems. Religious renewal, many Americans in the 1970s said, was necessary in the face of what they considered to be negative social change in the late 1960s. Even some former hippies and radicals advocated what one scholar called "getting saved from the 60s."

The socially conservative among Jewish, Christian, and Muslim revival advocates denounced what they believed was an absence of traditional family values such as sexual restraint and clean living. High inflation, the failure to prevent the communist takeover of Vietnam, and legalized abortion were signs of how moral corruption led to societal decay, according to these critics. Personal responsibility, they said, had been replaced by ineffective government programs that addressed the economic and social problems that only individuals, families, and local communities could effectively solve. In LOS ANGELES in the early 1990s, for example, W. D. Mohammed appeared at a meeting with Roman Catholic Cardinal Roger Mahony and Jewish radio personality Dennis Praeger to discuss religious solutions to abortion, drugs, and homelessness.

In the midst of sometimes utopian dreams of a better world, some Muslim Americans literally called for the United States to become an Islamic state, but this was rare. Most Muslim Americans rejected this view, hoping to participate as full partners alongside Jews, Christians, and others in creating a tolerant, if strengthened nation. Even as some missionary organizations, such as the TABLIGHI JAMAʿAT, wished to convert more Americans to the religion of Islam, they did not wish to become involved in electoral POLITICS.

Perhaps one of the most significant elements of the revival was its emphasis on individual Muslims studying and interpreting the Qur'an for themselves. For most of Islamic history, Muslims had memorized various passages of the Qur'an and recited them as part of their prayers and other religious rituals, but left its interpretation up to scholars who devoted their lives full time to its study. By the end of the 20th century, that had changed.

The Qur'an became something of a handbook for daily life, and Muslims at the grassroots would meet in each other's homes as well as in mosques and Islamic centers to discuss its meanings. In Los Angeles, for instance, anthropologist Carolyn Rouse met with many African-American Sunni women in the early 1990s whose informal study of the Qur'an circulated from house to house in South Central Los Angeles. Looking to the women of the seventh century for inspiration, these women debated the unfaithfulness of men, divorce, domestic violence, and the wearing of a HIJAB, or a head scarf. Women would use what they learned to influence their families and their religious leaders, often challenging patriarchy on the basis of their conclusion.

CONCLUSION

In everyday American speech, religious revivalism has come to be associated with another, more often used term, fundamentalism. For the first half of the 20th century, fundamentalism was a strictly Christian term that referred to beliefs in the inerrancy of the Bible, the virgin birth of JESUS, and faith in Jesus Christ as the sole path to heavenly salvation. By the end of the 20th century, however, the meaning of the term fundamentalism had been broadened to include a far greater range of beliefs and behaviors, including socially conservative values, closed-mindedness, and even political violence.

Despite its popularity, the word *fundamentalism* does not capture the complex, interrelated phenomena that characterized the Islamic-American awakening of the late 20th century. While perhaps more than a million Muslim Americans publicly demonstrated a renewed commitment to Islam in the way they talked, dressed, and even ate, they did not agree on any single political platform or even any one version of the Islamic faith. But Muslims from different racial, ethnic, and national origins did contribute to the rich and sometimes contradictory expectations, ideas, and practices that gave new meaning to their identity as Muslims. Even as they argued about some of the basic tenets of their faith, these Muslims created a shared world inspired by the hope that Islam would improve their own lives and make the world a better place.

Edward E. Curtis IV and Shannon Dunn

Further Reading

Curtis, Edward E., IV. "Islamism and Its African American Muslim Critics: Black Muslims in the Era of the Cold War." *American Quarterly* (2004): 684–709.
———. *Muslims in America: A Short History.* New York: Oxford University Press, 2009.
Dannin, Robert. *Black Pilgrimage to Islam.* New York: Oxford University Press, 2002.
Ernst, Carl W. *Following Muhammad: Rethinking Islam in the Contemporary World.* Chapel Hill: University of North Carolina Press, 2003.
Haddad, Yvonne Yazbeck, ed. *The Muslims of America.* New York: Oxford University Press, 1991.
Tipton, Steven M. *Getting Saved from the Sixties: Moral Meaning in Conversion and Cultural Change.* Berkeley: University of California Press, 1982.

Ross, North Dakota   See NORTH DAKOTA.

S

Said, Nicholas (Mohammed Ali ben Said)
(ca. 1831–1882) *slave, traveler, Civil War soldier, teacher, author*

Born the son of a respected general in Bornou (near the modern-day borders of Libya, Chad, and Sudan) around 1831, Mohammed Ali ben Said (later renamed Nicholas Said) was enslaved as a young boy, served princes and diplomats, traveled on five continents, learned to speak seven languages, fought for the Union Army during the U.S. Civil War (1861–65), and authored the longest English AUTOBIOGRAPHY of any AFRICAN-AMERICAN MUSLIM SLAVE. After journeying across Africa, Europe, and the Middle East for a series of masters, Said crossed the Atlantic as a paid servant for a married couple from Dutch Guiana (now Suriname). However, the couple swindled him, leaving Said stranded and penniless in Canada. Undaunted, he went to work as a teacher and a soldier, living briefly in Michigan, Ohio, and South Carolina before settling permanently in St. Stephens, Alabama.

Despite his ARABIC name, Mohammed Ali ben Said was not raised as a Muslim. In his 1873 *Autobiography of Nicholas Said; a Native of Bournou, Eastern Soudan, Central Africa,* he described the religion of his native land as "fetish, without human sacrifices." In fact, Said associated the introduction of Islam into Central Africa with desolation and ruin, because an invading army from Bagirmey had killed his father and three brothers when Said was 12 or 13 years old. The invasion, Said explained, resulted in the destruction of cities and the enslavement of thousands. Following this military defeat, Said went to live with Malam Katory, a stern but effective educator who taught him and other boys from elite families to write and speak Arabic. Approximately two years later, Said was captured and enslaved by a "marauding tribe" of Kindills (also known as Tuaregs), who transported him by horseback across the Sahara desert and sold him to an African Arab named Abd El-Kader. Said describes the torturous journey, during which he suffered from extreme heat and thirst, concluding that the "Sahara must be seen and felt to be realized."

After learning that Said was the son of a general, Abd El-Kader treated him well and eventually honored his request to be sold to Abdy-Aga, a young officer in the Ottoman Army. The Turkish officer was a kind master, as was his father, Hadji Daoud. Said accompanied Daoud on the old man's fourth HAJJ, or pilgrimage to the holy cities of Mecca and Medina. Together they journeyed from Tripoli to Alexandria, to Cairo, to Khartoum, across Abyssinia (now Ethiopia) to port cities in modern-day Eritrea and Somalia, and finally to the Arabian Peninsula. Observing trains and railroads for the first time in Egypt, Said recalled that he "had seen so many wonderful and unexpected sights within the few previous years that I think my organ of marvellousness had gone to sleep from sheer surfeit and exhaustion."

In his *Autobiography,* Said described Mecca as an attractive, brightly lit city with wide streets and three-story stone houses, though he noted that many of the city's residents seemed indifferent to the pilgrims' pious enthusiasm. Said also explained some rituals of the hajj, including the procession around the Ka'ba and the kissing of the "black stone." Because he was a slave, Said wrote, "it was construed that I did not go there voluntarily, and consequently, I was debarred the felicity of saluting the petrified angel." Said described Medina as "by far, the handsomest city I ever saw in the East," and found Medina's residents to be more serious and studious than those of Mecca. Said's account of the hajj is emblematic of his paradoxical stance toward Islam in general: On one hand, he expressed interest in and attentiveness to Muslim teachings, while on the other hand, he criticized Muslims who did not adhere to those teachings. Even in his comment about being unable to salute the "petrified angel," we can read both disappointment at being excluded from a sacred Muslim ritual and a measured cynicism in his description of the black stone. In reading this passage, however, we should also remember that Said's intended reading public primarily consisted of non-Muslim, white Americans.

When Daoud and Said returned from the hajj, Daoud's store had burned to the ground, rendering him bankrupt, and he was compelled to sell Said to Fuad Pacha, then Minister of the Interior for the Ottoman Empire. Said was taken to Constantinople, where the Pacha presented him as a gift to his brother-in-law, Reschid. "I began . . . to think that it was

In 1862, during the Civil War, Nicholas Said, a former African slave who traveled on five continents and completed the pilgrimage to Mecca, enlisted in the 55th Regiment of the Massachusetts Colored Volunteers. He later wrote an English-language autobiography about his remarkable life, including his experiences in the South during Reconstruction. *(Massachusetts Historical Society)*

my fate to pass from hand to hand, with never a sure and definite resting place," Said recalled. His fears were again realized when a Russian diplomat, Prince Anatole Mentchikoff, convinced Reschid Pacha to transfer Said to his possession. In 1854, Mentchikoff brought Said to Odessa, a city on the Black Sea (now part of the Ukraine) and procured a tutor to teach Said Russian, which he later described as the most difficult language he ever learned. After finding the treatment by Mentchikoff's other servants intolerable, Said entered the service of Prince Nicholas Vassilievitch Troubetzköy, a member of an eminent St. Petersburg family. One day as he was walking in the city, Said observed "a distinguished looking individual, in full Russian uniform, approaching." When Said removed his fez and stood at attention like a soldier, the individual—who turned out to be Czar Nicholas I—clapped him on the shoulder and commented, *Malodetz*," which translates as "smart boy."

Prince Troubetzköy proved to be a demanding master, requiring Said to learn French and to convert to Orthodox Christianity. Though he initially resisted "that vivacious tongue" and what he called "the Greek faith," at length Said succumbed to both, and he was baptized as a Christian in November 1855. This ceremony also marked his official name change from Mohammed Ali Ben Said to Nicholas Said. But after the baptism was over, when Said "thought the job was complete," the priest required him to kneel on a rock-hard surface for hours, begging forgiveness for his past sins. Said recalled that he was "in perfect agony for the greater portion of the time, and became so enraged with the papa, that I fear I committed more sins during that space of time than I had done in days before. In fact . . . a few ungainly Mohammedan asperities of language bubbled up to my lips. But I managed to get through without any overt act of rebellion." Said's conversion to Orthodox Christianity is described as an act of violence and power, placing him "in perfect agony" and causing him to become "enraged." Indeed, the Arabic phrases which "bubbled up" in this moment suggest that Said placed more stock in Muslim beliefs than his *Autobiography* elsewhere concedes. They also call the validity of this second conversion into question—for the lack of "any overt act of rebellion" suggests that Said opted for more covert forms of resistance.

Over the next several years, Said accompanied the prince as he toured Europe's great cities, including Vienna, Dresden, Munich, Heidelberg, Rome, Paris, and London. Said's travel notes regarding European politics, crime in Italian culture, comparative architectural styles, and potential successors to the papacy indicate the breadth and depth of his curiosity. In exchange for his services, Prince Troubetzköy granted Said permission to visit his native land in Africa for one year, granting him 300 pounds for the voyage. However, a colonial traveler prevailed upon Said to accompany him to the Americas, and as Said explained it, his fondness for travel won him over. Therefore, he set sail with De Sanddrost I. J. Rochussen of Dutch Guiana and his new wife, landing in the United States a few weeks later (probably in 1860). After sailing around the Caribbean, Said and the Rochussens traveled north to New York and proceeded into Canada. In a small town north of Ottawa, Rochussen asked Said for a loan, claiming that his "remittance" was behind schedule. Rochussen promptly disappeared with all 300 pounds, leaving Said penniless. A local pastor loaned him 10 dollars and advised him to seek help in Detroit or Buffalo, where he might find support from those cities' sizable black communities.

In 1862, Said worked as a teacher in Detroit, and the following year he joined the 55th Regiment of Massachusetts Colored Volunteers—the sister unit to the 54th Regiment, the first black regiment recruited in the North during the Civil War. Little is known about Said's military service, partly because he did not discuss it in his autobiography. After he was discharged in South Carolina in 1865, Said reportedly married, traveled around the South teaching and speaking, and finally settled in St. Stephens, Alabama. "I felt an insurmountable desire to put an end to my peregrinations," he explained. Said's autobiography concludes with a tribute to the importance of education and self-denial and restates his desire to assist with the project of racial uplift in the United States.

Nicholas Said's life raises intriguing questions about how much control enslaved Africans and African Americans had over their own lives. By the act of writing his life, Said exerted a form of self-mastery over his past, even though he spent much of it in servitude of one form or another. His story also reveals the ways that religious practice and identity both challenged and supported the power of those who owned him: Said's religious conversions were simultaneously acts of submission to and resistance against the dominant culture in which he was living at the time. In his *Autobiography*, Said lamented that "Africa has been, through prejudice and ignorance, so sadly misrepresented, that anything like intelligence, industry, etc. is believed not to exist among its natives." His text and others like it work to rectify this misconception.

Patrick E. Horn

Further Reading

Al-Ahari, Muhammad A., ed. *Five Classic Muslim Slave Narratives*. Chicago: Magribine Press, 2006.

Austin, Allan D. *African Muslims in Antebellum America: A Sourcebook*. New York: Garland Publishing, Inc., 1984.

"Evolution of the Map of Africa." Princeton University Library Digital Collections. Available online. URL: http://libweb5. princeton.edu/visual_materials/maps/websites/africa/ maps-continent/continent. html. Accessed October 15, 2008.

Khair, Tabish. *Other Routes: 1500 Years of African and Asian Travel Writing*. Bloomington: Indiana University Press, 2005.

McQueen, James. *A Geographical Survey of Africa: Its Rivers, Lakes, Mountains, Productions, States, Populations, &c.* London: Frank Cass and Company, 1840.

Said, Nicholas. *Autobiography of Nicholas Said; a Native of Bournou, Eastern Soudan, Central Africa*. Memphis: Shotwell & Co., 1873. Available online. URL: http://docsouth.unc. edu/neh/said/menu.html. Accessed October 15, 2008.

Autobiography of Nicholas Said (1873)

After being captured as a teenager in his native West Africa, Mohammed Ali ben Said (ca. 1831–82) spent the next 20 years traveling through Africa, Asia, Europe, and South America. According to his own account, he arrived in the United States in 1867, though Said actually came to North America at least ten years earlier and served in the Union Army during the Civil War from 1863 to 1865. Said, who changed his first name to Nicholas and lived in the South after the war, likely expunged his service in the Union Army from his autobiography in order to protect himself from any retribution from white Southerners unhappy with the outcome of the war. This excerpt from his autobiography picks up Said's journey in the United States during the Reconstruction era of U.S. history. Said explains how he went from the North to the South. Said's account of Reconstruction reveals how unsafe travel could be for black people, even with the Union Army still occupying the South. He praises black schoolchildren but criticized some of the black "carpetbaggers," Northern African Americans who had come South to pursue work in education, business, and politics.

While in Sandusky City [Ohio], I conceived the idea to go South, where I could be of great use to my benighted people in the capacity of a teacher.

I selected Charleston, South Carolina as the basis of my operation. Accordingly I left Sandusky City for Cleveland, Ohio, thence to Buffalo, Rochester, Albany, Troy, Poughkeepsie and New York City, and embarked for the port of my destination.

Having taken up my quarters at Mrs. Cobb's boarding house in Calhoune Street, I soon became acquainted with Wright, Langston, Randolph, Bozeman, Ransier, and a host of other less notable Northern colored men who came there for political purposes.

All the above named were very able men, but, with the exception of the last named, who was truly a very good and honest man, I have a very little opinion of their honesty.

I soon got into employment as a teacher, and taught here about a year.

I am proud to say that I have gained the esteem of numerous white friends in Charleston, among which are Messrs. General Simmons, Kanapaux, Dr. Ogier, Sim, De Saussure, Chazal, Cohen, and a host of others who have shown me a great deal of favor.

I left Charleston for Savannah, Georgia, in the commencement of 1870, and only remaining here three days I left for Thomasville, Thomas County, Georgia.

While here I conceived the idea of writing my Biography or rather adventures. Several of my well-wishers to whom I communicated my idea said it was a very good thing.

The Editor of the *Thomasville Enterprise* gave me a most flattering notice in his paper, by which I gained many friends.

I accordingly set to work and wrote an essay to that effect consisting of about one hundred pages. When I completed that, I proposed to give lectures on "Africa and Its Resources." I made my debut in Thomasville, then at Bainbridge, Albany, Americus, Macon, Griffin, and Atlanta. I soon got tired of that business which in fact did not yield me much profit, I left Atlanta, and got down to Forsyth in Monroe, where I took up a school sixteen miles from here in a village called Culloden.

I taught here six months and then retraced my steps to Thomasville where I had left my effects with a colored friend of mine, Solomon Harvey by name. To my no small disappointment he had left for Texas taking my goods with him.

After making arrangements as to the publication of my book, I started on a new plan, that of raising means by which to defray expenses of publication by *voluntary subscriptions.*

I have got a great many subscribers from Thomasville, Bainbridge, Quitman, Valdosta, Ga., Monticello, Madison, Tallahassee and Quincy, Florida. From Quincy I returned to Bainbridge thence to Early county Georgia, always meeting with success and good treatment from the white and black people.

While in Georgia and Florida, I had heard from the black people that Alabama was a very dangerous State and filled with Ku-Klux that the freedmen there did not know what freedom was owing to the oppression of the whites under which they were situated.

I was advised not to go to that State my life, they said, would be in great danger. My own common sense dictated to me, of course, that it was not possible that such a state of affairs could exist in Alabama, besides that, there were good and bad in all countries.

I shall here say, however, that it was thought by the blacks and a good number of whites I traveled for the purpose of spying through the country. Blacks were sent at times to pick me, but I had nothing to tell them excepting that I traveled for my own amusement and gratification, at the same time, making a little something which I hoped would enable me to publish my Adventures.

Some said I was harmless and quiet, and others that I was a Yankee emissary and a scoundrel.

I crossed the Chattahooche into Henry county, Alabama, and to my great surprise, was received with respect and kindness. I shall truly say, that I have never had such a reception heretofore.

I shall never forget the kindness and attention paid to my humble self by that most intelligent

and most gentlemanly Mr. M. Smith, of Columbia. When I left that place, after ten days stay, and was going to Abbeville, the county-seat, that kind man recommended me to Col. Oates, of that town:

COLUMBIA, ALA., July 21, 1871.
Colonel Oates:

The bearer, Nicholas Said, who is without a shadow of a doubt, a native African, and whose ostensible object in traveling through this country, is to obtain subscribers to his Autobiography, lectured here to-day.

And I am glad to say, gave entire satisfaction to his audience, which was composed of a goodly number of white and black people. He is, by far, the most intelligent, and the best educated man of the African race, with whom I have ever conversed, etc.

Any attention paid to Mr. Said will be thankfully received.

I am, Colonel,
Yours, most truly,
M. SMITH.

This letter did me an immense good in Abbeville, where I remained, and taught school until October of that year. I then went to Eufawla, Clayton, Troy, Montgomery, Selma, Greenville, Pineapple, Monroeville, Claiborne, Gainesville, and, finally to St. Stephens, Washington county, [Alabama] where I conceived the idea of *settling myself for life.*

On the 20th day of March, 1872, I found myself in St. Stephens, the county-seat of Washington County, Alabama, situated a few miles from the right bank of the Tombigbee river.

Here I felt an insurmountable desire to put an end to my peregrinations, that, is at least for a season; for I was perfectly exhausted, and as I had a notion to enlarge my Biography, and as the manuscript had become worn out, by constant handling; I had nothing better to do than to take a school somewhere, in order to accomplish my desired end.

Accordingly, on inquiry, I found that I could get one in the neighborhood of St. Stephens, and was suggested by Mr.—, one of the Trustees, to see one Dr. W. H. Coleman, who, it was said, lived six miles above that place on the road to Bladen Springs, in Choctaw county, Alabama.

This gentleman was, it was said, one of the county supervisors, whose duty it was to examine teachers, as to their qualifications.

Consequently, having received a note from Mr. Bailey, which ran thus:

Dr. W. H. Coleman:

SIR: The bearer, Nicholas Said, desires a situation in our neighborhood as a teacher, please to examine him and oblige,

Yours,
Most respectfully,
THOMAS BAILEY.

Armed with this document, I proceeded onward to Dr. Coleman's.

On entering the paling enclosure, I was informed that the Doctor was in the garden, and would be back in a few minutes.

Presently I saw him coming, and I asked him whether he was Dr. Coleman, and on being answered affirmatively, I presented the paper to him.

The Doctor appeared to be a man of about fifty years of age, with a kind and gentlemanly looking face and highly polished manners, and in stature something above the medium height.

His reception of me was quite flattering, for after my examination, I was asked whether I had been to breakfast; I told him I had not, whereupon "Bright," the servant girl, was called and instructed to furnish me with my breakfast.

This most kind and hospitable gentleman furthermore promised to *protect* me during my stay in his neighborhood; and I can truly say did more than he promised.

Shortly after I opened my school, the Doctor loaned me $5.00, thereby showing that he had confidence in my honesty. Through his instrumentality, my name has become popular through Washington and Choctaw counties.

I shall, so long as life lasts, remember him with unfailing gratitude, and shall render myself not unworthy of his confidence and good opinion of me.

The colored people in this section of the country should certainly be grateful to him for his unwearied zeal in causing a school to be established in their midst.

But alas! Though painful to say, it is sadly true that my people here appreciate but slightly the benefits of education.

My honest and ardent desire is to render myself useful to my race wherever it may be. I have no aspirations for fame, nor anything of the sort. But I shall always prefer at all times to find myself in the midst of the most ignorant of my race, and endeavor to teach the rising generation the advantages of education.

Self-denial is now-a-days so rare, that it is thought only individuals of insane mind can speak of it. A person who tries to live only for others, and puts himself in the second place, is hooted at, and considered a fit inmate for the asylum.

The man who artfully extorts the earning of his fellow-man, and who seems to have no feeling for his daily wants, is, by a strange perversion, deemed the wise.

To me, it is impossible to conceive how a human being can be happy through any other channel, than to do as much good as possible to his fellow-man in this world.

Source: Autobiography of Nicholas Said; a Native of Bornou, Eastern Soudan, Central Africa. Memphis: Shotwell & Co., 1873, pp. 202–213.

Said, Omar ibn (ca. 1770–1864) *African-American Muslim slave and author*

Omar ibn Said is the author of the only surviving ARABIC slave AUTOBIOGRAPHY written in the United States. Born in Futa Toro, Senegal, in 1770 (the exact date is unknown), he was a student for 25 years, then a teacher, trader, and soldier. In 1807, one year before the United States outlawed the trans-Atlantic slave trade, he was captured in war, enslaved, shipped to Charleston, South Carolina, and sold to work on a rice plantation. He escaped but was arrested and jailed in Fayetteville, North Carolina.

Soon, citizens flocked to see a slave who wrote in a strange script on the walls of his cell. His mysterious reputation attracted James Owen, brother of North Carolina's former governor. Owen purchased ibn Said in 1811 and employed him as a gardener and house servant. He was also encouraged to write—a practice that soon became illegal for North Carolina's slaves. The Owen family preserved some of ibn Said's manuscripts and gave some to friends as gifts. Most of the writings consisted of inscriptions of Qur'anic verses, Arabic translations of the Lord's Prayer and the Twenty-third Psalm, and lists of the Owen family members. The family appeared to cherish their roles as benefactors to the exotic scholar. They especially welcomed numerous visits by Christian missionaries who were eager to talk to him, and presented him as a model African convert to Christianity.

With such visits came ibn Said's relative fame, which brought him an opportunity to correspond with Lamen Kebe, a West African coreligionist who lived at the time in NEW YORK CITY. Before slavery, both men had lived in Kaba, Mali, and quite possibly had shared acquaintances. As slaves, both tried to survive and perhaps return home. Both converted to Christianity, or at least presented themselves as converts. Unlike ibn Said, who remained in captivity with the Owen family until his death in 1864, Kebe was eventually freed after nearly 40 years of slavery. At the time of their correspondence, Kebe was trying to convince the American Colonization Society (ACS) to send him to Africa as a Christian missionary.

Ibn Said's conversion from Islam to Christianity reportedly took place in 1821. He attended a Presbyterian church but still visibly maintained some Muslim practices. In 1831, ibn Said wrote his autobiography while prompted by somebody he referred to as "Sheikh Hunter," possibly a visiting ACS member. He later sent it to Kebe, who in turn gave the manuscript to Theodore Dwight, an advocate of the Free Soil movement, which opposed the introduction of slavery in Western states, and a founder of the American Ethnological Society. Dwight arranged for the first English translation of ibn Said's manuscript in 1848, part of which was published in 1864.

The autobiography is the only source on ibn Said's life in which he writes extensively about himself. His descriptions are terse. He does not mention, for example, whether he was married or had children back in Africa (he had no family while in the United States). Neither does he provide any details of the military conflict that brought about his captivity. Although it is possible to speculate that he was captured during a series of armed conflicts that involved Abdul Kader Kane, Futa Toro's ruler, and that the French may have been involved in some way, the precise circumstances of his capture are unclear.

What is most striking about his autobiography is that ibn Said appears to put in doubt whether he ever relinquished his identity as a religious Muslim. Rather than beginning his documents with a Christian PRAYER or a passage from the Bible, he reproduced Qur'anic Sura al-Mulk, the chapter of "God's Dominion," a powerful statement that God alone is the master over creation. He continues with a short account of his life that emphasizes his Muslim piety and scholarship. He writes about his education, his parents and siblings, his teachers, his annual charitable donations, his participation in military expeditions against his ethnic group's enemies, and the pilgrimage to Mecca. While showering his current captors with compliments, he notes the abuse he suffered at the hands of his first slaveholder and stresses that "I reside in our country here because of the great harm." He appears to address two audiences: whites, who he probably thought would gain access to a translation of the text, and his "brothers"—perhaps other African Muslims. The references he makes to his possible conversion are highly ambiguous. What is unambiguous is that he saturates the text with Muslim prayers and excerpts from the QUR'AN. He continued to do so in his other writings. In his last known manuscript, written in 1857, he was asked to inscribe the Lord's Prayer, which he had done before on numerous occasions. Instead, he wrote the Qur'anic Sura al-Nasr, the chapter of "Victory," and signed: "My name is Omar."

Because ibn Said's Arabic shielded him from the full control of his captors/benefactors, his writings provide a rare glimpse into enslaved Africans' strategies of resistance. He is monumentally important in the history of Islam in America, recognized by Muslims in Fayetteville who named one of their mosques after him. His autobiography had been missing for most of the last century but was rediscovered in 1995 in an old trunk in Virginia and sold at an auction to Tariq Beard, a prominent African-American collector, who has offered it for public viewing in BOSTON, New York, and in 2008 in Jackson, Mississippi.

Timur Yuskaev

Further Reading

Austin, Allan D. *African Muslims in Antebellum America: Trans-atlantic Stories and Spiritual Struggles.* New York: Routledge, 1997.

Diouf, Sylviane A. *Servants of Allah: African Muslims Enslaved in the Americas.* New York: New York University Press, 1998.

Said, Omar ibn. "The Life of Omar ibn Said, Written by Himself." Translated and introduced by Ala A. Alryyes. In *The Multilingual Anthology of American Literature,* edited by Marc Shell and Wernor Sollors, 58–93. New York: New York University Press, 2000.

"The Life of Omar ibn Said, Written by Himself" (1831)

As a Muslim adolescent who came of age in West Africa, Omar ibn Said (pronounced Sayyid, ca. 1770–1864) had intensively studied the Qur'an and other Islamic texts. In 1807, he was captured, enslaved, and transported to South Carolina. His autobiography, which he wrote in Arabic in 1831, several years after he officially converted to Christianity, is the only surviving slave autobiography written in Arabic. It is a short document, most of which is reprinted below. Its origins are obscure. Prompted to write it by a man he referred to as "Sheikh Hunter," ibn Said later sent it to his friend Lamen Kebe, who in turn gave it to ethnologist Theodore Dwight, who had it translated in 1848 and published in 1864. Although nominally a Christian, ibn Said begins his autobiography not with a quote from the Bible but with ayat, *or verses, from* Sura al-Mulk, *the 67th chapter of the Qur'an, which explains God's dominion over the heavens and the earth. This strategically placed preface may have been ibn Said's way of saying that though he was temporarily enslaved by a human, everything in creation was ultimately the property of God. The comments in brackets were added by translator and editor, Ala A. Alryyes.*

⬥

In the name of Allah, the Gracious, the Merciful. Thanks be to Allah, for his goodness of old, his generosity and favor. To him is majesty due. Thanks be to Him who created the creation for His worship, so He may judge their deeds and words.

From Omar to Sheikh Hunter: You asked me to write my life. I cannot write my life for I have forgotten much of my talk [language] as well as the talk of the Arabs. Also I know little grammar and little vocabulary. O my brothers, I ask you in the name of Allah, not to blame me for my eye is weak and so is my body.

My name is Omar Ibn Said; my birthplace if Fut Tur, between the two rivers [or seas]. I sought knowledge according to the instructions [original reads *wujod* or presence] of a Sheikh called Mohammad Said, my brother, and Sheikh Suleiman Kimba and Sheikh Jebril [i.e., Gabriel] Abdal. I continued seeking knowledge for twenty-five years, [then] I came to my place [and stayed] for six years. [Then there] came to our country a big army. It killed many people, it took me, and walked me to the big Sea, and sold me into the hand of a Christian man *(Nasrani)* who bought me and walked me to the big Ship in the big Sea.

We sailed in the big Sea for a month and a half until we came to a place called Charleston. And in a Christian language, they sold me. A weak, small, evil man called Johnson, and infidel *(Kafir)* who did not fear Allah at all, bought me.

I am a small man who cannot do hard work; I escape[d], from the hands of Johnson after a month, and walked to a place called Faydel. I saw houses after a month; I entered the houses to pray. I saw a young man who was riding horses, then his father came to the place. He spoke to his father that he saw a Sudanese man in the house. A man called Hindah together with another man riding a horse with many dogs took me walking with them for twelve miles to a place called Faydel. They took me to a big house [building]. I could not come out of the big house—called *jeel* [i.e., jail] in the Christian language—for sixteen days and nights.

On Friday, a man came and opened the door of the big house, and I saw many men whose language was Christian. They called to me; is not your name Omar, is it not Said? I did not understand [hear] the Christian language. I saw a man called Bob Mumford speaking [to the jailer?]. He took me out of the big house. I consented very much to walk with them to their place. I stayed in Mumford's place for four days and nights. A man called Jim Owen, the husband of Mumford's daughter, Betsy Mumford, asked me: "Do you consent to walk to a place called Bladen?" I said, "Yes." I agreed to walk with them I have stayed in Jim Owen's place until now.

Before I came into the hands of General Owen, a man called Mitchell came to buy me. Mitchell asked me: "Would you walk to a place called Charleston?" I said: "No, no, no, no, no, no, no—I will not walk to the place Charleston; I will stay in the hands of Jim Owen."

O, people of North Carolina; o, people of South Carolina; o, people of America, all of you; are there among you men as good as Jim Owen and [his brother] John Owen? They are good men for whatever they eat, eat; and whatever they wear they give me to wear. Jim with his brother read from the Bible *(Ingeel)* that Allah is our Lord, our Creator, and our Owner and the restorer of our condition, health and wealth by grace and not duty. [According?] to my ability, open my heart to the right path, to the path of Jesus Christ, to a great light.

Before I came to the Christian country, my religion was/is the religion of Mohammad, the prophet of Allah, may Allah bless him and grant him peace. I used to walk to the mosque *(masjid)* before dawn, and to wash my face, hands, feet. I [also] used to hold the noon prayers, the afternoon prayers, the sunset prayers, the night prayers.

I used to give alms *(zakat)* every year in gold, silver, harvest, cattle, sheep, goats, rice, wheat and barley—all I used to give in alms. I used to join the *Jihad* every year against the infidels *(Kuffar)*. I used to walk to Mecca and Medinah as did those who were able. My father had six sons and five daughters, and my mother had three sons and one daughter. When I left my country, I was thirty-seven years old. I have been residing in the Christian country for twenty-four years.

In the year eight hundred and thirty and one (1831) [after] Jesus Christ.

O, people of North Carolina; O, people of South Carolina; O, people of America, all of you: The first son of Jim Owen is called Thomas and his sister is called Maas Jen [Martha Jane?].

This is a good generation *(Geel)*. Tom Owen and Nell Owen had two sons and one daughter. The first boy is called Jim and the other John; the girl is called Melissa. Master *(Sayyid)* Jim and his wife Betsy Owen have two sons and five daughters. They are Tom, John, Martha, Miriam, Sophia, Margaret and Lisa. This generation is a very good generation.

And John Owen's wife is called Lucy. A good wife, she had three children and then two. Three died and two remained.

O, people of America; O, people of North Carolina: do you have, do you have, do you have, do you have such a good generation that fears Allah so much?

I am Omar, I love to read the book, the Great Koran.

General Jim Owen and his wife used to read the Bible, they used to read the Bible to me a lot. Allah is our Lord, our Creator, and our Owner and the restorer of our condition, health and wealth by grace and not duty. [According?] to my ability, open my heart to the Bible, to the path of righteousness. Praise be to Allah, the Lord of Worlds, many thanks for he grants bounty in abundance.

Because the law *(Shara')* was to Moses given, but grace and truth were by Jesus the Messiah.

First, [following] Mohammed. To pray, I said: "Praise be to Allah, Lord of the Worlds; the Compassionate, the Merciful; Sovereign *(Malik)* of the Day of Judgment; It is you we worship, and to you we turn for help; Guide us to the straight path; The path of those whom you have favored with grace; Not of those who have incurred Your wrath; Nor of those who have strayed. Amen."

And [but?] now, I pray in the words of our Lord Jesus the Messiah: "Our Father, who art in heaven, hallowed be thy name, thy Kingdom come, thy Will be done, on earth as it is in Heaven. Give us this day our daily bread and forgive us our trespasses as we forgive those who trespass against us, and lead us not into temptation but deliver us from the evil one for thine is the Kingdom, the power, and the glory for ever and ever. Amen."

I reside in our country here because of the great harm. The infidels took me unjustly and sold me into the hands of the Christian man *(Nasrani)* who bought me. We sailed on the big sea for a month and a half to a place called Charleston in the Christian language. I fell into the hands of a small, weak, and wicked man who did not fear Allah at all, nor did he read nor pray. I was afraid to stay with such a wicked man who committed many evil deeds so I escaped. After a month, Allah our Lord presented us into the hands of a righteous man who fears Allah, and who loves to do good deeds and whose name is General Jim Owen and whose brother is called Colonel John Owen. These are two righteous men. I am in a place called Bladen County.

I continue in the hands of Jim Owen who does not beat me, nor calls me bad names, nor subjects me to hunger, nakedness, or hard work. I cannot do hard work for I am a small, ill man. During the last twenty years I have not seen any harm at the hands of Jim Owen.

Source: Ala A. Alryyes, trans. "The Life of Omar ibn Said, Written by Himself." In *The Multilingual Anthology of American Literature,* edited by Marc Shell and Wernor Sollors, 75–93. New York: New York University Press, 2000.

Salafi Muslims

A social movement within Sunni Islam, Salafi Muslims are a global REVIVALISM movement. Taking their name from *al-salaf al-salih,* the "pious predecessors" of the first three generations of Muslims, contemporary Salafi Muslims seek to recover the original Islam that they believe has been corrupted by centuries of unsanctioned change. Less than 10 percent of Muslim Americans are Salafis. Their DRESS, views on gender relations, RELIGIOUS LIFE, and views on POLITICS are socially conservative. While certainly countercultural, however, most Salafi Muslim Americans explicitly oppose violence and radical movements such as al-Qaeda.

ORIGINS OF SALAFISM

While Salafis themselves see their origins extending back to the seventh century, historians date the inception of Salafism to late 19th-century Egypt. Spearheaded by scholars such as Muhammad 'Abduh and Jamal al-Din al-Afghani, Salafism was a reform movement that sought to make Islam compatible with modernity. By the end of the 20th century, however, Salafi Muslims had become increasingly separatist, generally choosing to remain aloof from the secular institutions and civic practices of the modern world.

From the Salafi perspective, Salafism is not a modern movement; rather, it is a return to the fixed, timeless, authentic Islam practiced at the time of the prophet MUHAMMAD but marginalized thereafter. Seeing themselves as fierce defenders of *tawhid*—or monotheism, the belief in one God—Salafi Muslims police Islamic practice from the influence of *bid'ah,* or impermissible innovation, and *shirk,* the sin of placing someone or something on par with God. Challenging the traditional authority of the four Sunni schools of law, Salafi Muslims see their jurisprudence as rooted directly in the authority of the Qur'an and the Sunna, or the tradition of the prophet Muhammad. In practice, however, Salafi reading of scripture and tradition is heavily influenced by the Hanbali school of LAW, in particular by 14th-century scholar Ibn Taymiyya and 18th-century reformer Muhammad ibn Abd al-Wahhab, as well as by contemporary Saudi Arabian jurists.

On account of Salafism's literalist, populist approach to scripture and its conservative social ethos, Western scholars often draw analogies between Salafism and American Christianity, describing the movement in terms such as "the Protestant reformers of Islam," "Puritan Islam," "Evangelical," and "neo-Fundamentalist." Salafi Muslims reject such categorizations. Some Salafi would also reject the more commonly used designation, WAHHABISM, though critics such as KHALED ABOU EL FADL (1963–) maintain that there is by now little difference between the two identities.

AMERICAN SALAFIS

Precursors to present-day Salafism can be located on American shores as early as 1939 or before, when Daoud Ahmad Faisal founded the Islamic Mission of America in Brooklyn, New York. In dialogue with immigrant Muslims and African-American converts, Faisal confrontationally promoted Islam as an antidote to the excesses of commercialism, corrupt political power, and imperialism. In subsequent decades, Salafi ideas and practices trickled in with students, visitors, and refugees from the Middle East, contributing to the hodgepodge of forms that during the 1950s and 1960s were grouped under the category of "orthodox."

It was not until the 1970s that Muslim Americans began to identify themselves or their ISLAMIC THOUGHT as Salafi. The early adopters were AFRICAN-AMERICAN MUSLIMS who traveled to Saudi Arabia to study Islam. Some of these Muslims, such as Jamaican-born Abu Ameenah Bilal Phillips, translated key Salafi texts from Arabic into English and authored original scholarship as well. By the 1990s, Salafi ideas and practices were spread through the annual conferences of smaller organizations such as the Islamic Assembly of North America and the Qur'an and Sunnah Society of North America. From the days of Faisal's mission before WORLD WAR II to the early 21st century, Salafism's growth in the United States has been driven by Saudi funding, both public and private, which has sponsored American exchange scholars, mosque-building, and the distribution of books and curriculums.

While Salafi Muslims can be found across the United States, the phenomenon is largely an East Coast one. Salafi mosques, bookstores, and schools can be found in largest numbers in urban centers such as NEW YORK CITY, East Orange, New Jersey, PHILADELPHIA, and Washington, D.C. According to a poll conducted by University of Kentucky professor Ihsan Bagby, 8 percent of practicing Muslim Americans favored Salafism over other interpretations of Islam, and the majority of these were African American.

PRACTICE AND CONFLICT

On account of their separatist ethos, converts to Salafi Islam are known to have fractured relationships with the non-Muslim members of their families. Similarly, in their zeal to purge Islamic practice of all nonoriginal elements, Salafi Muslims do not always foster the easiest of relations to other Muslims. Rather, they are often resented for what is perceived as their legalism, their antagonistic style and their alleged propensity for *takfir,* the labeling of others as infidels. Because Salafi Muslims regard the Qur'an and Sunna as providing a comprehensive guide for how to live Islamically, disputes with other Muslims are not limited to the specifics of ritual practice but cross over into the cultural realm as well. From a staunch Salafi perspective, just as exchanging a Ramadan greeting not explicitly used in the seventh century is an innovation, listening to popular music runs the risk of placing something on par with God.

In their pursuit of Islamic authenticity and in a way of marking themselves as distinct, Salafi Muslim Americans dress in a distinctly Arabian style. Salafi men tend to grow their beards long and don either a *thobe*—an Arabian one-piece garment—or hem their pant legs above the ankle, a practice known as *isbaal.* Salafi women generally wear black *niqabs,* one-piece garments that cover everything but the eyes. By means of their alternative styles of dress, Salafi Muslims offer a critique of American consumer culture even as they adopt the same consumerist techniques to enact their identity.

Somewhat ironically, given Salafism's pervasive critique of modern, secular culture, Salafi Muslims have been especially deft at exploiting the tools of new media to disseminate their ideas. In the 1980s and 1990s, Salafi doctrine was spread by cassette tape with the selling and trading of recorded sermons and lectures. Since the 1990s, Salafi Muslims have used the INTERNET to disseminate their message, broadcasting their missionary call around the country and the globe at Web sites such as salafipublications.com and SalafiTalk.net.

Since the al-Qaeda attacks of SEPTEMBER 11, 2001, a key goal of such Web sites has been to distinguish Salafism from the violent extremism of al-Qaeda and the Taliban. A key text in this effort has been Haneef James Oliver's *The 'Wahhabi' Myth* (2009), whose subtitle promises to "dispel . . . prevalent fallacies and the fictitious link with [Osama]

Bin Laden." The post-9/11 era has been difficult for Salafi Americans. The most prominent example was the 2003–04 prosecutions of the so-called paintball Jihadists of the "Virginia Jihad Network," in which 11 men were charged and nine convicted of various terrorism-related offenses. In 2005, Iraqi-American biologist and prominent Salafi lecturer Ali al-Timimi was sentenced to life in prison for exhorting his followers to wage holy war. As a consequence of this fraught political climate, it is generally thought that the Salafi movement in America is on the wane.

Joshua Dubler

Further Reading

Abou El Fadl, Khaled. "The Ugly Modern and the Modern Ugly." In *Progressive Muslims,* edited by Omid Safi. Oxford: Oneworld, 2003.

Curtis, Edward E., IV. "Islamism and Its African American Muslim Critics: Black Muslims in the Era of the Arab Cold War." *American Quarterly* 59, no. 3 (2007): 683–709.

Lee, Umar. *The Rise and Fall of the Salafi Dawah in the United States.* Available online. URL: http://www.archive.org/details/TheRiseAndFallOfTheSalafiDawahInTheUnited States. Accessed January 29, 2009.

Murphy, Caryle. "Five Years Later: Salafi Islam; For Conservative Muslims, Goal of Isolation a Challenge; 9/11 Put Strict Adherents on the Defensive," *Washington Post.* Available online. URL: http://www.washingtonpost.com/wp-dyn/content/article/2006/09/04/AR2006090401107.html. Accessed September 5, 2006.

Oliver, Haneef James. *The 'Wahhabi' Myth: Dispelling Prevalent Fallacies and the Fictitious Link with Bin Laden.* Available online. URL: http://www.thewahhabimyth.com. Accessed January 29, 2009.

Roy, Olivier. *Globalized Islam: The Search for the New Ummah.* New York: Columbia University Press, 2004.

as-Salafi, Abu 'Iyad. "A Brief Introduction to the Salafi Dawah." Available online. URL: http://www.salafipublications.com/sps/sp.cfm?subsecID=SLF02&articleID=SLF020001&articlePages=1. Accessed January 29, 2009.

Wiktorowicz, Quintan. "The Salafi Movement: Violence and the Fragmentation of a Community." In *Muslim Networks: From Hajj to Hip Hop,* edited by miriam cooke and Bruce B. Lawrence, 208–234. Chapel Hill: University of North Carolina Press, 2005.

Sambo   See MOUNT VERNON.

Saviour's Day

Celebrated every year on February 26, Saviour's Day is a Muslim-American HOLIDAY, instituted by NATION OF ISLAM (NOI) leader ELIJAH MUHAMMAD in 1950 to commemorate the life and work of W. D. FARD, the founder of the NOI, who members believed was God. Beginning in the 1950s, NOI members traveled from their temples across the United States to attend the annual convention in CHICAGO, ILLINOIS. By 1975, the mayors of many cities, such as Chicago; Oakland; Berkeley; LOS ANGELES; Gary; NEWARK, NEW JERSEY; and ATLANTA, among others, proclaimed Saviour's Day to be Nation of Islam Day because of the movement's popularity among their residents.

Celebrations of Saviour's Day began with the customary Opening PRAYER (in English rather than ARABIC), which is the first chapter of the QUR'AN, called *al-fatiha.* This was followed by high-spirited speakers who would each say a few words as part of the service, reminding people of the blessed day. They encouraged participants to give to charity and to purchase the line of items sold by community members. Like many conventions, Saviour's Day included sales of goods: for example, believers purchased pork-free meals, new editions of the community newspaper, MUHAMMAD SPEAKS, and literature, in the bazaarlike atmosphere outside the main speech area. In addition, informal networking between members from across the country took place on business matters.

The main speaker at Saviour's Day gatherings was the Honorable Elijah Muhammad, who outlined Fard's teachings for the benefit of members and non-Muslim visitors. He generally spoke for about an hour at the convention on such themes as the origins of the NOI, the mission story of Fard, the legitimacy of the group, leadership, and the loyalty and generosity of followers. The goal of attendees was to demonstrate loyalty to Muhammad's mission to achieve "freedom, justice, and equality" for all black people. Every element of the ritual, from the DRESS people wore to the speeches given, was designed to create a happy spirit of unity and peace of mind to any onlooker listening to the greetings of the believers of *as-salaam alaikum* (Peace be unto you) and the reply of *wa alaikum as-salaam* (and Peace be unto you) in the Arabic language. Female members wore long, flowing white gowns and white head scarves as they sat together, creating the vision of a sea of white for the onlooker. Most men displayed their FRUIT OF ISLAM (FOI) blue uniforms, although some wore brown ones, with bow ties and long ties. They sat together, also creating an air of discipline, particularly with their demonstration of a more public role in the convention. The FOI provided security for the event, carefully monitoring the stage area and managing the crowd, attempting to create an orderly and safe environment in the convention center where the event was held.

The commemoration of Saviour's Day continued in the NOI after Elijah Muhammad's death in 1975 until his son, W. D. MOHAMMED, put an end to it in 1978. Mohammed,

Members of the Nation of Islam attend a Saviour's Day convention in Chicago in 1972.   *(AP Images)*

who was attempting to lead NOI members toward a Sunni interpretation of Islam, acknowledged the contributions of NOI founder W. D. Fard but explicitly rejected the notion that Fard was God in the flesh, a belief that other Muslim Americans found heretical. Minister LOUIS FARRAKHAN disagreed with Mohammed's changes, however, and in 1978 recreated a version of the NOI based on the original teachings of Elijah Muhammad, including the belief that Fard was God. Farrakhan also rejuvenated the commemoration of Saviour's Day. Another claimant to the legacy of Elijah Muhammad, Minister Silis Muhammad, did so as well, and the practice of this uniquely Muslim-American holiday thus continued in the late 20th and early 21st centuries.

Fareed Z. Munir

Further Reading

Curtis, Edward E., IV. *Black Muslim Religion in the Nation of Islam, 1960–1975.* Chapel Hill: University of North Carolina Press, 2006.
Essen-Udom, E. U. *Black Nationalism: A Search for an Identity in America.* Chicago: University of Chicago Press, 1962.
Malcolm X, with Alex Haley. *The Autobiography of Malcolm X.* New York: Ballantine Books, 1965.
Muhammad, Attorney General Misshaki. "A Thumbnail Sketch of Mr. Silis Muhammad." Available online. URL: www.silismuhammad.com/muhammad.html. Accessed February 9, 2010.
Muhammad, Warith Deen. *As the Light Shineth from the East.* Chicago: WDM Publishing Company, 1980.

Schuon, Frithjof (1907–1998) *founder of the Maryamiyya Sufi Order*

Frithjof Schuon, known among his followers as 'Isa Nur al-Din, was an author, poet, painter, and Sufi teacher who founded the MARYAMIYYA SUFI ORDER. An outgrowth of the 'Alawiyya-Shadhiliyya, a North African Sufi lineage into which Schuon was initiated in Algeria, the Maryamiyya as a distinct order seems to have emerged from a series of powerful visions of the Virgin Mary that occurred to Schuon beginning in 1965.

Born in Basle, Switzerland, on June 18, 1907, into a German Catholic family, Schuon became interested in spiritual matters at an early age and first encountered Islam while working as a textile designer in Paris. Late in 1932, he traveled to Algeria where the next year he was initiated into Sufism by the Shadhili Sufi master Ahmad al-'Alawi. For many years Schuon led a small, secretive group of European Sufi disciples based mainly in Lausanne and Basle, although he counted followers from across Europe.

In 1946, Schuon was declared an independent master by his disciples rather than just a *muqaddam*, or "deputy," of the Algerian Sufi order into which he was originally initiated. In effect, this allowed Schuon to create his own Sufi order. He traveled widely from the 1950s to the early 1970s, a period during which he studied Native American art, religion, and culture among the Sioux and Crow Indians in the western United States. In 1980, Schuon and his wife, Catherine, moved from Switzerland to Bloomington, Indiana, where he quietly taught a small circle of American followers in a forested residential community called Inverness Farms.

On Christmas Eve 1985, Schuon experienced a particularly powerful vision of the Virgin Mary in which she appeared to him disrobed, an experience that appears to have led Schuon to begin promoting mystical exercises involving ritual nudity among his disciples. In 1991, a disillusioned member of the order brought a legal case against Schuon, who was subsequently indicted by a grand jury on felony charges of child molestation and sexual battery. A number of Schuon's more prominent followers vocally denounced the charges as false in the local press, and the prosecutor eventually dropped the case, citing insufficient evidence. Schuon died in his home at Inverness Farms in Bloomington on May 5, 1998.

Schuon was a prolific author, and his works have had a marked, although not always explicit, impact on the Western academic study of Sufism and other mystical traditions as well as, to a lesser extent, on Muslim intellectualist circles in the West, largely through the aegis of scholars such as Seyyed Hossein Nasr and Houston Smith. Deeply influenced by the thought of the French metaphysician René Guénon, Schuon's writings championed two interrelated ideas. First, there was the doctrine of the *sophia perennis*, or the "perennial wisdom" that was understood to animate all authentic systems of religious expression. This is normally called Perennialism. Second, there was the idea that secular modern life must be rejected in favor of traditional sacred doctrines. This is normally called Traditionalism. Among his many works addressing Islam, his *Understanding Islam* (1963) was particularly well received in both the Muslim world and the West.

Erik S. Ohlander

Further Reading

Aymard, Jean-Baptiste, and Patrick Laude. *Frithjof Schuon: Life and Teachings.* Albany: State University of New York Press, 2004.

Frithjof Schuon Estate. Available online. URL: http://www.frith jof-schuon.com. Accessed February 25, 2009.

Schuon, Frithjof. *Understanding Islam.* London: Allen and Unwin, 1963.

Sedgwick, Mark. *Against the Modern World: Traditionalism and the Secret Intellectual History of the Twentieth Century.* New York: Oxford University Press, 2004, pp. 84–93, 145–177.

sema

Sema, literally "audition," is a meditative dance practiced most commonly by members of the MEVLEVI SUFI ORDER, a group of Islamic mystics. Jalal ad-Din Muhammad Rumi, a Persian poet and theologian, inspired the movement in 13th-century Turkey, and according to traditional accounts, his son Sultan Veled established the Mevlevi Order and began the practice of *sema* on the day of Rumi's death on December 17, 1273.

Sema is a form of DHIKR, or remembrance of God. Those who perform the *sema*, known as *semazens*, have often been referred to as "whirling dervishes," because they spin round and round as part of the prayer ritual. *Semazens* wear *tennure*, a traditional costume, made of long white robes and a tall hat. The *semazens* rotate counterclockwise within a group of others, pivoting on the left foot. Each rotates counterclockwise around an axis and the *halka*, or circle. *Semazens* begin with their arms folded, then spread them wide with the right palm up and the left palm down. During this dance, *semazens* become closer to God by opening themselves up to his presence and letting the stresses of life fade away.

Since the early 1950s, Americans have observed *sema* both abroad and at home. Though some Sufi lodges and religious orders were banned in Turkey in 1925, later republican governments of Turkey allowed *sema* to be practiced in the form of public shows controlled by the Ministry of Culture. In 1953, the show was commercialized in the West and traveled to sold-out performances in the United States and Europe. The term *whirling dervish* had been used widely since the 1800s to denote spiritual ecstasy and even mystical madness, and audiences flocked to see the "authentic" stage performance of the ritual. The Mevlevi presence in the United States most likely existed in some form earlier, but the Mevlevi Order of America offered professional *sema* lessons in the 1970s, furthering the practice of *sema* in American culture. Mevlevi Master Suleyman Hayati Dede traveled from Konya, Turkey, to teach in the West, especially in the United States. In 1978, Dede's son, Sheikh Jelaluddin Loras, traveled to Northern California to begin American Mevlevi training and founded the order. The Mevlevi Order of America offered regular classes and seminars and held public events and holiday celebrations. The largest was *Shebi Aruz,* the anniversary of Rumi's death.

American versions of the *sema* attempt to engage the uninitiated in the ritual. As American Sufi master SAMUEL LEWIS, also known as Sufi Sam, put it: "The watcher is the prayerful devotee; the dancer is Divine." In Shakina Reinhertz's book, *Women Called to the Path of Rumi: The Way of the Whirling Dervish* (2001), she describes the *semazen* and the audience as blending into a transformed space where human and divine meet. The audience feels the connection to the divine; Reinhertz attributes to this how many observers come into the tradition.

The entrance of *sema* into American culture came first as an exotic wonder that could be marketed and sold as entertainment. But during the countercultural movements of the 1960s and 1970s, more and more Americans began to understand the ritual as a legitimate method of spiritual practice. The Mevlevi Order of America is but one of many established Sufi organizations that now serve local communities and has made the seemingly foreign religious ritual of *sema* a regular feature of American culture.

Andrew O'Brien

Further Reading

Mevlevi Order of America. Available online. URL: http://www.hayatidede.org/. Accessed May 18, 2008.

Reinhertz, Shakina. *Women Called to the Path of Rumi: The Way of the Whirling Dervish.* Prescott, Ariz.: Hohm Press, 2001.

Threshold Society. Available online. URL: http://www.sufism.org/society/sema/index.html. Accessed May 18, 2008.

September 11, 2001

On the morning of September 11, 2001, 19 Saudi Arabian and Egyptian members of al-Qaeda, a radical and violent Muslim political group that opposes the United States, Israel, and most Muslim governments, hijacked and crashed two large passenger jets into both towers of the World Trade Center in NEW YORK CITY and one into the Pentagon, the Department of Defense headquarters in Arlington, Virginia, near Washington, D.C. A fourth hijacked jet, apparently bound for the White House or the U.S. Capitol, crashed in Pennsylvania. Approximately 3,000 people were murdered that day. The attack destroyed the twin towers—the tallest buildings in New York—and caused considerable damage to the Pentagon. Osama bin Laden, the leader of al-Qaeda, later explained that the attacks were revenge for the suffering caused by U.S. foreign policy in the Middle East. Both before and after the terrorist attacks of 9/11, as the day came to be

known, al-Qaeda leaders justified what they called a jihad, or struggle, against the United States because of its strong support of Israel, its leadership of the war against Iraq in 1991, its military bases in the Persian Gulf, and its support for corrupt regimes in the Middle East.

Muslim-American leaders immediately denounced the attacks. The American Muslim Political Coordination Council, which represented the COUNCIL ON AMERICAN-ISLAMIC RELATIONS (CAIR), the MUSLIM PUBLIC AFFAIRS COUNCIL, the ISLAMIC SOCIETY OF NORTH AMERICA, and other groups plainly stated that "American Muslims utterly condemn what are apparently vicious and cowardly acts of terrorism against innocent civilians. We join with all Americans in calling for the swift apprehension and punishment of the perpetrators. No political cause could ever be assisted by such immoral acts." The ISLAMIC CIRCLE OF NORTH AMERICA said that "Islam does not permit such unjust acts." Individual Muslim Americans also expressed their dismay over the attacks, laying flowers outside the Muslim Council Center in Washington, D.C., donating blood to Red Cross blood drives across the nation, raising money for the mayor's 9/11 fund in

Mohammad Chowdhury, who waited tables at Windows on the World, a restaurant atop the North Tower of the World Trade Center in New York City, was killed in the terrorist attacks of September 11, 2001. His wife, Baraheen Ashrafi, gave birth two days later to their son Farqad Chowdhury, who is pictured here along with his sister, Fahina Chowdhury. *(Erica Berger/Corbis)*

New York, and flying the U.S. flag in solidarity outside their homes and places of worship.

Muslim Americans across the country also harbored a great deal of fear of the DISCRIMINATION and retributive violence that they might face as a result of the attacks. Despite their pleas, and those of many non-Muslim leaders, including President George W. Bush, for calm and compassion, the negative reaction against Muslim Americans, and those who "looked" Muslim, was immediate. In a hate crime in Mesa, Arizona, on September 15, 2001, Balbir Singh Sodhi, a gas station owner, became the first person to be killed in revenge for the attacks, even though he was not a Muslim but a Sikh. Immediately before the murder, a man named Frank Roque was heard at a local bar saying that he was going to "kill the rag heads responsible for September 11." Perhaps as many as seven others were murdered in the immediate aftermath of 9/11.

According to the Federal Bureau of Investigation (FBI), hate crimes against Muslims and Arabs in the United States rose 1,700 percent from 2000 to 2001. The Council on American-Islamic Relations received reports of 1,062 violent, threatening, and harassing incidents during the initial onslaught of the post-9/11 backlash and counted 2,250 victims of bias-motivated harassment and violence during their 2001/2002 reporting year. The AMERICAN-ARAB ANTI-DISCRIMINATION COMMITTEE reported more than 700 violent incidents targeting Arab and Muslim Americans, or those perceived to be, in the first nine weeks after the attacks and another 165 occurring between January 1 and October 11, 2002. The risk of death was highest in the first few weeks after the attacks; over time minor assaults, verbal harassment, and vandalism of private property and institutions, especially mosques, became the most prominent form of backlash. Muslim women wearing head scarves proved to be particularly vulnerable to public attack.

Seven days after the 9/11 attacks, U.S. Attorney General John Ashcroft announced that the FBI had received more than 96,000 tips and potential leads to terrorists from the American public, many of which targeted Muslim Americans. This broad public response serves as a good indicator of the collective suspicion that was cast on Muslim Americans. Government agents followed up on these tips, resulting in tens of thousands of FBI and police visits to Muslim-American homes and places of employment. Public fears and suspicion were kept at a high pitch during the first few years after the attacks as the mainstream American media remained focused on the potential presence of terrorist sleeper cells hiding in Muslim-American communities. The Bush administration also implemented a wide range of domestic security policies after the attacks that focused on Muslim-American and Arab-American communities. These included mass arrests, preventive detentions, FBI interviews,

registration and fingerprinting of male foreign nationals, widespread wiretapping, secret hearings, criminal indictments, and reviews of private Internet, telecommunication, and financial records. Of the 37 security-related initiatives launched between September 12, 2001, and mid-2003, 25 of them focused, either directly or indirectly, on Muslim and Arab Americans. First to be caught in the post-9/11 dragnet were some 1,200 Muslim and Arab males (presumably noncitizens) arrested across the country, but especially in cities such as DETROIT and LOS ANGELES, where there was a high percentage of first-generation Muslim Americans, permanent residents, and foreign visitors.

Many of the detainees, who did not have access to legal counsel or their families, were mistreated, according to a 2003 report from the Department of Justice's Office of Inspector General. The report, which officially censured the FBI's handling of the cases, found a pattern of abuse including "unnecessary" body searches—including cavity searches—that appeared "intended to punish." The exact identities and final fates of these persons remain unknown because the U.S. government has not released information about them; what is known is that none were charged with having terrorist connections. Other government programs—such as the special registration of some 80,000 Muslims and Arabs on temporary visas, FBI interviews of tens of thousands of Muslims living permanently in the United States, and 5,000 preventive detentions—also failed to net a single conviction for a terrorist crime, although thousands were deported for visa violations in what legal scholar David Cole has called the "most aggressive national campaign of ethnic profiling since WORLD WAR II."

While the U.S. government claimed to have broken up domestic terrorist cells in or around Buffalo, Detroit, Portland, Seattle, and northern Virginia, none of these groups had proven plans to inflict damage on the United States, and only one, the so-called Lackawanna Six, from Lackawanna, New York, near Buffalo, had an arguable al-Qaeda connection. Criminal indictments in "terrorism-related" cases concluded between 2001 and 2005 showed 200 convictions from more than 400 indictments, but very few of these convictions were for terrorism. Perhaps the most embarrassing of these cases for the FBI was the detention of Oregon lawyer BRANDON MAYFIELD, who was wrongly accused of aiding the 2004 bombings of commuter trains in Madrid, Spain. In November 2006, the FBI apologized to Mayfield for its mistake and paid him $2 million in restitution.

The United States Treasury Department closed six Muslim-American charities and seized their assets after the 9/11 attacks. Of the six, only one, the Holy Land Foundation, faced charges for support of terrorism, and in 2008, five of its officials were found guilty of terrorism-related charges stemming from their $12.4 million donation to Hamas, the

Palestinian political party. Criminal charges were dropped against two other Muslim-American charities, and no charges were filed for the other three. Despite the lack of charges and convictions against these organizations, the assets of all of these charities remained frozen by the government.

The U.S. government's handling of Muslim and Arab Americans provoked distrust, fear, and alienation in these communities, which were repeatedly charged with being unsupportive of government antiterrorism strategies—a claim that members of these communities firmly rejected. Indeed, prominent Muslim-American leaders and organizations called on the government to work with them rather than harass them. Muslim Americans were also negatively affected by the stereotyping and broad suspicion cast upon them by the government and media and felt the silent stares of stigma, suspicion, and hatred in their workplaces and on the streets.

Despite all the negative trends, Muslim Americans had varying post-9/11 experiences at the individual and local community levels, where Muslim Americans were often the subjects of compassion and empathy rather than fear or anger. Many Americans rejected notions of collective guilt or of a Muslim threat to American culture, and some members of the American public organized to protect Muslim Americans and their institutions and to protest unfair treatment. In TOLEDO, OHIO, for example, 2,000 community members, both Muslims and non-Muslims, joined hands outside the Islamic Center of Toledo, whose stained-glass windows had been damaged by gunfire in retribution for the 9/11 attacks. Led by Cheriffe Kadri, the president of the mosque, they prayed for peace and protection. Many non-Muslim Americans showed a rising interest in learning about Islam and Muslims, while Muslim Americans sought increased religious knowledge as well, in order to advance their capacity to answer the queries of others as well as their own questions.

In many locations across the United States since 9/11, Muslim Americans have experienced a level of community mobilization, civic engagement, and coalition participation nearly unprecedented in Muslim-American history. While the Muslim-American capacity to influence government policies at levels higher than the local remained quite limited, a broad multiracial and multiethnic Muslim-American assertion of civic responsibilities and demand for civil rights became stronger than ever before. On the national level, the American Civil Liberties Union, the American Friends Service Committee, and other public interest groups joined Muslim-American organizations in filing lawsuits or advocating for the civil rights of Muslim Americans. On the local level, Americans committed to INTERFAITH MOVEMENTS became part of each other's lives; in Indianapolis, Indiana, for example, the Peace Learning Center and Indiana, Purdue University Indianapolis School of Education organized an exchange of students among three parochial schools: one Jewish, one Christian, one Muslim.

These seeds of optimism for Muslim Americans were direct outcomes of the government policies, popular backlash, and enhanced anti-Muslim rhetoric that followed the 9/11 attacks, as Muslims and non-Muslims rose up to challenge undemocratic policies, popular political violence, and Islamophobia. The 9/11 attacks and the official and popular responses to them crystallized a sociopolitical crisis for Muslim Americans, a crisis whose eventual denouement would be positive in the view of many Muslim Americans. When Muslim Americans mobilized to defend and protect their community members and institutions, their civil rights, immigrant rights, and religious rights, they intersected with other groups in American society in new and deeper ways. At their meeting point, "us" and "them" merged symbolically into new and different configurations.

Hate crimes and attacks on Muslim institutions spurred the immediate activism of neighborhood, regional, and national coalitions, all of which embraced Muslim-American organizations. The work of many other groups left a handprint on this post-9/11 mobilization story: human rights organizations investigating abuses of prisoners, private philanthropies supporting community defense work, civil rights attorneys defending the falsely accused, immigrant coalitions marching in protest against government excesses, ethnic organizations calling for an end to collective profiling, community organizers conducting civil rights teach-ins and special registration monitoring, mosques organizing open houses, neighborhood organizations forming mosque defense committees, interfaith groups speaking out against hate crimes, school girls exchanging solidarity visits, and local and national Muslim-American organizations taking on a broader range of tasks than ever before under emergency conditions. The support of others for Muslim-American claims to full national belonging and citizenship pulled them in from the margins of social exclusion, accelerating their social integration into American society. Muslim Americans not only worked in coalition with other groups; they increasingly became part of them, hired as staff and recruited as volunteers.

Overall, the post-9/11 Muslim American experience was paradoxical: pushed out by some and embraced by others in American society. While Muslim Americans experienced extensive institutional discrimination, civil rights abuses, stereotyping, government targeting, and public attack, they also experienced enhanced inclusion in civil society organizations. Muslim Americans of all racial and ethnic origins, their organizations, and institutions became visible players in the American public square to a greater degree than ever before. This civic inclusion was by no means evenly distributed across the nation nor was it uncontested, but it was nonetheless palpable. This perhaps unexpected positive outcome emerged from the dynamic that was put into motion when state repression, public attacks, and popular vilification rather quickly reached a level that was intolerable to Muslim Americans and to some American institutions and individuals. Muslim Americans emerged from the terrorist attacks of September 11, 2001, in a much different social position from that they held prior to the attacks.

Louise Cainkar and Edward E. Curtis IV

Further Reading

Al-Marayati, Laila. "American Muslim Charities: Easy Targets in the War on Terror." *Pace Law Review* 25 (2005): 321–338.

Amnesty International. *Threat and Humiliation: Racial Profiling, Domestic Security, and Human Rights in the United States.* New York: Amnesty International, 2004.

Council on American-Islamic Relations. *Response to September 11, 2001 Attacks.* Washington, D.C.: CAIR, 2007.

Goodstein, Laurie. "Stereotyping Rankles Silent, Secular Majority of American Muslims," *New York Times,* 23 December 2001, p. A20.

Human Rights Watch. "We Are Not the Enemy: Hate Crimes against Arabs, Muslims and Those Perceived to Be Arab or Muslim after September 11." Vol. 14, no. 6 (G), November 2002.

National Commission on Terrorist Attacks. *The 9/11 Commission Report.* New York: W. W. Norton, 2004.

Tsao, Fred, and Rhoda Rae Gutierrez. *Losing Ground.* Chicago: Illinois Coalition for Immigrant and Refugees Right, 2003.

Suheir Hammad
"first writing since" (2001)

Suheir Hamad (1973–   ) was already well known among New York's literary circles before the al-Qaeda attacks of September 11, 2001, but she became a national literary figure after publishing "first writing since" on November 7, 2001. In 2003, she received a Tony Award for her writing and performance in Russell Simmons Presents Def Comedy Jam on Broadway. *Since then, her poetry has been anthologized in dozens of collections. "first writing since" captured her feelings as a person of multiple identities in the wake of the 9/11 attacks: a New Yorker who had been traumatized by the event, a Palestinian called on to explain the actions of the terrorists, a humanist concerned about New Yorkers' collective howl for revenge, the sister of a U.S. military member concerned about going to war, and a critic angry about the hypocrisy of U.S. foreign policy.*

1. there have been no words.
i have not written one word.
no poetry in the ashes south of canal street.

no prose in the refrigerated trucks driving debris
    and dna.
not one word.

today is a week, and seven is of heavens, gods,
    science.
evident out my kitchen window is an abstract
    reality.
sky where once was steel.
smoke where once was flesh.

fire in the city air and i feared for my sister's life
    in a way never
before. and then, and now, i fear for the rest of us.

first, please god, let it be a mistake, the pilot's
    heart failed, the plane's engine died.
then please god, let it be a nightmare, wake me
    now.
please god, after the second plane, please, don't
    let it be anyone who looks like my brothers.

i do not know how bad a life has to break in
    order to kill.
i have never been so hungry that i willed hunger
i have never been so angry as to want to control
    a gun over a pen.
not really.
even as a woman, as a palestinian, as a broken
    human being.
never this broken.

more than ever, i believe there is no difference.
the most privileged nation, most americans do
    not know
the difference between indians, afghanis, syrians,
    muslims, sikhs, hindus.
more than ever, there is no difference.

2. thank you korea for kimchi and bibim bob,
    and corn tea and the genteel smiles of the wait
    staff at wonjo—the smiles never revealing the
    heat of the food or how tired they must be
    working long midtown shifts. thank you korea,
    for the belly craving that brought me into the
    city late the night before and diverted my daily
    train ride into the world trade center.

there are plenty of thank yous in ny right now.
    thank you for my lazy procrastinating late ass.
    thank you to the germs that had me call in
    sick. thank you, my attitude, you had me fired
    the week before. thank you for the train that
    never came, the rude nyer who stole my cab
    going downtown. thank you for the sense my

mama gave me to run. thank you for my legs, my eyes, my life.

3. the dead are called lost and their families hold up shaky printouts in front of us through screens smoked up.

we are looking for iris, mother of three. please call with any information. we are searching for priti, last seen on the 103rd floor. she was talking to her husband on the phone and the line went. please help us find george, also known as adel. his family is waiting for him with his favorite meal. i am looking for my son, who was delivering coffee. i am looking for my sister girl, she started her job on monday. i am looking for peace. i am looking for mercy. i am looking for evidence of compassion. any evidence of life. i am looking for life.

4. ricardo on the radio said in his accent thick as yuca, "i will feel so much better when the first bombs drop over there. and my friends feel the same way."

on my block, a woman was crying in a car parked and stranded in hurt. i offered comfort, extended a hand she did not see before she said, "we're gonna burn them so bad, i swear, so bad." my hand went to my head and my head went to the numbers within it of the dead iraqi children, the dead in nicaragua. the dead in rwanda who had to vie with fake sport wrestling for america's attention.

yet when people sent emails saying, this was bound to happen, lets not forget u.s. transgressions, for half a second i felt resentful. hold up with that, cause i live here, these are my friends and fam, and it could have been me in those buildings, and we're not bad people, do not support america's bullying. can i just have a half second to feel bad?

if i can find through this exhaust people who were left behind to mourn and to resist mass murder, i might be alright.

thank you to the woman who saw me brinking my cool and blinking back tears. she opened her arms before she asked "do you want a hug?" a big white woman, and her embrace was the kind only people with the warmth of flesh can offer. i wasn't about to say no to any comfort. "my brother's in the navy," i

said. "and we're arabs." "wow, you got double trouble." word.

5. one more person ask me if i knew the hijackers. one more motherf****r ask me what navy my brother is in. one more person assume no arabs or muslims were killed. one more person assume they know me, or that i represent a people. or that a people represent an evil. or that evil is as simple as a flag and words on a page.

we did not vilify all white men when mcveigh bombed oklahoma. america did not give out his family's addresses or where he went to church. or blame the bible or pat robertson.

and when the networks air footage of palestinians dancing in the street, there is no apology that hungry children are bribed with sweets that turn their teeth brown. that correspondents edit images. that archives are there to facilitate lazy and inaccurate journalism.

and when we talk about holy books and hooded men and death, why do we never mention the kkk?

if there are any people on earth who understand how new york is feeling right now, they are in the west bank and the gaza strip.

6. today it is ten days. last night bush waged war on a man once openly funded by the cia. i do not know who is responsible. read too many books, know too many people to believe what i am told. i don't give a f*** about bin laden. his vision of the world does not include me or those i love. and petitions have been going around for years trying to get the u.s. sponsored taliban out of power. sh*t is complicated, and i don't know what to think.

but i know for sure who will pay.

in the world, it will be women, mostly colored and poor. women will have to bury children, and support themselves through grief. "either you are with us, or with the terrorists" meaning keep your people under control and your resistance censored. meaning we got the loot and the nukes.

in america, it will be those amongst us who refuse blanket attacks on the shivering. those of us who work toward social justice, in support of civil liberties, in opposition to hateful foreign policies.

i have never felt less american and more new yorker, particularly brooklyn, than these past days. the stars and stripes on all these cars and apartment windows represent the dead as citizens first not family members, not lovers.

i feel like my skin is real thin, and that my eyes are only going to get darker. the future holds little light.

my baby brother is a man now, and on alert, and praying five times a day that the orders he will take in a few days time are righteous and will not weigh his soul down from the afterlife he deserves.

both my brothers—my heart stops when i try to pray—not a beat to disturb my fear. one a rock god, the other a sergeant, and both palestin- ian, practicing muslim, gentle men. both born in brooklyn and their faces are of the arche- typal arab man, all eyelashes and nose and beautiful color and stubborn hair.

what will their lives be like now?
over there is over here.

7. all day, across the river, the smell of burning rubber and limbs floats through. the sirens have stopped now. the advertisers are back on the air. the rescue workers are traumatized. the skyline is brought back to human size. no lon- ger taunting the gods with its height.

i have not cried at all while writing this. i cried when i saw those buildings collapse on them- selves like a broken heart. i have never owned pain that needs to spread like that. and i cry daily that my brothers return to our mother safe and whole.

there is no poetry in this. there are causes and effects. there are symbols and ideologies. mad conspiracy here, and information we will never know. there is death here, and there are prom- ises of more.

there is life here. anyone reading this is breath- ing, maybe hurting, but breathing for sure. and if there is any light to come, it will shine from the eyes of those who look for peace and justice after the rubble and rhetoric are cleared and the phoenix has risen.

affirm life.
affirm life.
we got to carry each other now.
you are either with life, or against it.
affirm life.

Source: Suheir Hammad. "first writing since." In *Zaatar Diva.* New York: Cypher Books, 2005. © 2005 by Suheir Hammad. Used by arrangement with Cypher Books.

Shabazz, El Hajj Malik   See MALCOLM X.

Shadhili Sufi Order

The Shadhili Sufi Order began in North Africa in the 13th century. Abu-l-Hasan al-Shadhili, after whom the order is named, was born in the 13th century in modern-day Morocco and buried in Egypt, the country where the order began to take root in the 13th and 14th centuries, specifi- cally under the auspices of Abu-l-'Abbas al-Mursi and Ibn 'Ata' Allah.

The presence of Shadhili SUFISM in the United States has been diverse. Like many Sufi orders, the Shadhilis, also known as the Shadhiliyya, have established many branches since first coming to the United States in the early part of the 20th century (according to the earliest known written record) when students of Ahmad al-'Alawi, an Algerian Sufi *shaykh,* or teacher, came to the country.

Originating in what is now Morocco, the Shadhili order spread across the globe, leaving its footprints from Africa to the Arabian Peninsula and the Levant, as well as in South Asia, China, Indonesia, Europe, and North America. There has arguably never been a single unitive element among the various branches, in part due to geo- graphical and cultural diversity. However, according to an American Shadhili *shaykh,* Abdullah Nooruddeen Durkee, one thing that has characterized Shadhilis across time and space is their engagement with society (as opposed to renunciant tendencies) and a focus on gnosis, or personal understanding.

The perhaps best-known expression of the Shadhiliyya in the United States has been the MARYAMIYYA, which was headed by FRITHJOF SCHUON until his death in 1998. Privately known as Sheikh 'Isa Nur al-Din, he was originally from Switzerland and moved to Bloomington, Indiana, in the 1970s. Schuon first came to the United States in 1959, and in terms of available evidence, he was one of the first transmitters, if not the first, of Shadhili Sufism in the United States. However, since records have not necessarily existed documenting the presence of Shadhili Sufism in the United States, the dates of such origins can only be speculative. There could very well have been a presence since the arrival of African Muslim slaves in the 17th century.

Schuon was initiated into the Shadhiliyya-'Alawiyya Sufi order of Algeria via Ahmad al-'Alawi, and soon after studying with him, Schuon had visionary inspiration to connect with Mary and JESUS in his spiritual practices. Since that time his movement has been known as the Maryamiyya. Schuon was also connected with the perennialist/traditionalist school of philosophy, which holds that despite their external difference all religions share an inner core of spiritual and ethical values. Schuon was also an intellectual descendent of René Guénon, another European intellectual who was associated with the Shadhiliyya. While the practices of the Maryamiyya order have been Islamic in nature, they have also incorporated Christian, Hindu, and Native American practices and terminology.

Schuon did not lecture publicly, though he published many written works. His legacy has also been perpetuated by the Muslim-American professor Seyyed Hossein Nasr, who has published several books about Schuon. Other prominent scholars of Islam, such as Titus Burckhardt and Martin Lings, have also been associated with Schuon's teachings. Lings wrote a seminal work on Ahmad al-'Alawi in 1961, entitled *A Sufi Saint of the Twentieth Century.*

The Darqawiyya-Habibiyya, another branch of the Shadhiliyya, was formed in 1976 by 'Abd al-Qadir al-Murabit, formerly known as Ian Dallas. A British author and actor, he was initiated by Moroccan Sufi Sheikh Muhammad ibn al-Habib al-Darqawi in 1967, and by the middle 1970s, he had established a Sufi community in Norwich, England. He first brought the movement to the United States in 1973, and his followers established a center in Berkeley, California, in 1977. The order spread to other countries, notably Spain, and domestically his community spread from Berkeley to Southern California and North Carolina. 'Abd al-Qadir most notably influenced the famous American sheikh, Hamza Yusuf.

Sheikh Fadhlalla Haeri, an Iraqi engineer and a SHI'A MUSLIM AMERICAN who had been affiliated with the Habibiyya during the 1970s established a Sufi community in Blanco, Texas, near San Antonio in 1980. By the late 1980s, Haeri had relocated to England and eventually settled in South Africa. He started the magazine *Nuradeen* and has authored many books. Gray Henry, founder of Fons Vitae, a publishing house for books on Islamic spirituality, was also initiated into a Shadhili order. Fons Vitae has published many important translations of Shadhili texts—perhaps most notably *The Hikm* of Ibn 'Ata' Allah. Another American branch of the Shadhiliyya, the Burhaniyya, was founded by Sheikh Mohamed 'Uthman. Its centers spread to NEW YORK CITY and Montreal.

Muhammad al-Jamal, a Palestinian Shadhili *shaykh* from Jerusalem first started visiting the United States in 1992. Since that time he has visited at least once a year. By 1995, he had initiated approximately 300 students, and according to records from the Shadhiliyya Sufi Center of Northern California, 1,953 people had been formally initiated as of March 2008. Students of al-Jamal have often been introduced to his message through the work of Robert Ibrahim Jaffe, a medical doctor and one of al-Jamal's first students in the United States. In 2005, Jaffe founded the University of Spiritual Healing and Sufism (USHS), which meets quarterly and trains students in spiritual healing, all the while incorporating Sufi-Islamic practices, and the vast majority of the school's students have been initiated into al-Jamal's branch of the Shadhiliyya. USHS was previously known as the Jaffe Institute of Spiritual and Medical Healing (founded in 2000) and, before that, the School of Energy Mastery (founded in 1991).

Abdullah Nooruddeen Durkee, founder of the Green Mountain School and of the Noor Educational Foundation and translator of the *Tajwidi Qur'an,* has also contributed to a significant Shadhiliyya presence in the United States and has shared ties with al-Jamal's community. A convert and spiritual representative of his Egyptian Shadhili teacher, Ibrahim al-Battawi, Durkee has worked closely with the community of Muhammad al-Jamal for the past several years, teaching al-Jamal's students ARABIC, the QUR'AN, and about the historical development of the order. Although a native to the United States, Durkee spent several years in Egypt studying and teaching Sufism before returning to the United States in the late 1970s, eventually settling in Virginia. In addition to writing a number of published pamphlets, he also translated from Arabic into English *The School of the Shadhdhuliyyah,* a work by Abdu-l-Halim Mahmud, a former rector at al-Azhar University during the 20th century.

Nuh Keller, an American convert and Shadhili *shaykh,* has also established a significant community in the United States and has remained involved with Islamic learning institutions in the country, such as Sunni Path. Though he has lived in Amman, Jordan, for several years, many of his students have remained in the United States. In 1991, he translated *The Reliance of the Traveller,* a manual of Islamic law by the 14th-century author Ahmad ibn Naqib al-Misri.

American expressions of Sufism, in general, have often emphasized universal qualities of God and religion, making Sufism attractive to many Americans who consider themselves "spiritual but not religious." Mainstream expressions of Sufism, throughout history, have fallen in line with Sunni Islamic teachings and have simultaneously demonstrated a malleability and emphasis on inner dimensions of worship. This tendency has become magnified in American expressions of Sufism—among them the Shadhiliyya—and in this way they have reflected a new wave in the evolution of Sufism.

Elliott Bazzano

Further Reading
Durkee, Abdullah Nooruddeen. "The History and Practice of the Tariqat ash-Shadhuli." Available online. URL: http://www.sufimuslimcouncil.org/hr/Spirituality/PDF/Microsoft%20Word%20-%20Shadhul i.pdf. Accessed October 12, 2008.

Hermansen, Marcia. "Hybrid Identity Formations in Muslim America." *Muslim World* 90, no. 1 (Spring 2000): 158–198.

———. "The Other Shadhilis of the West." In *Une Voie Soufie dans le Monde: la Shadhiliyya*, 481–500. Paris: Maisonneure & Larose, 2005.

———. "Sufi Orders and Movements: United States." In *Encyclopedia of Women and Islamic Cultures*, Vol. 3. Leiden: Brill, 2005.

Malik, Jamal, and John Hinnels, eds. *Sufism in the West*. New York: Routledge, 2006.

Sedgewick, Mark. *Against the Modern World: Traditionalism and the Secret Intellectual History of the Twentieth Century*. New York: Oxford University Press, 2004.

Westerlund, David, ed. *Sufism in Europe and North America*. New York: RoutledgeCurzon, 2004.

Shakir, Zaid (1956–) *religious scholar*

The life of African-American Muslim religious scholar Zaid Shakir is a story of a person who grew up in federal housing projects and went on to become a leading scholar of Islam in the United States.

Born on May 24, 1956, in Berkeley, California, Zaid Shakir was the second of seven children. When he was young, his mother and father separated, and his mother moved the family to Carver Homes in southwest ATLANTA, GEORGIA. He moved again around the time he was in fourth grade to Pinnacle Heights, another housing project, in New Britain, Connecticut. Shakir was influenced during his childhood most deeply by his mother, a woman who, while having to rely on welfare to raise her children, wrote and published criticisms of white colonialism and imperialism in the *New Britain Herald* and *Hartford Courant*.

Growing up in the projects, Shakir witnessed police brutality toward blacks and Hispanics and was also dismayed by the illegal drug use, alcoholism, and broken homes in his neighborhood. Playing football and running track provided him a refuge, though a shoulder injury kept him from pursuing his love for sports. He felt little connection to the Baptist church in which his mother had raised him. He became an atheist.

In January 1975, as a first-year student at Connecticut State University, Shakir was influenced by the struggle for black liberation and especially its leftist critiques of Christianity as a religion that oppressed black people. But constant questioning of materialism and his mother's death in the spring of 1975 led him to reconsider his stance on God. He felt an urge to connect with some form of spirituality.

After dropping out of college later in 1975, however, Shakir became homeless. Out of desperation, he enlisted in the UNITED STATES MILITARY in 1976. First experimenting with transcendental meditation, which he found unsatisfying, he read a book on Islam by Egyptian author Hammouda Abdul Ati. In 1977, Shakir converted to Islam at a mosque associated with Sunni Muslim-American leader W. D. MOHAMMED (1933–2008).

After finishing his enlistment in the U.S. Air Force, he enrolled in the American University in Washington, D.C., where he earned a B.A. in international relations in 1983. In 1986, he received a master's in political science from Rutgers University, leaving after his graduation to study ARABIC in Cairo, Egypt, for a year.

In 1987, Shakir became an adjunct professor in political science at Southern Connecticut State University and served as imam, or religious leader, of a mosque in New Haven. Masjid al-Islam, the mosque of Islam, was socially active, campaigning against drug dealers in New Haven and supporting New York leader Siraj Wahhaj's efforts to shut down crack houses in Brooklyn. Shakir's followers also patrolled housing projects in New Haven. But Shakir was not satisfied with his knowledge of Islam and decided to deepen it by leaving to study Islam in Syria.

In 1994, Shakir commenced an intensive seven-year study of the QUR'AN, SHARI'A, or Islamic LAW and ethics, and other religious subjects. Graduating from the Islamic studies program at Damascus's Abu Noor University in 2001, Shakir returned to Connecticut, where he resumed his duties as imam of Masjid al-Islam.

In 2003, he was invited by the ZAYTUNA INSTITUTE to become a lecturer and scholar-in-residence at a new Islamic studies center led by HAMZA YUSUF in Hayward, California. In 2005, he published his first book of essays, *Scattered Pictures*. Shakir also emerged as a popular guest speaker both on college campuses and among Muslim-American audiences across the country, where he applied his vast knowledge of Islamic studies to a wide range of contemporary issues from terrorism and U.S. foreign policy to gender equality and poverty.

Edward E. Curtis IV

Further Reading
Shakir, Zaid. *Scattered Pictures: Reflections of an American Muslim*. Hayward, Calif.: Zaytuna Institute, 2005.

shari'a

Shari'a, or Islamic LAW and ethics, is not codified, and Muslims in the United States have held often widely divergent views about how shari'a is to be interpreted and its proper role in daily life. Based primarily on the QUR'AN and supplemented as necessary by the example, or Sunna, of the prophet Muhammad during his lifetime, shari'a is a human attempt to interpret the Divine Will in all aspects of life. As such, shari'a offers a complete guide for living that goes well beyond strictly legal doctrines to encompass even mundane aspects of everyday life, including religious worship, business relations, ethics and manners, and belief.

Although theoretically the shari'a applies to all Muslims, regardless of when or where they may live, as a practical matter, the degree to which individuals have wanted to or been able to live in strict accordance with the shari'a has varied considerably. This has been the case throughout the world, but has been especially true in the United States, where Muslims have been a religious minority and have often had to struggle to maintain their beliefs and practices, including the observance of shari'a.

AFRICAN MUSLIMS IN AMERICA

The first Muslims to reach the shores of North America in significant numbers were those kidnapped from their homes in West Africa and sold into slavery from the 17th through the 19th centuries. The brutal realities of life in slavery placed these enslaved Muslims at the mercy of a new law, one that reduced them to chattel and severely restricted the ability of even the most dedicated to observe even the basics of shari'a. (This is graphically illustrated in the 1997 movie *Amistad,* which shows a group of slaves attempting to perform one of the five daily prayers while chained together on board the slave ship.) Once they reached the shores of North America, Muslim slaves faced the additional hardship of being sold off and separated from their coreligionists. Isolated from each other and subjugated to the will of their masters within a society that deemed Islam a pagan religion, most Muslim slaves faced a lonely struggle to maintain their faith and religious practices.

Yet anecdotal evidence indicates that at least some Muslim slaves attempted to observe the shari'a as faithfully as their situations would allow. Salih Bilali, for example, a slave on a plantation in St. Simon's Island in Georgia, was described by his owner in the early 19th century as a "strict Mahometan; [he] abstains from spirituous liquors, and keeps various fasts, particularly that of the Rhamadan." Salih's friend and contemporary, Bilali Mohamed, who worked on a plantation in nearby Sapelo Island, had been trained in Islamic law back in Africa and was noted for praying five times a day facing east, fasting during the month of Ramadan, and celebrating the two major Islamic holidays (see BILALI OF SAPELO ISLAND). He was the author of a 13-page Arabic text, currently housed at the University of Georgia Library, based on a West African legal treatise from the Maliki school of Islamic jurisprudence and setting out the rules for ritual ablution and prayer.

Bilali Mohamed was considered the imam, or leader, of Sapelo Island's Muslim slave community, and the unusually large numbers of Muslims in close proximity to each other, combined with the island's geographic isolation, enabled at least some aspects of Islamic belief and practice to be passed on to future generations. One of his modern-day descendants, Cornelia Walker Bailey (a likely corruption of the original "Bilali"), has described being taught as a child to say her prayers facing the east, unknowingly following the Muslim practice of facing the holy city of Mecca to pray.

For most Muslim slaves, however, the need to survive had to take precedence over their desire to observe the shari'a. Unable to obtain HALAL, or permissible, foods, for example, even a devout Muslim would eat otherwise *haram,* or forbidden, food such as pork, knowing that the shari'a required them to eat what was available in order to survive. A slave whose owner refused to allow him or her to perform the five-times-daily prayer ritual might combine prayers and perform them in secret. While the shari'a is flexible enough to allow for such accommodations when necessary, slave owners' generally open hostility to Islamic practices and efforts to convert slaves to Christianity, as well the loss of any connection with the rest of the Muslim world, meant that for most slaves any knowledge of shari'a or its requirements generally disappeared within a generation or two.

EARLY IMMIGRANTS

Beginning in 1875, new groups of Muslims began to arrive in the United States as immigrants in search of economic opportunity. These new arrivals hailed mostly from the Middle East (Turkey, Syria, Lebanon, and Palestine) and Eastern Europe (Albania, Russia, Poland, and other countries) and found work as factory workers, farmers, itinerant peddlers, or small shopkeepers. Many of these new immigrants had little opportunity—or desire—to live according to the shari'a and assimilated into mainstream American society. Others held on to some shari'a practices but not others, for example eschewing pork but not worrying whether other meat was halal. The experience described by the son of Fazel Khan, who immigrated to Boston from present-day Pakistan in 1912, was in many ways typical: "[My father] married Mabel Smith, a devout Methodist. We were Americans . . . but we listened to Pakistani folk tunes, played on a flute, [and] learned Muslim prayers. . . . In our family life, East not only met but lived in reasonably good terms with West. . . . We children attended a Methodist church with our mother.

My father, who could find neither a mosque nor a Muslim community in Boston, prayed alone on his [prayer] rug every Friday evening."

Sometimes, however, larger groups of immigrants from the same part of the Muslim world formed communities where they could better maintain their cultural and religious practices. The heart of many such communities was the local mosque. As early as 1915, Muslim immigrants from Albania working in the local mills may have used the Peppermell Counting House in Biddeford, Maine, as a mosque; one of the oldest mosques in the United States built for that purpose was constructed in 1929 by immigrant Syrian farmers living in Ross, NORTH DAKOTA. Although the five daily prayers could be performed privately in any space that was ritually clean, the mosques provided early immigrant Muslims and their descendants a space in which to conduct the weekly congregational, or *juma,* prayer required every Friday. HOLIDAY observances, including the monthlong fast of Ramadan, were also important. So many Syrian Muslims worked at the Pullman car factory in Michigan City that when they celebrated Eid al-Fitr at the end of Ramadan, it had to close down.

Few of these early Muslim immigrants had had formal religious education before coming to the United States, and although many were keen to pass on their religious values to their children and grandchildren, they often made little distinction between shari'a-based practices and those that were based on a cultural norm. In addition, the geographic separation of these ethnic immigrant communities from one another and the rest of the Muslim world, combined with the lack of trained religious leaders, made it difficult to observe the shari'a as a complete way of life. Individual Muslims found their own ways of adapting to the challenge of living as a religious minority in a non-Muslim society. For many, this meant living their lives according to what they felt were the basic principles of Islam, including justice, respect, honesty, and dignity, rather than specific religious laws derived from shari'a.

MID-TWENTIETH-CENTURY MOVEMENTS AND MISSIONARIES

The influx of new Muslim immigrants slowed to a trickle with the passage of the Immigration Acts of 1917 and 1924, which explicitly barred almost all immigrants from Asia and set up a quota system that severely restricted immigration from the Middle East. Around this same time, however, a number of Islamic movements arose in the African-American community. Although the beliefs and practices of some of these diverged from traditional Islamic doctrines, they often adapted some shari'a practices. The MOORISH SCIENCE TEMPLE of America, for example, taught its members to pray three times a day facing the east. And ELIJAH MUHAMMAD,

the leader of NATION OF ISLAM, instructed his followers to pray in a traditionally Sunni manner and adopted dietary restrictions on pork and alcohol, but interpreted the meaning of these practices through his own black nationalist form of Islam.

Although generally considered a heretical sect because of its belief that another prophet followed the prophet MUHAMMAD, the Ahmadi movement did much to introduce more mainstream forms of Islam in the United States, especially among African Americans, and to demonstrate how shari'a could often harmonize with U.S. law. When immigration officials sought to bar entry to Muhammad Sadiq, an Ahmadiyya missionary who sailed from England to the United States in 1920, on the grounds that he was a "representative of a religious group that practiced polygamy," he responded, "I have not come here to teach plurality of wives. If a Moslem will ever preach or practice polygamy in America he will be committing a sin against his religion." Sadiq based his argument on a distinction between what is required by shari'a and what is permitted, maintaining that Muslims must avoid practices, such as polygamy, that are merely permitted—but not required—by shari'a when they contradict the law of the country in which they live.

Another missionary group was the Islamic Mission of America, founded by Sheikh Daoud Ahmed Faisal, which sought to propagate Sunni Islam. Muslims affiliated with his organization fasted during Ramadan, prayed five times daily, and endeavored to make the hajj pilgrimage. In 1962, a group of African Americans who had been attending the Islamic Mission's State Street Mosque in New York became dissatisfied with Sheikh Daoud, in part because they felt he was too interested in "being accepted by America" and unwilling to challenge the status quo. In response, they created the Darul-Islam movement, seeking to create a community of Muslims dedicated to an Islamic lifestyle according to what they considered to be an orthodox Sunni interpretation of shari'a, and in 1963 a group of 40 to 50 men signed the following *ba'yah,* or pledge: "In the name of Allah, the Gracious, the Merciful; Allah is the Greatest; Bearing witness that there is no God but Allah and that Muhammad (peace be on him) is His Messenger, and being a follower of the last Prophet and Messenger of Allah, I hereby pledge myself to the Shariah and to those who are joined by this pledge." Differences in interpretation of the shari'a led to friction within the movement, however. One key point of contention was in the proper understanding of the shari'a prohibition against intoxicants. Some members argued that they could continue to smoke marijuana because it was not mentioned specifically in the Qur'an, or that differences in the Qur'anic passages on intoxicants meant that they had the right to withdraw gradually from drinking alcoholic beverages, as the first Muslims did.

EFFECT OF 1960s IMMIGRATION REFORM

The number and diversity of Muslim Americans dramatically increased following the passage of the IMMIGRATION ACT OF 1965 amendments, which did away with the 1924 act's national-origin quota system that had disproportionately favored European immigration. As the number of Muslim immigrants from all parts of the world began to increase, the interaction of these new arrivals and their American-born children with indigenous Muslims and converts created many new challenges, as well as new opportunities to facilitate shari'a observance.

Many of the immigrants who arrived in the United States after 1965 and their descendants, much like previous generations, quickly adopted lifestyles that were not substantially different from mainstream America. This did not necessarily mean, however, that they renounced their Muslim identity or rejected shari'a totally. Some accepted shari'a in principle but would often choose not to observe aspects of it that they found inconvenient or that might attract negative attention. For example, one Muslim immigrant in the 1980s Midwest who owned and operated liquor stores and bars for 20 years observed, "Myself, I know as a Muslim we are not supposed to serve or drink or be in the bar business. A Muslim shouldn't do those things. But I never stopped to think I shouldn't do that when I was working." Other liquor store owners maintained that shari'a allowed them to sell liquor so long as their customers were non-Muslims. Women often avoided wearing Islamic clothing such as long skirts and head coverings in public because people stared at them. Still other Muslims lived according to their personal understanding of shari'a, such as a young American-born woman who stated, "Now I think women who go to the mosque to pray should be covered. . . . But how women dress outside of the mosque is their own private business. I don't want to go to college with my head covered, and wearing a short skirt does not make me a bad Muslim."

Yet even Muslims who sought to follow shari'a rigorously in all aspects of their lives faced a host of challenges and were often forced to make compromises. When halal meat was not available, Muslims would often buy kosher meat from a Jewish butcher or delicatessen, or they would buy non-halal meat so long as it was not pork. Work and school schedules often made it difficult to perform the five daily prayers at their prescribed times or to attend the Friday congregational prayer. Because prayer requires a thorough ritual ablution, which includes washing the face, hands, and feet, and a clean area without pictures or other adornments on the wall, many employers and schools simply did not have proper facilities to accommodate prayers. Often Muslims were hesitant to even ask for such accommodations or for time off to attend Friday prayers at a mosque or Islamic center, fearing that by doing so they might jeopardize their jobs or create friction with their non-Muslim coworkers.

Financial dealings also posed a challenge to Muslims because of the shari'a's prohibition against *riba,* or interest. While some Muslims interpreted this as prohibiting only usury, or the lending of money at an exorbitant rate of interest, others understood it as a complete bar against the paying or earning of interest. Muslims who followed a stricter interpretation were therefore faced with a dilemma. For example, as one Muslim businessman observed: "We know that Allah said that interest is *haram* and that we should not partake in that, but we are in a country whereby if we don't, then the Muslims will be left behind. So many times we have Muslims who are trying to buy a home, trying to get into business, trying to compete with the business man in this country. Often times we do have to take loans and we do have to pay interest on them. I don't believe Allah will hold that against us. We are not the one making the interest on that loan."

ACCOMMODATING SHARI'A IN AMERICAN LIFE

By the beginning of the 21st century, the growth of the Muslim-American community had begun to make it easier for those Muslims who wished to follow shari'a to do so in nearly every aspect of their lives. Employers and schools increasingly began to make accommodations for Muslims' prayers, arranging work schedules to allow for prayer time, or permitting students to pray during noninstructional time. Public venues used by large numbers of Muslims, such as universities and airports, sometimes added foot-washing facilities in restrooms for health and safety reasons.

Muslims who fasted during Ramadan became increasingly visible and accepted. Schools often allowed fasting students to spend their lunch period in the library rather than having to sit in the cafeteria while their classmates ate. When possible, student and professional athletes adjusted their schedules to accommodate the rigors of fasting. When that was not possible, many continued to fast anyway. In October 2007, even though most of their players had spent the last three weeks abstaining from food or drink all day due to the fast, Michigan's Fordson High School football team chalked up their first win during Ramadan, beating crosstown rival Dearborn High 16-14. "No Excuses" read the special T-shirts worn by the team's fans and team assistants at the game.

To facilitate the observance of shari'a dietary requirements, organizations such as the Islamic Food and Nutrition Council of America began to develop halal certification programs, allowing manufacturers to affix special symbols on packages to indicate that none of a product's ingredients and preparation were *haram,* or forbidden. In addition, some states began to pass truth-in-advertising laws that would allow them to levy fines against vendors caught falsely labeling products as halal, similar to laws designed to protect consumers from falsely labeled kosher products. It also became easier for Muslims to engage in "shari'a compliant" financial dealings, with a growing number of banks and mutual funds such as HSBC Amanah and Guidance Financial Group advertising mortgages and investment options specially designed to avoid *riba,* or interest, or investment in companies involved in liquor, pornography, gambling, or other activities considered *haram,* or forbidden, under shari'a.

An increasing number of Muslim communities began to establish their own cemeteries to ensure that burial services could be conducted in accordance with shari'a, which requires that the body be washed, shrouded, and buried within 24 hours of death. The body would be placed in the grave without a coffin, where local law permitted, on his or her right side, facing Mecca. Muslims who wished to bypass state inheritance laws and follow the elaborate shari'a rules of inheritance could easily do so by writing a will to that effect.

It was important to many Muslims to follow the shari'a when it came to questions of marriage, divorce, or custody arrangements, although most generally did so within the framework of U.S. law. Couples getting married frequently drew up a marriage contract specifying the dowry, known as *mahr* or *sadaq,* that the shari'a required the groom to give as a gift to the bride. The type or amount of dowry varied according to custom or the wishes of the party, ranging from a token amount to large sums of money. Muslim women increasingly began to use these marriage contracts as a way to ensure their rights, adding terms that would allow them to continue their education or work outside the home, or to initiate a divorce. While the vast majority of Muslim marriages in America, like in the rest of the world, were monogamous, a small number of Muslim men did marry more than one wife as allowed by shari'a. While religiously valid under shari'a, these marriages were not recognized by U.S. law.

When Muslim Americans had questions about the shari'a and how to apply it in their own lives and within their communities, they increasingly turned away from "imported" muftis, or religious authorities, and toward home-grown scholars, trained in Islamic law but born or raised in the United States, who could better understand the realities Muslim Americans faced as a religious minority. For example, in 2006, the Fiqh Council of North America, which is made up of scholars who have at least five years of residence in North America, issued a decision to use astronomical calculations to determine the start of Ramadan and the dates of Muslim holidays rather than moon sightings traditionally used. One basis for this change was to avoid the "hardship, chaos and confusion" that often resulted when the U.S. community relied on moon sightings by scholars in foreign countries, which made the start date unpredictable and often led to different Muslim groups within the United States—sometimes in the same city—celebrating on differ-

ent days. In addition, the Fiqh Council's methodology was mindful of the status of Muslims as a religious minority for whom advanced notice of Islamic dates would make it easier to request time off from work or school, or to have their holidays officially recognized.

Organizations such as the Fiqh Council or local scholars, known as muftis, also delivered fatwas, or religious rulings, responding to questions related to shari'a and its interpretation and practical application in the United States. In addition, individuals and communities increasingly began to use mediation and arbitration services available through the Fiqh Council or local mosques and Islamic centers to resolve disputes and disagreements according to shari'a principles. However, while the growing size of the U.S. Muslim population afforded Muslims with expanded opportunities to observe shari'a more completely than ever, individual decisions on its correct interpretation and what—if any—aspects of shari'a to follow continued to reflect the immense diversity among Muslims in the United States.

Lee Ann Bambach

Further Reading

Bakhtiar, Laleh. *Encyclopedia of Islamic Law: A Compendium of the Views of the Major Schools.* Chicago: Kazi Publications, 1996.

Curtis, Edward E., IV. *Islam in Black America: Identity, Liberation, and Difference in African-American Islamic Thought.* Albany: State University of New York Press, 2002.

Diouf, Sylviane A. *Servants of Allah: African Muslims Enslaved in the Americas.* New York: New York University Press, 1998.

Fiqh Council of North America. Available online. URL: http://www.fiqhcouncil.org/. Accessed April 3, 2008.

Gardell, Mattias. "Urban Muslims: The Formation of the Dar ul-Islam Movement." In *Muslim Communities in North America,* edited by Yvonne Yazbeck Haddad and Jane I. Smith. Albany: State University of New York Press, 1994.

Guidance Financial Group. Available online. URL: http://www.guidanceresidential.com/. Accessed April 3, 2008.

Haddad, Yvonne Yazbeck, and Adair T. Lummis. *Islamic Values in the United States: A Comparative Study.* New York: Oxford University Press, 1987.

Hallaq, Wael B. *A History of Islamic Legal Theories: An Introduction to Sunni Usul al-Fiqh.* New York: Cambridge University Press, 1997.

HSBC Amana Islamic Banking. Available online. URL: http://www.hsbcamanah.com/1/2/hsbc-amanah/. Accessed April 3, 2008.

Islamic Food and Nutrition Council of America. Available online. URL: http://www.ifanca.org/index.php. Accessed April 3, 2008.

Khalidi, Omar. *Indian Muslims in North America.* Watertown, Mass.: South Asia Press, 1990.

Lewin, Tamar. "Some U.S. Universities Install Foot Baths for Muslim Students," *International Herald Tribune*, 7 August 2007. Available online. URL: http://www.iht.com/articles/2007/08/07/america/muslims.php. Accessed February 10, 2010.

McCloud, Aminah Beverly. *African American Islam*. New York: Routledge, 1995.

Moore, Kathleen M. *Al-Mughtaribun: American Law and the Transformation of Muslim Life in the United States*. New York: State University of New York Press, 1995.

Orfalea, Gregory. *The Arab Americans: A History*. Northampton, Mass.: Olive Branch Press, 2006.

Wariko, Niraj. "While Fasting, Fordson High Football Players Get Upset Win," *Detroit Free Press*, 6 October 2007.

Azizah al-Hibri on the Islamic Legal Rights of Married Women (2002)

Azizah al-Hibri (1943–   ), a Lebanese-American law and philosophy professor at the University of Richmond, has published more than 30 books and articles in addition to leading the charge for Muslim women's legal rights both in the United States and abroad. The founder of Karamah, Muslim Women Lawyers for Human Rights, al-Hibri has attempted to convince non-Muslim and Muslim Americans that the shari'a, or Islamic law and ethics, can be a basis for (rather than an impediment to) the struggle for women's equality. Some Muslim Americans and Muslims abroad find her interpretations of the shari'a to be too liberal, though many Muslims, whether liberal or conservative, agree with her interpretations of the rights of married women explained below.

Marriage Relations in Islam

Historically, marriage has been an institution that favored men over women. Through this institution, basic women's rights such as the right to education, financial independence, and freedom of self-fulfillment were usually denied. A fulfilled woman was, in fact, viewed as one who married, served her husband well, and bore him children. This view, although less common today, continues to exist both in the West and in Muslim countries. Yet it is in total contradiction to the Islamic view of women and marriage.

Islam guarantees for women, among other things, the right to an education similar to that of the male, the right to financial independence, and even the right to engage in *ijtihad* [independent legal reasoning]. Islam also views marriage as an institution in which human beings find tranquility and affection with each other. It is for this reason that some prominent traditional Muslim scholars have argued that a woman is not required to serve her husband, prepare his food, or clean his house. In fact, the husband is obligated to bring his wife prepared food, for example. This assertion is based on the recognition that the Muslim wife is a companion to her husband and not a maid. Many jurists also defined the purpose of marriage institution in terms of sexual enjoyment (as distinguished from reproduction). They clearly stated that a Muslim woman has a right to sexual enjoyment within the marriage. This view has important consequences in areas such as contraception and divorce.

It is these rights and views, which are derived from the Qur'an and classical *ijtihad*, that we must actively reclaim. . . . So long as patriarchal (hierarchal/authoritarian) logic prevails, Muslim women will be denied their God-given rights. Qur'anic concepts of family relations must be more adequately recognized and enforced in Muslim countries and communities to abolish the authoritarian structure of the marriage institution.

In striving for this result we must recognize the fact that patriarchal logic is deeply entrenched in all societies and is quite resistant to being uprooted. If we, however, follow the Qur'anic approach to change, we will receive the support of many Muslim men and achieve a great measure of success without sacrificing the social cohesion of Muslim communities.

In fostering change the Qur'an resorts to what has been known recently in the West as affirmative action. In a patriarchal society even a general declaration of equal rights is not sufficient to protect women. Consequently, divine wisdom gave women further protections. Paramount among these protections is the ability of the Muslim woman to negotiate her marriage contract and place in it any conditions that do not contradict its purpose. For example, she could place in her marriage contract a condition forbidding her husband from moving her away from her own city or town. She could also insert a condition requiring him to support her in the pursuit of her education after marriage. She could also use the marriage contract to ensure that her marriage would foster, rather than destroy, her financial independence. This goal is usually achieved by requiring a substantial *mahr* [the dower].

The *Mahr* Requirement

Despite many patriarchal and Orientalist [stereotypical] interpretations that have distorted and even damaged the Muslim woman's rights in this area, the law of *mahr* was made clear quite early. The *mahr* is a requirement imposed by God upon men entering marriage as a sign of their serious commitment and a gesture of goodwill, a matter of great concern to women living in this patriarchal world. In fact, the giving of *mahr* is not much different from the Western custom of giving an engagement ring to signal commitment. Islamic law, however, preserved for the prospective wife the right to specify to her prospective husband the type of *mahr* she prefers. One woman may prefer cash, another property, depending on her relative needs or even taste. A third woman may choose something intangible (nonmaterial) as her *mahr,* such as education. That is acceptable also. A woman of meager means may prefer to ask for capital that she could immediately invest in a business. In fact, she could even use that capital to start her own business. Her husband would have no access to either the capital or income from that business even if he were in need because legally, her *mahr* belongs to her alone. . . .

Mahr, therefore, is not a "bride price" as some have erroneously described it. It is not money the woman pays to obtain a husband nor money [that] the husband pays to obtain a wife. It is part of a civil contract that specifies the conditions under which a woman is willing to abandon her status as a single woman and its related opportunities in order to marry a prospective husband and start a family. Consequently, as in Western prenuptial and nuptial agreements, the contract addresses matters of concern to the prospective wife and provides her with financial and other assurances. In short, it is a vehicle for ensuring the continued well-being of women entering matrimonial life in a world of patriarchal injustice and inequality. . . .

Family Planning

Another measure for guarding the interests of women in particular and the Muslim community in general is provided in the area of family planning. Islam values the family structure and, like Judaism and Christianity, encourages procreation. Islamic law, nevertheless, differs from both traditions in its liberal approach to family planning.

It shares with some Judeo-Christian traditions the view that contraception is permissible. Coitus interruptus *(al-'azl)* was practiced by members of the Muslim community during the time of Prophet Muhammad. Indeed, the Prophet knew that some of his companions, including his cousin Ali, practiced it, yet he did not prohibit it.

Al-Ghazali, a prominent fifteenth-century jurist, argues that contraception is always permitted. He makes an analogy between intercourse and a contract. A contract consists of an offer and acceptance. So long as the offer has not been accepted, he notes, it can be withdrawn. He even suggests that a woman can engage in contraception to preserve her beauty but adds that it is disliked *(makrouh)* if used to avoid female offspring. Jurists have, however, conditioned the practice of *al-'azl* upon the consent of the wife. Some even argue that if the husband practices *al-'azl* without the wife's permission, he has to pay her a fine because he has detracted from her sexual enjoyment, her established right.

Until recently, the majority of traditional jurists have taken a relatively liberal view toward abortion that properly balances the rights of the mother and the rights of the child. They recognized a period of early pregnancy that could be terminated at will and a subsequent period in which the embryo became ensouled. The jurists argued that when the embryo became ensouled, increasingly stringent criteria should be used to justify abortion (such as the health of the mother). More recently, relying on medical data, jurists have adopted the view that the embryo is ensouled soon after conception. It is desirable that Muslim women physicians and jurists reexamine this recent conclusion to determine its validity.

Maintenance

Classical Islamic jurisprudence entitles the woman to maintenance by her husband. Even if fully financially independent, she is not required to spend any of her money except as she wishes. Furthermore, the wife is under no duty to do any housework although she may engage in such work on a volunteer basis. Some traditional jurists suggested that the wife was entitled to monetary compensation for her volunteer housework activity.

The law of maintenance is based on the Qur'an, but unfortunately it has been used to assert the general superiority of men over women. The relevant Qur'anic verse simply states that men may gain *qiwamah* (advisory, caretaking status) vis-à-vis women if only they satisfy two preconditions.

First, the male must be the (financial) maintainer of the woman. In other words, if he is not carrying her financial responsibility, then he has no standing to interfere in her affairs by providing unsolicited advice. Second, the male must also possess qualities (such as financial acumen, real estate expertise, etc.) that the advised woman needs to reach a particular decision but lacks (at that point). Without these two qualifications (which, incidentally, may change from time to time and from one decision to another), men may not even presume to provide advice or be caretakers *(qawwamun)*.

Because the Qur'an was revealed in a world that was and continues to be highly patriarchal, it engaged in affirmative action to protect women. The revelation about maintenance provided women against poverty. It also made clear that maintenance alone does not suffice for a man to claim *qiwamah* over a woman. . . .

Despite all the rights and guarantees offered by Islam to women, most men still use women as uncompensated laborers in their households. Furthermore, they not only expect them to produce heirs but also to nurse these heirs. . . . Yet most Muslim jurists do not require Muslim women to nurse their children except to save the life of the child. Instead, the husband is required to hire a wet nurse (or buy milk formula) if the mother does not want to nurse. If the husband divorces the wife, and she nurses the child after the divorce, jurists agree that she is entitled to monetary compensation for that nursing. Hence, while masquerading as Islamic family law, a significant amount of the present family law in Muslim countries is influenced by local custom and patriarchal tradition.

Polygyny

Western writers have treated polygyny as one of the most controversial Islamic practices. Thus, it may be surprising to discover that Qur'anic reasoning clearly favors monogamy. The major Qur'anic verses at issue are two. One *ayah* [verse] states: "If you fear that you shall not be able to deal justly with the orphans, marry women of your choice, two, or three, or four; But if you fear that you shall not be able to deal justly (with them),

then only one or that which your right hand possesses. That will be more suitable to prevent you from doing injustice." The other *ayah* states that men cannot deal justly with their wives when they marry more than one woman [4:129].

Some Muslim jurists have interpreted the first *ayah* to mean that a man has the right to marry up to four wives as long as he is equally just with each of them. In providing this interpretation, these jurists ignored the first part of the *ayah* which conditions the permission upon a certain context that obtained at the time of its revelation, namely, one of justice and fairness concerning the treatment of orphaned wives. Secondly, these jurists ignored that last part of the *ayah*, which states that (even in that context) justice considerations make it preferable to marry only one wife. Consequently, this highly conditional and fact-specific verse was interpreted as if it articulated a general rule. Of the two conditions, the first was ignored altogether, whereas the second was reduced to the duty of exercising fairness in treatment and maintenance among the wives. These same jurists also ignored the second *ayah*, which flatly states that men are incapable of satisfying the condition precedent for engaging in polygyny, namely, justice and fairness.

Other traditional jurists, however, concluded that the Qur'an is clear in advocating monogamy as the general rule. They also added that insofar as polygyny causes the first wife harm, it is forbidden altogether *(haram)*. Several traditional jurists also recognized the right of the woman to place in the marriage contract a condition barring the prospective husband from additional (polygynous) marriages.

Yet practices of polygyny continue in some Muslim societies as a sign of economic or sexual power. As such, they are similar to the Western practice of having concubines or extramarital lovers. It is part of patriarchal custom and not religion. But religious scholars who attempt to criticize the practice or change the law are criticized for succumbing to Western influences.

Western neoorientalist critiques of Islam, thinly disguised as "feminist" critiques, have managed only to complicate the task of Muslim women. These critiques tend to be motivated more by a feeling of superiority and a desire for cultural hegemony than by a desire to help the female "Other" (in this case, the Muslim woman). The neoorientalist attitude is evidenced by the fact that only negative and distorted stereotypes of Muslim women are propagated in international fora. Furthermore, these Western "liberators" have taken it upon themselves to "explain" Islam, criticize the Qur'an, and redefine and prioritize the demands of Muslim women over these women's objections. This attack on Islam by unqualified biased commentators offends the religious sensibilities of all Muslims, male and female, regardless of their points of view.

Significantly, while Muslim women struggled repeatedly in international fora to raise basic issues of survival and development, such as hunger, water, war, and disease, patriarchal Western women have insisted on making the veil, clitoridectomy, and polygyny their primary preoccupations instead. They have even selected and funded some secular "Muslim" women to act as spokeswomen for the rest of the Muslim women. Needless to say, this neoorientalist attack on Islam has adversely impacted the civil rights of Muslims in Western countries and has poisoned the well for Muslim women seeking to regain their God-given Islamic rights in their own societies. Unfortunately, this state of affairs has alienated many Muslim women from the Western feminist movement.

Source: Azizah al-Hibri. "An Introduction to Muslim Women's Rights." In *Windows of Faith: Muslim Women Scholar-Activists in North America,* edited by Gisela Webb, 57–60, 62–68. Syracuse, N.Y.: Syracuse University Press, 2002.

Shi'a Muslim Americans

The term Shi'a refers to the partisans of Ali, the cousin and son-in-law of MUHAMMAD. After the Prophet died in 632 C.E., the early Shi'a claimed that Ali, the cousin and son-in law of the Prophet, was the only legitimate successor to the prophet Muhammad. They also believed that only family members of the Prophet, the *ahl al-bayt,* were qualified to lead the Muslim community after him. These leaders were called imams, and all of them were descendants of the Prophet from the line of Ali and Fatima, the daughter of the Prophet. The Shi'as believed that the rights of Ali and the family of the Prophet were usurped by the companions of Muhammad. This meant that, from the very beginning, Shi'a Islam rose as a dissenting group in opposition to the Muslim majority.

With the coming of Ali to power in 656, Shi'ism emerged as an effective religious movement. The massacre of Husayn, the son of Ali, and his forces at Karbala during his uprising against the Caliph Yazid in 681 was an important milestone in Shi'a history, as it affirmed notions of injustices endured by the progeny of the Prophet and exacerbated a passion for martyrdom.

Shi'a theology and jurisprudence took definitive shape in the times of the fifth and sixth imams, Muhammad al-Baqir, who died in the 730s, and Ja'far al-Sadiq, who died in 765. The latter, in particular, was largely responsible for the construction of a Shi'a legal edifice and the formulation of the Shi'a doctrine of the imamate. The true imam, al-Sadiq stated, had to be divinely appointed. The imam was also believed to be infallible and was empowered to provide authoritative interpretation of Islamic revelation. Designation and infallibility were complemented by the imam's possession of special knowledge that was either transmitted from the Prophet or derived from inherited scrolls. It was this notion of the divinely inspired and charismatic leadership of the imams that distinguished Shi'ism from the majority Sunnis.

Three major Shi'a groups, the Twelver Shi'a, the Nizari, and the Bohra Isma'ili communities, compose the Shi'a Muslim American population. The Nizari and the Bohra Isma'ilis branched off from the mainstream Shi'a community after the death of the sixth Shi'a imam, Ja'far al-Sadiq, proclaiming his son Isma'il to be his successor. The majority of the Shi'as maintained that al-Sadiq had appointed another son, Musa al-Kazim, to succeed him.

In 1094, when the eighth Fatimid caliph, al-Muntanhir, died, there was a dispute regarding his successor. The Isma'ilis became divided into the Musta'li (now called Bohra) and Nizari (now called Aga Khani) groups. Most of the Nizari Isma'ilis in America arrived since the 1970s. A highly organized and disciplined community, under the guidance of their spiritual leader, the AGA KHAN, they have established infrastructures in different fields like education, housing, and economic uplift for the community.

There are about 25,000 Bohras in America. Most migrated here since the 1970s and have settled in such cities as DETROIT, CHICAGO, and NEW YORK CITY. There are further subdivisions within the Bohra community. The first DAUDI BOHRA mosque was built in 1982 in Detroit. Even in America, most Bohras observe a strict DRESS code and prefer to communicate in their native language, Gujarati.

THE TWELVER SHI'A IN THE UNITED STATES

Among the early Muslim immigrants to America in the 1880s were Twelver Shi'as from what was then Greater Syria. Between 1900 and 1914, several hundred Shi'a newcomers settled in all parts of country, but especially in the Midwest. Many sought work at Detroit's Ford Motor Company. There was also a Shi'a settlement in Michigan City, Indiana. Early Lebanese Shi'as also settled in New York City; Quincy,

Massachusetts; Chicago; CEDAR RAPIDS IOWA; TOLEDO, OHIO; Sioux Falls, South Dakota; and Ross, NORTH DAKOTA. By 1922, a larger community of Shi'as started to crystallize, especially in Detroit.

The early Shi'a immigrants, most of whom were Lebanese, were quite liberal in their lifestyles and often assimilated to mainstream white American culture. They did not mark important dates in the Shi'a calendar, like ASHURA, when Husayn, the grandson of the Prophet, was killed in Karbala. The steady influx of immigrants led to the establishment of Shi'a institutions and centers of worship. The first Shi'a mosque was perhaps built in Michigan City in 1924. A booklet published by the Islamic Center of Michigan City states that the center was first organized on April 26, 1914, under the name of "The Bader Elmoneer Society of Michigan City, Indiana." In the early 1920s, the Bader Elmoneer Society purchased land and erected a building.

In the 1940s, Shi'as in Detroit purchased a bank, which they converted to a meeting place called the Hashemite hall. They gathered there to mark religious and social occasions. The first Shi'a scholar to come to America was Imam MOHAMAD JAWAD CHIRRI in 1949. Under his guidance, the Shi'as in Dearborn established the Islamic Center of America in 1963. With a population of about 75,000 Lebanese, Iraqi, and Iranian immigrants, Dearborn presently has one of the largest Shi'a Muslim communities in the United States.

Sensing the needs of the Shi'a American community, the most prominent Shi'a spiritual leader of the time, Ayatullah al-Khu'i (?–1992) sent an emissary to establish a center in Jamaica, New York, in 1976. This marked the beginning of an epoch in which the Shi'a religious leadership would be actively engaged in furnishing religious guidance to its followers in the West. Gradually, the Shi'a community established religious centers and infrastructures that would protect and perpetuate the identity of its members. There are 200 Shi'a centers and institutions in the United States.

Unlike the earlier immigrants, Shi'a Muslims who arrived after 1965 were ethnically, linguistically, and culturally diverse, though the majority likely came from Iran. The dramatic growth in Shi'a population was also due to adverse sociopolitical conditions in the Middle East, Africa, and South Asia. The 1979 Islamic revolution in Iran, the repressive social and political situation in Iraq, civil strife in Pakistan, the independence of Bangladesh, the civil war in Lebanon, adverse socioeconomic conditions in East Africa, and the establishment of the anti-Shi'a Taliban regime in Afghanistan have all contributed to the increased Shi'a presence. In addition, beginning in the 1970s, some African Americans began to convert to Shi'a Islam. There are at least three Shi'a Sufi organizations within the Iranian community in California.

As the Shi'a community became more diverse, it also fractured along ethnic and cultural lines. Major cities like New York, LOS ANGELES, Houston, Detroit, and Chicago are characterized by disparate Shi'a centers established along ethnic lines. The ethnic division within the Shi'a community has been further accentuated by the absence of a singular, centralized authority that could provide religious identity and cohesion to encompass different ethnic affiliations. To date, there has been no institution that could act as a unifying factor for all Shi'a groups.

ISLAMIC-AMERICAN RELIGIOUS DIVERSITY

Some early Muslim immigrants from the Middle East and South Asia sought to keep their faith intact and perform their religious obligations together. They also felt the need to socialize and maintain regular contact with their religious brethren. Since they were a minority, they often stressed their Islamic, rather than sectarian, identity. So, despite their doctrinal and juridical differences, the early Shi'a and Sunni Muslims cooperated with one another. They often intermarried, worshipped in the same mosques, marked social occasions together, and represented Islam to the non-Muslim community.

In 1963, the MUSLIM STUDENTS ASSOCIATION (MSA) was formed by students at the University of Illinois, Urbana-Champaign. The students' overall commitment to Islam overrode sectarian considerations, with Sunni and Shi'a students worshipping together. Four early MSA presidents were Shi'as.

The Islamic revolution in Iran in 1979 and the emergence of conservative Sunni Islamic movements in the United States increased sectarian tensions. Religious difference was imported by foreign-based Sunni movements such as the Salafis, Wahhabis, Hizb al-Tahrir, and the Tablighi Jama'at. Many of these movements have declared Shi'as to be non-Muslims (kafirs). The Shi'as also contributed to the conflict. Especially in South Asian centers, many speakers have derided and reviled the companions of the Prophet and his wife, Aisha. They have also published literature that disparages figures that Sunnis hold in high esteem.

Tensions between Sunnis and Shi'as increased in mosques, on campuses, on the INTERNET, and even in correctional facilities. Shi'a inmates often complain that they are victimized more by fellow Muslims than by non-Muslims. The U.S. invasion of Iraq in 2003 and subsequent sectarian clashes there further escalated tensions between the two groups, and the bombing of the Golden Mosque, a Shi'a holy shrine, in Samarra, Iraq, in February, 2006, made them even worse.

In some ways, the United States provided an ideal environment for the growth of religious diversity among Muslim Americans. Just as Christian Americans had split into a large variety of denominations in the 19th century, Muslim Americans in the 20th century gave birth to a vast array of different religious ideas, communities, and practices. Without a central state authority endorsing one form of Islam over another, Muslim Americans used Friday sermons, lectures, workshops, religious bookstores, tapes, CDs, the Internet, and print media to articulate their religious differences. Fundamentalist and progressive groups alike used the same media to compete for followers.

Religious leaders in both communities have called for reconciliation. In 2007, Sunni and Shi'a imams in Southern California launched a nationwide movement to promote unity among different branches of the faith and help prevent acts of violence in America. In a ceremony that was later repeated in Detroit and at a 2007 conference in Chicago, a number of prominent Sunni and Shi'a religious scholars in Southern California signed a "code of honor" that offered strategies for overcoming and avoiding divisions within the community. The code opposed the circulation of literature that incites sectarian hatred and encouraged balanced and objective dialogue among Sunni and Shi'a scholars.

SHI'A MUSLIM AMERICAN LEADERSHIP

The Shi'a experience has differed from the Sunni experience due to the influence exerted by Shi'a scholars and the institution of *marja'iyya*. A *marji'* is the most learned juridical authority in the Shi'a community, and his pronouncements on Islamic LAW are followed by those who acknowledge him as the religious guide. During the absence of the 12th Shi'a imam, who is believed to be the promised messiah, the *marji'* is seen by the Shi'as as invested with the authority of interpreting the relevance of Islamic norms for the modern era, thereby enabling him to influence the religious and social lives of his followers. The process of following the juridical rulings of the most learned jurist is called *taqlid* (literally, imitation).

The obligation to follow the religious dictates of the *marji'* has meant that the interpretations and pronouncements of the *maraji'* (pl. of *marji'*), formulated in the Muslim lands, are seen as both normative and legally binding on their followers. Such a structured system of religious leadership and imitation of the most learned is lacking in Sunni Islam, where there is no recognized clergy that can claim sole monopoly of the interpretation of religious texts. The obligation to follow the rulings of the *maraji'* has required American Shi'as to be allied to the *maraji'* rather than to any foreign government. It has also acted as a catalyst for unity in the Shi'a community by fostering ties among different Shi'as who have often been divided by culture, ethnicity, and language.

In recent years, the *maraji'* have become more accessible to their followers. Besides establishing religious centers and Internet sites, they have sent emissaries to visit them. Ayatullah Seestani, for example, who lives in Iraq, regularly sends his representative to monitor the progress of and report on the social and other needs of the American community. The Imam Mahdi Association of Marjaeya (IMAM), located in Los Angeles, is currently the liaison office of Ayatullah Seestani in the United States. The appointment by the *maraji'* of financial and religious deputies has enabled community members to provide facilities for religious education for the Shi'a community and has generated the confidence to engage in major projects such as the construction of mosques, Islamic centers, and seminaries considered necessary for the continued religious and spiritual well-being of the Shi'a community. In addition to establishing religious institutions and community centers, the *maraji'* have tried to meet the needs of their followers by responding to their questions and issuing juridical rulings that respond to the everyday concerns of Muslim Americans.

Apart from the *maraji'*, authority in the American Shi'a community has also been wielded by local religious scholars, or ulama. Most Shi'a ulama have immigrated to the United States since the 1980s and originated from the Middle East or South Asia. By 2010, there were approximately 150 such scholars in North America. The majority of these scholars work within Islamic centers and perform basic religious functions such as leading prayers, delivering sermons, and presiding at marriages and funerals. In an effort to unite the diverse ethnic groups that make up the American Shi'a community, an indigenous Council of Shi'a 'Ulama was formed in 1993. The council has met frequently since then.

SHI'A OUTREACH AND POLITICAL ACTIVITIES IN AMERICA

As more Shi'a immigrants settled in the United States, they came to view America as a fertile place for seeking converts. The 1980s saw the establishment of Shi'a privately run institutions that both served the needs of the Shi'a community and sought closer relations with non-Muslim Americans. But most American Shi'as have been more concerned with maintaining their distinct communal and sectarian identity than with engaging in dialogue with other faith groups. Since they form a small percentage of the wider Muslim-American community, their primary focus has been the preservation rather than extension of their religious and spiritual boundaries.

Since the events of SEPTEMBER 11, 2001, there has been greater engagement with U.S. POLITICS and the public sphere more generally. The presidential election of 2004 proved to the Shi'a community that political cooperation with Sunnis would benefit both groups. Sunnis and Shi'as supported voter registration drives and voted in record numbers that year. Shi'as have also cooperated with Sunnis to build a Muslim voting bloc that would unseat Republican and other politicians whom many Muslim Americans consider unsympathetic toward the Muslim world.

American Shi'as have often felt the need to voice their opposition to U.S. foreign policy regarding Iraq and Iran. Such instances have forced American Shi'as to abandon their traditionally ambivalent, even quietistic stance toward political activity. The Shi'as also came to the realization that civic engagement may be the most powerful way to fulfill their political aspirations. While seeking the strong support of other Muslim Americans, most of these candidates have avoided any formal association with Shi'a religious institutions. Shi'a politicians and citizens have also attempted to influence local political races by cooperating with Sunnis. Shi'a institutions have encouraged such coalition building, emphasizing the need to support a common candidate for school boards, the mayor's office, and the state legislature.

CONCLUSION

The past decade has witnessed diverse Shi'a communities emigrating to the United States. The major challenge that the community has faced is translating a majority religion to an area in which it is a nascent minority. The struggle among American Shi'as for the definition of the self, to give meaning to their new identity as Muslim Americans, and to the new sociopolitical context of their existence is manifesting itself in tensions between the traditional and modern, intellectual and conservative, indigenous and immigrant, young and old, and between Sunni and Shi'a Muslims. The community also comprises youths and African-American converts who identify with an American culture. Indigenous conflicts have arisen due to an immigrant community's having to come to terms with an alien culture.

Liyakat Takim

Further Reading
Abdo, Geneive. *Mecca and Main Street: Muslim Life in America after 9/11.* New York: Oxford University Press, 2006.

Bukhari, Zahid, Sulayman S. Nyang, Mumtaz Ahmad, and John L. Esposito, eds. *Muslims' Place in the American Public Square: Hope, Fears, and Aspirations.* Walnut Creek, Calif.: AltaMira Press, 2004.

Denny, Frederick. "Church/Sect Theory and Emerging North American Muslim Communities: Issues and Trends." In *The Shaping of an American Islamic Discourse: A Memorial to Fazlur Rahman,* edited by Earle Waugh and Frederick Denny. Atlanta, Ga.: Scholars Press, 1998.

Haddad, Yvonne. "The Impact of the Islamic Revolution in Iran on the Syrian Muslims of Montreal." In *The Muslim Community in North America,* edited by Earle Waugh, Baha Abu-Laban, and Regula Qureshi. Edmonton: University of Alberta, 1987.

———. *The Muslims of America.* New York: Oxford University Press, 1991.

Haddad, Yvonne, ed. *Muslims in the West: From Sojourners to Citizens.* New York: Oxford University Press, 2002.

Sachedina, Abdulaziz. "A Minority within a Minority: The Case of the Shi'a in North America." In *Muslim Communities in North America,* edited by Yvonne Yazbeck Haddad and Jane Idleman Smith. New York: Oxford University Press, 1991.

Schubel, Vernon. *Religious Performance in Contemporary Islam: Shi'i Devotional Rituals in South Asia.* Columbia: University of South Carolina Press, 1993.

Smith, Jane I. *Islam in America.* New York: Columbia University Press, 1999.

Walbridge, Linda. *Without Forgetting the Imam: Lebanese Shi'ism in an American Community.* Detroit: Wayne State University Press, 1997.

Siddiqi, Muzammil H. (ca. 1943–) *religious leader, activist*

During the late 20th and early 21st centuries, Muzammil H. Siddiqi emerged as one of the most prominent Muslim-American leaders in the United States, serving as president of the ISLAMIC SOCIETY OF NORTH AMERICA (ISNA) from 1996 to 2000 as well as chair of the FIQH COUNCIL OF NORTH AMERICA (FCNA) during the first decade of the 21st century.

Born in 1943 (the exact date is unknown), he studied at two of the most prominent Islamic institutions in India: the Aligarh Muslim University and Dar al-'Ulum Nadwa in Lucknow. In 1965, Siddiqi graduated from the University of Medina in Saudi Arabia with a degree in ARABIC and Islamic Studies and in 1974 received a Ph.D. from Harvard Divinity School, for which he wrote a dissertation entitled "Muslim Views of Christianity in the Middle Ages: An Analytical Study of Ibn Taymiyah's Work on Christianity."

From 1976 to 1980, Siddiqi served as chair of the Department of Religious Affairs at the Muslim World League, a Saudi-funded missionary organization. He also was chair of the Religious Affairs Committee of the MUSLIM STUDENTS ASSOCIATION of the United States and Canada. Since the early 1980s, Siddiqi has written a column for the *Pakistan Link* and has broadcast a weekly radio program from Southern California, where he has also been a director of the Islamic Society in Orange County. In 1996, he was elected to lead ISNA and, after stepping down in 2000, took a post as chair of the FCNA, a position from which he could influence the application of SHARI'A, Islamic law and ethics, to Muslim-American life.

Siddiqi's former association with Saudi-funded organizations such as the Muslim World League and his criticisms of certain aspects of UNITED STATES FOREIGN RELATIONS with the Muslim world, including U.S. policy toward Palestine, have led some conservative critics to accuse him of supporting terrorism. Yet interfaith activists and even politicians have cultivated close ties with Siddiqi. Siddiqi has been active in various INTERFAITH MOVEMENTS, attending meetings of the World Council of Churches and participating in more than 200 joint academic presentations with Jewish and Christian colleagues.

Among his many published works is an extended interfaith conversation entitled *The Abraham Connection* (1994).

After the terrorist attacks of SEPTEMBER 11, 2001, President George W. Bush invited him to deliver a Muslim prayer at the national memorial service held in the National Cathedral in Washington, D.C. From his position as chair of FCNA, he led a national effort to condemn all forms of terrorism committed in the name of Islamic religion after 9/11.

Mashal Saif

Further Reading

Hubbard, Benjamin, David M. Gordis, George Benedict Grose, Muzammil Siddiqi, and Benjamin Jerome. *The Abraham Connection: A Jew, Christian, and Muslim in Dialogue: An Encounter between Dr. David Gordis, Dr. George Grose and Dr. Muzammil Siddiqi.* Notre Dame, Ind.: Cross Cultural Publications, Cross Roads Books, 1994.

Siddiqi, Muzammil H. "Global Ethics and Dialogue among World Religions: An Islamic Viewpoint." In *Ethics, Religion, and the Good Society: New Directions in a Pluralistic World,* edited by Joseph Runzo. Louisville, Ky.: Westminster/John Knox Press, 1992.

slaves   See AFRICAN-AMERICAN MUSLIM SLAVES.

Sikander, Shahzia (1969–) *artist, MacArthur Award winner*

A prominent artist in the United States, Shahzia Sikander was named a MacArthur fellow in 2006, a prestigious award given by the John D. and Catherine T. MacArthur Foundation recognizing outstanding achievement in a variety of fields and disciplines. The "genius" award, as the MacArthur is often called, recognized her contributions to the world as an artist, working in the painstaking and labor-intensive medium of Indo-Persian miniature painting. In addition to painting, Sikander's work traverses a variety of media, including drawings, large-scale wall installations, digital animation, and video.

Born in 1969 in Lahore, Pakistan, Sikander was trained at the Department of Miniature Painting at Lahore's National College of Arts, where she received her B.F.A. in 1992, and continued her studies at the Rhode Island School of Design, in Providence, Rhode Island, earning an M.F.A. in 1995. She later became a fellow of the Glassell School of Art's Core Program in Houston (1995–97) and an artist-in-residence at Otis College of Art and Design in Los Angeles (2005).

Sikander's experimental approach to the genre of miniature painting in the mid-1980s in Lahore was seen as anachronistic, though her own creative expressions combined the genre with contemporary art practices. Her work launched a renewed commitment to the art of miniature painting

and gained a substantial following in Lahore, where the Department of Miniature Painting at the National College of Arts has seen a dramatic increase in the number of young artists now pursuing majors in the Fine Arts program.

Sikander's work recasts the formal artistic debates about the conventional methods of addressing traditional miniature paintings. Using her various geographic locations as a positive experience, she reassembled her miniature paintings to expand the formal properties of the artistic practice often classified as craft, even as she questions the materials and scale of the work. Using wit, irony, and paradox, Sikander's artwork draws upon a variety of media to push the boundaries of the miniature tradition. As much as her work is interested in the formal aspects and properties of artistic practices, the content of Sikander's work addresses themes of Islam, Pakistan, India, Hindu/Muslim relations, imagery and iconography, as well as notions of tradition and modernity, East and West, hybridity, and women.

Although based in New York, Sikander works in various locations and often these are visually reflected in her work. Her works can be found in major collections at institutions such as the Museum of Modern Art, the Whitney Museum of American Art, and the Solomon R. Guggenheim Museum, all in New York. Collections in California include those of the Museum of Contemporary Art, Los Angeles; San Francisco Museum of Modern Art; and San Diego Museum of Art.

Sikander's work has appeared in countless solo and group shows in the United States and around the world. Her work was featured in solo exhibitions at the Irish Museum of Modern Art, Dublin, in 2007; the Museum of Contemporary Art, Sydney, from 2007 to 2008; and Ikon Gallery in Birmingham, England, in 2008. Group shows include various exhibits and biennales around the world, including "Shahzia Sikander Selects: Works from the Permanent Collection," exhibited at the Cooper-Hewitt National Design Museum, New York, from March to September 2009.

In addition to winning the MacArthur Award, Sikander was named a Young Global Leader by the World Economic Forum in Davos in 2006. She received the Tamgha-e-Imtiaz, National Medal of Honor, from the Government of Pakistan, in 2005 and the Commendation Award from the Mayor's Office, New York City, in 2003. Her work has been reviewed in numerous art and other publications including *Artforum, ARTnews,* the *New York Times,* the *Wall Street Journal,* and *Time,* and in numerous academic journals and publications.

Munir Jiwa

Further Reading

Anderson, Maxwell. *American Visionaries: Selections from the Whitney Museum of American Art.* New York: Harry N. Abrams, Inc., 2001.

Azimi, Negar. "Interview—Shahzia Sikander." *Bidoun* 1, no. 3 (Winter 2005): 104–108.

Chambers, Kristin. *Threads of Vision: Toward a New Feminine Poetics.* Cleveland: Center for Contemporary Art, 2001.

Daftari, Fereshteh. *Without Boundary: Seventeen Ways of Looking.* New York: Museum of Modern Art, 2006.

social workers

According to the International Federation of Social Workers, social work "promotes social change, problem solving in human relationships, and the empowerment and liberation of people to enhance well-being." Though Muslim-American social workers as a trained class of professionals emerged only in the late 20th century, the first Muslim-American social service providers to work for social change and more healthy human relationships were arguably the many AFRICAN-AMERICAN MUSLIM groups that began in the 1920s and 1930s. Often focused on expanding economic opportunity, establishing stronger relationships among family members, challenging unfair laws, and battling ideas that black people were inferior, African-American Muslim leaders such as NOBLE DREW ALI (1886–1929), W. D. FARD (ca. 1877–ca. 1934), WALI AKRAM (1904–94), and MUHAMMAD EZALDEEN (ca. 1880–1957) saw Islam, variously defined, as a source of personal, political, and social liberation.

From the 1930s to the 1960s, a period in which the vast majority of converts to Islam in the United States were African-American, most African-American Muslim groups attempted to address themselves to the "whole person," that is, to find solutions to their members' political, economic, social, and cultural concerns. The NATION OF ISLAM (NOI), which grew quickly under the leadership of ELIJAH MUHAMMAD (1897–1975) and MALCOLM X (1925–65) from the 1930s through the 1960s, was the best known of these groups. For many members, the NOI provided a complete way of life, structuring members' daily lives around various business activities, religious rituals, social voluntarism, and educational programs. Other African-American Muslim groups, including the ISLAMIC PARTY OF NORTH AMERICA (IPNA), acted in a similar fashion, and IPNA launched neighborhood cleanup drives, conducted a prison ministry and food drives, and offered classes in crafts, sewing, and hygiene.

Though immigrant Muslims had performed social services informally within their local communities for a century, one of the first immigrant-led social work agencies was the Arab Community Center for Economic and Social Services (ACCESS), established in 1971. Housed in a storefront building located on Vernor Highway in Dearborn, Michigan, ACCESS was led by Muslim-American ALIYA HASSEN, a pioneering female leader. As the organization grew and Michigan's Arab population increased, ACCESS provided services related to job referral, translation, health emergencies, immigration, and legal aid to thousands of new Muslim and non-Muslim immigrants.

By the late 20th century, the number of formal Muslim-American social service agencies and licensed Muslim-American social workers had dramatically increased. In 1993, for example, the ISLAMIC CIRCLE OF NORTH AMERICA (ICNA) initiated a domestic assistance program to develop a network of local agencies under the larger umbrella of the ICNA. As part of its network, ICNA sponsored Muslim Family Services, United Muslim Movement against Homelessness, Muslim Women's Help Network, Housing Outreach for Muslim Sisters, and the Crescent Social Assistance Agency.

In 1998, Belkis Altareb, Maryam Funchess, Aneesah Nadir, and Shahina Siddiqui formed the Islamic Social Services Association, attempting to bring together Muslims working in fields of social work, service delivery, and mental health to discuss and coordinate their activities. Social services pioneers Sharifa Alkhateeb, Abu Jamal Teague, Imam Khalid Griggs, Iman Elkadi, Altaf Hussain, and Mohamed Magid were among 60 participants in a 1999 conference that aimed to raise awareness of the social service needs of Muslim Americans in the United States and Canada. The U.S.-based branch of the movement went on to offer workshops on marriage, caring for Muslim patients, and family violence prevention.

A number of Muslim-American organizations committed to reducing domestic violence among Muslim Americans began in this period. In 1997, for example, Hadayai Majeed helped to begin the Baitul Salaam (Peaceful House) Network in ATLANTA, seeking to raise awareness and provide counsel and shelter to victims of domestic violence. By 2007, the program had sheltered 591 women and children, answered more than 9,000 phone calls, and indirectly supported the creation of a dozen domestic violence awareness organizations and support groups.

Other Muslim-American advocates of mental health began to offer free mental health services to the poor. In 1995, Dr. Basheer Ahmed, a psychiatrist, helped to establish the Muslim Community Center for Human Services (MCCHS) in Fort Worth, Texas, which offered free counseling services, a domestic violence hotline, health fairs, and other services to those in need. In October 1998, MCCHS expanded its services by opening the Al-Shifa medical clinic to provide culturally and religiously sensitive primary care to underserved populations. Later, in 2007, female physicians and a pediatrician volunteered at a women's clinic for those female patients who preferred to see female health-care providers. Between 2006 and 2008, Al-Shifa clinic served a total of 1,200 to 1,800 patients, most of whom would have had no other source for treatment.

Muslim-American social workers in this period also focused on the challenges faced by displaced persons, including Muslims, who settled in the United States. From 1988 to 2003, approximately 15 percent of all refugees who arrived in the United States were Muslim—a total of 210,000 people. They came from 77 different countries, spoke dozens of languages, and, in many cases, arrived from the war-torn countries of Bosnia, Afghanistan, Iraq, and Somalia. Fariyal Ross-Sheriff, director of the Ph.D. program in social work at Howard University, became an expert on their lives and, in addition to her many academic articles on the subject, co-authored *Muslim Refugees in the United States: A Guide for Service Providers* (2003).

The al-Qaeda attacks against the United States on SEPTEMBER 11, 2001, posed special challenges for Muslim-American social workers as they sought to address the needs of both Muslim and non-Muslim Americans. In addition, the attacks resulted in a broad backlash against Muslim Americans, including physical assaults, deadly threats, stereotyping, and discrimination at work, in school, and on the street. One study of Arab-American experience by Wahiba Abu-Ras, a social work educator at Adelphi University, and Soleman H. Abu-Bader, a social work educator at Howard University, illustrated that social workers needed to help Muslims and Arabs cope with victimization since 9/11 and pointed out that many social work professionals lacked the cultural and linguistic competencies needed to address these issues.

From its informal origins in the early 20th century, Muslim-American social work has evolved into a broad network of providers and advocates that now includes religious leaders, Muslim-American organizations, secular and religious social service agencies, volunteers, and professional social workers. Muslim social workers have assisted individuals with problems related to poverty, marital struggles, aging, disability, substance abuse, grief and loss, domestic violence, mental health, child abuse, refugee and resettlement adjustment, parent-teen relations, cultural conflicts, mediation, blood vengeance, incarceration, discrimination, and translation needs. They have also attempted to serve as advocates or liaisons between their clients and service providers.

Pamela Aneesah Nadir, Khadija Khaja, and
Irene Queiro-Tajalli

Further Reading

Abu Ras, Wahiba, and Soleman Abu-Bader. "The Impact of September 11, 2001, Attacks on the Well-Being of Arab Americans in New York City." *Journal of Muslim Mental Health* 3, no. 2 (September 2008): 217–239.

Haque, Amber. "Religion and Mental Health: The Case of American Muslims." *Journal of Religion and Mental Health* 43, no. 1 (2004): 45–58.

Hodge, David R. "Social Work and the House of Islam: Orienting Practitioners to the Beliefs and Values of Muslims in the United States." *Social Work* 50, no. 2 (April 2005): 162–173.

Khaja, Khadija, and Chelsea Frederick. "Reflection on Teaching Effective Social Work Practice for Working with Muslim Communities." *Advances in Social Work* 9, no. 1 (Spring 2008): 1–7.

Maloof, Patricia S., and Fariyal Ross-Sheriff. *Muslim Refugees in the United States: A Guide for Service Providers.* Culture Profile No. 17. Washington, D.C.: Center for Applied Linguistics, 2003.

Ross-Sheriff, Fariyal. "Elderly Muslim Immigrants: Needs, Challenges, and Strategies for Program Development." In *Muslim Communities in North America,* edited by Yvonne Y. Haddad and Jane I. Smith, 404–421. Albany: State University of New York Press, 1994.

Saidah A. Sharif is leader of a social service agency in Newark, New Jersey, that aids Muslim victims of domestic violence. *(Jerry McCrea/Star Ledger/Corbis)*

Somali Muslim immigrants

Although Somali citizens have been immigrating to the United States since WORLD WAR II, moving predominantly to NEW YORK CITY and other East Coast cities, the 1991 civil war in Somalia, a nation in East Africa, accelerated refugee immigration throughout the 1990s. By 2010, approximately 150,000 Somali citizens had come to the United States. The largest concentration of refugees settled in Minnesota and Ohio, with smaller populations dispersing to 34 other states. U.S. government statistics indicate that approximately 25,000 immigrants moved to Minnesota, and the Somali Community

Association of Ohio (SCAO) estimated that 45,000 Somali immigrants settled in central Ohio.

Since only an estimated 7 percent of immigrants could speak English well enough to gain and keep English-speaking jobs in the 1990s, refugee families struggled to find adequate employment. Family members relied on aid, entrepreneurial activity, and personal savings. Many populated the service industry and other jobs that required little formal English-language education. Approximately 120 Somali employees, for example, found jobs at Viracon, which fabricates glass for large-scale architectural projects. Primarily located in Owatonna, Minnesota, Viracon also has facilities in Statesboro, Georgia, and St. George, Utah. Because Viracon accommodated the employees' religious practices, especially the *salat,* or ritual prayer, Somali Muslim employees became loyal to Viracon and recruited other Somalis to the company.

Where Somali refugees were geographically concentrated, they established various advocacy groups, including educational organizations and community bridge groups. The SCAO was founded in 1996 in an effort to aid new immigrants with the challenges of ASSIMILATION. Immigrant residents in Minnesota have also established the Somali American Media Association (SAMA), a multilingual news organization dedicated to keeping the Somali immigrant population informed about major events occurring both locally and around the world. Originally meant to promote communication between Somalis and non-Somalis in addition to providing news from home, SAMA has become a venue for Somali participation in American society. By broadcasting their own television program three nights per week in both Somali and English, SAMA has nurtured communication between Somali American immigrants and other local residents.

Similarly, a number of Somali immigrants have been successful in establishing business ventures often related to helping others in need. Washington, D.C., resident Mohamed Ali, for instance, a devout Muslim who attends prayer services at the ISLAMIC CENTER OF WASHINGTON, D.C., is the president and CEO of IDEA, Inc. IDEA, which stands for International Development Enterprise Access, is headquartered in Herndon, Virginia. Its purpose is to help provide health and educational services to developing countries as well as to African immigrants to the United States. Consistent with the Islamic tradition of *sadaqah,* wherein an observant Muslim does what he or she can to act in a morally just way, IDEA seeks to assist with the improvement of the standard of living for developing nations.

Like many other refugee and recent immigrants, Somali immigrants have maintained strong ties to their homeland. Much of their community activism has remained focused on local immigrant and refugee issues, or on international events. The Confederation of Somali Communities was founded in Minneapolis, Minnesota, in 1994 for the purpose of helping refugees navigate between contributing to American society and maintaining their own culture. Similarly, the Somali-American Political Engagement Committee and Somali Intellectual League were designed to promote civic participation and academic success, respectively.

Kim Dieser

Further Reading
Cagle, Jeff. "Portrait: No Longer Taboo," *Owatonna People's Press,* 31 March 2007, pp. 8–13.

Haddad, Yvonne. *Muslims in the West: From Sojourners to Citizens.* London: Oxford University Press, 2002.

Shepard, Raynel. *Cultural Adaptation of Somali Refugee Youth.* New York: LFB Scholarly Publishers, 2008.

South Asian–American Muslims

South Asians are one of the three largest groups of Muslims in the United States. The other two are African Americans and Arab Americans. South Asia includes people from India, Pakistan, Bangladesh, Sri Lanka, Nepal, Bhutan, the Maldive Islands, and even, according to some, Afghanistan. The current U.S. Census includes most South Asians under the category "Asian Indian." Before 1947, the Census counted "East Indians," a category that included people from present-day India, Pakistan, and Bangladesh. India and Pakistan gained their independence from Britain in 1947, and Bangladesh split off from Pakistan in 1971.

South Asian Muslims have immigrated to the United States in three different periods: the late 19th and early 20th centuries, the 1920s, and from 1965 to the present. In the late 19th and early 20th centuries, several dozen Muslim farmers from British India's northwestern province Punjab came to California and adjacent states and became farm laborers and, in a few cases, landowners. At the same time, small numbers of Indian Muslim sailors from India's eastern province of Bengal were leaving British merchant marine vessels to settle in the port cities of New Orleans and New York. These early immigrant Muslims married local women, primarily Mexican and Mexican-American women in California (most of whom were Catholic) and African American and Puerto Rican women in New Orleans and NEW YORK CITY. In only some cases did these families pass on a strong religious identity to their children.

South Asian Muslim men in the American West entrusted the religious training of the children to their largely Catholic mothers, while the families in New Orleans and New York often emphasized their racial heritage as "men of color." These pioneer South Asian Muslim men established families that were Muslim-descended, primarily working class, and racially or ethnically mixed. Their descendants identified more as Punjabis or Bengalis than as Muslims, at least until the partition of British India in 1947 into India and Pakistan. At that time, consciousness of their Muslim identity increased among some of the descendants. These two groups of pioneer South Asian Muslims have been largely overlooked by later South Asian Muslim immigrants.

In contrast, the second movement of South Asian Muslims to the United States, although even smaller in number, had a major impact on strands of Islam in America. By the 1920s, several South Asian Muslim religious preachers from the Ahmadi movement, a late 19th-century Islamic movement based in India's Punjab, had arrived in the United States. These men addressed themselves primarily to African Americans because it was African-American Muslims who were the first to organize on the basis of the Islamic religion in the United States in the early 20th century. (Arab immigrants who arrived in the late 19th century, the majority of them Christian, organized on the basis of national origin rather than religion.)

At the same time, the evolving African-American Muslim communities had limited contact with immigrant and foreign Islamic traditions, for the most part did not know ARABIC, and developed their own versions of Islam, defining themselves as different and emphatically separate from the dominant Anglo- and Christian-American culture. The well-educated Ahmadi missionaries were the first to reach out to African-American Muslims, bringing them English translations of the QUR'AN and publishing the *Muslim Sunrise,* the first English-language Muslim magazine in America, in the 1920s. They told the early African-American groups about the five pillars of Islam and directed their attention to mainstream Sunni teachings.

Despite the importance of race in American history and Islam's promise of racial equality, this early connection between indigenous and immigrant Muslims in the United States has received little attention, and efforts have been made to suppress or erase it. Following political decisions taken in Pakistan to declare Ahmadis non-Muslims, some post-1965 South Asian Muslim immigrants have reflected homeland prejudices and policies against Ahmadis in the United States. Disavowing the Ahmadis has negative implications for contemporary immigrant Muslim relationships with the sizeable African-American Muslim constituency, a constituency that won early legal victories that have broadened the rights of all Muslims in the United States. Yet there is an apparent unwillingness on the part of many immigrant Muslims, not only South Asians, to acknowledge African-American Muslims fully and to work with their heritage.

The third major movement of South Asian Muslims to the United States came when the IMMIGRATION ACT OF 1965 redressed the historic discrimination against Asians. The 1965 act vastly increased the numbers of immigrants from all of Asia, and it set preferences for well-educated, professional people. The South Asian Muslims emigrating to the United States after 1965 have been able to make significant contributions to Muslim-American institutional development because of their high educational and occupational qualifications and their homeland political experience. Like other South Asian immigrants, they brought with them long-standing traditions of cultural pluralism in the Indian subcontinent and political experience with democracy.

In the 1980s and 1990s, Muslims from South Asia came forward as key leaders of ambitious efforts to unite all Muslims in the United States. Earlier, Arab political organizations had included both Christians and Muslims, and although the FEDERATION OF ISLAMIC ASSOCIATIONS (FIA) IN THE UNITED STATES and CANADA had established a successful national network of mosques and even Muslim summer camps in the 1950s, many post-1965 immigrants and students sometimes deemed the FIA and its leadership to be insufficient. As they joined Arab Americans of the post-1965 generation, South Asian–American Muslims became some of the most prominent spokespersons for Muslim communities in the United States.

The highly qualified and ambitious new South Asian Muslim immigrants contrasted with Arab-Muslim immigrants, also a growing group after 1965, in several ways. The South Asians speak many languages, but most were well educated in English. Most also shared a British colonial heritage and post-independence histories that included some degree of experience with democratic political processes. The South Asian newcomers represented many religions, and religious diversity has long been accepted in South Asian societies. The historical experience of the subcontinent until 1947 featured religious pluralism, and the numerically dominant group, from India, brought familiarity with pluralism as well as democracy (immigrants from India include Hindus, Muslims, Buddhists, Christians, Sikhs, and Parsis or Zoroastrians). Diversity within Islam has always been striking in South Asia, and South Asian Muslim immigrants represented many strands of Islamic beliefs and practices and many kinds of Sunnis, Shi'as, and Sufis, especially from India. Muslims being a substantial minority, some 12–13 percent, in India, Muslims probably constituted about that percentage of Indian immigrants in the United States.

These post-1965 South Asian Muslim immigrants have had the means to import and maintain many elements of their cultural and religious traditions. The Asian Indian 1990 and 2000 census profiles give an idea of the resources of Muslims from India and Pakistan. Those immigrants born in India had the highest median household income, family income, and per capita income of any foreign-born group in the 1990 Census. In the 2000 Census, immigrants born in India had the third-highest median household income (behind only South Africans and Britishers), the second-highest median family income (behind South Africans), and the second-highest median per capita income (behind Britishers) of foreign-born groups. In both 1990 and 2000, Asian Indians had the highest percentage with a bachelor's degree or higher and were among the highest percentages in managerial and professional fields. The largest ethnic body of doctors in the United States is the American Association of Physicians from India, and one estimate puts Indian doctors at more than 20,000, or nearly 4 percent of the nation's medical doctors. There is also an Association of Pakistani Physicians of North America.

A spurt of mosque-building was initiated by the post-1965 Indian and Pakistani Muslims, and many post-1965 South Asian Muslim professionals have played major roles in interpreting SHARI'A, or Islamic law and ethics, and establishing religious institutions and political organizations in the United States. Analysis of the leadership of national Muslim and Islamic organizations of the 1980s and 1990s shows that Indian and Pakistani Muslims were at least equally if not more prominent than Arabs and African Americans, and national coalitions to mobilize the Muslim vote in both 2000 and 2004 were led by a Pakistani-American political scientist.

Arguably, South Asian Muslims offered new and relatively fresh political opportunities for Muslims in the United States. The Luce-Celler Bill of 1946 granted the rights of citizenship to South Asian and Filipino Americans. As a result, the Punjabi pioneers helped elect Dalip Singh Saund, a Sikh from California's Imperial Valley, the first congressman born in India (as well as Asia) in 1956. The post-1965 South Asian immigrants, including Muslims, were becoming naturalized U.S. citizens and plunging into American politics by the end of the 20th century. South Asian Muslims were active in both Democratic and Republican party political funding and campaigning. Some were organizing on the basis of religion and trying to mobilize a Muslim bloc vote for whichever party seemed more promising on issues of interest to them.

Some South Asian Muslims have been leaders in various progressive Muslim movements. In response to the strict gender segregation of some South Asian mosques, South Asian–American women have sometimes led what has been called the gender jihad. A woman of Indian origin, Asra Nomani, has been a public figure in the struggle to hold mixed-gender Friday prayers. Other South Asian–Muslim Americans have been relatively open to discussion of sexual issues, and some have joined various LESBIAN, GAY, BISEXUAL AND TRANSGENDER MUSLIM organizations such as Al-Fatiha, Queer Jihad, and Trikone.

In summary, for more than a century, South Asian Muslims have contributed significantly to Muslim-American and, ultimately, to American politics and social life in several ways. First, those who came in the early 20th century, the Punjabi farmers and Bengali ex-sailors, married local women of Hispanic and African-American background, their diasporic encounters leading to intermixture and cultural accommodation. Second, Muslim missionaries from India established linkages with indigenous African-American Muslims in the 1920s that strongly influenced the directions taken by African-American Muslims. Third, the more recent, post-1965 South Asian Muslim immigrants have brought ambitious and well-qualified new leadership to the developing Muslim-American religious and political organizations. Relatively new on the political scene, South Asian–Muslim Americans have been building bridges among Muslims and to the broader American public.

Karen Isaksen Leonard

Further Reading

Allen, Ernest, Jr. "Identity and Destiny: The Formative Views of the Moorish Science Temple and the Nation of Islam." In *Muslims on the Americanization Path?* Edited by Yvonne Yazbeck Haddad and John L. Esposito. Atlanta, Ga.: Scholars Press, 1998.

Bagby, Ihsan. *A Portrait of Detroit Mosques: Muslim Views on Policy, Politics and Religion.* Clinton Township, Mich.: Institute for Social Policy and Understanding, 2004.

Bald, Vivek. "Overlapping Diasporas, Multiracial Lives: South Asian Muslims in U.S. Communities of Color, 1880–1950." *Souls* 8, no. 4 (December 2006): 3–18.

Khan, Mohommed A. Muqtedar. *American Muslims: Bridging Faith and Freedom.* Beltsville, Md.: Amana, 2002.

Kurien, Prema. "To Be or Not to Be South Asian." *Journal of Asian American Studies* 6, no. 3 (October 2003): 261–288.

Leonard, Karen. "South Asian Leadership of American Muslims." In *Muslims in the West: From Sojourners to Citizens,* edited by Yvonne Yazbeck Haddad, 233–249. New York: Oxford University Press, 2002.

Leonard, Karen Isaksen. *Making Ethnic Choices: California's Punjabi Mexican Americans.* Philadelphia: Temple University Press, 1992.

———. *Muslims in the United States: The State of Research.* New York: Russell Sage, 2003.

Lincoln, C. Eric. *The Black Muslims in America.* Boston: Beacon Press, 1961.

Mahmud, Tayyab. "Freedom of Religion and Religious Minorities in Pakistan: a Study of Judicial Practice." *Fordham International Law Journal* 19, no. 1 (October 1995): 40–100.

McCloud, Aminah Beverly. *African American Islam.* New York: Routledge, 1995.

Moore, Kathleen M. *Al-Mughtaribun: American Law and the Transformation of Muslim Life in the United States.* Albany: State University of New York Press, 1995.

Staton, Dakota (Aliyah Rabia) (1930–2007) *jazz singer*

One of the most underrated JAZZ vocalists of the 20th century, Dakota Staton was born on June 3, 1930, in Pittsburgh (some sources give the date of her birth as 1932). She attended Pittsburgh's George Westinghouse High School, where one of her classmates was pianist AHMAD JAMAL. Staton began her formal musical instruction at the Filion School of Music in Pittsburgh. Her first steady singing gig was with the Pittsburgh-based Joe Wespray Orchestra. After spending several years performing in such Midwestern and Canadian cities as Indianapolis, CLEVELAND, DETROIT, St. Louis, Minneapolis, Toronto, and Montreal, Staton eventually made her way to NEW YORK CITY, landing a gig with the Baby Grand nightclub.

At the Baby Grand, she was discovered by David Cavanaugh, a producer for Capitol Records who promptly signed Staton to the Capitol Records label. Staton's first single, released in 1954, was "What Do You Know About Love." Quickly gaining the attention of the jazz press, Staton won *Down Beat* magazine's "Most Promising New Comer" award in 1955. Two years later, Staton released her most popular recording to date, "The Late, Late Show." The album of the same name reached as high as number 4 on the *Billboard* album charts. The success of "The Late, Late Show" led to a string of acclaimed albums, such as *In the Night* (1957), a collaboration with pianist George Shearing; *Dynamic!* (1958); and *Dakota at Storyville* (1961).

In 1958, Staton married Muslim trumpeter Talib Ahmad Dawud, a native Antiguan who had played with such jazz greats as Duke Ellington, Louis Armstrong, and Dizzy Gillespie. Staton converted to Islam and adopted the Muslim name Aliyah Rabia, retaining her original name professionally. As a newly converted AHMADI MUSLIM AMERICAN, Staton, along with her husband, was an outspoken critic of ELIJAH MUHAMMAD (1897–1975) and the NATION OF ISLAM, which they considered to be a heretical Muslim movement.

In the 1960s, Staton relocated to England for a time but continued to record and perform. After ending her association with Capitol Records in 1962, Staton went on to record for such labels as United Artists, Groove Merchant, and Muse. Much of this material, however, remains out of print. Staton's singing style possessed elements of pop and R&B, so much so that Staton often shared the bill with rock and roll acts such as Fats Domino. Though she had a long career, her overtures to pop music and R&B may have been one reason that she was overshadowed by such performers as Dinah Washington, Sarah Vaughn, and Ella Fitzgerald, at least in the minds of many jazz critics.

Well into the 1990s, Staton continued to record and perform live. In her later years, Staton began to incorporate more gospel and blues elements in her singing style. Dakota Staton died at the age of 76 in New York on April 10, 2007. She was survived by her brother, saxophonist Fred Staton. Her legacy was as a singer whose style bridged the gap between traditional jazz singers and contemporary pop divas.

Jason E. Housley

Further Reading

Berendt, Joachim. *The Jazz Book: From Ragtime to Fusion and Beyond.* New York: Lawrence Hill Books, 1992.

Bogdanov, Vladimir, Chris Woodstra, and Stephen Thomas Erlewine. *All Music Guide to Jazz: The Definitive Guide to Jazz Music.* San Francisco: Backbeat Books, 2002.

stereotypes

Stereotypes are oversimplified, unquestioned assumptions about an entire group of people. Though they are not necessarily negative and do not necessarily lead toward the mistreatment of other human beings, historians and other scholars of Muslim-American history are in wide agreement that the stereotyping of Muslims in the United States, like that of other religious and ethnic minorities such as blacks, Indians, and Latina/os, is generally negative and harmful, leading to various forms of DISCRIMINATION. Sometimes characterized as "Islamophobia," or the fear of Islam, anti-Muslim stereotypes have included the assumptions that Muslims are generally violent, fanatical, exotic, untrustworthy, and in the case of Muslim women, oppressed.

In *Islamophobia: Making Muslims the Enemy* (2008), religious studies scholars Peter Gottschalk and Gabriel Greenberg define "Islamophobia" as "a *social* anxiety toward Islam and Muslim cultures that is largely unexamined by, yet deeply ingrained in, Americans." Its roots can be traced from conflicts between Christians and Muslims in the European Middle Ages and the colonial era of American history to UNITED STATES FOREIGN RELATIONS with Muslim-majority empires and nations in the 19th and 20th centuries. In many cases, the stereotyping of Muslim people in the Thirteen Colonies and the United States has been directly related to the social, political, and economic interaction of American institutions and people with Muslims abroad. Such interactions have fueled the negative stereotype that "they" are not like "us," leading to portrayals of Muslims that embody religious, racial, and ethnic prejudice.

FROM THE COLONIAL ERA TO THE EARLY AMERICAN REPUBLIC

Anglo Americans in the colonial period inherited many negative stereotypes of Muslims from Europe. These stereotypes were developed in the Middle Ages during the age of Muslim expansion into Spain and during the Crusades, when Roman Catholic popes and other religious and political leaders from Europe waged war against Muslims in the holy land of Palestine. The relatively stronger Muslim states and empires of this era struck fear or caused anxiety in the hearts of many Europeans, who saw Islam as competition to their own creed of Christianity, which dominated much of Europe.

The prophet Muhammad was subject to especially virulent stereotyping, since he was blamed for creating what was considered by European Christians to be a false and misleading religion (Muslims themselves believed that Abraham, not Muhammad, was the first Muslim). In his 14th-century allegorical poem *Inferno,* the Italian poet Dante placed Muhammad in the second-lowest circle of hell, where the prophet was condemned to a horrible torture: For creating a religious schism in the church, he was to be split from his anus to his chin in perpetuity.

Though Anglo-American colonists inherited these negative views of Islam, their stereotypes of Muslims were also shaped by the more immediate seizure of British ships along the North African or "Barbary" coast in the late 17th century. In 1671, for example, Captain William Foster from Roxbury, Massachusetts, was captured by pirates and ransomed. Reacting to similar events, American preacher Cotton Mather criticized such pirates as the "fierce monsters of Africa," and as "Mahometan [Muhammadan] Turks and Moors, and Devils." Depicted as cruel, licentious, and brutish, Muslims were held up as the mirror image of the civilized, compassionate, and gentle Christian.

In addition to being viewed as brutish, uncivilized, and tyrannical, Muslims were depicted in the Thirteen Colonies and the early United States as symbols of the anti-Christ, the figure who, according to Christian doctrine, will appear at the end of the world to battle, unsuccessfully, with Christ. Beginning in the late 17th century—and continuing until the 21st century—prophetic teachers of Christianity attempted to interpret political events and natural disasters in the Middle East and Muslim world more generally as signs that the end time was near, often comparing real world happenings to biblical prophecies in Isaiah, Revelation, and other biblical scriptures.

From the colonial era to the early republic, American politicians would regularly use "Muslim" as an epithet, meant to discredit an opponent in the heat of argument. During and immediately after the American Revolution (1775–83), Islam and Muslims were often cited as examples of despotism and tyranny. In 1790, for example, Vice President John Adams voiced his disapproval of the 1789 French Revolution by saying that it would lead to fanaticism among the French people, who would follow "the first mad despot, who, with the enthusiasm of another Mahomet [Muhammad]" would

try to lead them. Later, critics of Adams returned the favor. After Adams became president in 1797 and then signed the Sedition Act of 1798—a law effectively making criticism of the government illegal—one person called Adams the "new Muhammad," meaning that he was a true tyrant.

The association of Islam and Muslims with tyranny in this period of U.S. history was furthered by conflicts with North African Muslim states. The United States' first foreign war was fought with the North African principality of Tripoli from 1801 to 1805. After the 1783 Treaty of Paris granted the United States independence from Great Britain, U.S.-flagged ships no longer enjoyed safe passage granted to British ships in the Mediterranean by the North African states of Algiers, Morocco, Tunis, and Tripoli. After several ships were taken captive by Algiers in 1785, the cash-strapped U.S. government attempted to negotiate with the dey of Algiers and raise the necessary funds to secure the release of the captives. But in 1801, newly elected President Thomas Jefferson, who had long disagreed with the policy of paying tribute, decided instead to wage war. Though the new U.S. Navy largely dominated the seas during the conflict, U.S. sailors on the U.S.S. *Philadelphia* were taken prisoner in 1803. The war continued until 1805, when the parties signed a treaty releasing the captives in exchange for $60,000 in ransom.

Many Americans, whether they were Democratic Republicans, Federalists, or of some other political persuasion, believed that Islamic religion was at fault for the behavior of the North Africans. The sailors' captivity—this fundamental denial of their liberty—was a result, it was said, of Islamic despotism. Islamic religion was blamed for bad government, social backwardness, ignorance, indolence, and unrestrained passion.

Though the linking of Islam and North African Muslims with bondage was a view entertained by the vast majority of Americans, there were a few dissenters. Exceptional writings such as Royall Tyler's *Algerine Captive* (1797) and the anonymously written *Humanity in Algiers* (1801) pointed out the hypocrisy of American views toward Muslims: How could one see the captivity of hundreds of hostages in North Africa as a travesty, they asked, while simultaneously allowing the enslavement of almost a million black people in the United States? In these novels, Muslims become the voice of generosity, freedom, and salvation. Such captivity narratives, especially James Riley's *Authentic Narrative of the Loss of the American Brig Commerce* (1817), would eventually play a larger role in the antislavery movement in the United States. When asked what books had most influenced him, for example, President Abraham Lincoln named six; one of them was Riley's novel, a story of how the captive and the man who once held him in captivity were able to achieve redemption.

NINETEENTH-CENTURY AND EARLY TWENTIETH-CENTURY INNOVATIONS

In the 1800s, the themes that had characterized stereotyping of Muslims and Islam in the colonial and revolutionary eras of American history remained potent. The Second Great Awakening, a period of religious REVIVALISM that occurred in the first half of the 19th century, led to an even greater proliferation of prophecy teachings about Muslims and Islam. A widespread belief that the world would come to an end in 1844, for example, prominently featured observations about the imminent decline of the Ottoman (Muslim) Empire. Muslim societies continued to be viewed in terms of iniquity.

But as Muslim lands were eclipsed first by European economic power and then by direct European imperialism, older stereotypes of the Muslim as powerful tyrant—though still in existence—gave way to a more complicated and ambiguous set of stereotypes about Muslims and Islam. In the slaveholding South, for example, a deep interest in ethnology, the study of people's racial and ethnic origins, led to the white "discovery" of AFRICAN-AMERICAN MUSLIM SLAVES. Impressed, if not befuddled, by the high levels of ARABIC literacy and education among slaves such as ABDUL RAHMAN IBRAHIMA (ca. 1762–1829) and OMAR IBN SAID (ca. 1770–1864), slave owners, journalists, Christian missionaries, and politicians insisted that such men were not wholly African but of mixed black and Arab, Moorish, or Turkish ancestry.

Since slaveholding was based at least partly on the widespread belief among Anglo Americans in the intellectual inferiority of black people, it was believed that such slaves could not possibly be "pure Africans." At the same time, some slave owners specifically sought Muslim or "Mandingo" slaves, whom they believed would make excellent overseers of other slaves due to their relatively higher intelligence. There is some evidence that Muslim slaves such as BILALI OF SAPELO ISLAND emphasized their Muslim identities so that they might take advantage of the privileges offered to overseers of slave gangs in places such as the GEORGIA SEACOAST.

The idea that Muslims possessed a certain level of civilization challenged the widely held notion in the revolutionary era that Islamic religion made people backward and slothful. This was one of several ambiguous images that appeared in the 19th-century American catalog of stereotypes about Muslims. Another image (if not entirely new) that gained currency in the 19th century was the association of Muslims with sexual licentiousness. In Anglo-American male culture, for example, the Turkish harem became a place of sexual fantasy. As depicted in European and American paintings, the Muslim harem was a seductive space where men could dominate women.

This rendering of the harem as a whorehouse had little to do with the reality of Middle Eastern women who happened to live in such domestic spaces but became attractive to the many Anglo-American men who traveled to the Middle East as tourists in search of such titillation and sensuous experience, sometimes literally wearing the clothes of a Turkish pasha as a way of acting out their fantasies. Called "howadjis," a play on the Arabic word *hajji*, or pilgrim, these white American men included figures such as Bayard Taylor, author of *Poems of the Orient* (1854), who was painted proudly wearing a turban and smoking a water pipe. "The howadji," wrote Timothy Marr in *The Cultural Roots of American Islamicism* (2008), set out to experience "such Eastern pleasures as dressing in loose oriental garb, smoking Turkish pipes, visiting public baths and slave markets, touring ruins from biblical times, and tenting with Bedouins and camels."

In the middle and latter parts of the 19th century, stereotypes of Muslims and Islam became more playful for the Anglo Americans who created such images. There was no better institutional example of this playfulness than the Shriners, a male fraternal organization founded in the late 1870s by New York actor William Florence that utilized Muslim texts, artistic symbols, clothes, and aspects of SUFISM, tracing their lineage to the prophet Muhammad and ancient Egyptian empires. Known for their conical headgear—called the fez—the Ancient Arabic Order of the Nobles of the Mystic Shrine, or Shriners, held secret fraternal meetings, built large and ornate lodges named after Muslim historical figures such as Abu Bakr, and marched—fully dressed in their "oriental" garb—in the nation's various summertime parades.

By the early 20th century, the Muslim Orient—that is, the places in Africa and Asia where Muslims lived as majority populations—might be depicted, simultaneously, as violent, misogynistic, evil, pathetic, and even funny. This complicated storehouse of stereotypes was used as a source of inspiration for American literature, poetry, and especially FILM. Various images of the Muslim Orient were favorite topics of the silent movies that appeared in the 1920s, and none was more popular than *The Sheik* (1921), a tale of seduction in which a British woman was abducted by an Arab *shaykh*, or leader, and despite her efforts, gave in to his irresistible charms.

Consumer culture was similarly saturated with images of the Muslim Orient, often used to sell a product that was sensuous or even miraculous. Cigarette makers, for example, marketed a number of brands that incorporated images of Muslims or Islam, including Camel, Mecca, Fatima, and Omar. Members of the MOORISH SCIENCE TEMPLE of America in the late 1920s sold Moorish Mineral and Healing Oil, and Moorish Body Builder and Blood Purifier, a tonic for "rheumatism, lung trouble, rundown constitutions, indigestion, and loss of manhood."

FROM THE IMAGINATIVE PLAYGROUND TO COLD WAR BATTLEGROUND

The development of the cold war between the United States and the Soviet Union after 1945, the year in which WORLD WAR II ended, changed the social and cultural dynamics in which the more playful strain of Muslim stereotypes was embraced. After World War II, the United States emerged as the world's preeminent economic and military power, locked in a cold war with the Soviet Union. In this period, the United States took unprecedented actions to ensure that countries in Africa, Asia, and Latin America, including many Muslim-majority countries, were led by governments that were friendly to U.S. political and economic interests.

The U.S. government sought to ensure the supply of oil from Saudi Arabia and the Persian Gulf to the United States and its allies, to support the fledging state of Israel, to prevent the spread of communism, and to overthrow or minimize the power of leaders who opposed any part of this agenda. In 1953, for example, the U.S. government assisted in overthrowing Mohammad Mossadeq, the democratically elected prime minister of Iran who had nationalized the Anglo-Iranian Oil Company. In his place, the U.S. and British governments supported the shah of Iran, a pro-Western monarch.

Growing numbers of people in Asia, Africa, and Latin America—from Vietnamese to Egyptians—hoped to pursue their own national interests, often calling for a "third way" between U.S.-backed capitalism and Soviet-supported communism. These "third way" or "third world" countries entered both formal and informal alliances in the 1950s and 1960s in order to support each other's bids for national self-determination. The attempt to achieve national independence became the most popular method for social or ethnic groups, especially ethnic minorities, to express hopes for personal liberty and social justice.

During this era, some revolutionaries who had no state or territory of their own or wished to expand their territorial homelands used violence as a way to achieve their goals. Activists in Northern Ireland, Puerto Rico, the Philippines, Israel, and other places committed violent acts against civilians to further their respective bids for national self-determination. In the United States and in other countries, such people were generally thought of as terrorists. Though nation-states frequently killed civilians in the course of waging war or in maintaining domestic peace, this use of violence was generally more acceptable according to both international law experts and popular American opinion.

In this age of nationalist terrorism, Muslims and Islam were not yet synonymous in American culture with terrorism. Through the 1970s, Americans were more likely to associate terrorism with Arabs, especially Palestinians, than with Muslims more generally. In 1972, for example, Black September, a Palestinian terrorist group, kidnapped and murdered 11 Israeli athletes at the Summer Olympics in Munich, West Germany. Though Muslims were part of the Black September group, its actions were not understood to be those of an Islamic group, but of an Arab group seeking national independence for Palestinians. It was often "the Arab" rather than "the Muslim" who was stereotyped as the violent, fanatical, and uncivilized "bad guy" of American political cartoons, movies, and TV shows during the 1970s.

REEMERGENCE OF THE "MUSLIM ENEMY" BEFORE AND AFTER 9/11

By the end of the 20th century, however, an important shift had occurred in the stereotyping of Muslims and Islam that cast them in American culture as central villains in both fictional and nonfictional struggles against tyranny, oppression, and senseless violence. Islam and Muslims in the American popular imagination and in U.S. foreign policy came to be understood primarily not as labels for a religion and a religious group of people but as symbols of incomprehensible and evil terror. Terrorism and Islam became synonymous in the minds of millions of Americans.

This change reflected the politics of an era in which the U.S. government emerged victorious in its cold war with the Soviet Union and at the same time realized the limits of its power to control the fate of other nations, especially in the developing world. In the early 1970s, the U.S. government decided to end its prosecution of the VIETNAM WAR and, in 1975, withdrew its last troops from the U.S. embassy in Saigon. The sting of failure in Vietnam was still fresh in Americans' minds when, amid the Iranian Revolution in 1979, several sectors of Iranian society joined together to oust the U.S.-backed shah, and the Islamic groups leading this anti-shah coalition took 52 Americans hostage for a total of 444 days.

This event and its fallout marked an important turning point in the history of stereotyping of Muslims and Islam in the United States. Some Americans mistakenly thought of Iranians, most of whom are of Persian ethnicity, as Arabs, but the Islamic nature of Iran's revolution soon emerged as the key identifier of these hostage takers. U.S. citizens were angry, and the Iranian hostage crisis emerged as a daily concern for millions of them.

CBS News anchor Walter Cronkite, rated by one poll in 1979 to be the most trusted man in America, signed off each evening news broadcast by informing viewers how many days the hostages had been held in captivity, and Ted Koppel, host of ABC News' *Nightline* program, brought the story into Americans' homes each night, making many feel as if they, too, had been taken hostage. Harkening back to colonial-

With the rise of anti-Muslim attitudes in the United States after the end of the cold war, Muslims and their allies protested against the increased stereotyping of them as terrorists. *(Les Stone/Sygma/Corbis)*

and revolutionary-era captivity narratives about the Barbary pirates, many Americans felt vulnerable, even helpless, especially when a 1980 U.S. military rescue operation failed to rescue the hostages and instead resulted in the deaths of eight members of the military.

Though the hostages were safely released on January 20, 1981, the same day that Ronald Reagan was inaugurated as U.S. president, the damage on the American psyche had been profound. In analyzing the Iranian revolution, many U.S. foreign policy makers and analysts began to discuss the Iranian revolution not as a reaction to U.S. policy in Iran so much as an example of what they considered to be a new trend: the emergence of Muslim militant groups bent on opposing the United States and its allies for religious reasons.

In one sense, these analysts were right to fear an increasing threat to U.S. power emanating from groups that based their political platform on Islamic ideas. In this era of reli-

gious revivalism, many in Muslim-majority countries articulated their deepest hopes in terms that resonated with Islamic ideas and symbols. In addition, many political parties and activist groups organized around Islamic themes and institutions, often because they lived in politically repressive countries where the government did not allow for freedom of assembly, association, or speech in other venues.

Religious organizations and religious sites were among the last places where people could congregate and by default provided a space for political protest. In the Arab world, for example, where the nationalist rhetoric of Egyptian president Gamal Abdel Nasser failed to deliver a promised victory over the Israelis in the 1967 war or the development of a large middle class, many Egyptians felt that the renewal of their country depended upon a renewal of Islamic values. A minority of these people formed violent groups committed both to the overthrow of their own government and to military resistance against the United States and Israel, who were seen as imperial, occupying forces in the Middle East.

U.S. foreign policy analysts correctly feared and predicted the rise of terrorism as a technique that would be used increasingly by such radical groups. But their analysis degenerated into irrational fear when they associated all Muslims with terrorist organizations, which were relatively few in number. For some, fighting terrorism became synonymous with fighting Islamic religion and by extension every Muslim. For example, according to the 1987 best seller, *Terrorism: How the West Can Win,* edited by Israeli politician (and later Prime Minister) Benjamin Netanyahu, the "world of Islam" had invented terrorism in the Middle Ages and, even in the modern world, remained "medieval" in its outlook. In addition, the book claimed, Islam was, at its very heart, antidemocratic and intolerant of diversity. Ironically, such criticism of Islam and Muslims was itself medieval, having emerged as a product of the Crusades.

This stereotyping of Muslims as the enemy was reflected in popular culture as well. In many best-selling novels and popular films of the 1980s, the Iranian hostage crisis was rewritten with a more positive outcome for those concerned about the limits of U.S. power. For example, Ken Follett's *On the Wings of Eagles* (1983), which became a best seller, was marketed as the story of an American rescue operation in Iran that actually worked. The book dramatically recounted the rescue operation led by billionaire H. Ross Perot to free two of his imprisoned business associates in Iran. Similarly, the movie *Delta Force* (1986) was the story of how an American commando and Vietnam veteran, played by Chuck Norris, rescued hostages aboard an airliner that had been hijacked by Muslim militants. The film ends with the bloodthirsty enactment of symbolic revenge against a hijacker by Norris and the happy reunion of hostages with members of their families.

After the Berlin Wall fell in 1989 and the Soviet Union formally came to an end in 1991, such stereotypes of "the Muslim as enemy" became even more prominent among U.S. foreign policy makers. Throughout the 1990s, Harvard professor and former National Security Council official Samuel P. Huntington popularized the thesis that conflict in the post–cold war era would occur along religious and cultural lines. Huntington argued that Islamic and other non-Western civilizations were fundamentally irreconcilable with Western civilization. In *The Clash of Civilizations and the Remaking of the World Order* (1998), Huntington claimed that "the fundamental problem for the West is not Islamic fundamentalism. It is Islam, a different civilization whose people are convinced of the superiority of their culture and are obsessed with the inferiority of their power."

In one stroke of the pen, Huntington had stereotyped more than 1 billion Muslims—and hundreds of millions of non-Muslims—ignoring the diversity of languages, religious beliefs, ethnic backgrounds, political orientations, and social classes that characterized these populations. It was a pattern that would be repeated by many foreign policy analysts who chose, consciously or unconsciously, to discuss terrorism as a typically Muslim activity. Some analysts warned that there was a vast and coordinated Islamic conspiracy against U.S. interests and American citizens, an idea that either ignored or was ignorant of the facts that many of these Muslim groups had differing agendas and few organizational ties to one another, and some had worked with the United States against a common enemy in Afghanistan, where the U.S. government funded and armed Muslim resistance to the Soviet occupation throughout the 1980s.

When al-Qaeda attacked the United States on SEPTEMBER 11, 2001, Americans had little but stereotypes available to answer questions about who the attackers were, why this particular group of Muslim radicals "hated us," and why they had committed the murders of more than 2,700 innocent people. Even as non-Muslim Americans attempted to go beyond superficial and stereotypical understandings of Islam and Muslims, and as Muslim Americans made massive efforts to battle stereotyping, the weight of the previous two decades was difficult to shed. Though there were important movements toward mutual understanding and compassion, the immediate aftermath of 9/11 was characterized by a hardening of negative attitudes toward Muslims and Islam.

As Gottschalk and Greenberg's *Islamophobia* has shown, the typical symbols of Islam already in the historical storehouse of American culture—from the veil to the scimitar, a curved sword—were used frequently after 9/11 not only to depict Muslims in a negative light but simultaneously to define Muslims as the exact opposite of Americans. These mirror images included the notion that Muslims were two-faced or untrustworthy, while Americans were truthful; Muslims were medieval, while Americans were modern; and Muslims oppressed women, while Americans liberated them.

In addition, many post-9/11 stereotypes portrayed Americans as moderate and normal, while representing Muslims as extreme and exotic. In cartoons, film, and on television, Muslims were often represented as overly religious, while Americans achieved a balance between freedom of religion and the separation of church and state. Muslim men were seen as hypermasculine or effeminate, while Americans were properly masculine. Even on the spate of post-9/11 television shows that broached the issue of stereotyping and discrimination against Muslims, many shows concluded that such prejudice was justified. "The right to be racist and suspicious of Arab and Muslim Americans is affirmed" in these shows, asserted American-studies scholar Evelyn Alsultany, "and the government practices to profile racially, detain, deport, and terrorize Arabs and Muslims are accepted."

Alsultany's concerns about the potentially damaging nature of anti-Muslim stereotyping seemed to be echoed in many public opinion polls after 9/11. A 2004 poll conducted by Cornell University's Media and Society Research Group, for example, found that 44 percent of Americans surveyed believed that the civil liberties of Muslim Americans should be curtailed, and 27 percent said that all Muslims should be required to register their whereabouts with federal authorities. A 2006 CBS News poll found that only 19 percent of respondents had a favorable impression of Islam, while 45 percent had an unfavorable impression. In 2007, 25 percent of those surveyed by *Newsweek* said that they supported the mass detentions of Muslim Americans in the event of another terrorist attack. Throughout the first decade of the 21st century, Muslim Americans feared that these attitudes would become even more widespread.

Muslim Americans fought such stereotyping through PHILANTHROPY, POLITICS, INTERFAITH MOVEMENTS, and other forms of civic engagement. They also fought it through comedy. Like many religious and ethnic minorities, Muslim-American comics began to make fun of the stereotypes by revealing their absurdity. For example, during his comedy routine, Azhar Usman, a South Asian American, criticized the fact that some Muslim countries still have monarchies rather than democratic forms of government. "Can you imagine living in a country where they choose the leader based on who his daddy was?" asked Usman, mocking not only Muslim monarchies but also the presidency of George W. Bush, son of the 41st president, George H. W. Bush.

In 2008, Usman, along with African-American comic Preacher Moss and Palestinian-American Mo Amer, turned their 2004 comedy tour, "Allah Made Me Funny," into an independent movie, which opened on 14 movie screens across the United States. Similarly, several Muslim- and Arab-American comedians have created the "Axis of Evil Comedy Tour" (2006) and the "Arab American Comedy Tour" (2006). One of them, Ahmed Ahmed, appeared on the *Tonight Show* in 2008, talking about the discrimination faced by Muslim Americans after 9/11: "Right after September 11th, hate crimes against Middle Eastern people and Muslims went up over 1000 percent. You believe that?" he asked, incredulously. "Which still puts us in fourth place behind blacks, gays, and Jews." Waiting for the laughter and applause to subside, Ahmed asked, "So what do we have to do?" Continuing with his routine, he described his experiences flying after 9/11. "I always know who the air marshal is," he deadpanned. "It's always the guy holding the *People* magazine upside down looking right at me."

CONCLUSION

Though Muslim Americans, like other American religious and ethnic minorities, have been vulnerable to negative stereotyping from the colonial era to the 21st century, such stereotyping is not inevitable. Instead, anti-Muslim stereotypes have been the product of complex historical processes that have revolved largely around U.S. interests in the Islamic world and Muslims abroad. Little attention has been paid to the fact that Muslims have contributed to the making of American society and culture since the colonial era, since the idea of a history that is simultaneously Muslim and American challenges basic notions of "us" and "them." Muslim Americans have had only modest success in altering negative stereotypes, but in their local communities, through their public affairs organizations, and on stage, they have attempted to blunt the force of negative and inaccurate images, sometimes by laughing at them.

Edward E. Curtis IV

Further Reading

Allison, Robert J. *The Crescent Obscured: The United States and the Muslim World, 1776–1815.* Chicago: University of Chicago Press, 1995.

Alsultany, Evelyn. "The Prime Time Plight of the Arab Muslim American after 9/11." In *Race and Arab Americans before and after 9/11*, edited by Amaney Jamal and Nadine Naber, 204–228. Syracuse, N.Y.: Syracuse University Press, 2008.

CBS News. "Poll: Sinking Perceptions of Islam." Available online. URL: http://www.cbsnews.com/stories/2006/04/12/national/main1494697.shtml. Accessed March 24, 2009.

Center for Media and Society Research Group. "Restrictions on Civil Liberties, Views of Islam, and Muslim Americans." December 2004. Available online. URL: http://www.comm.cornell.edu/msrg/report1a.pdf. Accessed March 24, 2009.

Gottschalk, Peter, and Gabriel Greenberg. *Islamophobia: Making Muslims the Enemy.* Lanham, Md.: Rowman and Littlefield, 2008.

Huntington, Samuel P. *The Clash of Civilizations and the Remaking of the World Order.* New York: Simon & Schuster, 1998.

Kidd, Thomas S. *American Christians and Islam: Evangelical Culture and Muslims from the Colonial Period to the Age of Terrorism.* Princeton, N.J.: Princeton University Press, 2009.

Lockman, Zachary. *Contending Visions of the Middle East: The History and Politics of Orientalism.* New York: Cambridge University Press, 2004.

Marr, Timothy. *The Cultural Roots of American Islamicism.* New York: Cambridge University Press, 2006.

McAlister, Melani. *Epic Encounters: Culture, Media, and U.S. Interests in the Middle East, 1945–2000.* Berkeley: University of California Press, 2001.

MSNBC. "Poll: Americans Are Mixed on U.S. Muslims." Available online. URL: http://www.msnbc.msn.com/id/19874703/site/newsweek/print/1/displaymode/1098/. Accessed March 24, 2009.

Netanyahu, Benjamin, ed. *Terrorism: How the West Can Win.* New York: Avon Books, 1987.

Shaheen, Jack G. *Reel Bad Arabs: How Hollywood Vilifies a People.* New York: Olive Branch Press, 2001.

Sufi Order of the West

The Sufi Order of the West, as an organization, developed from Indian Muslim INAYAT KHAN's vision of SUFISM for the western world. Though founded in 1912 in San Francisco as the "Sufi Order in America," the organization remained small after Khan left for a European tour the same year. It eventually developed several different branches in the United States, where, for almost a century, this pioneering organization has attempted to spread a peaceful, contemplative, and inclusive version of Islamic spiritual teachings.

Inayat Khan was born in India in 1882 to a family of musicians and first came to the United States in 1910 with his brother Maheboob and cousin Ali after first stopping in Europe. Another of Khan's brothers, Musherraff, joined them shortly thereafter. Inayat Khan left India under the auspices of his spiritual teacher, Muhammad Abu Hashim Madani, who entrusted him to spread the message of Sufism in the West. Though Inayat Khan was initiated into multiple Sufi orders in India, his primary affiliation was with the CHISHTI SUFI ORDER. The family of musicians made themselves known in the United States through lectures and musical performances, and Inayat Khan, the spiritual leader of the group, began to attract students. His first address in America was at Columbia University in NEW YORK CITY, where he was received with warmth and interest.

Though Inayat Khan came from a practicing Muslim family in India, he never required his students to become Muslims—nor, subsequently, did he require them to observe Islamic rituals such as the prescribed prayer or fasting during Ramadan. *Inayati* Sufism, or universal Sufism, has been largely characterized by an aversion to formal doctrine, emphasizing the idea that the religions of the world are ultimately united by underlying principles and that Sufism, in truth, seeks to point the aspirant toward that realization, rather than espouse a particular religion. Sufism, according to Inayat Khan, was not a religion. Since Khan was conversant with not only Sufism but also Hinduism and other religions, universal ideals permeated his teachings. *Inayati* Sufism necessarily evolved in relation to spiritual traditions of the world and placed great emphasis not only on their philosophical unity but also incorporated a ritual to commemorate the ideal. One of the order's primary practices, the universal worship service, has involved lighting candles dedicated to the world's religions, symbolizing their underlying unity. Lighting a single candle for unnamed religions has also been a part of the practice.

Most of these teachings were first broadcast to Europe, not America. According to Khan, however, the "time for the message was not yet ripe" for the spread of Sufism in the United States in 1910. He criticized American racism and the hustle and bustle of American life. In 1912, he appointed his student Rabia Martin as his representative in the United States and left for a European tour. Though he returned to America in the 1920s, and managed to commission another student, SAMUEL LEWIS (1896–1971), the movement remained much larger in Europe for the following four decades. During his career, Inayat Khan initiated perhaps 200 to 300 members into his organization, though thousands more were influenced by his teachings in the United States and Europe.

In the early 1960s, Inayat Khan's son, VILAYAT INAYAT KHAN (1916–2004) attempted to revive the remnants of the Sufi Order in America and find new persons sympathetic to his father's teachings. From 1968 to 1977 Vilayat Khan's Sufi Order of the West, which eventually became Sufi Order International, cooperated with the San Francisco–based SUFI RUHANIAT INTERNATIONAL group of Samuel Lewis, another Muslim-American Sufi who had once been taught by Inayat Khan.

In 1975, Vilayat Khan opened his own residential community and retreat center in New Lebanon, New York, called the Abode of the Message. This community, in tandem with centers in Seattle, Washington, and Sante Fe, New Mexico, often served as the headquarters of the American followers of Vilayat Khan. Perhaps as many as 100 centers affiliated with the teachings of Khan across the United States and Canada opened in the next two decades. The Omega Institute for Holistic Studies, located in Rhinebeck, New York, published Sufi Order International's many books and pamphlets in this period.

According to the Sufi Order, 10,000 people in North America were initiated into the organization by Vilayat Inayat Khan. In 1997, the North American section of the Sufi Order International said that it had 1,200 dues-paying members and a total circulation for its quarterly magazine, *Hearts & Wings,* of approximately 3,000. Sufi Order's mailing list had 8,000 individuals by the end of the 20th century.

In 2004, the organization was formally taken over by Zia Inayat Khan (1971–   ), the son of Vilayat Khan. Like his grandfather, Zia Khan has lived a spiritually eclectic life and studied Buddhism in addition to classical Chishti Sufism and its western adaptations. He has maintained, in line with his father and grandfather, that Sufism is ultimately beyond the limitations of religion and is instead a spiritual reality that is accessible to all, regardless of creed or affiliation. Zia Khan, moreover, has interacted with other American Sufi movements, including his participation in a conference in 2000 entitled the *Meeting of Five Shaykhs,* with Sheikh Hashim Kabban of the NAQSHBANDI SUFI ORDER and others.

Elliott Bazzano

Further Reading

Hermansen, Marcia. "Hybrid Identity Formations in Muslim America." *Muslim World* 90, no. 1 (Spring 2000): 158–198.

Khan, Pir Vilayat Inayat. *The Message of Our Time: The Life and Teachings of the Sufi Master Pir-O-Murshid Inayat Khan.* San Francisco: Harper & Row, 1978.

Malik, Jamal, and John Hinnels, eds. *Sufism in the West.* New York: Routledge, 2006.

Miller, Timothy, ed. *America's Alternative Religions.* New York: State University of New York Press, 1995.

Sufi Islamia Ruhaniat Society. *Introduction to Spiritual Dance and Walk: From the Work of Samuel L. Lewis.* Novato, Calif.: Prophecy Pressworks, 1972.

Westerlund, David, ed. *Sufism in Europe and North America.* New York: RoutledgeCurzon, 2004.

Inayat Khan
"America, 1910–1912" (ca. 1925)

Shortly before World War I, Indian musician and Sufi master Inayat Khan (1882–1927) toured the United States, performing South Asian music and lecturing about the spiritual side of Islam. In this passage from his memoirs, written around 1925, Khan expresses his admiration for Americans but criticizes them as racist and materialistic. His organization, the Sufi Order in the West, had its greatest initial success in Europe, though it would later grow and spread in the United States.

I was transported by destiny from the world of lyric and poetry to the world of industry and commerce, on the 13th of September 1910. I bade farewell to my motherland, the soil of India, the land of the sun, for America the land of my future, wondering: "perhaps I shall return some day," and yet I did not know how long it would be before I should return. The ocean that I had to cross seemed to me a gulf between the life that was passed and the life which was to begin. I spent my moments on the ship looking at the rising and falling of the waves and realizing in this rise and fall the picture of life reflected, the life of individuals, of nations, of races, and of the world. I tried to think where I was going, why I was going, what I was going to do, what was in store for me. "How shall I set to work? Will the people be favorable or unfavorable to the Message which I am taking from one end of the world to the other?" It seemed my mind moved curiously on these questions, but my heart refused to ponder upon them even for a moment, answering apart one constant voice I always heard coming from within, urging me constantly onward to my task, saying: "Thou art sent on Our service, and it is We Who will make thy way clear." This alone was my consolation. . . .

Now before me there was the question: how to set to work and in what direction? For the Message the time was not yet ripe, as I was at that time rather studying the psychology of the people than teaching. . . .

My first address to the people of America was arranged at Columbia University in New York by Dr. Reebner, and there I found a great response. Dr. Reebner, the Head of Music at the University was most interested in Indian music and we became friends. Among the audience was Miss Ruth St. Denis who invented Indian dances of her own and was making a speciality of it, and for whom our music became as a color and fragrance to an imitation flower. She tried to introduce the Indian music on the program of her performance, which was to me as a means to an end. We had an interesting tour together throughout the States, and yet for the public, which was for amusement, our music became merely an entertainment. This was an amusement for them, and therefore painful for us. Also it was not satisfactory to combine

real with imitation. However it helped to keep the wolf away from our door. . . .

Before ending our tour in the States I spoke at the University of Los Angeles, and to a very large audience at the Berkeley University of San Francisco where I met with a very great response, and where my lectures on, and my representation of Indian music and the presentation of its ideal met with a great interest.

At the end of my tour through the United States, when I arrived at San Francisco, I found the meaning of the scheme of Providence, that I was meant to come to San Francisco, a land full of psychic powers and cosmic currents, and begin from there the work of my Message. It is here that I found my first *mureed* [student] Mrs. Ada Martin. I was welcomed by Swami Trigunatita and his collaborator Swami Paramananda, who requested me to speak on Indian music to their friends at the Hindu temple, and was presented with a gold medal and an address. . . .

During my stay in America for more than two years there was not much done in the furtherance of the Sufi Movement. From my stay in America I began to learn the psychology of the people in the West and the way in which my mission should be set to work. If I can recall any great achievement in America, it was to have found the soul who was destined to be my life's partner.

With the liberal idea of freedom in all directions of life and in spite of Abraham Lincoln's liberal example and reform, there is still to be found in America a prejudice against color which is particularly shown to the Negroes who were for a long time in slavery, and since their freedom the prejudice has become still greater. It seems almost impossible to think that in a country which is most up-to-date in civilization, there should be a population so looked down upon. Yes, in India there are *shudras*, lower castes who are called untouchable. Yet there have been scientific reasons, from a hygienic point of view, for not touching them, and the attitude of the high caste towards them has never been that of hatred. The men and women of that pariah class in India are called by others *mehter*, which means master. Yes, the people in America have their reason for it. They think Negroes are too backward in evolution to associate with. But to me it seems that the coming race will be the race of Negroes; they are showing it from now. In whatever walk of life they find an opportunity, they come forward in competition. Not only in wrestling or boxing, but also on the stage the Negroes show their splendor, and the most surprising thing to me was that, conscious of all the prejudice against the Negro from all around, he does not allow his ego to be affected by it. In every position of outward humiliation he is put to, he stands upright with a marvelous spirit, which I only wished the man in the East had, who has become as a soil worn-out after a thousand harvests. The spirit in the East seemed to me deadened, being weighed down by autocratic influences, tramped upon by foreign powers, crucified by high moral and spiritual ideals, and long starved by poverty.

An ordinary man in America confuses an Indian with brown skin with the Negro. Even if he does not think that he is a Negro, still he is accustomed to look with contempt at a dark skin, in spite of the many most unclean, ignorant and ill-mannered specimens of white people who are to be found there on the spot. I did not find so much prejudice existing in America against a Japanese, of which so much has been said. Still in answer to the unchristian attitude of theirs, the government of Japan has all along threatened them with the Mosaic law, and is ready to return the same when the Americans visit Japan. Indians, when insulted abroad, can do nothing but bear it patiently. The color prejudice in some nations of Europe is even more, but it is often hidden under the garb of politeness and not so freely expressed as in America; the difference is between a grown-up person and a child in his expression of prejudice.

An American as a friend is very agreeable and desirable and most sociable. One feels affection, spontaneity in his feelings, although the business faculty is most pronounced in him, yet together with it he is most generous. The American readily responds to the idea of universal brotherhood. He is open to study any religion or philosophy, although it is a question if he would like to follow a certain religion long enough, because freedom, which is the goal, by many in America is taken as the way, and therefore, before starting the journey towards spiritual freedom, they want the way also to be a way of freedom, which is impossible. I have seen among Americans people of a thorough good nature and their life itself a religion, people of principle and gentleness. The broad outlook of the people in America gave me a great hope and a faith that it is this spirit which in time must bring the universal idea to the view of the world. It is most admirable for a great nation to bring forward the idea of world disarmament, when many other nations are fully absorbed in covetousness, and submerged in their own interests. This idea of disarmament brought out by President Harding, was responded to by the public there. This shows the bent of their mind. Besides, to friends or enemies, in their trouble, whenever the occasion has arisen, America has most generously come first to their rescue.

With all the modern spirit in America I found among the people love for knowledge, search for truth, and tendency to unity. I found them full of life, enthusiasm, and goodwill, which promises that this modern nation, although it is now in its childhood, will become a youth who will lead the world towards progress.

Source: Hazrat Inayat Khan. "America, 1910–1912." Available online. URL: http://wahiduddin.net/mv2/bio/Autobiography_1.htm. Accessed August 23, 2006.

Sufi Ruhaniat International

The Sufi Ruhaniat International (SRI) was founded in 1971 shortly before the death of its founder, SAMUEL LEWIS (1896–1971), who was also known as Murshid Sam and Sufi Sam (an acronym for Sufi Ahmad Murad). SRI formed as a splinter group of followers of INAYAT KHAN (1882–1927), a Muslim Indian mystic who first visited the United States in 1910. Initially called the Sufi Islamia Ruhaniat Society, the organization officially changed to SRI in 2002, eliminating the word Islamia from its title because the order did not mandate adherence to Sunni and Shi'a practices. Still, an increasing number of SRI's members in the 21st century came to consider themselves Muslim. Since the organization's beginnings, members of SRI have represented a wide range of religious traditions, and relinquishing those affiliations has not been a prerequisite for membership.

In 1923, Samuel Lewis received initiation into Inayat Khan's order and went on to propagate Khan's message, which included writing commentaries on his work and developing a form of spiritual dance. Lewis was also deeply influenced by Ruth St. Denis (1879–1968), a pioneer of the modern dance movement in America and Europe. Following Inayat Khan's death in 1927, the question of spiritual succession was contested among Khan's students and family, marking the first steps in splinter groups of *Inayati*, or universal, Sufism. In part because of his eclecticism and inclusive worldview, Lewis represented one of the forerunners of the New Age movement, which developed more succinctly in the late 1970s.

Spiritual walks and dances have primarily characterized SRI, though other branches of *Inayati* Sufism have also practiced the dances. The first dances began in the late 1960s and were known as "Dervish Dances," involving the repetition of sacred ARABIC phrases. The next forms were called "Mantric Dances" and usually involved Sanskrit phrases, taken from Yogic and Buddhist traditions. The conglomeration of these dances became known as the Dances of Universal Peace, or Sufi Dancing. They have since been practiced across the United States and in other countries as well. In 1972, the Sufi Islamia Ruhaniat Society published "Introduction to Spiritual Walk and Dance," a pamphlet that outlined the philosophy of the dances in addition to some of their particular forms.

Thousands of dances have been developed since their onset, and SRI has encouraged their transmission from teachers to students, rather than learning them individually. According to Lewis, the purpose of the dances was both for moral development and spiritual purification. Lewis said he created the dances to show young people how to deepen their spirituality and as a way to help them find bliss without the use of drugs. While Lewis and Inayat Khan's son, VILAYAT INAYAT KHAN (1916–2004), worked together for some time, one of the reasons Lewis separated from Vilayat's group was due to the latter's prohibition against drugs. While Lewis never advocated drug use, he was not comfortable setting a formal doctrine against it. Weariness of overly doctrinal stances has been characteristic of *Inayati* Sufism in general. Inayat Khan emphasized that SUFISM was not a religion, and one member of SRI who has resided in Arcata, California, put it this way: "The religion of the heart can't be claimed exclusively by any religion, but it can be claimed by all religions."

Upon the death of Samuel Lewis in 1971, Moineddin Jablonski assumed leadership of the SRI until he died in 2001. Shabda Khan became the next spiritual successor. In a similar light to Lewis, Shabda Khan has had eclectic training, having studied with a Tibetan Buddhist and Hindu teacher prior to his leadership role in SRI. As of 2009, he has remained the head of the organization. SRI has continued to grow, and by 2008, its U.S. membership had reached 1,317 and its international membership—comprised of 33 countries—1,708 members.

Elliott Bazzano

Further Reading

Clark, Peter, ed. *New Trends in the Developments in the World of Islam*. London: Luzac Oriental, 1998.

Halman, Hugh Talat. "Sufism in the West: Islam in an Interspiritual Age." In *Voices of Islam*, Vol. 5, edited by John Esposito and Omid Safi, 169–188. Westport, Conn.: Praeger, 2007.

Hermansen, Marcia. "Hybrid Identity Formations in Muslim America." *Muslim World* 90, no. 1 (Spring 2000): 158–198.

Khan, Pir Vilayat Inayat. *The Message of Our Time: The Life and Teachings of the Sufi Master Pir-O-Murshid Inayat Khan*. San Francisco: Harper & Row, 1978.

Malik, Jamal, and John Hinnels, eds. *Sufism in the West*. New York: Routledge, 2006.

Miller, Timothy, ed. *America's Alternative Religions*. Albany: State University of New York Press, 1995.

Sufi Islamia Ruhaniat Society. *Introduction to Spiritual Dance and Walk: From the Work of Samuel L. Lewis*. Novato, Calif.: Prophecy Pressworks, 1972.

Van Bruinessen, Martin, and Julia Day Howell, eds. *Sufism and the 'Modern' in Islam*. New York: I. B. Taurus, 2007.

Westerlund, David, ed. *Sufism in Europe and North America*. New York: RoutledgeCurzon, 2004.

Sufism

Sufism is the mystical or inner dimension of the Islamic tradition. For most Muslims, it provides a path to a closer and more intimate relationship with God. While some Muslims have rejected Sufism as un-Islamic, the historical development and spread of Islamic religion throughout Africa, Europe, and Asia was often due to the success of Sufi leaders and institutions. Sufis have been credited with major roles in bringing Islamic teachings to regions such as South and Southeast Asia, where they learned the local languages and conveyed Islamic and mystical teachings through vernacular poetry. In these various regions, Sufi practices often took on the local color, incorporating musical performance in the case of the Indian Chishti Order or engaging in shamanistic feats among certain Central Asian groups.

Sufi Muslims claim to derive their practices and concepts from the fundamental Islamic sources, the QUR'AN and Sunna, the practice of the prophet Muhammad. In addition to performing the five daily prayers and observing other elements of Sunni Islam, Sufis often focus their religious practice on directly experiencing the presence of God through the use of meditation. Called DHIKR, or the remembrance of God, this meditation can take several forms. Sufis may recite the names of God over and over, or proclaim God's greatness. They may also dance, sing, or recite religious poetry in their effort to experience God's presence. Some practitioners attempt to be absorbed entirely in God's love, seeking annihilation in the Divine.

Sufi dancers, New Mexico, 1974. Sufism, the mystical branch of Islam, increased in popularity during the 1970s as many Jewish and Christian Americans experimented with new forms of spiritual practice.   *(Jeff Albertson/CORBIS)*

Fundamental to the history of Sufism has been the role of the Sufi teacher, called the *shaykh* in the Arabic language or the *pir* in the Persian language. Traditionally, the Sufi student or disciple took allegiance to this teacher and was to obey him or her unquestioningly. Initiates in spiritual lineages were said to be following a *tariqa* (a way or a method), which crystallized into specific sets of religious practices within the various Sufi orders. Many of these orders were named after prominent Sufi saints of the past who were credited with formulating specific litanies and ritual practices. Some Sufi movements, such as the QADIRI-RIFA'I SUFI ORDER, named for 12th-century teacher Abd al-Qadir Jilani, became diffused worldwide, while others had more local reach.

SUFISM IN THE UNITED STATES

The introduction of Sufism to America as a lived religious practice may have occurred through what appear to be Sufi-inspired practices among West African slaves along the Georgia coast. Using long strings of prayer beads, or rosaries, AFRICAN-AMERICAN MUSLIM SLAVES may have recited vari-

ous litanies that they learned as students of Sufism. White Americans, however, took little notice of Sufism until the late 19th century, when middle- and upper-class individuals became attracted to Sufi philosophy as an alternative to Christian thought and practice. In 1893, Islam's most prominent American missionary of the time, ALEXANDER RUSSELL WEBB, appeared at the Chicago World's Fair, where he extolled Islam's virtues as a rational and scientific religion as part of the World's Parliament of Religions. In his writings on Islam, Webb stressed that Islam contained practical, concrete religious elements as well as more spiritual, esoteric religious elements.

The first documented Sufi teacher to come to the United States was INAYAT KHAN (1882–1927), who arrived from what was then British India in 1910 while on tour as a Hindustani musician. After declaring in 1912 that the United States was "not yet ripe" for the Sufi message, Khan moved to Europe. He later returned to the United States for a short period of time in the 1920s. Eventually, a group of followers successfully established his teachings in the SUFI ORDER OF THE WEST, which combined Khan's training in the India-based CHISHTI SUFI ORDER, with broader practices drawn from other religions.

The development of Sufi institutions in the United States remained limited, however, until after WORLD WAR II. In 1953, Albanian Muslim Americans established a BEKTASHI SUFI lodge in Michigan. Then, the countercultural movements of the 1960s and concomitant interest in Eastern spirituality brought renewed interest in Inayat Khan's teachings. His son, VILAYAT INAYAT KHAN, revived the movement in the 1960s under the names "Sufi Order in the West" or the "Message in Our Time." In 1975, Vilayat Khan established a center known as the Abode of the Message in New Lebanon, New York. The organization later adopted the name Sufi Order International, reflecting the more transnational currents of the time. Inayat Khan's grandson, Zia Inayat Khan, was invested with the succession of the order in 2000 and has since been conducting teachings based at the Abode.

DIVERSITY IN AMERICAN SUFISM

In the United States, various Sufi movements emerged in the late 20th century. One strand of movements, more universalistic in outlook, invoked Sufism and some aspects of Muslim tradition but did not demand formal conversion to Islam of its adherents. For example, Samuel Lewis was an early student of Inayat Khan who also followed Zen and Yogic paths and teachers. His brand of Sufism was transmitted to a smaller circle of disciples in San Francisco during the 1960s. He developed, in particular, practices of "spiritual" movement and "Sufi dancing," utilizing circle and round dances in group settings accompanied by the chanting of litanies drawn from various religious traditions, including the Islamic profession of faith. The disciples that "Sufi Sam," as Lewis was nicknamed, passed on to Vilayat Khan infused the latter's group with new leadership and energy in the early 1970s. Many disciples chose to remain within a distinct group called the Sufi Islamia Ruhaniat Society, whose name was changed in 2002 to SUFI RUHANIAT INTERNATIONAL. Another legacy of Samuel Lewis is an international movement practicing the Dances of Universal Peace.

Other Sufi orders, while largely recruiting among Americans, had a grounding in the Islamic SHARI'A, or Islamic law and ethics, and understood being Muslim as essential to spiritual progress within the Sufi tradition. Most of the leaders of these movements have been immigrants from Muslim societies. Notable among these have been the NAQSHBANDI SUFI ORDER led by the Cypriot *shaykh*, Nazim. This group has been directed in the United States by Sheikh MUHAMMAD HISHAM KABBANI. Other groups included the Turkish Helveti Jerrahi Order brought by Sheikh Muzaffer Ozak in 1980 and the BAWA MUHAIYADDEEN FELLOWSHIP established by a Sinhalese teacher, Muhammad Raheem

Bawa Muhaiyaddeen, and several branches of the Turkish MEVLEVI SUFI ORDER under Kabir Helminski or Jalaluddin Loras.

College and university professors associated with American Sufi movements, such as Huston Smith and Seyyed Hossein Nasr, have advocated the pursuit of a perennial truth and sympathetically presented Islamic teachings in the light of inner or mystical understandings. FRITHJOF SCHUON, a Swiss professor who ultimately settled in Bloomington, Indiana, was also influential in disseminating this "perennialist" or "traditionalist" understanding of Sufism. At the same time, he functioned as the head of the MARYAMIYYA SUFI ORDER, a branch of the SHADHILI SUFI ORDER, a movement popular in North Africa and the Arab Middle East.

American Sufi movements have included pockets of immigrants from Muslim societies, particularly found in larger urban centers such as NEW YORK CITY, CHICAGO, and LOS ANGELES, who follow Sufism in ways very similar to practices in their home societies. In the case of the West African Sufi orders such as the Murudiyya and the Tijaniyya, African immigrants have welcomed African-American Muslims into their Sufi meditation centers and mosques. Some African-American Muslims, drawn to West African Sufism for both spiritual and ethnic reasons, have developed transatlantic ties to Sufi teachers, institutions, and shrines in West Africa. The African American Islamic Institute in Kaolack, Senegal, for example, is home to black American Muslims studying under the guidance of Sheikh Hassan Cisse. In addition to the study of Islamic texts and ritual practices, practitioners contribute time and money to social services and a Qur'an school for children in the town of Kaolack.

The constituencies and membership of the various American Sufi movements have varied, since they represent diverse religious and social orientations. The Sufi Order of the West and the Idries Shah Movement have had a broader impact on mainstream American popular culture due to their publishing activities and outreach to broader communities through interests such as transpersonal psychology, holistic health, and Sufi dancing. Members did not have to make radical lifestyle or social adjustments and have tended to be white, middle- and upper-class spiritual seekers. Interest in these movements may have peaked in the mid-1970s. While the Sufi Order International has claimed that 10,000 persons took an initiation with Vilayat Khan, many more Americans had contact with its teachings through attending Sufi seminars and camps or reading publications.

SUFISM AND AMERICAN CULTURE

By the late 20th century, Sufi ideas and practices made a significant impact on American popular culture. Americans listened to Sufi musician Nusrat Fateh Khan's collaboration with rocker Eddie Vedder on the soundtrack to Sean Penn's film *Dead Man Walking*. Coleman Barks's translations of Jalaluddin Rumi, the medieval Sufi poet, became best sellers. Television and audio cassette evocations of Rumi's work were also promoted by celebrities such as the singer Madonna and the guru of holistic health Deepak Chopra.

In the case of the Islamic-American Sufi movements, impact on mainstream American culture has been less significant since the ideas propounded are more specific to Muslim concerns. Since some Sufi interpretations of Islam, such as the idea of charismatic leadership and the intercession of pious saints, were not accepted by all Muslims, it should not be thought that such movements have been supported by the entire Muslim American community. At the same time, many non-Sufi Muslims have appreciated the success of Sufi movements in drawing Americans to Islam. Beginning in the late 1990s, a strand of Sufism heavily grounded in traditional Islamic learning began to achieve popularity in the United States, especially among the generation of Muslims born to immigrant Muslim parents from South Asia or the Middle East. Teachers such as Hamza Yusuf Hanson (1960–) and Nuh Ha Mim Keller (1954–), both Euro-American converts to Islam, have attracted followers who espoused Islamic spirituality through meticulous practice of the norms of Islamic LAW. This type of renewed Islamic Sufism has also proved more broadly acceptable in the major Islamic-American organizations.

Sufism is practiced in both the Shi'a and Sunni branches of Islam and a number of Shi'a orders, including the NIMATULLAHI SUFI ORDER and the Oveyssi-Shahmaghsoudi, have developed followings among both the Iranian émigré and the American community. The son of Shah Maghsoud, Saleheddin Ali Nader Angha, heads an organization known as the MTO (Maktab Tarighat Oveyssi) or the Shahmaghsoudi School of Islamic Sufism, which claimed more than 39 centers in North America in 2008. Women have had a high degree of leadership within this movement, running a number of the local centers, giving lessons and teaching Sufi practices.

In many ways, the varieties of Sufi movements, ideas, and traditions in the United States express the diversity of Muslim-American communities and individuals as a whole. Sufi Muslim Americans hold differing ideas about how to develop a closer relationship with God, and they practice different rituals in their attempt to experience God's presence. Some Sufi groups do not seek ties to non-Sufi Muslims; others see themselves as part of a worldwide community of Muslim believers, whether Sufi or not. Sufi Muslims sometimes cross racial and ethnic lines; other times, they seek to strengthen such communal ties. Some Americans, who think of themselves as Sufis and may care little for other aspects of Islam, are simply lovers of Rumi's poetry. There is no one kind of Sufi, just as there is no one kind of Muslim.

Marcia Hermansen

Further Reading
Hermansen, Marcia K. "Hybrid Identity Formations in Muslim America: The Case of American Sufi Movements." *Muslim World* 90, nos. 1&2 (Spring 2000): 158–197.

———. "In the Garden of American Sufi Movements: Hybrids and Perennials." In *New Trends and Developments in the World of Islam,* edited by Peter B. Clarke, 155–178. London: Luzac Oriental, 1997.

Jervis, James. "The Sufi Order in the West and Pir Vilayat Inayat Khan." In *New Trends and Developments in the World of Islam,* edited by Peter B. Clarke. London: Luzac Oriental, 1997.

Rawlinson, Andrew. *The Book of Enlightened Masters: Western Teachers in Eastern Traditions.* Chicago: Open Court, 1997.

Webb, Gisela. "Sufism in America." In *America's Alternative Religions,* edited by Timothy Miller and Harold Coward. Albany: State University of New York Press, 1995.

———. "Tradition and Innovation in Contemporary American Islamic Spirituality: The Bawa Muhaiyadeen Fellowship." In *Muslim Communities in North America,* edited by Yvonne Y. Haddad and Jane I. Smith. Albany: State University of New York Press, 1994.

sunna   See ISLAMIC THOUGHT; RELIGIOUS LIFE; SHARI'A; SUNNI MUSLIM AMERICANS.

Sunni Muslim Americans

Sunni Muslims constitute the majority of Muslims worldwide, accounting for approximately 80 to 85 percent of the global Muslim population. They trace their origins to a seventh-century dispute over the question of who was best qualified to lead the Muslim community after the death of the prophet MUHAMMAD in 632 C.E. While Shi'a Muslims believed that only members of the family of the prophet Muhammad should lead the community, Sunni Muslims rejected this view and supported the ascension of Abu Bakr, a companion of Muhammad but not a relative, as the first caliph, or vice-regent, of the Muslim community.

While today's Sunni Muslims locate the origins of their communal identities in the seventh century, the term "Sunni," which simply means "traditional," was not used widely until the eighth century. Employed at first to merely emphasize continuity with the practices of the Prophet and his companions, "Sunni" has taken on additional meanings since the classical age of Islam. For some Muslims, Sunni

Islam came to be distinguished from SUFISM, or the mystical tradition of Islam; for others, including the great 11th to 12th century Islamic legal scholar and mystic al-Ghazali, the heart of Sunni Islam was Sufi Islam. Some came to define Sunni to mean those Muslims who not only follow the QUR'AN and the sunna, or traditions of the Prophet, but also the SHARI'A, the body of Islamic law and ethics developed by Islamic scholars; others have eschewed the legal tradition or de-emphasized it.

Sunni Muslims in the United States have accounted for the majority of the Muslim-American population since slave times. They have been diverse in every way—from their country of origin to their language, their socioeconomic status, their race or ethnicity, and even in their interpretation of Islamic religion. But they have shared certain religious practices throughout American history. From the time of slavery until today, Sunni Muslims have committed themselves to upholding traditions such as the practice of daily prayers; the recitation of the Qur'an, the holy scripture; the giving of charity; the observance of dietary guidelines; and fasting during Ramadan.

AFRICAN SLAVES

The Sunni Muslim presence in the Americas can be traced to the colonial era. Sunni Muslim slaves were taken against their will from West Africa, stretching from present-day Senegal to Nigeria, where, by the 17th and 18th centuries, Sunni Islam was already established. In some of those regions, Sunni Muslims were a majority, while in others they were a minority ruled by non-Muslim leaders. It has been estimated that almost 30,000 Sunni Muslim slaves were transported to America, representing 10 percent of all the West Africans who arrived in the Thirteen Colonies and United States from 1711 to 1808, the year the U.S. government banned the importation of slaves.

Most of the Sunni Muslim Africans were young men and women whose ages ranged between 18 and 30 years. Many came from the urban-ruling elite of West Africa, and some of them were highly educated. A considerable number of them were Qur'anic teachers and students who had received Islamic education in the centers of learning. Likewise, some other Sunni Muslim slaves were clerics, traders, and noble people. A few were from the ruling dynasties in their countries—persons such as ABDUL RAHMAN IBRAHIMA, who was abducted in 1788. Sunni Muslim slaves found America a hostile environment for the practice of their religion. White owners and Christian missionaries expressed a desire to wipe out any trace of "Muhammadanism," or Islamic religion, in the slaves. Some were forced to convert to Christianity.

Despite the challenge of being Muslim in America, however, some Sunni slaves in the 18th and 19th centuries managed to maintain ties to their faith. JOB BEN SOLOMON (1701–73) risked his personal safety to prostate himself in daily prayer toward Mecca, and he refused to eat pork or drink liquor, following the Islamic prohibition against their consumption. Slaves such as OMAR IBN SAID (ca. 1770–1864) practiced the rituals of their faith secretly, writing chapters of the Qur'an in ARABIC on the paper provided by the Christian missionaries attempting to convert them. Some Muslim slaves kept up Islamic traditions of PHILANTHROPY through the sharing of FOOD with their fellow slaves.

IMMIGRANTS FROM THE MIDDLE EAST AND SOUTH ASIA

In the 1870s, but especially from 1890 to World War I, a new wave of immigrants from the Middle East, largely from Syria, Lebanon, Jordan, and Palestine, arrived in the United States. These immigrants were for the most part uneducated and came from rural areas. Perhaps 90 percent of them were Christian, but the Muslims who did come—most of them Sunni—worked as peddlers and dockworkers, and also in factories, mines, and railroad construction. They settled all over the country but were concentrated in cities and towns, including DETROIT, MICHIGAN; CEDAR RAPIDS, IOWA; NEW YORK CITY; TOLEDO, OHIO; BOSTON, MASSACHUSETTS; and, perhaps most surprisingly, Ross, NORTH DAKOTA.

At first, many came with the hope to earn money and then return to their home countries. Toward the beginning of WORLD WAR I in 1914, however, an increasing number of these Sunni Muslim immigrants had settled for good in the United States. In addition to saying their daily prayers, some of the religiously observant among them fasted from dawn until sunset during the month of Ramadan. By the beginning of the 20th century, they began to rent halls where they could hold Friday congregational prayers or celebrate the birth of a child. They celebrated their major feasts such as Eid al-Fitr, marking the end of Ramadan, and Eid al-Adha, marking the end of the pilgrimage to Mecca. In Detroit, North Dakota, and other places, they purchased land where they could bury their dead in an Islamic fashion, placing the body directly in the ground, wrapped only in a simple white cloth.

During this same period, from 1880 to World War I, Sunni Muslims arrived from South Asia, including the modern-day countries of Bangladesh, India, and Pakistan. Many of those from the South Asian region called the Punjab became agricultural workers in California, while sailors from the region called Bengal left their ships to settle in New Orleans and New York. Although many of them, especially the agricultural workers in California who married Mexican Catholic women, did not continue to practice Sunni Islam in America, others passed on their religious traditions to their children.

AFTER WORLD WAR II

After WORLD WAR II ended in 1945, Sunni Muslim immigrant communities in the United States established stronger links with their countries of origin. One tangible example of these ties was the building of the ISLAMIC CENTER OF WASHINGTON, D.C., completed in 1957, which was a cooperative venture between Muslim Americans and foreign Muslims. Financed by the governments of 14 Muslim countries, the Islamic Center played host to various imams, or religious leaders, from Egypt's al-Azhar University, one of the oldest and most prestigious Sunni Islamic educational institutions.

In 1952, Muslim Americans founded the FEDERATION OF ISLAMIC ASSOCIATIONS IN THE UNITED STATES AND CANADA (FIA), which was later supported partly by Egyptian president Gamal Abdel Nasser. The FIA arranged for the placement of various al-Azhar-trained imams in the growing number of mosques around the United States. Muslim-American immigrants, concerned that their children and grandchildren did not know the Qur'an, the sunna, and Islamic history, asked these imams to teach their children these basics in Islamic Sunday school sessions.

In 1963, foreign students at the University of Illinois, Urbana, established the MUSLIM STUDENTS ASSOCIATION, which sought to teach non-Muslims about Islam, provide a community for Muslims on college campuses, and relate the fundamentals of Islamic thought to American and modern life. The MSA also became the organization through which various foreign Muslim organizations and leaders promoted a reformist version of Islam that stressed Islam's rationality and its applicability in all realms of life, including politics. Applying their interpretations of the sunna to everyday life, some Sunni Muslim Americans espoused the idea that Islam was a whole way of life that gave instructions on everything from the proper relations between husbands and wives to how one should lead a movement for social change.

After the IMMIGRATION ACT OF 1965 allowed many more nonwhite persons to immigrate to the United States, additional numbers of Sunni Muslims, especially from the Middle East and South Asia, came to the country. Many of them were highly educated, professional Muslims, who were willing to contribute substantial sums to the building of new MOSQUES AND ISLAMIC CENTERS and schools. Other post-1965 Sunni Muslim immigrants were refugees seeking shelter from wars and conflicts in countries such as Algeria, Iraq, Lebanon, Somalia, and Palestine. For both the refugees and other immigrants, the practice of Sunni Islamic traditions often became an important part of their new American identities. Some Muslims became more pious and prayed, fasted, donated money, read the Qur'an, and performed other religious duties more fervently than they had in their home countries.

In the 1980s, the number of Sunni Muslims continued to increase due to the influx of new immigrants, including professionals and middle-class people, from sub-Saharan Africa, Latin America, Central Asia, Europe, and Southeast Asia, as well as South Asia and the Middle East. Muslim-American immigrants established various businesses meant to cater to the religious needs of the community, from providing Islamic DRESS to serving Islamic FOOD. Expressing one's Sunni Muslim identity came to include not only fasting, praying, giving charity, and going on pilgrimage but also expressing one's belief in God and the prophet Muhammad by placing a bumper sticker on one's car or reading Islamic magazines.

INDIGENOUS SUNNI MUSLIMS

Though the first prominent convert to Sunni Islam in the United States was likely ALEXANDER RUSSELL WEBB, a white diplomat and newspaperman who became Muslim in the late 19th century, most American converts to Sunni Islam were African Americans. At first, AFRICAN-AMERICAN MUSLIMS created their own Islamic movements such as the MOORISH SCIENCE TEMPLE of America, founded in Chicago in 1925. They also joined the non-Sunni Ahmadiyya movement in the 1920s. But by the late 1920s and 1930s, they were also becoming Sunni Muslims. The Islamic Mission of America in New York City and the First Mosque of Pittsburgh led the way.

Influenced at least in part by immigrant Sunni Muslim communities as well as Muslim visitors from Africa and Asia, these black Muslims prostrated their bodies in the direction of Mecca when they prayed. They altered their diets to exclude pork, met for Friday congregational prayers, and, in some cases, such as that of MUHAMMAD EZALDEEN, they began to travel abroad to study the Qur'an or other parts of Islamic tradition. They also began to dress in ways that marked themselves as Muslims. Some women wore a HIJAB, or head scarf, while men often donned a kufi or turban, male forms of head cover.

Despite the presence of Sunni Muslims in the African-American Muslim community, however, it is unlikely that most black Muslims were Sunni in the 1950s. In the years after World War II, the NATION OF ISLAM became the predominant Muslim group among black Americans. But when MALCOLM X, a former leader of the Nation of Islam, formally converted to a Sunni interpretation of Islam in 1964, other African Americans followed. Malcolm X's journeys to Muslim countries in the Middle East and his performance of the pilgrimage to Mecca were the subject of intense press coverage and interest, and some African-American Muslims followed along, mostly figuratively, some physically, his path to Sunni Islam.

However, it was not until 1975 that the majority of Nation of Islam members would become Sunni Muslims. That year, W. D. MOHAMMED, the son of longtime leader

ELIJAH MUHAMMAD, became the leader of the Nation of Islam after the death of his father. He rejected those doctrines and practices that contradicted basic Sunni teachings and encouraged his followers to pray five times a day, observe the dawn-to-dusk fast during the month of Ramadan, and go to Mecca for the hajj, or pilgrimage, if they could afford to do so. Mohammed, who took on the title of imam, or leader, also encouraged followers to read and study the Qur'an and apply it to the concerns of everyday life. Until his death in 2008, he presided over a network of mosques devoted to spreading Sunni Islamic principles in the black community.

As pivotal as Imam Mohammed was to the spread of Sunni Islam among African Americans in the late 20th century, other African-American Sunni leaders became important voices in the Sunni community. University of Michigan professor Sherman Jackson joined the FIQH COUNCIL OF NORTH AMERICA, helping to interpret shari'a for the North American context. JAMIL ABDULLAH AL-AMIN led a network of approximately 20 Sunni mosques that composed the group called Darul Islam. Imam SIRAJ WAHHAJ of New York became especially popular as an African-American Sunni spokesperson among immigrant Muslims in the 1980s.

African-American Sunni Muslims were among the most socially conservative or pious practitioners of Islamic religion in the late 20th century. In addition to wearing the *hijab,* African-American Sunni women sometimes donned a face veil, covering all but their eyes; some wore the burka, covering their entire bodies. Those who wore such dress explained, like many Catholic nuns, that they loved God, and they wore such clothing to honor and obey Allah. Some African-American Sunni women also entered polygamous marriages, saying that the Qur'an permitted a man up to four wives—and adding that there were too few black men available for marriage. Most other African-American Sunni Muslims expressed their religious piety during this period in terms of increased adherence to the pillars of Islamic practice and especially to the reading and studying of the Qur'an.

By the 1970s, there were also a substantial number of white and Hispanic converts to Sunni Islam. While many whites first became attracted to Islam by studying or practicing Sufism, the mystical branch of Islam, many of those Sufis and those who had nothing to do with Sufism began to embrace what they called the deep spirituality and discipline of Sunni Islam. Other whites and Hispanics came to Sunni Islam through marriage, as husbands and particularly wives came to adopt the religion of their immigrant Muslim spouses. These converts or their children assumed positions of leadership in the Sunni Muslim–American community by the 1990s. For example, the white Sunni imam HAMZA YUSUF, who had studied for years under both Sunni and Sufi teachers in the Islamic world, became a national and international spokesperson for a peaceful, pious, and pluralistic form of Sunni Islam, especially after SEPTEMBER 11, 2001.

CONCLUSION

Though religion and its practices and institutions are sometimes assumed to be elements of human culture that do not change over time, the history of religion, including the history of Sunni Islam among Muslim Americans, tells a different story. When Africans were abducted and brought to the Americas in the colonial era and early period of U.S. history, they did not have the economic resources or the political right to establish their own Muslim institutions for learning or worship. In this environment, keeping some of the prayers and occasionally fasting were as much as some Muslims could do. With the voluntary waves of immigration during the late 19th and 20th centuries, both indigenous and immigrant Muslims had the opportunity to build the religious institutions vital to the practice of any religious tradition. They also developed a religious subculture where their Sunni identities could be expressed in all realms of American life, both private and public.

Sameh Mustafa Asal and Edward E. Curtis IV

Further Reading

Ba-Yunus, Ilyas, and Kassim Kone. *Muslims in the United States.* Westport, Conn., and London: Greenwood Press, 2006.

Diouf, Sylviane A. *Servants of Allah: African Muslims Enslaved in the Americas.* New York: New York University Press, 1998.

Hodgson, Marshall G. S. *The Venture of Islam: Conscience and History in a World Civilization,* Vol. 1. Chicago: University of Chicago Press, 1974.

Leonard, Karen. *Muslims in the United States: The State of Research.* New York: Russell Sage Foundation, 2003.

Lovell, Emily. *Islam in the United States: Past and Present.* Alberta, Canada: University of Alberta Press, 1983.

March, Clifton E. *From Black Muslims to Muslims.* London: Scarecrow Press, 1996.

Richardson, E. Allen. *Islamic Cultures in North America: Patterns of Belief and Devotion of Muslims from Asian Countries in the United States and Canada.* New York: Pilgrim Press, 1981.

Smith, Jane. *Islam in America.* New York: Columbia University Press, 1999.

Tablighi Jama'at

The Tablighi Jama'at, or the "Society of Conveying" (the message of Islam), is an Islamic movement that began in British India in the 1920s. The founder of the movement, Mawlana Muhammad Ilyas (1885–1944), a graduate of the religious seminary in Deoband, India, was disillusioned by the traditional educational system and wanted to project Islam in a more substantial and obvious manner. Consequently, he launched the Tablighi Jama'at movement to preach Islam to Muslims who were deviating from what he considered to be the correct teachings of the faith and slacking in their commitment to the religion.

The program of the Tablighi Jama'at was officially launched in 1934 after a meeting of village notables was held in the Indian district of Mewat. Attendees of the 1934 meeting reached the consensus that the propagation and preaching of Islam was the duty of all Muslims and not just the religious elite. This focus on missionary work as the duty of all Muslims continues to be the defining feature of the movement to this day. Initially, the Tablighi Jama'at operated under two limitations: First, its geographical scope was restricted to within the Indian subcontinent and, second, its members limited their preaching to individuals who already identified as Muslim. However, for over half a century now, the Jama'at has become a transnational phenomenon and no longer only aims at helping Muslims strengthen their faith but also tries to convert non-Muslims to Islam.

The Tablighi Jama'at's activities first began in the United States in 1952 when *jama'ats* (small groups of Tablighi workers) journeyed to America. Part of the aim of these initial *jama'ats* was to recruit Muslim Americans to return with them to the Indian subcontinent to be trained as Tablighi missionaries. Members of these early *jama'ats* in the United States stayed in motels and ventured into urban areas in search of mosques receptive to their message. They also targeted university campuses and searched telephone directories in search of Muslim Americans.

Despite their fervor, it was only after the United States passed the IMMIGRATION ACT OF 1965 that a support network was established, an audience for preaching was clearly identified, and the pace of Tablighi activity picked up. Tablighi Jama'at members from the Indian subcontinent established themselves in cities such as DETROIT, CHICAGO, NEW YORK CITY, and PHILADELPHIA, among other places.

In the 1970s, a substantial number of AFRICAN-AMERICAN MUSLIMS became members of the movement. In order to facilitate their initiation into the Jama'at, these new members were advised to travel to the three largest nations on the Indian subcontinent: India, Pakistan, and Bangladesh. They were told that they should spend approximately 40 days in each country, making sure to visit the Nizamuddin center in Delhi, India; the Tablighi Jama'at center in Raiwind, Lahore, Pakistan; and the Jama'at center in Dhaka, Bangladesh.

In the late 1970s and early 1980s, the number of immigrant South Asian Muslims who had been involved in Tablighi efforts increased, and they helped to spread the Tablighi message to CLEVELAND, Indianapolis, Nashville, New Orleans, and BOSTON. In 1980, the first annual international gathering of the Tablighi Jama'at in North America was held in Detroit. Another international gathering was also held in Detroit in 1985.

As many as 10,000 participants attended these meetings, some of the largest gatherings of Muslims in U.S. history. Both were attended by the then *amir,* or leader, of the Tablighi Jama'at, Mawlana In'amul Hasan (1918–95). Hasan established a *shura,* or council of elders, committee of the Jama'at in North America to coordinate Tablighi activities across the continent.

In the middle 1980s, in order to facilitate the smooth running of the organization, the Tablighis divided the United States into eight zones. Each zone is further divided into circles. Within each circle there are cities, and within each city are the mosques that are targeted as bases by the Tablighis. Although the Tablighi Jama'at movement aimed at propagating its message by the indiscriminate use of all mosques as bases, over time, specific institutions have come to be associated with Tablighi activities. A survey published in 1987 showed 25 mosques in the United States affiliated with the Tablighi Jama'at.

One of the defining characteristics of the Tablighi Jama'at is its resistance to bureaucratic organization. Consequently, the Jama'at has not incorporated itself as a legal entity in any state and has not established a physical headquarters, maintained a paid staff, published a newsletter, or even opened a central bank account. Instead, the Jama'at operates as a result of highly motivated and organized volunteers. The volunteers form temporary "delegations" with a leader. These delegations set out to perform a defined task—such as to preach in a certain region of the United States for a certain period of time—and disband after accomplishing their task. They do not leave behind any permanent structure, and if they are foreign visitors, they return to their country of origin, generally in India. By remaining loyal to its central leadership in India and maintaining a focus on personal face-to-face contact, the Tablighi Jama'at has been able to work and expand in a substantial manner in the United States.

Mashal Saif

Further Reading

Masud, Muhammad Khalid, ed. *Travellers in Faith: Studies of the Tablighi Jamaat as a Transnational Islamic Movement for Faith Renewal.* Leiden: Brill, 2000.
Metcalf, Barbara Daly. "New Medinas: The Tablighi Jama'at in America and Europe." In *Making Muslim Space in North America and Europe,* edited by Barbara Daly Metcalf. Berkeley: University of California Press, 1996.

taqwacore

Taqwacore, a community of punk musical artists, is an amalgam of the Islamic term *taqwa* ("God-consciousness") and *core,* the common suffix for punk subgenres, such as hardcore, grindcore, and emocore. Expressing a variety of perspectives, experiences, and relationships to Islam and the West, taqwacore bands often resist categorization as members of a "movement" or "scene" with its own codified ideology. Even the basic definition of taqwacore as "Muslim punk rock" is viewed as inadequate and misleading. Punk music itself emerged in the 1970s in the United Kingdom and the United States, led by such hard-driving, antiestablishment bands as the Sex Pistols and the Clash.

The earliest taqwacore artist, Kourosh Poursalehi of San Antonio, Texas, started his one-man band, Vote Hezbollah, in 2004 at the age of 15. Poursalehi, an Iranian-American who wore a silkscreened image of the Ayatollah Khomeini on his spiked vest, made it clear to journalists that the band's name was a joking response to anti-Islamic bigotry. Rather than attempt to adapt himself to mainstream America, he followed the punk ethos of celebrating alienation and deliberately provoking hostility.

A similar approach was taken by Basim Usmani, a Pakistani-American punk singer in Lowell, Massachusetts, who would attend white-supremacist punk shows while wearing a Pakistani flag on his leather jacket. In 2004, Usmani and Shahjehan Khan named their own taqwacore band the Kominas, for a Punjabi word commonly translated as "bastards" or "low-born."

Influenced in equal parts by punk's shock aesthetic and the militant pose of rap groups such as Public Enemy, the Kominas became known for provocatively titled songs such as "Suicide Bomb the Gap" (2006). One song, "Shari'a Law in the USA" (2006), evokes the Sex Pistols' "Anarchy in the UK" with its title and opening verse: "I am an Islamist, I am the Anti-Christ." While suspected by politically conservative critics of literally espousing violence, the Kominas also courted controversy among the Muslim-American community. The band's first song, "Rumi Was a Homo (But Wahhaj Is a Fag)," released in 2004, was an assault on Islamic homophobia. Specifically targeting Siraj Wahhaj, a New York imam who had allegedly justified the burning of a gay-friendly mosque, the song's lyrics refer to him as a "fag" while portraying Rumi as a model of queer-positive Islam.

Later recruiting two Hindu musicians and describing the band's sound as "Bollywood punk," the Kominas have emphasized their shared experience as South Asian Americans, frequently incorporating Punjabi lyrics and references to Indian films. In 2006, the band helped organize a fund-raiser on behalf of a vandalized Hindu temple in Minnesota. Usmani touches upon his relationship to Pakistan in songs such as "Rabyah," written while he worked as volunteer relief after the 2005 earthquake, and "Par Desi," written after he was attacked by white youths in Boston. The song "9,000 Miles" addresses the estrangements and longings of the South Asian diaspora, while borrowing expressions of this theme from African-American Islamic movements: the lines, "He likes the devil because the devil gives him nothing," "that makes him other than his own self," and "they wanted to go back home, but could not swim 9,000 miles" are taken from a Nation of Islam text. Reference is also made to Noble Drew Ali, who taught that African Americans must recognize their proper birthright as "Moors."

The name of Syrian-American Marwan Kamel's Chicago band, Al-Thawra, translates as "the revolution." Al-Thawra's content finds inspiration from the longtime association of punk with anarchism, most notably with Crass, and *rai* music, which Kamel calls the "punk of the Middle East." This political emphasis is shared by Secret Trial Five, an all-female band from Vancouver named in honor of five Muslim men who had been held in a Canadian prison for six years without any charges, much of it in solitary confinement, based on alleged evidence that neither they nor their lawyers were allowed to see. For singer Sena Hussain, a primary concern over the "Muslim punk" label was the possibility that her work would be mistaken for devotional or conventionally religious music. For Al-Thawra and Secret Trial Five, taqwacore served as a secular response to political injustice, as opposed to "Christian rock" or other attempts to make organized religion seem "hip."

Media confusion over taqwacore's true meaning and purpose became common as the artists found coverage in the *Boston Globe*, London *Guardian, Newsweek*, Toronto *Globe and Mail,* and *Rolling Stone,* with articles falling under titles such as "Slam Dancing for Allah." *Newsweek's* labeling of Washington-based Diacritical as an "Islamic band" in 2007, despite its having only one Muslim member, created tensions within the group that led to its breakup. A classically trained sitar player, Diacritical's Omar Waqar later pursued a solo project, *Sarmust,* to combine his backgrounds of punk rock and Sufi *qawwali* music.

In August 2007, the Kominas, Secret Trial Five, Al-Thawra, Vote Hezbollah, and Omar Waqar toured the northeastern United States in a green school bus. Nicknamed the "Taqwa-tour," the tour concluded at the annual convention of the ISLAMIC SOCIETY OF NORTH AMERICA (ISNA) in Chicago, where the bands signed to take part in an open-mic event. The performance of Secret Trial Five, the first instance of a woman singing onstage at an ISNA event, caused the event's organizers to call Chicago police and shut down the show.

Shortly after the tour, the Kominas were sued for defamation by author Asma Gull Hasan over a satirical reference to her in "Rumi Was a Homo." The song's attacks on both Hasan, who was well known in the Muslim community for her support of President George W. Bush and the war in Iraq, and Siraj Wahhaj, who had been named as a potential unindicted conspirator in the 1993 attack on the World Trade Center, express the twin alienations of many taqwacore punks, marginalized by the political climates of both North America and the Muslim community.

Michael Muhammad Knight

Further Reading

Knight, Michael Muhammad. *The Taqwacores.* New York: Autonomedia, 2004.

Toledo, Ohio

Located in close proximity to Michigan's southern border and on the southwestern edge of Lake Erie, Toledo is home to one of the oldest and most diverse Muslim communities in the state of Ohio. In the early 21st century, the population of Muslims living in the Toledo area numbered above 6,000 people out of a total population of approximately 300,000. Its members, consisting of more than 500 extended families,

represented at least 23 nationalities and included both Sunni and Shi'a Muslims.

Although Muslims lived in various hamlets throughout Ohio since the late 1800s, the first Muslim family—the Shoushers—may have come to Toledo in 1902, emigrating from Lebanon. More families followed, but the Muslim population remained small for many years. Muslims moving to and living in Toledo increased after WORLD WAR I. These Muslims were immigrants from the Middle East, primarily coming from either Syria or Lebanon. The Toledo Muslim community formed its first Muslim society in 1939 and was given an official charter in 1943, but the society eventually disbanded due to a lack of funds. A second organization, the Syrian American Muslim Society, was formed in 1951. The Syrian American Muslim Society hosted the second FEDERATION OF ISLAMIC ASSOCIATIONS IN THE UNITED STATES AND CANADA at a Toledo hotel in 1953 and helped to establish the first Islamic center in Toledo.

As the Muslim population began to grow, so did the need for a communal space for worship. Under the leadership of Abul Jalil Abdo Fakih, the Muslim community purchased land on Bancroft Street to build a mosque. Toledo's Muslim community opened the first mosque in Toledo history in 1954, which at the time was one of only a dozen or so mosques in the United States. After the construction of this mosque, more second-generation Muslims came to settle in Toledo.

The migration of these American-born Muslims to Toledo included an influx of Muslims from nationalities other than Syrian and Lebanese. For instance, in late 1954, the community embraced the first group of Indian Muslims who moved to the city. With the addition of these new non-Middle Eastern Muslims to the Toledo community, the Syrian American Muslim Society and their leader, Yehiya Shousher, decided to change the name of the society to the American Muslim Society.

In *The Arab Moslems in the United States,* a comparative study of Toledo and DETROIT in the 1960s, sociologist Abdo Elkholy was the first person to fully explore the Muslim community of Toledo and record the community's ability to adjust to life in the United States and embrace American culture. Elkholy noted how the Toledo Muslim community lived freely among their non-Muslim neighbors, whereas, at least according to Elkholy, the Muslims of Detroit isolated themselves in ghettos away from their non-Muslim neighbors.

By living among non-Muslims, Elkholy observed, the Toledo community had a better understanding of their neighbors. By maintaining one mosque, Muslims of Toledo also eliminated the tension that often occurs among different sects of Muslims, such as the Shi'a and the Sunni. In addition to residential integration, the Muslims of Toledo operated their businesses among non-Muslim businesses as

A bus that transports children to and from the Islamic School of Greater Toledo waits outside the Islamic Center of Greater Toledo. *(photolibrary)*

well. Intermarriage was also accepted and welcomed by the Muslims of Toledo. Welcoming converts greatly helped the Toledo community to grow in numbers and in their relationship with citizens of Toledo at large. All of these factors earned the Muslims of Toledo a great deal of respect and admiration from non-Muslims.

A curious occupation for the early Muslim community of Toledo was its involvement in the bar and liquor industry in the city. Prior to the 1970s, Muslims worked as merchants in the distribution and sale of alcohol in Toledo. In the late 1950s, Muslims owned 127 of Toledo's 400 bars—nearly 30 percent—along with liquor stores, carryout businesses, and restaurants that served alcohol. Muslims were active in other business ventures as well, but none as well documented as their participation in the alcohol industry of Toledo.

Elkholy believed that Muslim involvement with liquor-related businesses was the result of their Americanization. But this interpretation ignored the fact that temperance, or total abstinence from alcohol, was itself a mainstream American value and had been since the 1820s. If immigrants wished to assimilate into Anglo-American Protestant Christian culture, they may have been as likely to avoid alcohol as to consume or sell it.

Another explanation is that Toledo's Muslims did not identify alcohol-related businesses as sinful until the spread of Islamic religious REVIVALISM in the late 1960s and 1970s.

In the late 1950s, Elkholy thought that the barkeepers likely felt "subconscious religious guilt" over their liquor profiteering, but the proprietors themselves never admitted to feeling guilty about their work. These first- and second-generation Arab immigrants may have been practicing Muslims, but they were not scholars of the SHARI'A, or Islamic law and ethics. Liquor, while denounced by religious scholars, had been a part of Arabs' everyday lives for centuries. In fact, Middle Eastern Muslims had practically invented the distillation of hard alcohol and gave it its name (the English word alcohol is derived from an ARABIC word). Temperance may not have been universally accepted as a central aspect of Muslim-American identity when Elkholy did his interviews in Toledo.

The Toledo Muslim community continued to grow through the 1960s and 1970s to the extent that by 1978 the first mosque was no longer sufficient for the community's needs. The community purchased land in Perrysburg, a suburb in the southwestern section of Toledo, and completed construction of the Islamic Center of Toledo in 1983. The mosque was designed by a Turkish architect, Talat Itil. The Islamic Center was built with two 135-foot minarets, a prayer room able to accommodate 1,000 people, windows featuring verses from the Qur'an and Arabic calligraphy, and a 500-person sermon hall.

Since its creation, the Islamic Center has served as the main center of worship for the Muslim community. However,

550 Tribe of Ishmael

the Islamic Center of Toledo, also known as the Islamic Center of Greater Toledo, was not the only Islamic institution established in the Toledo area. Masjid Saad Foundation was founded by University of Toledo students in 1979, and in 2006, the organization purchased an old church and converted it to a mosque able to fit 1,000 people.

Masjid al-Islam, another Toledo Muslim organization, was originally comprised of NATION OF ISLAM adherents who converted to Sunni Islam. Its members were mainly African-American converts and were led by Imam Ibrahim Abdul-Rahim. Imam Ali Mosque and Masjid Qur'an wa Sunnah were also established as places of worship for Toledo's Muslim population. In 1994, the Toledo Islamic Academy, the first Islamic school founded in Toledo, began to offer classes from preschool to 12th grade, providing students with standard academic classes alongside a religious education including classes on QUR'AN and Muslim history. Besides the Islamic Academy, the University of Toledo, in 1999, established the Imam Khattab Endowed Chair of Islamic Studies.

The 21st-century Muslim community has gained national prestige for its progressive religious outlook. In 2001, the Islamic Center elected the first female president, Cherrefe Kadri, who, with Farooq Aboelzahab, the imam of the Islamic center, has promoted the importance of open-mindedness and independent reasoning in religion. Kadri emphasized interaction with people and good intentions over what she called dogmatic principles as the governing ethos of Islam. She believed that this strategy enabled the community to be seen as part of the entire Toledo community rather than a separate entity unto itself.

The strong bond the Muslim community has developed with its different groups and non-Muslim neighbors was shown in a number of communal events and gatherings. After the al-Qaeda attacks of SEPTEMBER 11, 2001, an interfaith prayer service was scheduled at the Islamic Center to show support for the Muslim community of Toledo. Only a few hundred were expected, but nearly 1,500 people from different religious faiths came to support the Muslim community. Zaid Hummos, who was the president of Masjid Saad, mentioned that in 2006 many non-Muslims in Toledo were taking extra efforts to inform themselves about Islam.

The Muslim community of Toledo has continued to expand over the years. A number of new organizations, such as the United Muslim Association of Toledo, have been established along with Web sites, such as ToledoMuslims.com, to provide information on events and news about the community.

Matthew Long

Further Reading

Elkholy, Abdo A. *The Arab Moslems in the United States.* New Haven, Conn.: College and University Press, 1966.

Khan, Meena. "Islam." In *Religions in Ohio: Profiles of Faith Communities,* edited by Tarunjit Singh Butalia and Dianne P. Small. Athens: Ohio University Press, 2004.

Lampman, Jane. "A Mosque in America's Heartland," *Christian Science Monitor,* 6 September 2007. Available online. URL: http://www.csmonitor.com/2007/0906/p13s01-lire.html. Accessed December 9, 2008.

Yonke, David. "Deep Roots Help Muslims Blend into Community," *The Toledo Blade,* December 2007. Available online. URL: http://www.toledoblade.com/apps/pbcs.dll/article?AID=/20071215/NEWS10/71215001. Accessed February 6, 2009.

Tribe of Ishmael   See ISHMAELITES.

Turkish-American Muslims

The Republic of Turkey was established on October 29, 1923, succeeding the six-century-long Ottoman Empire (1299–1923). Originally established by Turks who migrated from Central Asia to Anatolia and accepted Islam in the 10th century, the Ottoman Empire dominated southeastern Europe, the Middle East, and northern Africa and ultimately became host to some 23 ethnicities. It was ruled primarily by Islamic LAW that was applied to the Muslim subjects of the empire, namely Turks and converts from acquired lands. Modern Turkey was founded upon the collapse of the Ottoman Empire after WORLD WAR I and accepted secular law. It has had a highly homogenous population religiously, with more than 99 percent of Turkish citizens being Muslim.

Immigration to America from the multiethnic Ottoman Empire began much later than that of Europeans and the forced arrival of Africans. Large-scale immigration began only in the late 19th century as a response to the increased labor demand due to industrialization in the United States. From 1860 to 1920, 60,000 to 100,000 Ottoman subjects arrived in the United States. Although no statistics reveal what portion of these Ottomans were Muslim, the majority, given their ethnicities, were not Muslims. Most of these initial Ottoman immigrants were ethnic Armenians and Greeks—both of which were not Muslims—and Arabs, who were not ethnic Turks. Those Ottoman Turks who did immigrate to America probably worked as unskilled laborers at factories in the Midwest and Northeast. Approximately 7,000 Ottoman subjects worked for the Ford Motor Company in DETROIT, MICHIGAN, in the first two decades of the 20th century. While most of these Ottoman subjects would have been ethnic Arabs, there were a sufficient number of ethnic Turks to establish several Turkish communal institutions.

Young single Turkish males who worked for Ford's Highland Park plant, which opened in 1907, established boardinghouses where men could pass their leisure time by playing backgammon or asking one of their literate companions to write a letter back home. By 1924, Turks had established the first of several COFFEEHOUSES in Detroit. During this period, they also supported a Detroit chapter of the Turkish Red Crescent Society, a philanthropic organization that provided aid to Muslims in the United States and in Turkey. Around 1,000 members paid monthly dues of $2 and were required to attend one meeting per year. By 1929, the group owned 538 plots in the Roselawn Cemetery and purchased an additional 200 plots in three nearby CEMETERIES for their members. Detroit's Turkish Muslims also sustained a chapter of the Turkish Orphans' Association, whose purpose was to aid children who had been orphaned during World War I.

According to an Armenian researcher, M. M. Aijian, writing in 1920, Turkish speakers in Chicago were divided along religious, national, and ethnic lines in this era. After World War I, Anatolian, Balkan, and Kurdish speakers of Turkish established enclaves that always included a coffeehouse and sometimes included lodging, restaurants, and pool halls. Aijian also reported that despite Prohibition, he observed Turks drinking beer one Sunday afternoon on Chicago's north side, lustily singing love songs in Turkish to the accompaniment of a small band. One of the first Turkish-American newspapers, *Sedai Vatar,* or Call of the Fatherland, was established in NEW YORK CITY after World War I. In 1933, Turkish New Yorkers established the Turkish Cultural Alliance of New York, later renamed the Federation of Turkish American Associations.

After WORLD WAR II ended in 1945, a small number of Turks immigrated to the United States: 798 Turks came during the 1940s, 3,519 during the 1950s, and 10,142 during the 1960s. These Turks tended to be highly educated medical doctors, engineers, and scientists or students pursuing higher education, a trend that accelerated in the 1970s. By 1990, half of the Turks living in the United States were foreign-born and the average age was 32. By 1996, there were 64,350 Turks living in the United States. Approximately half of these Turks were between the ages of 15 and 34. The 2000 U.S. Census counted 117,575 Americans of Turkish descent.

This more recent generation of Turkish Americans has continued the earlier trend of establishing cultural institutions that linked them with one another and with developments in Turkey. Turkish restaurants and markets have been established across the United States, and Turkish media outlets are available in most cities. Turkish Americans often use satellite dishes to watch Ebru TV, the first Turkish 24-hour television channel broadcast via satellite. Popular print media in the community have included the *Turkish Daily News,* the *Turkish Times,* and *Zaman.* By the 21st century, there were approximately 100 Turkish-American groups, including 70 Turkish Student Associations on university campuses around the country.

Despite the relative financial and social success of Turkish Americans, they have not made a visible impact on U.S. POLITICS. Especially before the 1970s, Turkish-American involvement in American politics was rare. The Turkish invasion of Cyprus in 1974 mobilized many Turks to lobby the U.S. government to change its pro-Greek policies, but their voices were generally drowned out by the much larger and stronger Greek-American community.

Many of the most significant contributions to American society by Turkish Americans have come from secular Muslims. For instance, AHMET ERTEGUN (1923–2006), the leader of Atlantic Records and the cofounder of the Rock and Roll Hall of Fame, became one of the most influential music producers in the United States. Feza Gursey (1921–93) was the J. Willard Gibbs Professor of Physics at Yale University and won the prestigious Oppenheimer Prize and Wigner Medal. Muzafer Sherif (1906–88) was one of the founders of social psychology who helped develop social judgment theory and realistic conflict theory. Tunc Yalman, the artistic director of the Milwaukee Repertory Theater, and Osman Karakas, who received the 1991 National Press Award for best news photography, have been examples of Turkish-American Muslims' contribution to the arts.

Though many Turkish-American Muslims are secular, others are actively engaged in Muslim-American affairs and especially in INTERFAITH MOVEMENTS. The most noteworthy religious contribution of Turkish Americans has been the GÜLEN MOVEMENT, a Turkish Islamic movement created by Fethullah Gülen, who was born in Erzurum, Turkey, in 1941. Gülen, who has inspired millions of Turks around the world to commit or recommit themselves to an Islamic religious life, has lived in the United States since 1999. His vision has inspired many Turkish-American Muslims as well as non-Muslims to community service. The main focus of the movement has been establishing educational centers to serve the general public in increasing intercultural and interreligious dialogue and understanding around the United States.

Eren Tatari

Further Reading

Aijian, M. M. "Mohammedans in the United States." *The Moslem World* 10 (1920): 30–35.

Bilgé, Barbara. "Voluntary Associations in the Old Turkish Community of Metropolitan Detroit." In *Muslim Communities in North America,* edited by Yvonne Y. Haddad and Jane I. Smith, 381–405. Albany: State University of New York Press, 1994.

Kaya, Ilhan. "Turkish-American Immigration History and Identity Formations." *Journal of Muslim Minority Affairs* 24, no. 2 (October 2004): 295–308.

Micallef, Roberta. "Turkish Americans: Performing Identities in a Transnational Setting." *Journal of Muslim Minority Affairs* 24, no. 2 (October 2004): 233–241.

Tyner, McCoy (Alfred, Sulaimon Saud)
(1938–) *jazz pianist*

A legend of the hard bop style of JAZZ, McCoy Tyner is renowned for providing musical support to jazz great John Coltrane as well as for his seminal work as leader of his own ensemble.

Jazz pianist McCoy Tyner was born on December 11, 1938, in PHILADELPHIA, PENNSYLVANIA. Tyner grew up in the same Philadelphia neighborhood as fellow jazz pianists Bobby Timmons and brothers Bud and Richie Powell, as well as bassist Reggie Workman and trumpeter Lee Morgan. Tyner's mother, a beautician, encouraged him to take up the piano. She also allowed the Powell brothers to practice on her piano, since they had none. Tyner's brother Jarvis would earn a degree of notoriety when he emerged as a prominent official in the American Communist Party. While attending West Philadelphia High School, McCoy Tyner jammed with Lee Morgan, Reggie Workman, and other local musicians.

As a teenager, Tyner began to practice Sunni Islam and adopted the name Sulaimon Saud, retaining his birth name professionally. At some point—it is not clear when—he stopped practicing Islam. In 1959, while holding down a factory job, Tyner formed the Jazztet with Art Farmer and Benny Golson. This ensemble was short-lived, but it resulted in the hit recording "Killer Joe" in 1960. Tyner soon received an invitation to join the ensemble of renowned saxophonist John Coltrane and appeared on such classic Coltrane albums as *Coltrane's Sound* (1960), *My Favorite Things* (1961), and *A Love Supreme* (1964).

During this period, Tyner also recorded several albums as a leader, including *Inception* (1962), *Reaching Fourth* (1963), *Today and Tomorrow* (1964), and *McCoy Tyner Plays Ellington* (1965). Additionally, Tyner served as sideman on the albums of fellow musicians Wayne Shorter and his former high school classmate Lee Morgan. Tyner left Coltrane's band in 1965 and was replaced with Coltrane's wife, Alice. He signed with Blue Note Records where he recorded *The Real McCoy* (1967) with former Coltrane bandmate Elvin Jones and *Assante* (1970).

In the 1970s, Tyner began to incorporate strings as well as elements of African, Latin, and Asian music in his performances. These newfound influences resulted in the Grammy-nominated album *Sahara* (1972). Despite such artistic success, the commercial aspects of jazz in the 1970s were such that Tyner spent time as a sideman for soul singers Ike and Tina Turner.

Throughout the 1980s and 1990s, Tyner recorded prolifically, often with the younger generation of jazz players. Several of his recordings were tributes to his former bandleader John Coltrane. In 2002, Tyner was named a Jazz Master by the United States National Endowment for the Arts and, in 2003, received a Heroes Award from the Philadelphia Chapter of the Recording Academy. In 2005, he was granted an honorary doctorate of music from Berklee College of Music in Boston, Massachusetts. The recipient of five Grammy Awards (most recently in 2004 for *Illuminations*), he continued to perform in the 21st century with a big band as well as his trio, featuring bassist Avery Sharpe and drummer Aaron Scott.

Jason E. Housley

Further Reading
Cook, Richard, and Brian Morton. *The Penguin Guide to Jazz Recordings.* London: Penguin, 2006.

Yanow, Scott. *Jazz on Record: The First Sixty Years.* San Francisco: Backbeat Books, 2003.

United States foreign relations

Muslim Americans have been involved in the foreign policy of the United States since the beginning of the republic. From the entanglement of an AFRICAN-AMERICAN MUSLIM SLAVE in U.S. conflicts with the Barbary pirates in the early 19th century to the targeting of Muslim Americans as part of the "war on terror" launched by President George W. Bush after SEPTEMBER 11, 2001, Muslim Americans have played both highly visible and largely unsung roles in the story of U.S. relationships with foreign nations and powers. A persistent theme in this history has been Muslim-American vulnerability to accusations of disloyalty to the United States, particularly in U.S. relations with Muslim countries. Despite their presence in North America since the 16th century, Muslim Americans have often been viewed, like Japanese, Roman Catholics, and other nonwhite and non-Protestant Christian groups, as foreign and thus potentially disloyal.

Though some Muslim Americans have opposed various foreign policy positions of the U.S. government, particularly the U.S. role in the Vietnam War, pro-Israel policies after 1967, and the more recent 2003 war in Iraq, many Muslim Americans also have been ardent supporters of U.S. policy abroad. Some have been staunchly opposed to communism, taking the side of the United States in its cold war with the Soviet Union. Still other Muslim Americans have become members of the foreign service of the United States. No matter what their views of U.S. involvement abroad, thousands of Muslim Americans have also joined the U.S. military, willingly sacrificing their lives to implement the foreign policy of the government.

LATE EIGHTEENTH TO
EARLY TWENTIETH CENTURY

The first military action conducted by the United States after the American Revolution (1775–83) was against the Barbary states, small semiautonomous Muslim countries in North Africa that were of little danger to France and England but regularly captured the naval vessels of weaker nations such as the United States in order to ransom the ships' cargo crews. From 1785 to 1815, Algiers, Tripoli, Morocco, and Tunis captured 35 American ships and took more than 700 sailors captive. From 1801 to 1805, President Thomas Jefferson prosecuted a successful naval war against Tripoli, but even after this victory, American ships and sailors continued to be captured and ransomed.

The plight of the captives caused anxiety in the United States—partly because their captivity invited comparison with the million African-American human beings who were forcibly enslaved in the country at the time. But insult was added to injury when some of the captured sailors "turned Turk." That is, they converted to Islam. Five of the 300 captives from the U.S.S. *Philadelphia*, which ran aground outside of Tripoli in 1803, became Muslims, acts many Americans interpreted as "disgracing the flag." And sometime between 1810 and 1813, a sailor named Walker from Baltimore abandoned "his country, his family, and religion" to live with the Muslim "horde of barbarians," according to a U.S. diplomat in Algiers. The conversion of Americans to Islam, in other words, was seen in this important formative period as an act of political disloyalty, religious heresy, and sheer madness.

To be sure, however, the foreign policy of the young republic was not always bellicose toward the Muslim world, as exemplified by the strange case of ABDUL RAHMAN IBRAHIMA, a Muslim slave who was the beneficiary of the U.S. attempts to make peace, one way or another, with the Barbary states. Ibrahima, who had claimed he was a Moroccan, had written in ARABIC to the leader of Morocco in the 1820s asking for help in securing his freedom. His letter made its way from a U.S. senator to a U.S. diplomat in Tangier and finally to the desk of Secretary of State Henry Clay and President John Quincy Adams, who decided to support the request. Remarkably, Clay offered "the Moor" transportation back to Africa if his owner would free him. Ibrahima did return to Africa, but to the western part of Africa from which American slaves had come, not to the North African Barbary coast.

Ibrahima's case and the cases of the converted sailors were unusual in this period. The direct involvement of Muslim Americans in U.S. foreign relations in the 19th century was limited. Since most Muslims in the country were

African-American Muslim slaves, they had little chance to influence the outcomes of American relations with the rest of the world. Policy makers did not concern themselves with persons who were neither citizens nor, according to many white Americans at the time, even full human beings.

The most prominent Muslim-American voice on foreign affairs of the late 19th and early 20th centuries was, instead, a white convert. ALEXANDER RUSSELL WEBB, the former U.S. consul to the Philippines who converted to Islam in 1888, spoke on behalf of Islam at the World Parliament of Religions held at the COLUMBIAN EXPOSITION OF 1893 in CHICAGO, where he advocated strong relationships among the Muslim nations and the United States. With temporary financial support from some South Asian Muslims, he also established a Muslim mission in Manhattan and a Muslim-American journal in 1893. As a pamphleteer, Webb defended the (Muslim) Ottoman Empire's role in the Armenian massacres and attempted to convince his readers that the burgeoning movement to defend Armenians against the Ottoman Empire was "anti-American." In addition to receiving some financial support from the Ottoman Empire, Webb was appointed an honorary consul for Ottoman Sultan Abdul Hamid II's government in 1901.

EARLY MUSLIM-AMERICAN OPPOSITION TO ZIONISM

If there has been one issue on which the vast majority of Muslim Americans have consistently criticized U.S. foreign policy, it has been the Israeli-Palestinian conflict. Opposition to Zionism, the late 19th- and 20th-century political movement to establish a Jewish national home in Palestine, has deep roots among Muslim Americans. In 1917, British foreign secretary Arthur Balfour expressed the commitment of the British government, which was the colonial master of Palestine at the time, to establish a national home for Jews there. News of this declaration generated opposition in many quarters, especially among Arab communities. Arab-American leaders, most of whom were Christian in this period, attempted to convince the U.S. government to oppose the creation of a Jewish state in Palestine. They were not alone—some Reform Jewish Americans, concerned that their citizenship rights in the United States would be threatened by the creation of a Jewish state in the Middle East, also registered their opposition to Zionism during this time.

On December 8, 1917, the Palestine Antizionism Society and the Ramallah Young Men's Society staged a demonstration that drew 500 protesters to the Bossert Hotel in Brooklyn, New York. The organizers issued a resolution that (1) objected to the formation of any nation "based on religious principles, by a minority [of Jews], contrary to the principles of the majority [of Muslim and Christian Arabs]"; (2) warned that Jewish immigrants, who were largely European, would

use their wealth to buy up Palestinian lands and homes; and (3) stated that Jewish immigration would force an "emigration of the rightful inhabitants" of Palestine. The leaders of this movement appealed directly to Secretary of State Robert Lansing and President Woodrow Wilson and, in 1919, following WORLD WAR I, sent a delegation to debate the fate of the Middle East at the Paris Peace Conference.

Throughout the 1920s and into the 1930s, Arab Americans continued their organized and sometimes high-profile opposition to Zionism. The Palestine Antizionism Society, which became the Palestine National League (PNL), published a book entitled *The Case against Zionism* in 1921. In 1922, movement leader Fuad Shatara faced off against representatives of the American Zionist Organization at a hearing of the Committee on Foreign Affairs in the House of Representatives. As violent disturbances between Palestinian Arabs and the growing number of Jews in Palestine occurred in 1929, Arab-American activists also debated American Zionists in some of America's most prestigious periodicals, including the *Nation* and *Current History*. On September 9, 1929, the Young Men's Moslem Association, an organization led by Abd M. Kateeb, joined the PNL and the New Syria Party to demand self-determination for Palestinians in a meeting with Secretary of State Henry L. Stimson.

Though such efforts would continue, ARAB-AMERICAN MUSLIMS and Christians failed to prevent the creation of the State of Israel in 1948. U.S. secretary of state George Marshall was swayed by the arguments that the establishment of a Jewish state was contrary to U.S. interests, but President Harry S. Truman overruled him and immediately recognized the independence of Israel. For Muslims and Arabs, both in the United States and abroad, these events were what they called a "catastrophe," a disaster that they would fight for the rest of the 20th century.

BLACK MUSLIMS BETWEEN WORLD WAR I AND WORLD WAR II

As African Americans converted to various forms of Islam in the 1920s and 1930s, they identified their religious and political solidarity with Muslims and other persons under colonial rule in Africa and Asia. Nearly all African-American social movements of the time, but especially those that stressed either communist leanings or sympathies for non-Western countries, were viewed as potentially subversive and tracked carefully by the Federal Bureau of Investigation (FBI). On the eve of WORLD WAR II, as the United States and Empire of Japan prepared for war, AFRICAN-AMERICAN MUSLIMS, like many African Americans, were critical of U.S. claims to be fighting for freedom abroad when they were still discriminated against at home. Some African-American Muslims, like other black Americans, defended the Empire of Japan's

United States foreign relations 555

expansion in Asia, identifying with the Japanese as fellow people of color.

Sympathy for the Japanese among working-class and middle-class African Americans had been building since Japan defeated Russia in 1905. In the midst of the Great Depression, black Muslims, black Jews, advocates of black emigration to Africa, and black advocates for pan-Asian solidarity openly expressed sympathies for a fellow "colored" nation, and a Japanese national, Major Satokata Takahashi, created a "Development of Our Own" group to organize and consolidate such sentiments in DETROIT, Chicago, and St. Louis.

Various African-American leaders incorporated Takahashi's ideas into their own political platforms. In 1932, Mittie Maud Lena Gordon, a former member of Marcus Garvey's Universal Negro Improvement Association, established the Peace Movement of Ethiopia (PME), which advocated the repatriation of black Americans to Africa while also defending the war objectives of Japan. The organization's stationery included an Islamic star and a crescent, and in a June 14, 1942, meeting, Gordon said that the PME was affiliated with "Islam." Another Chicago-based organization established in 1932 with anticolonial, pro-Japanese leanings was the Pacific Movement of the Eastern World (PMEW), which sought help from the Japanese to advance African-American interests. Led from 1934 to 1940 by Rev. David D. Ervin, a Holiness pastor of the Triumph, the Church of the New Age, the PMEW sometimes advocated a Japanese invasion of the United States in order to secure African-American equality, while at other times put forward the idea of blacks migrating to Japan.

As the expectation spread among thousands of African Americans that the Empire of Japan would save them from American racism in the early 1940s, the U.S. government began a systematic roundup of the black leaders thought responsible for such feelings. Among the 25 leaders arrested for sedition was ELIJAH MUHAMMAD, the leader of the Nation of Islam. Acquitted of the sedition charge, Muhammad was convicted for refusing to register for the military draft. The incident foreshadowed a pattern of African-American Muslim protest that would emerge after World War II: While black Americans would seldom engage in any truly treasonous activity against the United States, they would use their association with foreign powers and "foreign" traditions like Islam to protest the domestic and foreign policies of the U.S. government toward people of color.

AFTER WORLD WAR II

As the United States emerged as the world's preeminent military and political power after 1945, Muslim Americans expressed a wide array of views toward U.S. foreign policy. The community was now so diverse that it was unlikely to agree about U.S. involvement in and often control over so many countries and regions. Instead, Muslim-American concerns often echoed the interests of the racial, ethnic, or national group with which they felt solidarity. Most Albanian Muslim Americans, for example, opposed the post–World War II Communist takeover of their Muslim-majority country in Southeastern Europe. After 1945, many sought refuge in the United States, which they viewed as a land of political and religious freedom. In Detroit and their other ethnically Albanian enclaves, these Muslim Americans were fierce proponents of the cold war with the Soviet Union, hoping one day to free their country from the Soviet sphere of influence.

While Arab-American Muslims similarly viewed the United States as a land of freedom and opportunity, they also lobbied for the United States to change its policies toward Israel and Palestine. The Palestinian refugee crisis created by the Arab-Israeli war of 1948 elicited a strong desire among Arab Americans to aid the refugees. The FEDERATION OF ISLAMIC ASSOCIATIONS IN THE UNITED STATES AND CANADA (FIA) contributed to this effort, donating money for but also raising awareness about the plight of Palestinians. Though the FIA and other organizations hoped for a change in U.S. policy toward Israel, they often advocated for their position using the "soft language" of U.S. interests. As early opponents of Zionism had stated, they said, it was in the best interest of the United States to support Palestinian rights.

After World War II, it was not immigrant but indigenous Muslims who fiercely challenged the morality of U.S. foreign policy. And the focus of their opposition was not U.S. policy toward the Soviet Union but policy toward the newly independent states of Asia and Africa. As the imperial powers of France, Great Britain, the Netherlands, Belgium, the United States, Italy, and others began to recognize the political independence of their colonies in Latin America, Asia, and Africa after World War II, these colonial powers simultaneously attempted to retain indirect control over political and economic affairs in the newly independent states. As the cold war developed alongside this new form of colonialism, the Soviet Union and United States also attempted to draw these countries into their respective spheres of influence and directly interfered in electoral politics to ensure the outcomes they desired.

In the midst of this struggle for power in what came to be called the "Third World," the most public Muslim-American criticism of U.S. foreign policy came from members of the NATION OF ISLAM (NOI). According to the historian Penny Von Eschen in her book *Race against Empire,* the NOI "permitted a space—for the most part unthinkable in the Cold War era—for an anti-American critique of the Cold War." NOI leader Elijah Muhammad and his spokesperson, MALCOLM X, lauded the rise of independent Muslim-majority nations and sought to become allies of Third-World Muslim leaders, especially Gamal Abdel Nasser, the president of Egypt who had successfully faced down the invasion of the British, French, and Israelis during the Suez crisis of 1956. Malcolm X had recently praised the 1955 Afro-Asian Conference of developing countries in Bandung, Indonesia, as a turning point in the affairs of the world, as people of color vowed to reject the political and mental control of outsiders. Nasser would later sponsor the education of Elijah Muhammad's son Akbar Muhammad at the University of al-Azhar in Cairo, and in 1958 cabled Elijah Muhammad extending his "best wishes to our brothers of Africa and Asia living in the West."

The NOI continued its role as the Muslim voice of dissent against U.S. foreign policy in the 1960s as NOI member and heavyweight boxing champion MUHAMMAD ALI became America's most recognizable symbol of protest against the VIETNAM WAR. In 1966, at the height of the military conflict in Vietnam, Ali proclaimed he was willing to give up his boxing crown and go to jail rather than be inducted into the UNITED STATES MILITARY. He said that he was a conscientious objector whose religion prohibited the killing of innocents. Casting the Vietnam War as a racist and immoral conflict, Ali also stated that the U.S. participation was hypocritical: Quipping that "no Vietcong ever called me nigger," Ali pointed out the irony of the United States defending freedom abroad when it still had its own problems with racial equality at home. In 1967, he was convicted of draft evasion and stripped of his boxing title, though a 1971 Supreme Court decision, *CLAY, A/K/A ALI V. UNITED STATES*, overturned the decision and allowed Ali to return to the boxing ring.

U.S. MIDDLE EAST POLICY AFTER 1967

The 1967 victory of Israel in the Six-Day War over its Arab neighbors Jordan, Syria, and Egypt amplified pro-Palestinian feelings among most Muslims in the world, including in the United States. As a result of the Arab defeat, Jordan lost control of the holy places in the Old City of Jerusalem, and a new wave of Palestinian refugees fanned out across the Middle East, and when possible, also settled in the United States and Europe. Palestinians who remained in the West Bank came under what by 2010 was the longest-lasting military occupation of the 20th and 21st centuries. In the wake of the embarrassing defeat in 1967, Egyptian president Nasser's blustery rhetoric seemed hollow, and many Muslims and Arabs questioned about what had gone wrong. An increasing number of Arabs and Muslims felt that they could no longer rely on their elected or appointed leaders to advance the interests of Palestinians and began to assume more individual responsibility for the Palestinian struggle for self-determination.

In the United States, though many Muslim Americans would become more politically organized in the 1990s around

foreign policy issues such as the BOSNIAN WAR of 1992 and Russian repression in the region of Chechnya, it was nonreligious Arab-American organizations that took the lead in attempting to improve the image of Arabs in the United States. In late 1967 and early 1968, the Arab American University Graduates, a newly formed public affairs group that included Muslims but was not organized around Islamic concerns, sought to influence public opinion about Arab affairs by generating scholarship and awareness about the Middle East. In 1972, the National Association of Arab Americans began to lobby Congress directly on foreign affairs, endorsing initiatives such as the Camp David Accords, a peace treaty signed by Egypt and Israel in 1978.

That endorsement made clear that, at times, the interests of the U.S. government and some Muslim Americans converged. In Afghanistan, for example, the United States took an active but covert role in supporting the Afghan resistance against the Soviet invasion in 1979, a move that pleased at least some, if not many, Muslim Americans. Joining Saudi Arabia, and cooperating with Pakistan, Egypt, and even Israel, the United States funded Afghan militias in their struggle to expel the Soviet army. ROBERT DICKSON CRANE, a white American convert to Islam and former Nixon administration official, was appointed U.S. ambassador to the United Arab Emirates in 1981 to strengthen the clandestine alliance supporting the Afghan resistance. Secretary of State Alexander Haig's opposition to Crane's appointment, however, led to Crane's dismissal within the year.

Crane's quick departure was symbolic of the lack of access Muslim Americans would have in the 1980s and 1990s to the White House and its policies toward nations with significant Muslim populations. When Israel invaded Lebanon in 1982, Muslim and Arab Americans lobbied the Congress to restrict the use of U.S.-made armaments in what was, according to most experts in international law, an illegal invasion of a sovereign country. Though Senator Mark Hatfield and a few other legislators, including Arab-American Christians Nick Jo Rahall (D-W.Va.) and Mary Rose Oakar (D-Ohio), also protested the use of American weapons, the vast majority of the Congress defended Israel's policy. The United States became further entangled in Lebanon in 1982 when President Ronald Reagan sent a peacekeeping force there to oversee the evacuation of the Palestine Liberation Organization from Beirut. Though U.S. forces were theoretically neutral in the war, they eventually became mired in the conflict, suffered significant casualties, and were completely withdrawn by 1984.

The United States' next overt military operation in the Middle East was the Gulf War of 1991. After Iraqi president Saddam Hussein invaded Kuwait in 1990, President George H. W. Bush led an international coalition to expel the Iraqi army from Kuwait. The Muslim Public Affairs

Committee (MPAC), founded in 1988 in Los Angeles, condemned the Iraqi invasion of Kuwait but simultaneously called for the withdrawal of U.S. troops from the region. Though the majority of Muslim Americans favored nonmilitary solutions to this conflict, a vocal minority of Muslim Americans, including Muslim-American leader W. D. Mohammed, supported the war. Many Shi'a Muslim Americans with Iraqi roots also spoke out in favor of the removal of the Iraqi army from Kuwait and favored the overthrow of Hussein's regime.

When Israel and the Palestine Liberation Organization signed the Oslo Accords on the White House lawn in 1993, some Muslim Americans expressed their reservations, but most Muslim-American leaders and the American Muslim Council (AMC), a prominent lobbying group formed in 1990, endorsed the peace agreement. They later criticized Israel for refusing to withdraw its military forces from the Palestinian territories. The AMC was equally critical of nominally Muslim regimes that did not live up to the ideals of Islam. So, after 1991, when the Taliban, the ruling government of Afghanistan, began to restrict female access to education and female participation in the workplace, the AMC condemned such activities as un-Islamic.

In the 1990s, the AMC and MPAC joined nearly every other Muslim-American public affairs group, including the African-American followers of W. D. Mohammed, in lobbying the U.S. government to recognize Palestinian claims to Jerusalem. Their motivation was at once religious and political in nature. In a 1999 issue of *Islamic Horizons,* Islamic Society of North America (ISNA) president Muzammil H. Siddiqi outlined the religious centrality of Jerusalem's Dome of the Rock to Muslims everywhere. Noting that it is considered the third holiest site in Islam, Siddiqi explained that it is from this place that the prophet Muhammad is believed to have ascended into the heavens during the *mi'raj,* or Night Journey.

On October 29, 2000, approximately 10,000 Muslim Americans and their allies converged on Washington's Lafayette Park to support the claims of Palestinians to Jerusalem. The event was cosponsored by more than 20 Muslim- and Arab-American organizations. Then, on April 20, 2002, in what was the largest pro-Palestinian rally ever held in the United States, approximately 50,000 Arab and Muslim Americans protested the ongoing Israeli occupation of the Palestinian territories. Though these were significant political watersheds for Muslim Americans, the protests did not result in any substantive changes in U.S. policy toward the Israeli-Palestinian conflict.

THE WAR ON TERROR

In the presidential election of 2000, while the majority of African-American Muslims, like African Americans more generally, voted for Democratic candidate Al Gore, most Arab- and South Asian–American Muslims favored Republican George W. Bush. Some were attracted to Bush because he was a social conservative and had criticized the use of secret evidence in the prosecution of terror-related cases. Some also applauded his criticism of the Clinton administration's frequent use of the military to engage in "nation-building."

The Bush administration's response to the al-Qaeda attacks of September 11, 2001, however, disappointed those Muslim-American voters, as Bush embraced the very policies he had criticized before. In addition to relying on military intervention and secret evidence, Bush's "war on terror" included extraordinary rendition (that is, the transfer of detainees from U.S. custody to the custody of other governments) and the suspension of habeas corpus for enemy combatants (that is, detainees were not allowed to challenge their detention in a court of law).

While Muslim Americans were overwhelmingly in favor of apprehending and punishing the 9/11 attackers, they were split on the question of how much force should be used against the Taliban government of Afghanistan, which provided haven for al-Qaeda. Muslim Americans were also concerned about President Bush's framing of the war on terror as a "crusade," a good-versus-evil campaign in which countries were either "with us or against us." As the scope of the war on terror expanded, Muslim Americans became overwhelmingly critical of U.S. policy. In 2003, the United States invaded Iraq and overthrew the government of Saddam Hussein. According to one poll, only 13 percent of Muslim Americans initially supported the Iraq War. Like many non-Muslim Americans, most Muslims did not believe that the Bush administration had established a link between Hussein's regime and al-Qaeda, and they rejected the idea that the Iraq War was a legitimate part of the war on terror. A 2007 Pew poll found that 71 percent of Muslim Americans surveyed said that they did not believe the war on terror was a genuine effort to reduce terrorism.

CONCLUSION

Muslim Americans have long been central participants in the foreign relations of the United States. They have been, alternately, vocal opponents and loyal supporters of U.S. foreign policy. After the attacks of September 11, 2001, some critics of Muslim Americans, repeating old stereotypes, said that Muslims were a dangerous and potentially disloyal force inside the country that needed to be watched. Such overt prejudice, which echoed earlier views about German Americans during World War I and Japanese Americans during World War II, ignored the history of Muslims in America. That history showed that while Muslims have often questioned, deeply and sincerely, the foreign policy of the United States, all but a

As part of its public diplomacy campaign after the terrorist attacks of September 11, 2001, the U.S. government sought to publicize the relative freedom and success of Muslims in America. In 2002, a woman in Kuala Lumpur, Malaysia, reviewed an advertisement in a local publication that was part of the campaign.   *(Zainal ABD Halim/Reuters/Landov)*

few have sought to use the means that the U.S. Constitution provides to change the policies of the country.

Edward E. Curtis IV

Further Reading

Abd-Allah, Umar F. *A Muslim in Victorian America: The Life of Alexander Russell Webb.* New York: Oxford University Press, 2006.

Allen, Ernst, Jr. "When Japan Was 'Champion of the Darker Races': Satokata Takahashi and the Flowering of Black Messianic Nationalism." *Black Scholar* 24 (Winter 1994): 23–46.

Allison, Robert J. *The Crescent Obscured: The United States and the Muslim World, 1776–1815.* Chicago: University of Chicago Press, 1995.

Curtis, Edward E., IV. "Islamism and Its African American Critics: Black Muslims in the Era of the Arab Cold War." In *Religion and Politics in the Contemporary United States,* edited by R. Marie Griffith and Melani McAlister, 157–183. Baltimore: Johns Hopkins University Press, 2008.

———. *Muslims in America.* New York: Oxford University Press, 2009.

Davidson, Lawrence. "Debating Palestine: Arab-American Challenges to Zionism, 1917–1932." In *Arabs in America: Building a New Future,* edited by Michael W. Suleiman, 227–240. Philadelphia: Temple University Press, 1999.

Nimer, Mohamed. *The North American Muslim Resource Guide: Muslim Community Life in the United States and Canada.* New York: Routledge, 2002.

Orfalea, Gregory. *The Arab Americans: A History.* Northampton, Mass.: Olive Branch Press, 2006.

Von Eschen, Penny M. *Race against Empire: Black Americans and Anticolonialism, 1937–1957.* Ithaca, N.Y.: Cornell University Press, 1997.

Dusé Mohamed Ali
"Awakening of Islam" (1922)

Writer and activist Dusé Mohamed Ali (1866–1945) was an intellectual who believed that racial and ethnic minorities in the West should take an active interest in Western foreign policy toward the "colored world," which included Asia, Africa, and Latin America. The founder in 1912 of the London-based African Times and Orient Review, *a monthly journal that sought to articulate the "aims, desires, and intentions of the Black, Brown, and Yellow races," Ali was an Egyptian-born Muslim who immigrated at an early age to Great Britain, where he received an English-language education. In 1921, he moved to New York and became a foreign affairs columnist for the* Negro World, *the official newspaper of the Universal Negro Improvement Association (UNIA). Both echoing and shaping UNIA leader Marcus Garvey's call for the unity of all colonized people against their Western oppressors, Ali furthered the idea, already beginning to grow among black Americans, that*

Islamic religion and Muslim nations were black people's natural allies in the struggle for freedom and equality. Ali also expressed the idea, popular among many Muslim Americans throughout the 20th century, that the West should adopt a friendlier foreign policy toward Muslim nations. In this 1922 Negro World *column on the "awakening of Islam," Ali criticized the attempts of the West to carve up Turkey after the defeat of the Ottoman Empire in World War I in addition to decrying other Western geopolitical schemes to control the rest of the world.*

For over three hundred years the Turks have been fighting a defensive battle against aggressive Christianity and they have not progressed because they have never had time to set their house in order. Yet, when and where they had the opportunity, the Turks have shown themselves capable administrators for they not only succeeded in maintaining peace in the Balkans during their period of overlordship, but they also managed to establish a condition of order among the contending Christian factions in Jerusalem who were ready to show their Christ-like attributes by their wanton and bloody rioting about the Church of the Holy Sepulchre at Eastertide and but for the efforts of the Turkish soldiery, these upholders of the cross would have turned the Holy City into a veritable shambles.

Having observed the injustice which has been meted out to Turkey, first by Czarist Russia and then by Great Britain after the Crimean War, and subsequently by Austria, Italy and the Balkan States, the Muslim world realized that commercial Christendom with the assistance of its governments meant to humiliate Turkey and seize all those rich lands in Asia Minor which were ripe for exploitation and which were held by the despised Turk. It was furthermore intended by the "Great Powers" to wipe out Islam, even as Judaism had been wiped out by Titus, making of the Muslim a wanderer on the face of the earth, even as was the case of the Jews. Now the European Christian has never appeared to realize that . . . the degradation of Turkey meant the humiliation of the Muslims throughout the world. It is direct opposition to Islam to assume that it is aggressive. On the contrary, the Muslim world is specifically enjoined by our Prophet to be on the defensive rather than the offensive.

Turkey, after her early conquest of Europe under the first Sultan, ending with the reign of

Sulieman the Magnificent [in 1566], never was the offender. She has been on the defensive ever since that distant day when she was driven back from the gates of Vienna.

Meanwhile Muslims noted the unfriendly attitude of Great Britain which began with the attacks made by Mr. W. E. Gladstone [British Prime Minister] on Abdul Hamid [Ottoman Sultan]; the Bulgarian assumption of autonomy backed by Russia; Britain and the great powers; the seizure of Tunis by France in 1881; that of Egypt by England in 1882; the unwarranted occupation of Mussawa and other towns on the Red Sea littoral by Italy and France, which formed part of the Turkish Empire, by reason of the fact that, although nominally Egyptian territory, the late Khedive, Ismail, was, after all, only a vassal to the Sultan of Turkey.

Equatorial Africa was handed over to the ruthlessness of Belgium and its Red King, and Austria decided to take a hand in the game of spoliation by annexing Bosnia and Herzegovina. England then arrived at an understanding with France which resulted in . . . the establishment of a French protectorate over Morocco—the Riff being assigned to Spain—and the deposition of its sultan, and the former power, after privily aiding the young Turks in their revolution and the dethronement of [Ottoman Sultan] Abdul Hamid, shed a benevolent smile upon an intriguing Russia, who engineered the first Balkan war immediately after Turkey's unsuccessful effort to save Tripoli from the powers of Italy.

The first Balkan war having materialized, although Sir Edward Grey had previously assured the late Kamel Pasha, Turkey's Grand Vizier, that the powers would see to it that Bulgaria should not be allowed to disturb the peace of the Balkans; England's Minister for Foreign Affairs declared that whatever the result of the war, the status quo ante bellum would be maintained. This was because the powers thought Turkey strong enough to defeat the Balkan confederation. When, however, Turkey was beaten by the Balkan States with the covert assistance of Russia, the treaty of London was made which deprived Turkey of her possessions in Thrace and Macedonia. And the Turkish-European line was drawn between Enos and Midia. Russia, finding that Ferdinand of Bulgaria had Constantinople within his grasp, demanded that the capital of Islam should be handed over to the Muscovite; but Ferdinand having objected,

Russia immediately set Serbia and Greece upon Bulgaria and the second Balkan war was put into operation, resulting in the defeat of Bulgaria, the reoccupation of Adrianople by Turkey and the treaty of Bucharest, which restored a portion of Thrace and Macedonia to Turkey.

The great war [World War I (1914–18)] followed quickly upon the heels of the Balkan imbroglio, and Russia, who still hankered after Constantinople, by bombarding several Turkish Black Sea towns with her Black Sea Fleet, brought Turkey into the war because of her reprisals. The terms of the unjust treaty of Sevres is fresh in the minds of all those interested in this question. The Muslims of the world have become dissatisfied with the treatment Islam has received at the hands of the "Big Four" [United States, United Kingdom, France, and Italy]. It has discovered that if it does not "hang together" it must "hang separately," and the Indian Hindu, reaching out for a much-advertised self-determination, joined hands with the Indian Muslim in his efforts to restore to Turkey a fair share of those possessions which were wrested from her.

There are 500,000,000 Asiatic and Negro Muslims in the world. These Muslims have become tired of European aggression. They mean to be up and doing in defense of their religious freedom and the Khalifate [the institution, located in Istanbul, in nominal control of the Sunni Muslim world]. Turkey is the Khalifate and the Khalifate is Turkey. Muslims are not on the offensive; they are on the defensive. If, however, Britain shall continue her anti-Muslim and anti-Turkish policy, so much the worse for the British Empire, for the unstemmed march of Islamic conversion is reaching out to the four corners of the earth. Even leading Englishmen and Englishwomen have embraced the Faith in "Christian England."

Source: Dusé Mohamed Ali. "Foreign Affairs: Awakening of Islam," *Negro World,* 12, no. 7 (April 1, 1922): 4–5.

United States military

From the American Revolution to the war on terror, Muslims have fought in almost every conflict involving the United States military. By the early 21st century, there were thousands of Muslim-American men and women serving in the nation's armed forces. Their sacrifices for a country so often seen in the Islamic world as anti-Muslim—at least during the first decade of the 21st century—has been symbolically important. In an age characterized by military actions against Muslim-majority nations, Muslim-American soldiers have received recognition that was absent for much of U.S. military history.

AMERICAN REVOLUTION

At least four Americans who may have been Muslim served in the American Revolution (1775–83): Bampett Muhamed; Yusuf Ben Ali, whose slave name was Joseph Benhaley; Salem Poor; and Peter Salem, whose slave name was Peter Buckminster. Muhamed, who was a corporal by rank, served from 1775 to 1783 in Virginia, while Ali's record is unclear.

U.S. postage stamps have commemorated both Salem and Poor, whose Muslim identities are less certain. Peter Salem, freed by his master, may have fired the shot at the Battle of Bunker Hill that killed British major John Pitcairn on June 17, 1775. Salem reenlisted in the Continental Army in 1776 and served at the Battles of Saratoga and Stony Point. He died at Framingham, Massachusetts, in 1816. Salem Poor, with whom Peter Salem has sometimes been confused, purchased his freedom in 1769 and enlisted in 1775. He also fought at Bunker Hill, where he distinguished himself on the field. Subsequently, officers penned a commendation describing him as an "excellent" and "experienced" officer, concluding that "in the Person of this Negro Centers a Brave & gallant Soldier."

Turning to records of the War of 1812, three men with Muslim last names can be identified from enlistment records. These were Bilali Muhammad, or BILALI OF SAPELO ISLAND, Jacob Amin, and John Hamin, who served as a corporal in the Fourth Company of the Virginia Militia. Bilali Muhammad was an overseer of other slaves on Sapelo Island, where he reportedly led a group of them ready to defend the GEORGIA SEACOAST against British invasion.

Much of the research on Muslims in the military depends on identifying Muslim last names. This does not guarantee that the bearer was a Muslim, since some may have converted to Christianity or have had no religious beliefs. Similarly, those with Muslim first and last names cannot automatically be taken to be Muslim, although a Muslim identity is highly likely. In the case of the name Muhammad or Ali, the likelihood of Christian rather than Muslim identity dramatically diminishes.

CIVIL WAR ERA

In 1856, Hajji Ali (ca. 1828–1903) was recruited from the Ottoman Empire by the U.S. government to drive camels for the U.S. Army. He arrived on the USS *Supply* and worked with the U.S. Camel Corps until it was disbanded in 1864. The army imported 60 camels to use in the arid Southwest. Ali died in 1902, having acquired U.S. citizenship in 1880. He was also known as Hi Jolly and was perhaps a convert to Islam from a Greek Christian family.

According to Amir N. Muhammad's *Muslim Veterans of American Wars* (2007), as many as 292 Muslim last names appear in troop listings for the Civil War (1861–65). Of these, 10 fought in the Confederate Army, and four served in the racially segregated Union Army. In the Union Army, the highest-ranked Muslim officer was Captain Moses Osman, who served with the 104th Illinois Infantry. The first person with a Muslim last name buried in a national military cemetery was W. B. Osman (no known relation to Moses Osman), who died in 1865 and was interred in Poplar Grove National Cemetery in Petersburg, Virginia.

NICHOLAS SAID (ca. 1831–82), also known as Mohammed Ali ben Said, served in the Civil War from 1863 until 1865. Born in Bornou (near the modern-day borders of Libya, Chad, and Sudan) around 1831, he was raised to practice African traditional religion and later converted to Islam. Then, in the 1850s, he converted, probably under duress, to the Russian Orthodox Christianity of his master. He spoke several languages, traveled widely, and arrived in the United States as a freedman, although he had been a slave in three previous continents (Africa, Asia, and Europe). He reached the rank of sergeant in the Union Army.

WORLD WAR I TO THE VIETNAM WAR

The onset of WORLD WAR I, which the United States entered in 1917, saw a dramatic rise in the probable number of Muslim recruits and conscripts. Military records contain a total of 5,470 people with Muslim-sounding last names, with Muhammad—the most common—spelled in 41 different ways. The number of Muslims serving from 1917 to 1918 could be higher, given the claim that 13,965 Syrian Americans served in the U.S. armed forces, and a substantial percentage—from 10 to 25 percent—would likely have been Muslim. World War I veterans with Muslim names include Rashid Abdul, originally from Turkey, Mohamed Ali, born in Syria in 1893, and Mohammed Allah, from Arabia, born in 1892.

WORLD WAR II (1941–45) saw fewer recruits with Muslim last names, but 1,555 men and women so far have been identified. Of these, 58 had the name Muhammad, which was spelled in 17 different ways. Many American servicemen and servicewomen with Muslim last names, including many with Muslim first names, had emigrated from all parts of the Muslim world, though some were born in the United States.

One World War II veteran, Abdullah Igram from CEDAR RAPIDS, IOWA, was a prominent member of the city's Lebanese Muslim community. After the war, he convened the first national meeting of the FEDERATION OF ISLAMIC

ASSOCIATIONS IN THE UNITED STATES AND CANADA in 1952. In 1953, he wrote to President Dwight D. Eisenhower, former supreme commander of Allied Forces in World War II, requesting that Muslim servicemen and servicewomen be permitted to have the letter *I*, for Islam, printed on their dog tags, the identification tags worn by military personnel. Christians were identified with a *C*, and Jews with an *H* (for Hebrew), but this section of the tag was left blank for Muslims. Consequently, a Muslim solider killed in action might not receive the correct burial rite.

Eisenhower initially declined Igram's request but later the Department of Defense agreed, and during the 1950s "I" became an official category. For the first time, Muslims serving in the U.S. armed forces who chose to declare their religion could be officially recognized and counted as Muslim. During the Korean War (1950–53), several Muslims were captured and imprisoned by the North Koreans, and others died on the battlefield. The latter include Wilbur C. Islam, killed in November 1951, and Dirk Robert Abbas, killed on October 2, 1952.

According to the Combat Area Casualties Current File, at least 12 Muslim Americans died in the VIETNAM WAR. One of them, Keith A. Rahman, was awarded the Joint Services Commendation Medal on April 2, 1971, probably the highest award honoring a Muslim in the U.S. military to this point in time. Some Muslims opposed America's involvement in Vietnam, especially members of the NATION OF ISLAM (NOI), which asserted that blacks should not fight in an army that failed to treat them equally. Like other African-American civil rights groups, the NOI pointed out that blacks were much more likely than whites to be killed in action, arguing that they were treated as expendable and more likely to be placed in greater danger. Famously, the heavyweight boxing champion and NOI member MUHAMMAD ALI (1942–   ) was sentenced to five years in prison for draft evasion in 1967, although the Supreme Court rescinded this sentence in 1971. Almost 100 NOI members were jailed for resisting the draft.

AFTER THE COLD WAR

Following the end of the cold war in the early 1990s, the U.S. military was deployed to several Muslim-majority nations for a variety of purposes, including peacekeeping missions in Somalia and during the BOSNIAN WAR. During the Gulf War from 1990 to 1991, the military hosted a visit in Saudi Arabia from W. D. MOHAMMED (1933–2008), the leader who transformed the original Nation of Islam into the WORLD COMMUNITY OF AL-ISLAM IN THE WEST, to offer advice on religious orientation for troops stationed there. Mohammed was credited with assisting the military in accommodating Muslims and persuading the Department of Defense to introduce Muslim CHAPLAINS.

Major James Ahearn, probably the most decorated Muslim-American soldier in U.S. history. *(U.S. Army/AP Images)*

The military has deliberately recruited Muslim troops since 1990 in hopes that these Muslims will assist other personnel in better understanding and relating to Muslim populations. By the 21st century, there were as few as 3,700 and as many as 20,000 Muslims in the U.S. military. The dramatic range in the estimate is due to two factors: The Department of Defense does not publish a specific figure, and Muslims in the military often choose not to identify their religious affiliation. Since the 1990s, several organizations have been established to support Muslims in the military, including the Muslim Veterans Association, Muslim Military Members, the American Muslim Armed Forces and Veterans Affairs Council, and the Muslim American Military Chaplains Association.

Many Muslim Americans served with distinction and lost their lives during the Gulf War (1990–91), Afghanistan War, and IRAQ WAR. By 2010, Section 60 of Arlington National Cemetery, where those killed in Iraq and Afghanistan have been buried, included Captain Humayun S. M. Khan, who died June 8, 2004, when he diverted a suicide bomber from his unit. He was posthumously awarded the Bronze Star and the Purple Heart. Colleagues spoke of him as a "peacemaker" whose ambition was to become a military lawyer.

The same honors were awarded to another Muslim casualty of the war in Iraq, U.S. Army specialist Kareem Rashid Sultan Khan, killed August 6, 2007, and buried in Arlington National Cemetery. Among the many eulogies that Khan received, perhaps the most symbolically important was from Secretary of State Colin Powell, who on October 19, 2008, discussed the meaning of Khan's death on NBC's *Meet the Press*. Responding to rumors that Democratic presidential candidate Barack Obama was secretly Muslim, Powell reminded viewers that Obama was a practicing Christian. But Powell, who endorsed Obama, also asked, "What if he is? Is there something wrong with being a Muslim in this country? The answer's no, that's not America. Is there something wrong with some seven-year-old Muslim-American kid believing that he or she could be president?" Powell went on to describe a photograph of Khan's mother, who was mourning at her son's grave site. He was moved, he indicated, by the scene. "He was 14 years old at the time of 9/11," said Powell, "and he waited until he can go serve his country, and he gave his life."

The highest-ranking Muslim fatality in Iraq was the death of Major James Ahearn October 7, 2007. Ahearn, who converted to Islam in Iraq, was married to an Iraqi wife. During his service, Major Ahearn received a Bronze Star for Valor, two Meritorious Service Medals, a second Bronze Star, five Army Commendation Medals, a Humanitarian Service Medal, two National Defense Service Medals, an Air Reserve Forces Meritorious Service Medal, a Kuwait Liberation Medal from the Kingdom of Saudi Arabia, a Presidential Unit citation, a Valorous Unit Award, a Global War on Terrorism Service Medal and an Army Service Medal—probably making him the most highly decorated Muslim in U.S. military history.

Muslim-American soldiers, like soldiers of all faiths, have also been discharged or faced court-martial for violations of their oaths or for the commission of crimes while in uniform. Army Sergeant Asan Akbar was found guilty of murder by a court-martial and sentenced to death on April 21, 2005, for rolling grenades into a tent on his base in Iraq. While some military observers said that Akbar's attack was evidence that Muslim soldiers could not be trusted, others pointed out that this man's attack was an isolated and atypical incident. In 2004, another member of the military, Senior Airman Ahmad I. Al-Halabi, was accused of espionage, though he pled guilty to lesser charges of disobeying orders, lying, and misconduct. Assigned to Camp Delta in GUANTÁNAMO BAY in Cuba, where the detainees were almost all Muslim, Al-Halabi was sentenced to 295 days confinement, demoted, and discharged.

As of early 2009, the highest-ranking Muslim officer serving in the U.S. military was Colonel Douglas Burpee, a Marine stationed in Afghanistan as a helicopter pilot whose call sign was "Hadji," or Pilgrim. Born in Pakistan, Burpee immigrated to the United States in 1981. He has said that his military service to his country is an expression of his Islamic faith, since Islam opposes the actions of terrorist groups such as al-Qaeda.

The first Muslim to command an operational aviation squadron in the navy was Commander Muhammad Muzzafar F. Khan, who took over from Commander Timothy Langdon of Sea Control Squadron (VS) 31 in May 2004.

MUSLIM MILITARY CHAPLAINS

Several significant events relating to Muslims in the U.S. military followed from the decision to commission Muslim chaplains. In 1993, the crescent symbol was authorized for Muslim chaplains to wear on their lapels. That year, Army Captain Abdul-Rasheed Muhammad, based at Walter Reed Army Medical Center, Washington, D.C., became the first Muslim military chaplain after graduating from the Graduate School of Islamic and Social Sciences in Leesburg, Virginia, the only school recognized for such training. After the terrorist attacks of SEPTEMBER 11, 2001, Muhammad wrote to various Muslim scholars to solicit their opinions on whether Muslims in the U.S. military could deploy to a Muslim country where they might find themselves fighting and killing fellow Muslims.

This act resulted in considerable controversy due to the diverse opinions and responses that were received. Several eminent Muslim scholars, including Yusuf al-Qaradawi of Qatar, signed a FATWA, or religious opinion, which stated, "It's acceptable—God willing—for the Muslim-American military personnel to partake in the fighting in the upcoming battles, against whomever, their country decides, has perpetrated terrorism against them." Some scholars declared that Muslims could deploy to a Muslim country only in a noncombatant capacity. In 2003, Abdullah Webster refused to serve in Iraq, citing conscientious objections on religious grounds in defense. He was tried and convicted by a military court-martial for refusing to serve and sentenced to 295 days incarceration. Amnesty International declared him a prisoner of conscience. Webster was dishonorably discharged and released in April 2005.

The first army Muslim chaplain was followed by the appointment of Navy Lt. M. Malik Abd al-Mut'a Ali Noel, Jr., commissioned as a chaplain in 1996. A year later, a mosque was opened at the Norfolk Navy Base, and in 1998, a crescent was added to the Christian cross and Jewish Star of David on the exterior of the military chapel at the National Naval Medical Center in Bethesda, Maryland. The Chaplains Board has issued advice to senior officers that they should allow Muslims, when possible, to leave duty early when fasting during the month of Ramadan and to grant leave during the Muslim HOLIDAYS, including the feast days following Ramadan and hajj, the season of pilgrimage.

In 1999, Navy Lt. Saif-ul-Islam became the first Muslim chaplain assigned to the U.S. Marines. Achieving the rank of Lieutenant Commander by 2008, Islam has twice received the Joint Services Commendation Medal. In 1998, an Islamic prayer hall was opened in Fort Lewis, Washington, home of the 29th Signal Battalion, where Captain JAMES YEE (1968–   ) was stationed at the time. There were a dozen Muslim soldiers in its ranks. Yee estimated that between 100 and 150 soldiers at Fort Lewis and McChord Air Force Base were Muslim.

In 2000, the air force followed the army and navy when it appointed Abdullah Hamza Al-Mubarak as the first Muslim chaplain. A commissioned officer since 1997, he had also served in the air force reserve. In September 2005, stationed at Ramstein Air Base, Germany, Captain Al-Mubarak took part in the opening of the air forces' first prayer space designated for Jewish and Muslim worship.

On November 21, 2006, West Point opened a Muslim prayer hall for the 30 or so regular Muslim military attendees at Friday prayers. Also during 2006, the Naval Academy in Annapolis, Maryland, hosted its first celebration of Eid al-Fitr, the feast that concludes the month of dawn-to-sunset fasting during Ramadan. Senior officers and Pentagon officials have started to attend Muslim celebrations in what has been described as a bid to attract more Muslim recruits, though some soldiers have reported that the military can be a difficult environment for Muslims. Chaplain Captain Abdullah Hulwe was the only Muslim chaplain deployed in Iraq, where he has said that he had to educate fellow soldiers on how to treat Iraqi detainees with respect. He also reported that his wife has faced discrimination at military bases in the United States.

CONCLUSION

In the course of U.S. history, Muslim-American members of the military have gone from being highly invisible to highly visible. Despite the fact that thousands of Muslims fought in the American Revolution, the War of 1812, the Civil War, World War I, World War II, and the Korean War, there was no official recognition that they existed until the 1950s, when Muslim-American activists successfully lobbied for an identification tag that marked them as members of the Islamic religion. That grudging recognition changed by the late 20th century, however, as UNITED STATES FOREIGN RELATIONS and military activities focused primarily on Muslim-majority nations. During the Gulf War and war on terror, the services and sacrifices of Muslim soldiers became symbols in a war for the hearts and minds of Muslims all around the globe. President George W. Bush cited the mere presence of Muslims in the U.S. military as proof that the war on terror was not a war on Islam and Muslims. Muslim-American activists stated that the presence of Muslim servicemen and servicewomen evidenced how much Muslims had contributed to the country. Muslim-American soldiers themselves amassed impressive records of service and, like soldiers of many other faiths, have given their lives for their country.

Clinton Bennett

Further Reading

Avlon, John. "Our Islamic Soldiers: Healing Force in the War on Terror." *Radical Middle Newsletter.* 1 May 2006. Available online. URL: http://www.radicalmiddle.com/x_avlon_soldiers.htm. Accessed February 10, 2010.

Barner, Mike. "Muslims in the US Military Are as Loyal as Any, Chaplain Says," *Seattle-Post Intelligencer,* 20 October 2001. Available online. URL: http://seattlepi.nwsource.com/attack/43546_chaplains20.shtml. Accessed February 10, 2010.

Garamone, Jim. "Islam Growing in America, US Military." American Forces Press Service. October 4, 2002. Available online. URL: http://www.defenselink.mil/news/newsarticle.aspx?id=44689. Accessed February 10, 2010.

Hitti, Philip K. *The Syrians in America.* New York: George H. Doran Co., 1924.

Kjelgaard, Jim. *Hi Jolly.* New York: Dodd, Mead, 1959.

Lanning, Michael Lee. *African Americans in the Revolutionary War.* New York: Citadel Press, 2005.

Muhammad, Amir N. *Muslim Veterans of American Wars: Revolutionary War, War of 1812, Civil War, World War I & II.* Washington, D.C.: FreeMan Publications, 2007.

al-Qaradawi, Yusuf, et al. "Statement of September 27, 2001." Available online. URL: http://www.unc.edu/~kurzman/Qaradawi_et_al.htm. Accessed February 10, 2010.

Said, Nicholas. *Autobiography of Nicholas Said; a Native of Bournou, Eastern Soudan, Central Africa.* Memphis: Shotwell & Co., 1873. Available online. URL: http://docsouth.unc.edu/neh/said/menu.html. Accessed October 15, 2008.

United States Department of Veterans Affairs. Burial and Memorials. Available online. URL: http://gravelocator.cem.va.gov/j2ee/servlet/NGL_v1. Accessed March 29, 2009.

Whittle, Richard. "Uncle Sam Wants US Muslims to Serve." *Christian Science Monitor,* 27 December 2006. Available online. URL: http://www.csmonitor.com/2006/1227/p03s01-usmi.html. Accessed March 29, 2009.

USA PATRIOT Act

U.S. Public Law 107–56, passed October 26, 2001, and officially entitled "Uniting and Strengthening America by Providing Appropriate Tools Required to Intercept and Obstruct Terrorism," is best known by its acronym, the USA PATRIOT Act. In response to the events of SEPTEMBER 11, 2001, this law sought to enhance domestic security, increase the ability of law enforcement agencies to monitor potential terrorists, increase border security, and "deter and punish terrorist acts in the United States and around the world." The PATRIOT Act authorized the Department of Justice to detain people it considered terrorist suspects with no probable cause as "material witnesses" to crimes. The Department of Justice was not required to release the names of these individuals taken into custody.

The law and its enforcement had an immediate impact on the lives of thousands of Muslim Americans and Muslim visa holders in the United States. In November 2001, guidelines for the "voluntary" interviews of more than 5,000 noncitizen men in the United States on nonimmigrant visas from either Arab or Muslim countries were issued to all U.S. attorneys and all law enforcement agencies. These guidelines encouraged law enforcement officials to ask a series of questions meant to draw out the potential suspect's links to terrorism, including such queries as: "How did you feel when you heard the news about the World Trade Center attacks?" It was thought that such interviews might generate leads in the prosecution of terrorists. Men ages 18 to 33 who had been living in the United States on student, work, or tourist visas since January 2000 were sent letters asking them to volunteer for questioning. Even though the interviews were said to be voluntary, there were implications that visas could be revoked for failing to volunteer.

In November 2001, the Department of State slowed visa processing for men from Arab and Muslim countries. Soon after, students from countries with terrorist affiliation were arrested on visa violations. In January 2002, the Immigration and Naturalization Service (INS) started tracking down and deporting more than 6,000 noncitizen males who had been ordered by a judge to leave the United States but had not done so. According to the U.S. government, there were more than 314,000 "absconders" in the United States, but less than 2 percent were Middle Eastern. To critics of the USA PATRIOT Act, the government's focus on Middle Eastern and other Muslim males over other absconders was clear evidence of racial and religious profiling and bias.

In May 2002, the Enhanced Border Security and Visa Entry Reform Act required all airlines to submit a list of passengers who have boarded a plane bound for the United States. This act also required strict monitoring of foreign students. By June 2002, the Department of Justice requested that U.S. customs officials "seek out and search all Yemenis, including American citizens, entering the U.S." This action resulted in Yemeni Americans being removed from planes and boarding lines. In July 2002, the INS started enforcing the Immigration and Nationality Act of 1952, which requires all aliens to register changes of address within 10 days of moving. In response to this act, a legal Palestinian immigrant from North Carolina was arrested for driving four miles over the speed limit and detained for two months, charged with failing to register his new address. In August 2002, a fingerprinting and registry initiative was announced for persons from select Arab and Muslim countries. This policy, which expanded to include all other foreigners, requires all visa-holding foreign visitors to be fingerprinted, photographed, and registered upon entry to the United States.

Since passage of the PATRIOT Act, it is estimated that at least 50 Muslim men have been arrested as "material witnesses." For example, Abdallah Higazy, an Egyptian-born student, was arrested on December 17, 2001, as a material witness in the 9/11 case when a pilot's radio had been reportedly found in his hotel room that overlooked the World Trade Center. While detained, Higazy was coerced to give a false confession as officials threatened Higazy and his family. The charges against Higazy were dropped when evidence surfaced that the radio did not belong to him and that a hotel security guard had lied about the situation. BRANDON MAYFIELD, an American-born Muslim living in Oregon, was also arrested as a material witness in connection with the 2004 Madrid, Spain, train bombings when a fingerprint was erroneously matched with Mayfield's. Mayfield had been subjected to warrantless surveillance in accordance with the PATRIOT Act prior to his arrest. Upon his arrest, his home and law office were searched and his computer and files seized. Mayfield was released when Spanish authorities announced that the latent fingerprint reported to be Mayfield's actually belonged to an Algerian national.

According to Muslim-American advocacy groups, since the USA PATRIOT Act was implemented, Muslim Americans, Arab and non-Arab alike, have been denied some of their most basic constitutional rights, including Fourth Amendment rights that protect U.S. citizens against unreasonable searches and seizures without probable cause. According to its critics, the PATRIOT Act has such broad parameters that the U.S. government can take away people's most basic human, civil, and constitutional rights whenever it chooses, with no probable cause, simply on the suspicion of possible terrorist ties. The act's passage and implementation have brought together a coalition of civil rights and civil liberties groups, including the non-Muslim American Civil Liberties Union and the Muslim COUNCIL ON AMERICAN-ISLAMIC RELATIONS, who continue to challenge the act in the courts and among the general public.

Britney J. McMahan

Further Reading

Akram, Susan M. "The Aftermath of September 11, 2001: The Targeting of Arabs and Muslims in America." *Arab Studies Quarterly* 24, no. 2/3 (Spring/Summer 2002): 61. Available online. URL: http://www.ebscohost.com. Accessed April 13, 2008.

"Brandon Mayfield." *National Association of Criminal Defense Lawyers.* Available online. URL: http://www.nacdl.org. Accessed April 13, 2008.

Cainker, Louise. "No Longer Invisible: Arab and Muslim Exclusion after September 11." *Middle East Report* 224 (Autumn 2002): 22–29. Available online. URL: http://www.jstor.org/stable/1559419. Accessed April 13, 2008.

Malhotra, Anjana. "Material Witness Law Is Being Abused." *Washington Report on Middle East Affairs* 23, no. 6 (July/August 2004): 69. Available online. URL: http://www.ebscohost.com. Accessed April 14, 2008.

Moore, Kathleen. "A Part of US or Apart from US?: Post-September 11 Attitudes towards Muslims and Civil Liberties." *Middle East Report* 224 (Autumn 2002): 32–35. Available online. URL: http://www.jstor.org/stable/1559421. Accessed April 13, 2008.

"USA Patriot Act 2001." *Findlaw.* Available online. URL: http://www.findlaw.com. Accessed April 12, 2008.

values   See ISLAMIC THOUGHT; RELIGIOUS LIFE; SHARIʿA.

Vietnam War

The Vietnam War, often called "America's longest war," took place between communist North Vietnam and U.S.-backed South Vietnam from 1954 to 1975, with the United States first sending troops in the early 1960s and large numbers in the mid-1960s. Viewed in the context of the cold war, U.S. involvement was predicated on stopping the spread of communism throughout Southeast Asia. The human costs were enormous. An estimated 2 million North and South Vietnamese civilians and soldiers died, and 58,200 members of the UNITED STATES MILITARY perished in the conflict. From 1954 to 1972, successive U.S. presidential administrations offered support to various South Vietnamese regimes in their struggle against North Vietnam. In 1972, President Richard Nixon announced a policy of "Vietnamization," meaning that U.S. troops would gradually be withdrawn and the South Vietnamese would be primarily responsible for waging the war. In 1975, North Vietnamese forces reunited the country under communist rule.

As they had done in WORLD WAR I and WORLD WAR II, Muslim Americans fought and died in the U.S. military during the Vietnam War. At least 12 Muslim Americans gave their lives, according to the Combat Area Casualties Current File. In many ways, however, the most important contribution that Muslim Americans, especially AFRICAN-AMERICAN MUSLIMS, made to the war effort was to oppose it. The Vietnam War generated more opposition in the United States than any other war in American history, and African-American Muslim leaders were among the war's vocal opponents, attracting the attention and often admiration of many non-Muslim and Muslim-American YOUTH. One Muslim American—MUHAMMAD ALI—became the face of anti-Vietnam protest.

MUSLIM-AMERICAN TROOPS

Of the 12 Muslims that died in the conflict, 11 served in the U.S. Army and one in the U.S. Marines. They held military grades from private first class to sergeant, and their ages ranged from 20 to 38. Six were listed as having gunshot wounds, and two died in helicopter crashes. Of the remaining four, two were listed as "accidental self destruction," one as "accidental homicide," and the last as "other."

Islam Ozger, from New York, died on April 5, 1969, just shy of his 22nd birthday. A marine, Ozger had been in Vietnam less than a month before falling to small arms fire. As a part of India Company conducting sweeps in Quang Nam Province, he fell under heavy fire and was one of nine killed.

Eugene Miley was one of the victims of a helicopter engine failure during takeoff from Phouc Vinh in December, 1967. Staff Sergeant Sanford Ira Finger was the other Muslim-American helicopter casualty on "Warrior 143," which crashed offshore in October 1971 as it flew from Tuy Hoa to Cam Rahn Bay. The condition of the debris recovered indicated that the aircraft had struck the water at high speed during inclement weather. Only four of the crew members' bodies were found, not including Finger's.

OPPOSITION TO THE WAR

Though the NATION OF ISLAM (NOI) was not formally a pacifist organization, its antiwar tradition nevertheless dated back to the 1930s, when it prohibited members from serving in the armed forces. During World War II (1941–45), NOI leader ELIJAH MUHAMMAD (1897–1975) went to federal prison in 1942 on charges of draft evasion, and his son, W. D. MOHAMMED (1933–2008), was later sent to prison for refusing service in the Korean War (1950–53). Such antiwar sentiment did not change with the conflict in Vietnam.

MUHAMMAD SPEAKS, the NOI newspaper, became one of the most popular media sources among all African Americans opposed to the war and to Western interference in the developing world more generally. During the 1960s, the paper, which had a weekly circulation of 60,000, regularly featured articles, interviews, and political cartoons opposing the war. *Muhammad Speaks* presented the war as part of America's racial struggles, highlighting racial inequalities in the armed forces, especially in the disproportionate casualty rate among blacks and other minorities.

When NOI members applied for conscientious objector status, claiming that their religious beliefs prevented them from serving in the military, they were generally denied on the basis that the NOI was not a legitimate religious group. In 1965, for example, Stanley L. Garland cited his Muslim religious views when he refused to take the physical examination required of all those drafted into the military before formal induction. After two years of court battles, Garland was convicted and sentenced to three years in federal prison for draft evasion. Garland was one of almost 100 NOI members who served prison sentences for resisting the draft during the Vietnam War.

The most publicized case of defying the draft came from the African-American boxing champion Muhammad Ali, who applied for conscientious objector status on August 23, 1966. In doing so, he pointed to his membership in the NOI and explained why he refused to serve in the military: "I ain't got no quarrel with the Viet Cong," he said, referring to the military forces of the North Vietnamese. "No Viet Cong ever called me a nigger." Later, he added that he refused to go "10,000 miles to help murder, kill, and burn other people to simply help continue the domination of white slave masters over dark people the world over. This is the day and age when such evil injustice must come to an end."

On April 28, 1967, Ali was arrested on charges of violating the Selective Service Act, the law that authorized the draft. He was stripped of his boxing license and heavyweight title by the New York State Athletic Commission and the World Boxing Association. Later he told *Sports Illustrated*: "I'm giving up my title, my wealth, maybe my future. Many great men have been tested for their religious beliefs. If I pass this test, I'll come out stronger than ever."

On June 20, 1967, Ali was convicted of draft evasion, sentenced to five years in prison, and fined $10,000. But in 1971, the Supreme Court unanimously overturned Ali's conviction in *CLAY, A/K/A ALI V. UNITED STATES*. Muhammad Ali's public stance was a lightning rod for public debate and resulted in both admiration and outright scorn. Martin Luther King, Jr., praised his actions, whereas Representative Frank Clark (D-Pa.) found Ali to be a "complete and total disgrace." Detractors also included many black soldiers.

Another influential African-American Muslim critic of the war was MALCOLM X (1925–65), the NOI leader who became a Sunni Muslim after separating from Elijah Muhammad in 1964. As early as 1954, Malcolm linked the struggles of Vietnamese, Kenyans, African Americans, and others as people of color toiling under the yoke of Western colonialism and imperialism. Malcolm believed that the Vietnam War was just another in a long series of U.S. military actions designed to bring the country more political power and wealth. He encouraged black Americans to be in solidarity with "little rice farmers" and to follow their example as freedom fighters.

In late 1964, Malcolm X lashed out at the U.S. government, calling it the most "hypocritical since the world began," because it "was supposed to be a democracy, supposed to be for freedom." Condemning the fact that many African Americans were disenfranchised in the United States, Malcolm stated: "They want to draft you . . . and send you to Saigon to fight for them," while the "right to register and vote without being murdered" was of little concern. After Malcolm was assassinated on February 21, 1965, it was discovered that he had kept in his address book a North Vietnamese stamp depicting a U.S. helicopter being shot down by North Vietnamese forces—a symbol of his solidarity with the North Vietnamese.

The memory of Malcolm X became a rallying point for soldiers opposed to the war. "GIs United Against the War," established in 1969 at Fort Jackson, South Carolina, and the "Malcolm X Society," established in 1970 at Vandenberg Air Force Base, cited the legacy of Malcolm X's opposition to the war as their inspiration. Malcolm X Society members claimed that "Malcolm X was the most appropriate symbol . . . of the continuing struggle for change."

AFTERMATH

The high-profile opposition of many African-American Muslims to the Vietnam War had deep roots in the history of African-American Muslim groups' struggles for racial equality at home and Afro-Asian independence abroad. Such concerns about the impact of UNITED STATES FOREIGN RELATIONS on the developing world would continue after the last Americans pulled out of Vietnam in 1975. But many African-American Muslims would dramatically alter their relationship with the U.S. military in the final decades of the 20th century. Even as the memory of the Vietnam War lingered among Muslim Americans as a whole, an increasing number of them volunteered for military service.

The Vietnam War had other related consequences for Muslim-American history as well. The war caused a labor shortage at home, which prompted Congress to pass the IMMIGRATION ACT OF 1965, which permitted many more Muslims from Asia and Africa to immigrate to the United States beginning in 1968. Among the immigrants were thousands of doctors, scientists, and engineers, many of whom would become key figures in the sciences, information technology, and architecture in the late 20th century.

In addition, the Vietnam War, along with the era's widespread social protest, sexual revolution, and the Watergate crisis, was interpreted by many Muslim Americans, along with other spiritually and religiously minded Americans in the 1960s and 1970s, as a sign of the nation's moral decline. Many Muslim Americans supported the idea that the solution to America's moral, political, and economic problems was a return to religious values, and along with millions of

Christians and Jews, fueled the growth of religious REVIVAL-ISM in the late 1970s and late 20th century.

Bret Lewis

Further Reading

"African American Involvement in the Vietnam War." Available online. URL: http://www.aavw.org/. Accessed February 3, 2009.

CACCF Statistics. Available online. URL: http://www.archives.gov/research/vietnam-war/casualty-statistics.html. Accessed February 3, 2009.

Westheider, James E. *The African American Experience in Vietnam: Brothers in Arms.* New York: Rowman and Littlefield, 2008.

———. *Fighting on Two Fronts: African Americans and the Vietnam War.* New York: New York University Press, 1997.

voting   See POLITICS.

W

Wadud, Amina (1952–) *religious scholar and activist*

Amina Wadud, originally named Mary Teasley, is a scholar, teacher, and activist. Her life as an African-American Muslim woman directly informs her work as a scholar of the Qur'an and Islamic religious traditions. As a scholar, she is best known for her feminist interpretations of the Qur'an. As an activist, she is perhaps even more famous for serving as a PRAYER leader at a mixed-gender Friday service in NEW YORK CITY in 2005.

Wadud was born on September 25, 1952, and grew up in Washington, D.C., in the family of a Methodist minister. She converted to Sunni Islam in 1972 while an undergraduate student at the University of Pennsylvania. Shortly after that she changed her name. Conversion, to her, is a continuing act of transition, where being a Muslim is an ongoing process of "engaged surrender" to God. After graduating from college, she married, had children, and then studied and taught in Libya. After returning to the United States, she divorced, lived on welfare, and had a short career as a school teacher in Philadelphia. Later on, as a graduate student from 1982 to 1988 at the University of Michigan, she began her academic engagement with the Qur'an, and traveled to Egypt to learn ARABIC. She received her Ph.D. in Islamic Studies and Arabic in 1988. Between 1989 and 1992, Wadud taught at the International Islamic University in Malaysia. She joined Sisters in Islam, a fledging study circle of Muslim women, which became Malaysia's leading women's rights organization. Wadud helped formulate their Qur'an-based responses to shari'a courts. She returned to the United States in 1992 to teach at Virginia Commonwealth University. In 2006, she became Visiting Scholar at Starr King School for the Ministry in Berkeley, California.

Wadud published her seminal work, *Qur'an and Woman: Rereading the Sacred Text from a Woman's Perspective,* in Malaysia in 1992. In that book, she developed a line of argument characteristic of her academic work overall. Echoing Christian and Jewish feminist theologians, she suggested that sacred texts yield different meanings when read through the lens of gender equality. *Qur'an and Woman* attempts to provide a holistic reading of the Qur'an that emphasizes the justice and mercy of God. It deemphasizes or reinterprets particular Qur'anic verses that have been used to sanction patriarchy. In her interpretive approach, Wadud relied on FAZLUR RAHMAN, a Pakistani-American scholar. She analyzed the Qur'an as the transcendent word of God revealed in the particular environment of seventh-century Arabia. Because it is transcendent, she claimed, it has universal applications. Because it was contextually situated, she continued, its meanings must be reexamined for new audiences and new conditions.

According to Wadud, to be faithful to the revelation, new interpretations must adhere to the Qur'an's principles but not necessarily to its individual legal injunctions. As Wadud provocatively states in her later work, *Inside the Gender Jihad: Women's Reform in Islam* (2006), sometimes Muslims have to "say 'no' to the text" in order to live by its ethical vision. This has far-reaching practical implications, as in the case of her call for radical reexamination of legal norms regulating Muslim family life. She emphasizes the Qur'anic designation of the human being, male and female, as God's *khalifah,* "moral agent." If God is just and humans are God's equal agents, they must strive for equality in all aspects of life, religious and profane, public and private.

Wadud has consistently combined her academic work with local and global advocacy for the rights of women, ethnic minorities, and people living with HIV/AIDS. She has spearheaded a movement for full inclusion of women in religious public life, including as leaders of communal prayers. In 1994, she delivered what she intended to be a *khutbah,* or Friday sermon, in front of a mixed congregation in the Claremont Main Street Mosque in Cape Town, South Africa. She spoke about equality of women and men in family life. She challenged Muslim orthodoxy further by leading a mixed-gender Friday prayer service in March 2005 in New York City. Local mosques approached by the organizers of this event declined to cooperate. The service instead was held in Manhattan at the Episcopalian Cathedral of St. John the Divine. It stirred international controversy, with many Muslim authorities asserting that traditionally only men can lead mixed-gender prayers. To Wadud, however, this was a logical continuation of her interpretation of the Qur'an. In her sermon, she once again reminded Muslims about the equality of human beings in the eyes of God. With the act of leading this prayer, she sought to establish a precedent against exclusion of women from public religious roles, including the most visible role of a congregational prayer leader.

The impact of Wadud's struggle for gender equality—what she calls her "gender jihad"—goes far beyond these more controversial activities. Perhaps most important is her contribution in putting gender at the top of the Muslim-American agenda. She is one of the leading reminders of the turn Muslim feminists have made away from secular approaches toward finding gender equality within the Islamic tradition. Wadud has been an American voice in international Muslim debates on women's rights. Other Muslims, women and men, scholars and everyday interpreters, have emulated her efforts of reading the Qur'an as a liberating text.

Timur Yuskaev

Further Reading

Wadud, Amina. "American Muslim Identity: Race and Ethnicity in Progressive Islam." In *Progressive Muslims: On Justice, Gender and Pluralism,* edited by Omid Safi, 270–285. Oxford: Oneworld, 2003.

———. *Inside the Gender Jihad: Women's Reform in Islam.* Oxford: Oneworld, 2006.

———. *Qur'an and Woman: Rereading the Sacred Text from a Woman's Perspective.* New York: Oxford University Press, 1999.

Wahhabism

Wahhabism is a major reform movement in Saudi Arabia founded by Muhammad ibn Abd al-Wahhab (1703–87), a Muslim religious scholar with whom the Saudi extended family made a strategic alliance in order to spread its political domains in the 18th century. The term *Wahhabism* was created by outsiders, in particular the opponents of this movement. Saudis themselves have refused to be labeled Wahhabi. The followers prefer the term *al-muwahhidun,* or Unitarians, or *ahl al-tawhid,* the people of Divine unity.

Muhammad ibn Abd al-Wahhab, a trained scholar, writer, and jurist, believed that correct belief (or orthodoxy) must be accompanied by correct behavior (orthopraxy) in both private and public life. He stressed the doctrine of *tawhid,* or monotheism, and condemned many popular Muslim religious practices, especially those associated with SUFISM, as impermissible innovations to God's revelations in the QUR'AN and to the sunna, or traditions of the prophet Muhammad. Sometimes called a "puritan" by outsiders, al-Wahhab believed that a moral revival and by extension a social revival depended upon the stricter and more disciplined adherence to Islam. He also believed that Islamic scriptures should be read literally and that Islam, properly practiced, offered the sole path to salvation.

Like SALAFI MUSLIMS, Wahhabi Muslims have sought to "purify" Islam and to follow strictly the practices of the *salaf,* or pious Muslim ancestors who lived in the seventh century. But Salafis, in general, have not automatically followed FATWAS issued by Saudi religious authorities, instead choosing the guidance of religious leaders in Jordan, Yemen, Syria, and Egypt. While the Wahhabis have considered themselves to be Salafis, some scholars differentiate them by emphasizing that Wahhabism is the more conservative form of Salafism and that Wahhabism is a term that has been used to identify Salafi movements in Saudi Arabia.

Because Osama bin Laden is a Saudi citizen—and because 15 of the 19 al-Qaeda members who staged the terrorist attacks on SEPTEMBER 11, 2001, were Saudis as well—it is sometimes assumed their violent interpretation of Islam is a product of Wahhabism. However, the root of bin Laden's violent ideology, especially global jihad (meaning struggle or war) and the absolute division of the world into Muslims versus non-Muslims, is based on the ISLAMIC THOUGHT of the jurist Ibn Taymiyya (1263–1328), not that of al-Wahhab. After the death of al-Wahhab, some Wahhabis incorporated Ibn Taymiyya's view and became a more militant wing. Most Wahhabis, however, rejected an offensive interpretation of jihad, insisting that it could only be defensive in nature—the majority position in the SHARI'A, or Islamic law and ethics, since the Middle Ages. According to a 2007 poll, for example, the majority of Saudis did not approve of the violent terrorist activities of al-Qaeda, and 88 percent supported the government efforts to eliminate the group.

WAHHABISM IN AMERICA

The history of Wahhabism in the United States has been influenced by the larger history of UNITED STATES FOREIGN RELATIONS with the Kingdom of Saudi Arabia. U.S.-Saudi contacts began as early as 1919 when Saudi Prince Faisal and President Woodrow Wilson met after WORLD WAR I at the Paris Peace Conference at Versailles, though full diplomatic relations were not established until 1933. Both countries' foreign policies were deeply intertwined for the rest of the 20th century, as the United States became the guarantor of Saudi security in exchange for full access to Saudi oil reserves—estimated at various points to be the largest in the world. Saudi Arabia is also home to Mecca, the holiest city in Islam, and destination of the hajj, or annual pilgrimage.

Wahhabi influences in the United States first appeared during the era of the "Arab Cold War" between Saudi Arabia and Egypt from roughly 1954 to 1967. In this battle between the revolutionary nationalist forces of Egyptian leader Gamal

Abdel Nasser and the monarchical government of Saudi Arabia, the Saudi regime attempted to increase its influence in the West and throughout the world by promoting Wahhabi interpretations of Islam. The University of Medina, established in 1961, and the Muslim World League, created in 1962, trained and funded Muslim missionaries throughout the world, including the United States, and Saudi Arabia also supported the MUSLIM STUDENTS ASSOCIATION (MSA), founded in 1963 at Champaign, Illinois.

MALCOLM X (1925–65), a leading member of the NATION OF ISLAM, also benefited from the Saudi largesse, becoming an official guest of the state during his pilgrimage in 1964 and returning to Saudi Arabia later that year to receive missionary training by the Muslim World League. But he disagreed with his Wahhabi and Salafi allies over the best strategy for the liberation of black people: They advocated an Islamic religious revival, whereas Malcolm favored pan-Africanism and black revolution.

From the 1960s until the end of the 20th century, the Saudi government and the agencies that it supported also funded the publication of various pamphlets and books that advocated a socially conservative, often Wahhabi or Salafi interpretation of Islam. In 2000, Saudi Arabia successfully distributed 138 million copies of Saudi-approved translations of the QUR'AN to countries throughout the globe, including the United States. In addition, it continued to support Wahhabi missionaries such as University of Medina graduate Abu Muslimah, who led the Islamic Center of America (ICOA) project in East Orange, New Jersey, in the 1980s.

Wahhabi teachings about the need for Islamic reform could also be found in relatively small organizations such as the Qur'an and Sunnah Society of North America. This organization presented the view that Islam was the sole path to earthly and heavenly salvation, emphasizing the need to convert all non-Muslims to Islam. It also presented a socially conservative view of morality that included the need for the separation of men and women in public venues. Another such Wahhabi-influenced institution was the Institute of Islamic and Arabic Sciences, an adjunct campus of Al-Imam Muhammad ibn Saud Islamic University in Riyadh, Saudi Arabia, which was established in Fairfax, Virginia, in 1988. The chairman of its board was Prince Bandar bin Sultan, the Saudi ambassador to the United States.

Saudi Arabia also provided financial aid to more than a dozen MOSQUES AND ISLAMIC CENTERS and ISLAMIC SCHOOLS in the United States. In 1998, the King Fahd Mosque in Culver City, a suburb of LOS ANGELES, was built with $8 million in private donations from the son of the King, Prince Abdul Aziz bin Fahd. Al-Haramain Islamic Foundation, a Saudi-based nonprofit organization, established a U.S.-based branch in October 1997 in Ashland, Oregon.

Accepting Saudi support, however, did not automatically mean accepting Wahhabi interpretations of Islam. For example, Saudi Arabia hosted many Muslim-American leaders, including W. D. MOHAMMED (1933–2008). Still, Mohammed, like most Muslim Americans, never adopted Wahhabism as a school of thought. Mohammed, perhaps the most popular leader of African-American Muslims in the 1980s, often disagreed with Wahhabi interpretation of various issues, such as the relationship of Muslims to people of other faiths and the relationships of men to women—issues on which he took a far more liberal stance. Unlike most Wahhabi-influenced preachers, for example, Mohammed participated in INTERFAITH MOVEMENTS that sought to respect religious pluralism rather than convert everyone to the same religion.

AFTER 9/11

After the terrorist attacks of September 11, 2001, the U.S. government suspected that some Muslim extremists had used Saudi charitable funds to support their activities and sought to expose, cut off, and shut down institutions that it suspected of possible ties. In February 2004, for example, the FBI froze the assets of al-Haramain, a Saudi nonprofit group active in the United States. The Saudi government followed suit, closing the Saudi-based foundation in October.

Such prosecutions contributed to the decline of Wahhabism in the United States during the first decade of the 20th century. In 2000, 21 percent of the mosque leaders surveyed said they or their congregations were influenced by Wahhabi interpretations of Islam. Polls taken later in the decade indicated that fewer than 10 percent of Muslim-American individuals identified with similar Salafi ideas—probably meaning that an even smaller number found Wahhabism to be attractive. There were still Muslim Americans committed to Wahhabi notions of an Islamic reformation based on the original teachings of the first generation of Muslims. But the association of Wahhabism with terrorism—however incorrect in reality—had led many Muslim Americans sympathetic to Wahhabi ideas to eschew the label.

See also REVIVALISM.

Eva F. Amrullah

Further Reading

Al-Yaqeen, Ain. "Saudi Government Paper: 'Billions Spent by Saudi Royal Family to Spread Islam to Every Corner of the Globe.'" The Islamic Supreme Council of America. Available online. URL: http://www.islamicsupremecouncil. org/bin/site/wrappers/media-show_clips_wahhabi-8466X. html. Posted March 26, 2002.

Delong-Bas, Natana J. *Wahhabi Islam: From Revival and Reform to Global Jihad.* New York: Oxford University Press, 2004.

Murphy, Caryle. "Five Years Later: Salafi Islam; For Conservative Muslims, Goal of Isolation a Challenge; 9/11 Put Strict Adherents on the Defensive," *Washington Post.* Available online. URL: http://www.washingtonpost.com/wp-dyn/content/article/2006/09/04/AR2006090401107.html. Accessed February 11, 2010.

Oliver, Haneef James. "The 'Wahhabi' Myth: Dispelling Prevalent Fallacies and the Fictitious Link with Bin Laden." The Wahhabi Myth. Available online. URL: http://www.thewahhabimyth.com. Accessed March 18, 2009.

Wahhaj, Siraj (1950–) *religious leader and activist*

Siraj Wahhaj is a leading Muslim-American preacher. He is also a community builder, serving as the imam of Masjid al-Taqwa in Bedford-Stuyvesant, Brooklyn, and as the head of the Muslim Alliance of North America (MANA). A husband and father of nine children, Wahhaj was the first African-American vice president of the Islamic Society of North America and, as he explained in an interview with this author, sees himself "as a bridge" between African-American and immigrant Muslims.

Born on March 11, 1950, and originally named Jeffrey Kearse, Wahhaj grew up in a Baptist family in Brooklyn's public housing. He had a particular knack for religion and teaching: Encouraged by his mother, he won perfect attendance awards and taught Sunday school in his parents' church. A gifted artist and athlete, in 1968 he enrolled in New York University on a partial basketball scholarship, planning to become a math teacher.

Wahhaj converted to Elijah Muhammad's Nation of Islam (NOI) and adopted the name Jeffrey 12X in 1969. This was a result of a spiritual and political crisis prompted by the assassination of Martin Luther King, Jr., in 1968. Wahhaj recollects that his choice was the Nation of Islam or the Black Panthers. He became a "one hundred percent soldier of the Nation," he wrote, selling record numbers of *Muhammad Speaks,* the NOI newspaper. He studied under the tutelage of Louis Farrakhan, eventually serving as his assistant minister at Harlem's Mosque No. 7, and later as minister of Mosque No. 7C in Brooklyn.

In 1975, he followed the transformation toward Sunni orthodoxy spearheaded by W. D. Mohammed and adopted the name Siraj Wahhaj, "radiant light." In 1978, he attended a four-month course in Mecca at King Abdul Aziz University and returned to Brooklyn with a zeal to "teach total indoctrination in the Sunnah," or the traditions of the prophet Muhammad of Arabia. He left W. D. Mohammed's community in 1981 because he was disappointed with the pace of the organization's reform, later reflecting that he might have been "a bit impatient."

Encouraged by Sheikh Ahmad Tawfiq, a student of Malcolm X and the head of the Mosque of Islamic Brotherhood in Harlem, Wahhaj established Masjid al-Taqwa, which quickly grew from a congregation of 25 people into a New York City Muslim landmark. Wahhaj envisioned his mosque as a partner in community development. Cooperating with the local New York City Police Department precinct, the mosque led a neighborhood campaign to close down 15 crack houses in 1988. Wahhaj has also served as a police clergy liaison. In recognition of his efforts, Brooklyn borough president Marty Markowitz declared August 15, 2003, Siraj Wahhaj Day. He is also known as the first Muslim to offer an opening prayer at the U.S. House of Representatives, in 1991.

Wahhaj's primary legacy is that of Muslim-centered religious leader. A consistent theme in his speeches has been unity of Muslim Americans through uncompromising allegiance to Sunni orthodox beliefs and practices. His interpretation of what orthodoxy entails has been markedly conservative; he has been, for example, criticized for employing antigay language, which he shares with many Muslim and non-Muslim religious social conservatives. In the early 1980s, he became the first African-American spokesperson to achieve prominence among immigrant Muslim audiences. He constantly crisscrossed the country, speaking at dozens of national and regional gatherings and raising funds for countless immigrant mosques and community centers. His recorded speeches became best sellers in Muslim stores in North America and Europe.

At the same time, his activism has focused consistently on the issues affecting African Americans, reflected in his role as an architect of MANA. Taking on the legacy of the NOI's "do for self" ideology, he has preached Muslim self-reliance and pride. He has been consistently critical of the U.S. government domestic and international policies—a stance, he has stressed, that he inherited from King and Malcolm X. His critics often mention that the prosecutor in the 1993 World Trade Center bombing trial included Wahhaj's name in a very long list of individuals who might be named as coconspirators. Wahhaj, however, was never indicted or formally tied to the terrorist act. Before and after this incident, in Muslim gatherings and courtroom testimonies, he has repeatedly spoken against terrorism. After the terrorist attacks of September 11, 2001, he called on Muslim Americans to develop more responsible language of interaction with non-Muslim Americans and to seek productive cooperation. When asked to summarize his role in the national Muslim life, Wahhaj describes himself as a teacher instructing Muslim Americans "how to live an Islamic life in this country."

Timur Yuskaev

Further Reading

Barrett, Paul M. *American Islam: The Struggle for the Soul of Religion.* New York: Farrar, Straus and Giroux, 2007.

"The Shaykh of Da'wah in the West: Imam Siraj Wahhaj." Sha-keenah.org. Available online. URL: http://www.sakeenah.org/celebrate2.shtml. Accessed December 20, 2007.

Siraj Wahhaj
First Muslim Invocation in Congress (1991)

On June 25, 1991, Siraj Wahhaj became the first Muslim to pray before a session of the U.S. Congress. Imam Wahhaj offered a prayer in the House of Representatives. The next year, the Senate followed suit by inviting W. D. Mohammed to open a session of the upper body with prayer. The tradition of offering prayer at the opening of Congressional sessions traces its roots to the Continental Congress, which in 1774 decided, after heated debate, to begin its meetings with a prayer. The House of Representatives, which was formed in 1789, continued the tradition, generally employing a Protestant Christian chaplain for the task. By the late 20th and early 21st centuries, however, representatives of all world religions, including Judaism, Hinduism, and Islam, were invited to give the prayer. Siraj Wahhaj, an African-American Sunni Muslim leader from Brooklyn, New York, was suggested by the American Muslim Council, an immigrant-led organization, as the first Muslim. His prayer drew mainly from the words of the first sura, *or chapter, of the Qur'an entitled* al-Fatiha, *or the Opening, though it incorporates a few phrases from other Qur'anic verses and Wahhaj himself. He was welcomed to the House by Nick Jo Rahall, an Arab-American Christian Congressman from West Virginia.*

Imam Siraj Wahhaj, member, American Muslim Council, Washington, DC, offered the following prayer:

In the name of God, most gracious, most merciful:

Praise belongs to Thee alone, Oh God, Lord, and Creator of all the worlds;

Praise belongs to Thee who shaped us and colored us in the wombs of our mothers; colored us black and white, brown, red, and yellow;

Praise belongs to Thee, who created us from males and females and made us into nations and tribes that we may know each other;

Most gracious, most merciful, all knowing, all wise, just God;

Master of the day of judgment, Thee alone do we worship and from Thee alone do we seek help;

Guide the leaders of this Nation, who have been given a great responsibility in worldly affairs, guide them and grant them righteousness and wisdom;

Guide them and us on the straight path, the path of those whom Thou hast bestowed Thy favors, the path of Your inspired servants, the path of Noah, Abraham, Moses, Jesus, and Muhammad;

Guide them and us not on the path of the disobedient ones who have earned Your wrath and displeasure. Amen.

* * *

Mr. RAHALL. Mr. Speaker, it is an honor for me to welcome to the House Chamber as guest chaplain, the Imam of Masjid al-Taqwa, Siraj Wahhaj, of Brooklyn, NY.

He is the first Muslim leader to work in cooperation with the New York City Police Department, and he is nationally known for his leadership in establishing a drug-free zone in his drug-laden neighborhood of Bedford-Stuyvesant in Brooklyn. Siraj Wahaj works well within the community in which he was born, and where he has lived for 41 years.

Siraj Wahhaj's leadership extends far beyond his local community. In addition to being a member of the Masjid al-Shura, the consultative committee of New York City, he serves on the advisory board of the Islamic Society of North America, and is a member of the board of directors of the American Muslim Council in Washington, DC.

Siraj Wahhaj was one of the first Muslims to address Christians from the pulpit. His weekly radio program on WWRL-AM is popular with non-Muslims as well as with Muslims.

As he prayed for the Members of this body today, and the people we represent, I know his words entered the minds and will remain in the hearts of all those within the sound of his voice and the reading of his words.

Source: Congressional Record (House), vol. 137, no. 99, 102d Congress 1st Session, June 25, 1991, H4947.

Webb, Alexander Russell (Mohammed Alexander Russell Webb) (1846–1916) *American journalist and convert to Islam*

Alexander Russell Webb, also known as Mohammed Alexander Russell Webb, was one of the first known American converts to Islam. His conversion from Presbyterianism to Islam in the late 19th century intrigued those Americans who came in contact with him since most Westerners in the 1890s associated Islam with violence, the Turkish harem, and religious heresy. Webb was the first "respectable" white American citizen to establish a Muslim mission in the United States, and his journalistic writings on Islam remain an irreplaceable record of American religious history in the late 19th and early 20th centuries.

Alexander Webb was born on November 9, 1846, in Hudson, New York. He attended the Home School in Glendale, Massachusetts, and Claverack College in New York. He then followed in the footsteps of his father, Alexander Nelson Webb, and entered the newspaper business. Heading west, the young Webb purchased a weekly newspaper in Unionville, Missouri, and later took on a series of editorships in Missouri.

In 1872, at the age of 25, Webb abandoned his childhood religion of Presbyterianism. He had grown disillusioned with Christianity and what he saw to be its moral and philosophical shortcomings. Webb explored theosophy, a movement that amalgamated spiritual wisdom from all world religions. He also began reading about and practicing Buddhism. Webb described this period of his life as a time of intense study, and he spent anywhere from four to seven hours a day studying Eastern religions. Eventually, Webb's interest turned to Islam, which was seen by many Americans of the period as an Eastern religion.

But Webb did not convert to Islam until 1887, when he moved to the Philippines. A strong supporter of Democratic politics in the Gilded Age, Webb sought a post in the diplomatic service. In 1887, President Grover Cleveland appointed him to be U.S. consul in Manila, Philippines. This assignment delighted Webb, who thought that he might meet with Muslims from the East in the Philippines. Though his only serious contact with Muslims was through a correspondence with Indian Muslim businessman Hajee Abdulla Arab, Webb's commitment to Islam grew during this time, and in 1888, he publicly announced that he was going to convert to Islam. Webb developed close relationships with other Indian Muslims, and frustrated with the bureaucratic nature of his government post, Webb embarked on a tour of India. Webb took on a new first name—Mohammed—and transformed his appearance with the deliberate adoption of Turkish DRESS and hairstyle. Webb's converted zeal impressed Muslims who prized devotion to the QUR'AN and to God. His lectures, delivered in 1892 throughout India, exuded religious devotion and the hope that his audiences would subsidize the establishment of an Islamic mission in the United States. Webb believed Americans would convert quickly and in large numbers to the Islamic faith. Webb's enthusiastic embrace of Islamic LAW and lifestyle captured the attention of Americans, especially newspaper reporters, upon his return to the United States in 1893. Webb's deliberate refashioning of his appearance and his will-

ingness to condone non-Western traditions such as polygamy revealed his rejection of American culture and his belief that Islam provided a morally superior way of life.

Webb published the pro-Islamic lectures that he had delivered overseas, providing a defense of Islam and a critique of Christianity. Webb also increased his proselytizing efforts by founding a mission, the American Islamic Mission, in NEW YORK CITY immediately upon his return to the United States in February 1893. Webb believed that by his educating Americans about the practical benefits of Islam a large number of Americans would reject Christianity like he had and embrace Islam. Webb's optimism caught the attention of newspaper reporters, but he failed to meet his financial goals and the converts were small in number. So Webb was forced to move the mission's location in Manhattan three times in two years due to financial strain.

Webb saw potential for proselytizing when he was asked to speak on behalf of Islam at the World's Parliament of Religions, an interfaith gathering of representatives from religious traditions from around the world held in CHICAGO in September 1893. Webb presented an oddly exotic figure to the primarily American, Protestant audience. Every other representative for Eastern religions at the parliament was a foreigner. Webb, on the other hand, had rejected the predominant religion of his home country for a religious system often considered at odds with his American identity. This made Webb a mini-celebrity at the parliament, as journalists were eager to interview him, and the Parliamentary Hall was filled to capacity when he spoke. Webb gave two lectures at the parliament. His first address, "The Spirit of Islam," included a brief history and theological lesson for his predominantly Western audience. His second lecture, "The Influence of Islam on Social Conditions," was a description of Islam's positive effects upon the moral conditions of Muslim societies spread throughout the Middle and Far East. Webb's primary theme in both speeches was the benefits of Islam for modern, Western society. Stressing what he considered Islam's rationality and superiority in ethics, personal piety, and treatment of the poor, Webb contended that if Islamic morals were followed in the United States, many of America's social problems, such as urban poverty, alcoholism, and prostitution, would diminish.

Webb enjoyed steady news coverage of his efforts to convert Americans to Islam. Newspapers had already made the announcement of the American Islamic Mission, and Webb encountered little public opposition to his work. But Webb's suggestion at the parliament that the Islamic practice of polygamy would put an end to the immoral behavior of Americans may have hindered his ability to promote Islam in the United States. Onlookers did not criticize Webb's conversion to Islam, but there were many vocal critics of his comments about polygamy during his lecture, "The Spirit of Islam." Despite the rejection of his mildly pro-polygamy remarks, Webb was frequently applauded when he announced his American Islamic Mission and publication office headquartered in Manhattan, and he also received applause when he described the virtues of the prophet Muhammad and the moral discipline of Muslims around the world.

After the parliament adjourned, newspapers used a more critical tone when describing Webb's activities. Newspapers no longer described his conversion and mission to America in relatively friendly tones, and they abandoned their depiction of Webb as a dignified and intelligent man. Webb's attempts to relocate Muslims to colonies in the southern United States had already met reactions of doubt and even fear. The national press's notable change in attitude toward Webb revealed the limits of the nation's religious tolerance in the 1890s, and Webb's willingness to adopt Eastern practices and openly attack Western traditions led some to publicly criticize Webb.

His optimism for converting Americans to Islam was not realized in his lifetime, and he soon encountered financial troubles that forced him to close his Manhattan mission in 1894 and relocate it to his home in Ulster, New York. Webb's financial troubles increased, despite his cost-cutting, and eventually he closed the mission. He remained a Muslim despite these setbacks, and in 1898 he moved to Rutherford, New Jersey, where he struggled to find foreign or domestic funding for his Muslim-American periodicals.

In 1901, Sultan Abdul Hamid II of the Ottoman Empire appointed Webb an honorary consul general to the United States. This position provided further grounds for criticism and charges of Webb's anti-Americanism. The former U.S. consul to the Philippines now represented the interests of a foreign nation. Webb may have caught the Sultan's attention as the likely author of *The Armenian Troubles and Where the Responsibility Lies,* an anonymous pro-Ottoman pamphlet that blamed American missionaries and their converts in Armenia as the perpetrators of Ottoman political unrest. Webb's position as Ottoman consul, however, was strictly honorary. He received no salary or tangible benefits for his service. Webb died on October 1, 1916, in his simple Rutherford, New Jersey, home, with little wealth.

Though his impressive legacy would not be celebrated by Muslim Americans for decades, Webb has recently emerged as a historical figure of symbolic importance in Muslim America. Many American converts and Muslim immigrants alike now recognize Webb's role in promoting an American Islamic community. His unapologetic embrace of both his Muslim and American identities, and his tolerant and open-minded attitudes toward people of other faiths, make him a model for some Muslim Americans seeking to craft a unique Muslim-American identity.

Sarah Miglio

Further Reading

Abd-Allah, Umar F. *A Muslim in Victorian America: The Life of Alexander Russell Webb.* New York: Oxford University Press, 2006.

Singleton, Brent D., ed. *Yankee Muslim: The Asian Travels of Mohammed Alexander Russell Webb.* Rockville, Md.: Borgo/Wildside Press, 2007.

Alexander Russell Webb
Islam in America (1893)

The most famous white American convert to Islam in the 19th century, Alexander Russell Webb (1846–1916) defended Islam against various stereotypes that characterized the religion among his fellow citizens. He praised Islam as a progressive, scientific, and rational force for good, a religion that shared much in common with the universal values of Judaism and Christianity. In 1893, the same year that Webb addressed the World's Parliament of Religions in Chicago, he wrote Islam in America, *one of the first Muslim-American publications meant to explain the faith to non-Muslims. In this excerpt, Webb explains why he became a Muslim.*

I have been frequently asked why I, an American, born in a country which is nominally Christian, and reared, "under the drippings" of an orthodox Presbyterian pulpit, came to adopt the faith of Islam as my guide in life. A reply to this question may be of interest now to that large body of independent thinkers, who are manifesting a desire to know what the Islamic system really is. I am not vain enough to believe that I am the only American in this vast and progressive country capable of comprehending the system taught by the inspired Prophet of Arabia, and of appreciating its beauty and perfection. Nor do I believe that I am so deficient mentally as to accept, as truth, a religion which no one else in this country would be foolish enough to accept. But whether those who do accept it are wise or foolish in the estimation of their fellow men, I feel quite confident that at least a few may be benefited by my experience.

I was not born, as some boys seem to be, with a fervently religious strain in my character. I was emotional in later years, but not mawkishly sentimental, and always demanded a reason for everything. I will not even go so far as to assert that I was a good boy, such as fond and prejudiced mothers sometimes point out as shining examples for their own sons. I attended the Presbyterian Sunday school of my native town—when I couldn't avoid it—and listened with weariness and impatience to the long, abstruse discourses of the minister, while I longed to get out into the glad sunshine, and hear the more satisfying sermons preached by God Himself, through the murmuring brooks, the gorgeous flowers and the joyous birds. I listened incredulously to the story of the immaculate conception; and the dramatic tale of the vicarious atonement failed to arouse in me a thrill of tearful emotion, because I doubted the truth of both dogmas. Of course the narrow-minded church Christian will say at once, that the scriptural bogey-man, Satan, had me in his clutches as soon as I was born.

When I reached the age of twenty, and became, practically, my own master, I was so weary of the restraint and dullness of the church that I wandered away from it, and never returned to it. As a boy I found nothing in the system taught me in church and Sunday-school calculated to win me to it, nor did I find it any more attractive in later years, when I came to investigate it carefully and thoroughly. I found its moral ethics most commendable, but no different from those of every other system, while its superstitions, its grave errors, and its inefficiency as a means of securing salvation, or of elevating and purifying the human character, caused me to wonder why any thoughtful, honest and intelligent person could accept it seriously. Fortunately I was of an enquiring turn of mind—I wanted a reasonable foundation for everything—and I found that neither laymen nor clergy could give me any rational explanation of their faith; that when I asked them about God and the trinity, and life and death, they told me either that such things were mysteries, or were beyond the comprehension of ordinary mortals.

After trying in vain to find something in the Christian system to satisfy the longings of my soul and meet the demands of reason, I drifted into materialism; and, for several years, had no religion at all except the golden rule, which I followed about as closely as the average Christian follows it.

About eleven years ago I became interested in the study of the Oriental religions, beginning with Buddhism, as students of the Eastern systems usually do, and finding much to interest me in the Theosophical literature, which was not easy to be obtained in this country at that time. So intensely absorbed did I become in my studies and experiments, that I devoted four and five hours a day to them, often taking for that purpose time that I really needed for sleep. My mind was in a peculiarly receptive, yet exacting and analytical condition, absolutely free from the prejudices of all creeds, and ready to absorb the truth, no matter where it might be found. I was intensely in earnest in my efforts to solve the mysteries of life and death, and to know what relation the religious systems of the world bore to these mysteries. I reasoned that if there was no life beyond the grave, no religion was necessary to mankind; while if, as was claimed by many, there was a post-mortem life of far greater duration than the earthly existence, the nature and conditions of which were governed by our life on this globe, then it was of the greatest importance to know what course of life here would produce the most satisfying results in the next world.

Firmly materialistic, I looked at first to the advanced school of materialistic science, and found that it was just as completely immersed in the darkness of ignorance concerning spiritual things, as I was. It could tell me the name of every bone, muscle, nerve and organ of the human body, as well as its position, and (with one exception) its purpose of function; but it could not tell me the real difference between a living man and a dead one. It could tell me the name of every tree, plant and flower, and designate the species to which each belonged, as well as its apparent properties of attributes; but it could not tell me how and why the tree grew and flower bloomed. It was absolutely certain that man was born of woman, lived a brief period, and died; but whence he came, and whither he went were riddles which it confessed itself utterly unable to solve.

"Those matters belong to the church," said a scientist to me.

"But the church knows nothing of them," I replied.

"Nor do I, nor does science," was the helpless, hopeless way in which he dismissed the question from the conversation.

I saw Mill and Locke, and Kant and Hegel, and Fichte and Huxley, and many other more or less learned writers, discoursing, with a great show of wisdom, concerning protoplasm, and protogen, and monads, and yet not one of them could tell me what the soul was, or what becomes of it after death.

"But no one can tell you that," I fancy I hear someone say.

That is one of the greatest errors that poor, blind humanity ever made. There are people who have solved this mystery, but they are not the blind, credulous, materialistic followers of materialistic creeds.

I have spoken thus much of myself in order to show the reader that my adoption of Islam was not the result of misguided sentiment, blind credulity or sudden emotional impulse, but that it followed an earnest, honest, persistent, unprejudiced study and investigation, and an intense desire to know the truth.

After I had fully satisfied myself of the immortality of the soul, and that the conditions of the life beyond the grave were regulated by the thoughts, deeds and acts of the earth life; that man was, in a sense, his own savior and redeemer, and that the intercession of anyone between him and his God could be of no benefit to him, I began to compare the various religions, in order to ascertain which was the best and most efficacious as a means of securing happiness in the next life. To do this it was necessary to apply to each system, not only the tests of reason, but certain truths which I had learned during my long course of study and experiment outside the lines of orthodoxy, and in fields which priest and preacher usually avoid. . . .

There is no religious system known to humanity that is and has been, for centuries, so grossly misrepresented and thoroughly misunderstood by so-called Christians as that taught by the Prophet of Islam. The prejudice against it is so strong among the English-speaking people of the globe, that even the suggestion that it may possibly be the true faith and at least, worthy of a careful, unprejudiced investigation, is usually received with a contemptuous smile, as if such a thing was too palpably absurd to be considered seriously. It is this stubborn, unreasoning prejudice that prevents Europeans and Americans, who visit the East, from acquiring any accurate knowledge of Mohammedan social and religious life, or of the true doctrines of Islam. The air of superiority and self-sufficiency which they usually carry with them, repels the better and more enlightened classes of Mussulmans, and what is acquired from the lower classes cannot be taken as in any sense reliable. And yet it is this class of information that furnishes the inspiration for the magazine articles and books upon Mohammedan social life and beliefs which circulate in Europe and America. . . .

My study and observation among the Mussulmans [Muslims] of the East have led me to confidently believe that it is the most perfect system of soul-development ever given to man, and the only one applicable to all classes of humanity. It is founded upon that eternal truth, which has been handed down to man from age to age by the chosen prophets of God, from Moses to Mohammed. It is the only system known to man that is strictly in harmony with reason and science. It is free from degrading superstitions, and appeals directly to human rationality and intelligence. It makes every man individually responsible for every act he commits and every thought he thinks, and does not encourage him to sin by teaching him a vicarious atonement. It is elevating and refining in its tendencies, and develops the higher, nobler elements of humanity when it is faithfully, wisely and intelligently followed.

Source: Alexander Russell Webb. *Islam in America: A Brief Statement of Mohammedanism [sic] and an Outline of the American Islamic Propaganda.* New York: Oriental Publishing Company, 1893, pp. 11–14, 23–24.

whirling dervishes   See MEVLEVI SUFI ORDER.

white Muslim Americans

Using a broad definition, white Muslim Americans include European-American converts to Islam, Caucasian European Muslim immigrants such as BOSNIAN-AMERICAN MUSLIMS and some TURKISH-AMERICAN MUSLIMS, and ARAB-AMERICAN MUSLIMS, all of whom are considered to be "white" according to the U.S. Census. In recent times, many Muslim Americans themselves have adopted these racial criteria, and in a 2007 Pew poll, 38 percent of all Muslim Americans described themselves as white.

However, a historical approach to the question of "who is a white Muslim American" suggests a different conclusion. Many Southern and Eastern European Muslims and Middle Eastern Muslims have faced a history of legal and informal discrimination that makes their experiences different from those of Muslim Americans of northern European heritage who have chosen to become Muslims.

In the 2007 Pew poll, among Muslim Americans who have converted to Islam, 34 percent identified themselves as white, meaning that by the beginning of the 21st century, there were at least 200,000 to 250,000 white Muslim converts in the United States.

Their history and experiences reflect the larger story of religion in the United States since the 19th century. Like other white Americans dissatisfied with Christianity, Judaism, and other faiths, many of them have been religious seekers, searching for spiritual experience and communal identifications different from the traditions in which they were raised. As a result of their seeking, they have transformed the nature of SUFISM in the United States and by the late 20th century had also become some of the most prestigious and learned scholars of Islam in the United States.

ALEXANDER RUSSELL WEBB

The 19th century was a period of religious ferment and innovation in the United States, especially in New England. New religious movements emerged or expanded, such as the Church of Jesus Christ of Latter Day Saints (Mormons), Shakers, Seventh-Day Adventists, and Christian Scientists. Many Americans weary of traditional Christian denominations explored both these "home-grown" traditions as well as "exotic" traditions from the East, including Buddhism, Hinduism, and Islam. Transcendentalists and theosophists were especially interested in the "secret knowledge" available from Eastern religious traditions. They studied available texts and traveled to gain greater access to this knowledge. However, this fascination with the East also included fears and misperceptions about the politics and culture of foreign countries, stoked by travelogues and Christian missionary accounts.

In this context, ALEXANDER RUSSELL WEBB (1846–1916), a white, Presbyterian journalist from Hudson, New York, began his journey to Islam. Webb was disillusioned with Christianity, finding its doctrines of atonement—the belief that Jesus's crucifixion led to salvation for all—and the Trinity—the belief that God was One but was also three persons: Father, Son, and Holy Spirit—irrational. He began searching for a new religious tradition in the early 1880s, exploring Buddhism, materialism, and theosophy before declaring his conversion to Islam in 1888, one year after his appointment to the U.S. consulate in the Philippines. After studying Islam under several guides, Webb resigned from his position at the consulate and began planning to serve as a missionary for Islam in America.

In 1893, Webb returned to the United States and immediately began his mission work. He founded the American Moslem Brotherhood in NEW YORK CITY and instituted study circles in various cities. He also established American Islamic Propaganda publications, which produced the journals *Moslem World* and *Voice of Islam*. His major publications included *Islam in America* (1893), which described his conversion, outlined basic Muslim beliefs and practices, and appealed to Americans to convert. In lectures and writings he argued that the ideals of Islam were perfectly consistent with the best attributes of progressive America and liberal religion, such as fraternalism, tolerance, monotheism, prohibition, engagement with science, concern for the poor, cleanliness, and rationalism. At the World's Parliament of Religion, held at Chicago's COLUMBIAN EXPOSITION OF 1893, Webb was the primary representative of Islam, delivering two lectures. Despite his prominence and institutional development, Webb largely disappeared from public view by 1896, after the *New York Times* published several negative articles about conflicts over his finances and fund-raising.

Webb was not the first white Muslim American—some whites converted to Islam during the course of the Barbary wars in the early 19th century—but he was clearly the most prominent early white convert. He served as a liaison between white Americans and the international Muslim community, recognized the importance of establishing institutions for community-building, used publications to target Americans by highlighting Islam's embodiment of American ideals, and produced a conversion narrative serving multiple purposes. His work foreshadowed developments and experiences common to later converts.

SUFISM

In the early and mid-19th century, Transcendentalists explored Islam, among other traditions, to find sources of mysticism and meditation. Their appreciation for Sufi poets, especially the 13th-century Persian poet and jurist Rumi, in addition to Sufism's self-reflective practices and experiential focus, provided the groundwork for interest in Islam during the 20th century. From 1910 to 1912, Hazrat INAYAT KHAN, an Indian musician and mystic, brought Sufism to the West and conducted a series of lectures in the United States. After moving to Europe, he established the SUFI ORDER OF THE WEST (now Sufi Order International). In addition to his white American wife, Khan found a few receptive audiences among college students, theosophists, and general religious seekers in America. His message focused on religious liberalism, toleration, meditation, mystical experiences, and universal brotherhood. His ideas also included a critique of American racism and capitalism. Khan's son, Pir VILAYAT INAYAT KHAN, inherited leadership of the Sufi order after his father's death. Vilayat Khan saw increased interest in Sufism among white Americans in the 1960s, during a new wave of religious seeking. He expanded his teachings to include psychotherapy and healing, explicitly incorporating the psychological ideas of Carl Jung. Vilayat Khan's followers included SAMUEL LEWIS, who founded the SUFI RUHANIAT INTERNATIONAL. This group focused on dance as practice (most notably the Dance of Universal Peace), but they incorporated a blend of practices beyond Sufism.

The 1960s and 1970s produced several other prominent Sufi groups that appealed to white Americans. In 1971, a graduate student invited Sri Lankan Sufi Bawa Muhaiyaddeen to PHILADELPHIA, where he founded the BAWA MUHAIYADDEEN FELLOWSHIP of North America. Initially functioning more as a teacher and counselor, Muhaiyaddeen promoted peace, religious pluralism, and an end to racial distinctions. The order grew increasingly formal over the late 1970s and early 1980s. They incorporated practices such as the DHIKR, a ritualized remembrance of God, and *salat,* daily ritual prayers, which is the second pillar of Islam. Due to its explicit non-racial commitments, the fellowship has been a location for increased interaction among white, African-American, and immigrant Muslims. Another Sufi order, the MEVLEVI SUFI ORDER of America (Whirling Dervishes) was founded after Sheikh Seleyman Hayati Dede visited America during the 1970s and sent his son, Jelaluddin Loras, to teach in the West. The Mevlevi Order appeals to converts through lectures, workshops, and classes. Many women have expressed particular appreciation for their ability to participate equally in the practice of meditative whirling.

Characterizing "Sufism" among white Americans in the 21st century is challenging. The range of Sufi groups and practices has varied significantly, from the most universalistic and New Age or metaphysical to those that strictly follow the SHARI'A, the legal, ethical, and behavioral rules based on the QUR'AN and Muslim tradition. The lines between Sufism and New Age, New Religious Movements, mysticism, religious healing, and therapy have been increasingly blurred. This has led some immigrants to critique white Sufi practices and self-identification as not "truly" Muslim.

Religious studies scholar Marcia Hermansen has estimated that approximately 25,000 white Americans practice Sufism in the United States. They tend to form smaller communities, some of which are consciously interracial, that easily adapt to local contexts. Most groups develop a blend of traditional ISLAMIC THOUGHT and practice with Western ideas and concerns. These practitioners emphasize their spiritual journeys and often believe there are multiple paths to God. Sufism appeals specifically to some female converts since it is seen as less legalistic, posits parallel rights and responsibilities for men and women, and provides women with more opportunities for participation in rituals (even among the more traditional groups). Despite small numbers, Sufi practice among white Americans has influenced broader American popular culture, permeating MUSIC, POETRY, dance, therapy, and psychology.

THE CONVERSION EXPERIENCE
Interaction and Organization

While Sufis were among the first Muslim immigrants to specifically focus on converting Americans, other Muslims soon followed. Early groups included the Ahmadiyya Community in the 1920s and the Islamic Mission of America for the Propagation of Islam and Defense of the Faith and the Faithful in the late 1930s. Both groups admitted whites but tended to focus their efforts on Americans of African and Asian descent.

Declining restrictions on immigration and an even greater emphasis on organizational development in the middle of the 20th century laid the groundwork for increased white American conversion. As immigration increased during the 1950s and 1960s, more white Americans interacted with Muslims. This interaction resulted in higher numbers of intermarriages. Male international students and second-generation sons began marrying white women. These spouses were not required to convert if they were Christian or Jewish, but they were expected to raise their children as Muslims and learn their husbands' customs, community, and religion. This exposure to Islam often led women to conversion, either immediately before or soon after marriage. This trend has continued even as the number of white men marrying Muslim immigrant women has begun to increase.

While personal interaction through marriage stimulated many white conversions, organizations provided the materials, support, and structure for more sustained and systemic conversion efforts. Most significantly for white Americans, the MUSLIM STUDENTS ASSOCIATION (MSA) formed in 1963. It provided accessible English literature to white Americans. In the middle 1970s, the MSA began to focus its efforts more specifically on non-Muslims. Targeting college students, whom they considered to be the most open-minded and receptive Americans, MSA's missionary work expanded beyond sustaining immigrant communities. Along with the MSA, numerous local and national organizations increased their focus in the 1980s on conversion by providing personal contacts and information to potential converts. Prominent organizations in these efforts include the ISLAMIC SOCIETY OF NORTH AMERICA (ISNA) and the ISLAMIC CIRCLE OF NORTH AMERICA. International efforts to reach non-Muslims in the West also shaped mission efforts to white Americans. Khurram Murad, a disciple of Mawlana Maududi working in the United Kingdom, used literature and visits to the United States in the 1970s to give practical advice and theoretical justifications for engaging non-Muslims.

The Conversion Narrative

American converts often provide narratives of their experiences. Like Alexander Russell Webb's early narrative in 1893, these accounts serve multiple roles, including the solidification of personal identity, outreach to other potential converts, and assertions of the compatibility of American and Muslim identities. Conversion narratives are available in mission literature, scholarly analyses, and on the INTERNET. Ranging from a few paragraphs to complete books, they usually describe converts' motivations for considering conversion, the appeal of Islam, and the consequences of their decisions. Some converts describe themselves as "reverts," reflecting the belief that all people are Muslim at birth.

White Americans offer many reasons for conversion common to other Muslim American converts. These motivations include disillusionment with their own religious traditions, positive experiences with other Muslims, and gratifying engagements with Islam in their school studies or religious seeking. Most white American converts do not emphasize resistance to racism, a prominent idea in other Americans' conversion narratives. While Islam's appeal varies among converts, their narratives often cite spirituality, mysticism, social justice, moral responsibility, family, and community as significant in their decision. Narratives also highlight the ease of conversion and the rationality of the faith (including an embrace of science) in explaining the draw of Islam.

The conversion experience often affects the outward appearance and behavior of American converts. Possible changes include restricting behaviors when socializing with the opposite sex, celebrating different HOLIDAYS, and modifying one's diet. The most visible and politically charged change is often DRESS. Many converts change their clothing to signal a new emphasis on modesty, including the *hijab,* the female head covering, and the kufi or turban, the male head covering. While the *hijab* is often portrayed as a symbol of oppression, converts wearing it risk potential violence and discrimination to reflect their new identity, indicate their obedience to God, and challenge stereotypes. These types of changes lead to a wide range of reactions from converts' families and friends. Some converts receive broad acceptance, while others face concerns or even outright rejection. While relations often relax over time, many converts experience continuing conflicts with families and friends regarding clothing, holidays, and child-rearing.

Along with these challenges, many white Muslims experience tensions regarding their place inside the Muslim-American community. Some AFRICAN-AMERICAN MUSLIMS openly critique a perceived preference among immigrants for white converts. Single white Muslim women may face criticism from immigrants as competition for marriage. These women may also feel alienated since many activities for women are family-oriented. Finally, some immigrants voice concerns about the disproportionate impact of white American converts on identity and practices, including gender relations and Sufism.

A POWERFUL MINORITY

White Muslim Americans have been a minority of Muslim converts since the 19th century, but they have made a significant impact on Islam in the United States. They have been Muslim-American missionaries, Islamic scholars, and leaders. They have also contributed to Muslim-American poetry, media, and the struggle for gender equality. When white Muslim-American Ingrid Mattson was elected in 2006 to lead ISNA, for example, Muslim Americans proudly hailed the event as a sign of their commitment to women's rights and a version of Islam that did not pay attention to race.

White Muslim Americans have also served as powerful defenders of Muslim interests in the United States. They have asserted the compatibility of Islam with common American values: a dedication to God and PHILANTHROPY, an emphasis on family, good deeds, and discipline, and a focus on education and religious freedom. They have publicly defended their choice to convert, stressing that their decision was rational and justified, as math professor JEFFREY LANG (1954–   ) did in his memoir *Struggling to Surrender* (1994). They have also attempted to influence UNITED STATES FOREIGN RELATIONS toward the Muslim world, as can be observed in the lobbying and writing of former Nixon administration official and U.S. ambassador ROBERT DICKSON CRANE (1929–   ).

White Muslim-American leaders have been a bridge between Muslim and non-Muslim Americans. After the terrorist attacks of SEPTEMBER 11, 2001, for example, religious leader HAMZA YUSUF (1960–   ) appeared at the White House with President George W. Bush to condemn the attacks as an abuse of Islamic religion and show Muslim-American solidarity with all Americans.

From defending the interests of Muslims to leading Muslim efforts after 9/11, the white minority of Muslim Americans has helped to shape the larger story of Muslim America. As the United States has become an increasingly important location of interaction and discussion in global Islam, white Muslim Americans are likely to continue their role in shaping the engagement between Islam and the broader American culture.

Alyson L. Dickson

Further Reading

Abd-Allah, Umar F. *A Muslim in Victorian America: The Life of Alexander Russell Webb.* New York: Oxford University Press, 2006.

Anway, Carol L. *Daughters of Another Path: Experiences of American Women Choosing Islam.* Lee's Summit, Mo.: Yawna Publications, 1996.

Curtis Edward E., IV, ed. *The Columbia Sourcebook of Muslims in the United States.* New York: Columbia Press, 2008.

Haddad, Yvonne Yazbeck, and Jane I. Smith. *Muslim Communities in North America.* Albany: State University of New York Press, 1994.

Haddad, Yvonne Yazbeck, Jane I. Smith, and Kathleen M. Moore. *Muslim Women in America: The Challenge of Islamic Identity Today.* New York: Oxford University Press, 2006.

Hermansen, Marcia K. "Dimensions of Islamic Religious Healing in America." In *Religion and Healing in America,* edited by Linda L. Barnes and Susan S. Sered. New York: Oxford University Press, 2005.

———. "Roads to Mecca: Conversion Narratives of European and Euro-American Muslims." *Muslim World* 89, no. 1 (January 1999): 56–89.

Lang, Jeffrey. *Struggling to Surrender: Some Impressions of an American Convert to Islam.* Beltsville, Md.: Amana, 1994.

Malik, Jamal, and John Hinnells. *Sufism in the West.* London: Routledge, 2006.

Nieuwkerk, Karin van, ed. *Women Embracing Islam: Gender and Conversion in the West.* Austin: University of Texas Press, 2006.

Nimer, Mohammed. *The North American Muslim Resource Guide: Muslim Community Life in the United States and Canada.* New York: Routledge, 2002.

Pew Research Center. "Muslim Americans: Middle Class and Mostly Mainstream." Washington, D.C.: Pew Research Center, 2007.

Poston, Larry. *Islamic Da'wah in the West: Muslim Missionary Activity and the Dynamics of Conversion to Islam.* New York: Oxford University Press, 1992.

Reinhertz, Shakina. *Women Called to the Path of Rumi: The Way of the Whirling Dervish.* Prescott, Ariz.: Hohm Press, 2001.

Smith, Jane I. *Islam in America.* New York: Columbia University Press, 1999.

women

The United States has long been a gendered society. A person's gender shapes his or her economic opportunities, political identity, cultural assumptions, and religious life. Like most other societies in the modern era, American society has been patriarchal, meaning that the society has been organized to grant men certain powers and privileges over women.

Muslim-American communities, like many other religious communities in the United States, have used gender as a "fundamental principle" in organizing their worship, their homes, and other aspects of their lives. While some progressive and liberal Muslim Americans have challenged the organization of the community life along lines of gender, most Muslim Americans, like Americans in general, have defended the idea that there is a "common sense" difference between men and women. What almost all Muslim Americans have agreed on was the ideal that gender should not limit a person's educational or career opportunities. Men and women may be different, most Muslim Americans believe, but they are also equal.

Though it has been often assumed that women in Muslim communities are silent and oppressed, Muslim-American women have been essential partners in the building of Muslim-American institutions and culture from the beginning of their history. Muslim-American women have often challenged the gender hierarchy of their religious communities, while also continuing to work with men to advance the interests of the entire community. Muslim-American men have not often given up their privilege willingly, sometimes preferring to speak *for* women rather than *to* them. But by the late 20th century, most Muslim-American men had begun to alter their gendered views, often accepting Muslim-American women's determination to share power and authority at home, in the mosque, and in the workplace.

EARLY FEMALE LEADERS

Though men were the public face of Muslim-American religious communities for much of the 20th century, women played vital behind-the-scenes roles in developing and sustaining Muslim communities. This was especially true in AFRICAN-AMERICAN MUSLIM communities, who generally comprised the single largest ethnic group of Muslim Americans in the 20th century. In some instances, African-American women achieved public recognition as leaders.

For example, from its origins in 1925, NOBLE DREW ALI's MOORISH SCIENCE TEMPLE of America (MSTA) celebrated the leadership gifts of women and men, appointing leaders of both genders equally to positions on the local, state, and national levels. According to MSTA member Delores Weaver-Bey of Lockport, Illinois, the MSTA founder never told women "what we could not do." Ali dispatched dozens of followers, many of whom were women, as urban ministers to develop and head temples in both the North and the South. M. Whitehead-El was one of the three officials who filed documents in August 1928 to incorporate the national body and permit it to assume its current name. Two years later, she was promoted to the position of governor, a job that indicated authority over believers within a state or large region. Women continued to serve at all levels of the MSTA even as the organization declined in membership during the second half of the 20th century.

In ELIJAH MUHAMMAD's NATION OF ISLAM (NOI), his wife, CLARA MUHAMMAD, was, in the words of son and successor, W. D. MOHAMMED (1933–2008), "the glue that kept the movement together" for four decades. Soon after her husband moved the headquarters of the NOI from Detroit to CHICAGO in the 1930s, Clara Muhammad assumed the position of supreme secretary, a post that enabled her to more visibly "define, represent, and model budding Islamic womanhood," according to Mohammed. While directing the activities of men who were previously unaccustomed to taking orders from a woman, Clara became the lesser-known leader of the NOI.

In the 1930s and 1940s, NOI leaders created both the MUSLIM GIRLS TRAINING (MGT) and its male counterpart, the FRUIT OF ISLAM (FOI). Though Clara also pioneered the Islamic school system, now named in her honor as the Sister Clara Muhammad Schools, core teachings of the original NOI implied that women's work was confined to the domestic sphere, and that strong and stable family units were primarily the responsibility of female members.

In immigrant communities such as TOLEDO, OHIO, and BOSTON, MASSACHUSETTS, Muslim women similarly played essential, if behind-the-scenes, roles in sustaining religious communities. But by the 1960s, several immigrant Muslim women challenged such roles and insisted on more power in determining the course of their congregations. In 1965, Aliya Hassen, an Arab-American Muslim woman born in South Dakota, wrote a series of articles for the *FIA Journal,* the official periodical of the FEDERATION OF ISLAMIC ASSOCIATIONS IN THE UNITED STATES AND CANADA (FIA), at the time the largest of the national immigrant-led organizations. She insisted that Muslim men, not Islam itself, were the source of gender inequality. Later, in the 1970s, Zahia Khalil would be elected president of the FIA, the first time a Muslim-American woman had ascended to such a post.

Even as some Muslim-American groups became more socially conservative during the Islamic revival of the 1970s and 1980s, other leaders questioned the rigid gender separation and social hierarchy. In 1975, W. D. Mohammed, who took over the NOI that year, preached about the equality of men and women, announcing that he had studied the role of Arab women during the lifetime of the prophet MUHAMMAD in the sixth and seventh centuries and concluded that Islam did not justify "rigid divisions between men and women." While African-American Muslim women also confronted gender stereotypes that limited their roles to caring and nurturing their spouses and children in the domestic sphere, under Mohammed's leadership they experienced fewer gender challenges than their counterparts in immigrant mosques, especially in regard to mosque access and leadership opportunities. As with African-American Christian women, African-American Muslim women were a "backbone" of their religious communities. Thus, they rarely battled their male counterparts for adequate or equal access to space in the mosque.

WOMEN'S ACTIVISM
As in majority-Muslim societies, the mosque has been a central gathering place for Muslim Americans. In this communal space where rituals are observed, relationships sustained and nurtured, and beliefs legitimated, Muslim-American women have confronted patriarchal gender beliefs that have limited their roles, marginalized them physically, and dehumanized them spiritually. From the 1980s into the 21st century, many Muslim-American women fought for access to clean and adequate space in the mosque as part of a larger struggle for

gender justice or what Islamic studies scholar AMINA WADUD (1952–) labeled "gender mainstreaming," the inclusion of women in all aspects of Muslim practice, performance, and leadership.

According to "The Mosque in America: A National Portrait," a comprehensive examination of the roughly 1,625 American mosques sponsored by four organizations (three Muslim, one academic) released in 2001, most mosques are "healthy and vital." The report tied growth to "steady" conversion rates, and findings indicated that each mosque welcomed an average of 16 new Muslims every year. Yet in this report, women were said to represent only 15 percent of the estimated weekly participants at the Friday congregational prayers. The figure was surely low, given the estimated number of Muslim-American women, though it may have also reflected the nonattendance of women who felt unequally treated by their male-led communities. For most Muslims, prayer requires space for physical movement. Most women make their prayers in a space different from men, sometimes forced, sometimes choosing to pray behind curtains, screens, on balconies, behind panes of glass, or in basements or separate rooms from which they can neither see nor hear as well as men on the main floor can.

Rather than view this spatial differentiation as an act of gender modesty for all participants, a growing number of women and men characterized such practices as gender injustice. "Barriers that are placed in front of women are barriers to full participation and leadership in our communities," argues Asra Nomani, an Indian American who led a revolt at the West Virginia mosque she attends by insisting to pray in the same area with, though behind, men. According to Nomani, mosques that deny women full access place the Muslim-American community at a "crossroads," where the choices are either to mirror the egalitarian practices of the prophet Muhammad or be reduced to "the lowest fears we've got."

GENDERED INTERPRETATIONS OF TRADITIONAL SOURCES
Another aspect of the struggle for gender justice in the late 20th and early 21st centuries was female-inclusive readings of the QUR'AN. In her books, *Qur'an and Woman* (1999) and *Inside the Gender Jihad: Women's Reform in Islam* (2006), Amina Wadud argued that the sources of Islam, especially the Qur'an, had been misinterpreted by men as patriarchal texts. Wadud insisted instead that they were scriptures of gender liberation. To Wadud, such "spiritual activism" enabled Muslim women to use the same textual weapons against gender oppression that others have employed to maintain exclusive male control over "what is considered 'Islam.'"

Alongside other scholars who have used their research in Islamic texts to eradicate gender oppression from within the Islamic tradition—a group including Lois Lamya al-Faruqi,

Fatima Mernissi, Asma Barlas, and Kecia Ali—Wadud asserted that neither Islamic scriptures nor the legal opinions derived from those sources are static. Thus, for Wadud, "rereading and radically interpreting" them are both permissible and necessary tasks to separate Islamic religion from sexual oppression. By reinterpreting the texts through the lens of God's emphasis on justice, these scholars and activists have insisted that Islamic rituals performed only by men, such as leading the prayers or performing a wedding ceremony, could also be conducted by women.

MORE INCLUSIVE LEADERSHIP

A final part of the struggle for gender justice in the late 20th and early 21st centuries was the fight for more inclusive leadership in Muslim-American organizations. Muslim-American women assumed positions of leadership in various chapters of the MUSLIM STUDENTS ASSOCIATION. Women also created female-led organizations where there would be no barrier to their advancement in the community. For example, the California-based Muslim Women's League and the International League of Muslim Women (headquartered in DETROIT, MICHIGAN) nurtured and encouraged the leadership of women in every aspect of the community's affairs, including women's leadership in local mosques.

In 1998, NOI leader LOUIS FARRAKHAN promoted Ava Muhammad to lead Atlanta's Muhammad Mosque No. 15. She became the first female minister in the Nation of Islam and perhaps the first Muslim-American woman to lead a mosque. Farrakhan later named Muhammad his national spokesperson, a position both Farrakhan and MALCOLM X once held in the Nation of Islam. While some under Farrakhan's leadership viewed Muhammad as their imam, or spiritual leader, others, including former NOI leader W. D. Mohammed, discounted the characterization, in part because holding Friday prayers was not at the time a widespread practice in the NOI and Muhammad did not lead her Atlanta mosque in PRAYER.

When Canadian-born Hartford Seminary professor INGRID MATTSON was elected president of the ISLAMIC SOCIETY OF NORTH AMERICA (ISNA) in 2006, she became the most prominent female leader of a mainstream Islamic body in the country. As leader of the 20,000-member group that represented Muslim student, social, and political organizations and was an accepted source for religious interpretation, Mattson made public her own interpretations of SHARI'A, or Islamic law and ethics. As ISNA president and director of the seminary's Islamic Chaplaincy Program, she also advocated more equality in leadership of mosques and in female prayer spaces, while also defending the traditional role for men as prayer leaders.

By the 1990s, Muslim-American women were also becoming leaders in other arenas of American life. For example, Sheila Abdus-Salaam became the first female Muslim judge to serve on the New York State Supreme Court when she was elected in 1993. Yaphett El-Amin was elected to the Missouri State House of Representatives in 2001 and came in second in her bid for a Democratic nomination for a Missouri State Senate seat six years later. Individually and collectively, in private and public settings, Muslim-American women across the nation continued to provide persuasive evidence that women's rights were an issue facing both Muslim and American communities. Acting both individually and collectively, Muslim-American women were reshaping the boundaries of gender identities and transforming their roles and positions in the Muslim-American community.

Debra Majeed

Further Reading

Bagny, Ihsan, et al. "The Mosque in America: A National Portrait." Washington, D.C.: Council on American-Islamic Relations, 2001.

Barlas, Lois Asma. *"Believing Women" in Islam: Unreading Patriarchal Interpretations of the Qur'an.* Austin: University of Texas Press, 2002.

Curtis, Edward E., IV, ed. *The Columbia University Sourcebook on Muslims in the United States.* New York: Columbia University Press, 2008.

McCloud, Aminah. *Transnational Muslims in American Society.* Gainesville: University Press of Florida, 2006.

Mernissi, Fatima. *The Veil and the Male Elite: A Feminist Interpretation of Women's Rights in Islam.* Cambridge, Mass.: Perseus Books, 1991.

Wadud, Amina. *Insider Gender Jihad: Women's Reform in Islam.* Oxford: Oneworld, 2006.

———. *Qur'an and Woman: Rereading the Sacred Text from a Woman's Perspective.* New York: Oxford University Press, 1999.

Webb, Gisela, ed. *Windows of Faith: Muslim Women Scholar-Activists in North America.* Syracuse, N.Y.: Syracuse University Press, 2000.

Aliya Al-Ogdie Hassen
"Feminine Participation in Islamic Affairs" (1965)

A pioneering Muslim-American leader, Aliya Al-Ogdie Hassen (1910–90) not only advocated for women's leadership among immigrant Muslims, she also challenged the generational and racial divides that arose in the 1960s as many new Muslim immigrants arrived in the United States. Born on April 30, 1910, in Kadoka, South Dakota, to a first-generation Arab-American Muslim family from Lebanon, she left to attend the Briggs Boarding School in Detroit in 1925. In the 1950s, she moved to New York City, where she led a group of African Americans on a tour to meet Gamal Abdel Nasser, president of Egypt, and in the 1960s, assisted Malcolm X

(1925–65) in planning for his historic 1964 hajj, or pilgrimage to Mecca. In 1972, Hassen moved back to Detroit where she became a leading figure in the Arab Community Center for Economic and Social Services (ACCESS), which supplied recently arrived immigrants from Yemen, Palestine, and Lebanon with food, housing, and education in addition to helping them utilize government social services.

Hassen was a Muslim American who defied stereotypes and easy categorization. A religious Muslim, she regularly prayed, taught others how to wash the bodies of the dead in preparation for an Islamic burial, and went on the hajj. But she also enjoyed gambling and asked to be cremated upon her own death in May 1990, in defiance of shari'a, or Islamic law. In the excerpts below from a three-part series in the FIA Journal, *an official publication of the Federation of Islamic Associations of the United States and Canada, Hassen makes a case, long before 21st-century Muslim-American feminists, that Muslim women in the classical age of Islam were leaders in public affairs until Muslim men used the Qur'an as an excuse to oppress them. They became "petted and pampered playmates," she said, only after the capital of the Muslim empire moved from Damascus to Baghdad in the eighth century, more than a century after the death of the prophet Muhammad.*

Muslim women, from the very inception of Islam, participated in business affairs, in religious affairs, in educational affairs, in the social services of their community and in national emergencies. That they also participated in state affairs is also a fact. However, it is timely to offer some evidence that even in political affairs, women were not discriminated against.

Two of the most tragic civil wars in Islam were political wars and women participated in both. Aisha, wife of Muhammad participated in the political affairs which were climaxed by the Battle of Al-Jamal, and Zainab, granddaughter of Muhammad, participated in the political affairs of the tragic Battle of Karbala. . . .

No name is more renowned among the Arabs than that of [Tamudir Al-] Khansa, as a poetess before Islam and as one of Islam's most glorious daughters after she was converted to Islam. Few women, or men for that matter, exemplify the piety, courage and love of country that this woman did.

Shortly after Muhammad's Hejra [hijra, or emigration] to Medina, Khansa came with a number of the members of her tribe to learn about Islam, and were converted to the faith. She became one of Muhammad's favorite friends. He loved to listen to her recite her poems and she loved to recite them for him. Many were the encouraging poems she composed to cheer on and encourage the men going into battle. I believe the best known of her poems translated into English, composed in pagan Arab days, is her lament for her brother, the youthful king of their tribe. Who has read it and not wept, as she no doubt wept when she composed it? Yet this woman was not to weep years later after her absolute submission to God's will, when her four sons were slain.

During the battle of Qadiysia, she had accompanied her sons to war. On the eve of the battle she exhorted her sons thusly, "O my sons. You embraced Islam of your own free will. You stand here on the eve of battle, of your own free will. I swear to you by God, the one and only Deity, that you my sons, are sons of the same father and of the same mother. I never betrayed your father, or your maternal uncle. I never allowed a blot on your noble birth, nor is there any kind of pollution in your pedigree. You know the rewards of God, for those who fight in His cause and in His behalf. Remember the life of this world is but a transitory thing in nature. But remember, the life in the hereafter is everlasting. God says in His Book.

"O ye who believe, endure. Outdo each other in perseverance and be ever ready to observe your duty unto God, if you are to succeed.

"Now then, my sons, when you awaken in the morning, be prepared to contribute your very best in the battle. Fear not. March forward without hesitation into the enemy lines and know that God is beside you. Face the enemy chiefs without fear and God willing, should you fall, your abode shall be Paradise."

The next morning Khansa helped her four sons buckle on their war gear and sent them off. They sallied forth singing her poems and her last exhortations to them. Khansa remained in the rear of the battalion along with the wives, mothers, sisters and daughters of the soldiers, ready after the first onslaught to move in and tend to the wounded and dying. Sometimes during the din of battle she could hear the beloved voices of one or the other, singing or challenging the enemy's most renowned chiefs and warriors to fight. Later, news was brought to her that all four sons had perished in the battle. She was still a moment and then said, "Praise be to God. Glory be to God, who has honored me by His acceptance of my sons, in His cause. It is now my only hope that out of His infinite mercy, that God will reunite me with them in the abode of His mercy." Having thus spoken she went on tending to the wounded.

Of such material were these seventh century Muslims. Such were the examples they set for the Muslims to come after them. Their deeds should have served all our women in all times. They guided such renowned women as Rabiaha, Shuhda, Zubaida, Velda, Aisha, Labana and Algaznaia. Women who lived in various parts of the Muslim Empire, from Iraq, to Persia, to North Africa and Spain. Perhaps some of them even influenced Shagarat Al-Dur, who ruled over Egypt for a time, without a single man from among the Ulama, raising a voice against her rule over men, on the grounds that she was a female.

With such impressive examples to follow, how did the position and status of Muslim women degenerate? How did it come about that the women allowed themselves to be veiled and secluded from public life and participation in Islamic affairs? Where did the vicious circle begin?

In my opinion it had its beginning after the Capitol of the Caliph was moved to Persia. By this time the Muslim Empire was far flung and every Governor of every province and all the Muslim chiefs, became a Croesus. In Persia, the sophisticated began to slowly absorb and emulate the pagan customs of the Babylonians. Women became petted and pampered playmates, instead of helpmates, veiled to reserve their beauty from the gaze of lesser beings. Soon, when the inactivity atrophied their zeal, like kittens waiting to be fed and petted, they reverted to the subservient role they had been cast into in pagan Arab days. Once more, the male was superior to the female of the species. This status was in time to be enforced upon women in every land, by their men, who copied the sophistry of Muslim men of Persia.

More damaging than the imitations of Babylon civilization and its customs, was the interpretations that men later made of Qur'anic quotations. Interpretations which made it incumbent upon women to accept their lot on religious grounds, which were alleged to be rules laid down by God, detailing the proper deportment for them. These quotations, used to inhibit and restrain women from activities common to women of the seventh century, were narrowly interpreted that they might serve the ends of the now inflated male ego. Passages that were meant to protect and avert

harm from a woman's pathway, in the times when the Medina was a trouble spot, like Qur'an 33:59: "O Prophet. Inform your wives and daughters and the believing women that they should wear an outer cloak over their selves when traveling about, that they may be identified and not molested," began to be interpreted to mean far more than it was intended to mean.

In the days of sedition and expectancy of war between the Muslims and the Hypocrites, a number of Muslim women going about, dressed in the revealing type dress of that day, were molested and many incidents took place. To avoid further incidences, women were advised to wear a concealing outer cloak, distinctive of respectability. Most certainly it was never intended to confine them prisoners in their home, or hooded, veiled and hobbled, away from home. The same verse is as equally protective and applicable today, as it was when revealed under the same set of circumstances . . . verses like Qur'an 24:31,

"And say to the believing women that they should lower their gaze and guard their chastity and that they should not exhibit their beauty, except what is normally exposed. That they should draw a veil covering their bosoms. . . ."

These injunctions like the former are as good now as they were then, under the same mode of clothing, peculiar to that time. It was immodest to reveal most of a woman's bosom then and it is still immodest today. Exposure of breasts, waists and thighs, cause men just as much temptation today as it did then and just as many women receive insults because of such immodest dress today and run the risk of being molested because of their immodesty, as they did then.

Had the style of women's dresses been modest even in today's standard, the admonition would not have been necessary.

The Bikinis and short shorts and skin-tight pants of today that women of ultra sophistication wear, draw lewd insults to those who wear them, as well as danger of molestation, and those who place themselves in such a position, have themselves alone to blame. Modesty of dress could have avoided insult and harm to them. But men of the day we are discussing, neglected to remember the underlying reasons for these injunctions, just as they neglected to remember that in the Qur'an 24:30, it also instructed the men to, "Say to the believing men that they should lower their gaze and guard their chastity. . . ." Had not temptations been placed before their eyes by the immodest apparel of that day, they too would not have been warned to avoid sin by looking away and thinking purely, when such sights met their gaze.

Aisha tells us of an incident which took place in her home, during the visit of her step sister Asma. It seems that Asma, dressed in the mode of the sophisticated city woman, was reclining in a relaxed manner, chatting with her and Muhammad, when he finally had to turn his face away from Asma and say to her, "O Asma. When women come of age, it is no longer proper for her to leave exposed so many parts of her body." Had Muhammad believed that women should wear nun-like habits and completely veil themselves, he was most assuredly articulate enough to have said so. Instead, he simply stressed the need for adult women to attire themselves modestly—advice which holds true in every day and age.

What was the mode of dress that Muhammad thought objectionable? Several styles were in vogue in that day. One style was that typical to our screen's version of the "Belly Dancers." This costume was highly ornamented with beads, jewels, or embroidery, or plain in the case of some slaves, at the brassiere-like vest, which called attention to bosoms more exposed than concealed. Also at the waist and girdle, calling attention to waist, hips and thighs. Add to this a number of bracelets to arms and ankles, filled with charms and bells which jingled as they walked to call attention to them and you have a sight which would stop men in their tracks today, as it did then. After all, human nature has not changed that much.

This then was the at-home wear even of the aristocratic ladies. Older women added to the above costume a voluptuous, or full shift-like, low necked kimono sleeved, long MuMu [a long dress that hangs from the shoulders], which was embroidered at neck, sleeves and hem. This was made from a net-like or diaphanous material of one or two layers and worn over all. This was not always confined to older women, but to more conservative women when going about in public. From this, we may rightly assume that a need for a change in dress was called for. For it is and always has been, that through modesty of dress and deportment, that the chastity and morals of both men and women have been safeguarded.

All of these "excuses" contributed heavily towards the segregation of women from public life and secular affairs. Further, when the Emirs [princes] and Governors of the various provinces of the Muslim Empire, destroyed the idealism and unity of Islam, with their struggle for power, the decline and fall of the Muslim Empire began. When this came to pass, it became inevitable that the keys to emancipation which freed Muslim women, be lost in the seas of retrogression. The men who were once masters of most of the known world and its seas, now added, "it's for your own protection, my dears," to the multiple excuses of the past. Protection indeed! But it happened and it came to pass that the helpmate, the Amazon, the educator, the business woman, the social service worker, the spirited companion, became the decorative but spineless hothouse flower relegated to obscurity behind veils and barred doors—a position she did not emerge from again until the twentieth century.

In this century a few brave Egyptian women, rediscovered their rights and began a stupendous fight to regain them. They were most fortunate to find exceptionally courageous and enlightened men to support them in their struggle. Thanks to these suffragists, women, in Egypt are once again participating in every field of human endeavor beneficial to God and country . . . are being employed in the Ministry of Education, the Public Health Services and all Social Services. Once again they are practicing law, medicine, surgery and entering into every scientific field to work in complete equality beside their men. This re-emancipation is not confined solely to Egyptian women. They only started the ball rolling. Now Muslim women in every Muslim land have almost totally emerged from behind the veil and the cloister and are slowly and steadily taking their rightful places besides their men, as helpmates, friends and patrons to each other.

The points presented thus far have shown that beyond a shadow of a doubt that men and women are spiritual equals before God and the law. Shown that they have equal responsibilities towards each other, the Muslim family, the community and the nation. This leaves us with a last point of contention. Which sex is "superior" to the other? What is the natural position of the sexes?

The Qur'an 4:34 states, "Men are the protectors and providers of women, because by nature God gave to men a greater degree of strength (physical strength) than women." However, translated it simply implies that men are superior to women only on a physical, or biological basis.

This makes him the "natural head" of the family. It therefore becomes his bounden duty as the sire of the family, to shield, guide, protect and provide for the family. He alone is its natural breadwinner. Therefore, it is because of this position in the human family that men became much more prominent in public life and secular affairs.

Consequently he is "superior" to women in this sense and in this sense alone.

We now turn to the natural position in which the female stars. Since time immemorial, with rare exceptions, her position physically and biologically is that of mother, wife, helpmate, supplementary guide and protectoress of the home and its offspring. Her first duty is to them. However, once she fulfills this obligatory duty, if she had the time, the talent and the desire for an avocation in life apart from her immediate family, she has every right to do so according to Islam.

If this shows that men are "superior" to women, it is the only type of superiority over women, recognized by Islam. Now then, should the laws of inheritance seem unjust to women, due to the fact that men do receive twice the share of a female, this is only seemingly unjust. Actually aside from the fact that before Muhammad's time, women inherited nothing and had no property rights, real or personal, there is a fine equity even in this law. Why? Because the male is obligated to completely maintain and provide for the home and family, out of every resource available to him, earned or inherited. This however, does not apply to women. No woman is compelled to spend one cent of her earnings or her dowry, or her inheritance, upon the family. She may do so of her own free will. However, it is not incumbent upon her. These facts erase the seeming injustice.

In conclusion, O daughters of Islam, where do you go from here? Your status and position in the faith has been stripped of the artifices which relegated you to obscurantism. Your eyes have been opened by the examples set for you by Muslims of the seventh century, who lived in the lifetime of Muhammad, your Prophet. Lived in a day when had the precedences of their deeds and actions been contrary to Islam or what was expected of them, they most certainly would never have been allowed to participate in every religious and secular affair of their times. But they were not discriminated against and therefore participated in every aspect of Islamic affairs. The beacon light which they lit and held high to guide your future, is still re-lit. You may again follow its rays. But first know yourself.

Know your capabilities, your potentials, your limitations and your strength, before deciding what you want out of life, or what you have to offer life. If happily married and content with your role as wife and mother, be sure that this noble career as queen of your home is life's most noble one. If married and you still feel the need or the desire for an avocation apart from the family, which can be compensational to yourself, or in the services of God, the community or the nation, as long as you fulfill the obligations to the home and family, allow nothing to hinder you from seeking it. If you are unmarried and long for a career, go forth and seek it. One day it may be greatly beneficial to family and community.

However you decide, remember as you participate in Islamic or secular affairs, of community of nation, the spirit of Islam's "First Ladies," will lovingly shadow you and cheer you onward towards your goal.

Source: Aliya Al-Ogdie Hassen. "Feminine Participation in Islamic Affairs." *FIA Journal* 1, no. 3 (June 1965): 18–26.

Works Progress Administration

The Works Progress Administration (WPA) was one of President Franklin Delano Roosevelt's New Deal programs during the GREAT DEPRESSION that sought to provide work in order to alleviate economic distress. Established in 1935, the WPA provided work for both blue- and white-collar workers. One of the tasks for unemployed authors and teachers was to conduct oral history interviews of various marginalized social groups within society. Two of the groups that were the subjects of these interviews were Muslim Americans and those with Muslim-American ancestry: the GULLAH people of the GEORGIA SEACOAST and Syrian-Lebanese immigrants to NORTH DAKOTA.

The book *Drums and Shadows* (1940) was a production of the WPA's Georgia Writers' Project. The goal of *Drums and Shadows* was twofold: to provide work for unemployed writers and to record the oral histories of the inhabitants of the Georgia seacoast, many of whom were elderly former slaves by the 1930s. *Drums and Shadows* forms the first major attempt at a public history of the Gullah culture. Although the work of the WPA writers in Georgia was in many ways superseded by other researchers such as Lorenzo Dow Turner, this oral history project succeeded in preserving many of the traditional stories of the Gullah culture. Among the discoveries that *Drums and Shadows* exposed to a broader public was the multigenerational presence of Muslims in the United States. The memory of Muslim RELIGIOUS LIFE along the Georgia Seacoast was recalled in the 1930s, as the grandchildren of Muslims told interviewers about African-Islamic traditions of PRAYER, FOOD, and DRESS they learned about in their youth.

Another oral history project of the WPA recorded the experiences of Muslim Americans in North Dakota. This project provided a wealth of information concerning the immigration, employment, and settlement patterns of Muslim immigrants from Syria and Lebanon in the late 19th and early 20th centuries. These records suggest that while Muslims in North Dakota may have hated the harsh winters of the upper Midwest, they did not fear their non-Muslim neighbors or feel the need to conceal their religious faith. In the town of Ross, Muslims developed an Islamic cemetery and a mosque. They butchered meat according to rules of Islamic tradition, invited guest religious leaders to marry their children and bury their dead, and observed various Muslim HOLIDAYS, including the dawn-to-dusk fasting during Ramadan.

The efforts of the WPA writers' projects produced a vast array of data, marking the first effort to systematically collect oral histories on a national scale. None of the projects aimed explicitly to record aspects of Muslim-American life. But the data collected from both immigrants and former slaves revealed that Islam had been a noteworthy part of America's past.

Patrick Callaway

Further Reading

Georgia Writers' Project. *Drums and Shadows*. Athens: University of Georgia Press, 1940.

Sherman, William C., Paul L. Whitney, and John Guerrero. *Prairie Peddlers: The Syrian-Lebanese in North Dakota*. Bismarck, N.Dak.: University of Mary Press, 2002.

World Community of al-Islam in the West

The World Community of al-Islam in the West was the reorganized NATION OF ISLAM (NOI) under the leadership of W. D. MOHAMMED (1933–2008), the seventh son and named successor of NOI leader ELIJAH MUHAMMAD (1897–1975). After succeeding to the NOI leadership upon his father's death in 1975, Mohammed announced his intention to lead the NOI membership into Sunni Islam, the branch of Islam practiced by 80 to 85 percent of the world's Muslims, and the Nation of Islam became the World Community of al-Islam in the West (WCIW) in 1976. His program for Sunni reform was comprehensive and sought to address all religious teach-

ings and movement symbols that were viewed as religiously illegitimate by its SUNNI MUSLIM AMERICAN critics.

When Elijah Muhammad died in 1975, he left behind one of the largest Muslim religious organizations in the United States. Valued at approximately $60 million, the Nation of Islam "empire," which was personally owned by Muhammad, included approximately 75 mosques, a weekly newspaper, a multimillion-dollar fish import business, a small bank, trucks, a clothing factory, farms, and homes. In addition to offering its members a strict moral code, a strong sense of communal solidarity, and what members believed was the guidance of a living prophet—Elijah Muhammad—the NOI became successful because of its message of racial self-determination. Like many black organizations in the past, it stressed the need for African Americans to be economically independent from the white-dominated marketplace.

W. D. Mohammed preserved or improvised on many of these themes, though he hoped to take the organization in a radically different direction. In many ways, the conditions that helped to make the NOI so successful had begun to change. The victories of the civil rights movement, the end of legal segregation, and rise of incomes among many African Americans had expanded the black middle class, the presence of which blunted some of the impact of the NOI's radical political call for a separate black nation. Religious REVIVALISM in the era was dominated by Sunni Muslim organizations led by both immigrants and African Americans, and more African Americans outside the NOI were coming to associate with Sunni Islam.

W. D. Mohammed responded to these large cultural and social changes by transforming the NOI into a Sunni religious organization geared toward black cultural pride rather than racial separatism. He began his program of reforms by changing movement nomenclature: Temples became mosques, ministers became imams, and the Nation of Islam became the World Community of al-Islam in the West. Mohammed gave up his own title of "Supreme Minister" for "Imam," or religious leader. The name of the NOI newspaper, *MUHAMMAD SPEAKS*, was changed to *Bilalian News*, in recognition of Bilal, Islam's first muezzin, or prayer caller. Dozens of University of Islam girls' schools were renamed Sister CLARA MUHAMMAD schools to honor his mother, a key figure in the NOI's early history.

As in the past, Mohammed honored the dignity of work, the centrality of family, social responsibility, and the rehabilitation of ex-convicts. But to this list, he added loyalty to the United States. Beginning in 1976, the WCIW celebrated July 4 with patriotic speeches, parades, and articles, officially recognizing Independence Day. The NOI's former call for a separate nation was rejected.

By 1980, *Bilalian News* published the addresses of 163 mosques associated with the WCIW. One hundred twenty-four affiliated radio stations were also listed. The WCIW was international in outlook, regarding itself as a full member of the world Muslim community. *Bilalian News* carried regular articles on what was happening throughout the globe with frequent references to the Muslim World League, the Saudi-funded Sunni missionary organization, and the Organization of Islamic Conference, a semigovernmental organization with official status at the United Nations. The paper also covered the antiapartheid struggle in South Africa, the Rhodesian Bush War, the Soviet invasion of Afghanistan, human rights issues, and issues on human development. Finally, like *Muhammad Speaks, Bilalian News* addressed family life, morality, and the arts.

From 1976 until 1985, the word *Bilalian* was used not only for members of the movement but also for African Americans whose achievements the newspaper celebrated. Almost any Bilalian "first" was reported. The newspaper's aims included addressing impediments to Bilalian accomplishments, critiquing discriminatory practice that denied anyone the opportunity to grow and develop in their "balanced human form," and supporting the financial development of all deprived communities. Some aims were specifically concerned with improving the welfare and public image of African Americans.

One aspect of Elijah Muhammad's legacy that remained central to the WCIW was his concern to encourage pride in African-American heritage. Other aims expressed solidarity with all oppressed and disadvantaged people, regardless of race or creed. At local mosques, WCIW members ran social service and welfare programs such as the Ilm Foundation, sponsored by the Masjid Ibadillah in Los Angeles. Youth leadership training, food programs, free clothing, annual health checkups, and work with ex-offenders have all characterized the organization's philanthropic work.

Mohammed became a key participant in Focolare, an international interfaith movement established by a Roman Catholic nun. Human beings, said Mohammed in 1980, were not to be distinguished by the religious label that they wear but by their moral conduct. Following his example, imams and mosques also participated in various INTERFAITH MOVEMENTS. The *Bilalian News* regularly reported on local interfaith dinners and international meetings alike.

In 1980, the WCIW changed its name to the American Muslim Mission, reflecting the growing identification as an American mission of a global religion. In 1985, the organization's national leadership council, headed by Mohammed, was disbanded, with each mosque becoming independent and self-governing. Imams were elected by mosque memberships rather than being centrally appointed. Then, in 1997, the movement became known as the Muslim American Society and, in 2002, as the American Society of Muslims. The *Bilalian News,* discontinued in 1981, was revived as the *Muslim Journal.*

W. D. Mohammed retired as president of the American Society of Muslims in 2003, establishing a new charity called Mosque Cares. He expressed disappointment that many imams had failed to gain the requisite knowledge of Islam and of ARABIC needed to convey the authentic tradition and that some opposed integration into Sunni Islam. While officially open to anyone, the membership remained almost entirely African-American. Nevertheless, he remained the de facto head of the American Society of Muslims.

When Mohammed died in 2008, the American Society of Muslims may have commanded the interest of 100,000 to 250,000 people, but its future direction was uncertain. While there were other strong leaders inside the movement, including Imam Plemon T. El-Amin of Atlanta, Mohammed had not named a successor. It was not clear to its members that the movement even needed a single leader since it had evolved into a grassroots, community-based organization that welcomed national and international ties but remained focused on the local activism and individual piety of its members.

Clinton Bennett

Further Reading

Ba-Yunus, Ilyas, and Kassim Kone. *Muslims in the United States.* Westport, Conn.: Greenwood Press, 2006.

Bukhari, Zahid Hussain. *Muslims' Place in the American Public Square: Hope, Fears, and Aspirations.* Walnut Creek, Calif.: AltaMira Press, 2004.

Curtis, Edward E., IV. *Islam in Black America: Identity, Liberation, and Difference in African-American Islamic Thought.* Albany: State University of New York Press, 2002.

Haddad, Yvonne Yazbeck, and Jane I. Smith. *Muslim Minorities in the West: Visible and Invisible.* Walnut Creek, Calif.: AltaMira Press, 2002.

Terry, Don. "Black Muslims Enter the Mainstream," *New York Times,* 3 May 1993.

Watanabe, Teresa. "Influential Islamic Leader Steps Down," *Los Angeles Times,* 13 September 2003, p. B24.

World Wide Web   See INTERNET.

World Trade Center bombing of 1993

On February 26, 1993, at 12:18 P.M. a car bomb exploded below the World Trade Center in NEW YORK CITY. The World Trade Center was a complex of offices, public space, and restaurants whose twin towers rising 100 stories dominated the skyline of downtown Manhattan's financial district. The structure withstood the shock even though the blast ripped a hole through four sublevels of concrete. The blast killed six people and wounded 1,042 others. The bombing was the first successful attack by terrorists linked to al-Qaeda, an Islamic extremist group, in the United States.

THE CONSPIRACY

Ramzi Yousef, a Kuwaiti-born electrical engineer of Pakistani descent, planned the attacks with Mahmud Abouhalima, Ahmed Ajaj, Nidal Ayyad, Mohammad Salameh, and Abdul Rahman Yasin. They came from a variety of backgrounds. Abouhalima had belonged to the outlawed Muslim Brotherhood as an adolescent in Egypt. He applied successfully for amnesty in the United States in 1986. Between 1986 and 1991 he drove a cab in Brooklyn, New York, while volunteering for a nonprofit charity that raised money for the Afghan resistance, which, with U.S. assistance, successfully expelled the Soviet army from Afghanistan.

Salameh, a Palestinian from a refugee family, grew up in Jordan. He came to the United States in 1986, where he worked at a number of short-term menial jobs in New York. Yasin was born to an Iraqi family in Bloomington, Indiana, while his father attended Indiana University. He grew up in Iraq but used his U.S. citizenship to return to the United States in 1992. Ayyad, a Palestinian raised in Kuwait, graduated from Rutgers University with a degree in chemical engineering in 1991. A naturalized American citizen, Ayyad took a job at Allied Signal, an engineering firm that allowed him to obtain some of the chemicals used in the bomb.

Yousef, who had studied bomb-making at training camps in Afghanistan, and Ajaj boarded a flight from Pakistan to New York on September 2, 1992. The two men sat separately. Both carried false passports, which roused the suspicion of customs officials in New York. An inspection of Ajaj's luggage revealed material and instructions for building a bomb and other weapons. Ajaj was arrested and sent to a facility in Queens, where he remained in telephone contact with Yousef. Yousef, traveling under a false Iraqi passport, claimed to be the victim of political persecution in Iraq and asked for asylum. Customs officials released Yousef pending a hearing scheduled for December 2, 1992. Yousef took up residence in Jersey City, New Jersey, just across the Hudson River from lower Manhattan.

Yousef contacted Sheikh OMAR ABDEL-RAHMAN, a controversial cleric preaching at the Al-Farooq mosque in Brooklyn. Abdel-Rahman, like Abouhalima, had been a member of the Muslim Brotherhood in Egypt. He had been arrested and tortured in Egypt on suspicion of inciting the murder of Egyptian leader Anwar Sadat in 1981. Although he was acquitted of these charges, the Egyptian government expelled him upon his release from prison. Abdel-Rahman introduced Yousef to the remaining conspirators. Yousef's uncle, Khalid Sheikh Mohammed, provided the conspirators with advice and $660.00. According to the 9/11 Report, released in 2004, Khalid Sheik Mohammed was the chief architect of the second terrorist attack on the World Trade Center on SEPTEMBER 11, 2001.

By the end of 1992, the conspirators were assembling material and conducting reconnaissance of the World Trade Center. On two occasions, they were nearly exposed when Salameh, who served as a driver for the other members of group, got into car accidents. On January 21, 1993, Salameh's first accident left Yousef in the hospital in Rahway, New Jersey. With his neck in a brace, Yousef ordered chemicals for the bomb from the hospital telephone. A few weeks later Salameh crashed the car again as he drove Ayyad home from mapping the garage of the World Trade Center. Looking for a less accident-prone driver, Yousef enlisted Jordanian Eyad Ismoil (Ismail), an old friend. Just before the attack, Yousef mailed letters to the major newspapers denouncing Israel as a terrorist state and warning that more attacks would follow the bombing of the World Trade Center unless the United States abandoned support for Israel.

Around noon on February 26, 1993, Yousef and Ismoil drove a rented Ryder truck loaded with explosives to the parking garage under the World Trade Center. The 1,310-pound device, which Yousef and Yasin had constructed together, consisted of four boxes, each packed with a mixture of newspaper, urea, and nitric acid (fertilizer), three canisters of compressed hydrogen, and four containers of nitroglycerin. Yousef lit the fuse and fled. The bomb exploded, causing tremendous damage and widespread panic as people attempted to flee the building. Several of hours after the bombing, Yousef boarded a plane bound for Pakistan.

Yousef intended to destabilize Tower One, sending it crashing it into Tower Two. But the towers (which were constructed using the tube-frame structural design pioneered by Muslim-American architect FAZLUR RAHMAN KHAN) withstood the blast. Yousef also intended to suffocate the people inside the towers. Most of the 1,042 people injured in the attack suffered from falling debris and smoke inhalation during the evacuation rather than from the blast itself. Thick, greasy smoke penetrated as high as the 93rd floor and filled the stairwells. The blast cut off electricity, trapping hundreds of people, including a kindergarten class, in the elevators. Without guiding lights or official instructions, more than 50,000 people evacuated the building successfully.

INVESTIGATION

Investigators recovered the vehicle identification number of the Ryder truck from the debris. Using this number, they traced the Ryder truck to a rental company in Jersey City. They arrested Salameh when he returned to the rental company to claim the deposit on the truck, which he had reported stolen. With Salameh in custody, the police had no trouble finding Yasin, who had helped Yousef construct the bomb. Yasin was interrogated at FBI headquarters in NEWARK, NEW

JERSEY. He was quickly released and allowed to return to Iraq, apparently after providing extensive information about the bombing. After the second attack on the World Trade Center on September 11, 2001, the FBI placed Yasin on its list of Most Wanted Terrorists.

Salameh, Abouhalima, Ayyad, and Ajaj went on trial later in the year and, found guilty, were sentenced to life imprisonment in May 1994 for their roles in the World Trade Center bombing. On February 7, 1995, Pakistani intelligence agents and members of the American Diplomatic Security Service arrested Yousef in Islamabad, Pakistan. Yousef was tried in a U.S. District Court in New York, and on September 5, 1996, Judge Kevin Duffy sentenced Yousef to life in prison for his role in the aborted Bojinka plot, a plot to blow up 11 airplanes en route from Asia to the United States. On November 12, 1997, Yousef was also found guilty of "seditious conspiracy" for the World Trade Center bombing. The Jordanian government extradited Eyad Ismoil, who had driven the Ryder truck to the World Trade Center, to the United States. On April 3, 1998, Eyad was sentenced to 210 years in prison.

MUSLIM-AMERICAN RESPONSE

The AMERICAN MUSLIM COUNCIL and other Muslim-American agencies immediately condemned the attack as an unjustified assault on a nation where Muslims live in peace and security. The AMERICAN-ARAB ANTI-DISCRIMINATION COMMITTEE urged Americans not to blame all Arabs for the actions of a few. Fearing a rise in violence against Arabs and Muslims, the Muslim community condemned the bombing while inviting the media to present a complex view of Islam. At the same time, they called for greater attention to the grievances that apparently inspired the attack, including the ongoing Israeli-Palestinian conflict.

Sonja Spear with John Schrumpf

Further Reading

National Commission on Terrorist Attacks upon the United States. *The 9/11 Commission Report.* New York: W. W. Norton, 2004.

U.S. House of Representatives, 103rd Congress, First Session. *World Trade Center Bombing.* Washington, D.C.: U.S. Government Printing Office, 1994.

World's Fair   See COLUMBIAN EXPOSITION OF 1893.

World War I

Though World War I was fought mainly in Europe from 1914 to 1918 and U.S. troops entered the "Great War" only in 1917, about a year and a half before it ended, the war had a critical impact on the unfolding history of Muslim America.

Hundreds, if not thousands of Muslim Americans, mostly ARAB-AMERICAN MUSLIMS, fought in the war as part of the American Expeditionary Force. According to the War Department, at least 13,965 or 7 percent of Syrian Americans served in uniform. Of these, 10 percent or more were Muslims. In North Dakota, where approximately one-third of all Arab Americans were Muslims, at least one-quarter of Syrian-American troops were Muslim. They included Private Omer Otmen, a 29-year-old who was inducted into the army on April 29, 1918, and sent to Camp Dodge, Iowa, where he was assigned to Company I of the 350th Infantry. He was deployed overseas from July 6, 1918, to June 7, 1919, and was present during the Meuse-Argonne Offensive, a bloody 1918 battle that pitted American and other allied troops against German forces and resulted in 125,000 American casualties. Otmen survived and was discharged on June 14, 1919.

The impact of the war on Arab-American Muslim identity was profound. Immigration from the Middle East and Southeastern Europe, lands controlled by the Ottoman Empire, came to a virtual halt after the beginning of the war in 1914. According to historian Philip Hitti, Arab Americans began to think of themselves less as visitors and more as permanent residents and citizens of the United States. U.S. patriotism among the new immigrants increased as Arab Americans on the home front supported the war effort. In Quincy, Massachusetts, Hitti wrote, a group of Syrian Americans that likely included at least some Muslims built ships, establishing a world record for "driving 2,805 oil-tight rivets into the hull of a steel ship in a nine-hour stretch." In the New York areas, 4,800 Arab Americans purchased war bonds worth $1.2 million.

Though there were very few Muslim-American converts to Islam at the time, U.S. participation in the war also fueled the social conditions and political environment in which hundreds, if not thousands, of African Americans would become Muslims in the 1920s. This was one of the unforeseen consequences of the war. Black soldiers served in a war that President Woodrow Wilson had said would make the world "safe for democracy." As African-American leaders such as W. E. B. DuBois closed ranks to support the United States, they also expected that African-American involvement in a campaign for democracy would lead to racial equality in the United States.

Pan-African Muslim intellectual DUSÉ MOHAMED ALI (1866–1945), editor of the *African Times and Orient Review,* wrote in 1918 that "President Wilson will be forced to see that those men who have fought for the freedom of small nationalities in Europe and elsewhere shall not be denied that freedom to which they are so justly entitled in the United States." The hopes of African-American troops for equality were high, especially for those who had served alongside French troops who treated them with relative respect.

Such expectations went unfulfilled. The UNITED STATES MILITARY remained segregated during the war, and when black soldiers returned from the fight in 1919, they discovered that little had changed in American race relations. They organized politically, lending support to the call of the Universal Negro Improvement Association (UNIA) for racial self-determination and emigration to a free Africa. Muslim intellectuals such as Dusé Mohamed Ali, who by 1922 had become foreign affairs correspondent for the UNIA's *Negro World,* urged African Americans to cultivate political relationships with other "colored races" seeking freedom from colonization in Africa and Asia. Ali's linking of black hopes to Asian and African independence had ripples in African-American RELIGIOUS LIFE as well. During the 1920s and early 1930s, AHMADI MUSLIM missionary Muhammad Sadiq, MOORISH SCIENCE TEMPLE of America founder NOBLE DREW ALI, and NATION OF ISLAM founder W. D. FARD urged African Americans to practice Islam, which, they said, was a rightful religious inheritance that offered black people freedom and equality—unlike the Christianity of white Americans.

Though World War I did not directly cause the flowering of Islam among African Americans, it unleashed a series of events and conditions that led some African Americans to associate Islam with political freedom and cultural pride. World War I had a different effect among Arab Americans, many of whom came to associate more closely with the United States as a result of the war. In both cases, the war altered the course of Muslim-American history.

Edward E. Curtis IV

Further Reading

Duffield, Ian. "Some American Influences on Dusé Mohamed Ali." In *Pan-African Biography,* edited by Robert A. Hill, 11–56. Los Angeles: Crossroads Press, 1987.

Hitti, Philip K. *The Syrians in America.* New York: George H. Doran Company, 1924.

Sherman, William C. *Prairie Peddlers: The Syrian-Lebanese in North Dakota.* Bismarck, N.Dak.: University of Mary Press, 2002.

World War II

World War II, fought primarily by the Axis powers of Germany and Japan against the Allied powers of the United States, the Soviet Union, Great Britain, and the French resistance from 1939 to 1945, had important repercussions for Muslim-American history. As in WORLD WAR I, the implications of the war, which the United States entered in 1941, were neither uniform nor predictable for Muslim Americans. On the one hand, the war provided an opportunity for both foreign-born and native-born ARAB-AMERICAN MUSLIMS and other immigrant Muslims to demonstrate their loyalty to the United States. On the other hand, some of black America's most vociferous opponents to U.S. participation were AFRICAN-AMERICAN MUSLIMS who sided with the Empire of Japan.

Though no reliable estimate exists on the number of Muslims who volunteered to serve in the UNITED STATES MILITARY during World War II, at least 1,555 men and women with identifiably Muslim names volunteered. This estimate of those who served is likely low, because it does not include African-American Muslims with non-Muslim names and Muslim immigrants who had adopted Anglo-sounding names. Perhaps as many as 5,000 or more Muslims served in the war. Of these, 58 had the name Muhammad, spelled in 17 different ways. Ally A. Mohammed, for example, whose race was classified as "Native American" in enlistment records, signed up on July 20, 1942, when he was 33 or 34. He was a divorced waiter from Louisiana with a grade-school education. Shrieff Mohammed from NEW YORK CITY, who likely emigrated from South Asia, enlisted on February 6, 1943. This 37- or 38-year old had little education, no listed occupation, and did not yet have American citizenship.

Enlisting on April 20, 1943, John R. Omar (1924–2007), the son of Syrian-Lebanese immigrant Mohammed Omar and a resident of Quincy, Massachusetts, served as a top turret gunner on a B-24 Liberator bomber. Assigned to the 491st bombardment group of the Eighth Air Force in Europe, Omar participated in 29 missions, including the Battle of the Bulge (1944–45), a German offensive that resulted in a decisive Allied victory. During a mission over Madgeburg, Germany, Omar managed to open his B-24's bomb doors manually after the hydraulic system was damaged by German antiaircraft fire. While doing so, he was hit by shrapnel in his right foot. He was later awarded a Purple Heart medal whose citation read: "For meritorious achievement in accomplishing aerial operations missions over enemy-occupied Continental Europe, Omar's actions reflect great credit upon himself and the armed forces of the United States." After the war, Sergeant Omar founded Omar's Auto Body Shop in Quincy, a business he operated for more than five decades until his retirement in 1989. He was also a member of the Islamic Center of New England and later adopted the title Haj to indicate that he had performed the PILGRIMAGE to Mecca.

Arab-American Muslim Abdullah Igram of CEDAR RAPIDS, IOWA, enlisted on December 4, 1942, and was stationed in the Philippines until the end of the war. Returning home to Iowa in 1946, Igram joined other Muslim-American leaders in asserting that their participation in the war was evidence that Islam deserved to be recognized as a legitimately American religion. In 1952, he founded the FEDERATION OF ISLAMIC ASSOCIATIONS IN THE UNITED STATES AND CANADA, and in 1953 Igram petitioned the

Eisenhower administration to recognize the right of Muslims in the military to indicate their religious identity on their identification tags, or dog tags. In the wake of World War II and the burgeoning cold war between the United States and the Soviet Union, immigrant mosque-goers in Toledo, Ohio, also stressed the ideological parallels between Islamic and American values, seeing them as complementary and mutually reinforcing. It has also been argued by scholars of Arab-American history that after World War II, Arab Americans were increasingly identified as having white ETHNICITY, which was the ultimate sign of acceptance as a mainstream American community.

Among African-American Muslims, World War II had far different repercussions. Muslim-American leaders such as WALI AKRAM (1904–94) apparently encouraged his congregants in CLEVELAND, OHIO, to volunteer for the armed services, and members of the ADDEYNU ALLAHE UNIVERSAL ARABIC ASSOCIATION used their wages from work at war-related industries around Buffalo, New York, to develop their Muslim community in West Valley, New York. However, black Muslim leaders such as ELIJAH MUHAMMAD (1897–1975), leader of the NATION OF ISLAM, was among the approximately 25 black leaders—Muslim and non-Muslim—targeted by the Federal Bureau of Investigation for encouraging pro-Japanese sympathies among African Americans. Part of a grassroots African-American movement, these Muslims saw the Japanese as fellow people of color, hoping that a Japanese victory in the war would translate into freedom from racism and oppression in the United States. Though accused of sedition, Muhammad was convicted only of draft evasion and was imprisoned in a federal correctional facility in Milan, Michigan, from 1943 to 1946.

Soon after World War II, the Nation of Islam and its main spokesperson, Malcolm X (1925–65), emerged as powerful critics of the Civil Rights movement and U.S. FOREIGN RELATIONS. The Nation of Islam joined African and Asian leaders in criticizing the United States for its cold war policy of meddling in the affairs of the newly independent nations of Asia and Africa, citing CIA-backed coups in Latin America and the Middle East as examples of white racism toward people of color. This anticolonial stance was also attractive to Muslim-American immigrants, who increasingly articulated their hopes that the United States would support self-determination in their former homelands, and especially for Palestinians, who had been left without a state as a result of the Arab-Israeli war of 1948. Unlike Elijah Muhammad and Malcolm X, however, many Muslim-American immigrants rejected the idea that America was hopelessly flawed, instead asking that the United States simply apply its principles of freedom and democracy when dealing with Muslims abroad.

Edward E. Curtis IV

Further Reading

Allen, Ernst, Jr. "When Japan Was 'Champion of the Darker Races': Satokata Takahashi and the Flowering of Black Messianic Nationalism." *Black Scholar* 24 (Winter 1994): 23–46.

National Archives. "Access to Archival Databases (AAD)." Available online. URL: http://aad.archives.gov/aad/. Accessed October 19, 2009.

Orfalea, Gregory. *The Arab Americans: A History.* Northampton, Mass.: Olive Branch Press, 2006.

wrestlers

American professional wrestling has long made use of political and social tensions to drive its storylines and shape its characters. In this milieu, Muslims have been typically portrayed as "heels," or villains. Like a great villain in the movies, the heel is the person the audience loves to hate. Successful heels have large fan bases and over the years become so cherished by fans that they have become a type of "babyface," or hero. Some Muslim-American wrestling fans have appropriated the negative stereotype with irony and pride, turning the heels into heroes.

In the 19th century, stock villains included the "Terrible Turks," thereby initiating negative stereotypes of Muslims within the genre. In the mid-1950s, during the height of the cold war, literary critic Roland Barthes wrote that "in America wrestling represents a sort of mythological fight between Good and Evil (of a quasipolitical nature, the 'bad' wrestler always being supposed to be a Red [Communist])." This sentiment was echoed by the Canadian wrestler Bret "Hitman" Hart, who wrote in his 2007 autobiography: "Wrestling storylines have always exploited wartime animosities: first the American good guy versus the Germans and the Japanese, and now it was the Russians and the Iranians."

The first modern American wrestler to become famous using a Muslim persona (or "gimmick") was Edward "The Sheikh" Farhat (1926–2003). The wrestler's real life identity may bear little resemblance to the gimmick he or she adopts. Farhat was born into a Christian Lebanese immigrant family in Lansing, Michigan. Beginning his wrestling career in 1949, Farhat was billed as "The Sheikh of Araby" who hailed from "the Syrian desert." Hardly an enemy of America, Farhat had served in the U.S. Army in WORLD WAR II. The Sheikh was "managed" in the ring by Ernie Roth, a Jewish American from Canton, Ohio. Roth portrayed the character of Abdullah "the Weasel" Farouk, often wearing a turban or a fez. As implied by his nickname of "Weasel," Farouk's character was also a heel, who would often smuggle foreign objects to the Sheikh. The Sheikh would enter the ring, rant in Arabic gibberish, and attempt to "maim" his opponent. Often, the Sheikh would bloody his opponent, sometimes using the foreign objects (usually pencils) he received from the Weasel. The Sheikh would also hurl fireballs into the face of his opponent before finishing off his "victim" with a submission hold, usually the "camel clutch." In what was an interesting prefiguring of tensions among Muslim Americans, the Sheikh's most noted "feud" in the 1960s and early 1970s was with African-American wrestler Bobo Brazil (Houston Harris). This feud, along with other matches in the Sheikh's career, is captured in Donald Jackson's 1985 documentary film *I Like to Hurt People*. Ed Farhat was inducted posthumously into the World Wrestling Entertainment's Hall of Fame in 2007.

The next major Muslim character was Abdullah the Butcher (nicknamed "the Madman from Sudan"), who began wrestling under that name in the 1960s. Like the Sheikh, Abdullah was portrayed by another Christian, Lawrence Shreve, who was born in Canada. Wrestler Bret Hart remembers his father Stu Hart, a wrestling promoter, launching the Abdullah character: "Then [in 1969] Stu lucked out, bringing in a three-hundred-pound black school janitor out of Windsor, Ontario, who called himself Abdullah The Butcher and was billed as hailing from Khartoum. I watched this monster, unlike any I'd ever seen in wrestling, sell out week after week telling violent, bloody stories. Around the house, we called him Abbie." Abdullah became one of the most famous "hardcore" wrestlers, who like the Sheikh became famous for using foreign objects (in Abdullah's case, usually a fork) to draw blood from his opponents and himself. Also like the Sheikh, he continued the portrayal of the Muslim character as villainous, sadistic, and brutal.

Perhaps the first Muslim character to be portrayed by a Muslim was that of the Iron Sheikh (born Hossein Vaziri in Tehran). Undoubtedly due to stereotypes, the original name of the character was Hossein the Arab, ironic when one realizes that the wrestler was not only Iranian (and thus not an Arab) but had wrestled for his country. After the Iranian Revolution in 1979, his character was re-created as the Iron Sheikh (both a play on "Iran" and to distinguish himself from the "original" Sheikh). The Iron Sheikh was also a heel, who in 1983 defeated the all-American babyface Bob Backlund for the World Wrestling Federation championship. He also teamed with the Russian character of Nikolai Volkoff, a nod to the dual threats of Iran and Russia in the last days of the cold war. In thick Iranian accent, the Iron Sheikh would usually address the crowd with the following words: "Iran, number one. Russia, number one. USA, hack phooey." The team was managed by "Classy" Freddie Blassie, who then took on the nickname of "Ayatollah" Blassie. In 2005, the Iron Sheikh was inducted into the World Wrestling Entertainment Hall of Fame.

Another "hardcore" Muslim character was that of Sabu, originally billed as being from Saudi Arabia. The character was portrayed by Terry Brunk, who was trained by his real-life uncle, Ed Farhat. Lest there be any doubt that Sabu was also a heel, the usual tagline applied to him was "homicidal, genocidal, and suicidal." Sabu would often be brought to his matches strapped to a gurney in the fashion of a dangerous, mentally ill patient, his bonds loosened by his manager to wreak havoc on both his opponent and himself.

A controversial wrestler was Muhammad Hassan, played by Italian-American Mark Copani. The character debuted in 2004 as an Arab American who was fed up with the prejudice against Arab Americans since the terrorist attacks of SEPTEMBER 11, 2001. Hassan would then offer praises to Allah, a practice that was protested by Muslim Americans. His manager, Khosrow Daivari (played by Iranian-American Shawn Daivari), would then translate Hassan's words into "Arabic," which was actually Farsi. Again, this seemed to play upon the stereotypes of those who were ignorant of the differences between the two languages.

In an episode taped on July 4, 2005, after Daivari was defeated by his opponent, the Undertaker, Hassan called out five masked "terrorists" to defeat the Undertaker. Three days later came the deadly terrorist bombings in London. The clip was shown on North American television but was removed from broadcasts in the United Kingdom. The controversy over the clip was widely covered in the U.S. media, and as a result, the Muhammad Hassan character was taken off the air. The Daivari character continues to wrestle.

Stereotypical characters are not limited to the men in wrestling. Recently, the character of Raisha Saeed, manager to female heel wrestler Awesome Kong, has been developed. Saeed is billed as being from Damascus, speaks in an Arabic accent, and wears almost a full burka covering that leaves only her eyes exposed. Ironically, the character is portrayed by Melissa Anderson, whose first wrestling gimmick was as the all-American girl, Cheerleader Melissa.

American Muslim author Michael Muhammad Knight incorporates images and characters from professional wrestling in his works. In 2005, he orchestrated the performance piece "Taqwamania 2005: The Brawl for It All" in which he wrestled a proxy for conservative Muslim-American leader Ibrahim Hooper of the COUNCIL ON AMERICAN-ISLAMIC RELATIONS (CAIR). Knight's character blended professional wrestling personas such as Hulk Hogan, the Sheik, and the Iron Sheik with Islamic symbols. Knight's manager was Rabeya, a burka'd riot girl—that is, a veiled woman connected to the Islamic punk movement—taken from the pages of his novel *The Taqwacores* and portrayed in the match by religious studies professor Laury Silvers. Inspired by the feminist Muslim potential in Rabeya and professional wrestling, Silvers went on to train as an independent professional wrestler and debuted as Mumita: The Destroyer in full *hijab* and *niqab*.

Clearly, there are negative images of Muslims reflected in the Muslim characters in American professional wrestling.

All of them are heels, and with the exception of Muhammad Hassan (who spoke of the problems associated with being an Arab American), all of them are not just anti-American but violently so. However, they may also be viewed very differently by Muslim Americans. Some Muslim Americans have also watched and cheered for the Muslim wrestlers, who were often the only Muslim characters they saw on television in the 1970s and 1980s.

Amir Hussain

Further Reading

Barthes, Roland. *Mythologies,* translated by Annette Lavers. London: Jonathan Cape, 1972.

Beekman, Scott. *Ringside: A History of Professional Wrestling in America.* Westport, Conn.: Praeger, 2006.

Hart, Bret. *Hitman: My Real Life in the Cartoon World of Wrestling.* Toronto: Random House Canada, 2007.

Knight, Michael Muhammad. *The Taqwacores: A Novel.* New York: Autonomedia, 2005.

Sammond, Nicholas, ed. *Steel Chair to the Head: The Pleasure and Pain of Professional Wrestling.* Durham, N.C.: Duke University Press, 2005.

Wu-Tang Clan

The Wu-Tang Clan is a HIP-HOP group that emerged in NEW YORK CITY during the early 1990s. Their groundbreaking 1993 album *Enter the Wu-Tang (36 Chambers)* revolutionized the sound of hip-hop with its stark and aggressive production. Led by Robert Diggs, known as RZA, the nine-member group's name was inspired by a film about a powerful group of kung fu warriors, and this imagery was often referenced lyrically, along with graphic stories about street life in New York.

The group's second single, "C.R.E.A.M.," in 1994 gave Wu-Tang the financial success they had sought and allowed them to realize an ambitious business plan to secure solo album projects for many members in the coming years. The group achieved mainstream success throughout the 1990s, expanding their brand beyond music to include a clothing line, comic book, video game, and acting roles in movies and television.

The group was initially based around the energies of RZA and his two cousins, Gary Grice (GZA), and Russell Jones (Ol' Dirty Bastard). In 1981, GZA introduced RZA to emceeing and to the religion of Islam. GZA taught his cousin about the Supreme Mathematics, a Nation of Islam teaching that was adapted by the FIVE PERCENTERS, a group formed by CLARENCE 13X (1928–69). Ol' Dirty Bastard and most other Wu-Tang members claimed membership in the Five Percenters, and most had at least one alias with an explicit Five Percenter connection, including Sun God, Shallah, and Universal God of Law. The RZA alias stands for Ruler-Knowledge-Wisdom-and-Understanding, terms referring to the Five Percenters' "Supreme Alphabet," in which each letter has an esoteric and powerful meaning. Despite their use of Islamic motifs, Five Percenters, including Wu-Tang, do not see themselves as Muslims but instead claim that Islam is a way of life, rather than a religion.

Beyond Wu-Tang aliases, Five Percenter terms and expressions can be found mixed in with the martial arts and street stories in the group's lyrics. Five Percenter references can be understood only by those "in the know." For example, the casual listener may not register the references to Five Percenters when Method Man declares in the Ol' Dirty Bastard song: "I fear for the 85 that don't got a clue." Method alludes in this verse to the Five Percenter breakdown of humanity: 5 percent righteous, 10 percent knowledgeable but ill-intentioned, and 85 percent who live in ignorance. RZA's lyrics include mentions of the QUR'AN, and the lyrics "I Self Lord and Master" and "Arm Leg Leg Arm Head" in the song to "Born a Prince" are the Supreme Alphabet meanings for the "Islam" and "Allah." Both are Five Percenter teachings on the "Godhood" of humankind.

Beyond lyrics and aliases, Wu-Tang members used Five Percenter teachings to understand everything from a member's jail time and righteous living to the timing of the release of the albums. DJ Allah Mathematics designed an early version of the Wu-Tang logo with a sword and book. The sword represented RZA's tongue, and the book, wisdom. RZA wrote in the *Wu-Tang Manual* that "it's like you either go with the book, and have it peaceful, or you got the sword. That's the same idea of the Muslim flag's sword. It's saying, 'We gave you knowledge, the Holy Koran, and we'll cut your . . . head off if you act savage.'" Later the sword and book would be removed, leaving the stylized "W" (for Wu-Tang), one of the most famous logos in hip-hop. The Islamic motifs are present but not binding for the Wu-Tang Clan. RZA claims he is not a Muslim, but that his "way of life" is Islam: "Or as I like to say, I Stimulate Light and Matter. You have to realize that *you* stimulate everything around you. Everything else is only a reflection."

Bruce Burnside

Further Reading

Bogdanov, Vladimir, ed. *All Music Guide to Hip-Hop: The Definitive Guide to Rap & Hip-Hop.* San Francisco: Backbeat Books, 2003.

Knight, Michael Muhammad. *The Five Percenters: Islam, Hip Hop and the Gods of New York.* Oxford: Oneworld, 2007.

RZA. *The Wu-Tang Manual.* New York: Riverhead Books, 2005.

Y

Yee, James (**Yusuf Yee**) (1968–) *former U.S. Army captain and Muslim chaplain*

James Yee was a Muslim chaplain serving the UNITED STATES MILITARY at GUANTÁNAMO BAY, Cuba, who was wrongly accused of mutiny and sedition in 2003. His record was later cleared, and he wrote a book recounting his experiences and criticizing U.S. treatment of Guantánamo detainees.

James Yee was born in 1968 in Springfield, New Jersey, to second-generation Chinese Lutheran Americans. Yee was an excellent student and athlete in high school, which gained him admission to the U.S. Military Academy at West Point. After graduating from West Point, he served briefly as a post–Gulf War army officer in Saudi Arabia. Converting to Islam in 1991, he left the military to pursue four years of studies in the Islamic sciences and ARABIC at the Abu Nour Islamic Foundation in Syria. When Yee returned to the military, he was endorsed by the American Muslim Armed Forces and Veterans Affairs Council and appointed one of the first Muslim CHAPLAINS in the U.S. Army in January 2001.

Initially stationed at Fort Lewis, Washington, Yee, as demanded of all army chaplains, counseled soldiers and families of all religious backgrounds. The aftermath of the terrorist attacks of SEPTEMBER 11, 2001, changed his work considerably, as he was asked to give "debriefing seminars"

U.S. Army captain James Yee, a Muslim chaplain who served detainees at the U.S. Naval base in Guantánamo Bay, Cuba, speaks with his wife, Huda, and daughter Sarah at Fort Benning, Georgia, in 2005. *(Billy Smith II/Stringer/Reuters/Corbis)*

on Islam to American soldiers and to offer guidance to Muslim soldiers assigned to overseas missions. Television and radio stations requested interviews, and Yee found himself in high demand as the "spokesperson" on Islam from the military. In 2002, he was appointed to serve as Muslim chaplain at Guantánamo Bay, Cuba, where he ministered to Muslim soldiers and translators and provided for detainees' religious needs. His most important duties, though, were to advise camp commanders on religious and cultural issues and to ease tensions between guards and inmates, for which he received praise in his performance evaluations.

In September 2003, Yee took a routine leave from Guantánamo. On his way to his family in Seattle, he was arrested and taken into custody at the Jacksonville, Florida, airport. Charged with mutiny, sedition, aiding the enemy, and espionage with potential of a death penalty, Yee was transferred in shackles, blackened goggles, and earmuffs to a maximum-security brig in South Carolina. Held in solitary confinement for a total of 76 days, Yee was subjected to sensory deprivation techniques similar to those used against the prisoners at Guantánamo.

After a month of investigation found no evidence, the military reduced his charges to "mishandling classified documents," claiming that a list of Guantánamo detainees, their cell locations and interrogators, was found among his belongings. In the end, this material was evaluated as necessary for his job, the entire case was dropped, and Yee's record was cleared. Yee returned to duty as a chaplain at Fort Lewis, but he put in his resignation shortly thereafter and received an Honorable Discharge in January 2005.

Yee published an account of his experiences entitled *For God and Country: Faith and Patriotism under Fire,* in which he argued that most of the Guantánamo detainees had little or no "intelligence value," yet camp commanders routinely incited the guards against the prisoners. Yee alleged that guards taunted prisoners about their religion and that their grave mishandlings of the QUR'AN provoked hunger strikes and suicide attempts among the inmates. Yee also wrote that he arrived at Guantánamo with the hope that he would be useful to the military's mission, but he concluded that the mission was in fact to break the detainees' spirits. He said his mediation was sometimes tolerated but more often resented. He argued as well that the detention facility and operations at Guantánamo Bay should be closed, or at least opened to the media for greater transparency. Yee recommended that this would send a message to the world that the United States renounced torture and abuse. Yee also began to give lectures about his ordeal, religious diversity issues, and the challenges of protecting national security and civil liberties. He made presentations at many universities and on Capitol Hill to congressional staff. As of 2009, he was still hoping for an official apology for his detention but doubted

it would come. Since Yee's arrest in 2003, there has been no other Muslim chaplain assigned to the Guantánamo staff and detainees.

Karima W. Abidine

Further Reading

American Muslim Armed Forces and Veteran Affairs Council. Available online. URL: http://www.amafandvac.org/cms/. Accessed June 2008.

"Ex-Army Chaplain Says Religion Made Him Target," *Ventura County Star.* 25 April 2007. Available online. URL: http://www.vcstar.com/news/2007/apr/25/ex-army-chaplain-says-religion-made-him-target/. Accessed February 16, 2010.

"How Dubious Evidence Spurred Relentless Guantánamo Spy Hunt," *New York Times,* 19 December 2004. Available online. URL: http://www.nytimes.com/2004/12/19/politics/19gitmo.html. Accessed February 16, 2010.

James Yee Official Website. Available online. URL: http://www.justiceforyee.com. Accessed June 2008.

Lelyveld, Joseph. "The Strange Case of Chaplain Yee." *New York Review of Books* 52, no. 20 (December 15, 2005). Available online. URL: http://www.nybooks.com/articles/article-preview?article_id=18550. Accessed February 16, 2010.

"The Ordeal of Chaplain Yee," *USA Today* 16 May 2004. Available online. URL: http://www.usatoday.com/news/nation/2004-05-16-yee-cover_x.htm. Accessed February 16, 2010.

PBS Religion & Ethics News Weekly, Episode No. 906. "Interview: James Yee," October 7, 2005. Available online. URL: http://www.pbs.org/wnet/religionandethics/week906/interview.htm. Accessed February 16, 2010.

"Suspicion in the Ranks: Inside the Spy Investigation of Captain James Yee," *Seattle Times.* 9–16 January 2005. Available online. URL: http://seattletimes.nwsource.com/news/nation-world/jamesyee/. Accessed February 16, 2010.

Yee, James, and Aimee Molloy. *For God and Country: Faith and Patriotism under Fire.* New York: Public Affairs, 2005.

youth

Since the early 20th century, the identities of Muslim-American youth have been characterized by a diversity of lifestyles and life choices. Muslim-American youth experience, like that of Muslim-American history as a whole, has been shaped by different religious, racial, ethnic, national, and gender identities. Some Muslim-American youth have rejected the religious heritage of their parents, while many others have attempted to merge the religious values and cultural practices of their parents with similar and divergent practices and values. For some Muslim-American youth, a blended identity has been empowering and emboldening, sharpening their sense of self. For others, it has been a struggle in which they feel caught between multiple worlds.

NINETEENTH- AND EARLY
TWENTIETH-CENTURY ORIGINS

Adolescence, as typically understood today—teenage years marked by the struggle for autonomy—is a largely modern phenomenon. Until the middle to late 1800s, most Americans under the age of 18 spent little time in school, if any at all, and were expected to contribute to family farming. During the 19th century, however, the U.S. economy became increasingly industrialized, and the mass migration to cities and immigration from overseas changed the structure of American families. Coupled with the rise of child labor laws and mandatory schooling, this change in American social life marked the creation of "youth" as an age group afforded its own distinct legal and social status in the United States.

Public EDUCATION, which became increasingly compulsory in the late 19th century, played a central role in the lives of Muslim-American youth. School has been a vital American institution, because, along with technical and intellectual training, schools have been primary sites of socialization for young people. ARAB-AMERICAN MUSLIM communities in NORTH DAKOTA, for example, sent their children to public schools in the early 20th century. Taught to be patriotic American citizens and to assimilate into white, Anglo-Protestant culture, Muslims such as Charlie Juma, likely one of the first Muslim Americans born in western North Dakota, learned to speak ARABIC but also began to attend the local Lutheran church and converted to Christianity. A similar result was obtained in California when in this period SOUTH ASIAN–AMERICAN MUSLIM agricultural workers married Roman Catholic Mexican-American women and left the education of their children to their wives. A generational and cultural gap was created between many first-generation immigrants and their American children, a phenomenon common in many immigrant families of whatever religious or ethnic background.

During the era of WORLD WAR I, however, Muslims, both parents and children, came to identify more strongly as Americans and with the U.S. efforts to win the war. Arab Americans, composed mostly of Christians but including some Muslims, enrolled their children in the Boy Scouts and the Girl Scouts, and more than a thousand Muslim-American youths joined the UNITED STATES MILITARY fighting in Europe. The sacrifice required in the war further cemented the identification of Muslim-American youth with the United States as their home country. Some saw a contradiction between their American and Muslim identities and, in some instances, gave up the practice of Islam. Others, especially Muslim-American youth in cities with larger Muslim populations such as TOLEDO, OHIO, and NEW YORK CITY, began to view Islam as an American creed, sometimes describing the mosque to their non-Muslim neighbors as their "church."

At the same time that many second-generation Muslim-American youths were consciously attempting to assimilate into white Protestant-American culture, AFRICAN-AMERICAN MUSLIMS were striving to keep from being harmed by it. The reemergence of Islam as a religious tradition among African Americans in the 1920s and 1930s was defined by the effort to resist and counter white supremacy. For the African-American Muslims who joined the Ahmadi movement, the MOORISH SCIENCE TEMPLE of America, various Sunni mosques, and the NATION OF ISLAM (NOI), conversion to Islam was not only a matter of individual spirituality but was also the basis of a movement to establish new community life and institutions, from MOSQUES and newspapers to ISLAMIC SCHOOLS, all of which were designed to instill pride within African Americans, especially youth.

MUSLIM-AMERICAN YOUTH INSTITUTIONS
SINCE THE 1930s

Since the 1930s, full-time Islamic schools, Sunday religious classes, and youth organizations have sought to teach adolescents about community norms. In public schools and in their relationship to non-Muslim friends, teachers, and neighbors, they have been exposed to a different set of standards, and through the arts youth have created new identities that sometimes resist but often blend their sense of being fully American and fully Muslim.

Schooling

African-American Muslims founded the first institutions for Islamic education in the United States. In 1932, W. D. FARD, founder of the NOI, established the first University of Islam in Detroit. Universities of Islam were developed as an alternative education system to public schools, many of which discriminated against African Americans at the time. Universities of Islam sought to inculcate Muslim children and youth with self-esteem and good moral character. These schools taught kindergarten through 12th grade but were named "University" by longtime NOI leader ELIJAH MUHAMMAD (1897–1975) because of the high expectations and standards held for students and the comprehensive nature of the curriculum.

As the NOI community grew, so did its schools, and by the middle 1970s, there were 41 such institutions across the United States, teaching primary and secondary instruction. After the death of Muhammad in 1975, his son, W. D. MOHAMMED (1933–2008), took the helm of the community and renamed the Universities of Islam after the schools' very first teacher, who was also his mother, CLARA MUHAMMAD (1899–1972). The Clara Muhammad Schools retained the dual emphasis on education and self-pride but also incorporated Sunni Islamic thought and traditions into classroom instruction.

Two of the most successful schools have been the Sister Clara Muhammad elementary school and W. D. Mohammed high school in ATLANTA. W. D. Mohammed high school has offered its students the chance to participate in extra-curricular activities such as mock trial, a celebrated step team, and the *Lady Caliphs,* an all-women varsity basketball team that competed for a national high school championship in 2006. After reviving the Nation of Islam in the late 1970s, LOUIS FARRAKHAN (1933–) reestablished the Universities of Islam in 1989. Like their predecessors, these institutions have attended to the intellectual and personal growth of students in grades kindergarten through 12 in a number of cities across the country, including CHICAGO, Baton Rouge, and San Francisco.

The type of community-building that African-American Muslims embarked upon in the 1920s and 1930s has also been taken up by their immigrant counterparts. Although Clara Muhammad Schools have educated non-African-American youth, the majority of youth from immigrant Muslim families who attended Islamic school did so at schools established within their own ethnic communities. These schools were first established in the 1980s by Muslim immigrant parents who sought to address the need for institutions to help their children retain their cultural and religious identity. In addition to the inclusion of Arabic and Islamic Studies in school curriculums, these schools have enforced conservative moral codes to govern gender relations and modesty. Islamic schools within Muslim immigrant communities have grown steadily, and a number of schools, such as Al-Ihsan Academy established by Guyanese immigrants in New York City, have conducted large fund-raising efforts to support state-of-the-art computer labs and athletic facilities.

Islamic schools have become part of a broader system of institutions that help Muslim youth develop the skills to navigate being members of a religious minority in the United States. Graduates of these schools have gone on to excel at the nation's most prestigious colleges and universities, yet most full-time Islamic schools have struggled to remain open. These schools depend on tuition to operate and are often confronted with parents who are either unable to afford school fees or lack confidence in these nascent institutions.

Most Muslim-American adolescents have received formal religious education at the mosque Sunday school. Patterned on the Sunday school tradition of American Christian churches, a number of Muslim-American communities have held Sunday religious classes since the 1950s. Teaching young students basic religious duties, Islamic history, and religious and cultural etiquette, these schools attempt to protect and preserve the religious and cultural identities of Muslim youth. This is a formidable challenge for Sunday school administrators and teachers who meet with students for only a fraction of the time young Muslims spend in the nation's public schools.

The vast majority of Muslim youth in the 20th and 21st centuries have attended public middle schools and high schools. In these settings, Muslim youth have been confronted with many beliefs and practices that call into question those norms and values they have been taught by their families and communities. As religious and sometimes racial minorities within public school settings, Muslim youth have also experienced various forms of anti-Muslim STEREOTYPES and DISCRIMINATION. In 2005, 17-year-old Hassan Rahgozar was beaten by fellow students in a California high school bathroom in a racially motivated attack. Rahgozar sued the West Contra Costa Unified School District for failing to respond to threats against him made before the assault. Similarly, Jana Elhifny, a former Reno-area high school student, was awarded a settlement in 2009 after suing school officials for not protecting her from anti-Muslim harassment.

Although discrimination has been on the rise since the attacks of SEPTEMBER 11, 2001, for Muslim youth the experience with prejudice has differed depending on their race, class, and relationship to non-Muslims. In New York City, where Muslims make up 12 percent of public school students, oral histories of Muslim high school students have revealed that Muslim students are keenly aware of and often frustrated by discrimination, but they are not paralyzed by it. They have envisioned their generation as best equipped to eliminate prejudice against Muslims and expressed a desire to work against discrimination through a network of local and national youth groups and organizations.

Youth Organizations

Youth-oriented groups and activities have played an important role in the development of identity among Muslim-American youth since World War I. Prior to the establishment of formal youth organizations targeted toward Muslim Americans, early immigrant communities created activities specifically designed for youth. This first generation of youth activities, such as the Bosnian Women Singers Club founded by Ulfeta Sarich in Chicago in the 1930s, replicated contemporary practices of broader American society.

In the 1950s, the FEDERATION OF ISLAMIC ASSOCIATIONS IN THE UNITED STATES AND CANADA (FIA), a coalition of dozens of immigrant-led mosques in the United States and Canada, formed the Islamic Youth Organization. The FIA sponsored summer youth camps and youth conventions in which hundreds of Muslim Americans participated. In 1957, the Islamic Youth Organization, then led by Joe Mallad and Mary Caudry (who was also cochair of the Detroit Islamic Council), participated in the annual convention of the FIA, which featured panel discussions, prayer, and evening dances.

The 1965 convention of the FIA included more events specifically geared toward youth, including a "Youth Jam Session."

All-Muslim BOY SCOUT and GIRL SCOUT troops also began in the 1970s. Drawing on sayings of the prophet Muhammad that endorsed sports and physical activity, the Darul Islam movement, a federation of African-American Sunni Muslim mosques established in 1967, created Islamic scouting organizations and a sports tournament. In the late 1970s, members of the Darul Islam established the *Jawalah* (ranger) *Scouts* for males, the *Banaatul Muslimeen* (Muslim daughters), a scouting group for girls and young women, and the *Riyaadah,* Arabic for sports, an annual athletic competition. Since that time these activities have been key community institutions aimed at the development of Islamic character among Muslim-American youth.

In 1978, the Atlanta Masjid of Islam created one of the first all-Muslim Girl Scout troops in the United States. In 1982, W. D. Mohammed, Pakistani-American Boy Scout official Syed Ehtesham Haider Naqvi, Boy Scout Chief Executive Ben Love, Turkish diplomat Engin Ansay, and Guinean diplomat Youssouf Sylla founded the Islamic Council on Scouting in North America (ICSNA). In addition to promoting athletic and other skills, Muslim scouting has encouraged a sense of belonging and a strong religious identity. By 2006, there were at least 1,000 Muslim-American Girl Scouts and 2,000 Boy Scouts.

As religious REVIVALISM continued to spread in the last two decades of the 20th century, many new Muslim-American youth organizations emphasized the importance of religious piety and a socially conservative view of Muslim morality. Since the middle 1980s, for example, youth organizations such as Muslim Youth of North America (MYNA), Young Muslims (YM), and Muslim American Society-Youth (MAS Youth) were created by the ISLAMIC SOCIETY OF NORTH AMERICA, the ISLAMIC CIRCLE OF NORTH AMERICA, and the MUSLIM AMERICAN SOCIETY, respectively. Their organizational structure and goals, as well as ethnic makeup and religious perspective, tended to replicate those of their parent organizations. These organizations have also focused on civic engagement and religious training. Activities such as religious study circles and leadership retreats have sought to mold young Muslims into Muslim-American leaders who are fully competent and religiously grounded.

Because these more socially conservative organizations have often encouraged modest DRESS and gender-segregated activities, a religious outlook that some youth find unattractive, some groups have begun to take more open positions toward youth-oriented programs, particularly around the arts. Importantly, these efforts were preceded by other local and national groups, like those within the ministry of W. D. Mohammed that took a different attitude toward youth activities, maintaining similar notions of morality but embracing MUSIC and performance as positive forms of youth expression.

Art and Muslim Identity

Since the late 20th century, an arts movement has begun to flower among young Muslim Americans. HIP-HOP, which has historically been informed by notions of black consciousness and moral discipline articulated by African-American Muslims, has emerged as an important catalyst in this movement. Seen as an extension of the Islamic poetic tradition, hip-hop has become a key medium of self-expression through which youth celebrate their identities as Muslim Americans.

This budding arts movement has also created its own market and series of superstars where Muslim artists well-known in mainstream popular culture, as well as local community hip-hop artists, become icons of an accessible, affirming, and "cool" notion of being Muslim. Although hip-hop has dominated the Muslim-American popular arts, Muslim youth have also listened to and produced *nasheeds* (Islamic songs), inspired by the harmonies of R&B, and Islamic punk and country music, as well as visual and performance art.

Bringing together popular culture, religion and youth, this arts movement has underscored anxieties within Muslim-American communities about sex and gender relations among Muslim youth. Fears about premarital sex, pregnancies to unwed parents, and sexually transmitted disease have characterized the attitudes of many adults who see popular culture as encouraging immoral behavior. These fears have a particularly strong impact on young Muslim women, often placing them under greater scrutiny and restriction.

In a 2005 ethnographic study on Yemeni-American high school students by Loukia Sarroub, young women expressed significant feelings of anxiety and depression about the future as their professional ambitions were circumscribed by notions of chastity, MARRIAGE, and conservatism within their communities. The young men in this study reported no similar feelings. This particular case reflected a differing set of expectations for MEN and WOMEN that have characterized a number of Muslim communities and extended into the realm of artistic performance. Female hip-hop artists, for example, have been confronted with religious criticism and limited opportunities to perform within some Muslim-American communities because of their gender. In response, some Muslim-American groups have sought to support female performances. For example, in 2007 the Sisterhood of the Mosque of Islamic Brotherhood located in Harlem, New York, and Muslims in Hip Hop, an online Muslim hip-hop collective, held a hip-hop concert at New York City's Aaron Davis Hall that featured female Muslim artists.

Despite adult fears and gender inequalities, Muslim youth have continued to participate in the arts and popular culture.

Significantly, Muslim youth participation in the arts has enabled many youth to embrace their diversity and blended identities as assets rather than abnormalities. Through artistic expression and consumption, young Muslims have defined Islam for themselves and resisted demands to conform to the ideals or expectations of adults, Muslim and non-Muslim. For example, Chicago's Inner-city Muslim Action Network (IMAN), founded by Muslim college students, has advanced an advocacy and social service agenda that focuses on empowering communities in urban neighborhoods and has also made the arts a central element of its organizational mission. The appointment of Muslim-American youth to its Board of Directors and its bimonthly Community Café showcase for Muslim artists, male and female, are just a few of the ways IMAN has challenged traditional attitudes toward youth espoused by Muslim Americans, as well as within broader American society.

CONCLUSION

Throughout Muslim-American history, youth have been and continue to be the epicenter of Muslim life in the United States. Some of the first and most durable American Muslim institutions were created for Muslim youth, from early 20th-century associations to later 20th- and 21st-century Islamic schools. Muslim-American youth have lived in diverse contexts, yet shared the experience of coming of age as Muslims in the United States. As a part of this experience, they have moved between different worlds—public, private, religious, and secular. Through their familiarity in multiple contexts, Muslim-American youth have acted as bridges between their local communities and broader American society. Furthermore, through the benefit of living with blended identities they have charted a course for themselves and their communities defined on their own terms.

Suad Abdul Khabeer

Further Reading

Abdul-Ghafur, Saleemah, ed. *Living Islam Out Loud: American Muslim Women Speak.* Boston: Beacon Press, 2005.

Aidi, Hishaam. "'Verily, There Is Only One Hip-Hop Umma': Islam, Cultural Protest and Urban Marginality." *Socialism and Democracy* 18, no. 2 (2004): 107–126.

Bing-Canar, Jennifer, and Mary Zerkel. *Banaat Chicago/Daughter of Chicago: Growing Up Arab and Female in Chicago.* VHS. Seattle: Arab Film Distribution, 1996.

Cristillo, Louis, et al. *This Is Where I Need to Be: Oral Histories of Muslim Youth in New York City.* New York: Columbia Teacher's College Student Press Initiative, 2008.

Elkholy, Abdo A. *The Arab Moslems in the United States: Religion and Assimilation.* New Haven, Conn.: College and University Press, 1966.

Kahf, Mohja. *Girl in the Tangerine Scarf: A Novel.* New York: Carroll and Graf, 2006.

Karim, Jamillah. *American Muslim Women: Negotiating Race, Class, and Gender within the Ummah.* New York: New York University Press, 2008.

———. "Between Immigrant Islam and Black Liberation: Young Muslims Inherit Global Muslim and African American Legacies." *Muslim World* 95, no. 4 (October 2005): 497–513.

Khabeer, Suad A. "Rep That Islam: The Rhyme and Reason of American Islamic Hip Hop." *Muslim World* 97, no. 1 (January 2007): 125–141.

Rashid, Hakim M., and Zakiyyah Muhammad. "The Sister Clara Muhammad Schools: Pioneers in the Development of Islamic Education in America." *Journal of Negro Education* 61, no. 2 (Spring 1992): 178–185.

Sarroub, Loukia K. *All American Yemeni Girls: Being Muslim in a Public School.* Philadelphia: University of Pennsylvania Press, 2005.

Sirin, Selcuk R., and Michelle Fine. *Muslim American Youth: Understanding Hyphenated Identities through Multiple Methods.* New York: New York University Press, 2008.

Yusuf, Hamza (Mark Hanson) (1960–)
preacher and educator

By the early 21st century, Hamza Yusuf had become one of Muslim America's most popular religious scholars, educators, and spokespeople. After the al-Qaeda attacks of SEPTEMBER 11, 2001, Yusuf was propelled onto the national stage as a spokesperson for Muslim Americans. He met with President George W. Bush and became an outspoken critic of both state and vigilante terrorism. In his public speaking, Yusuf combined an impassioned and charismatic speaking style with substantive references to popular culture, Western literature, and medieval ISLAMIC THOUGHT. Defending traditional Islamic religious literature and teaching methods, including those in the mystical branch of Islam called SUFISM, he cofounded the ZAYTUNA INSTITUTE, which aimed to offer traditional Islamic training to Muslim Americans in order to produce an indigenous form of American Islam.

Hamza Yusuf was born Mark Hanson in 1960 to a family of Greek Orthodox and Catholic background. He was born in Walla Walla, Washington, and raised in Marin County, California. Both of Yusuf's parents were well educated and active in the civil rights movement and in antiwar activism. Hanson considered joining the Greek Orthodox priesthood until a near-fatal car accident in 1977 prompted him to reconsider his life path.

After reading the QUR'AN, Yusuf has said, he decided to convert to Islam at the age of 17 in 1977. Shortly after, he traveled to the United Kingdom, where he studied Islam and

ARABIC. During this period, he met Abdullah Ali Mahmood from Sharjah, one of the small emirates, or principalities, in the Persian Gulf. Mahmood, a religious scholar, encouraged Yusuf to study Islam in the United Arab Emirates, where Yusuf spent four years. Yusuf also traveled to Saudi Arabia, Mauritania, Algeria, Morocco, and Egypt, studying under prominent Islamic scholars who licensed him to teach what he learned. During his 10-year sojourn, he became the first American lecturer to teach in the prestigious Karaouine University in Fes, Morocco.

Upon returning to the United States in the late 1980s, Yusuf traveled widely, speaking about Islam to a growing following in Muslim communities and on college campuses. In 1996, Yusuf cofounded Zaytuna Institute, which was modeled partly on the traditional methods of studying and teaching Islam that Yusuf had learned during his 10 years abroad. Unlike some advocates of modern Islamic REVIVALISM who stressed the need to rid Islam of centuries of accumulated traditions, Hanson explicitly embraced both the classical and medieval traditions of Islam. He preserved a central place for Sufi interpretations of Islam in the curriculum of Zaytuna, located in Hayward, California, and devoted himself to translating Sufi texts, such as *Purification of the Heart: Signs, Symptoms and Cures of the Spiritual Diseases of the Heart* (2004), into English. But while committed to preserving both classical and medieval Islamic traditions, Yusuf also hoped to produce a body of Islamic knowledge that was relevant to the contemporary world.

In his early years as a lecturer in the United States, Yusuf's speeches were frequently punctuated by harsh criticisms of American culture and POLITICS, as well as other religious traditions. In a frequently cited speech he made just two days before the events of SEPTEMBER 11, 2001, Yusuf was quoted as saying that "a great, great tribulation" is coming to America. Yusuf is also quoted in a 1995 speech stating that Judaism is a racist religion. He has since explained, in a September 2006 PBS *Frontline* interview, that he was "infected" with anti-Semitism during his time in "the Muslim world," and has since "(grown) out of it," realizing that it is incompatible with core Islamic values.

After the attacks of September 11, however, Yusuf changed the focus of his criticism, which became directed toward fellow Muslims. He was chosen by President George W. Bush to represent Muslim Americans in a public meeting at the White House on September 20, 2001. Yusuf accepted the invitation and arrived in typical western clothing, with trimmed beard and without what had become his standard turban. He reclaimed his given name, introducing himself as Hamza Yusuf Hanson, and articulated a message of conciliation, cross-religious and cross-cultural respect, and regret for the tone of his previous rhetoric. The October 8, 2001, issue of London's *Guardian* quotes Yusuf as saying, "September 11 was a wake-up call to me. . . . I don't want to contribute to the hate in any shape or form. I now regret in the past being silent about what I have heard in the Islamic discourse and being part of that with my own anger."

Yusuf increasingly emphasized the commonality between American and Islamic values. In the same interview he asserted, "I would rather live as a Muslim in the west than in most of the Muslim countries, because I think the way Muslims are allowed to live in the west is closer to the Muslim way." Though Yusuf did not back off completely from offering criticism of U.S. foreign policy, criticizing the use of all weapons of mass destruction, fear tactics, and racism, whether employed by states or individuals, his new focus was on what he saw as the abuse of Islamic tradition in justifying violence.

Yusuf received criticism from other Muslims for the sudden and dramatic change in his rhetoric and philosophical bent. The shock was compounded by the fiery rhetoric he used toward fellow Muslims who, Yusuf said, abused Islamic theology. Some, like Yusuf Estes, another popular Muslim-American figure, charged that, in his eagerness to appease the Western mainstream, Yusuf stretched the meaning of certain Islamic traditions and ignored others. Even so, Yusuf defended his approach and remained focused on building Muslim-American intellectual institutions that would produce an interpretation of the faith that was deeply informed by both its American identity and the Islamic intellectual heritage.

See also SHAKIR, ZAID.

Hanifa Abdul Sabur

Further Reading

Abdo, Geneive. *Mecca and Main Street: Muslim Life in America After 9/11.* New York: Oxford University Press, 2006.

# Z

Zakaria, Fareed (1964–) *foreign affairs journalist*

Indian-American Fareed Zakaria, a well-known journalist, commentator, and author specializing in international relations, was born on January 20, 1964, in Mumbai, India. His father was a leading politician in the Indian government and a scholar of Islamic religion. His mother was an editor for the *Times of India*. Raised a Muslim, Zakaria attended the Christian-run Cathedral and John Connon School in Mumbai, the most prestigious preparatory school in India. After preparatory school, he moved to the United States in order to attend Yale University, receiving a B.A. in 1986. He then attended the John F. Kennedy School of Government at Harvard University, which granted him a Ph.D. in government in 1993. Zakaria remained at Harvard after graduation to conduct research and teach courses on political science and government.

In 1992, Zakaria became the editor of the journal *Foreign Affairs,* sometimes contributing his own articles to the journal, including "Culture Is Destiny" in 1994 and "The Rise of Illiberal Democracy" in 1997. In 1993, he published his first book, *The Future of Freedom: Illiberal Democracy at Home and Abroad,* which examined the deficiencies and successes of democracy and democratic societies. The book, which enumerated steps the United States must take to revitalize its democracy, became a best seller and was translated into 20 languages.

In 1996, Zakaria became a contributing writer for *Newsweek* magazine, and then published his second book, *From Wealth to Power: The Unusual Origins of America's World Role* (1998). *From Wealth to Power* explored the relationships between a nation's central government and its ability to influence foreign affairs. Using examples from U.S. history, Zakaria claimed that when the federal government was weak, such as in the 19th century, the United States tended to be less engaged in aggressive foreign political maneuvers. But as the government became more powerful and performed additional functions during and after the Civil War, the United States increased its influence in foreign politics and its interests in foreign expansion.

In 2000, Zakaria resigned his position as editor of *Foreign Affairs* and became editor at *Newsweek International.* Perhaps his most influential article for *Newsweek* was his piece entitled, "The Politics of Rage: Why They Hate Us." Written shortly after the al-Qaeda attacks of SEPTEMBER 11, 2001, the article attempted to explain how political, social, economic, and religious contexts in the Middle East led to the attacks. Zakaria frequently commented on various aspects of the war on terror, including the IRAQ WAR and the domestic and foreign policies of the George W. Bush administration.

Surveying the changes in international relations after 9/11, Zakaria's third book, *The Post-American World* (2008), claimed that the world has entered a period in which the economic and military power of the United States has ebbed and other nations around the world, particularly China and India, were burgeoning. Zakaria said that this diminution of U.S. power was not a problem in and of itself, but that continued political strife and idleness among Americans affected the quality of life in the country.

In addition to writing books and articles, Zakaria has become a television personality. From 2005 to 2007, he hosted a weekly program called *Foreign Exchange* on PBS and then in 2008 launched *Fareed Zakaria GPS (Global Public Square),* a political talk show that examines policies and the foreign events affecting the world. Zakaria has interviewed a number of important political and public figures such as Barack Obama, Tony Blair, Condoleezza Rice, and Bill Gates.

Since the late 1990s, Zakaria's reputation as an intellectual and political expert has been recognized by numerous organizations and publications. He was recognized as one of the 21st century's most important people by *Esquire* magazine in 1999. He won the World Affairs Councils of America's Journalist Award in 2005, and in 2006 he was named one of the 100 most influential graduates of Harvard University. In 2007, Zakaria was named by both *Foreign Policy* and *Prospect* magazines as one of the top 100 public intellectuals in the world.

Zakaria has been outspoken on a number of issues but has rarely discussed his Muslim identity. In an interview with *Village Voice,* Zakaria stated that he understood certain aspects of the Muslim world through intuition—aspects, he said, that cannot be grasped by reading books or through study. However, he did not want to become a spokesman on behalf of the Muslim world. He felt as if his world and his life are different from the Muslim world because, "I'm not a religious guy."

Matthew Long

Further Reading

Hoge, James F., and Fareed Zakaria, eds. *The American Encounter: The United States and the Making of the Modern World Essays from 75 Years of Foreign Affairs.* New York: Basic Books, 1997.

Zakaria, Fareed. "Articles: Archive." Available online. URL: http://www.fareedzakaria.com/articles/archive.html. Accessed December 4, 2008.

———. *From Wealth to Power.* Princeton, N.J.: Princeton University Press, 1998.

———. *The Future of Freedom: Illiberal Democracy at Home and Abroad.* New York: W. W. Norton & Company, 2003.

———. *The Post-American World.* New York: W. W. Norton & Company, 2008.

Zaytuna Institute

Founded in 1996 by Hamza Yusuf and Hesham Alalusi in California, Zaytuna Institute has become one of the leading institutions of Islamic learning in the United States. Its expressed goal is to offer traditional forms and contents of Islamic knowledge to Muslim Americans. In 1998, the institute acquired a physical location in Hayward, California, and in 2007, with plans to found Tabari College as the first accredited Islamic seminary in the United States, it relocated to Berkeley, California.

Since its inception, Zaytuna has developed on-site courses and programs, distance-learning programs conducted online, and weekend intensive courses in various locations throughout the country, called "Minara Programs." Its educational approach has emphasized traditional forms of Islamic instruction, including intensive Arabic courses, introductions to the Qur'an, the sunna of the prophet Muhammad, and shari'a, or Islamic legal and ethical thought. These traditional subjects are adapted in order to make them relevant for the religious, political, and social contexts in which Muslim Americans find themselves. Many of Zaytuna's learning materials including books, a journal called "Seasons," many audio-visual materials, and several translations of classical Arabic texts have been marketed to and used by significant numbers of Muslims in North America.

Zaytuna's success can mainly be ascribed to the charismatic leadership of Hamza Yusuf, and later Zaid Shakir. In addition to these two leading scholars, Zaytuna has employed other Muslim scholars whose training in the Muslim world and in traditional Islamic sciences has formed the basis of their scholarly and instructional authority.

Hamza Yusuf grew up in a Greek Orthodox family in northern California and converted to Islam in his teens. He went on to study for 10 years in various parts of the Muslim world with traditional teachers. His definition of traditional Islamic knowledge is best described as an eclectic combination of classical Islamic doctrines, mystical interpretations, and modern Western sensibilities. Yusuf has been hailed as the leading Muslim American scholar on the one hand while being criticized for his stance with the Bush administration after September 11, 2001, on the other. Immediately after the attacks, Yusuf came out publicly, in various American and European media outlets, condemning the attacks and defending Islamic doctrine and identity as antithetical to such attacks. He has also been a signatory to several declarations of contemporary Muslim scholars against terrorism and for better interfaith relations, including the 2007 "Common Word" formulated in response to remarks by Pope Benedict XVI earlier the same year.

The second-leading figure of Zaytuna is Zaid Shakir, an African-American scholar who converted to Islam in 1977 and studied for several years in Syria and Morocco. Shakir has described his coming of age during the civil rights movements and has combined civil rights and political activism with deep involvement in Muslim community-building in the United States. He joined Zaytuna in 2003 as scholar-in-residence and lecturer. Shakir has become the second public face of Zaytuna and has spoken frequently to the media, public gatherings, and conferences.

In subtle ways, the curriculum and agenda of Zaytuna represented by Yusuf and Shakir as well as other teachers at the institute have been relatively conservative on many social and political issues while supporting Sufi perspectives and an indigenous American interpretation of Islam for Muslim Americans. This includes an emphasis on the compatibility of Islamic and American values, such as democracy and religious pluralism, and the unique position of Muslim Americans under conditions of religious freedom and freedom of speech that afford them unprecedented opportunities for rethinking the role of Islam in the modern world and the strengthening of a global Muslim identity.

Juliane Hammer

Further Reading

Shakir, Zaid. *Scattered Pictures: Reflections of an American Muslim.* New Islamic Directions Publishers, 2007.

Yusuf, Hamza, and Zaid Shakir. *Agenda to Change Our Condition.* Zaytuna Institute, 1999.

Zerhouni, Elias Adam (1951–) *medical researcher, director of the National Institutes of Health*

Elias Adam Zerhouni, a radiologist, invented scanning techniques that allowed doctors to see three-dimensional representations of internal organs. He also helped to create the Institute for Cell Engineering at Johns Hopkins University. He served as head of the National Institutes of Health (NIH) from 2002 to 2008.

Elias Zerhouni was born on April 12, 1951, in Nedrona, Algeria, where his father was a math professor and his maternal uncle was a radiologist. He swam competitively while studying medicine at the University of Algiers, where he met and married Nadia Azza, a fellow competitive swimmer. In 1975, the couple moved to Baltimore, Maryland. Zerhouni completed his residency in diagnostic radiology in 1978 at Johns Hopkins University, where he was an assistant professor.

While at Johns Hopkins, Zerhouni participated in studies of computed tomography (CT scan), a technique that produces a three-dimensional image of an object from a large number of two-dimensional X-ray scans along a single axis of rotation. The CT scan allowed doctors to identify tumors, especially in the lungs. In 1981, Zerhouni became vice-chairman of the department of radiology at Eastern Virginia Medical School before returning to Johns Hopkins in 1985, when he became codirector of the magnetic resonance imaging (MRI) division in 1988.

While Zerhouni was at Johns Hopkins in the late 1980s, he developed "myocardial tagging," an innovative procedure using magnetic resonance imaging to take three-dimensional moving pictures of the heart. Using a similar imaging technique, he created a method of diagnosing breast cancer that replaced a more invasive procedure.

In 1985, Zerhouni expanded his activities from research to health policy, becoming a consultant to the White House under Ronald Reagan and consultant to the World Health Organization in 1988. In 1996, Zerhouni became executive vice dean of the Johns Hopkins School of Medicine, just six years after becoming a naturalized American citizen. In 2000, he joined the Institute of Medicine, a component of the National Academy of Sciences that offers policy makers scientific advice on biomedical science and health.

In May 2002, President George W. Bush appointed Zerhouni director of the NIH after a two-year search for a director who shared President Bush's opposition to embryonic cell research. Zerhouni, who had helped create Johns Hopkins Institute for Cell Engineering in 2001, supported research that extended research to the less controversial field of adult stem cells. Under Zerhouni, the NIH doubled its budget to $27.3 billion, partly with the goal of creating a complete set of three-dimensional pictures of every protein in the body as the first step toward curing Alzheimer's disease and other disorders in which misshaped proteins play a role.

Zerhouni also fostered cooperation between the public and private sectors by creating a public database of pharmaceutical compounds and their properties. In 2005, Zerhouni responded to a congressional investigation of possible ethics violations at the NIH by banning NIH scientists from consulting for drug companies. In this period, federal support for the NIH stagnated, and some scientists complained that it was increasingly difficult to get NIH grants. In 2004 and 2005, Zerhouni informed Congress that the Bush administration's opposition to work on embryonic stem cells was slowing scientific research. Despite this comment, which seemed to support critics of the Bush policy on stem cell research, Zerhouni remained in his post.

Before the 2008 presidential election, Zerhouni resigned his position at the NIH to make way for a new administration. In 2009, he joined the board of trustees of the newly created King Abdullah University of Science and Technology in Jeddah, Saudi Arabia. He also joined the Bill and Melinda Gates Foundation as a senior fellow in the Global Health Initiative and as executive committee board member for the Foundation's Grand Challenges in Global Health program, which seeks to solve health problems in the world's poorest countries. Zerhouni's role has been as both a health policy and research adviser.

By the time Zerhouni stepped down from his post at the NIH in 2008, he had already amassed an impressive record. During a three-decade-long career, he had become one of the highest-ranking Muslim officials in the U.S. government, laid the foundation for future research into a number of chronic illnesses including Alzheimer's disease, and improved the diagnosis of heart disease through his research on magnetic resonance imaging.

Sonja Spear

Further Reading

Harris, Gardner. "Federal Health Official to Step Down," *New York Times,* 24 September 2008, p. A22.

"KAUST Announces New Board of Trustees." King Abdullah University of Science and Technology. Available online. URL: www.kaust.edu.sa/news-releases/board-of-trustees. aspx. Accessed March 3, 2009.

Stolberg, Sheryl Gay. "Man in the News: From Algeria to a Dream—Elias Adam Zerhouni," *New York Times,* 27 March 2002, p. A16.

Zewail, Ahmed Hasan (1946–) *chemist, Nobel Laureate*

Ahmed Hasan Zewail won the Nobel Prize in chemistry in 1999 for pioneering femtochemistry, an area of physical chemistry that uses extremely fast laser flashes to examine chemical reactions in process on a molecular level. This method allowed scientists to understand exactly what happens in a chemical reaction between stable states, giving scientists a powerful tool to interrogate some basic assumptions in the field of chemistry.

Ahmed Zewail was born in Damanhour, just outside of Alexandria, Egypt, on February 26, 1946. He grew up in the small Egyptian city of Disuq, where his father worked for the government and ran a small business importing and assembling bicycles and motorcycles. Zewail completed a master of science from the University of Alexandria in 1969. He received a scholarship to the University of Pennsylvania, where he completed a Ph.D. in chemistry in 1974. That same year he began postdoctoral work at the University of California at Berkeley, where he collaborated with Charles Harris using picosecond lasers, lasers flashing at intervals of only one-trillionth of a second. In 1976, he accepted a fac-

ulty position at the California Institute of Technology, commonly called Caltech, where he has remained for his entire career, rising to the Linus Pauling Chair in Chemical Physics and to director of Caltech's National Science Foundation's Laboratory for Molecular Sciences in 1990.

In 1989, Zewail received the King Faisal International Prize for science. While at the award ceremony in Riyadh, Saudi Arabia, Zewail met his future wife, Dema-al-Faham, whose father Shaker al-Faham was in Riyadh to accept the King Faisal International Prize for literature. Dema Zewail, who completed an M.D. from Damascus University and a master's in public health from the University of California, Los Angeles, in 1989 became an expert in public health. The couple had four children: Maha, Amani, Nabeel, and Hani.

Zewail has devoted his career to capturing the behavior of atoms as they combine into molecules in real time. Femtochemistry, for which he received the Nobel Prize, uses ultrafast lasers to take "snapshots" of chemical reactions at

In 1999, Ahmed Hasan Zewail received the Nobel Prize in chemistry for his use of extremely fast laser flashes to examine chemical reactions on a molecular level. *(Tobias Rostlund, Pool/AP Images)*

intervals of one femtosecond—one-millionth of a billionth of a second. To explain just how short a femtosecond is, Zewail's research team offered a helpful comparison: Though it takes one second for light to travel 180,000 miles—about three-quarters of the distance from the Earth to the Moon—it takes just one femtosecond for light to travel 1 percent of the thickness of a human hair. Taking "snapshots" at these intervals, Zewail's team developed a portrait of how atoms moved, creating a four-dimensional picture of atoms in both space and time. Zewail's work allowed scientists to see molecular bonds form and break in real time, on the same timescale that the reaction took place.

Most recently, Zewail has used this technique to study the workings of cells as they manufacture proteins. Under Zewail's direction, the Laboratory for Molecular Sciences has used femtochemistry to study how electrons move in DNA (deoxyribonucleic acid, the material that contains the genetic instructions used in the development of living organisms). This research promises insight into the ways in which DNA is damaged and repaired.

In a productive scholarly career, Zewail has written 13 books. He has also led a team of 250 researchers who have collectively published more than 500 papers. Zewail's most recent efforts to understand chemical changes in motion use the electron microscope.

Although Zewail became a naturalized American citizen in 1982, he has maintained his Egyptian citizenship and his connections to Egypt and the Arab Middle East. He offered a portion of his $937,300 Nobel Prize to his former school, now the Dr. Ahmed H. Zewail High School, in Disuq to improve its science instruction. He has also published works of popular science in ARABIC, including *Age of Science* (2005), *Time* (2007), and *Dialogue of Civilizations* (2007).

In 2001, Zewail, a trustee of the American University in Cairo, created the Ahmed H. Zewail Prize for graduating seniors who have demonstrated extraordinary commitment to scientific inquiry and humanistic values. The prize reflects Zewail's belief that scientific and technological advancement are crucial for the future development of Egypt and the Middle East. Zewail served as the jury president for the L'Oreal-UNESCO award for women in science in 2007. That year, he also joined the advisory boards of Egypt's Supreme Council for Science and Technology, the King Abdullah University of Science and Technology, and the Arab American National Museum.

Egypt has recognized Zewail's contributions to science by awarding him its highest honor, the Order of the Grand Collar of the Nile in 1999. Zewail appeared on Egyptian stamps in 1998 and 1999. He has also received the Benjamin Franklin Medal (1998), the Robert A. Welch Award (1997), and the Albert Einstein World Award (2006), among others.

Zewail has called on Arabs to regain their medieval preeminence in science and technology by investing in education and research. He has also advocated dialogue between the West and the Muslim world to promote mutual understanding and cooperation toward human and scientific progress. Zewail, whose professional affiliations include both Middle Eastern and American institutions, has exemplified this ideal of intellectual exchange.

Sonja Spear

Further Reading

Brown, Malcolm. "Snapshots Taken as Chemicals Bond," *New York Times*, 4 December 1987, p. A18.

Zewail, Ahmed H. *Voyage through Time: Walks of Life to the Nobel Prize*. Cairo: American University in Cairo, 2002.

Appendix

SPEECH BY PRESIDENT BARACK OBAMA, CAIRO, EGYPT
JUNE 4, 2009

Target of an anti-Muslim smear campaign during the 2008 presidential election, Democratic candidate Barack Obama, a professed Christian, constantly battled against the idea, spread by Internet rumor and some political operatives, that he was secretly a Muslim. Using the language of evangelical Christianity, he said that he believed in "Jesus Christ as our Lord and Savior," while others pointed to his long-standing membership in the United Church of Christ. In attempting to quell fears among the voting public that he would be a stealth Muslim president, he also maintained a studied distance from Muslim-American communities. Some Obama volunteers even asked some Muslim women wearing the hijab, or head scarf, at a June 2008 rally in Detroit to avoid being photographed with the candidate. Though the Obama campaign apologized for the act and some Muslim Americans complained about the ways in which they were being ignored by Obama, most Muslim Americans, well aware of the prejudices that Obama faced as the grandson of Kenyan Muslims and American Christians, took his campaign strategy in stride. In the end, according to one poll, approximately 90 percent of Muslim Americans voted for Obama, who won the election in November 2008.

Uniquely qualified to address the growing rift between the Muslim world and the United States, President Obama was far more open about the Muslim heritage of his father's family after being elected. Meeting leaders from Muslim nations, Obama greeted them with a traditional Islamic greeting, "Salam 'Alaykum" or "peace be to you." Addressing the Turkish parliament on April 6, 2009, Obama outlined his intention to work with Muslims toward common goals and interests, acknowledging his own connections to the Muslim community. Then, in a widely anticipated speech on June 4, 2009, at Cairo University in Cairo, Egypt, President Obama outlined his approach to repairing the damaged relationships between Muslims abroad and the United States. In preparing for the speech, the White House consulted with a large number of national security analysts, international affairs commentators, and Muslim-American business leaders and academics. Obama's remarks, which were translated into 13 different languages, were warmly received by people all around the world, though some critics noted that the speech announced no new policy proposals. In his speech, for which he received a standing ovation, Obama voiced the grievances of Muslims—from the U.S. role in the overthrow of the Iranian prime minister in 1953 to the ongoing suffering of Palestinians in the West Bank and Gaza Strip. Admitting to what he called past mistakes while also defending the essential goodness and interests of the United States, Barack Hussein Obama, as he referred to himself in the speech, also praised the role of Muslim Americans in the making of American culture and society and proposed to begin anew America's relationship with Muslims in Africa, Asia, and Europe.

Thank you very much. Good afternoon. I am honored to be in the timeless city of Cairo, and to be hosted by two remarkable institutions. For over a thousand years, Al-Azhar has stood as a beacon of Islamic learning; and for over a century, Cairo University has been a source of Egypt's advancement. And together, you represent the harmony between tradition and progress. I'm grateful for your hospitality, and the hospitality of the people of Egypt. And I'm also proud to carry with me the goodwill of the American people, and a greeting of peace from Muslim communities in my country: *Assalaamu alaykum.*

We meet at a time of great tension between the United States and Muslims around the world—tension rooted in historical forces that go beyond any current policy debate. The relationship between Islam and the West includes centuries of coexistence and cooperation, but also conflict and religious wars. More recently, tension has been fed by colonialism that denied rights and opportunities to many Muslims, and a Cold War in which Muslim-majority countries were too often treated as proxies without regard to their own aspirations. Moreover, the sweeping change brought by modernity and globalization led many Muslims to view the West as hostile to the traditions of Islam.

Violent extremists have exploited these tensions in a small but potent minority of Muslims. The attacks of September 11, 2001, and the continued efforts of these extremists to engage in violence against civilians has led some in my country to view Islam as inevitably hostile not only to America and Western countries, but also to human rights. All this has bred more fear and more mistrust.

So long as our relationship is defined by our differences, we will empower those who sow hatred rather than peace, those who promote conflict rather than the cooperation that can help all of our people achieve justice and prosperity. And this cycle of suspicion and discord must end.

I've come here to Cairo to seek a new beginning between the United States and Muslims around the world, one based on mutual interest and mutual respect, and one based upon the truth that America and Islam are not exclusive and need not be in competition. Instead, they overlap, and share common principles—principles of justice and progress; tolerance and the dignity of all human beings.

I do so recognizing that change cannot happen overnight. I know there's been a lot of publicity about this speech, but no single speech can eradicate years of mistrust, nor can I answer in the time that I have this afternoon all the complex questions that brought us to this point. But I am convinced that in order to move forward, we must say openly to each other the things we hold in our hearts and that too often are said only behind closed doors. There must be a sustained effort to listen to each other; to learn from each other; to respect one another; and to seek common ground. As the Holy Koran tells us, "Be conscious of God and speak always the truth." That is what I will try to do today—to speak the truth as best I can, humbled by the task before us, and firm in my belief that the interests we share as human beings are far more powerful than the forces that drive us apart.

Now part of this conviction is rooted in my own experience. I'm a Christian, but my father came from a Kenyan family that includes generations of Muslims. As a boy, I spent several years in Indonesia and heard the call of the *azaan* at the break of dawn and at the fall of dusk. As a young man, I worked in Chicago communities where many found dignity and peace in their Muslim faith.

As a student of history, I also know civilization's debt to Islam. It was Islam—at places like Al-Azhar—that carried the light of learning through so many centuries, paving the way for Europe's Renaissance and Enlightenment. It was innovation in Muslim communities—it was innovation in Muslim communities that developed the order of algebra; our magnetic compass and tools of navigation; our mastery of pens and printing; our understanding of how disease spreads and how it can be healed. Islamic culture has given us majestic arches and soaring spires; timeless poetry and cherished music; elegant calligraphy and places of peaceful contemplation. And throughout history, Islam has demonstrated through words and deeds the possibilities of religious tolerance and racial equality.

I also know that Islam has always been a part of America's story. The first nation to recognize my country was Morocco. In signing the Treaty of Tripoli in 1796, our second President, John Adams, wrote, "The United States has in itself no character of enmity against the laws, religion or tranquility of Muslims." And since our founding, American Muslims have enriched the United States. They have fought in our wars, they have served in our government, they have stood for civil rights, they have started businesses, they have taught at our universities, they've excelled in our sports arenas, they've won Nobel Prizes, built our tallest building, and lit the Olympic Torch. And when the first Muslim American was recently elected to Congress, he took the oath to defend our Constitution using the same Holy Koran that one of our Founding Fathers—Thomas Jefferson—kept in his personal library.

So I have known Islam on three continents before coming to the region where it was first revealed. That experience guides my conviction that partnership between America and Islam must be based on what Islam is, not what it isn't. And I consider it part of my responsibility as President of the United States to fight against negative stereotypes of Islam wherever they appear.

But that same principle must apply to Muslim perceptions of America. Just as Muslims do not fit a crude stereotype, America is not the crude stereotype of a self-interested empire. The United States has been one of the greatest sources of progress that the world has ever known. We were born out of revolution against an empire. We were founded upon the ideal that all are created equal, and we have shed blood and struggled for centuries to give meaning to those words—within our borders, and around the world. We are shaped by every culture, drawn from every end of the Earth, and dedicated to a simple concept: E pluribus unum—"Out of many, one."

Now, much has been made of the fact that an African American with the name Barack Hussein Obama could be elected President. But my personal story is not so unique. The dream of opportunity for all people has not come true for everyone in America, but its promise exists for all who come to our shores—and that includes nearly 7 million American Muslims in our country today who, by the way, enjoy incomes and educational levels that are higher than the American average.

Moreover, freedom in America is indivisible from the freedom to practice one's religion. That is why there is a mosque in every state in our union, and over 1,200 mosques within our borders. That's why the United States government has gone to court to protect the right of women and girls to wear the hijab and to punish those who would deny it.

So let there be no doubt: Islam is a part of America. And I believe that America holds within her the truth that regardless of race, religion, or station in life, all of us share common aspirations—to live in peace and security; to get an education and to work with dignity; to love our families, our communities, and our God. These things we share. This is the hope of all humanity.

Of course, recognizing our common humanity is only the beginning of our task. Words alone cannot meet the needs of our people. These needs will be met only if we act boldly in the years ahead; and if we understand that the challenges we face are shared, and our failure to meet them will hurt us all.

For we have learned from recent experience that when a financial system weakens in one country, prosperity is hurt everywhere. When a new flu infects one human being, all are at risk. When one nation pursues a nuclear weapon, the risk of nuclear attack rises for all nations. When violent extremists operate in one stretch of mountains, people are endangered across an ocean. When innocents in Bosnia and Darfur are slaughtered, that is a stain on our collective conscience. That is what it means to share this world in the 21st century. That is the responsibility we have to one another as human beings.

And this is a difficult responsibility to embrace. For human history has often been a record of nations and tribes—and, yes, religions—subjugating one another in pursuit of their own interests. Yet in this new age, such attitudes are self-defeating. Given our interdependence, any world order that elevates one nation or group of people over another will inevitably fail. So whatever we think of the past, we must not be prisoners to it. Our problems must be dealt with through partnership; our progress must be shared.

Now, that does not mean we should ignore sources of tension. Indeed, it suggests the opposite: We must face these tensions squarely. And so in that spirit, let me speak as clearly and as plainly as I can about some specific issues that I believe we must finally confront together.

The first issue that we have to confront is violent extremism in all of its forms.

In Ankara, I made clear that America is not—and never will be—at war with Islam. We will, however, relentlessly confront violent extremists who pose a grave threat to our security—because we reject the same thing that people of all faiths reject: the killing of innocent men, women, and children. And it is my first duty as President to protect the American people.

The situation in Afghanistan demonstrates America's goals, and our need to work together. Over seven years ago, the United States pursued al Qaeda and the Taliban with broad international support. We did not go by choice; we went because of necessity. I'm aware that there's still some who would question or even justify the events of 9/11. But let us be clear: Al Qaeda killed nearly 3,000 people on that day. The victims were innocent men, women and children from America and many other nations who had done nothing to harm anybody. And yet al Qaeda chose to ruthlessly murder these people, claimed credit for the attack, and even now states their determination to kill on a massive scale. They have affiliates in many countries and are trying to expand their reach. These are not opinions to be debated; these are facts to be dealt with.

Now, make no mistake: We do not want to keep our troops in Afghanistan. We see no military—we seek no military bases there. It is agonizing for America to lose our young men and women. It is costly and politically difficult to continue this conflict. We would gladly bring every single one of our troops home if we could be confident that there were not violent extremists in Afghanistan and now Pakistan determined to kill as many Americans as they possibly can. But that is not yet the case.

And that's why we're partnering with a coalition of 46 countries. And despite the costs involved, America's commitment will not weaken. Indeed, none of us should tolerate these extremists. They have killed in many countries. They have killed people of different faiths—but more than any other, they have killed Muslims. Their actions are irreconcilable with the rights of human beings, the progress of nations, and with Islam. The Holy Koran teaches that whoever kills an innocent is as—it is as if he has killed all mankind. And the Holy Koran also says whoever saves a person, it is as if he has saved all mankind. The enduring faith of over a billion people is so much bigger than the narrow hatred of a few. Islam is not part of the problem in combating violent extremism—it is an important part of promoting peace.

Now, we also know that military power alone is not going to solve the problems in Afghanistan and Pakistan. That's why we plan to invest $1.5 billion each year over the next five years to partner with Pakistanis to build schools and hospitals, roads and businesses, and hundreds of millions to help those who've been displaced. That's why we are providing more than $2.8 billion to help Afghans develop their economy and deliver services that people depend on.

Let me also address the issue of Iraq. Unlike Afghanistan, Iraq was a war of choice that provoked strong differences in my country and around the world. Although I believe that the Iraqi people are ultimately better off without the tyranny of Saddam Hussein, I also believe that events in Iraq have reminded America of the need to use diplomacy and build international consensus to resolve our problems whenever possible. Indeed, we can recall the words of Thomas Jefferson, who said: "I hope that our wisdom will grow with our power, and teach us that the less we use our power the greater it will be."

Today, America has a dual responsibility: to help Iraq forge a better future—and to leave Iraq to Iraqis. And I have made it clear to the Iraqi people—I have made it clear to the Iraqi people that we pursue no bases, and no claim on their territory or resources. Iraq's sovereignty is its own. And that's why I ordered the removal of our combat brigades by next August. That is why we will honor our agreement with Iraq's democratically elected government to remove combat troops from Iraqi cities by July, and to remove all of our troops from Iraq by 2012. We will help Iraq train its security forces and develop its economy. But we will support a secure and united Iraq as a partner, and never as a patron.

And finally, just as America can never tolerate violence by extremists, we must never alter or forget our principles. Nine-eleven was an enormous trauma to our country. The fear and anger that it provoked was understandable, but in some cases, it led us to act contrary to our traditions and our ideals. We are taking concrete actions to change course. I have unequivocally prohibited the use of torture by the United States, and I have ordered the prison at Guantánamo Bay closed by early next year.

So America will defend itself, respectful of the sovereignty of nations and the rule of law. And we will do so in partnership with Muslim communities which are also threatened. The sooner the extremists are isolated and unwelcome in Muslim communities, the sooner we will all be safer.

The second major source of tension that we need to discuss is the situation between Israelis, Palestinians and the Arab world.

America's strong bonds with Israel are well known. This bond is unbreakable. It is based upon cultural and historical ties, and the recognition that the aspiration for a Jewish homeland is rooted in a tragic history that cannot be denied.

Around the world, the Jewish people were persecuted for centuries, and anti-Semitism in Europe culminated in an unprecedented Holocaust. Tomorrow, I will visit Buchenwald, which was part of a network of camps where Jews were enslaved, tortured, shot and gassed to death by the Third Reich. Six million Jews were killed—more than the entire Jewish population of Israel today. Denying that fact is baseless, it is ignorant, and it is hateful. Threatening Israel with destruction—or repeating vile stereotypes about Jews—is deeply wrong, and only serves to evoke in the minds of Israelis this most painful of memories while preventing the peace that the people of this region deserve.

On the other hand, it is also undeniable that the Palestinian people—Muslims and Christians—have suffered in pursuit of a homeland. For more than 60 years they've endured the pain of dislocation. Many wait in refugee camps in the West Bank, Gaza, and neighboring lands for a life of peace and security that they have never been able to lead. They endure the daily humiliations—large and small—that come with occupation. So let there be no doubt: The situation for the Palestinian people is intolerable. And America will not turn our backs on the legitimate Palestinian aspiration for dignity, opportunity, and a state of their own.

For decades then, there has been a stalemate: two peoples with legitimate aspirations, each with a painful history that makes compromise elusive. It's easy to point fingers—for Palestinians to point to the displacement brought about by Israel's founding, and for Israelis to point to the constant hostility and attacks throughout its history from within its borders as well as beyond. But if we see this conflict only from one side or the other, then we will be blind to the truth: The only resolution is for the aspirations of both sides to be met through two states, where Israelis and Palestinians each live in peace and security.

That is in Israel's interest, Palestine's interest, America's interest, and the world's interest. And that is why I intend to personally pursue this outcome with all the patience and dedication that the task requires. The obligations—the obligations that the parties have agreed to under the road map are clear. For peace to come, it is time for them—and all of us—to live up to our responsibilities.

Palestinians must abandon violence. Resistance through violence and killing is wrong and it does not succeed. For centuries, black people in America suffered the lash of the whip as slaves and the humiliation of segregation. But it was not violence that won full and equal rights. It was a peaceful and determined insistence upon the ideals at the center of America's founding. This same story can be told by people from South Africa to South Asia; from Eastern Europe to Indonesia. It's a story with a simple truth: that violence is a dead end. It is a sign neither of courage nor power to shoot rockets at sleeping children, or to blow up old women on a bus. That's not how moral authority is claimed; that's how it is surrendered.

Now is the time for Palestinians to focus on what they can build. The Palestinian Authority must develop its capacity to govern, with institutions that serve the needs of its people. Hamas does have support among some Palestinians, but they also have to recognize they have responsibilities. To play a role in fulfilling Palestinian aspirations, to unify the Palestinian people, Hamas must put an end to violence, recognize past agreements, recognize Israel's right to exist.

At the same time, Israelis must acknowledge that just as Israel's right to exist cannot be denied, neither can Palestine's. The United States does not accept the legitimacy of continued Israeli settlements. This construction violates previous agreements and undermines efforts to achieve peace. It is time for these settlements to stop.

And Israel must also live up to its obligation to ensure that Palestinians can live and work and develop their society. Just as it devastates Palestinian families, the continuing humanitarian crisis in Gaza does not serve Israel's security; neither does the continuing lack of opportunity in the West Bank. Progress in the daily lives of the Palestinian people must be a critical part of a road to peace, and Israel must take concrete steps to enable such progress.

And finally, the Arab states must recognize that the Arab Peace Initiative was an important beginning, but not the end of their responsibilities. The Arab-Israeli conflict should no longer be used to distract the people of Arab nations from other problems. Instead, it must be a cause for action to help the Palestinian people develop the institutions that will sustain their state, to recognize Israel's legitimacy, and to choose progress over a self-defeating focus on the past.

America will align our policies with those who pursue peace, and we will say in public what we say in private to Israelis and Palestinians and Arabs. We cannot impose peace. But privately, many Muslims recognize that Israel will not go away. Likewise, many Israelis recognize the need for a Palestinian state. It is time for us to act on what everyone knows to be true.

Too many tears have been shed. Too much blood has been shed. All of us have a responsibility to work for the day when the mothers of Israelis and Palestinians can see their children grow up without fear; when the Holy Land of the three great faiths is the place of peace that God intended it to be; when Jerusalem is a secure and lasting home for Jews and Christians and Muslims, and a place for all of the children of Abraham to mingle peacefully together as in the story of Isra—as in the story of Isra, when Moses, Jesus, and Mohammed, peace be upon them, joined in prayer.

The third source of tension is our shared interest in the rights and responsibilities of nations on nuclear weapons.

This issue has been a source of tension between the United States and the Islamic Republic of Iran. For many years, Iran has defined itself in part by its opposition to my country, and there is in fact a tumultuous history between us. In the middle of the Cold War, the United States played a role in the overthrow of a democratically elected Iranian government. Since the Islamic Revolution, Iran has played a role in acts of hostage-taking and violence against U.S. troops and civilians. This history is well known. Rather than remain trapped in the past, I've made it clear to Iran's leaders and people that my country is prepared to move forward. The question now is not what Iran is against, but rather what future it wants to build.

I recognize it will be hard to overcome decades of mistrust, but we will proceed with courage, rectitude, and resolve. There will be many issues to discuss between our two countries, and we are willing to move forward without preconditions on the basis of mutual respect. But it is clear to all concerned that when it comes to nuclear weapons, we have reached a decisive point. This is not simply about America's interests. It's about preventing a nuclear arms race in the Middle East that could lead this region and the world down a hugely dangerous path.

I understand those who protest that some countries have weapons that others do not. No single nation should pick and choose which nation holds nuclear weapons. And that's why I strongly reaffirmed America's commitment to seek a world in which no nations hold nuclear weapons. And any nation—including Iran—should have the right to access peaceful nuclear power if it complies with its responsibilities under the nuclear Non-Proliferation Treaty. That commitment is at the core of the treaty, and it must be kept for all who fully abide by it. And I'm hopeful that all countries in the region can share in this goal.

The fourth issue that I will address is democracy.

I know—I know there has been controversy about the promotion of democracy in recent years, and much of this controversy is connected to the war in Iraq. So let me be clear: No system of government can or should be imposed by one nation by any other.

That does not lessen my commitment, however, to governments that reflect the will of the people. Each nation gives life to this principle in its own way, grounded in the traditions of its own people. America does not presume to know what is best for everyone, just as we would not presume to pick the outcome of a peaceful election. But I do have an unyielding belief that all people yearn for certain things: the ability to speak your mind and have a say in how you are governed; confidence in the rule of law and the equal administration of justice; government that is transparent and doesn't steal from the people; the freedom to live as you choose. These are not just American ideas; they are human rights. And that is why we will support them everywhere.

Now, there is no straight line to realize this promise. But this much is clear: Governments that protect these rights are ultimately more stable, successful and secure. Suppressing ideas never succeeds in making them go away. America respects the right of all peaceful and law-abiding voices to be heard around the world, even if we disagree with them. And we will welcome all elected, peaceful governments—provided they govern with respect for all their people.

This last point is important because there are some who advocate for democracy only when they're out of power;

once in power, they are ruthless in suppressing the rights of others. So no matter where it takes hold, government of the people and by the people sets a single standard for all who would hold power: You must maintain your power through consent, not coercion; you must respect the rights of minorities, and participate with a spirit of tolerance and compromise; you must place the interests of your people and the legitimate workings of the political process above your party. Without these ingredients, elections alone do not make true democracy.

The fifth issue that we must address together is religious freedom.

Islam has a proud tradition of tolerance. We see it in the history of Andalusia and Cordoba during the Inquisition. I saw it firsthand as a child in Indonesia, where devout Christians worshiped freely in an overwhelmingly Muslim country. That is the spirit we need today. People in every country should be free to choose and live their faith based upon the persuasion of the mind and the heart and the soul. This tolerance is essential for religion to thrive, but it's being challenged in many different ways.

Among some Muslims, there's a disturbing tendency to measure one's own faith by the rejection of somebody else's faith. The richness of religious diversity must be upheld—whether it is for Maronites in Lebanon or the Copts in Egypt. And if we are being honest, fault lines must be closed among Muslims, as well, as the divisions between Sunni and Shia have led to tragic violence, particularly in Iraq.

Freedom of religion is central to the ability of peoples to live together. We must always examine the ways in which we protect it. For instance, in the United States, rules on charitable giving have made it harder for Muslims to fulfill their religious obligation. That's why I'm committed to working with American Muslims to ensure that they can fulfill zakat.

Likewise, it is important for Western countries to avoid impeding Muslim citizens from practicing religion as they see fit—for instance, by dictating what clothes a Muslim woman should wear. We can't disguise hostility towards any religion behind the pretence of liberalism.

In fact, faith should bring us together. And that's why we're forging service projects in America to bring together Christians, Muslims, and Jews. That's why we welcome efforts like Saudi Arabian King Abdullah's interfaith dialogue and Turkey's leadership in the Alliance of Civilizations. Around the world, we can turn dialogue into interfaith service, so bridges between peoples lead to action—whether it is combating malaria in Africa, or providing relief after a natural disaster.

The sixth issue—the sixth issue that I want to address is women's rights. I know—I know—and you can tell from this audience, that there is a healthy debate about this issue. I reject the view of some in the West that a woman who chooses

to cover her hair is somehow less equal, but I do believe that a woman who is denied an education is denied equality. And it is no coincidence that countries where women are well educated are far more likely to be prosperous.

Now, let me be clear: Issues of women's equality are by no means simply an issue for Islam. In Turkey, Pakistan, Bangladesh, Indonesia, we've seen Muslim-majority countries elect a woman to lead. Meanwhile, the struggle for women's equality continues in many aspects of American life, and in countries around the world.

I am convinced that our daughters can contribute just as much to society as our sons. Our common prosperity will be advanced by allowing all humanity—men and women—to reach their full potential. I do not believe that women must make the same choices as men in order to be equal, and I respect those women who choose to live their lives in traditional roles. But it should be their choice. And that is why the United States will partner with any Muslim-majority country to support expanded literacy for girls, and to help young women pursue employment through micro-financing that helps people live their dreams.

Finally, I want to discuss economic development and opportunity.

I know that for many, the face of globalization is contradictory. The Internet and television can bring knowledge and information, but also offensive sexuality and mindless violence into the home. Trade can bring new wealth and opportunities, but also huge disruptions and change in communities. In all nations—including America—this change can bring fear. Fear that because of modernity we lose control over our economic choices, our politics, and most importantly our identities—those things we most cherish about our communities, our families, our traditions, and our faith.

But I also know that human progress cannot be denied. There need not be contradictions between development and tradition. Countries like Japan and South Korea grew their economies enormously while maintaining distinct cultures. The same is true for the astonishing progress within Muslim-majority countries from Kuala Lumpur to Dubai. In ancient times and in our times, Muslim communities have been at the forefront of innovation and education.

And this is important because no development strategy can be based only upon what comes out of the ground, nor can it be sustained while young people are out of work. Many Gulf states have enjoyed great wealth as a consequence of oil, and some are beginning to focus it on broader development. But all of us must recognize that education and innovation will be the currency of the 21st century—and in too many Muslim communities, there remains underinvestment in these areas. I'm emphasizing such investment within my own country. And while America in the past has focused on oil and gas when it comes to this part of the world, we now seek a broader engagement.

On education, we will expand exchange programs, and increase scholarships, like the one that brought my father to America. At the same time, we will encourage more Americans to study in Muslim communities. And we will match promising Muslim students with internships in America; invest in online learning for teachers and children around the world; and create a new online network, so a young person in Kansas can communicate instantly with a young person in Cairo.

On economic development, we will create a new corps of business volunteers to partner with counterparts in Muslim-majority countries. And I will host a Summit on Entrepreneurship this year to identify how we can deepen ties between business leaders, foundations and social entrepreneurs in the United States and Muslim communities around the world.

On science and technology, we will launch a new fund to support technological development in Muslim-majority countries, and to help transfer ideas to the marketplace so they can create more jobs. We'll open centers of scientific excellence in Africa, the Middle East and Southeast Asia, and appoint new science envoys to collaborate on programs that develop new sources of energy, create green jobs, digitize records, clean water, grow new crops. Today I'm announcing a new global effort with the Organization of the Islamic Conference to eradicate polio. And we will also expand partnerships with Muslim communities to promote child and maternal health.

All these things must be done in partnership. Americans are ready to join with citizens and governments; community organizations, religious leaders, and businesses in Muslim communities around the world to help our people pursue a better life.

The issues that I have described will not be easy to address. But we have a responsibility to join together on behalf of the world that we seek—a world where extremists no longer threaten our people, and American troops have come home; a world where Israelis and Palestinians are each secure in a state of their own, and nuclear energy is used for peaceful purposes; a world where governments serve their citizens, and the rights of all God's children are respected. Those are mutual interests. That is the world we seek. But we can only achieve it together.

I know there are many—Muslim and non-Muslim—who question whether we can forge this new beginning. Some are eager to stoke the flames of division, and to stand in the way of progress. Some suggest that it isn't worth the effort—that we are fated to disagree, and civilizations are doomed to clash. Many more are simply skeptical that real change can occur. There's so much fear, so much mistrust that has built up over the years. But if we choose to be bound by the past, we will never move forward. And I want to particularly say this to young people of every faith, in every country—you, more than anyone, have the ability to reimagine the world, to remake this world.

All of us share this world for but a brief moment in time. The question is whether we spend that time focused on what pushes us apart, or whether we commit ourselves to an effort—a sustained effort—to find common ground, to focus on the future we seek for our children, and to respect the dignity of all human beings.

It's easier to start wars than to end them. It's easier to blame others than to look inward. It's easier to see what is different about someone than to find the things we share. But we should choose the right path, not just the easy path. There's one rule that lies at the heart of every religion—that we do unto others as we would have them do unto us. This truth transcends nations and peoples—a belief that isn't new; that isn't black or white or brown; that isn't Christian or Muslim or Jew. It's a belief that pulsed in the cradle of civilization, and that still beats in the hearts of billions around the world. It's a faith in other people, and it's what brought me here today.

We have the power to make the world we seek, but only if we have the courage to make a new beginning, keeping in mind what has been written.

The Holy Koran tells us: "O mankind! We have created you male and a female; and we have made you into nations and tribes so that you may know one another."

The Talmud tells us: "The whole of the Torah is for the purpose of promoting peace."

The Holy Bible tells us: "Blessed are the peacemakers, for they shall be called sons of God."

The people of the world can live together in peace. We know that is God's vision. Now that must be our work here on Earth.

Thank you. And may God's peace be upon you. Thank you very much. Thank you.

Bibliography

Abd-Allah, Umar F. *A Muslim in Victorian America: The Life of Alexander Russell Webb.* New York: Oxford University Press, 2006.

Abdo, Geneive. *Mecca and Main Street: Muslim Life in America after 9/11.* New York: Oxford University Press, 2006.

Abdul-Ghafur, Saleemah, ed. *Living Islam Out Loud: American Muslim Women Speak.* Boston: Beacon Press, 2005.

Abdul-Jabbar, Kareem, and Peter Knobler. *Giant Steps: The Autobiography of Kareem Abdul-Jabbar.* Toronto: Bantam Books, 1983.

Abdul-Jabbar, Kareem, and Mignon McCarthy. *Kareem.* New York: Warner Books, 1990.

Abdul-Jabbar, Kareem, and Alan Steinberg. *Black Profiles in Courage: A Legacy of African-American Achievement.* New York: William Morrow, 1996.

Abdullah, Aslam, and Gasser Hathout. *The American Muslim Identity: Speaking for Ourselves.* Los Angeles: Islamic Society of Southern California, 2003.

Abdul Rauf, Feisal. *Islam: A Sacred Law.* Watsonville, Calif.: Threshold Books, 2000.

———. *Islam: A Search for Meaning.* Costa Mesa, Calif.: Mazda Publishers, 1996.

———. *What's Right with Islam: A New Vision for Muslims and the West.* New York: HarperCollins, 2004.

Abdul-Rauf, Muhammad. *History of the Islamic Center: From Dream to Reality.* Washington, D.C.: Islamic Center, 1978.

Abou El Fadl, Khaled. *And God Knows the Soldiers: The Authoritative and Authoritarian in Islamic Discourses.* Lanham, Md.: Rowman and Littlefield, 2001.

———. *The Great Theft: Wrestling Islam from the Extremists.* San Francisco: Harper San Francisco, 2005.

———. *Islam and the Challenge of Democracy.* Princeton, N.J.: Princeton University Press, 2004.

———. *The Place of Tolerance in Islam.* Boston: Beacon Press, 2002.

———. *The Search for Beauty in Islam: A Conference of the Books.* Lanham, Md.: Rowman and Littlefield, 2006.

———. *Speaking in God's Name: Islamic Law, Authority and Women.* Oxford: Oneworld, 2001.

Abraham, Nabeel, and Andrew Shryock, eds. *Arab Detroit: From Margin to Mainstream.* Detroit: Wayne State University Press, 2000.

Abu-Jaber, Diana. *Crescent.* New York: W. W. Norton, 2003.

———. *The Language of Baklava: A Memoir.* New York: Pantheon, 2005.

Abu Ras, Wahiba, and Soleman Abu Ras. "The Impact of September 11, 2001, Attacks on the Well-Being of Arab Americans in New York City." *Journal of Muslim Mental Health* 3, no. 2 (September 2008): 217–239.

Abu Shouk, Ahmed I., J. R. Hunwick, and R. S. O'Fahey. "A Sudanese Missionary to the United States: Satti Majid, Shaykh al-Islam in North America, and His Encounter with Noble Drew Ali, Prophet of the Moorish Science Temple." *Sudanic Africa* 8 (1997): 137–191.

Adorno, Rolena, and Patrick Charles Pautz. *Álvar Núñez Cabeza de Vaca: His Account, His Life, and the Expedition of Pánfilo de Narváez.* 3 vols. Lincoln: University of Nebraska Press, 1999.

Afzal-Khan, Fawzia, ed. *Shattering the Stereotypes: Muslim Women Speak Out.* Northampton, Mass.: Olive Branch Press, 2005.

Agha, Shahid Ali. *Call Me Ishmael Tonight: A Book of Ghazals.* New York: W. W. Norton, 2003.

———. *Rooms Are Never Finished.* New York: W. W. Norton, 2002.

———, ed. *Ravishing DisUnities: Real Ghazals in English.* Hanover, N.H.: University Press of New England, 2000.

Agic, Senad. *Immigration and Assimilation: The Bosnian Muslim Experience in Chicago.* Lima, Ohio: Wyndham Hall Press, 2004.

Ahmed, Leila. *A Border Passage: From Cairo to America—A Woman's Journey.* New York: Penguin, 2000.

Aidi, Hisham. "'Verily, There Is Only One Hip-Hop Umma': Islam, Cultural Protest and Urban Marginality." *Socialism and Democracy* 18, no. 2 (2004): 107–126.

Aijian, M. M. "Mohammedans in the United States." *Moslem World* 10 (1920): 30–35.

Akbari, Hamid, and Azar Khounani. *Iranians in Chicagoland.* Charleston, S.C.: Arcadia, 2005.

Al-Ahari, Muhammed. *A Heritage of East and West: The Writings of Imam Camil Avdic.* Chicago: Magribine Press, 2006.

———, ed. *Five Classic Muslim Slave Narratives.* Chicago: Magribine Press, 2006.

Al-Amin, Imam Jamil. *Revolution by the Book: The Rap Is Live.* Beltsville, Md.: Writers' Inc. International, 1994.

Alawani, Taha Jabir. *Towards a Fiqh for Minorities, Some Basic Reflections.* Herndon, Va.: International Institute of Islamic Thought, 2003.

Alba, Richard, and Victor Nee. *Remaking the American Mainstream: Assimilation and Contemporary Immigration.* Cambridge, Mass.: Harvard University Press, 2003.

Alexander, Amy, ed. *The Farrakhan Factor: African-American Writers on Leadership, Nationhood, and Minister Louis Farrakhan.* New York: Grove Press, 1998.

Alford, Terry. *Prince among Slaves: The True Story of an African Prince Sold into Slavery in the American South.* New York: Oxford University Press, 1977.

Ali, Dusé Mohamed. *In the Land of Pharaohs: A Short History of Egypt from the Fall of Ismail to the Assassination of Boutros Pasha.* London: Stanley Paul, 1911.

Ali, Kecia. *Sexual Ethics and Islam: Feminist Reflections on Qur'an, Hadith, and Jurisprudence.* Oxford: Oneworld, 2006.

Ali, Muhammad, with Hana Yasmeen Ali. *Soul of a Butterfly: Reflections on Life's Journey.* New York: Simon & Schuster, 2004.

Al-Jibali, Muhammad. *Islamic Perspective of Contraception and Abortion.* Arlington, Texas: Al-Kitaab & as-Sunnah Publishing, 2000.

Allen, Anne B. "Estevanico the Moor." *American History* 32, no. 3 (July 1997): 36–43.

Allen, Ernest, Jr. "Identity and Destiny: The Formative Views of the Moorish Science Temple and the Nation of Islam." In *Muslims on the Americanization Path?,* edited by Yvonne Yazbeck Haddad and John L. Esposito. Atlanta: Scholars Press, 1998.

———. "When Japan Was 'Champion of the Darker Races': Satokata Takahashi and the Flowering of Black Messianic Nationalism." *Black Scholar* 24 (Winter 1994): 23–46.

Allison, Robert J. *The Crescent Obscured: The United States and the Muslim World, 1776–1815.* Chicago: University of Chicago Press, 1995.

Al-Marayati, Laila. "American Muslim Charities: Easy Targets in the War on Terror." *Pace Law Review* 25 (2005): 321–338.

Ameri, Anan, and Yvonne Lockwood. *Arab Americans in Metro Detroit: A Pictorial History.* Chicago: Arcadia Publishing, 2001.

Ammar, Nawal H., Robert R. Weaver, and Sam Saxon. "Muslims in Prison: A Case Study from Ohio Prisons." *International Journal of Offender Therapy and Comparative Criminology* 48, no. 4 (2004): 414–428.

Amnesty International. *Threat and Humiliation: Racial Profiling, Domestic Security, and Human Rights in the United States.* New York: Amnesty International, 2004.

An-Na'im, Abdullahi. *Islam and the Secular State: Negotiating the Future of Shari'a.* Cambridge, Mass.: Harvard University Press, 2008.

Ansari, Es-Seyyid Es-Shaykh Taner. *Alternative Healing: The Sufi Way.* Nassau, N.Y.: Ansari Publications, 2007.

———. *The Sun Will Rise in the West.* Napa, Calif.: Ansari Publications, 2000.

———. *What About My Wood! 101 Sufi Stories.* Nassau, N.Y.: Ansari Publications, 2005.

Ansari, Es-Sayyid Es-Shaykh Taner, trans. *Grand Masters of Sufism: Abdul Qadir Geylani's* Secret of Secrets *and Ahmed er Rifai's* Guidance to Mysticism. Nassau, N.Y.: Ansari Publications, 2008.

Ansari, Tiel Aisha. *Knocking from Inside.* The Ecstatic Exchange, 2008.

Anway, Carol L. *Daughters of Another Path.* Lee's Summit, Mo.: Yawna Publications, 1996.

Arab American Institute. "Healing the Nation: The Arab American Experience after September 11." Washington, D.C.: Arab American Institute Foundation, 2002.

———. "Profiling and Pride: Arab American Attitudes and Behavior since September 11." Washington, D.C.: Arab American Institute Foundation, 2002.

Aswad, Barbara C., and Barbara Bilgé, eds. *Family and Gender among American Muslims: Issues Facing Middle Eastern Immigrants and Their Descendants.* Philadelphia: Temple University Press, 1996.

Athar, Shahid. *Islamic Medicine.* Karachi, Pakistan: Pan-Islamic Pub. House, 1989.

———. *Reflections of an American Muslim.* Chicago: Kazi Publications, 1994.

Atiyeh, Wadeeha. *Scheherezade Cooks!* New York: Gramercy, 1960.

Austin, Allan D. *African Muslims in Antebellum America: A Sourcebook.* New York: Garland, 1984.

———. *African Muslims in Antebellum America: Transatlantic Stories and Spiritual Struggles.* New York: Routledge, 1997.

Avdich, Kamil. *Survey of Islamic Doctrine.* Cedar Rapids, Iowa: Unity Pub. Company, 1979.

Avlon, John. "Our Islamic Soldiers: Healing Force in the War on Terror." *Radical Middle Newsletter,* May 1, 2006. Available online. URL: http://www.radicalmiddle.com/x_avlon_soldiers.htm.

Aymard, Jean-Baptiste, and Patrick Laude. *Frithjof Schuon: Life and Teachings.* Albany: State University of New York Press, 2004.

Ayubi, Zahra. "Facing the Divorce Stigma." *Azizah* 4, no. 3 (2007): 58–61.

———. "Specific Issues in Muslim Divorce." *The Family Law Review: Family Law Section of the Georgia State Bar* (December 2006): 1, 4–5.

Bagby, Ihsan. "The Mosque and the American Public Square." In *Muslims' Place in the American Public Square: Hope, Fears, and Aspirations,* edited by Zahid Hussain Bukhari et al., 323–346. Walnut Creek, Calif.: AltaMira Press, 2004.

Bagby, Ihsan, Paul M. Perl, and Bryan T. Froehle. *The Mosque in America: A National Portrait.* Washington, D.C.: Council on American-Islamic Relations, 2001.

Bakhtiar, Laleh. *Encyclopedia of Islamic Law: A Compendium of the Views of the Major Schools.* Chicago: Kazi Publications, 1996.

Bald, Vivek. "Overlapping Diasporas, Multiracial Lives: South Asian Muslims in U.S. Communities of Color, 1880–1950." *Souls* 8, no. 4 (December 2006): 3–18.

Baquaqua, Mahommah Gardo, and Samuel Moore. *Biography of Mahommah G. Baquaqua, a Native of Zoogoo, in the Interior of Africa.* Detroit: Geo. E. Pomeroy & Co., Tribune Office, 1854.

Baraka, Amiri. *The Autobiography of LeRoi Jones.* Chicago: Lawrence Hill, 1997.

Barboza, Steven. *American Jihad: Life after Malcolm X.* New York: Doubleday, 1994.

Barlas, Lois Asma. *"Believing Women" in Islam: Unreading Patriarchal Interpretations of the Qur'an.* Austin: University of Texas Press, 2002.

Barrett, Paul. *American Islam: The Struggle for the Soul of a Religion.* New York: Farrar, Straus and Giroux, 2007.

Bayoumi, Mustafa, "East of the Sun (West of the Moon): Islam, the Ahmadis, and African America." *Journal of Asian-American Studies* 4, no. 3 (October 2001): 251–263.

———. *How Does It Feel to Be a Problem? Being Young and Arab in America.* New York: Penguin, 2008.

Ba-Yunus, Ilyas, and Kassim Kone. *Muslims in the United States.* Westport, Conn., and London: Greenwood Press, 2006.

Bengalee, M. R. "What Would Muhammad Say to Chicago?" *Muslim Sunrise,* no. 7 (1930): 18–19.

Benson, Kathleen, and Philip M. Kayal, eds. *A Community of Many Worlds: Arab Americans in New York City.* New York: Museum of the City of New York/Syracuse University Press, 2002.

Berg, Herbert. *Elijah Muhammad and Islam.* New York: New York University Press, 2009.

Beynon, Erdmann Doane. "The Voodoo Cult among Negro Migrants in Detroit." *American Journal of Sociology* 42 (May 1938): 894–907.

Bilgé, Barbara. "Turkish-American Patterns of Intermarriage." In *Family and Gender among American Muslims,* edited by Barbara C. Aswad and Barbara Bilgé, 59–106. Philadelphia: Temple University Press, 1996.

———. "Voluntary Associations in the Old Turkish Community of Metropolitan Detroit." In *Muslim Communities in North America,* edited by Yvonne Y. Haddad and Jane I. Smith, 381–405. Albany: State University of New York Press, 1994.

Bing-Canar, Jennifer, and Mary Zerkel. *Banaat Chicago/Daughter of Chicago: Growing Up Arab and Female in Chicago.* Seattle: Arab Film Distribution, 1996.

Bingham, Howard, and Max Wallace. *Muhammad Ali's Greatest Fight: Cassius Clay vs. the United States of America.* New York: M. Evans, 2000.

Birchmeier, Jason. "Mos Def." In *All Music Guide to Hip-Hop: The Definitive Guide to Rap & Hip-Hop,* edited by Hal Leonard Corporation. San Francisco: Backbeat Books, 2003.

Blank, Jonah. *Mullahs on the Mainframe: Islam and Modernity among the Daudi Bohras.* Chicago: University of Chicago Press, 2001.

Bluett, Thomas. *Some Memoirs of the Life of Job, the Son of Solomon, the High Priest of Boonda in Africa; Who was a Slave About Two Years in Maryland; and Afterwards Being Brought to England, Was Set Free, and Sent to His Native Land in the Year 1734.* London: R. Ford, 1734.

Blyden, Edward W. *Christianity, Islam, and the Negro Race.* 1888. Reprint, Baltimore, Md.: Black Classic Press, 1994.

Bogdanov, Vladimir, ed. *All Music Guide to Hip-Hop: The Definitive Guide to Rap & Hip-Hop.* San Francisco: Backbeat Books, 2003.

Bogdanov, Vladimir, Chris Woodstra, and Stephen Thomas Erlewine. *All Music Guide to Jazz: The Definitive Guide to Jazz Music.* San Francisco: Backbeat Books, 2002.

Bookbird: Journal of International Children's Literature. Special Issue: Children's Literature of the Islamic World 35, no. 3 (Fall 1997).

Boosahda, Elizabeth. *Arab-American Faces and Voices.* Austin: University of Texas Press, 2003.

Bozorgmehr, Mehdi, Claudia Der-Martirosian, and Georges Sabagh. "Middle Easterners: A New Kind of Immigrant." In *Ethnic Los Angeles,* edited by Roger Waldinger and Mehdi Bozorgmehr, 345–378. New York: Russell Sage Foundation, 1996.

Bradford, Clare. "Representing Islam: Female Subjects in Suzanne Fisher Staples's Novels." *Children's Literature Association Quarterly* 32, no. 1 (Spring 2007): 47–62.

Breitman, George, ed. *Malcolm X Speaks.* New York: Grove Weidenfeld, 1965.

Brodeur, Patrice, and Sondra Myers, eds. *The Pluralist Paradigm.* Scranton, Pa.: University of Scranton Press, 2006.

Brown, Christopher. "Interview with Suheir Hammad." *The Electronic Intifada,* June 8, 2006. Available online. URL: http://electronicintifada.net/v2/article4788.shtml. Accessed March 4, 2009.

Brown, H. Rap. *Die, Nigger, Die: A Political Autobiography of Jamil Abdullah al-Amin.* Chicago: Lawrence Hill Books, 2002.

Bsisu, May. *The Arab Table: Recipes and Culinary Traditions.* New York: HarperCollins, 2005.

Bukhari, Zahid, Sulayman Nyang, Mumtaz Ahmad, and John L. Esposito, eds. *Muslims' Place in the American Public Square: Hopes, Fears, and Aspirations.* Lanham, Md.: AltaMira Press, 2004.

Bullock, Katherine. *Muslim Women Activists in North America: Speaking for Ourselves.* Austin: University of Texas Press, 2005.

Bunt, Gary. *Islam in the Digital Age.* London: Pluto Press, 2003.

———. *Virtually Islamic.* Cardiff: University of Wales Press, 2000.

Burkett, Randall K. *Black Redemption: Churchmen Speak for the Garvey Movement.* Philadelphia: Temple University Press, 1978.

———. *Garveyism as a Religious Movement: The Institutionalization of a Black Civil Religion.* Metuchen, N.J.: Scarecrow Press, 1978.

Bush, John. "A Tribe Called Quest." In *All Music Guide to Hip-Hop: The Definitive Guide to Rap & Hip-Hop,* edited by Hal Leonard Corporation. San Francisco: Backbeat Books, 2003.

Butler, Clark, ed. *Guantánamo Bay and the Judicial-Moral Treatment of the Other.* West Lafayette, Ind.: Purdue University Press, 2007.

Byng, Michelle D. "Mediating Discrimination: Resisting Oppression among African-American Muslim Women." *Society for the Study of Social Problems* 45, no. 4 (November 1998).

CACCF Statistics. Available online. URL: http://www.archives.gov/research/vietnam-war/casualty-statistics.html. Accessed February 3, 2009.

Cagle, Jeff. "Portraits: No Longer Taboo," *Owatonna People's Press,* 31 March 2007, pp. 8–13.

Cainkar, Louise. "The Deteriorating Ethnic Safety Net among Arabs in Chicago." In *Arabs in America: Building a New Future,* edited by Michael Suleiman, 192–206. Philadelphia: Temple University Press, 1999.

———. *Homeland Insecurity: The Arab American and Muslim American Experience after 9/11.* New York: Russell Sage Publications, 2009.

———. "The Impact of the September 11 Attacks on Arab and Muslim Communities in the United States." In *The Maze of Fear,* edited by John Tirman, 215–239. New York: Social Science Research Council, 2004.

———. "Islamic Revival among Second-generation Arab-American Muslims: The American Experience and Globalism Intersect." *Bulletin of the Royal Institute for Interfaith Studies* 6, no. 2 (Autumn/Winter 2004): 99–120.

———. "No Longer Invisible: Arab and Muslim Exclusion after September 11." *Middle East Report* 224 (Autumn 2002): 22–29.

Caldwell, Deborah. "The First Celebrity Muslim." Beliefnet. Available online. URL: http://www.beliefnet.com/story/96/story_9678_1.html. Accessed August 25, 2008.

———. "Hakeem Olajuwon: A Ramadan Interview." Beliefnet. Available online. URL: http://www.beliefnet.com/story/55/story_5556_1.html. Accessed July 8, 2008.

———. "Muhammad Ali's New Spiritual Quest." Beliefnet. Available online. URL: http://www.beliefnet.com/story/160/story_16045_1.html. Accessed August 25, 2008.

Cameron, Charles. "A Block from Woodward: Victor Avenue in Highland Park, Where Little Arabia Meets Little Persia," *Detroit Saturday Night,* 7 July 1926, pp. 11–12.

Campo, Juan E. "Islam in California: Views from the *Minaret.*" *Muslim World* 86 (1996): 294–312.

Carmi, Daniella. *Aamir and Yonathan.* New York: Levine Books, 2000.

Carson, Clayborne. *Malcolm X: The FBI File.* New York: Carroll & Graf, 1991.

Cateura, Linda Brandi. *Voices of American Muslims: 23 Profiles.* New York: Hippocrene Books, 2005.

Chang, Jeff. *Can't Stop, Won't Stop: A History of the Hip-Hop Generation.* New York: Picador, 2005.

Charara, Hayan. *Inclined to Speak: An Anthology of Contemporary Arab American Poetry.* Fayetteville: University of Arkansas Press, 2008.

Chirri, Mohamed Jawad. *Inquiries about Islam.* Rev. ed. Detroit: Islamic Center of America, 1996.

———. *The Shi'ites under Attack.* Detroit: Islamic Center of America, 1986.

Chishti, Abu Abdullah Ghulam. *The Book of Sufi Healing.* Rochester, Vt.: Inner Traditions International, 1991.

Chishti, G. M. *Natural Medicine.* New York: McGraw-Hill, 1978.

———. *The Traditional Healer's Handbook: A Classic Guide to the Medicine of Avicenna.* Rochester, Vt.: Healing Arts Press, 1991.

Chu, Jeff. "Duty, Honor and Allah." *Time,* 23 August 2005.

Clark, Peter, ed. *New Trends in the Developments in the World of Islam.* London: Luzac Oriental, 1998.

Clegg, Claude Andrew, III. *An Original Man: The Life and Times of Elijah Muhammad.* New York: St. Martin's Press, 1997.

cooke, miriam, and Bruce B. Lawrence, eds. *Muslim Networks from Hajj to Hip Hop.* Chapel Hill: University of North Carolina Press, 2005.

Cristillo, Louis, et al. *This Is Where I Need to Be: Oral Histories of Muslim Youth in NYC.* New York: Columbia Teacher's College Student Press Initiative, 2008.

Cronon, E. David. *Black Moses: The Story of Marcus Garvey and the Universal Negro Improvement Association.* Madison: University of Wisconsin Press, 1955.

Cross, Wilbur. *Gullah Culture in America.* Westport, Conn.: Praeger, 2008.

Curtin, Philip D. *Africa Remembered: Narratives by West Africans from the Era of the Slave Trade.* Madison: University of Wisconsin Press, 1967.

Curtis, Edward E., IV. *Black Muslim Religion in the Nation of Islam, 1960–1975.* Chapel Hill: University of North Carolina Press, 2006.

———. *Islam in Black America: Identity, Liberation, and Difference in African-American Islamic Thought.* Albany: State University of New York Press, 2002.

———. "Islamism and Its African American Critics: Black Muslims in the Era of the Arab Cold War." In *Religion and Politics in the Contemporary United States,* edited by R. Marie Griffith and Melani McAlister, 157–183. Baltimore: Johns Hopkins University Press, 2008.

———. *Muslims in America: A Short History.* New York: Oxford University Press, 2009.

———, ed. *The Columbia Sourcebook of Muslims in the United States.* New York: Columbia University Press, 2008.

Curtiss, Richard H. "Dr. Agha Saeed: Dynamic Leader of Expanding American Muslim Alliance." *Washington Report on Middle East Affairs,* no. 1297 (December 1997): 23–25.

Cushman, Thomas, and Stjepan Mestrovic. *This Time We Knew: Western Responses to Genocide in Bosnia.* New York: New York University Press, 1996.

DAAS Research Project. *Citizenship and Crisis: Arab Detroit after 9/11.* New York: Russell Sage Foundation Press, 2009.

Daftary, Farhad. *A Modern History of the Ismailis: Continuity and Change in a Muslim Community.* New York: Palgrave Macmillan, 2009.

D'Alisera, JoAnn. *An Imagined Geography: Sierra Leoneans in the United States.* Philadelphia: University of Pennsylvania Press, 2004.

Damrel, David. "Aspects of the Naqshbandi-Haqqani Order in North America." In *Sufism in the West,* edited by Jamal Malik and John Hinnells, 115–126. New York: Routledge, 2006.

Daniel, Norman. *Islam and the West: The Making of an Image.* Oxford: Oneworld, 1997.

Dannin, Robert. *Black Pilgrimage to Islam.* New York: Oxford University Press, 2002.

———. "The Greatest Migration?" In *Muslim Minorities in the West: Visible and Invisible,* edited by Yvonne Yazbeck Haddad and Jane I. Smith, 59–76. Walnut Creek, Calif.: AltaMira Press, 2002.

Darraj, Susan Muaddi, ed. *Scheherazade's Legacy: Arab and Arab American Women on Writing.* Westport, Conn.: Praeger Publishers, 2004.

Davidson, Lawrence. "Debating Palestine: Arab-American Challenges to Zionism, 1917–1932." In *Arabs in America: Building a New Future,* edited by Michael W. Suleiman, 227–240. Philadelphia: Temple University Press, 1999.

DeCaro, Louis A., Jr. *On the Side of My People: A Religious Life of Malcolm X.* New York: New York University, 1996.

de Jong-Keesing, Elisabeth. *Inayat Khan: A Biography.* Translated by Hayat Bouman and Penelope Goldschmidt. The Hague and London: East-West Publications Fonds B.V., 1974.

De La Cruz, G. Patricia, and Angela Brittingham. "The Arab Population: 2000." Washington, D.C.: U.S. Census Bureau, 2003.

DeLong-Bas, Natana. "Muhammad Ali." In *Notable Muslims: Muslim Builders of World Civilization and Culture.* Oxford: Oneworld, 2006.

———. *Wahhabi Islam: From Revival and Reform to Global Jihad.* New York: Oxford University Press, 2004.

Demi. *Muhammad.* New York: McElderry, 2003.

Denny, Frederick M. "The Legacy of Fazlur Rahman." In *Muslims of America,* edited by Yvonne Yazbeck Haddad, 96–108. New York: Oxford University Press, 1991.

Deutsch, Nathaniel. *The Tribe of Ishmael: Inventing America's "Worst" Family.* Berkeley: University of California Press, 2009.

Dickey, Christopher. *Securing the City: Inside America's Best Counterterror Force—the NYPD.* New York: Simon & Schuster, 2009.

Diouf, Sylviane A. *Servants of Allah: African Muslims Enslaved in the Americas.* New York: New York University Press, 1998.

———. "The West African Paradox." In *Muslims' Place in the American Public Square,* edited by Zahid H. Bukhari et al., 268–295. Lanham, Md.: AltaMira Press, 2004.

Dirks, Jerald F. *Muslims in American History: A Forgotten Legacy.* Beltsville, Md.: Amana, 2006.

Duffield, Ian. "Some American Influences on Dusé Mohamed Ali." In *Pan-African Biography,* edited by Robert A. Hill, 11–56. Los Angeles: Crossroads Press, 1987.

Eck, Diana. *A New Religious America.* San Francisco: Harper Collins, 2001.

Eickelman, Dave, and Jon Anderson, eds. *New Media in the Muslim World.* Bloomington: Indiana University Press, 2003.

Elkholy, Abdo A. *Arab Moslems in the United States: Religion and Assimilation.* New Haven, Conn.: College and University Press, 1966.

Ellis, Deborah. *Breadwinner.* Toronto: Groundwood, 2001.

———. *Mud City.* Toronto: Groundwood, 2004.

———. *Parvana's Journey.* Toronto: Groundwood, 2003.

Ernst, Carl E., and Bruce B. Lawrence. *Sufi Martyrs of Love: The Chishti Order in South Asia and Beyond.* New York: Palgrave Macmillan, 2002.

Ernst, Carl W. *The Shambhala Guide to Sufism.* Boston: Shambhala, 1997.

Ertegun, Ahmet. *What I'd Say: The Atlantic Story.* New York: Welcome Rain Publishers, 2001.

Esposito, John L., and John O. Voll. "Ismail al-Faruqi: Muslim Scholar-Activist." In *The Muslims of America,* edited by Yvonne Haddad, 65–79. New York: Oxford University Press, 1991.

Essien-Udom, E. U. *Black Nationalism: A Search for an Identity in America.* Chicago: University of Chicago Press, 1962.

Evanzz, Karl. *The Messenger: The Rise and Fall of Elijah Muhammad.* New York: Pantheon, 1999.

Faisal, Daoud Ahmed. *Islam, the True Faith: The Religion of Humanity.* Brooklyn: Islamic Mission of America, 1965.

Falkloff, Marc. *Poems from Guantánamo: The Detainees Speak.* Iowa City: University of Iowa Press, 2007.

Ferris, Marc. "To 'Achieve the Pleasure of Allah': Immigrant Muslim Communities in New York City, 1893–1991." In *Muslim Communities in North America,* edited by Yvonne Yazbeck

Haddad and Jane Idleman Smith, 209–230. Albany: State University of New York Press, 1994.

Fess, Margaret L. "Mohammedan Village Byproduct of Depression," *Buffalo Courier-Express,* 2 June 1946, p. 8D.

Foltz, Richard, Frederick Mathewson Denny, and Haji Baharuddin Azizan, eds. *Islam and Ecology: A Bestowed Trust.* Cambridge, Mass.: Harvard University Press, 2003.

Forrest, Leon. *Relocations of the Spirit.* Wakefield, R.I.: Asphodel Press, 2004.

Friedlander, Jonathan. "The Yemenis of Delano: A Profile of a Rural Islamic Community." In *Muslim Communities in North America,* edited by Yvonne Yazbeck Haddad and Jane Idleman Smith, 423–444. Albany: State University of New York Press, 1994.

———, ed. *Sojourners and Settlers: The Yemeni Immigrant Experience.* Salt Lake City: University of Utah Press, 1988.

Friedmann, Yohanan. *Prophecy Continuous: Aspects of Ahmadi Religious Thought and Its Medieval Background.* Berkeley: University of California Press, 1989.

Galvan, Juan. "Who Are Latino Muslims?" *Islamic Horizons* (July/August 2008): 26–30.

Gardell, Mattias. *In the Name of Elijah Muhammad: Louis Farrakhan and the Nation of Islam.* Durham, N.C.: Duke University Press, 1996.

Gehrke-White, Donna. *The Face Behind the Veil: The Extraordinary Lives of Muslim Women in America.* New York: Citadel Press, 2006.

Georgia Writers' Project. *Drums and Shadows.* Athens: University of Georgia Press, 1940.

Ghamari-Tabrizi, Behrooz. "Loving America and Longing for Home: Isma'il al-Faruqi and the Emergence of the Muslim Diaspora in North America." *International Migration* 42, no. 2 (2004): 61–84.

GhaneaBassiri, Kambiz. *Competing Visions of Islam in the United States.* Westport, Conn.: Greenwood, 1997.

Gillan, Maria Mazziotti, and Jennifer Gillan, eds. *Unsettling America: An Anthology of Contemporary Multicultural Poetry.* New York: Penguin, 1994.

Gomez, Michael A. *Black Crescent: The Experience and Legacy of African Muslims in the Americas.* Cambridge: Cambridge University Press, 2005.

———. *Exchanging Our Country Marks: The Transformation of African Identities in the Colonial and Antebellum South.* Chapel Hill: University of North Carolina Press, 1998.

———. "Muslims in Early America." *Journal of Southern History* (November 1994): 671–710.

Gottschalk, Marie. *The Prison and the Gallows: The Politics of Mass Incarceration in America.* New York: Cambridge University Press, 2006.

Gottschalk, Peter, and Gabriel Greenberg. *Islamophobia: Making Muslims the Enemy.* Lanham, Md.: Rowman and Littlefield, 2008.

Gourse, Leslie. *Art Blakey: Jazz Messenger.* New York: Schirmer Trade Books, 2002.

Griffith, R. Marie, and Melani McAlister, eds. *Religion and Politics in the Contemporary United States.* Baltimore: Johns Hopkins University Press, 2008.

Griggs, Khalid Fattah. *Come Let Us Change This World: A Brief History of the Islamic Party in North America, 1971–1991.* Winston-Salem, N.C.: Vision Media, 2007.

Gualtieri, Sarah M. A. *Between Arab and White: Race and Ethnicity in the Early Syrian American Diaspora.* Berkeley: University of California Press, 2009.

Haddad, Yvonne Y., ed. *Muslims in the West: From Sojourners to Citizens.* New York: Oxford University Press, 2002.

———. *The Muslims of America.* New York: Oxford University Press, 1991.

Haddad, Yvonne Yazbeck, and John Esposito, eds. *Muslims on the Americanization Path?* New York: Oxford University Press, 2000.

Haddad, Yvonne Yazbeck, and Adair T. Lummis. *Islamic Values in the United States: A Comparative Study.* New York: Oxford University Press, 1987.

Haddad, Yvonne Y., and Jane I. Smith. *Mission to America: Five Islamic Sectarian Communities in North America.* Gainesville: University Press of Florida, 1993.

Haddad, Yvonne Y., and Jane I. Smith, eds. *Muslim Communities in North America.* Albany: State University of New York Press, 1994.

———. *Muslim Minorities in the West: Visible and Invisible.* Walnut Creek, Calif.: AltaMira Press, 2002.

Haddad, Yvonne Yazbeck, Jane I. Smith, and Kathleen M. Moore. *Muslim Women in America: The Challenge of Islamic Identity Today.* New York: Oxford University Press, 2006.

Hakan, Yavuz, and John L. Esposito. *Turkish Islam and the Secular State: The Gulen Movement.* Syracuse, N.Y.: Syracuse University Press, 2003.

Halman, Hugh Talat. "Sufism in the West: Islam in an Interspiritual Age." In *Voices of Islam,* Vol. 5, edited by John Esposito and Omid Safi, 169–188. Westport, Conn.: Praeger, 2007.

Hammad, Suheir. *Born Palestinian, Born Black.* New York: Harlem River Press, 1996.

———. *Zataar Diva.* New York: Rattapallax Press, 2006.

Hamza, Doha R. "On Models of Hospital Chaplaincies: Which One Works Best for the Muslim Community?" *Journal of Muslim Mental Health* 2 (2007): 65–79.

Hanania, Ray. *Arabs of Chicagoland.* Charleston, S.C.: Arcadia, 2005.

Hansen, Joyce, and Gary McGowan. *Breaking Ground, Breaking Silence: The Story of New York's African Burial Ground.* New York: Henry Holt, 1998.

Haque, Amber. "Religion and Mental Health: The Case of American Muslims." *Journal of Religion and Mental Health* 43, no. 1 (2004): 45–58.

Hasan, Asma Gull. *American Muslims: The New Generation.* New York: Continuum, 2000.

———. *Red, White, and Muslim: My Story of Belief.* New York: HarperOne, 2009.

Hashaw, Tim. *Children of Perdition: Melungeons and the Struggle of Mixed America.* Macon, Ga.: Mercer University Press, 2006.

Hassouneh-Phillips, Dena Saadat. "'Marriage Is Half of Faith and the Rest Is Fear Allah': Marriage and Spousal Abuse among American Muslims." *Violence against Women* 7, no. 8 (August 2001): 927–947.

Hathout, Hassan. *Audible Silence, Thought and Remembrance of a Muslim Elder.* Cairo, Egypt: Shourouk Intl., 2006.

Hathout, Hassan, Maher Hathout, and Fathi Osman. *In Fraternity: A Message to Muslims in America.* Los Angeles: Minaret Publishing House, 1989.

Hathout, Hassan, and Samer Hathout. *Jihad versus Terrorism.* Pasadena, Calif.: Multimedia Vera International, 2002.

Hayden, Patrick, Tom Lansford, Robert P. Watson, eds. *America's War on Terror.* Burlington, Vt.: Ashgate, 2003.

Hayes, Kevin J. "How Thomas Jefferson Read the Qur'an." *Early American Literature* 39, no. 2 (2004): 247–261.

Heiligman, Deborah. *Holidays around the World: Celebrate Ramadan and Eid Al-Fitr: With Praying, Fasting, and Charity.* New York: National Geographic, 2006.

Hermansen, Marcia. "Hybrid Identity Formations in Muslim America: The Case of American Sufi Movements." *Muslim World* 20 (2000): 158–197.

———. "Roads to Mecca: Conversion Narratives of European and Euro-American Muslims." *Muslim World* 89, no. 1 (January 1999): 56–89.

Hirschman, Elizabeth Caldwell. *Melungeons: The Last Lost Tribe in America.* Macon, Ga.: Mercer University Press, 2005.

Hitti, Philip K. *The Syrians in America.* New York: George H. Doran Company, 1924.

Hodge, David R. "Social Work and the House of Islam: Orienting Practitioners to the Beliefs and Values of Muslims in the United States." *Social Work* 50, no. 2 (April 2005): 162–173.

Howell, Sally, and Amaney Jamal. "Detroit Exceptionalism and the Limits of Political Incorporation." In *Being and Belonging: Ethnography in American Muslim and Middle Eastern Populations after 9/11,* edited by Katherine Ewing, 47–49. New York: Russell Sage Foundation Press, 2008.

Human Rights Watch. "We Are Not the Enemy: Hate Crimes against Arabs, Muslims and Those Perceived to Be Arab or Muslim after September 11." Vol. 14, No. 6 (G), November 2002.

Husain, Amir. *Oil and Water: Two Faiths One God.* Kelowna, B.C., Canada: Copperhouse, 2006.

Husain, Asad, and Harold Vogelaar. "Activities of the Immigrant Muslim Communities in Chicago." In *Muslim Communities in North America,* edited by Yvonne Yazbeck Haddad and Jane Idleman Smith, 231–257. Albany: State University of New York, 1994.

———. "Recent Immigrant Religions in a Restructuring Metropolis: New Religious Landscapes in Chicago." *Journal of Cultural Geography* 17 (Fall/Winter 1997): 55–77.

Husain, Sarah, ed. *Voices of Resistance: Muslim Women on War, Faith, and Sexuality.* Berkeley: Seal Press, 2006.

Hussaini, Mohammad Mazhar, and Ahmed Hussain Sakr. *Islamic Dietary Laws and Practices.* Chicago: Islamic Food and Nutrition Council of America, 1984.

Idibly, Ranya, Suzanne Oliver, and Priscilla Warner. *The Faith Club: A Muslim, A Christian, A Jew—Three Women Search for Understanding.* New York: Free Press, 2006.

Ismail, Vehbi. *Muhammad, The Last Prophet.* Beltsville, Md.: Amana, 2001.

Jackson, Sherman A. *Islam and the Blackamerican: Looking toward the Third Resurrection.* New York: Oxford University Press, 2005.

Jamal, Amaney, and Nadine Naber, eds. *Race and Arab Americans before and after 9/11: From Invisible Citizens to Visible Subjects.* Syracuse, N.Y.: Syracuse University Press, 2008.

Jervis, James. "The Sufi Order in the West and Pīr Vilāyat 'Ināyat Khān: Space-Age Spirituality in Contemporary Euro-America." In *New Trends and Developments in the World of Islam,* edited by Peter B. Clarke, 211–259. London: Luzac Oriental, 1998.

Johnston, James H. "Mamout Yarrow: The Man in the Knit Cap," *The Washington Post,* 5 February 2006, p. W16. Available online. URL: http://www.washingtonpost.com/wp-dyn/content/article/2006/02/03/AR2006020300827_4.html. Posted February 3, 2006. Accessed April 7, 2009.

Jubran, Sulaiman. "Classical Elements in *Mahjar* Poetry." *Journal of Arabic Literature* 38, no. 1 (2007): 67–77.

Kahera, Akel Ismail. *Deconstructing the American Mosque: Space, Gender and Aesthetics.* Austin: University of Texas Press, 2002.

———. "A Mosque Between Significance and Style." *ISIM Review* (Autumn 2005): 56–57.

Kahf, Mohja. *The Girl in the Tangerine Scarf.* New York: Carroll and Graf, 2006.

Kamalipour, Yahya R., and Nancy Snow, eds. *War, Media, and Propaganda: A Global Perspective.* Lanham, Md.: Rowman and Littlefield, 2004.

Karim, Jamillah A. *American Muslim Women: Negotiating Race, Class, and Gender within the American Ummah.* New York: New York University Press, 2008.

———. "Between Immigrant Islam and Black Liberation: Young Muslims Inherit Global Muslim and African American Legacies." *Muslim World* 95, no. 4 (October 2005): 497–513.

———. "Voices of Faith, Faces of Beauty: Connecting American Muslim Women through *Azizah.*" In *Muslim Networks from Hajj to Hip Hop,* edited by miriam cooke and Bruce B. Lawrence, 169–188. Chapel Hill: University of North Carolina Press, 2005.

Karim, Persis. *Let Me Tell You Where I've Been: New Writing by Women of the Iranian Diaspora.* Fayetteville: University of Arkansas Press, 2006.

Kassam, Tazim R. "The Daily Prayer (*Du'a*) of Shi'a Isma'ili Muslims." In *Religions of the United States in Practice,* Vol. 2, edited by Colleen McDannell, 32–44. Princeton, N.J.: Princeton University Press.

Kassamali, Noor. "Healing Rituals and the Role of Fatima." In *Religious Healing in Boston: Body, Spirit, Community,* edited by Susan Sered, 43–45. Cambridge, Mass.: Center for the Study of World Religions, Harvard University, 2004.

Kaya, Ilhan. "Turkish-American Immigration History and Identity Formations." *Journal of Muslim Minority Affairs* 24, no. 2 (October 2004): 295–308.

Keller, Nuh Ha Mim. *Port in a Storm, A Fiqh Solution to the Qibla of North America.* Amman: Wakeel Books, 2001.

Kelley, Robin D. G. *Race Rebels: Culture, Politics, and the Black Working Class.* New York: Free Press, 1994.

Kelley, Ron, Jonathan Friedlander, et al., eds. *Irangeles: Iranians in Los Angeles.* Berkeley: University of California Press, 1993.

Kelly, Patricia. "Integration and Identity in Muslim Schools: Britain, United States and Montreal." *Islam and Christian-Muslim Relations* 10, no. 2 (1999): 197–217.

Kennedy, N. Brent. *The Melungeons: The Resurrection of a Proud People.* Macon, Ga.: Mercer University Press, 1997.

Keshavarz, Fatemeh. *Jasmine and Stars: Reading More Than Lolita in Tehran.* Chapel Hill: University of North Carolina Press, 2007.

Khabeer, Suad Abdul. "Rep that Islam: The Rhyme and Reason of American Islamic Hip Hop." *Muslim World* 97, no. 1 (2007): 125–141.

Khaja, Khadija, and Chelsea Frederick. "Reflection on Teaching Effective Social Work Practice for Working with Muslim Communities." *Advances in Social Work* 9, no. 1 (Spring 2008): 1–7.

Khalidi, Omar. *Indian Muslims in North America.* Watertown, Mass.: South Asia Press, 1990.

Khan, M. A. Muqtedar. *American Muslims: Bridging Faith and Freedom.* Beltsville, Md.: Amana, 2002.

———. "Constructing the American Muslim Community." In *Religion and Immigration: Christian, Jewish, and Muslim Experiences in the United States,* edited by Yvonne Yazbeck Haddad, Jane I. Smith, and John L. Esposito, 175–198. Walnut Creek, Calif.: AltaMira Press, 2003.

Khan, Pir Vilayat Inayat. *The Message of Our Time: The Life and Teachings of the Sufi Master Pir-O-Murshid Inayat Khan.* San Francisco: Harper and Row Publishers, 1978.

Khan, Shahnaz. *Muslim Women: Crafting a North American Identity.* Gainesville: University Press of Florida, 2000.

Khan, Yasmine. *Engineering Architecture: The Vision of Fazlur R. Khan.* New York: Norton, 2004.

Kidd, Thomas S. *American Christians and Islam: Evangelical Culture and Muslims from the Colonial Period to the Age of Terrorism.* Princeton, N.J.: Princeton University Press, 2009.

Kjelgaard, Jim. *Hi Jolly.* New York: Dodd, Mead, 1959.

Knight, Frederick. "Justifiable Homicide, Police Brutality, or Governmental Repression? The 1962 Los Angeles Police Shooting of Seven Members of the Nation of Islam." *Journal of Negro History* 79, no. 2 (Spring 1994): 182–196.

Knight, Michael Muhammad. *The Five Percenters: Islam, Hip Hop and the Gods of New York.* Oxford: Oneworld, 2007.

———. *The Taqwacores.* New York: Autonomedia, 2004.

Köszegi, Michael. "The Sufi Order in the West: Sufism's Encounter with the New Age." In *Islam in North America: A Sourcebook,* edited by Michael Köszegi and J. Gordon Melton, 213–220. New York: Garland, 1992.

Kubik, Gerhard. *Africa and the Blues.* Jackson: University Press of Mississippi, 1999.

Kukis, Mark. *"My Heart Became Attached": The Strange Odyssey of John Walker Lindh.* Dulles, Va.: Brassey's, 2003.

Kurien, Prema. "To Be or Not to Be South Asian." *Journal of Asian American Studies* 6, no. 3 (October 2003): 261–288.

Kusha, Hamid R. *Islam in American Prisons: Black Muslims' Challenge to American Penology.* Burlington, Vt.: Ashgate, 2009.

Laird, Lance D., et al. "Muslims and Health Disparities in the United States and United Kingdom." *Archives of Disease in Childhood* 92, no. 10 (2007): 922–926.

Laird, Lance D., and Wendy Cadge. "Caring for Our Neighbors: How Muslim Community-Based Health Organizations Are Bridging the Health Care Gap in America." Clinton Township, Mich.: Institute for Social Policy and Understanding, 2008.

Lang, Jeffrey. *Even Angels Ask: A Journey to Islam in America.* Beltsville, Md.: Amana, 1997.

———. *Losing My Religion: A Call for Help.* Beltsville, Md.: Amana, 2004.

———. *Struggling to Surrender: Some Impressions of an American Convert to Islam.* Beltsville, Md.: Amana, 1994.

Lanning, Michael Lee. *African Americans in the Revolutionary War.* New York: Citadel Press, 2005.

Larkin, Colin, ed. *The Virgin Encyclopedia of Jazz.* London: Virgin Books, 2004.

Lawrence, Bruce B. *New Faiths, Old Fears: Muslims and Other Asian Immigrants in American Religious Life.* New York: Columbia University Press, 2002.

Leaming, Hugo P. "The Ben Ishmael Tribe: A Fugitive 'Nation' of the Old Northwest." In *The Ethnic Frontier: Essays in Group Survival in Chicago and the Midwest,* edited by Melvin G. Holli and Peter d'A. Jones, 97–141. Grand Rapids, Mich.: Eerdmans Publishing, 1977.

Lee, Martha F. *The Nation of Islam: An American Millenarian Movement.* Syracuse, N.Y.: Syracuse University Press, 1996.

Leonard, Karen Isaksen. *Making Ethnic Choices: California's Punjabi Mexican Americans.* Philadelphia: Temple University Press, 1992.

———. *Muslims in the United States: The State of Research.* New York: Russell Sage Foundation, 2003.

———. "South Asian Leadership of American Muslims." In *Muslims in the West: From Sojourners to Citizens,* edited by Yvonne Yazbeck Haddad, 233–249. New York: Oxford, 2002.

Lesch, David W., ed. *The Middle East and the United States: A Historical and Political Reassessment.* Boulder, Colo.: Westview, 2007.

Lewis, Samuel. *Sufi Vision and Initiation: Meetings with Remarkable Beings.* San Francisco: Sufi Islamia/Prophecy Publications, 1986.

Lewisohn, Leonard. "Persian Sufism in the Contemporary West: Reflections on the Ni'matu'llahi Diaspora." In *Sufism in the West,* edited by Jamal Malik and John Hinnells, 49–70. New York: Routledge, 2006.

Lincoln, C. Eric. *The Black Muslims in America.* Boston: Beacon Press, 1961.

Lo, Mbaye. *Muslims in America: Race, Politics, and Community Building.* Beltsville, Md.: Amana, 2004.

Lockman, Zachary. *Contending Visions of the Middle East: The History and Politics of Orientalism.* New York: Cambridge University Press, 2004.

Lovell, Emily. *Islam in the United States: Past and Present.* Alberta, Canada: University of Alberta Press, 1983.

Macauley, David. *Mosque.* Boston: Houghton Mifflin, 2003.

Mahmud, Tayyab. "Freedom of Religion and Religious Minorities in Pakistan: A Study of Judicial Practice." *Fordham International Law Journal* 19, no. 1 (October 1995): 40–100.

Majeed, Debra Mubashshir. "The Battle Has Been Joined: Gay and Polygynous Marriages Are Out of the Closet and in Search of Legitimacy." *Cross Currents* 54, no. 2 (2004): 73–81.

Makarim, Sami Nasib. *The Druze Faith.* Delmar, N.Y.: Caravan Books, 1974.

Makda, Hajra. *Sweet 'n Easy: Recipes for the Islamic Household.* Leicester, England: Tropic Publications, 2001.

Malcolm X, with Alex Haley. *The Autobiography of Malcolm X.* New York: Ballantine Books, 1987.

Malik, Jamal, and John Hinnells, eds. *Sufism in the West.* New York: Routledge, 2006.

Malkawi, Fathi. "The Future of Muslim Education in the United States: An Agenda for Research." *American Journal of Islamic Social Sciences* 20, nos. 3 & 4 (2003): 46–82.

Maloof, Patricia S., and Fariyal Ross-Sherriff. *Muslim Refugees in the United States: A Guide for Service Providers.* Culture Profile No. 17. Washington, D.C.: Center for Applied Linguistics, 2003.

Mamdani, Mahmood. "Good Muslim, Bad Muslim: A Political Perspective on Culture and Terrorism." In *American Anthropologist* 104, no. 3 (2002): 766–775.

Mamiya, Lawrence H. "From Black Muslim to Muslim: The Evolution of a Movement." *Journal for the Scientific Study of Religion* 21, no. 2 (June 1982): 138–152.

Marable, Manning, and Hishaam D. Aidi, eds. *Black Routes to Islam.* New York: Palgrave Macmillan, 2009.

Marr, Timothy. *The Cultural Roots of American Islamicism.* New York: Cambridge University Press, 2006.

Marsh, Clifton E. *Black Muslims to Muslims: The Resurrection, Transformation, and Change of the Lost-Found Nation of Islam in America, 1930–1995.* 2d ed. Lanham, Md.: Scarecrow Press, 1996.

Marston, Elsa. "A Window in the Wall: Palestinians in Children's Literature." *Horn Book* 80, no. 6 (November-December 2004): 647–655.

Martin, B. G. "Sapelo Island's Arabic Document: The 'Bilali Diary' in Context." *Georgia Historical Quarterly* 77, no. 3 (Fall 1994): 589–601.

Masud, Muhammad Khalid, ed. *Travellers in Faith: Studies of the Tablighi Jamaat as a Transnational Islamic Movement for Faith Renewal.* Leiden: Brill, 2000.

Matthews, Mary. *Magid Fasts for Ramadan.* Illustrated by E. B. Lewis. New York: Clarion, 1996.

Mattson, Ingrid. *The Story of the Qur'an: Its History and Place in Muslim Life.* Malden, Mass.: Blackwell, 2008.

Maurer, Bill. "Faith in Form: Islamic Home Financing and 'American' Islamic Law." In *Being and Belonging: Muslims in the United States Since 9/11,* edited by Katherine Pratt Ewing, 178–199. New York: Russell Sage Foundation, 2008.

McAlister, Melani. *Epic Encounters: Culture, Media, and U.S. Interests in the Middle East, 1945–2000.* Berkeley: University of California Press, 2001.

McCarus, Ernest. *The Development of Arab-American Identity.* Ann Arbor: University of Michigan Press, 1994.

McChesney, Robert D. *Charity and Philanthropy in Islam: Institutionalizing the Call to Do Good.* Bloomington and Indianapolis: Indiana University Center on Philanthropy, 1995.

McCloud, Aminah Beverly. *African American Islam.* New York: Routledge, 1995.

———. *Transnational Muslims in American Society.* Gainesville: University Press of Florida, 2006.

McCloud, Aminah, and Frederick Thaufeer Al Deen. *A Question of Faith for Muslim Inmates.* Chicago: ABC International Group, 1999.

McCloud, Sean. *Making the American Religious Fringe: Exotics, Subversives, and Journalists, 1955–1993.* Chapel Hill: University of North Carolina Press, 2004.

Merry, Michael S., and Geert Driessen. "Islamic Schools in Three Western Countries: Policy and Procedure." *Comparative Education* 41, no. 4 (November 2005): 411–432.

Metcalf, Barbara Daly, ed. *Making Muslim Space in North America and Europe.* Berkeley: University of California Press, 1996.

Micallef, Roberta. "Turkish Americans: Performing Identities in a Transnational Setting." *Journal of Muslim Minority Affairs* 24, no. 2 (October 2004): 233–241.

Miller, Timothy, ed. *America's Alternative Religions.* Albany: State University of New York Press, 1995.

Mir, Ali. *Art of the Skyscraper: The Genius of Fazlur Khan.* New York: Rizzoli International Publications, 2001.

Miyakawa, Felicia M. *Five Percenter Rap: God Hop's Music, Message, and Black Muslim Mission.* Bloomington: Indiana University Press, 2005.

Mobin-Uddin, Asma. *The Best Eid Ever.* Illustrated by Laura Jacobson. Honesdale, Pa.: Boyds Mill, 2007.

Mohammad-Arif, Aminah. *Salaam America: South Asian Muslims in New York.* London: Anthem Press, 2002.

Monson, Ingrid. "Art Blakey's African Diaspora." In *The African Diaspora: A Musical Perspective,* edited by Ingrid Monson. New York: Routledge Books, 2003.

Moore, Daniel Abd al-Hayy. *Burnt Heart/Ode to the War Dead.* San Francisco: City Lights Books, 1971.

———. *The Chronicles of Akhira.* Santa Barbara, Calif.: Zilzal Press, 1986.

———. *The Ramadan Sonnets Long Days on Earth: Book V.* San Francisco: City Light Books, 1996.

Moore, Kathleen M. *Al-Mughtaribun: American Law and the Transformation of Muslim Life in the United States.* Albany: State University of New York Press, 1995.

———. "A Closer Look at Anti-Terrorism Law: *American-Arab Anti-Discrimination Committee v. Reno* and the Construction of Aliens' Rights." In *Arabs in America: Building a New Future,* edited by Michael W. Suleiman, 84–99. Philadelphia: Temple University Press, 1999.

———. "The *Hijab* and Religious Liberty: Anti-Discrimination Law and Muslim Women in the United States." In *Muslims on the Americanization Path?,* edited by Yvonne Y. Haddad and John L. Esposito, 105–127. New York: Oxford University Press, 2000.

———. "Muslims in Prison: Claims to Constitutional Protection of Religious Liberty." In *The Muslims of America,* edited by Yvonne Yazbeck Haddad, 136–156. New York: Oxford University Press, 1991.

———. "Representation of Islam in the Language of Law: Some Recent U.S. Cases." In *Muslims in the West: From Sojourners to Citizens,* edited by Yvonne Y. Haddad, 187–204. New York: Oxford University Press, 2002.

Moxley, Carolyn Rouse. *Engaged Surrender: African American Women and Islam.* Berkeley: University of California Press, 2004.

Mubashshir, Debra Washington. "Forgotten Fruit of the City: Chicago and the Moorish Science Temple of America." *Cross Currents* 51, no. 1 (Spring 2001): 6–20.

Muhaiyaddeen, M. R. Bawa, Shaikh. *God, His Prophets and His Children.* Philadelphia: Fellowship Press, 1978.

———. *Islam and World Peace: Explanations of a Sufi.* Philadelphia: Fellowship Press, 1987.

Muhammad, Amina. "The Sister-Wives: A Look at Polygyny." *Azizah* 4, no. 3 (2007): 45–50.

Muhammad, Amir N. *Muslim Veterans of American Wars: Revolutionary War, War of 1812, Civil War, World War I & II.* Washington, D.C.: FreeMan Publications, 2007.

Muhammad, Elijah. *How to Eat to Live: Book No. 2.* Reprint, Newport News, Va.: National Newport News and Commentator, n.d [1972].

———. *How to Eat to Live: Book One.* Atlanta: Messenger Elijah Muhammad Propagation Society, 1967.

———. *Message to the Blackman in America,* 1965. Reprint, Newport News, Va.: United Brothers Communications Systems, 1992.

———. *The Supreme Wisdom: The Solution to the So-Called Negroes' Problem.* Newport News, Va.: National Newport News and Commentator, 1957.

Muhammad, Warith Deen. *As the Light Shineth from the East.* Chicago: WDM Publishing Company, 1980.

Muhammad, Zakiyyah. "Islamic Education in America: An Historical Overview with Future Projections." *Religion & Education* 25, nos. 1 & 2 (1998): 87–96.

Murad, Khurram. *Da'wah among Non-Muslims in the West.* London: The Islamic Foundation, 1986.

Naff, Alixa. *Becoming American: The Early Arab Immigrant Experience.* Carbondale: Southern Illinois University Press, 1985.

Naficy, Hamid. *The Making of Exile Cultures: Iranian Television in Los Angeles.* Minneapolis: University of Minnesota Press, 1993.

Nance, Susan. "Mystery of the Moorish Science Temple: Southern Blacks and American Alternative Spirituality in 1920s Chicago." *Religion and American Culture* 12, no. 2 (Summer 2002): 123–166.

———. "Respectability and Representation: The Moorish Science Temple, Morocco, and Black Public Culture In 1920's Chicago." *American Quarterly* 4, no. 4 (December 2002): 623–659.

Nanji, Azim. "The Nizari Ismaili Muslim Community in North America: Background and Development." In *The Muslim Community in North America,* edited by Earle H. Waugh et al., 149–164. Edmonton: University of Alberta Press, 1983.

Nash, Michael. *Islam among Urban Blacks: Muslims in Newark, New Jersey, A Social History.* Lanham, Md.: University Press of America, 2008.

Nasr, Seyyed Hossein. *The Encounter of Man and Nature: The Spiritual Crisis of Modern Man.* London: Allen and Unwin, 1968.

———. *An Introduction to Islamic Cosmological Doctrines.* Cambridge, Mass.: Harvard University Press, 1964.

———. *Knowledge and the Sacred.* Edinburgh: Edinburgh University Press, 1981.

———. *The Spiritual and Religious Dimensions of the Environmental Crisis.* London: Temenos Academy, 1999.

National Commission on Terrorist Attacks. *The 9/11 Commission Report.* New York: W. W. Norton, 2004.

Netanyahu, Benjamin, ed. *Terrorism: How the West Can Win.* New York: Avon Books, 1987.

Netton, Ian Richard. *Sufi Ritual: The Parallel Universe.* Richmond, Surrey: Curzon, 2000.

Nieuwkerk, Karin van, ed. *Women Embracing Islam: Gender and Conversion in the West.* Austin: University of Texas Press, 2006.

Nimer, Mohamed. *The North American Muslim Resource Guide: Muslim Life in the United States and Canada.* New York: Routledge, 2002.

Nomani, Asqa Q. *Standing Alone in Mecca: An American Woman's Struggle for the Soul of Islam.* New York: HarperCollins, 2005.

Noor, Queen. *Leap of Faith: Memoirs of an Unexpected Life.* New York: Miramax, 2003.

Nuriddin, Jaludin, and Suliaman El-Hadi. *Vibes from the Scribes: Selected Poems.* Trenton, N.J.: Africa World Press, 1992.

Nuruddin, Yusuf. "The Five Percenters: A Teenage Nation of Gods and Earths." In *Muslim Communities in North America,* edited by Yvonne Y. Haddad and Jane I. Smith, 109–132. Albany: State University of New York Press, 1994.

Nyang, Sulayman S. *Islam in the United States of America.* Chicago: Kazi Publications, 1999.

Obajtek-Kirkwood, Anne-Marie, and Ernest Hakanen. *Signs of War: From Patriotism to Dissent.* New York: Palgrave Macmillan, 2007.

Oliver, Haneef James. *The 'Wahhabi' Myth: Dispelling Prevalent Fallacies and the Fictitious Link with Bin Laden.* Available online. URL: http://www.thewahhabimyth.com. Accessed January 29, 2009.

Omran, Abdel R. *Family Planning in the Legacy of Islam.* London and New York: Routledge, 1992.

O'Reilly, Kenneth. *Racial Matters: The FBI's Secret File on Black America, 1960–1972.* New York: Free Press, 1991.

Orfalea, Gregory. *The Arab Americans: A History.* Northampton, Mass.: Olive Branch Press, 2006.

———. *Before the Flames: A Quest for the History of Arab Americans.* Austin: University of Texas Press, 1988.

Orfalea, Gregory, and Sharif Elmusa. *Grape Leaves: A Century of Arab American Poetry.* Salt Lake City: University of Utah Press, 1988.

Oweis, Fayeq S. "Islamic Art as an Educational Tool about the Teaching of Islam." *Art Education* 55, no. 2 (March 2002): 18–24.

Oyewole, Abiodun, Umar Bin Hassan, and Kim Green. *The Last Poets on a Mission: Selected Poems and a History of the Last Poets.* New York: H. Holt, 1996.

Padhdiwala, Tasneem. "The Aging of the Moors." *Chicago Reader* 37, no. 8 (November 15, 2007). Available online. URL: http://www.chicagoreader.com/features/stories/moors/. Accessed March 1, 2009.

Padwick, Constance E. *Muslim Devotions: A Study of Prayer-Manuals in Common Use.* Oxford: Oneworld, 1996.

Patel, Eboo. *Acts of Faith: The Story of an American Muslim, the Struggle for the Soul of a Generation.* Boston: Beacon Press, 2007.

Patel, Eboo, and Patrice Brodeur, eds. *Building the Interfaith Youth Movement.* New York: Rowman and Littlefield, 2006.

Patterson Bible, Jean. *Melungeons: Yesterday and Today.* Rogersville, Tenn.: East Tennessee Printing Company, 1975.

Peery, Richard M. "Al-Hajj Wali Abdul Akram Founded the First," *Cleveland Plain-Dealer,* 3 August 1994, p. 8B.

Pew Research Center. "Muslim Americans: Middle Class and Mostly Mainstream." Washington, D.C.: Pew Research Center, 2007.

Poston, Larry. *Islamic Da'wah in the West.* New York: Oxford University Press, 1992.

Qaisi, Ghada G. "A Student Note: Religious Marriage Contracts: Judicial Enforcement of 'Mahr' Agreements in American Courts." *Journal of Law and Religion* 15, no. 1 (2000): 67–81.

Qazwini, Hassan. *American Crescent: A Muslim Cleric on the Power of his Faith, the Struggle against Prejudice, and the Future of Islam in America.* New York: Random House, 2007.

Quick, Abdullah H. "Al-Mu'allaqa: The Muslim Woman between Divorce and Real Marriage." *Journal of Islamic Law* 3, no. 1 (1998): 27–40.

———. *Deeper Roots: Muslims in the Americas and the Caribbean from before Columbus to the Present.* London: Ta-Ha Publishers, 1996.

———. *Islam and the African in America: The Sunni Experience.* Ontario, Canada: Islamic Academy of Canada, 1997.

Qutb, Sayyid. *Social Justice in Islam.* Rev. ed. Oneonta, N.Y.: Islamic Publications International, 2000.

Raboteau, Albert J. *Slave Religion: The "Invisible Institution" in the Antebellum South.* New York: Oxford University Press, 1978.

Rachanow, Shelly S. "The Effect of *O'Lone v. Estate of Shabazz* on the Free Exercise Rights of Prisoners." *Journal of Church and State* 40, no. 1 (1998): 125–149.

Rahman, F. "Amulets and Poems: One Healer's Beginnings." *Lancet* 350, no. 9094 (1997): 1,848–1,849.

Rahman, Fazlur. *Avicenna's Philosophy.* London: Oxford University Press, 1952.

———. *Health and Medicine in the Islamic Tradition.* New York: Crossroad, 1989.

———. *Major Themes of the Qur'an.* Minneapolis: Bibliotheca Islamica, 1980.

———. *Prophecy in Islam: Philosophy and Orthodoxy.* London: Allen and Unwin, 1958.

Rashad, Ahmad, and Peter Bodo. *Rashad: Vikes, Mikes, and Something on the Backside.* New York: Viking, 1988.

Rashid, Hakim M., and Zakiyyah Muhammad. "The Sister Clara Muhammad Schools: Pioneers in the Development of Islamic Education in America." *Journal of Negro Education* 61, no. 2 (Spring 1992): 178–185.

Rawlinson, Andrew. *The Book of Enlightened Masters: Western Teachers in Eastern Traditions.* Chicago: Open Court, 1997.

Reinhertz, Shakina. *Women Called to the Path of Rumi: The Way of the Whirling Dervish.* Prescott, Ariz.: Hohm Press: 2001.

Renard, John, ed. *Windows on the House of Islam: Muslim Sources on Spirituality and Religious Life.* Berkeley: University of California Press, 1998.

Rich, Richard, Terry L. Noss, Thomas J. Tobin, Brian Nissan, and William Kidd. *Muhammad (P.B.U.H.), The Last Prophet.* Bridgeview, Ill.: Distributed by Fine Media Group, 2007.

Richardson, E. Allen. *Islamic Cultures in North America: Patterns of Belief and Devotion of Muslims from Asian Countries in the United States and Canada.* New York: Pilgrim Press, 1981.

Riley, Carroll. "Blacks in the Early Southwest." *Ethnohistory* 19, no. 3 (Summer 1972): 247–260.

Rivera, Khadijah. "Empowering Latino Women." *Islamic Horizons* (July/August 2002): 37–38.

Rockwell, John. "Qawwali Music Stirs the Audience; Pakistanis Bring Drums and Chants to Carnegie," *New York Times,* 5 March 1975, p. 30.

Rose, David. *Guantánamo: The War on Human Rights.* New York: New Press, 2004.

Ross-Sheriff, Fariyal. "Elderly Muslim Immigrants: Needs, Challenges, and Strategies for Program Development." In *Muslim Communities in North America,* edited by Yvonne Y. Haddad and Jane I. Smith, 404–421. Albany: State University of New York Press, 1994.

Ross-Sheriff, Fariyal, and Azim Nanji. "Islamic Identity, Family, and Community: The Case of the Nizari Ismaili Community." In *Muslim Families in North America,* edited by Earle H. Waugh et al., 101–117. Edmonton: University of Alberta Press, 1992.

Rothschild, Jeffrey. *Bestower of Light: A Portrait of Dr. Javad Nurbakhsh, Master of the Nimatullahi Sufi Order.* New York: Khaniqahi Nimatullahi Publications, 1999.

Rouse, Carolyn Moxley. *Engaged Surrender: African American Women and Islam.* Berkeley: University of California, 2004.

Rowe, Amy. "Honey, Hadiths, and Health Day: A Spectrum of Healing in the Daily Life of Boston Muslims." In *Religious Healing in Boston: Body, Spirit, Community,* edited by Susan Sered, 35–41. Cambridge, Mass.: Center for the Study of World Religions, Harvard University, 2004.

Roy, Olivier. *Globalized Islam: The Search for the New Ummah.* New York: Columbia University Press, 2004.

Rustomji-Kerns, Roshni. *Living in America: Poetry and Fiction by South Asian American Writers.* Boulder, Colo.: Westview, 1995.

RZA. *The Wu-Tang Manual.* New York: Riverhead Books, 2005.

Saad, Lydia. "Anti-Muslim Sentiment Fairly Commonplace: Four in Ten Americans Admit Feeling Prejudice against Muslims." *Gallup.* August 10, 2006. Available online. URL: http://www.gallup.com/poll/24073/Anti-Muslim-Sentiments-Fairly-Commonplace.aspx. Accessed May 1, 2009.

Sabry, Nermin Said, and Katherine Richardson Bruna. "Learning from the Experience of Muslim Students in American Schools: Towards a Proactive Model of School-Community Cooperation." *Multicultural Perspectives* 9, no. 3 (2007): 44–50.

Sachs, Susan. "Conference Confronts the Difficulties of Being Muslim and Gay," *New York Times,* 30 May 1999, p. 23.

Safi, Omid, ed. *Progressive Muslims: On Justice, Gender, and Pluralism.* London: Oneworld, 2003.

Said, Edward. *Covering Islam: How the Media and the Experts Determine How We See the Rest of the World.* New York: Vantage Books, 1997.

Said, Nicholas. *Autobiography of Nicholas Said; a Native of Bournou, Eastern Soudan, Central Africa.* Memphis: Shotwell & Co., 1873.

Said, Omar ibn. "The Life of Omar ibn Said, Written by Himself." Translated and introduced by Ala A. Alryyes. In *The Multilingual Anthology of American Literature,* edited by Marc Shell and Wernor Sollors, 58–93. New York: New York University Press, 2000.

Sakr, Ahmad Hussain. *Muslim Guide Food Ingredients.* Foundation for Islamic Knowledge, 1997.

Salaam, Aliyyah. "Children of Polygamy Speak." *Azizah* (Summer 2002): 106.

Sanchez, Sonia. *A Blues Book for Blue Black Magical Women.* Detroit, Mich.: Broadside Press, 1974.

———. *Love Poems.* New York: Third Press, 1973.

Sarroub, Loukia K. *All American Yemeni Girls: Being Muslim in a Public School.* Philadelphia: University of Pennsylvania Press, 2005.

Satrapi, Marjane. *Persepolis.* New York: Pantheon, 2004.

Schmidt, Garbi. *Islam in Urban America: Sunni Muslims in Chicago.* Philadelphia: Temple University Press, 2004.

Schneider, Paul. *Brutal Journey: The Epic Story of the First Crossing of North America.* New York: H. Holt, 2006.

Schubel, Vernon James. "Karbala as Sacred Space among North American Shi'a: 'Every Day Is Ashura, Everywhere Is Karbala.'" In *Making Muslim Space in North America and Europe,* edited by Barbara Daly Metcalf. 186–203. Berkeley: University of California Press, 1996.

Schuon, Frithjof. *Understanding Islam.* London: Allen and Unwin, 1963.

Sedgwick, Mark. *Against the Modern World: Traditionalism and the Secret Intellectual History of the Twentieth Century.* New York: Oxford University Press, 2004.

Seidel, Kathleen. *Serving the Guest: A Sufi Cookbook.* Peterborough, N.H.: Superlumenal Enterprises, 1999.

Sells, Michael. *The Bridge Betrayed: Religion and Genocide in Bosnia.* Berkeley: University of California Press, 1998.

Semmerling, Tim. *"Evil" Arabs in American Popular Film: Orientalist Fear.* Austin: University of Texas, 2006.

Serageldin, Ismail, and Steele, James. *Architecture of the Contemporary Mosque: New Architectures.* London: Academy Editions, 1998.

Shaheen, Jack. *Reel Bad Arabs: How Hollywood Vilifies a People.* Northampton, Mass.: Media Foundation, 2006.

Shakir, Zaid. *Scattered Pictures: Reflections of an American Muslim.* Hayward, Calif.: Zaytuna Institute, 2005.

Shepard, Raynel. *Cultural Adaptation of Somali Refugee Youth.* New York: LFB Scholarly Publishers, 2008.

Sherman, William C. *Prairie Peddlers: The Syrian-Lebanese in North Dakota.* Bismarck, N.Dak.: University of Mary Press, 2002.

Siddiqui, Huma. *Jasmine in Her Hair: Culture and Cuisine from Pakistan.* Madison, Wisc.: Jasmine Press, 2003.

Singleton, Brent D. "Brothers at Odds: Rival Islamic Movements in Late Nineteenth Century New York City." *Journal of Muslim Minority Affairs* 27, no. 3 (December 2007): 473–486.

———, ed. *Yankee Muslim: The Asian Travels of Mohammed Alexander Russell Webb.* Rockville, Md.: Borgo/Wildside Press, 2007.

Sinno, Abdulkader H. *Muslims in Western Politics.* Bloomington: Indiana University Press, 2009.

Sirin, Selcuk R., and Michelle Fine. *Muslim American Youth: Understanding Hyphenated Identities through Multiple Methods.* New York: New York University Press, 2008.

Slyomovics, Susan. "The Muslim World Day Parade and 'Storefront' Mosques of New York City." In *Making Muslim Space in North America and Europe,* edited by Barbara Daly Metcalf, 204–216. Berkeley: University of California Press, 1996.

Smith, Jane I. *Islam in America.* New York: Columbia University Press, 1999.

Srikanth, Rajini. *The World Next Door: South Asian American Literature and the Idea of America.* Philadelphia: Temple University Press, 2004.

Stanley, Diane. *Saladin: Noble Prince of Islam.* New York: HarperCollins, 2002.

Staples, Suzanne Fisher. *Haveli*. New York: Knopf, 1993.

———. *Shabanu, Daughter of the Wind*. New York: Knopf, 1989.

Stolberg, Sheryl Gay. "Man in the News: From Algeria to a Dream—Elias Adam Zerhouni," *New York Times,* 27 March 2002, p. A16.

Stowe, David. *How Sweet the Sound: Music in the Spiritual Lives of Americans*. Cambridge, Mass.: Harvard University Press, 2004.

Strum, Philippa, and Danielle Tarantolo, eds. *Muslims in the United States*. Washington, D.C.: Woodrow Wilson International Center for Scholars, 2003.

Sufi Islamia Ruhaniat Society. *Introduction to Spiritual Dance and Walk: From the Work of Samuel L. Lewis*. Novato, Calif.: Prophecy Pressworks, 1972.

Suleiman, Michael W., ed. *Arabs in America: Building a New Future*. Philadelphia: Temple University Press, 1999.

Swanson, Jon. "Sojourners and Settlers in Yemen and America." In *Sojourners and Settlers: The Yemeni Immigrant Experience,* edited by Jonathan Friedlander, 49–68. Salt Lake City: University of Utah Press, 1988.

Tate, Sonsyrea. *Little X: Growing Up in the Nation of Islam*. San Francisco: HarperSanFrancisco, 1997.

Taylor, Arthur. *Notes and Tones: Musician-to-Musician Interviews*. New York: DaCapo Press, 1993.

Thobani, Akbarali. *Islam's Quiet Revolutionary: The Story of Aga Khan IV*. New York: Vantage Press, 1993.

Thompson, Mary V. "'And Procure for Themselves a Few Amenities': The Private Life of George Washington's Slaves." *Virginia Cavalcade* 48, no. 4 (Autumn 1999): 178–190.

———. "Religious Practice in the Slave Quarters at Mount Vernon." *Colonial Williamsburg Interpreter* 21, no. 1 (Spring 2000): 10–14.

Trix, Frances. "Bektashi Tekke and the Sunni Mosque of Albanian Muslims in America." In *Muslim Communities in North America,* edited by Yvonne Yazbeck Haddad and Jane Idleman Smith, 359–380. Albany: State University of New York, 1994.

———. *Spiritual Discourse: Learning with an Islamic Master*. Philadelphia: University of Pennsylvania Press, 1993.

Tsao, Fred, and Rhoda Rae Gutierrez. *Losing Ground*. Chicago: Illinois Coalition for Immigrant and Refugees Rights, 2003.

Turner, Richard Brent. *Islam in the African-American Experience*. 2d ed. Bloomington: Indiana University Press, 2003.

U.S. House of Representatives, 103rd Congress, First Session. *World Trade Center Bombing*. Washington, D.C.: U.S. Government Printing Office, 1994.

Van Sertima, Ivan. *They Came before Columbus*. New York: Random House, 1976.

Vincent, Rickey, and George Clinton. *Funk: The Music, the People, and the Rhythm of the One*. New York: Macmillan, 1996.

Viscidi, Lisa. "Latino Muslims a Growing Presence in America." *Washington Report on Middle East Affairs* (June 2003): 56, 58.

Von Eschen, Penny M. *Race against Empire: Black Americans and Anticolonialism, 1937–1957*. Ithaca, N.Y.: Cornell University Press, 1997.

———. *Satchmo Blows Up the World: Jazz Ambassadors Play the Cold War*. Cambridge, Mass.: Harvard University Press, 2004.

Wade, Dorothy, and Justine Picardie. *Music Man: Ahmet Ertegun, Atlantic Records, and the Triumph of Rock-n-Roll*. New York: W. W. Norton, 1990.

Wadud, Amina. "American Muslim Identity: Race and Ethnicity in Progressive Islam." In *Progressive Muslims: On Justice, Gender and Pluralism,* edited by Omid Safi, 270–285. Oxford: Oneworld, 2003.

———. *Inside the Gender Jihad: Women's Reform in Islam*. Oxford: Oneworld, 2006.

———. *Qur'an and Woman: Rereading the Sacred Text from a Woman's Perspective*. New York: Oxford University Press, 1999.

Wagoner, Jay J. *Early Arizona: Pre-History to the Civil War*. Tucson: University of Arizona Press, 1975.

Walbridge, Linda. *Without Forgetting the Imam: Lebanese Shi'ism in an American Community*. Detroit: Wayne State University Press, 1997.

Walker, Dennis. *Islam and the Search for African American Nationhood*. Atlanta, Ga.: Clarity Press, 2005.

Walsh, Lorena S. *From Calabar to Carter's Grove: The History of a Virginia Slave Community*. Charlottesville: University Press of Virginia, 1997.

Wariko, Niraj. "While Fasting, Fordson High Football Players Get Upset Win," *Detroit Free Press,* 6 October 2007.

Waugh, Earle H., and Baha Qureshi Regula Abu-Laban, eds. *The Muslim Community in North America*. Edmonton: University of Alberta Press, 1983.

Waugh, Earle H., and Frederick Denny, eds. *The Shaping of an American Islamic Discourse: A Memorial to Fazlur Rahman*. Atlanta: Scholars Press, 1998.

Waugh, Earle H., et al., eds. *Muslim Families in North America*. Edmonton: University of Alberta Press, 1991.

Webb, Alexander Russell. *Islam in America*. New York: Oriental Publishing Company, 1893.

Webb, Gisela. "Tradition and Innovation in Contemporary American Islamic Spirituality: The Bawa Muhaiyaddeen Fellowship." In *Muslim Communities in North America,* edited by Yvonne Yazbeck Haddad and Jane Idleman Smith, 75–108. Albany: State University of New York Press, 1994.

———, ed. *Windows of Faith: Women Muslim Scholar-Activists in North America*. Women and Gender in North America. Syracuse, N.Y.: Syracuse University Press, 2000.

Weiner, Leo. *Africa and the Discovery of America*. Philadelphia: Innes & Sons, 1920.

Weinstein, Norman. *A Night In Tunisia: Imaginings of Africa In Jazz*. Metuchen, N.J.: Scarecrow Press, 1992.

West, Cynthia S'thembile. "Revisiting Female Activism in the 1960s: The Newark Branch Nation of Islam." *Black Scholar* 26, no. 3-4 (1996): 41–48.

Westerlund, David, ed. *Sufism in Europe and North America*. New York: Routledge, 2004.

Westheider, James E. *The African American Experience in Vietnam: Brothers in Arms*. New York: Rowman and Littlefield, 2008.

———. *Fighting on Two Fronts: African Americans and the Vietnam War*. New York: New York University Press, 1997.

Wiktorowicz, Quintan. "The Salafi Movement: Violence and the Fragmentation of a Community." In *Muslim Networks: From Hajj to Hip Hop,* edited by miriam cooke and Bruce B. Lawrence, 208–234. Chapel Hill: University of North Carolina Press, 2005.

Williams, Raymond. *Religions of Immigrants from India and Pakistan*. Cambridge: Cambridge University Press, 1988.

Willis, John Ralph. *Studies in West African Islamic History: The Cultivators of Islam, The Evolution of Islamic Institutions and the Growth of Arabic Literature.* New York: Routledge, 1979.

Wilson, Peter Lamborn. *Sacred Drift: Essays on the Margins of Islam.* San Francisco: City Lights Books, 1993.

Winkler, Wayne. *Walking toward the Sunset: The Melungeons of Appalachia.* Macon, Ga.: Mercer University Press, 2004.

Wolf, C. Umhau. "Muslims in the Midwest." *Muslim World* 50, no. 1 (1960): 39–48.

Wolfe, Michael. *The Hadj: An American's Pilgrimage to Mecca.* New York: Grove Press, 1993.

Women of South Asian Descent Collective, eds. *Our Feet Walk the Sky: Women of the South Asian Diaspora.* San Francisco: Aunt Lute Books, 1993.

Woodard, Komozi. *A Nation within a Nation: Amiri Baraka (LeRoi Jones) & Black Power Politics.* Chapel Hill: University of North Carolina Press, 1999.

Wuthenau, Alexander Von. *Unexpected Faces in Ancient America: 1500 B.C.–A.D. 1500.* New York: Crown Publishing, 1975.

Yanow, Scott. *Jazz on Record: The First Sixty Years.* San Francisco: Backbeat Books, 2003.

Yee, James, and Aimee Molloy. *For God and Country.* New York: Public Affairs, 2005.

Younis, Mohamed. "Muslim Americans Exemplify Diversity, Potential Key Findings from a New Report by the Gallup Center for Muslim Studies." *Gallup.* March 2, 2009. Available online. URL: http://www.gallup.com/poll/116260/Muslim-Americans-Exemplify-Diversity-Potential.aspx. Accessed April 28, 2009.

Zakaria, Fareed. *The Post-American World.* New York: W. W. Norton, 2008.

Zewail, Ahmed H. *Voyage through Time: Walks of Life to the Nobel Prize.* Cairo, Egypt: American University in Cairo, 2002.

Zogby International. *Muslims in the American Public Square.* Washington, D.C.: Zogby International, 2001.

———. *Report on Muslims in the American Marketplace.* Washington, D.C.: Zogby International, 2001.

Index

A **boldface 1:** or **2:** denotes a volume number. Other **boldface** page numbers denote extensive treatement of a topic. *Italic* page numbers refer to illustrations; *c* refers to entries in chronology.

A

AAUAA. *See* Addeynu Allahe Universal Arabic Association

AAUG (Arab-American University Graduates) **1:**xxx*c*, 58

Abd al-Hamid II (Ottoman sultan) **1:**265; **2:**554, 560, 576

Abdallah, Mike **1:**27, 29–32, 206

Abd al-Mut'a Ali Noel, M. Malik, Jr. **1:**xxxiv*c*; **2:**563

Abdel-Rahman, Omar **1:**xxxiii*c*, **1–2; 2:**433, 591

Abdul-Jabbar, Kareem **1:**xxx*c*, xxxii*c*, *2*, **2–3**
  acting and writing **1:**3
  autobiography **1:**73–74
  college and professional basketball life **1:**2–3
  Khaalis, Hamaas Abdul **1:**325
  NBA **2:**417, 418
  religious life **1:**3

Abdul-Khabeer, Rashidah **1:**xxxiii*c*, 246, 248

Abdullah, Ackmed **1:**xxvi*c*, 198

Abdul-Malik, Ahmed **1:**xxix*c*, **4**

Abdul Malik, Daud **1:**24, 119

Abdul Rauf, Feisal **1:**4–5; **2:**432

Abdul-Rauf, Mahmoud **1:**xxxiv*c*, **5–6**, 302; **2:**418, 443

Abdul-Wahad, Tariq **1:**xxxiv*c*, **6–7**

Abdur-Rahim, Shareef **1:**7, 69; **2:**418

Abdus-Salaam, Sheila **1:**xxxiii*c*, **7–8; 2:**433, 461–462, 584

ablution **1:**xxxvi*c*, **8–9**

Abode of the Message **1:**xxxi*c*
  Chishti Sufi Order **1:**114
  Khan, Vilayat Inayat **1:**328, 329
  Sufi Order of the West **2:**536
  Sufism **2:**541

Abou El Fadl, Khaled **1:**xxxv*c*, **9–10**, 201; **2:**473, 500

Abouhalima, Mahmud **2:**591, 592

Abourezek, James **1:**xxxi*c*, 49, 58

Abu Bakr as-Siddiq **2:**400, 416

AbuSulayman, AbdulHamid **1:**67, 269

ACCESS. *See* Arab Community Center for Economic and Social Services

ACS. *See* American Colonization Society

Adams, John Quincy **1:**xxiii*c*, 256, 312; **2:**553

ADC. *See* American-Arab Anti-Discrimination Committee

Addeynu Allahe Universal Arabic Association (AAUAA) **1:**xxvii*c*, xxviii*c*, **10–11**
  Arabic **1:**62
  Ezaldeen, Muhammad **1:**175–176
  Great Depression **1:**219
  missionaries **2:**373
  Newark, New Jersey **2:**428
  Philadelphia, Pennsylvania **2:**447
  World War II **2:**594

adhan **1:**xxv*c*, **11–12**
  Arabic **1:**62
  Million Man March **2:**370
  Mohammed, W. D. **2:**377
  music **2:**404
  prayer **2:**468

ADS (American Druze Society) **1:**xxix*c*, 160

Afghanistan
  Abdel-Rahman, Omar **1:**1
  Kathwari, Farooq **1:**322
  Lindh, John Philip Walker **1:**342
  United States foreign relations **2:**556, 557
  United States military **2:**562

Afghanistan War (2001–)
  chaplains **1:**99
  Guantánamo Bay **1:**219
  Iraq War **1:**280
  Lindh, John Philip Walker **1:**342

Africa **1:**xxii*c*, xxxv*c*
  Baquaqua, Mahommah Gardo **1:**77

families **1:**177

food **1:**206

Ibrahima, Abdul Rahman **1:**255, 256

Ishmaelites **1:**283

African-American Muslims **1:**xvi–xvii, **12–19**, *13*
  African Muslim immigrants **1:**24
  agriculture **1:**26
  Arabic **1:**62
  black Sunni Muslim communities **1:**14–16
  Boston, Massachusetts **1:**88
  cemeteries **1:**98
  Chicago, Illinois **1:**102, 104
  demographics **1:**139
  Detroit, Michigan **1:**142
  dietary laws **1:**145–147
  dress **1:**157
  education **1:**168
  Ezaldeen, Muhammad **1:**175
  families **1:**177–179
  feminists **1:**195
  film **1:**198
  first black Muslims **1:**12–14
  food **1:**207, 208
  funerals **1:**213
  hajj **1:**226
  health care **1:**237
  HIV/AIDS **1:**246
  Immigration Act of 1965 **1:**261
  Islamic schools **1:**294–295
  Jesus **1:**313
  law **1:**336
  Los Angeles **1:**345
  Malcolm X **2:**351–352
  men **2:**367–368
  missionaries **2:**372
  Mohammed, W. D. **2:**377–378
  Muhammad Speaks **2:**402